Watson's Textile Design
and Colour

Watson's Textile Design and Colour

Elementary Weaves and Figured Fabrics

Z. GROSICKI

Department of Fibre Science, University of Strathclyde,
Royal College, George St., Glasgow C1

LONDON
NEWNES–BUTTERWORTHS

THE BUTTERWORTH GROUP

ENGLAND

Butterworth & Co (Publishers) Ltd
London: 88 Kingsway, WC2B 6AB

AUSTRALIA

Butterworths Pty Ltd
Sydney: 586 Pacific Highway, NSW 2067
Melbourne: 343 Little Collins Street, 3000
Brisbane: 240 Queen Street, 4000

CANADA

Butterworth & Co (Canada) Ltd
Scarborough: 2265 Midland Avenue, Ontario M1P 4S1

NEW ZEALAND

Butterworths of New Zealand Ltd
Wellington: 26–28 Waring Taylor Street, 1

SOUTH AFRICA

Butterworth & Co (South Africa) (Pty) Ltd
Durban: 152–154 Gale Street

First published by Longmans, Green & Co, 1912
Second Edition 1921
Third Edition 1931
Fourth Edition 1937
Fifth Edition 1946
Sixth Edition 1954
Seventh Edition published in 1975 by
Newnes–Butterworths, an imprint
of the Butterworth Group

© Butterworth & Co (Publishers) Ltd, 1975

ISBN 0 408 70515 9

Filmset by Filmtype Services Ltd,
Scarborough, Yorks

Printed in England by Hazell, Watson & Viney Ltd,
Aylesbury, Bucks

Preface

This book first appeared on the textile scene in 1912 when it was published by Longmans, Green & Co. Since then it has been revised several times, firstly by the original author, W. Watson, and later by E. G. Taylor and J. Buchan, all of whom occupied teaching posts in the Royal College of Science and Technology, Glasgow—a University College which a decade ago became the University of Strathclyde. Thus, following an apparently established law of succession, I have been asked and have undertaken with considerable satisfaction, a further modification of the original work.

This time however more than a simple revision was required. The book has been responsible for bringing up (most properly) several generations of Woven Cloth Designers in the past but modern thinking in this area demanded a good degree of modernisation of the subject matter. And so considerable portions have been entirely rewritten, the contents completely reorganised to achieve more logical progression, and several new approaches well proven in actual teaching practice have been introduced to permit clearer understanding of the nature of woven structures. Severe pruning of excessive verbosity and superfluous illustrations has resulted in a reduction of the original by about one hundred pages without, one hopes, compromising in the slightest the nature of this book as a comprehensive treatise on simple woven cloth construction and design.

All the structures dealt with in the body of this book are still being produced, some in traditional materials and settings, some in completely new guises, and it is felt that as long as woven fabric is manufactured this constructional variety and richness will remain. It is also felt that in this era of shrinking resources and proliferation of waste a technique which results in the creation of the longest lasting article, which at the same time is structurally soundest and aesthetically most satisfying can only improve its position in preference to the most wasteful ones. It is, therefore, mainly with this idea of serving to retain and to spread the knowledge of the 'mysteries' of weaving technology that the reborn version of the book is offered.

The glossary of textile terms in Appendix I has been changed only slightly and for the sake of completeness a number of items of historical rather than actual interest has been retained. In Appendix II a simple survey of properties and uses of man-made fibres is provided and an equally simple introduction to the subject of yarn and cloth relationships in a woven fabric is given in Appendix III. For those wishing to enquire further into matters surveyed in the appendices references are given to more exhaustive works on each subject. It is fully realised that the treatment of the subject matter in the appendices is somewhat simplistic but it is hoped that by providing such guide lines the new book might still serve as a designer's vade mecum today as it undoubtedly did in the past.

Encouragement in the work was received from many sources and sincere thanks are due to all my colleagues and particularly to E. G. Taylor, N. Peacock and H. Hodgkinson for their advice and help, and not least to my wife for putting up with my 'humours' during the preparation of this volume for printing.

Z.G.

Contents

1

Elements of Woven Design

CLASSIFICATION OF WOVEN FABRICS

Woven fabrics are composed of longitudinal or warp threads and transverse or weft threads, interlaced with one another according to the class of structure and form of design that are desired. The terms *chain* or *twist* are applied to the warp, and the warp threads are known individually as *ends*, while the terms *picks* and *filling* are applied to the weft threads. In the following the term threads is used in referring to warp and weft collectively, but in order to distinguish clearly one series from the other the warp threads are mostly described as 'ends', and the weft threads as 'picks'.

Woven structures may be conveniently divided into two principal categories, as follows:

(1) Simple structures, in which the ends and the picks intersect one another at right angles and in the cloth are respectively parallel with each other. In these constructions there is only one series of ends and one series of picks and all the constituent threads are equally responsible for both the aspect of utility or performance in a fabric and the aspect of aesthetic appeal.

(2) Compound structures, in which there may be more than one series of ends or picks some of which may be responsible for the 'body' of the fabric, such as ground yarns, whilst some may be employed entirely for ornamental purposes such as 'figuring', or 'face' yarns. In these cloths some threads may be found not to be in parallel formation one to another in either plane, and indeed, there are many pile surface constructions in which some threads may project out at right angles to the general plane of the fabric.

This book deals primarily with design in simple structures where *construction*, i.e. yarn interlacing, is frequently synonymous with *design* or the surface effect formed; in compound fabrics, however, the term 'construction' must be clearly separated from *ornamentation*, or *design* which may depend entirely on colour distribution and may, therefore, be independent of the construction itself.

BASIC OPERATIONS IN WOVEN CLOTH PRODUCTION

Cloth weaving is nowadays accomplished on sophisticated, high speed, precision machinery which in itself represents a field of intensive study for mechanical engineers. From the point of view of the designer the complicated operations of a weaving machine can be broken down into simple functions related to the process of cloth formation with particular reference to those functions which have the greatest influence upon the structure and the appearance of fabrics.

Figure 1.1 illustrates the lay-out of a weaving loom in the form of a simple, schematic diagram. The sheet of warp yarn, consisting of the required number of ends wound into a considerable length, is carried upon the

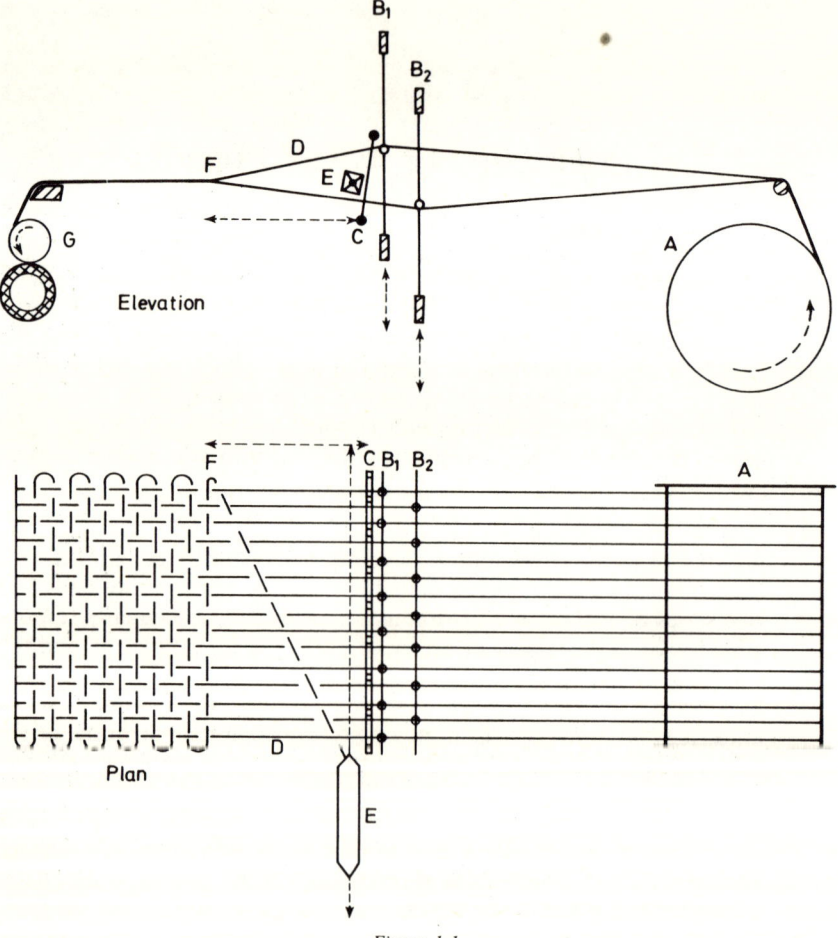

Figure 1.1

weaver's beam, A. The beam is made up according to instructions in a series of preparatory operations prior to its introduction into the loom. The specification for making the beam, in addition to stipulating the type of yarn, the number of ends, and the length of the warp, may also include a pattern if it is desired to produce a cloth with coloured stripes. The warp ends from the beam are then drawn through the healds, B_1 and B_2, threaded through the splits of the reed C and at the point D they become interlaced with the weft supplied by the shuttle E. The cloth is formed at the *fell* of the cloth, marked F, and is wound upon the cloth roller situated at the front of the loom.

The weaving process itself consists of three basic operations which form a continuous cycle whether in the simplest hand-loom, or in the most complex automatic machine. These primary motions can be described as follows:

(1) Shedding—the separation of the warp threads into upper and lower layers forming a *shed*, or a tunnel, through which the weft is passed.
(2) Picking—the insertion of the weft through the shed.
(3) Beating-up—the carrying forward of the last inserted pick of weft to the cloth already woven.

The picking and the beating-up operations are fixed no matter what type of fabric is being produced, but the shedding motion is variable and can be described as the heart of weaving as it is here that the nature of the interlacing, or the weave, is decided, and in order to be able to construct the desired effects the textile designer must have a very thorough knowledge and understanding of this primary operation.

In addition to the three principal operations, several ancillary motions are required for control purposes, and of these some are merely mechanical devices connected with the safety and the continuity of weaving operations, but some are of considerable interest to the designer as their influence can alter the cloth appearance to no lesser degree than the shedding. These are:

(1) Warp pay-off—This determines the rate at which the warp is fed forward and the tension of the warp yarn. The tension is largely responsible for the configuration of warp ends in the cloth and two fabrics of identical design but woven with varying degrees of tension may appear different and may possess different characteristics.
(2) The cloth take-up—this determines the speed of cloth withdrawal and, therefore, the density of spacing of the weft picks in the cloth.
(3) The weft colour selector—this device is only built into machines on which it is intended to weave fabrics with transverse, or 'cross-over', stripes consisting of different colours or kinds of weft. Modern machines may contain devices capable of introducing into the cloth up to eight different weft threads.

The shedding, during which the warp threads are manipulated to produce a given interlacing, is achieved by threading each end through an eye of a heald wire, and raising or lowering this wire dependent on whether it is required to lift the end above the weft, or to keep it below the weft during picking. In tappet and dobby shedding systems heald wires are not operated singly, but are attached to heald frames, or heald shafts, and each wire on a given shaft conforms to the movement of that shaft, rising or falling together with it (*Figure 1.2*). The tappet, or cam, system is used to control the shedding where, due to simplicity of interlacing, only few heald shafts, or healds, are required. Dobby shedding systems offer the designer a considerably greater scope for producing figured effects and are often capable of controlling up to 24 healds. In addition the dobby selection device offers the ease of pattern change, whereas the tappet assembly is quite rigid. Also, tappet shedding imposes a limit as to the length of the design whilst no such limits exist in the dobby system. For these reasons the tappet principle of shedding is employed mainly for high speed production of standard cloths where changes of structure are infrequent, and where its simplicity offers some advantages.

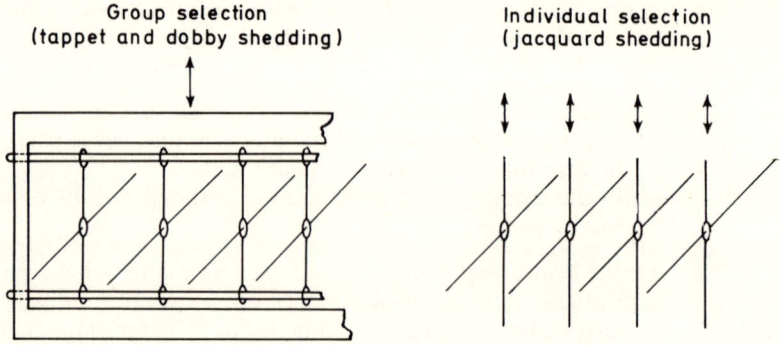

Figure 1.2

The dobby is used in the production of simple, figured fabrics, but ornate figured styles require a jacquard system of shedding in which heald wires can be manipulated individually be means of cords and not collectively through the agency of the heald frames (*Figure 1.2*).

METHODS OF FABRIC REPRESENTATION

The unit of woven fabric is the point of intersection of a warp end and a weft pick, the interlacing being of two possible kinds as shown in *Figure 1.3*. In either case the interlacing is achieved by the manipulation of the ends, these being raised to obtain the interlacing (a), or lowered to produce the interlacing (b). A number of these interlacings combined together in both

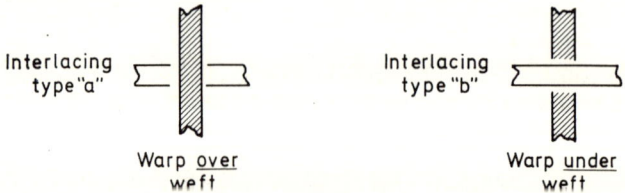

Figure 1.3

directions produces a unit of design, or one repeat of the weave. The simplest weave which can constitute a cloth requires two ends and two picks as a repeat of design, is known as the plain weave, and can be pictured as at A (*Figure 1.4*). In this diagram it will be seen that on pick 1 the first end is raised to produce the interlacing (a), whilst the second end is lowered to give the interlacing (b).

As the diagram represents a complete unit of design it must be understood that successive neighbouring units will be identical with the first as shown at B, *Figure 1.4*. In this diagram four repeats of the construction are shown but normally one unit is quite sufficient to depict the entire interlacing pattern of a cloth and, therefore, looking at the order of interlacing as shown at A, it will be taken that on pick one every odd end in the warp will be raised and every even one lowered, whilst on pick two the reverse takes place. Interlacing diagrams as shown in *Figure 1.4* are not normally employed in designing woven fabrics as they are too laborious to prepare especially when large designs are considered. They are occasionally used to depict cloths in which threads are displaced from the straight path, but in most cases design paper (point paper, squared paper) is employed, and offers an easy way of representing the interlacings in a quick and simple manner. The standard textile design

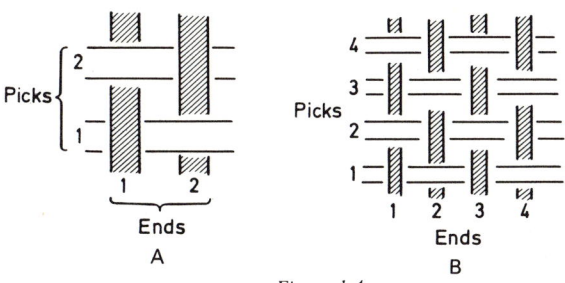

Figure 1.4

paper is ruled in groups of 8 × 8, these being separated by thicker bar lines as shown at A, in *Figure 1.5*.

Each vertical space is taken to represent a warp end and each horizontal space a weft pick, each square, therefore, indicates an intersection point of an end and a pick. At B in *Figure 1.5* square 'x' indicates the point of crossing of the second end with the second pick, whilst square 'y' is the point at which

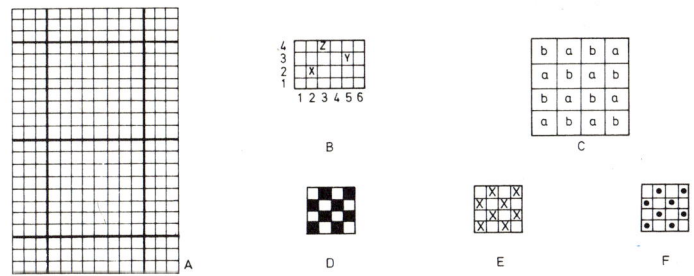

Figure 1.5

the fifth end crosses the third pick, and square 'z' shows where the third end intersects the fourth pick. Developing the idea of the two different types of interlacing, the diagram shown at B in *Figure 1.4* could be represented on design paper as at C, in *Figure 1.5*, which shows quite clearly the alternate occurrence of interlacings 'a' and 'b' in both directions. Even this method, though quicker than an interlacing diagram, suffers from the lack of definition so the normal convention, which satisfies the conditions of clarity and rapid execution, is to use *marks* to denote the interlacing 'a' (warp over weft), and *blanks* to denote the interlacing 'b' (warp under weft) as shown at D, E and F in *Figure 1.5*. As can be observed, any kind of mark is satisfactory and it will be seen later that several types of marks may be used in one design simultaneously to indicate that, perhaps, some ends differently marked vary in their thickness, colour, or function from the others. Certain designs may be more easily followed when the convention is reversed and in such cases it is easy to adopt the opposite procedure, i.e. use marks to denote 'warp under weft' and blanks to indicate 'warp over weft', but since this is contrary to the normally accepted convention it is advisable to indicate clearly that the reversal of the convention has taken place. Whichever system of marking is used it must be remembered that the point paper is not merely a general representation of the design but is a specific plan of the order of the interlacing of threads, and that each square is the point of intersection of a warp end and a weft pick. To interlace, the threads must cross one another and, therefore, in each full repeat of the weave every vertical space and every horizontal space must have at least one mark and at least one blank otherwise the threads do not interlace but merely form loose floats which do not become woven into the cloth. One such unacceptable design is illustrated at A, in *Figure 1.6*, where ends 1 and 5 are clearly not interlacing with the weft but simply lying on top of it, and pick three lies below all the warp ends without any interweaving.

Although the design on point paper conveys clearly the plan of interlacings in the repeat of a weave it cannot be used to indicate also the configuration of the threads in the cloth and in cases in which this is important the design may be supplemented by the fabric sections. In fact, many compound structures cannot be properly understood without the use of sectional diagrams. The use of such diagrams and their relationship with the design paper is shown in *Figure 1.6*. Design B represents an area of plain weave, whilst C shows a section of the cloth cut through the warp at pick one, and

 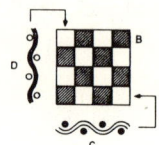 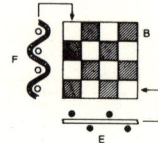

Figure 1.6

D, a section through the weft at end one in a fabric in which both the ends and the picks are equally displaced. The sections E and F are cut respectively at the same points with regard to the design as C and D, but although identical weave is used in each instance, different thread configuration is obtained, with the weft in this case lying quite straight and causing the warp to bend markedly. Of course, the different arrangement does not occur either spontaneously or at random but is dependent upon well defined conditions which are fully explained in the following chapters.

In the foregoing examples only the standard 8 × 8 design paper has been illustrated but in some cases, especially in connection with large figured designs, other orders of ruling are used and these are illustrated in *Figure 11.15*, and the reasons for their use are explained in Chapter 11.

WEAVE REPEAT UNIT

Any weave repeats on a definite number of ends and picks (or of vertical and horizontal spaces): generally only one repeat need be indicated on design paper. The number of ends and picks in a repeat may be equal, or unequal, but in every case the complete repeat must be in rectangular form on account of the threads interlacing at right angles. For instance, a weave cannot take the form shown at A in *Figure 1.7*; if, as shown in the example, any part of the complete repeat extends over 10 ends and 10 picks, every other portion must extend over 10 ends and 10 picks.

It is necessary for the marks and blanks to join correctly at the sides, and at the top and bottom of a design, in order that when the pattern is repeated in the loom from side to side and from end to end of the cloth an unbroken

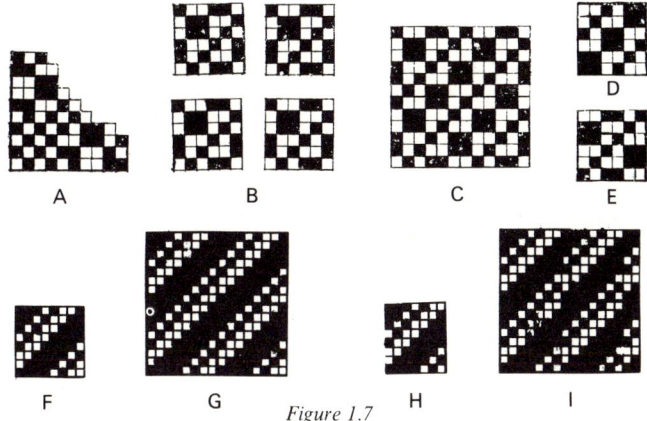

Figure 1.7

weave will result. The joining of the repeats of a weave is illustrated at B and C in *Figure 1.7*, in which B shows four complete repeats of a weave on 6 ends and 6 picks detached from each other. In each repeat the last end and pick respectively join correctly with the first end and pick, so that when the repeats are put together, as shown at C, a continuous and unbroken weave is formed. A warp 100 cm wide, with 30 ends per cm, will contain $100 \times 30 = 3000$ ends, which will give $3000 \div 6 = 500$ repeats of the weave B across the width of the cloth.

D and E in *Figure 1.7* show that a weave may appear different on account of being commenced in a different position, if only one repeat is shown, but such an alteration does not cause any change in the woven cloth, as either D or E will produce exactly the same effect as C.

Commencing a weave at a different position, as stated above, does not in any way affect the appearance of the cloth but whatever the starting point a full repeat must be invariably given. An incomplete repeat, if used as the basis for a design, results immediately in a faulty construction and this is clearly illustrated at H and I in *Figure 1.7*. F and G represent respectively the correct, full repeat and the effect of combining of several repeats to form a faultless cloth. H shows an incomplete repeat of the same weave and whilst the fault is not very obvious in the single unit it becomes immediately apparent when several of these faulty units are joined together as at I.

CONSTRUCTION OF DRAFTS AND LIFTING PLANS

A draft indicates the number of healds used to produce a given design and the order in which the warp ends are threaded through the mail eyes of the healds. (Note—the terms shafts, leaves, staves, cambs and heddles are synonymous with the term healds.)

Lifting plan (weaving or pegging plan) defines the selection of healds to be raised or lowered on each successive insertion of the pick of weft.

The weave or design depends entirely, as far as the interlacing of threads is concerned, upon the order of drafting in the healds combined with the order of lifting or lowering of the healds. Skill in drafting is particularly useful in designing for the tappet and the dobby shedding systems as these limit the number of different orders of interlacing to eight healds and to twenty-four healds respectively and in order to increase the width of the repeat beyond the eight or the twenty-four ends, the designer must depend upon skilful use of drafting. The length of the design is normally limited to eight picks in tappet shedding while this limitation does not exist in dobby shedding where, theoretically, designs of any length can be produced.

Methods of indicating drafts and lifting plans

Various methods of indicating drafts may be employed, as for instance—
(*a*) By ruling lines, as shown in *Figure 1.8* at A, B, and C, in which the horizontal lines represent the healds, and the vertical lines the warp threads, while the marks placed where the lines intersect indicate the healds upon which

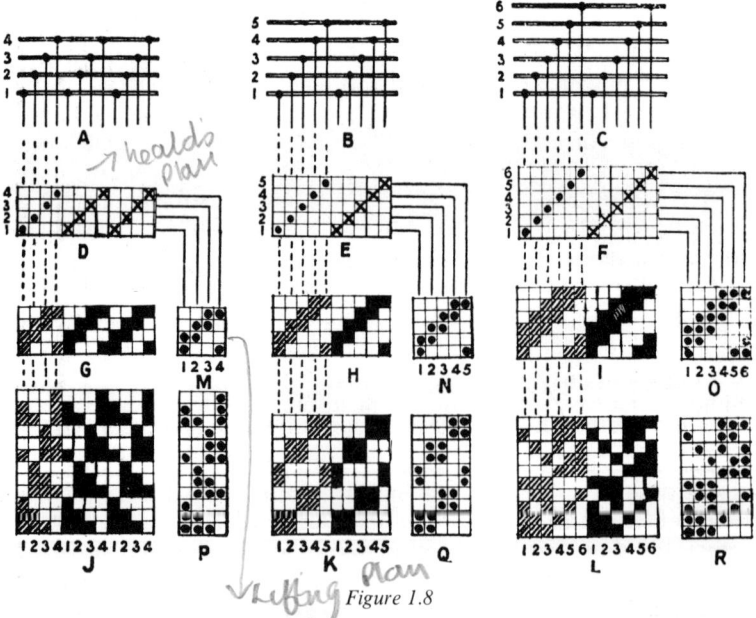

Figure 1.8

the respective threads are drawn. (*b*) By the use of design paper, as shown at D, E, and F in *Figure 1.8*, in which the horizontal spaces are taken to represent the healds, and the vertical spaces the warp threads. Marks are inserted upon the small squares to indicate the healds upon which the respective threads are drawn. This method is usually the most convenient. (*c*) By numbering, as shown by the numbers below the designs given at J, K, and L in *Figure 1.8*, which refer to the number of the healds (the front heald is number one). In this case the threads are successively drawn on the healds in the order indicated by the numbers.

The principle in drafting a pattern is that *ends which work in different orders require separate healds* and it should be obvious that as the heald is an entity all ends drawn through the eyes of a given heald must work alike. The converse of the above rule is not entirely applicable, and although it may be said that all ends which work alike *may* be placed on the same heald, it will be found later that occasionally it is more convenient to draw ends operating in identical fashion through different healds. Nevertheless, in order that the issue is not confused all examples shown in *Figure 1.8* employ the simple method of: separate healds for ends working differently, same healds for ends working alike. All the examples in *Figure 1.8* show the use of the most common and the simplest system of drafting known as *straight* drafting upon four, five, and six healds. In the straight draft, using a weave repeating upon four ends, successive ends of the repeat are drawn upon successive healds until the end of the repeat is reached whereupon the end number five which is the first end of the second repeat and, therefore, identical in its working with the first end of the first repeat, is drawn upon the first heald, and so on until the sequence is completed again (A and D in *Figure 1.8*). In this system of drafting the number of ends in the design repeat cannot exceed the number of healds employed, but it may be a factor of the number of healds. Thus, any weave, repeating upon two ends, or upon four ends, as shown at G and J in *Figure 1.8*, is suitable for the draft A; any weave on five ends such as H and K is suitable for the draft B, while weaves repeating on two, or three, or on six ends, as shown at I and L, can be woven on the draft C. For the purpose of illustration, in each example more than one repeat of the design and the draft are given (different marks are shown in the first repeat), but in practice it is necessary to show only one repeat. The draft is repeated in the healds across the full width of the warp (with the exception in some cases of the selvages), and if there are 2400 threads in the warp the draft A will be repeated 600 times, the draft B 480 times, and the draft C 400 times. It will be noted from the various examples given in *Figure 1.8* that the number of picks in a repeat is of no consequence as far as the draft is concerned, but will have to be considered carefully in connection with the lifting plan.

The examples M, N, O, P, Q, and R in *Figure 1.8* are the respective lifting plans for the designs alongside which they are placed; they indicate the order in which the healds are raised and depressed in forming the design. M, N, and O form designs suitable for tappet shedding on account of the low number of picks per repeat and in this instance the lifting plan is indicative of the shape and arrangement of shedding tappets or cams. Where a dobby is used, as it must be in cases of P, Q, and R due to the length of the repeat, the lifting plan indicates the order of pegging, or cutting the control lattice of the selection mechanism. The numbered vertical spaces of the lifting plans correspond with the numbers at the side of the drafts; the vertical space numbered 1 in the lifting plans indicates how the first heald is operated; that numbered 2, the second heald; that numbered 3, the third heald; and so on. The plans further show which healds are raised and depressed on succeeding picks; thus, M indicates that on the first pick the healds 1 and 4 of the draft D are raised, and the healds 2 and 3 depressed; on the second pick, the healds 1 and 2 are raised, and the healds 3 and 4 depressed; on the third pick numbers 2 and 3 are raised, and 1 and 4 depressed; and on the fourth pick numbers 3 and 4 are raised, and 1 and 2 depressed. In the same manner P indicates that on the first pick the healds 1, 2, and 3 are raised; on the second pick, the healds 1 and 2; on the third pick, the heald 1 and so on.

In each example given in *Figure 1.8* the lifting plan is exactly the same as the corresponding design, a feature which only occurs in straight drafts. The threads of a warp may be drawn straight from right to left instead of from left to right (this is not commonly done), which, unless allowed for in the lifting plan, will cause the direction of the design to be reversed.

Relations between design, draft, and lifting plan

The three factors upon which the construction of any woven fabric depends —the design, the draft, and the lifting plan—are very closely dependent on one another as already indicated. A thorough knowledge of this inter-dependence is very valuable to a designer upon whose skill severe mechanical limitations of the weaving loom may be imposed. In many cases it is only his intimate acquaintance with the drafting systems and the possibilities of manipulating the lifting orders which enables him to introduce variety into apparently rigid mechanical systems of operation. In normal practice the designer's brief is to produce a range of designs for looms with a known pattern scope. This usually also involves the draft and the lifting plan construction. A similar procedure is adopted when the designer is asked to reproduce a specific design from a sample. The weave in the sample is analysed and a suitable draft and lifting plan devised. Occasionally a more difficult task is encountered which is to construct designs and the correspond-ing drafts to suit a given lifting plan. This may occur in tappet shedding where the lifting order is fixed by the cam shape and all else must be subordinated to it, but an extension of the pattern range is desired. Yet another different exigency arises when the designer, engaged in the production of experimental pattern ranges, works with a dobby loom and wishes to design a series of patterns and the corresponding lifting plans to suit the existing draft in a warp that is in the loom. The following examples show the various procedures adopted in the different circumstances and emphasise the close inter-dependence of the three factors.

Construction of drafts and lifting plans from given designs

The construction of the draft and lifting plan for a given design is illustrated in stages in *Figure 1.9*. Following the rule stated earlier: The threads in a design, which are raised and depressed simultaneously—that is, are indicated the same in the design—may be drawn on the same heald; the threads that are different from each other must be drawn on different healds. As many healds are, therefore, required as there are threads working differently from each other in the repeat of a design; thus a 4-thread twill requires four healds, a 5-thread twill five healds, etc. In practice it is sometimes found advantageous to use more healds than the least possible number.

In constructing the draft for design A in *Figure 1.9* the first end is indicated on the first heald, then all the ends in the design, which work the same as the first end, are also indicated on the first heald, as shown at B. The working of the first heald is copied from the design A on to the first vertical space of the lifting plan, as shown at C. The second end in the design A works differently from the first end, and is, therefore, indicated on the second heald, and all the ends, which work like the second end, are indicated on the same heald, as shown at D; while the working of the second heald is copied from the design on to the second vertical space of the lifting plan, as indicated at E. The third end in the design A works differently from either the first or the second, and is, therefore, indicated on the third heald, and also all the corresponding ends, as shown at F; then the working of the third heald is indicated on the third vertical space of the lifting plan, as shown at G.

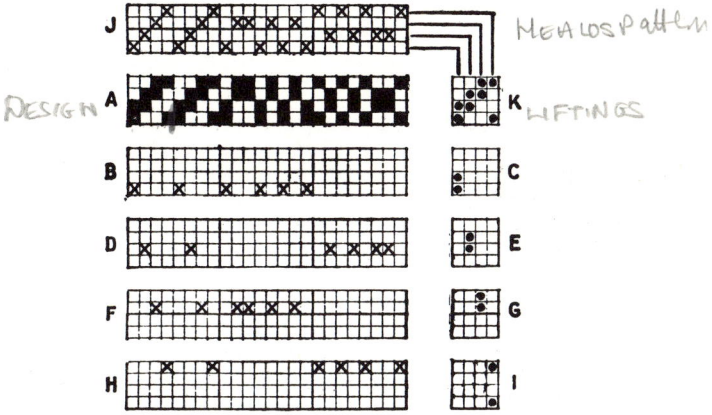

Figure 1.9

In the same manner the fourth end of the design, which works differently from either the first, second, or third, is indicated on the fourth heald, and also all the corresponding ends, as shown at H (this completes all the ends in the repeat), while the order of working is indicated on the fourth vertical space of the lifting plan, as shown at I. B, D, F, and H are shown combined at J, and C, E, G, and I at K, which thus respectively show the complete draft and lifting plan for the design A.

The foregoing system of constructing a draft and lifting plan fully illustrates the principles involved, but the usual method of procedure is that represented in stages at A to O in *Figure 1.10*, in which A shows the design. The draft is made first, the ends of the design being taken in succession, and commencing with the first end it is indicated on the first heald, as shown at B. (It does not follow, however, that the first end of a design should in all cases be indicated on the first heald, this being shown at G in *Figure 4.12*.) The second end is different from the first, hence it is indicated on the second heald, as shown at C in *Figure 1.10*; the third end is like the first, and is, therefore, indicated on the same heald as the first end, as shown at D; the fourth end is like the second, and is indicated on the same heald as the second end, as shown at E; the fifth end is like the first and third ends, and is indicated on the same heald, as shown at F; the sixth end is different from any of the preceding and is, therefore, indicated on the next heald (the third), as shown at G; the seventh end is different again, hence it is indicated on the fourth heald, as shown at H; the eighth end is like the sixth, and is indicated on the same heald, as shown at I; the ninth end is like the seventh, and is, therefore, indicated on the fourth heald, as shown at J; while the tenth end is like the sixth and eighth, and is indicated on the third heald, as shown at K.

In constructing the lifting plan, the healds are taken in succession from front to back, and the order of working of the corresponding ends is copied from the design on to successive vertical spaces from left to right. Thus, the working of the ends, drawn on the first heald, is indicated on the first vertical space of the lifting plan, as shown at L in *Figure 1.10*; of the ends, drawn on the second heald, on the second vertical space, as shown at M; while in the same manner the working of the third heald is indicated on the third vertical space, as shown at N, and of the fourth heald on the fourth vertical space, as represented at O. The lifting plan is complete on as many vertical spaces as there are healds in the draft, and on as many horizontal spaces as there are picks in the design. The threads are conveniently followed if the draft is placed directly above or below, and the pegging-plan alongside the design.

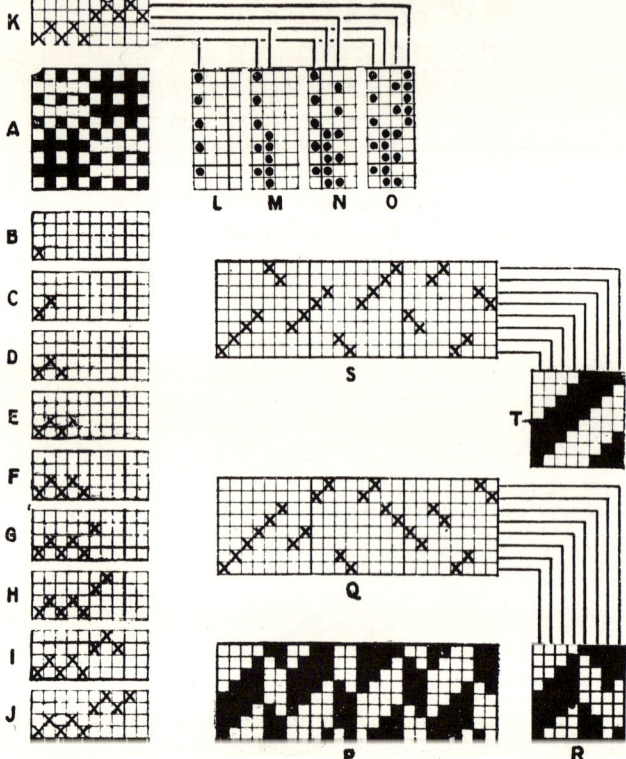

Figure 1.10

In drafting the ends of a design from the first to the last in successive order, it is not always advisable to indicate those which are different from each other in the same order on the healds as they are found in the design. A draft should be arranged in an order which can be easily followed and remembered by the drawer-in and weaver, and to accomplish this, in many cases, it is necessary for the order of drafting to correspond with the basis upon which the design is constructed. For example, P in *Figure 1.10* shows a design in which the threads are reversed in sections of four and two; if the threads which work differently from each other are indicated on the healds successively in the order in which they are found in the design, the draft will be as shown at Q, which is too irregular to be readily remembered. By indicating the draft to correspond with the arrangement of the design, as shown at S, however, the order of drawing in is simply four to right and two to left, with a break of four healds at each change. In the latter method the lifting plan also is more regular, as will be seen by comparing the plans R and T, which respectively correspond with the drafts Q and S. Certain designs can be drafted in different ways, but a change in the order of drafting necessitates a corresponding change in the lifting plan.

The healds for designs in which different weaves and different yarns are combined, may usually be divided into two or more distinct sections, which are put together to form the complete set of healds. The different sections should be placed in such positions relative to each other as will most contribute to successful weaving. There is no fixed rule that can be practised, but, generally, the healds should be placed nearest the front, which (*a*) carry the weakest yarn, (*b*) carry the threads which are subjected to the most strain (are most frequently interlaced), and (*c*) are the most crowded with the threads.

Construction of drafts from given designs and lifting plans

This process is illustrated in stages in *Figure 1.11*, in which K shows the design, and L the lifting plan. The first vertical space of L indicates that the first heald is raised on the picks 1 and 2, therefore all the threads of the design K, which are raised on the picks 1 and 2, are drawn on the first heald, as shown at M. The second vertical space of L shows that the second heald

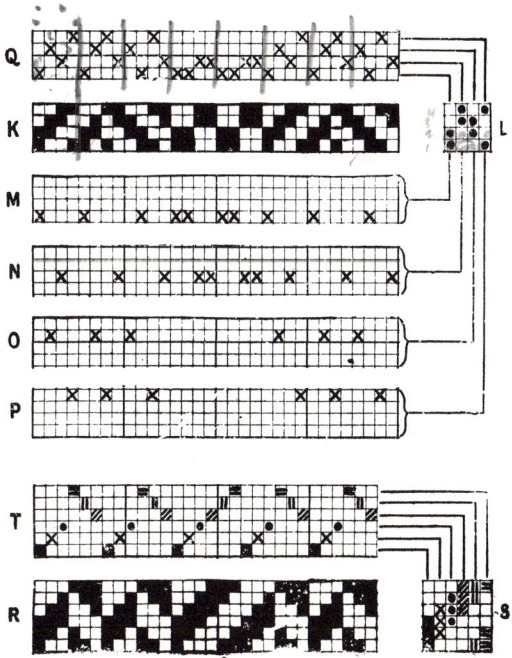

Figure 1.11

is raised on the picks 3 and 4, therefore all the threads in the design K that lift on the corresponding picks are drawn on the second heald, as shown at N. In the same manner, all the threads which are raised on the picks 2 and 3 to correspond with the third vertical space of L, are drawn on the third heald, as shown at O, and those that are raised on the picks 1 and 4, to correspond with the fourth vertical space of L, are drawn on the fourth heald, as indicated at P. Q shows the marks of M, N, O, and P combined, and thus indicates the draft, which will produce the design K if the lifting plan L is employed. The design K in *Figure 1.11* is similar to the design G in *Figure 1.12*, but the lifting plan L is different from the plan B, therefore in one case the draft Q is required in producing the design, and in the other case the draft A.

In further illustration, a design is given at R in *Figure 1.11* and a lifting plan at S, for which the draft indicated at T is required; the different marks will enable the successive stages in the construction of the draft to be followed.

Construction of designs from given drafts and lifting plans

The method of constructing the design from a given draft and lifting plan is illustrated in stages in *Figure 1.12*, in which A shows the draft and B the lifting plan. The vertical spaces in B, in the order of 1, 2, 3, and 4 respectively, indicate how the healds 1, 2, 3, and 4 are operated, and the marks of B indicate healds raised. Thus, the first vertical space of B shows that the first heald is raised on the picks 1 and 2, therefore all the threads that are drawn on the first heald will be correspondingly raised, as shown at C in *Figure 1.12*.

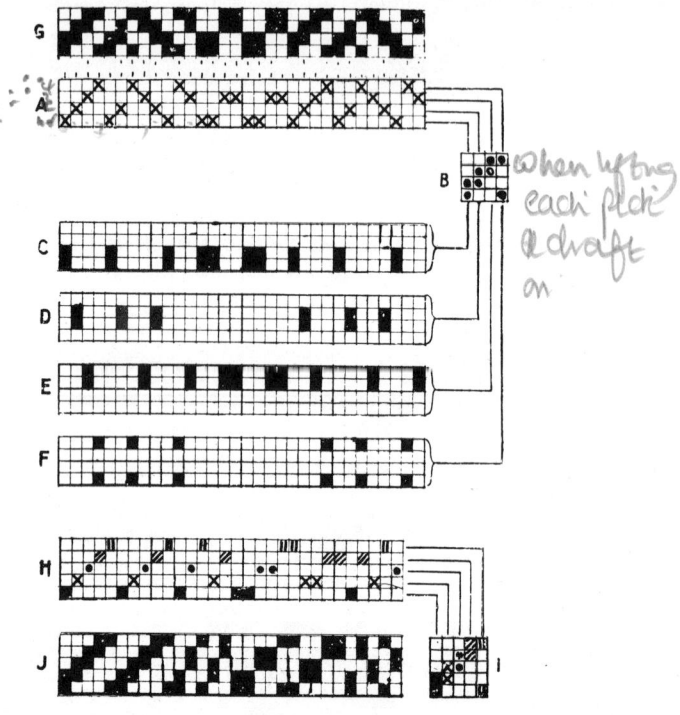

Figure 1.12

The second vertical space of B shows that the second heald is raised on the picks 2 and 3, all the threads drawn upon the second heald being, therefore, lifted, as shown at D. In the same manner the third heald is raised on the picks 3 and 4, and lifts the threads drawn upon it, as shown at E, while the fourth heald is raised on the picks 1 and 4, and produces the lifts indicated at F. The marks given in C, D, E, and F are shown combined at G, which thus indicates the design produced by the draft A and the lifting plan B.

As a further illustration a 5-heald draft is given at H, and the lifting plan at I, which produce the design shown at J; the ends upon each heald, and the corresponding order of working are represented by a different mark in order that the building up of the design J may be conveniently followed.

Systems of drafting

In addition to the straight drafts and the various mixed drafts which were illustrated in the preceding sections there exist several other well defined orders of drafting, such as: skip, point, sateen, herring-bone, reversed,

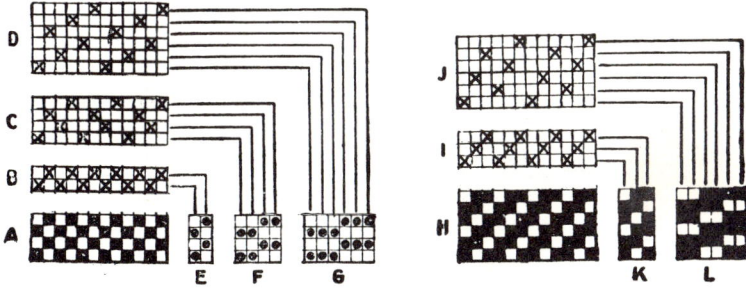

Figure 1.13

transposed, curved, combined, etc. Of these, the first three mentioned are most important and the remainder, though occurring reasonably often are usually formed as a natural outcome of following the design or the lifting plan for which they are arranged similar to the various mixed drafts shown above.

Skip drafts: this system is particularly useful in weaving very densely set fabrics where normally a small number of healds is required. In order that the mails will not be too crowded on the shafts and to reduce friction and rubbing between the ends it is customary to use more healds than the minimum necessary for the weave. For example, the plain weave indicated at A in *Figure 1.13*, may be drawn on two healds, as shown at B, if the cloth is coarse; or on four healds, as shown at C, if the cloth is of medium fineness; or on six healds, as indicated at D, if the cloth is very fine. Assuming in each case that there are 10 mails per cm on each shaft, draft B will give 20 ends per cm; draft C, 40 ends per cm; and draft D, 60 ends per cm. In tappet shedding, with the draft C the first and second healds are joined together, and the third and fourth together; and with the draft D the first, second, and third together, and the fourth, fifth, and sixth together. The operation of two plain tappets then lifts the odd threads on one pick, and the even threads on the next pick. In dobby shedding, the lifting plans for the drafts B, C, and D are as shown at E, F, and G respectively.

The design given at H in *Figure 1.13*, may be drawn on three healds as shown at I, or on six healds, as shown at J. In the latter case the healds 1 and 2 are coupled together, and 3 and 4, and 5 and 6, if the usual three tappets are employed; but in dobby shedding the lifting plans for the respective drafts are as shown at K and L.

Sateen drafts: the purpose of sateen draft is similar to skip draft in that each is used to reduce friction between adjacent warp ends and to alleviate the overcrowding of the mails. In sateen drafts, however, this result is not achieved by duplication of the healds but by staggering the end placing. The principle is illustrated in *Figure 1.14* in reference to a sateen draft on five healds, and it will be found useful to compare these examples with those shown in connection with the straight draft on five healds given in *Figure 1.8*.

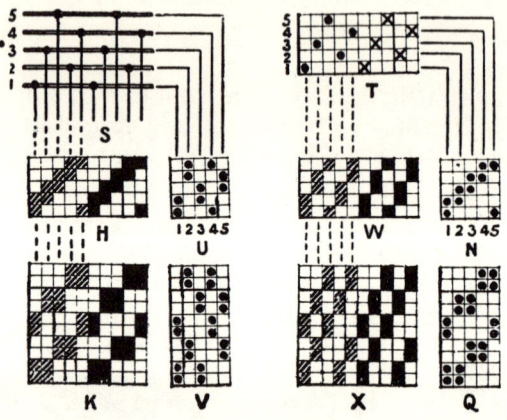

Figure 1.14

The examples which are alike in the two figures are lettered the same. As shown at S and T in *Figure 1.14*, the threads in the order of 1, 2, 3, 4, 5, are drawn on the healds in the order of 1, 3, 5, 2, 4, therefore the threads are not lifted in the same order as the healds are raised. Thus, in order to produce the design H, the lifting plan U is required, and to produce the design K, the lifting plan V. In the same manner the lifting plan N produces the design W, and the lifting plan Q, the design X. Further, the plan N indicates that on the first pick the healds 1 and 5 are raised, which lift the first and third ends in each repeat of the design W; on the second pick the healds 1 and 2 are raised, and lift the first and fourth ends; on the third pick the healds 2 and 3 lift the fourth and second ends, and so on, the design W thus resulting from the combination of the draft T and the lifting plan N. A draft is complete on the same number of ends, and a lifting plan on the same number of picks, as the design.

Point drafts: point drafts are used for weaves which are symmetrical about the centre, and they are frequently employed to produce waved or diamond effects. The main advantage of this system is that it allows the production of quite large effects economically which if attempted on the straight drafts would require almost twice the number of healds. Examples B and E in *Figure 1.15* show the method used to construct these drafts and it will be seen that to achieve a well defined point in the design the ends are drawn in straight order starting with heald 1 and finishing with the last heald in the number employed, whereupon the order of drawing-in of the consecutive ends is reversed. The first and the last healds carry only one end each, whilst all the healds in the middle carry two ends each per repeat of the draft. As a result, using this system of drafting the number of ends per repeat of the design is: 2 × (No. of healds) less 2. This is illustrated at A, where the waved design constructed on five healds repeats upon eight ends,

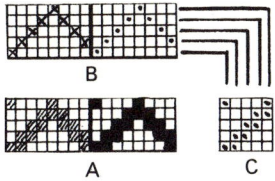

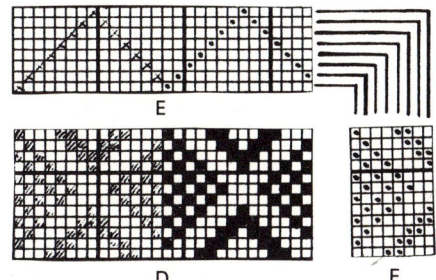

Figure 1.15

and at D, where the diamond effect using eight healds repeats upon fourteen ends. Further extension of design size is possible with special adaptations of the point draft and several examples of this are given in chapters devoted to waved twills and diamonds (*Figures 3.7* and *4.5*).

HEALD CALCULATIONS

There are two principal types of healds in use: the knitted healds in which the mails are fixed according to a definite pitch or density, and the slider wire healds in which the mails are free to move in either direction. In each group several sub-types could be enumerated, but their existence does not in any way prejudice the main argument. The knitted healds are cheaper but their useful life is shorter and they suffer from the rigidity of pitch, also, they have to be manufactured for a specific sett and a specific draft. As a result, they are nowadays only employed in certain special fields and the slider wire healds have become generally accepted in all branches of weaving where their adaptability and long lasting qualities are capable of offsetting the higher initial cost.

Whatever the type of healds used in constructing tappet and dobby designs, the draft should be considered carefully in order to avoid needlessly complicating the healds. A good design, however, should not be sacrificed in order to simplify the arrangement of the healds. An ideal draft, so far as regards the healds, is obtained when (*a*) an equal number of ends is drawn on each heald, and (*b*) the mails on each heald are evenly distributed across the width. The first point is illustrated by the examples given in *Figure 1.16*, in which two rather similar designs are given at A and C, each of which repeats on 42 ends, while the respective drafts are indicated at B and D. The design is constructed in such a manner that in the repeat the same number of ends—vis., 7—are drawn on each heald, as indicated in the draft B, hence all the healds are alike. Assuming that there are 42 ends per cm in the reed, each heald will have (42 ends ÷ 6 healds) = 7 mails per cm, and if the healds are 80 cm wide, each will contain (80 × 7) = 560 mails. In the design C,

however, the conditions are different, as will be seen from an examination
of the draft D, in which in the repeat of 42 ends, 8 ends are indicated on each
of the healds 1, 3, 4, and 6, as compared with 5 ends on healds 2 and 5.
Assuming, again, that there are 42 ends per cm in the reed, each of the healds
1, 3, 4, and 6 will require $(42 \times \frac{8}{42}) = 8$ mails per cm, while each of the
healds 2 and 5 will require $(42 \times \frac{5}{42}) = 5$ mails per cm. If the healds are
80 cm wide, each of the shafts 1, 3, 4, and 6 will contain $(80 \times 8) = 640$ mails,
and healds 2 and 5 $(80 \times 5) = 400$ mails.

In reference to the second point, while the distribution of the ends on
each heald, in the drafts B and D in *Figure 1.16*, is not perfectly uniform, it
is near enough to allow each heald to be knitted at a uniform rate. This last
condition is, of course, not valid in slider wire healds where the mails
assume automatically the correct position in respect of the reed, once the
warp ends are tightened in the loom.

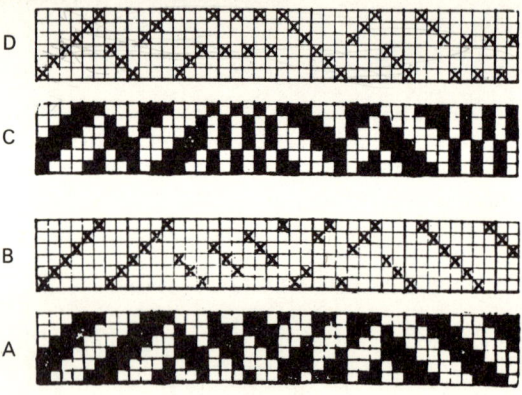

Figure 1.16

At one time efforts were frequently made to adapt healds knitted for high
sett fabrics to serve also lower sett fabrics if drafts were similar. The adaptation was achieved by casting-out in the healds, i.e. leaving empty certain
mail eyes at regular intervals. This procedure has been largely discontinued
as it makes drawing-in of ends very laborious, mitigates against the introduction of automatic in-drawing machinery, and increases labour costs
beyond the point at which a saving through the re-use of an existing set of
healds could be achieved. However, the techniques of casting out in the
healds are similar in principle to the casting out in jacquards, which process
is described in detail in Chapter 11.

DENTING

Warp ends during weaving are spaced out across the width of the warp
sheet according to a desired density by the wires of the reed. The most
frequent order of denting (drawing ends through a space—dent or split—
between two wires in the reed) is one, two, three, or four ends per dent
regularly across the width. There are some types of fabric, however, which
require an irregular order of denting to emphasise certain design features

and in such cases the order of arrangement of the ends in the reed becomes an essential part of the design and must be indicated carefully and in the correct relationship in respect of the weave and the draft. Circumstances which necessitate the use of the special denting orders are explained and illustrated, as they arise, in the subsequent chapters. At this point only the basic considerations involved are discussed and the various methods of indicating the denting are illustrated.

A in *Figure 1.17* shows a weave in which adjacent ends work alike, if these pairs of ends were drawn through the same split of the reed they would tend to roll over one another, in this way losing the clarity of the design. To

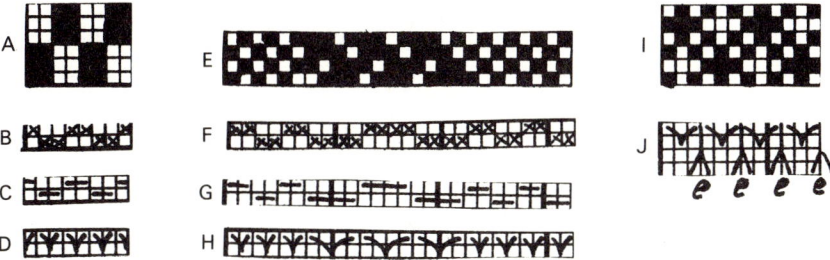

Figure 1.17

prevent this, the ends which work alike are drawn through different dents, and the reed wire which separates them ensures that no rolling takes place. B, C, and D show the different methods used to indicate the order of denting suitable for this weave. At E a crammed stripe design is illustrated in which the ends forming one weave stripe are less densely spaced (two per dent), than the ends forming a different weave stripe (four per dent). F, G, and H indicate how this order of denting could be marked. At I a different construction is shown and, here, the intention is to produce fine, dense lines with the ends crammed closely together separated by lines of open fabric. This is achieved by drawing three adjacent ends through the same split and leaving an empty dent in between each filled dent. J illustrates a convenient method of indicating this order with 'e' showing where a dent is left empty.

2

Construction of Elementary Weaves

PLAIN WEAVE

In plain weave the threads interlace in alternate order, and if the warp and weft threads are balanced—that is, are similar in thickness and number per unit space, the two series of threads bend about equally. This is illustrated at C in *Figure 2.1*, which shows how the first pick of A interlaces, and at D, which represents the interlacing of the last end of A. In this class of plain cloth each thread gives the maximum amount of support to the adjacent threads, and in proportion to the quantity of material employed, the texture is stronger and firmer than any other ordinary cloth. The weave is used for structures which range from very heavy and coarse canvas and blankets made of thick yarns to the lightest and finest cambrics and muslins made in extremely fine yarns. In the trade such terms as tabby, calico, alpaca, and taffeta are applied to plain cloth.

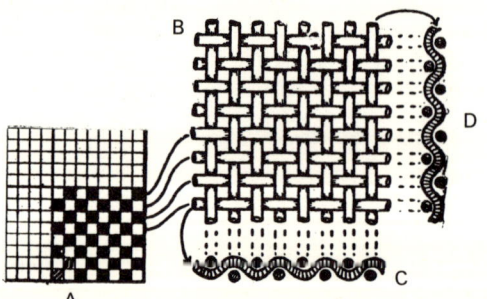

Figure 2.1

Plain weave produces the simplest form of interlacing, but it us used to a greater extent than any other weave, and diverse methods of ornamenting and of varying the structure are employed, as for example: Threads which are different in colour, material, thickness, or twist are combined; the number of threads per split of the reed, or of picks in a given space, is varied in succeeding portions of a cloth; the ends are brought from two or more warp beams which are differently tensioned, or are passed in sections over bars by which they are alternately slackened and tightened; while by means of a specially shaped reed which rises and falls the threads are caused to form zig-zag lines in the cloth. Two or more of the foregoing methods may be employed in the same cloth, and after weaving further variety may be produced by the processes of dyeing, printing, and finishing. A number of different kinds of plain cloth are illustrated in *Figure 2.3*. A represents a fine cotton muslin cloth; B shows a coarse jute hessian; in C threads of different colours are combined in check form; in D the threads in both warp and weft vary in colour and in thickness; E illustrates the use of fancy slub yarns; in F the pattern is formed by combining different orders of denting; G shows a seersucker stripe produced by using two warp beams which are differently tensioned; while H represents an all-over crepon effect that is due to the use of hard-twisted (crepon) weft which, when the cloth is scoured, shrinks irregularly.

Rib and cord effects produced in plain weave

Plain weave structures in which considerable difference exists between the warp and the weft threads as regards thickness and number per unit space result in rib and cord effects. (The term cord is frequently applied to ribs which run the length of the cloth in order to distinguish them from those that run horizontally.) In cloths where the number of ends per unit space largely

A B C

Figure 2.2

exceeds the number of picks, the latter tend to lie straight in the cloth with the former bending round them, and a warp rib structure results. If the opposite conditions prevail, the ends tend to lie straight with the picks bending round them, a weft rib structure being formed. In each case the prominence of the rib is accentuated if the straight threads are thicker than those which bend. These various constructional differences cannot be shown adequately by the design paper representation and their portrayal is best effected by the sectional diagrams as shown in *Figure 2.2*. At A one rib is shown in which all the warp threads are similar in thickness as also are the weft threads and the rib is formed due to greater number of ends than picks per unit space. In this type of fabric rib lines which are uniform in size appear on both sides of the cloth. A different form of rib structure is produced, however, if a thick and a fine thread alternately are employed in warp and weft, as shown at B. In forming a warp rib the thick ends always pass over

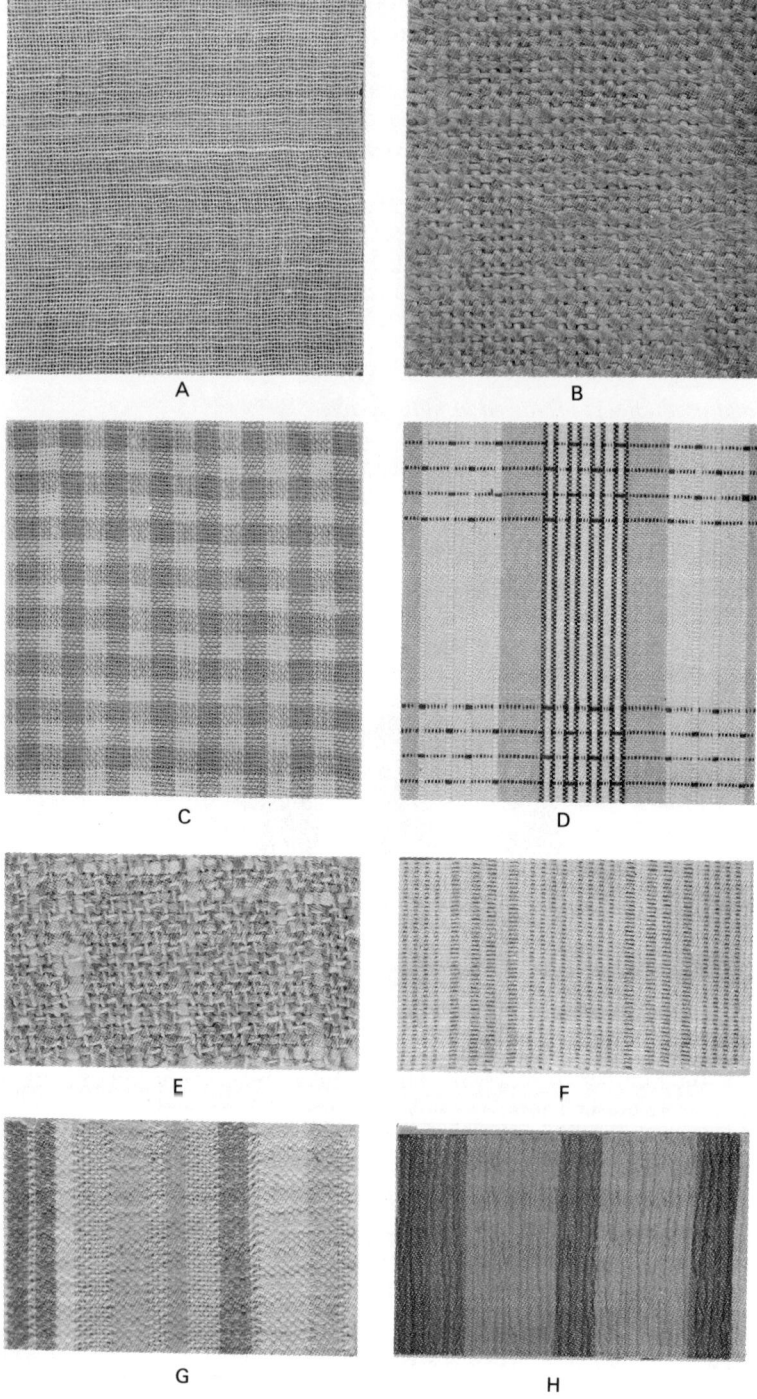

Figure 2.3

the thick picks, and under the fine picks; whereas in forming a weft rib, the thick picks always pass over the thick ends and under the fine ends. In the warp ribs there should be more ends per unit space than picks, and in the weft ribs more picks than ends. In this case, the rib lines, which are separated from each other by fine lines, show prominently on one side of the cloth only.

In another method of producing a warp rib structure in plain weave the odd ends are brought from one warp beam, and the even ends from another beam. One beam is much more heavily tensioned than the other, with the result that the heavily tensioned ends lie almost straight in the cloth and force the picks into two lines. The lightly tensioned ends are therefore compelled to bend round the picks in the manner illustrated at C, so that horizontal ridges and depressions are formed in the cloth. The rib formation is quite prominent if all the ends are equal in thickness, but it is still more pronounced if the lightly tensioned ends are thicker than the others.

SIMPLE OR REGULAR TWILL WEAVES

The twill order of interlacing causes diagonal lines to be formed in the cloth, as shown in the fabric represented in *Figure 2.4*. The weaves are employed for the purpose of ornamentation, and to enable a cloth of greater weight, closer setting, and better draping quality to be formed than can be produced in similar yarns in plain weave. Twilled effects can be made in various ways,

Figure 2.4

but in simple twills the points of intersection move one outward and one upward on succeeding picks. A twill cannot be made upon two threads, but upon any number that exceeds two; a simple twill is complete upon the same number of picks as ends. Twill lines are formed on both sides of the cloth, and the direction of the lines may be either to the right or to the left, but the direction on one side is opposite to that on the other side when the cloth is turned over. Warp and weft floats on one side of the cloth respectively coincide with weft and warp floats on the other side; thus, if warp float predominates on one side weft float will predominate in the same proportion on the other side.

Designation of twills

The order of interlacing of regular twills is the same for every thread in the repeat and, as stated above, the diagonal line is formed by advancing this order in steps of one in either direction. The fact that the interlacing order of all threads in the repeat is identical makes it possible to designate twills by describing the interlacing of the first thread, e.g.: -2 up, 2 down; 2- and -2; 2/2; or, more conveniently $\frac{2\cdot}{\cdot 2}$. This could be taken to indicate that on the first pick the first two ends are up, and the following two down; or, that the first end is raised for the first two picks and lowered for the following two. Either method could be equally well adopted to build up twills and both are shown in *Figure 2.5*, the first at A and B, and the second at C and D. Looking at several repeats of this weave shown side by side as at E it can be observed that it makes no difference to the appearance of the cloth whichever method is adopted in the construction.

The graphical method of designation described above has two further advantages. In regular twills it indicates at a glance the size of repeat, e.g. $\frac{2\cdot}{\cdot 2}$ twill gives a repeat of 4 ends × 4 picks, and $\frac{1\cdot 2\cdot}{\cdot 3\cdot 2}$ twill indicates a repeat of 8 ends × 8 picks. The rule to establish the size of repeat is to add all interlacings above the line (warp up) to the sum of interlacings below the line (warp down).

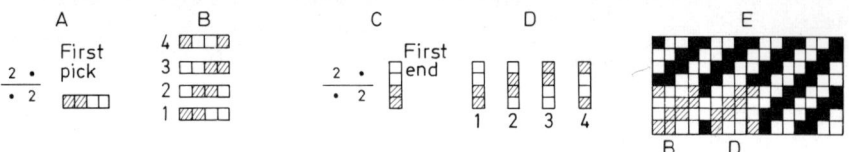

Figure 2.5

(warp down). The second advantage is that using this method it is possible to see immediately whether a twill has equal amounts of warp and weft showing on the face, e.g. $\frac{2\cdot}{\cdot 2}$; or, whether it is predominantly warp-faced, e.g. $\frac{3\cdot}{\cdot 1}$; or weft-faced, e.g. $\frac{1\cdot}{\cdot 3}$. Although it is correct to assume that a warp-faced twill when turned over becomes weft-faced, in practice, twills which are intended to show more warp on the face are constructed with a considerably greater number of ends per cm than picks per cm, and conversely, weft-faced twills are made with greater number of picks per cm than ends per cm. Therefore, even apart from the fact that most clothes are finished on the face side only, a mere reversal of the cloth will not automatically change the character of it as it will invariably appear improperly set on the reverse side.

Systematic construction of regular twills

The smallest number of threads on which it is possible to construct a twill is three and A, B, C and D in *Figure 2.6* illustrate all possible ways in which three-thread, or three-shaft, twills can be formed. Actually, only two interlacings are possible—the weft faced $\frac{1\cdot}{\cdot 2}$ (A and D) and the warp faced $\frac{2\cdot}{\cdot 1}$ (B and C), but as each of them can be used to make a twill running in either direction, four different effects can be produced. The terms *Cashmere, Jean, Jeanette,* and *Genoa* (q.v.) are applied to certain cloths made in the three-shaft twill weave.

On four threads three orders of interlacing can be made, viz., $\frac{1\cdot}{\cdot 3}$, $\frac{2\cdot}{\cdot 2}$, and $\frac{3\cdot}{\cdot 1}$, and as each of them may be inclined in either direction, six different effects can be formed. These are shown at E, F, G, H, I, and J in *Figure 2.6*. Next to plain weave, the $\frac{2}{2}$ twill is probably used more than any other weave, and is also known by the following trade terms: *serge*, *blanket*, *sheeting*, and *shalloon* (q.v.). The term 'drill' (q.v.) is frequently applied to the $\frac{3}{1}$ twill.

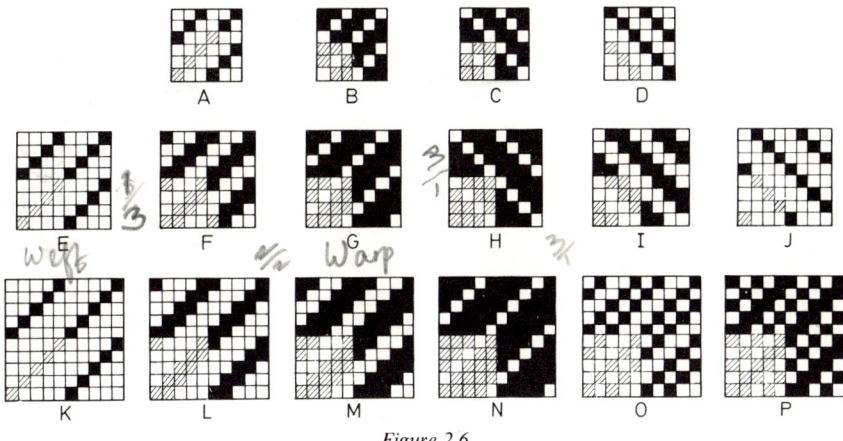

Figure 2.6

On five threads six twill weaves, running to the right, may be woven, as shown at K to P in *Figure 2.6*, while similar effects may be made twilling to the left. K and N are opposite to each other, and also L and M, and O and P; therefore, if one weave of a pair is formed on the face, the other weave will be formed on the reverse side, but twilling in the opposite direction, when the cloth is turned over.

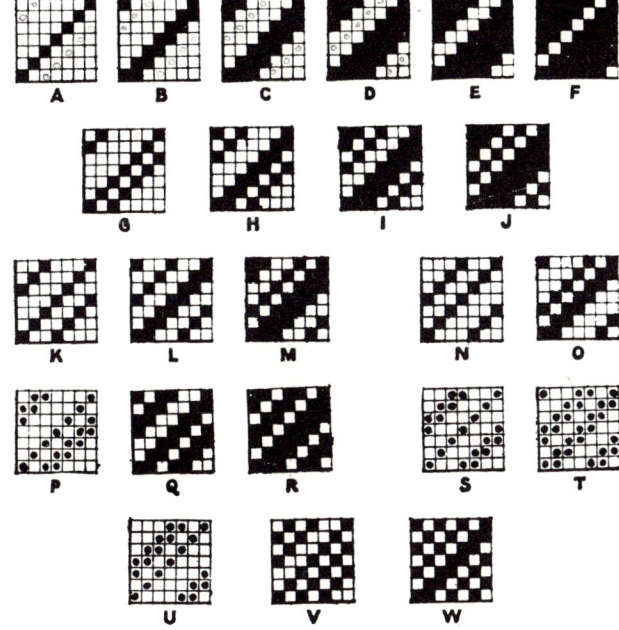

Figure 2.7

A systematic method of constructing simple twills is illustrated in *Figure 2.7*, which shows all the possible effects on seven threads. A single row of marks is inserted in the first weave A, then in each weave B to F a line of marks is successively added alongside. Commencing again with A, a single line of marks, separated by one space from the marks previously inserted, is added to A, B, C, and D, as shown at G, H, I, and J; then the single line is placed two spaces distant, as shown at K, L, and M; and afterwards three spaces apart, as indicated at N and O. A double line of marks is then added to A, B, and C with one space between, as shown respectively at P, Q, and R; then to A and B with two spaces between, as indicated at S and T; and afterwards to A with three spaces between, as shown at U. A commencement is again made with A, and two separate lines of marks are added, as shown at V and W.

The process may be carried still further in constructing twills on a larger number of threads, and by working systematically, as shown in the foregoing, it is possible to ensure that all the possible twills are obtained. It is necessary, however, to examine the weaves carefully, and weed out those that are duplicates of others. In *Figure 2.7*, for the purpose of illustration, duplicate weaves (which are indicated in dots) are included, and it will be found that H and U are alike, and so are O and P, L and S, and Q and T. The elimination of duplicate weaves still leaves 19 different twills and as each one of them could be made with the twill lines running in the opposite direction, a total of 38 effects could be achieved. This illustrates the considerable variety which it is possible to obtain even within a comparatively small size of the repeat. With further increases in the size of the repeat numerous new combinations arise and large twills based on 16, or 20 thread repeats offer almost infinite scope for experimentation. An examination of *Figure 2.7* will show that the various twills differ in the proportion of warp and weft visible on the face, and that they also differ with regard to the number of lines of the warp and the weft float which they contain. Designs A to F contain one warp and one weft float in the repeat and form two lines, whilst designs G to U form four lines, and designs V and W show six lines in the repeat.

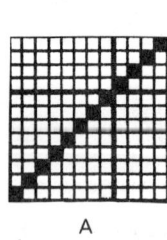 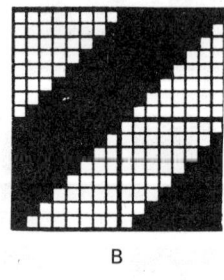 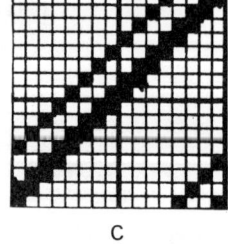

A   B   C

Figure 2.8

From the above examples it will be appreciated that the number of different interlacings which are possible increases with the increase in the size of the repeat. Not all of the constructions produced on a larger base are, however, suitable—many of the arrangements which are possible cannot be used in practice due to excessive length of float which results in a slack, poorly bound construction, unlikely to produce a serviceable fabric. Examples of such unsuitable arrangements are given at A, B, and C in *Figure 2.8*.

Large regular twills

Large twills are frequently also known as the *diagonals*, particularly those which show a prominent line, as in the example represented in *Figure 2.9*. In *Figure 2.10* a method of designing diagonals is illustrated, which can be employed in constructing twills upon any number of threads. It is first necessary to decide upon the number of threads in the repeat, and then to

Figure 2.9

consider the general prominence of the main line or lines of the twill, and whether warp or weft shall be brought chiefly to the surface. If the weft is superior to the warp, the weft float should predominate over the warp float, and vice versa, but if the warp and weft are similar in quality both may be floated equally. Frequently, however, a predominance of weft float is

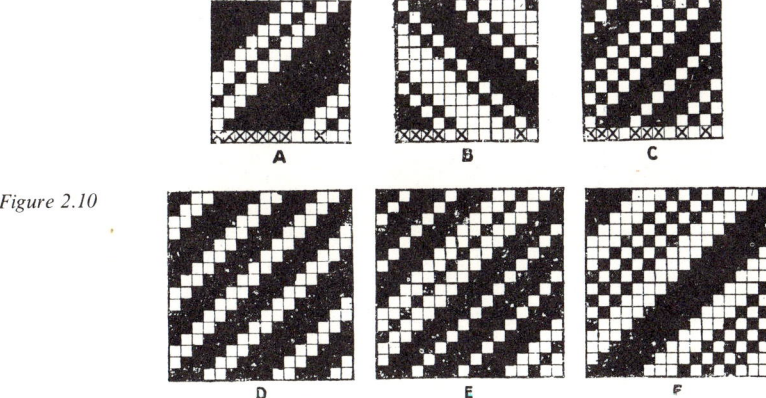

Figure 2.10

preferred, because as a rule, the weft is rather more lustrous than the warp on account of containing less twist. The next point to consider is the number of intersections in the repeat, which should be sufficient to give the cloth the proper firmness. The twill may then be arranged according to the pattern and structure required; and experiments can conveniently be made by indicating the marks in various ways on the first horizontal space of a number of plans, as shown by the crosses in the examples A, B, and C in *Figure 2.10*. Such arrangements as are considered satisfactory may then be carried out in full by copying the marks one square to the right on succeeding horizontal spaces, as shown at A and C, or one square to the left, as shown at B, according to the direction in which the twill is required to run. The marks are continued from one side to the other, and from the top to the bottom of the plan in such a manner that the twill lines will be unbroken in succeeding repeats; and when the design is completed the same number of marks will have been inserted upon each horizontal and each vertical space.

A and C in *Figure 2.10* represent warp-faced diagonals, whereas at B an even-sided construction is shown. As regards the number of intersections it may be considered advisable, in constructing a large twill, to obtain about the same degree of firmness as is produced by a smaller twill in the same cloth. Thus, A in *Figure 2.10* contains four intersections in twelve threads, and is, therefore, approximately equal in firmness to 3-and-3 twill, which contains two intersections in six threads. B contains six intersections in twelve threads, and is, therefore, similar in firmness to 2-and-2 twill, which contains two intersections in four threads, while C, in which there are eight intersections in twelve threads, corresponds in firmness to 1-and-2 twill, which has two intersections in three threads.

In constructing a large twill that contains a number of small lines in the repeat, it is necessary to avoid making the lines too much alike. The 16-thread twill, given at D in *Figure 2.10*, is defective in this respect, as it is very little different from a 5-thread twill which can be more economically woven. With a slight alteration, as shown at E, the weave appears distinctly as a 16-thread twill. F in *Figure 2.10*, which corresponds with the fabric represented in *Figure 2.9*, shows distinctly as a large twill, yet it is approximately equal in firmness to 2-and-2 twill.

Using the graphical method of designation the twills in *Figure 2.10* could be indicated as follows: A $\frac{7\cdot1\cdot}{\cdot2\cdot2}$; B $\frac{4\cdot1\cdot1\cdot}{\cdot1\cdot4\cdot1}$; C $\frac{3\cdot3\cdot1\cdot1\cdot}{\cdot1\cdot1\cdot1\cdot1}$; D $\frac{3\cdot4\cdot3\cdot}{\cdot2\cdot2\cdot2}$; E $\frac{3\cdot3\cdot3\cdot1\cdot}{\cdot1\cdot1\cdot2\cdot2}$; and F $\frac{5\cdot1\cdot1\cdot1\cdot}{\cdot3\cdot1\cdot1\cdot3}$.

Relative firmness of twill weaves

Where a weave changes from marks to blanks, and vice versa, the warp and weft threads correspondingly change from one side of the cloth to the other, or 'intersect' each other. Each thread must make at least two intersections in a complete repeat of a weave, one in passing from the face to the back, and another in passing from the back to the face; otherwise the thread will float continuously on one side of the cloth. The intersecting of the threads gives the cloth firmness, and (with certain exceptions) the more frequent the intersections are the firmer the cloth is. If a twill fabric is correctly built *on the square*—that is, with the warp and weft threads equal in thickness and in number per cm—each intersection causes the threads to be separated by about the thickness of a thread. Therefore, other things being equal, the more frequently the intersections occur the further apart should the threads be placed. This is illustrated in *Figure 2.11*, in which three 8-thread twill weaves are given at A, B, and C, while the interlacings of the first pick of the designs are represented at D, E, and F respectively. The dotted vertical lines are placed apart a distance equal to the diameter of a thread, and each intersection is taken to occupy a space equal to a diameter. (This is not strictly accurate, but is near enough for practical purposes.) Weave A repeats on eight threads, and each thread has two intersections, and thus occupies the space of ten diameters, as shown at D; the repeat of B contains eight threads and four intersections, and thus occupies the space of twelve diameters, as represented at E; while in the repeat of C there are eight threads and six intersections, which occupy the space of fourteen diameters, as indicated at F.

It will be readily understood that a cloth which is of suitable firmness when woven in the weave C, will be looser if woven in the weave B, and will be still more lacking in firmness if woven in the weave A. That is, assuming that the warp and weft threads are the same thickness in each case, B will require more threads per unit space than C, and A than B; the relative proportions being (approximately) A:B:C::14:12:10. On the other hand, assuming that the threads per unit space are the same in each case, thicker threads can

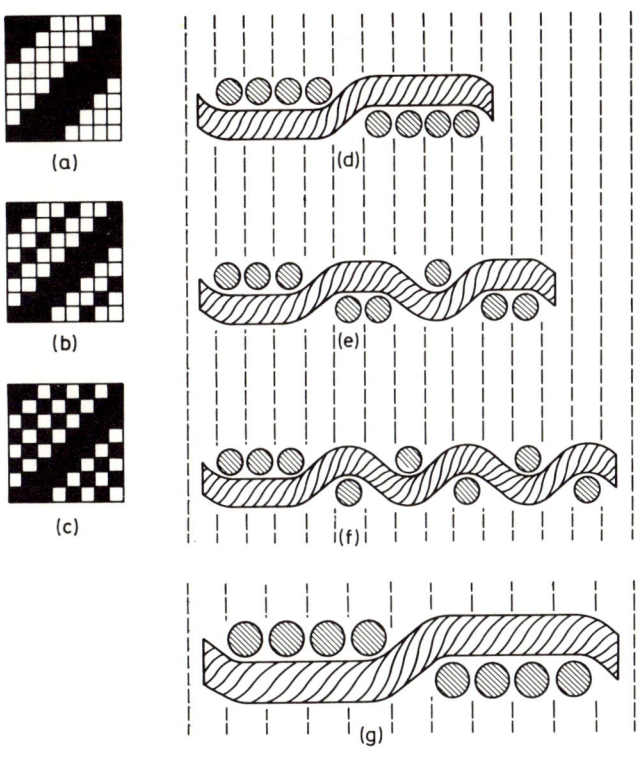

Figure 2.11

be employed for A than for B, and for B than for C. This is illustrated at G, which represents the thickness of the yarn (approximately) that can be employed for the weave A if the threads per unit space are the same as for the weave C. It will be seen that 10 diameters in G occupy the space of 14 diameters in F. A loose weave (such as A), therefore, allows more yarn to be put into a cloth than a firmer weave (such as B), and permits a heavier cloth to be formed. (See Appendix III.)

Influence of the twist of the yarns

The twist, which is put into yarns in order to bind the fibres together, affects the handle, strength, and wearing property of a cloth, and also has a considerable influence upon the appearance of a fabric in which any form of twill line is developed. Generally, just sufficient twist is inserted to enable the threads to withstand the strain of weaving. More turns per inch are required in fine than in thick threads, and for short than for long-fibred materials, while warp yarns are mostly harder twisted than weft yards. The twist, while strengthening the yarn, makes it harder, and reduces its lustre, and to many fabrics the necessary firmness of structure is imparted by the warp, and softness and brightness by the weft. For special purposes yarns are twisted more or less than the normal according to the effect required in the cloth; thus *voile* and *crepon* yarns are very hard twisted, whereas yarns for raised fabrics have less twist.

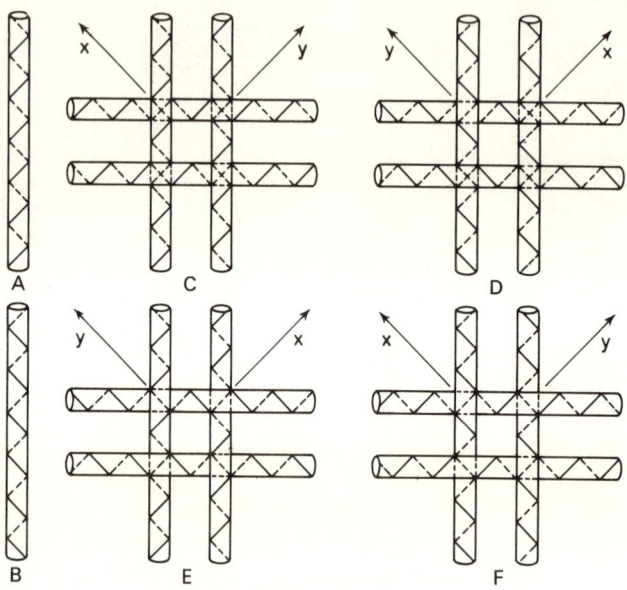

Figure 2.12

If the direction of the twist is to the right looking up the thread, as shown at A in *Figure 2.12*, it is termed 'open-band', or 'Z' twist, and if to the left as represented at B, 'cross-band', or 'S' twist. In cotton yarns A represents warp twist (twist way), and B weft twist (weft way), whereas in worsted yarns warp twist is as shown at B, and weft twist as shown at A. Single woollen yarn is almost invariably twisted, as indicated at B. In folded yarns the twist is mostly inserted in the opposite direction to that of the single threads, because this causes some of the twist to be taken out of the singles, and a softer folded yarn results than if the direction of the twist is the same in both twisting operations; the latter method increases the twist in the singles, and tends to make the folded yarn hard.

C, D, E, and F in *Figure 2.12* illustrate the different ways in which the warp and weft threads may be placed in relation to each other as regards the direction of the twist. In C the warp twist is as shown at A, and the weft twist as at B, the surface direction of the twist being to the right in both threads when the weft is laid at right angles to the warp. D is the exact opposite of C, the surface direction of the twist being to the left. In E both series of threads are twisted 'Z' way, and in F 'S' way. In C and D the direction of the twist, on the under side of the top thread, is opposite to that on the upper side of the lower thread, hence the threads do not readily bed into, but tend to stand off from each other, which assists in showing up the weave and structure of the cloth distinctly. In E and F, on the other hand, the twist on the underside of the top thread is in the same direction as that on the upper side of the lower thread, hence in this case the conditions are favourable for the threads to bed into each other and form a compact cloth in which the weave and thread structure are not distinct.

In twill fabrics the clearness and prominence of the twill lines are accentuated if their direction is opposite to the surface direction of the twist of the yarn. If, however, the lines of a twill are required to show indistinctly, the twill should run the same as the surface direction of the twist of the yarn. If one yarn predominates on the surface the twill should oppose, or run with, the twist of the surface threads according to whether the effect is required to show prominently or otherwise. Thus, in C and D in *Figure 2.12* the arrows X indicate the direction in which the twill should run if the lines are required to show boldly and clearly, and the arrows Y if an indistinct twill effect is desired. In E and F the arrows X show the proper direction for producing a bold twill, and the arrows Y for producing an indistinct twill if the weft yarn predominates on the surface. If, however, the warp forms the face of the cloth in E and F, the arrows Y indicate the proper direction for a bold twill effect, and the arrows X for an indistinct twill. Irrespective of the coincidence, or otherwise, of the direction of the twill with the direction of the twist the weaves appear more distinct in combinations C and D, than in E and F.

If a twill runs both to right and left in a cloth (a herring-bone twill), it shows more clearly in one direction than the other. Also, the difference in the appearance of right and left twist is sufficient to show clearly in a twill fabric in which the weave is continuous, and 'shadow' effects are produced in warp-face weaves by employing both kinds of twist in the warp threads.

SATEEN AND SATIN WEAVES

In pure sateen and satin weaves the surface of the cloth consists almost entirely either of weft or warp float, as in the repeat of a weave each thread of one series passes over all but one thread of the other series.

In addition, the interlacing points are so arranged as to allow the floating threads to slip and to cover the 'binding' point of one thread by the float of another. This results in the production of fabrics with a maximum degree of smoothness and lustre and without any prominent weave features. Very close packing of threads is possible and quite heavy constructions can be achieved with properly set cloths. Fabrics with insufficiently close thread spacing, however, exhibit poor seam strength in made up articles due to seam slippage arising on account of the excessive freedom of the threads.

The terms *sateen*, and *satin* tend to be used somewhat indiscriminately and are frequently confused one with another. Correctly, sateen indicates a weft faced construction, whilst satin is used with reference to a corresponding warp face structure. This difference is reflected in the settings of the respective cloths and sateens are constructed with a greater number of picks per cm than ends per cm, and, conversely, satins have more ends than picks per cm in order to achieve the desired solid surface effect.

Regular sateens and satins

The examples given in *Figure 2.13* will enable the construction of twills and regular sateens and satins to be compared. In twill weaves the distance from a mark on one thread to the corresponding mark on the next thread—termed a step, move, or count—is one, hence in the cloth the intersections support each other, and distinct twill lines are formed. In regular sateen weaves the step, move, or count is more than one, so that the intersections do not support each other, but as the distance moved each time is equal and regular a certain degree of twilling is formed in the cloth. The prominence of the twill line varies according to (a) the order in which the threads interlace; and (b) the direction of the twill line in relation to the direction of the twist of the yarn. In the best regular sateens the points of intersection are equally distributed over the repeat area, and if the twill lines and the twist run in the same direction, a smooth, lustrous, and almost untwilled surface is formed.

In *Figure 2.13*, A shows a 1 up, 4 down twill in which the marks are arranged in the order of 1, 2, 3, 4, and 5; in B the move or count is two to the right, hence the marks are indicated on the spaces in the order of 1, 3, 5, 2, and 4; while in C the count is three to the right, the order of arrangement being 1, 4, 2, 5, and 3. By counting one less than the number of threads in the repeat (in this case four) a reversed twill is produced, as shown at D in *Figure 2.13*.

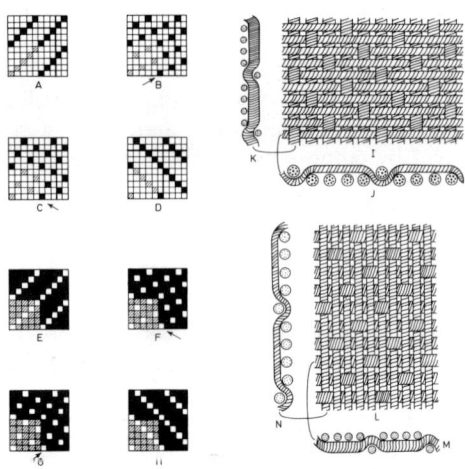

Figure 2.13

A similar procedure can be adopted to produce a corresponding warp faced satin starting with the 4 up, 1 down twill. This is indicated at E, F, G, and H in *Figure 2.13*. I in *Figure 2.13* shows a flat view of the plan B, while J represents the interlacing of the first pick, and K of the first end. If the twist in the yarn is in the direction indicated on the threads in I the twill lines will show indistinctly. The flat view, given at L in *Figure 2.13*, corresponds with the design F, the interlacing of the third pick being represented at M, and of the first end at N. In this case if the threads are twisted in the direction indicated, a rather distinct twill, running to the left will be formed. (In cotton cloths the term *drill* (q.v.) is frequently applied to this structure.)

The arrows under B, C, F, and G in *Figure 2.13* indicate in each case the direction in which twilling lines will tend to appear in sateens and satins if the twist in the yarns and the cloth settings are favourable towards it. In most cases, with the exception of 'drills', any tendency to form distinct twilling lines is avoided, and in subsequent diagrams it is shown that some superficially correct arrangements have to be rejected unless a distinct twill line is desired.

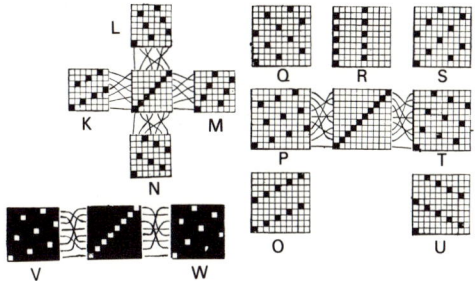

Figure 2.14

All the possible sateens on seven threads are given in *Figure 2.14* at K, L, M, and N, the threads of which are shown connected by lines with the 1-and-6 twill. K is constructed by counting two, L by counting three, M by counting four, and N by counting five, in each case to the right on succeeding picks. It will be seen from an examination of the foregoing weaves, that the move may be either upward or outward; thus, in K the count upwards is four; in L, five; in M, two; and in N three on succeeding ends. N is similar to K, and M to L, but twilling in the opposite direction. It will be noted that all seven thread sateen constructions result in a very obvious alignment of the points of intersection and for this reason the seven thread repeat is not normally employed.

O, P, Q, R, S, T, and U in *Figure 2.14* are constructed on ten threads by counting 2, 3, 4, 5, 6, 7, and 8 respectively, but only P (counting 3) and T (counting 7), which are similar but twilling in opposite directions, are proper weaves. In each of the others no marks are placed on some of the threads, hence 2, 4, 5, 6, and 8 cannot be counted in designing sateens on ten

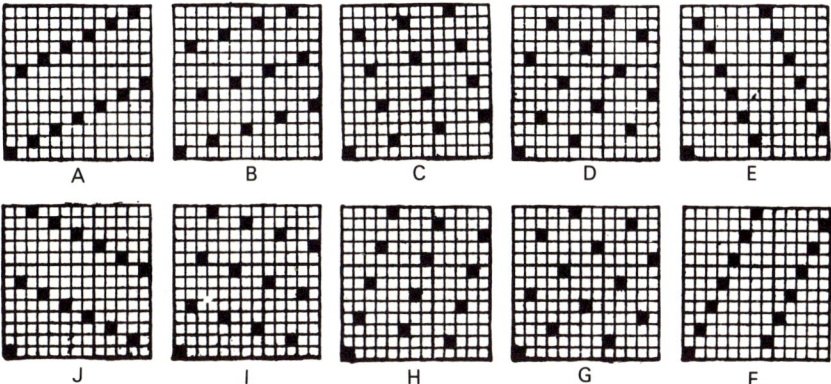

Figure 2.15

threads. From the example the following rule for the construction of regular sateens and satins may be drawn: any number (with the exception of one, and a number that is one less than the number of threads in the repeat) may be counted which has no common factor with the number of threads in the repeat of the wave. Quite similar effects which differ only in the direction of twilling will be produced by using *moves* which are by an equal number higher, or lower than half the number of threads in the repeat. Thus, on eight threads, where only moves of 3 and 5 can be used, the effects, in conformity with the rule established above, are similar and differ only in respect of the direction of twilling. This is shown at V and W in *Figure 2.14* where the two 'moves' suitable for an eight thread satin (or sateen) are clearly represented.

In *Figure 2.15* all the possible sateens on thirteen threads are given at A, B, C, D, E, F, G, H, I, and J, which are produced by counting 2, 3, 4, 5, 6, 7, 8, 9, 10, and 11 respectively. Similar sateens result from counting 2 and 11, 3 and 10, 4 and 9, 5 and 8, and 6 and 7, and in *Figure 2.15* the weaves are arranged in pairs one above the other to correspond. A, E, F, and J give poor sateen effects, because of the distinct twill lines that are formed; B, C, H, and I are better, but in each of these the marks form a more prominent line in one direction than in the other; in D and G, however, the distribution of the marks is perfect.

Although most of the examples given above on design paper represented the sateen weaves it must be understood that any rules in respect of *counting*, or *moving* of an interlacing point are equally applicable to the warp satin weaves.

Irregular Sateens and Satins

Regular sateens cannot be constructed on four and six threads, because no number can be counted which has not a common factor with four and six. An attempt to produce an effect similar to sateen on four threads is shown at A in *Figure 2.16*. This is based on the 1 up, 3 down twill with marks arranged in the order of 1, 2, 4 and 3. The term satinette is usually applied to this weave but from the point of view of correct classification of weaves it belongs to a group of structures known as broken twills (q.v.).

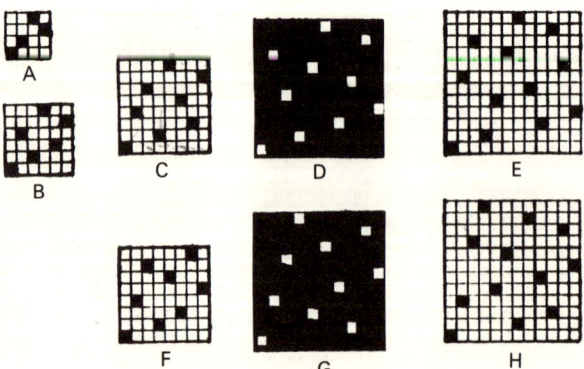

Figure 2.16

In the 6-thread sateen, given at **B** in *Figure 2.16*, the marks are arranged in the order of 1, 3, 5, 2, 6, and 4. Irregular sateens are entirely free from twill lines, a feature that frequently gives them an advantage over regular sateens, and for this reason sateens are arranged irregularly on eight, ten, twelve, etc., threads. C in *Figure 2.16* shows an irregular sateen on eight threads, in which 3 is counted to the right for four picks; on the fifth pick the count is equal to half the number of threads in the repeat—viz., 4—then on the succeeding picks 3 is counted to the left. A 10-thread irregular satin is given at D, in which the count is 3 for half the number of picks, then 5 is counted, and afterwards the move is in 3s to the left. In the 12-thread irregular sateen given at E the count is 3 and 5 alternately for six picks, then 6, and afterwards 3 and 5 alternately to the left. The weaves F, G, and H respectively correspond with C, D, and E, and are constructed in the same manner except that the count is upward instead of outward.

In sateens and satins it is only possible to introduce different colours effectively in the threads which form the surface. As a transverse stripe is rarely desired the introduction of coloured threads is in practice limited to warp satins. These are particularly suitable for displaying colours in stripe form and, if the warp threads are of good quality and free from irregularities, brilliant effects are produced because the lustrous and unbroken cloth surface enhances the brightness of the colours. Different materials can also be effectively combined in the warp and further variety can be achieved by combining satin with other weaves, particularly the plain and the various twills.

Sateen weft
Satin warp

3

Development of Weaves from Elementary Bases

PLAIN WEAVE DERIVATIVES

This group of structures comprises varied simple weaves which are all extensions of the plain weave and can be produced on two healds. The extension of the plain weave can proceed, either vertically, grouping together several picks in the same shed and resulting in warp ribs; or, horizontally, with groups of neighbouring ends working in tandem and producing weft ribs; or, in both directions simultaneously, resulting in mat, hopsack and basket weaves.

Warp rib weaves

Simple warp ribs can be produced in ordinary plain weave and their construction is illustrated in *Figure 2.2*. Other, more pronounced effects result from extending the plain weave vertically, as shown in the examples given at A to F in *Figure 3.1*. A, B, and C produce regular warp ribs in which each end passes alternately over and under 2, 3, and 4 picks respectively, and is brought prominently to the surface on both sides of the cloth. This is shown at G in *Figure 3.1*, which indicates how the ends interlace with the picks in the plan A. Lines or ribs, that are equal in size, are formed running the width of the cloth, as shown in *Figure 3.2*, which represents a fabric produced in the weave given at A in *Figure 3.1*.

D, E, and F in *Figure 3.1* are irregular warp ribs, which produce horizontal lines that are unequal in size. In D and E the odd ends are chiefly on the surface, while the even ends are mostly on the back, as shown at H, which represents the interlacing with the weave E. By using a good class of material for the odd ends, and a cheaper material for the even ends, a cloth with a good appearance may be economically produced in designs such as D and E. In the design F a wide rib alternates with two finer ribs, but in this case all the ends are equally on the surface.

In each of the examples given above the correct formation of the rib is dependent not only on the order of interlacing but also on the respective density of setting of the warp and the weft threads. Best results are obtained with a high warp sett in which the warp ends cover the weft almost entirely.

The ribs can be emphasised even more strongly by the use of alternate coarse and fine ends, slack and tight ends, and thick and fine picks as shown respectively at I, J, and K in *Figure 3.1*. Each of the above three combinations will produce a more prominent rib than that shown at H although there is no difference in the weave itself. Further increase in the prominence of

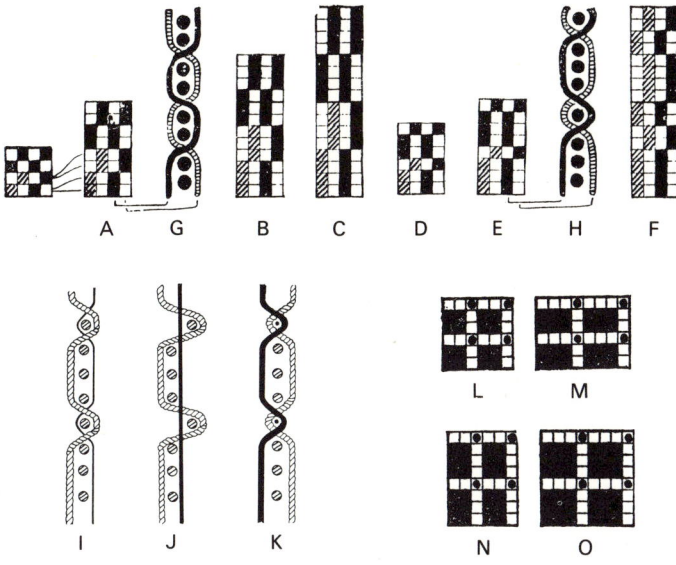

Figure 3.1

warp ribs can be achieved by grouping together several ends which work alike and raising them over a number of coarse picks and then passing them under one fine pick. Using this method with fine warps it is possible to achieve ribs equally prominent to those obtained by the use of alternate coarse and fine ends but of much smarter appearance. This type of construction is shown on design paper at L, M, N, and O in *Figure 3.1*. For looms with changing boxes at one side only, a 2-and-2 order of wefting may be employed for the designs N and O, one of the fine picks going into the same shed as the two thick picks. Many of the weaves illustrated are used extensively in the production of the various *grosgrain* cloths and also form the basis of the *matelasse* fabrics.

Weft rib weaves

These are opposite to warp rib weaves, and result from extending the plain weave horizontally, as shown in the examples A to F in *Figure 3.3*. In A, B, and C, which are regular weft ribs, each pick of weft passes alternately under and over 2, 3, and 4 ends respectively; the weft is brought prominently to the surface and forms lines running the length of the cloth on both sides. D, E, and F are irregular weft ribs, which produce longitudinal lines that are unequal in size. The diagrams G and H respectively correspond with the plans A and F, and show how the picks interlace with the ends. The fabric represented in *Figure 3.2*, if turned one-quarter round, will illustrate the appearance of a weft rib weave. As in the warp ribs, the appearance of the cloth also depends on the respective thread settings and to achieve good effects it is necessary to weave a weft rib with a high number of picks per inch and a comparatively low number of ends per inch. The prominence of the ribs can

Figure 3.2

be increased by suitable use of coarse and fine yarns as shown in the diagrams I and J in *Figure 3.3*. Construction J, which depends upon a suitable arrangement of coarse and fine ends, is more frequently employed as it does not require the use of a loom with multiple shuttle boxes which is necessary in the production of rib I where alternate coarse and fine picks are introduced. Weaving particulars to produce the weft rib J (also shown on design paper at D) in cotton yarns would be: Warp—2 coarse ends, 40/2 tex; 1 fine end, 15/1 tex; 20 ends per cm; weft—42 picks per cm of 30/1 tex.

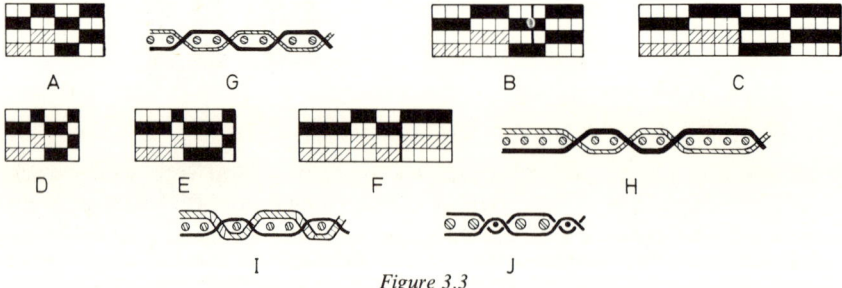

Figure 3.3

The dependence of all rib constructions upon the correct thread settings is very marked and the weave D, which in the circumstances illustrated above produces a distinct weft rib, can also be employed to give a warp rib if the following yarn counts and settings are used: Warp—18/1 tex cotton, 52 ends per cm with the two ends working together slack, and the single end tight; weft—38/1 tex cotton, 16 picks per cm. The warp rib obtained in this manner results in an effect which is similar to that achieved by means of the weave F in *Figure 3.1* but slightly less prominent.

Hopsack, mat, or basket weaves

These are constructed by extending the plain weave both vertically and horizontally, so that in both directions there are two or more threads working together in the same order. A, B, and C in *Figure 3.4* are regular hopsacks arranged respectively 2-and-2, 3-and-3, and 4-and-4; the warp and weft show equally on the surface of both sides of the cloth in the form of small equal-sized squares or rectangles. The interlacing diagram given at M represents the weave A, while a fabric to correspond is illustrated in *Figure*

3.5. D, E, and F in *Figure 3.4* are irregular hopsack weaves, which form unequal spaces in the cloth. On account of the loose method in which the threads interlace in ordinary hopsack weaves, large designs are only employed in fine fabrics. It is possible, however, to obtain well interlaced effects in coarser fabrics by combining hopsacks with warp and weft ribs to form constructions frequently referred to as fancy basket weaves. Some examples of these structures are shown at G to L in *Figure 3.4* and it will be observed

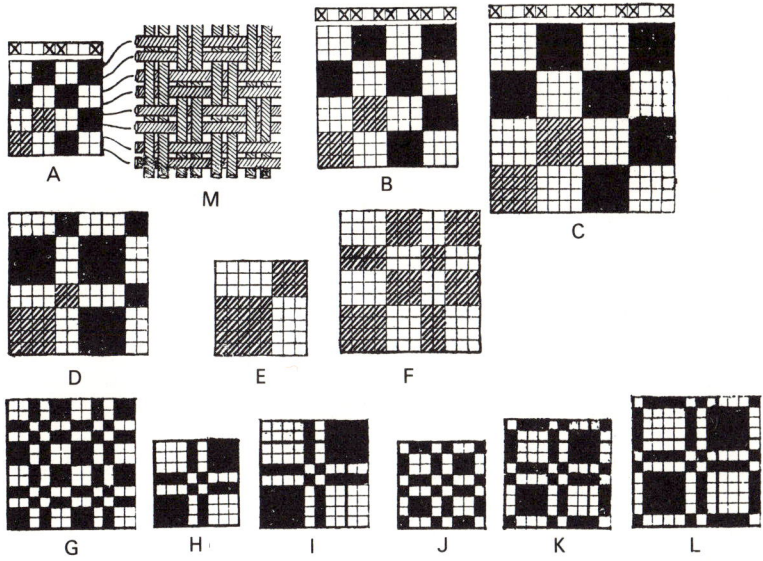

Figure 3.4

that although some repeats are quite large all effects can be produced on only two healds with the use of suitable drafts. The designs G to L are frequently woven with finer yarns for the rib ends and picks than for the hopsack threads. Thus, the design J may be arranged in the following manner: Warp—two double ends of 30/1 tex cotton (hopsack), and two single ends of 15/1 tex cotton (warp rib); Weft—two picks of 60/1 tex cotton (hopsack),

Figure 3.5

and two picks of 15/1 tex cotton (weft rib). All hopsack and basket weaves can be extended further to produce even larger and more prominent effects but, in order to avoid loose construction, it is necessary to modify the weaves considerably. Several examples of such modified hopsacks are given in *Figure 5.1*.

Denting of weft rib and hopsack weaves

The ends which work together tend to twist or roll round each other as the cloth is woven, and if this takes place the cloth suffers in appearance, while the weaving process is made more difficult. The twisting of the ends can be prevented by denting them in such a manner that those which work alike are separated by the wires of the reed. Above each plan A, B, and C in *Figure 3.4* a system of denting is given in which the marks and blanks indicate the order in which the ends are passed together through the reed, the threads of a group being passed through different splits. The same orders of denting are applicable to the weft rib weaves A, B, and C in *Figure 3.3*.

Mock rib effects

Occasionally cloths are produced in ordinary plain weave which resemble the design given at A in *Figure 3.1*. This is achieved by doubling up two threads of weft on a pirn and inserting the double weft in lieu of the two single picks which are necessary in the proper warp rib construction. A special effect is sometimes obtained by having differently coloured threads wound alongside each other on the pirns. The withdrawal of the weft in the direction of the length of the pirn causes the threads to make one twist round each other for every revolution made by them on the pirn or cop. The slight amount of twist thus inserted causes the colours to show intermittently in the cloth producing an irregular or streaky colour effect. Similarly, an imitation weft rib which resembles A in *Figure 3.3* can be obtained in plain weave by placing two ends in each mail, in which case, if they are differently coloured, the rolling of the threads round each other causes the colours to show intermittently in the cloth.

WEAVES CONSTRUCTED ON TWILL BASES

Regular twills are capable of a considerable degree of modification and serve frequently as the bases for the construction of new designs which superficially may appear to possess little in common with the original base.

Waved twills

One of the simplest forms of modified twill is the waved twill achieved by reversing the direction of the twill at suitable intervals. The reversal can occur either upon a warp end, in which case a horizontal wave is produced, or upon a weft pick which results in a vertical wave or a zig-zag effect.

The horizontal wave effects are economically produced in point drafts, and good styles may be woven on a few healds by means of twill tappets. The vertical line effects, however, mostly require a dobby shedding motion, because of the comparatively large number of picks in the lifting plan. *Figure 3.6* illustrates a horizontal wave pattern that corresponds with the weave given at D in *Figure 3.7* while by turning *Figure 3.6* one-quarter round a vertical effect is shown that corresponds with the weave L in *Figure 3.7*.

Figure 3.6

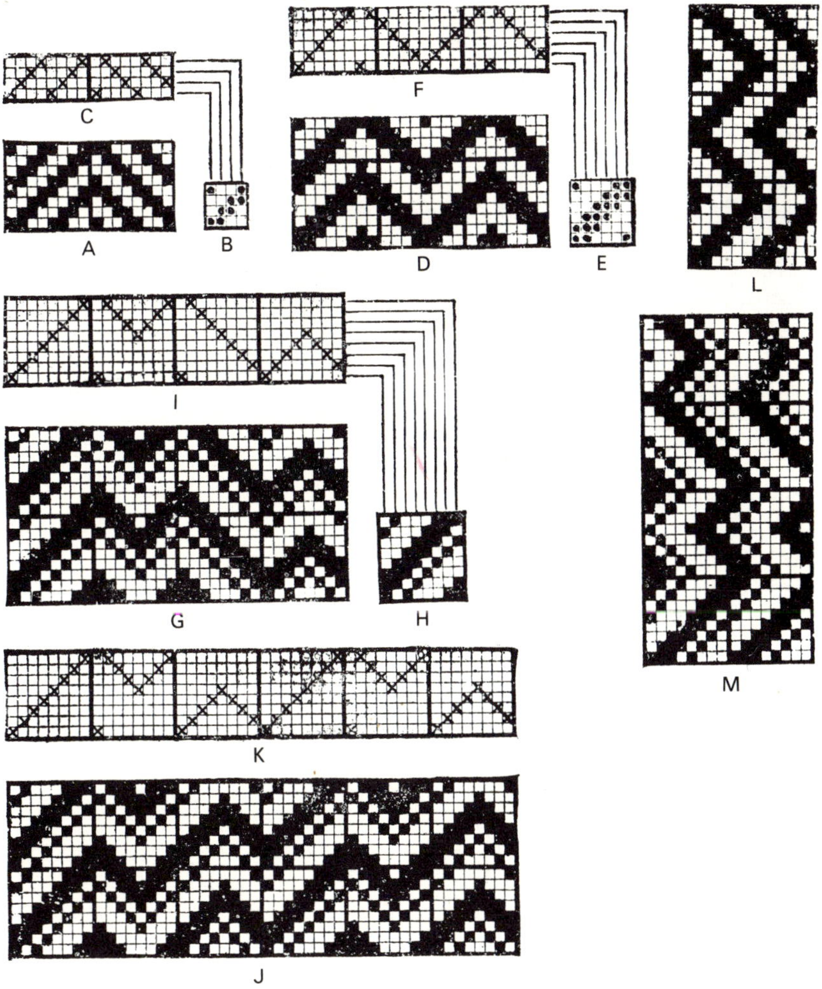

Figure 3.7

A in *Figure 3.7* shows the 2-and-2 twill given at B, arranged 8 ends to right and 8 ends to left, turning on the first and ninth ends, whilst D shows the 3-and-3 twill E running 6 ends to right and 6 ends to left, turning on the first and seventh ends. A more complex arrangement is illustrated at G, in which the 8-thread twill H is turned on the ends 1, 9, 13, 17, 25, and 29. In each case the design is, for convenience, so arranged that an equal number of ends is drawn on each heald, as shown in the point drafts C, F, and I, which respectively correspond with the designs A, D, and G.

In the designs A, D, and G, the twills run for as many threads to the right as to the left, so that each twill line returns to the level at which it commenced.

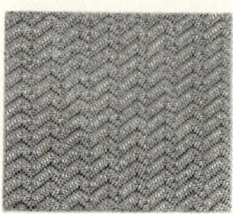

Figure 3.8

In the design J, however, for which K is the draft, the twill H is arranged to run 8 ends to the right and 4 ends to the left alternately, so that the zig-zag line gradually rises and runs at a flat angle from side to side of the cloth, as shown in the corresponding fabric represented in *Figure 3.8*.

The designs L and M in *Figure 3.7*, which correspond with D and G, illustrate the method of producing vertical waves in the cloth. In the former the twill turns on the picks 1 and 7, and in the latter on the picks 1, 9, 13, 17, 25, and 29. A defect of the pointed twill arrangement is the formation of an increased float where the weave turns, the long float occurring in the weft in the horizontal waved effects, and in the warp in the vertical patterns.

Herringbone twills

These twills, although they also depend upon the reversal of the direction to achieve the desired effect, are constructed in a different manner from the ordinary waved twills. Careful study of the designs and drafts in *Figure 3.9* will show the differences in construction. The twill does not come to a point where it changes the direction, but instead one twill line is said to 'cut' into

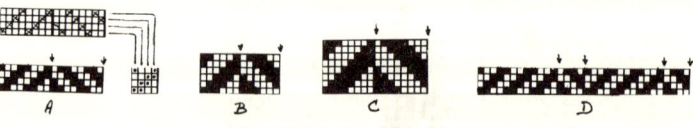

Figure 3.9

the other at the point of reversal. Example A in *Figure 3.9* shows the construction of a 2-and-2 twill herringbone quite clearly. The twill runs from left to right for a desired number of ends—in this case eight—whereupon the reversal of the direction takes place by introducing on the ninth end the marks which are exactly opposite to those of the eighth end, and commencing to run the twill from this point down in the reverse direction. The effect of

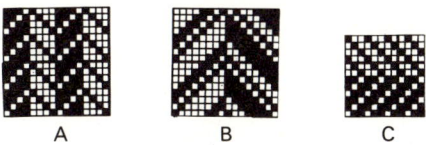

Figure 3.10

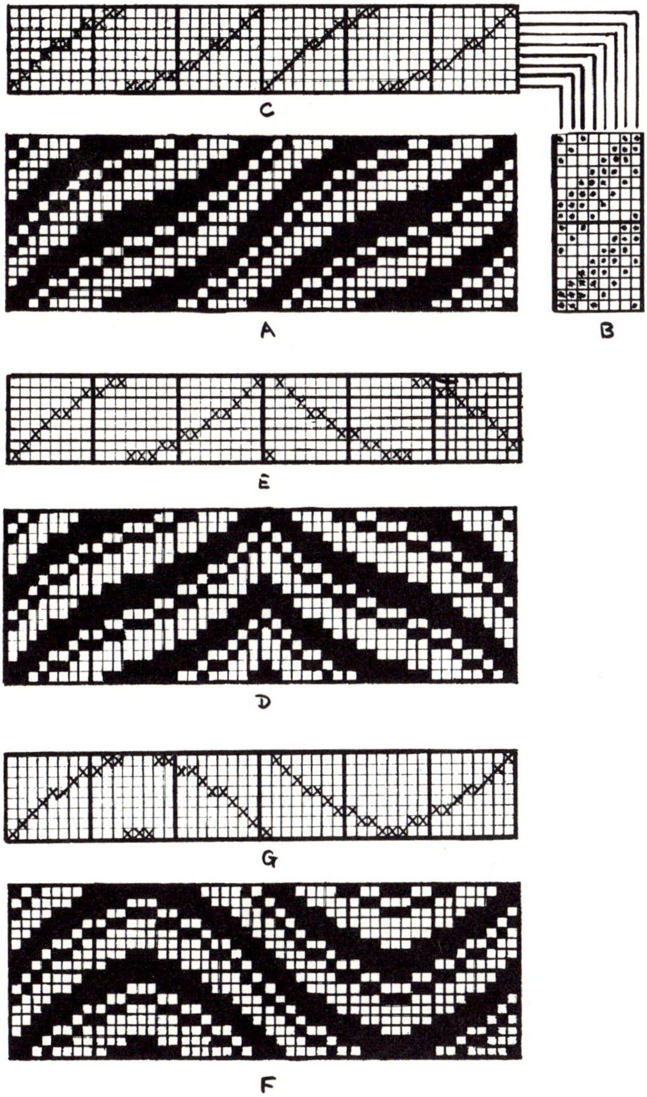

Figure 3.11

the diametrically opposite lifts at the reversal point is to throw the neighbour-ing ends apart from one another to produce what is commonly known as the 'break' or the 'cut' (indicated in *Figure 3.9* by arrows). This method of join-ing also tends to produce a distinct stripe effect, and prevents the formation of an extended float where the weave turns, which is an undesirable effect un-avoidably occurring in ordinary waved twills. Examples B and C in *Figure 3.9* show the 3-and-3, and 4-and-4 twills arranged on the herringbone basis, whilst D represents a 2-and-2 herringbone twill with unequal width of stripe. All the weaves shown in *Figure 3.9* are extensively used in the manufacture of suitings and overcoatings.

Figure 3.10 illustrates the very distinct effects which it is possible to achieve when, instead of even sided twills, use is made of either warp, or weft sided twills as the base for herringbones. Owing to the principle of opposing, on the point of reversal, a warp lift with a weft lift (and vice-versa), any warp faced twill is reconstituted in the form of a weft faced twill running in the reverse direction. A and B in *Figure 3.10* show this effect clearly. Where warp yarn is of different colour to the weft yarn very distinct stripes are formed. As the two twills formed in this manner are quite different a larger number of healds will be necessary to produce these effects than is normally required for the production of the herringbone effects from even-sided twills of similar size. In order to achieve equal degree of prominence in the warp, and in the weft faced stripe, these cloths must be woven in a *square* sett.

The above principle of construction can be used to produce transverse or cross-over stripes if the reversal of the direction is made upon a pick of weft as shown at C in *Figure 3.10*. This type of design is occasionally employed in cloths for hangings and other soft furnishings.

Curved twills

The principle of construction of curved twills will be understood from an examination of the design A in *Figure 3.11*, which is constructed from the 8-thread twill given at B on the basis of the curved draft indicated at C. This class of design is only used to a limited extent, as there is the disadvantage that the length of the weft float and the firmness of the cloth vary in different parts of the twill line.

Curved twills may be reversed in direction so as to form zig-zag effects in which each curve terminates in a point, as shown at D in *Figure 3.11*, and the corresponding draft E; or an undulating wave twill may be made, as indicated at F and the corresponding draft G.

Broken twills

A large variety of attractive effects, generally somewhat similar in appearance to herringbone twills, can be produced by *breaking* a regular twill. The *break* can be achieved in different ways and the designs in *Figure 3.12* illustrate the simplest method in which the continuity of the twill is stopped by frequent reversals of the direction. Designs A to E show the basic twills and side by side their corresponding broken twill counterparts are illustrated. Suitable drafts are indicated by crosses above each group of designs. The designs A_1

to E_1 are derived by stopping the orderly progression of the regular twill half-way through the repeat and running the ends in the second half of the repeat in reverse order. In the case of four shaft twills the new order of drafting is, therefore, 1, 2/4, 3; whilst in the eight thread twills the order is 1, 2, 3, 4/8, 7, 6, 5. The design A_1 represents the very popular 2-and-2 broken twill, and B_1 is the 1-and-3 broken twill which is also known as the satinette. Most even sided twills result in well balanced effects upon 'breaking', but some twills which are not even-sided sometimes give rise to the formation of inconsequential floats when broken half-way through the repeat. This is illustrated at E_1 which does not produce a pleasing effect due to the doubling-up of the floats at each 'break' point of the repeat.

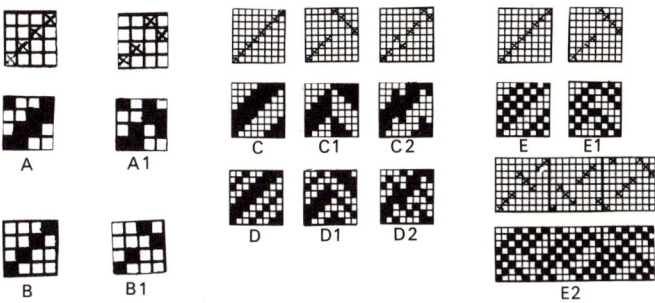

Figure 3.12

In addition to the *break and reversal* half-way through the repeat many other effects can be achieved by breaks of the draft at more frequent intervals and designs C_2 and D_2 show the effect of the draft broken in pairs: 1, 2/4, 3; 5, 6/8, 7—whilst E_2 results from the break and reversal of the design E in groups of 3: 1, 2, 3/6, 5, 4; 7, 8, 1/4, 3, 2; 5, 6, 7/2, 1, 8; 3, 4, 5/8, 7, 6. From the foregoing examples it will be clear that if the 'break' unit is a factor of the repeat of the original weave then the size of the new weave repeat is unaltered; if, however, the 'break' unit is not a factor of the original repeat size, then the new repeat size will be equal to the l.c.m. of the 'break' unit and the original repeat. In the example E_2 the relevant figures are 3 and 8 respectively, and, therefore, in accordance with the rule given above, the new design repeats upon 24 ends. The order of progression in these constructions is well illustrated by the example E_2 and upon studying it the following instructions could be formulated: 1. Run the twill in one direction for the required number of threads (in E_2—1, 2, 3); 2. Add to the number of the last thread the number of threads per 'break' and run the twill in the opposite direction (in E_2—3 + 3 = 6 ∴ 6, 5, 4); and so on, until the original starting point is reached again. In trying to reach arithmetical solutions it must be remembered that the number of threads per repeat represents a unit, and, therefore, in an eight thread repeat, thread number 9 is equal to number 1, thread number 10 to number 2, etc.

Another useful system of broken twill construction which is particularly applicable to twills that are composed of equal warp and weft float, consists of 'entering and skipping' the threads of an ordinary twill. Any number of threads may be entered and skipped respectively at a place, but generally the most suitable number to skip is one less than half the number of threads in the repeat of the twill. If the latter condition is observed in certain equal-sided twills, the warp and weft floats oppose each other, and a fine line or 'cut' is made where the twill is broken. As will be seen from the examples given in *Figure 3.13* the 'broken' portions of the twills are not in this method alternately reversed as in the previous system, but run in the same direction.

The method of entering-and-skipping is illustrated in *Figure 3.13*, in which three repeats of 2-and-2 twill are given at A, while at B the threads of A are shown arranged in the order of 2 entered and 1 skipped. C shows the draft for B, if a normal 2-and-2 twill lifting plan is employed; and it will be noted that the order of drawing in is 2 healds drawn and 1 heald skipped, and thus coincides with the basis upon which B is constructed.

D in *Figure 3.13* shows the 3-and-3 twill arranged in the order of 3 entered and 2 skipped; F the 4-and-4 twill arranged 4 entered and 3 skipped; and H a 10-thread twill arranged 4 entered and 4 skipped; while E, G, and I represent the bases of construction, and the drafts for the respective designs. The number of threads in the repeat of a design can be ascertained by noting the number of squares that corresponding positions of the weave are distant

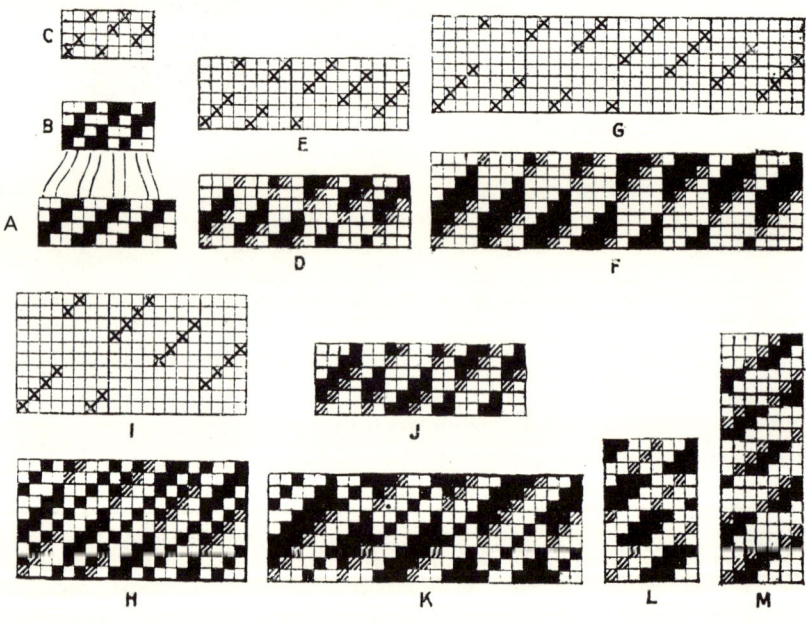

Figure 3.13

from each other. Thus, in F corresponding positions move one square downward and four squares outward each time; and as there are 8 picks in the weave there are: $(8 \div 1) \times 4 = 32$ ends in the repeat. In H there are 10 picks in the weave, and the move is 2 downward and 4 outward; therefore in the repeat there are: $(10 \div 2) \times 4 = 20$ ends.

The designs may be varied by entering unequal numbers of threads, as shown at J in *Figure 3.13*, in which the 3-and-3 twill is arranged 4 entered, 2 skipped, 2 entered, and 2 skipped. In the same manner, K shows a 9-thread twill arranged 6 entered, 3 skipped, 3 entered, and 3 skipped, and this example also illustrates that the system of construction is by no means limited to twills which are composed of equal warp and weft float, but can be used with good results in re-arranging the threads of almost any type of twill.

Designs can also be constructed by filling and skipping the picks, as shown at L and M in *Figure 3.13*; the former of which consists of an 8-thread twill arranged with 3 picks filled and 3 picks skipped, and the latter of a 7-thread twill arranged 3 picks filled and 2 skipped. Further, in either the warp or weft method, if the base marks are inserted first, as shown by the shaded squares in the designs given in *Figure 3.13*, marks may be added to them in any desired order.

In yet another method of constructing broken twills it is possible to create small mat or cord effects by combining the 'enter-and-skip' system with the repetition of similar lifts side by side, or with the reversal of direction. The

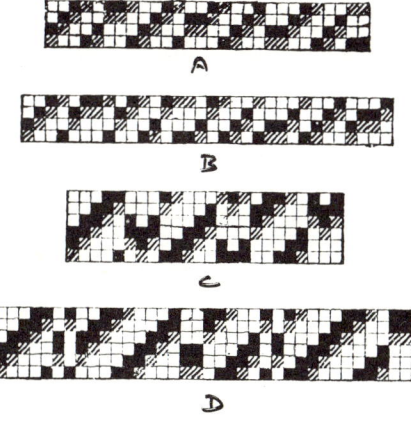

Figure 3.14

mat or cord effects can be made either to cut with the twill, or to join it in continuation, and some of these fancy broken constructions are shown in *Figure 3.14*. Designs A and B are based on the 2-and-2 twill, and designs C and D on the 3-and-3 twill. In A the small mat effect, produced by repetition of like lifts, cuts with the twill at one side, and joins it at the other side. In B four threads of the twill cut with four threads of the modified twill, whilst C and D show broken 3-and-3 twill designs in which the skipping, the repetition and the reversal of the order are arranged in various combinations. Threads which are different in colour or material may be effectively introduced at the places where a weave is broken. Also an advantage of the broken twill system of construction is that variety of design is produced with little or no effect upon the firmness of the structure, so that the yarns and settings which are suitable for an ordinary twill are equally suitable for the same twill broken.

Transposed or re-arranged twills

By means of transposition or re-arrangement of the original order of the threads in a regular twill many new and attractive designs can be created. The transposition results in the interruption of the continuous twill line and some transposed effects are very similar to broken twill designs. Re-arrangement of both the warp and the weft threads is possible and several systems of transposition are shown in *Figure 3.15.* The base line of a 12-thread ordinary twill is indicated at A, while at B the marks are transposed in groups of 2,

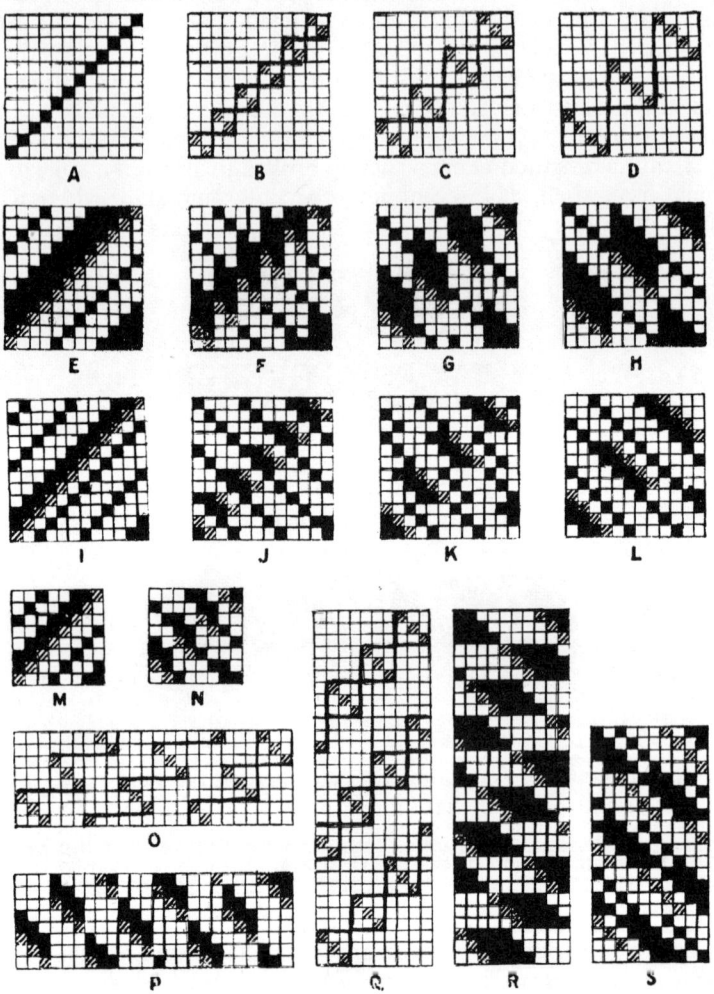

Figure 3.15

at C in groups of 3, and at D in groups of 4. In E, F, G, and H, and in I, J, K, and L, the shaded squares correspond with the base marks indicated in A, B, C, and D, respectively. At F, G, and H respectively the twill E is re-arranged in the warp according to the transposed bases B, C, and D; while J, K, and L similarly show the twill I re-arranged in the weft. A comparison will show that the ends of the ordinary twill E, taken consecutively from 1 to 12, are arranged in F in the order of 2, 1; 4, 3; 6, 5; 8, 7; 10, 9; 12, 11; in G in the order of 3, 2, 1; 6, 5, 4; 9, 8, 7; 12, 11, 10; and in H in the order of, 4, 3, 2, 1; 8, 7, 6, 5; 12, 11, 10, 9. In J, K, and L respectively the picks of the twill I are arranged in corresponding orders.

The design given at N in *Figure 3.15* corresponds with the fabric represented in *Figure 3.16*. The weave is termed the Mayo or Campbell, and is formed by transposing the ends of the 8-thread twill M in 2s. O and P illustrate the transposition of the ends of a 3-and-5 twill in 3s, in which it is necessary to extend the design over a number of ends, which is the l.c.m. of 8 and 3— i.e., 24. The ends of the twill are thus arranged in the order of 3, 2, 1; 6, 5, 4; 1, 8, 7; 4, 3, 2; 7, 6, 5; 2, 1, 8; 5, 4, 3; 8, 7, 6. In the same manner in transposing the picks of a 10-thread twill in 3s, as shown at Q and R, the repeat

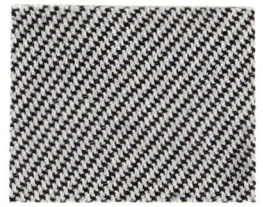

Figure 3.16

extends over 30 picks—the l.c.m. of 10 and 3; while in transposing a 10-thread twill in 4s, as shown at S, the repeat extends over 20 picks—the l.c.m. of 10 and 4.

A variation of the foregoing method consists of arranging the groups of threads in transposed and straight order alternately, as shown at A to D in *Figure 3.17*, and the corresponding designs E to H. The design H coincides

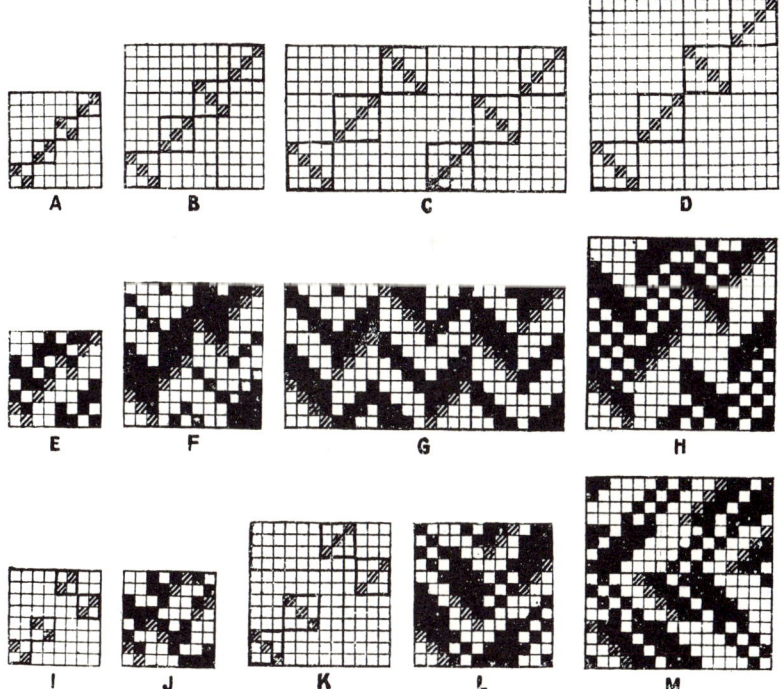

Figure 3.17

with the fabric represented in *Figure 3.18*. Designs J, L, and M in *Figure 3.17* are re-arranged in the order corresponding to the distribution of lifts in a 4 thread satinette and the bases of the first two are shown at I and K respectively. The design M, repeating on 16 threads, is arranged in the same manner except that the threads are in groups of four. It will be readily appreciated that this particular form of transposition is only suitable for such repeats which are divisible by four.

An entirely separate class of re-arranged twills is based on the sateen system of moves and most twills transposed in the sateen order tend to loose the distinctive diagonal line which is their feature in the original form. Both

Figure 3.18

the warp and the weft thread transposition is possible and the only limiting condition in the choice of twill is that it must repeat over the same number of threads as the sateen from which the order of the re-arrangement was derived. The method is illustrated in *Figure 3.19*, in which A and B represent two sateen re-arrangements of the ends, and C and D two similar re-arrangements of the picks, of a 9-thread twill with which they are shown connected by lines. The shaded squares show the bases of the designs. In A the 9-thread sateen base counting 2 outwards is employed, and in B counting 2 upwards, hence the ends, which in the twill are in the order of 1, 2, 3, 4, 5, 6, 7, 8, 9, are arranged in A in the order of 1, 6, 2, 7, 3, 8, 4, 9, 5, and in B in the order of 1, 3, 5, 7, 9, 2, 4, 6, 8. In the same manner, in C the picks of the twill are arranged in the order of 1, 3, 5, 7, 9, 2, 4, 6, 8, and in D in the order of 1, 6, 2, 7, 3, 8, 4, 9, 5.

A convenient method of re-arranging a twill in sateen order is illustrated at E to H in *Figure 3.19*. The sateen base is first inserted, as shown at F, then each sateen mark is taken to be one mark of the twill, and to it the other marks of the twill are added in regular order. In re-arranging the ends of the twill the marks are added above and below the base marks, as shown at G, whereas if the picks are re-arranged the marks are added alongside the base marks, as indicated at H. In each design G and H the marks and blanks are alike; also the weaves appear very similar on paper, but they yield quite different effects in the cloth because in G the principal floats are in the warp, and in H in the weft.

In some cases, a re-arranged weave produces a much looser structure than the original twill, as will be evident from a comparison of the twill I in *Figure*

3.19, and the sateen re-arrangement given at J. G and H, on the other hand, are quite as firm as the original twill E, on account of the manner in which the floats cut with each other. The original twills E and I, however, are similar in firmness, the only difference between them being that the latter contains more marks than the former, but this is sufficient to affect the firmness of the re-arranged weave very considerably. It will, therefore, be evident, from a comparison of the examples E, G, and H with I and J, that the re-arrangement of twills which are equally firm may result in structures being formed that

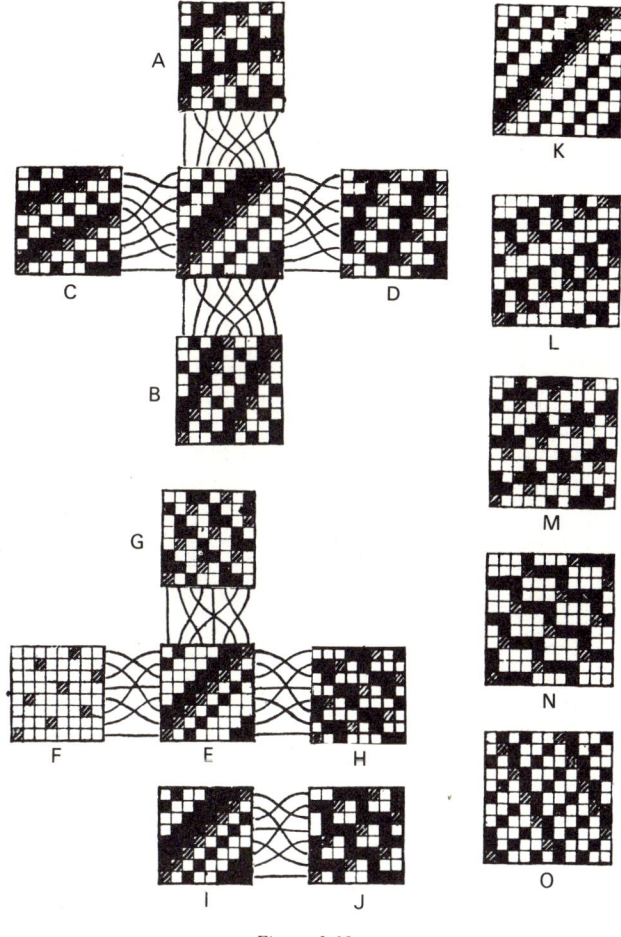

Figure 3.19

differ materially in firmness. Certain twills, of which I in *Figure 3.19* is an example, produce the same design whether they are re-arranged in the warp or in the weft.

Four sateen re-arrangements in the warp of the 11-thread twill K, are given in *Figure 3.19* at L, M, N, and O, in which the count is 2, 3, 4, and 5 respectively; it will be seen that the design O is much firmer than the others. By turning the designs one-quarter round, so that the vertical spaces become horizontal, four re-arrangements in the weft will be obtained. The examples are thus illustrative of the great variety of weaves that can be produced in the fore-going system, particularly if it be taken into account that a large number of different twills can be made on eleven threads, each of which will produce a different series of effects.

The chief disadvantage of constructing a new design by re-arranging the threads of a *given* twill is that the order of interlacing is governed by the twill, and the resulting design may be quite unsuitable for the cloth for which it is intended. The system, however, is useful, because a twill and a sateen re-arrangement in the warp can be woven in the same healds by means of straight and sateen drafting.

Elongated twills

The angle formed in the cloth by a twill weave depends upon: (a) the relative ratio of ends and picks per unit space; and (b) the rate of advance of one interlacing in respect of the following one.

If the ends and the picks per unit space are equal a regular twill advancing in steps of one as shown at A in *Figure 3.20* runs at an angle of 45°. If, how-ever, there are more ends than picks per inch in the cloth, the line of an

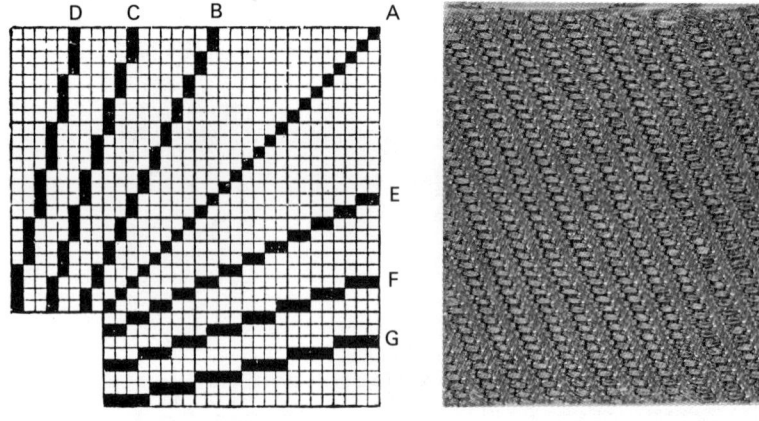

Figure 3.20   Figure 3.21

ordinary twill more nearly approaches the vertical; while if the picks exceed the ends the line becomes flatter. A fabric in which a steep twill is formed is represented in *Figure 3.21*, which, if turned one-quarter round, will also show the appearance of a flat twill.

Elongated twills, running at various angles, can also be constructed by advancing the points of intersection two or more threads in one direction to one thread in the other direction, as shown at B to G in *Figure 3.20*.

The relationship between the angle formed by a twill and the two sets of factors which determine it may be expressed by the following simple formula:

$$\tan \alpha = \frac{\text{Rate of advancement of twill upwards}}{\text{Rate of advancement of twill outwards}} \times \frac{\text{ends per cm}}{\text{picks per cm}}$$

The angle calculated is that from the horizontal and the following three examples illustrate the application of the formula.

(1) Rate of advancement (or step) of twill—1 in both directions. Square set cloth—24 threads per cm in both directions.

$$\tan \alpha = \frac{1}{1} \times \frac{24}{24} = 1$$

$$\alpha = 45°.$$

(2) Step upwards—2; step outwards—1.
Ends per cm—42; picks per cm—21.

$$\tan \alpha = \frac{2}{1} \times \frac{42}{21} = 4$$

$$\alpha = 76°.$$

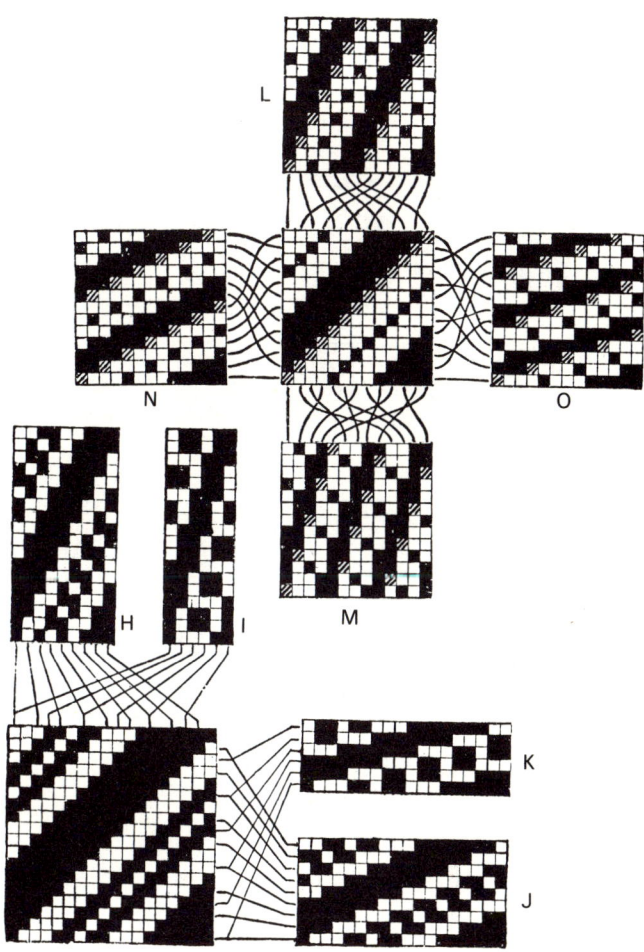

Figure 3.22

(3) Step upwards—1; step outwards—2.
Ends per cm—12; picks per cm—30.

$$\tan \alpha = \frac{1}{2} \times \frac{12}{30} = \frac{1}{5}$$

$$\alpha = 11°.$$

One method of designing elongated twills consists of selecting, or re-arranging the threads of a given ordinary twill in certain orders, as illustrated by the examples given in *Figure 3.22*. Each thread in the elongated twills is shown connected by a line with the corresponding thread in the original twill, and the four designs made from each twill correspond with the bases indicated at **B**, **C**, **E**, and **F** in *Figure 3.20*. Commencing with the first end of the given twill, the steep twill H is constructed by inserting every second end of the twill, and the steep twill I, by inserting every third end. Then, commencing with the first pick, the flat twill J is constructed by inserting every second pick

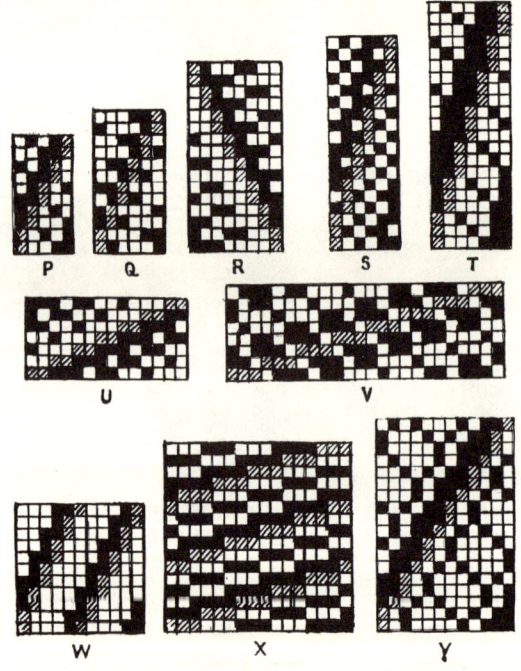

Figure 3.23

of the given twill, and K by inserting every third pick. As the number counted is in each case a factor of the number of threads in the given twill, the repeat of the new design in one direction is proportionally less.

The examples L to O illustrate the method of procedure when the number counted is not a factor of the number of threads in the given twill. The twill repeats on 13 threads, therefore, in counting 2, it is necessary to arrange the threads in the order of 1, 3, 5, 7, 9, 11, 13, 2, 4, 6, 8, 10, 12, as shown at L and N; while in counting 3, the threads are ultimately arranged in the order of 1, 4, 7, 10, 13, 3, 6, 9, 12, 2, 5, 8, 11, as indicated at M and O. It should be noted that in this case exactly the same designs would result from transposing the twill in sateen order, counting 2 and 3.

The foregoing method, though quite useful, may result in loose fabric, and generally it is preferable to construct elongated twills specifically designed for the purpose, starting with a base line of marks running at the desired angle, and repeating upon the required number of ends and picks. Other marks are then added systematically to the base marks, in the manner illustrated at P to Y in *Figure 3.23*. P, Q, and R are steep twills on 5, 6, and 8 ends respectively, counting 2 upward to 1 outward. The fabric, represented in *Figure 3.21*, corresponds with the design R. S and T are steep twills on 6 and 7 ends respectively, counting 3 upward to 1 outward; while U is a flat twill on 7 picks, counting 2 outward to 1 upward, and V a flat twill on 8 picks, counting 3 outward to 1 upward. W and X illustrate how the base marks are carried

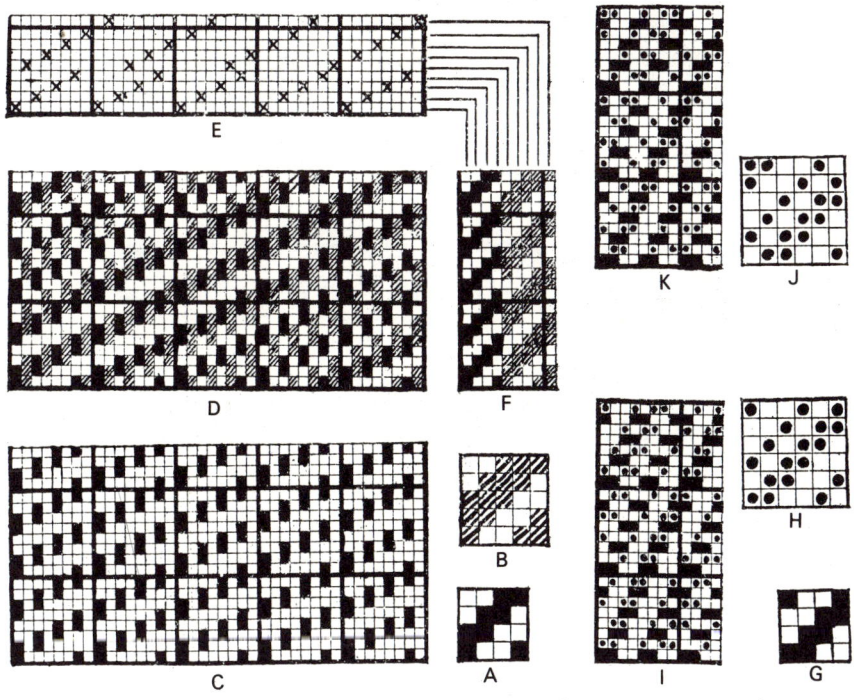

Figure 3.24

through a design, in order to obtain correct repetition, when the number counted is not a factor of the number of threads in the repeat. The design Y, in which the count is 2 and 1 alternately, will serve to illustrate how the angle of the twill line may be still further varied.

In steep twills the warp should, as a rule, show more prominently on the surface than the weft, and vice versa in flat twills. To conform with this rule the weaves U, V, and X in *Figure 3.23* should be regarded as the 'reversed convention' designs in which the marks indicate 'weft-up'. This method of construction is, in the above cases, preferable as it makes it easier to appreciate the development of the effect from the base marks. Steep twills, which produce distinct twill lines of warp in the cloth are termed 'whip cords'. The addition of marks to the edges of a line of warp float, as shown in Q and R, develops the prominence of the line.

Unless the cloth is firmly set the threads are liable to slip in elongated twill weaves. Firmness of texture can be obtained to some extent by inserting a suitable firm weave between the floating twill lines; thus 2-and-1 twill

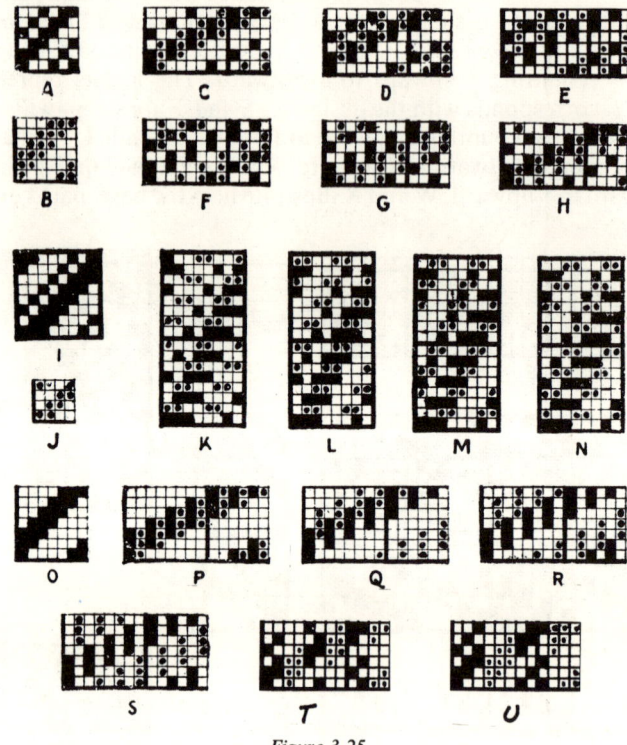

Figure 3.25

naturally fits a weave in which the count is 2, as shown at P in *Figure 3.23*, and plain weave or 1-and-3 twill, when the count is 3, as shown at S and T.

Elongated twills can be also produced by combining various twill weaves and a number of examples of these structures is shown in *Figure 3.24* and *3.25*.

Combination of twill weaves

Different methods of constructing designs by combining small ordinary twill weaves in the order of an end or a pick of each alternately are illustrated in *Figures 3.24, 3.25,* and *3.26*. In combining the 4 and 5-thread twills, given respectively at A and B in *Figure 3.24*, an end of each alternately, one twill— say A—is first indicated on the odd vertical spaces, as shown at C. Then, to complete the design, twill *B* is indicated on the even vertical spaces, as shown at D. Each twill must be carried out on 20 ends and picks—the l.c.m. of 4 and 5, hence the design D consists of 20 threads of A combined with 20 threads of B, and thus repeats on 40 ends and 20 picks.

The proper method of drafting the design D is illustrated at E in *Figure 3.24*, in which the ends of the 2-and-2 twill are indicated on four healds placed at the front of the five healds upon which the ends of the 3-and-2 twill are drawn. The arrangement enables the order of drawing in to be readily followed, while the most crowded healds are placed at the front and carry the ends which interweave most frequently. The lifting plan is given at F.

The 4- and 6-thread twills, given respectively at G and H in *Figure 3.24*, are shown combined—a pick of each alternately—at I, the 2-and-2 twill being inserted on the odd horizontal spaces, and the 6-thread twill on the

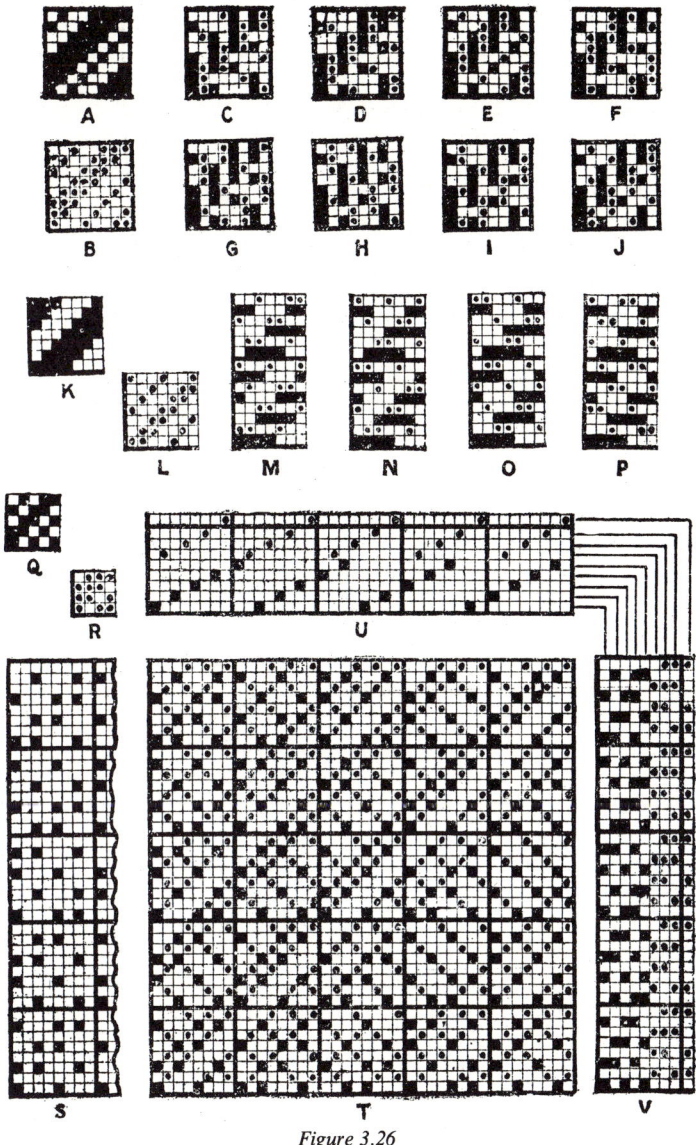

Figure 3.26

even horizontal spaces. In this case, as 12 is the l.c.m. of 4 and 6, each twill is extended over 12 ends and picks so that the design I consists of 12 picks of G combined with 12 picks of H, and repeats on 24 picks and 12 ends.

When the repeats of the twills that are combined have no factor in common only one design results in either the warp or the weft method of combination, as each twill gets into every possible relationship with the other twill. If, however, the repeats have a common factor more than one design can generally be constructed by altering the relative position of the two twills. Thus, 2 will divide into 4 and 6—the respective repeats of G and H in *Figure 3.24*, and it is therefore possible to produce a second design, as shown at K, by commencing the 6-thread twill in the position indicated at J, while retaining the 2-and-2 twill in the original position. It will be found by experiment that any further change in the relative position of the two twills will simply produce a duplicate of either I or K.

The construction of different designs by varying the relative position of two twills can be carried still further if the twills are equal in size or if one is double the size of the other. Thus, in combining the two six-thread twills given at A and B in *Figure 3.25*—an end of each alternately—six designs are obtained, as shown at C, D, E, F, G, and H; and, as 6 ends of one twill are combined with six ends of the other, each design repeats on 12 ends and 6 picks. One twill—say A—is inserted in the same position on the odd vertical spaces of each design, then the twill B is indicated on the even vertical spaces; commencing in the design C with the first end of B; in D with the second end; in E with the third end; in F with the fourth end; in G with the fifth end; and in H with the sixth end. The twills can be combined—a pick of each alternately—in the same manner, and the latter method has the advantage that each design only requires six healds, whereas each design C to H in *Figure 3.25* requires 12 healds.

The twills I and J are shown combined—a pick of each alternately—at K, L, M, and N in *Figure 3.25*, only four changes being possible in this case as J is on four threads. It is necessary, however, to use 8 threads of the weave J to conform with the repeat of I, hence the complete design repeats on 16 picks and 8 ends. The weave I is indicated in the same position on the odd horizontal spaces of K, L, M, and N; then the weave J is inserted on the even horizontal spaces commencing with the picks in turn in succeeding designs.

A still further development, which is illustrated by the examples O to S in *Figure 3.25*, consists of using the same twill for both the odd and the even threads. The weave O is indicated on the odd vertical spaces of the designs P, Q, R, and S, commencing each time with the first end; but in inserting the weave on the even vertical spaces, P commences with the first, Q with the third, R with the fourth, and S with the fifth end of O. In this weave any further change of position will produce a duplicate of one of the preceding. This method has the advantage that only half as many healds are required as there are ends in the repeat.

Further possibilities which exist in this group of structures are shown at T and U where the two original twills, A and B, have been combined by taking alternate pairs of ends from each, as at T, or combining in groups of three ends from each at a time, as at U. The possibilities of achieving novel effects by combination are virtually endless as one, or both, twills used could be first transposed and then used in combination either warp-wise or weft-wise; in single threads, in pairs, or in larger groups of threads.

In the foregoing combinations, flat or steep twills are respectively produced according to whether the ends or the picks are combined. The examples given in *Figure 3.26* illustrate methods of combining twills by which designs—

twilling at the angle of 45°—are formed. The designs C to J are constructed by first indicating *alternate* ends of the twill A on the odd vertical spaces in the same position in each design. Then *alternate* ends of the twill B are inserted on the even vertical spaces, commencing with the following end in each succeeding design. Thus C commences with the first end of B, D with the second end, E with the third end, and so on.

In the same manner, the designs M, N, O, and P in *Figure 3.26*, are constructed by inserting alternate picks of the twill K in the same position on the odd horizontal spaces; then alternate picks of the twill L, commencing each time with a different pick, are inserted on the even horizontal spaces. In this case as each twill repeats on an odd number of picks, all the picks must be combined, and the resulting designs therefore repeat on 14 picks and 7 ends. All the positions in which the twill L can be placed are not shown, as the remaining positions simply produce duplicates of M, N, and P; it will be found that duplicate designs result when the marks of the original twills are arranged symmetrically.

A useful method of employing two small twills in the construction of a large fancy twill running at the angle of 45° is illustrated by the examples Q, R, S, and T in *Figure 3.26*. One twill—say Q—is indicated where the *odd* vertical and horizontal spaces intersect, in the manner represented in the portion given at S, then the design is completed by inserting the second twill (*R*) where the *even* vertical and horizontal spaces intersect, as shown at T. The number of ends and picks in the repeat of the design is equal to twice the l.c.m. of the threads in the repeat of the twills—or $2 \times 5 \times 4 = 40$ ends and picks. Marks should largely predominate over the blanks in the twills that are combined, or the floats in the resulting designs will be too large. A warp or weft surface is produced according to whether the marks are taken to indicate weft or warp. The draft for the design T is given at U, and the lifting plan at V; and an important feature of the arrangement is the small number of healds that is required. In each of the foregoing systems of combination more than two twills can be employed which may be either unequal or equal in size.

WEAVES CONSTRUCTED ON SATIN OR SATEEN BASES

Simple developments

In simple derivatives the new design is built up by using the original satin or sateen as the base, and subtracting or adding marks as required, in the same relative position to each base mark. Thus, the *Venetian* weave, given at A in *Figure 3.27* is produced by indicating an additional weft float above each blank of the original 5-thread satin, while the 'Buckskin' weave shown at B is similarly constructed except that it is based on the 8-thread satin. The newly created additional weft floats are indicated on the design paper by means of dots. Similarly, new designs can be based on the weft sateens but in this case, the design is developed by introducing additional warp floats alongside the original interlacing points as indicated at C and D. These constructions are used in the production of very heavy weft-faced cotton fabrics that are employed as protective clothing in situations in which a considerable degree of wear is expected. By introducing comparatively few ends per inch a very large number of picks can be inserted, and a compact, strong cloth is produced, which generally has a soft, downy surface, formed by 'raising' the weft. A cloth may be woven with 40 ends per cm of 40/2 tex cotton warp, and from 60 to 80 picks per cm of from 30 to 44 tex cotton weft. The design E in *Figure 3.27* is reversible, and if heavily wefted the cloth has a dense weft surface on both sides. The various structures in this class of fabrics are known by such terms as 'swansdown', 'lambskin', and 'imperial'.

The examples F to J in *Figure 3.27* are constructed on a 10-thread sateen basis. It is usually convenient to commence a design by adding a few marks to each base mark, as shown at F, and to then add other marks in stages (if considered necessary), as indicated in the designs G, H, I, and J.

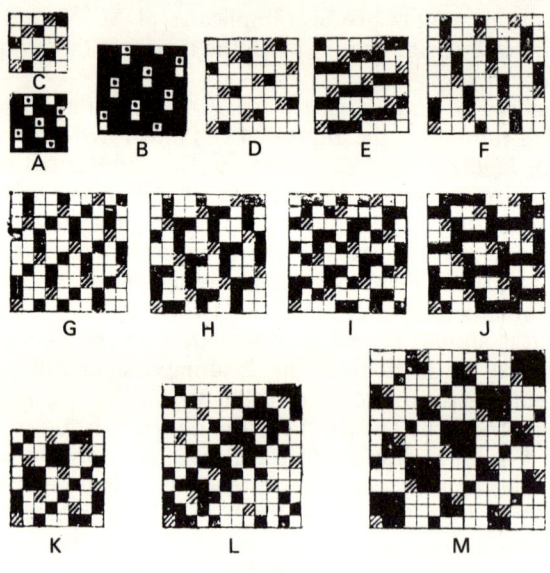

Figure 3.27

As a rule, in constructing small weaves the marks should be added in the same order to the base marks, in the manner represented at C to J in *Figure 3.27*. In the case of a few sateens, however, such as the 8, 12, and 15-thread weaves, in which the sateen marks run in line with each other at 45° angle, and join with each other in succeeding repeats, the method may be deviated from. Thus K, L, and M in *Figure 3.27* show interesting designs which result from the addition of marks in irregular order to the 8, 12, and 15-thread sateens respectively. (Examples of larger and more elaborate sateen derivatives are given in *Figure 4.2*.)

Extension of sateen weaves

Sateen weaves may be extended horizontally, as shown at A and D in *Figure 3.28*; or vertically, as indicated at B and E; or both horizontally and vertically, as represented at C and F; the examples illustrating the system in reference to the 5 and 8-thread sateens. Their chief value, when used in the forms shown at A to F is that with the same number of healds longer floats are formed on the surface of the cloth than is the case with ordinary sateens. For instance, the design A, which requires five healds, has a weft float of 8, and is a very suitable weave for displaying a lustrous weft stripe prominently on the surface of a cloth.

The extended sateens may be readily employed as bases in the construction of new weaves, which are usually of a bolder character than those produced upon ordinary sateen bases. Marks are added systematically to the base marks, as shown in the designs G to L in *Figure 3.28*, which respectively correspond with the plans A to F. Satin base can, of course, be equally well used, but as the development by 'subtraction' of marks is rather more difficult,

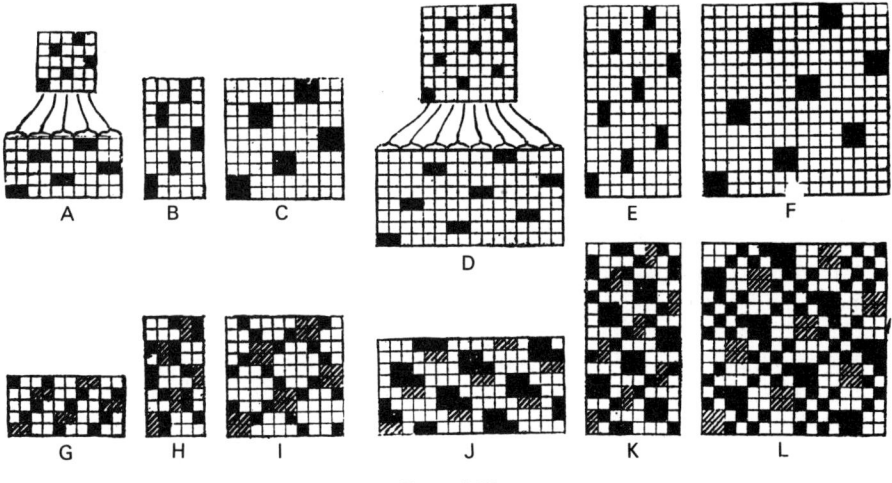

Figure 3.28

the sateens are generally preferred on the grounds of convenience. If desired, a warp faced character of the cloth is easily achieved by the addition of a sufficient number of marks to the original sateen.

Sateen base, or the particular system of moves adopted in a sateen, is also of value as a means of re-arranging certain weave orders. This has already been shown in connection with the transposed twills. In addition the weave serves frequently as the basis for the distribution of figures in isolated spot designs.

4

Fancy Twill, Diamond and Diaper Designs

FANCY TWILLS

Large diagonals

A method of constructing ordinary twills or diagonals by combining two or more small twills in diagonal form is illustrated at A and B in *Figure 4.1*. These diagonals, however, cannot be drafted on to a small number of healds. A is composed of 3-and-1 and 1-and-3 twills, while B is a compound of 3-and-3, 2-and-1, and 1-and-3 twills, the last twilling in the opposite direction to the diagonal. The chief points to note in constructing the weaves are that the twills are joined together in a suitable manner, that they are sufficiently different from each other, and that each is alloted enough space to give the large twill a distinctly diagonal appearance. By reversing one of the twills, as shown in B, the diagonal form is developed very clearly.

Shaded twills

These are designed, as shown at C, D, and E in *Figure 4.1*, by combining a number of small twills in which the floats increase or decrease in size. C is composed of five twills on six threads, which are arranged 5-and-1, 4-and-2, 3-and-3, 2-and-4, and 1-and-5. The term *single-shading* is applied to this style because each kind of float shades in one direction only. D is a *double-shaded* style which is composed of the 1-and-4, 2-and-3, 3-and-2, and 4-and-1 twills, the floats of which are arranged to shade in both directions. E is composed of 5-and-1, 4-and-1, 3-and-1, and 2-and-1 twills, which are so arranged as to form distinct warp and weft sections each of which is single shaded. The last style can be readily modified to produce warp and weft sections which are double-shaded.

Diagonals on sateen bases

These are constructed by combining two or more sateen derivatives, in the method illustrated in *Figure 4.2*. Certain sateens, such as the 8, 10, and 15-thread weaves, can be used in constructing diagonal designs running at 45°

angle. An example is shown at F in *Figure 4.2*, which is based on the 8-thread sateen counting 5. Sateens can also be selected which will yield steep twills, as shown at G, or flat twills, as shown at H. G is based on a 10-thread sateen counting 3, and H on a 7-thread sateen counting 2. According to the angle in

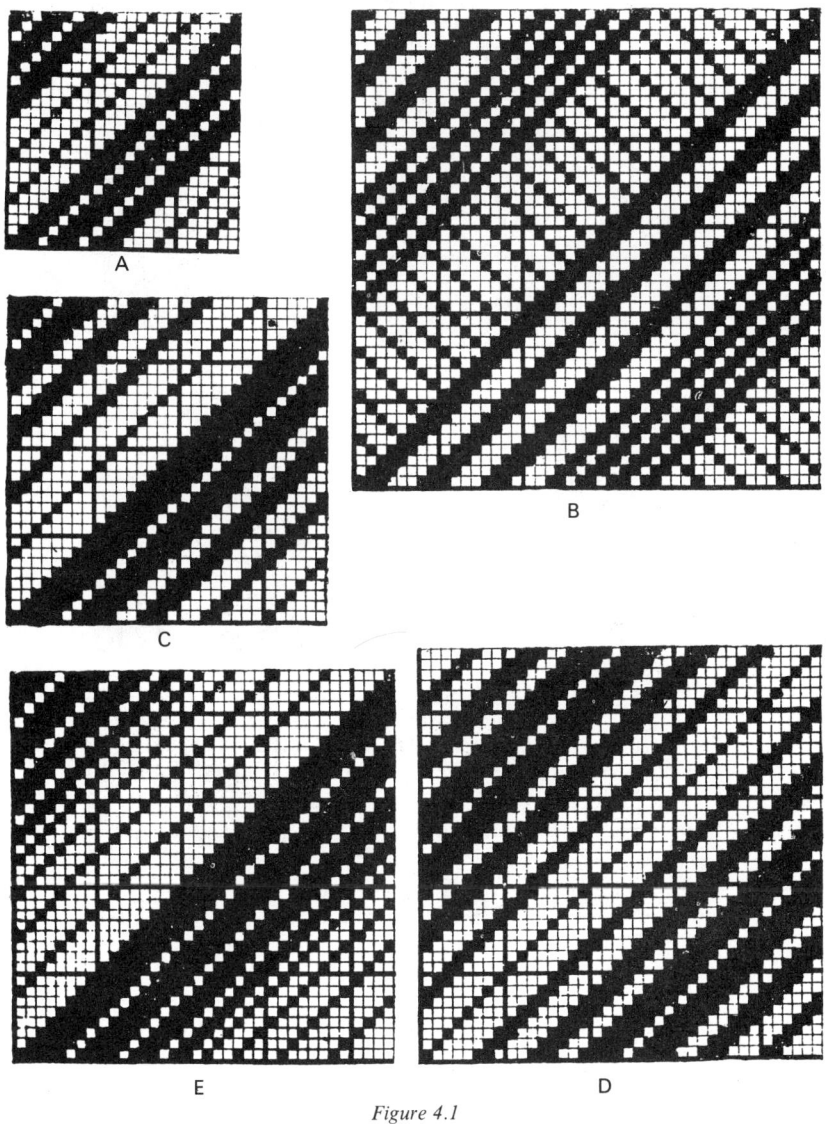

Figure 4.1

which the diagonal is required to run the sateen base is inserted over an equal or an unequal number of ends and picks; thus in F the ends and picks are equal; G is on three times as many picks as ends; and H on twice as many ends as picks. The number of ends and picks in a design must be a multiple of the number of threads in the repeat of the sateen. In adding marks to the sateen marks the weaves in the respective sections should be made sufficiently different from each other to show clearly, except when a shaded diagonal effect is formed, as shown at H, in which the weave is changed very gradually. Diagonal lines may be arranged to run at different angles in a design as shown at I, which is constructed on the 8-thread sateen basis. The development of

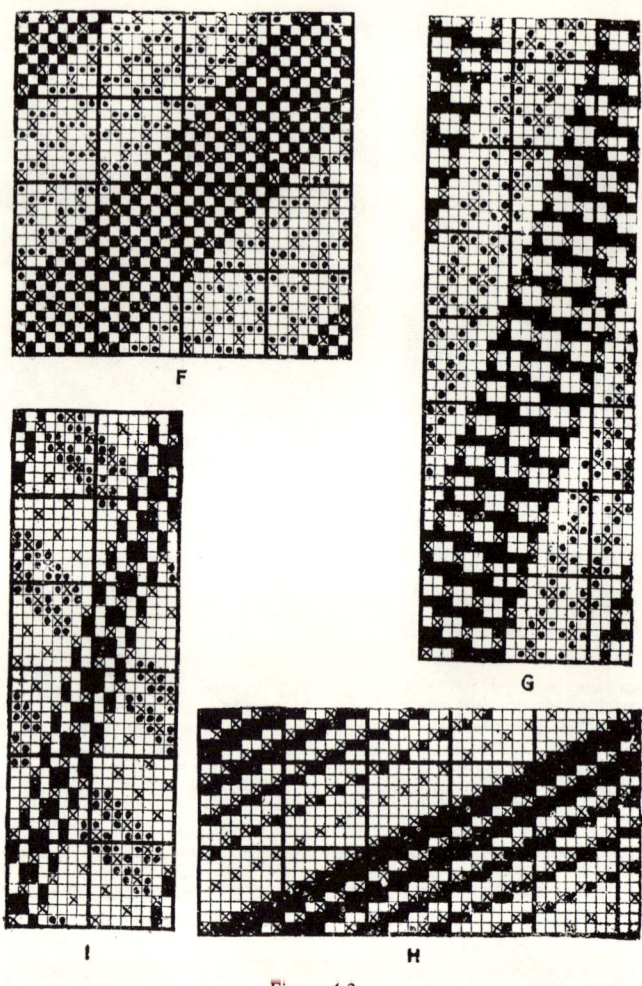

Figure 4.2

these constructions can be easily traced from the designs as the original sateen base marks are shown in the form of crosses, whilst the second stage extensions are indicated by the solid marks and the third stage work is represented by the dotted marks.

Figured twills

The examples, given at A, B, C, and D in *Figure 4.3*, illustrate the arrangement of small spots or figures in conjunction with, and running at the same angle, as ordinary twills. A spot may be repeated diagonally one or more times in each repeat of the twill lines; and in finding the repeat of a spot it is necessary to count the spaces diagonally. For example, in the design A the crosses, which indicate corresponding positions of the spots, occur on every third space—counted diagonally, and in order to show this clearly, dots are indicated between the crosses. The complete repeat of the twill is upon 12 threads or diagonal spaces, and the spot is therefore repeated four times. A representation of the design A, in the woven fabric, is given in *Figure 4.4*.

The twill in the design B in *Figure 4.3* repeats on 16 threads, and as the figure repeats on 8 diagonal spaces, as indicated by the crosses and dots, it is inserted twice in the complete design. In C the twill lines repeat upon 16 threads, but in this case the spot repeats on 6 spaces—counted diagonally, hence the complete repeat extends over 48 picks—the l.c.m. of 16 and 6. The design C could be arranged similarly to repeat upon 48 ends and 16 picks

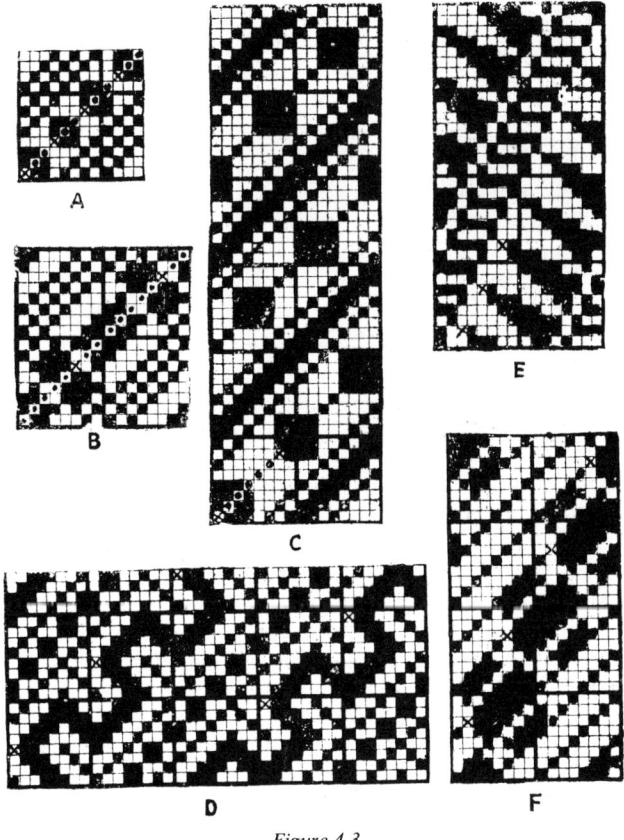

Figure 4.3

by extending the weave horizontally, and in the design D a figured twill is shown thus arranged. The twill repeats upon 20 threads, and the figure on 8 diagonal spaces, hence the complete design occupies 20 picks and 40 ends, the latter number being the l.c.m. of 20 and 8. In dobby shedding it is necessary to extend the designs vertically, but in jacquard weaving the horizontal method has the advantage that a saving of cards is effected. In designing figured twills it is convenient to first insert lightly a diagonal line of marks as a basis; the spaces occupied by the figure and the twill then require to be adjusted to the size of the repeat, or vice versa.

Small figures may be arranged in combination with steep or flat twills, and an example is given at E in *Figure 4.3* in which the twill repeats on 16 ends and 32 picks, while the distance between corresponding parts of the figure is

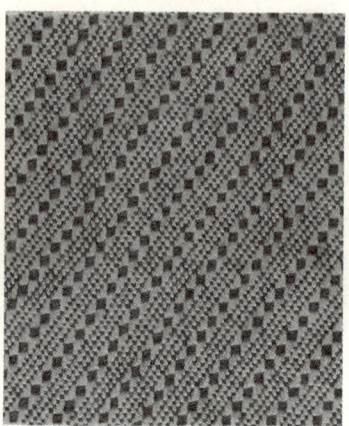

Figure 4.4

two spaces outward, and four spaces upward. The design F is inclined at the same angle as E, the distance between corresponding parts of the figure being four outward and eight upward, but in this case the space between the figures is simply filled in with 1-and-3 ordinary twill.

DIAMONDS AND DIAPERS

These designs, from the point of view of their construction, can be regarded as a further development of the twill weaves. Two different types can be distinguished: those that are symmetrical about their vertical and horizontal axes which can be produced with the aid of the point draft; and those that are not pointed which are symmetrical about their diagonal axes. The first type, in its simplest form, is a development of the waved twill, whilst many effects in the second group are based on the herringbone twill. The terms diamond or diaper are used somewhat indiscriminately, but it is more correct to apply the term diamond with reference to the first type, and the term diaper in respect of the second type.

Construction of diamond designs

True diamond shapes converge into a vertix and for this reason most designs of this type can be constructed economically on the point draft basis. The structure may be developed in the following two ways: (1) By employing a vertical waved twill or zig-zag as the lifting plan in conjunction with the point draft; (2) By indicating a diamond base and building up the design symmetrically on each side of the centre thread. The first method is illustrated at A, B,

C, and D in *Figure 4.5* in which A shows a 1-and-3 twill that is arranged at B as a horizontal waved twill in the order of 1, 2, 3, 4, 3, 2, while C represents the same twill arranged to zig-zag vertically in the order of 1, 2, 3, 4, 3, 2 (two repeats are given in each direction). If B be taken as a draft with C as the lifting plan, the small diamond design given at D will result.

In the same manner E, F, and G in *Figure 4.5*, illustrate the construction of a diamond design based upon 2-and-2 twill. The draft E turns on the first and ninth ends, and the lifting plan F, which, as shown by the crosses, runs in the

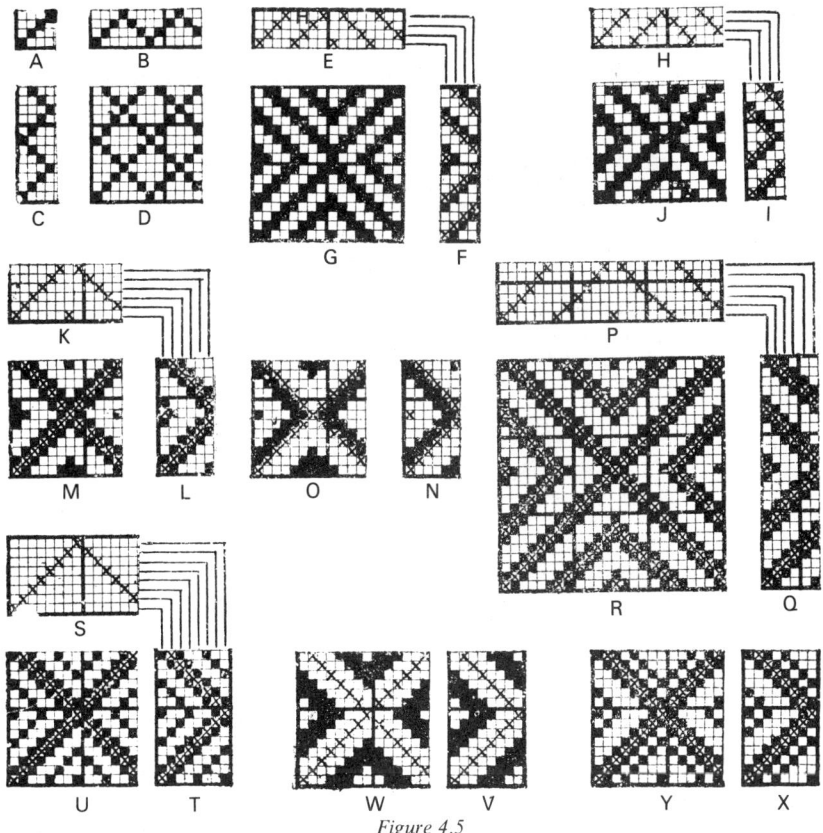

Figure 4.5

same order vertically as the draft is arranged horizontally, turns on the first and ninth picks. The combination of E and F produces the diamond design given at G, in which, however, it will be noted that the diamond spaces are not alike. This is due to the additional mark of the 2-and-2 twill being necessarily placed at one side of the base marks in the lifting plan. It is possible, however, to produce similar diamond spaces in the 2-and-2 twill by making the repeat two threads larger in one direction than in the other, as shown at H, I, and J. The design J corresponds with the woven pattern represented in *Figure 4.6*.

The construction of three diamond designs, based upon 3-and-3 twill weave, is illustrated at K to R in *Figure 4.5*. The draft K turns upon the first and seventh ends, and the corresponding lifting plan L upon the first and seventh picks. In the latter the base line (indicated by the crosses) forms the centre of the float of three, and the arrangement results in the formation of a perfectly symmetrical diamond design, as shown at M. A lifting plan for the draft K is given at N, however, in which the base line does not form the centre of the 3-and-3 twill weave, and this results in the production of a design, as represented at O, in which the diamond spaces are not alike. By employing more than one repeat of the twill in each direction, as shown at P, Q, and R in *Figure 4.5*, a larger diamond design is produced. If the base line of the lifting plan forms the centre of the marks of the twill weave, a continuous line of marks in each direction is formed which enclose the diamond spaces.

The drafts E, K, and P in *Figure 4.5* turn on the same heald (the first) each time, and the arrangement has the advantage that the same number of ends is drawn upon each heald. Pointed drafts, however, are frequently made to

Figure 4.6

turn on the first and last healds, which thus require half as many mails as the centre healds, as shown at S in *Figure 4.5*. In order to illustrate certain features in the designs, three lifting plans are given at T, V, and X, in each of which an 8-thread twill weave is reversed in the same order as the draft S, while the corresponding designs are indicated at U, W, and Y. The same twill weave is used in both T and V, and in both cases the base line of marks forms the centre of the twill. In the plan T, however, the base line is in the centre of the float of three, whereas in V it coincides with the single line of marks. The difference in the position of the twill results in the formation of two quite different designs, as will be seen from a comparison of U and W. In the lifting plan X the base line of marks is in the centre of the float of three, but the single line of marks is not in the centre of the space between, hence in the resulting design, given at Y, the two diamond spaces are dissimilar. This, however, is not necessarily a disadvantage.

Figure 4.7 shows the construction of a more elaborate diamond design than any of the foregoing, and also illustrates a method of using straight and waved twills in the production of bordered fabrics. A shows a straight draft, and B a fancy point draft on 8 healds, while C and D represent straight and waved twill lifting plans to correspond. The straight twill given at E results from the combination of A and C; the horizontal waved twill F from the combination of B and C; the vertical zig-zag twill G from the combination of A and D; and the diamond design H from the combination of B and D. By suitably repeating the respective sections a number of times a bordered fabric may be formed in which E forms the corners, F the cross-borders, G the side-borders, and H the centre.

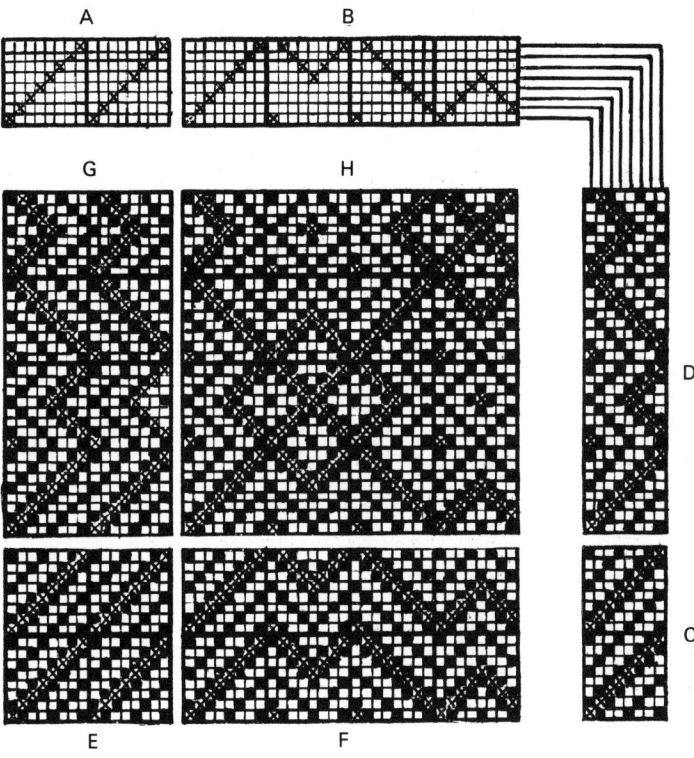

Figure 4.7

Figure 4.8 shows another form of diamond figure which repeats upon 90 ends and picks, and can be woven in 18 healds. The order of drafting is indicated by the black squares on the first 18 horizontal spaces of the design. The lifting plan, which is based on the weave given at A in *Figure 4.9*, is indicated on the first 18 vertical spaces of *Figure 4.8*; and, as shown by the solid marks, the order of reversing is the same as in the draft. A method of preventing the formation of an increased float where the twill reverses (which is common to pointed twills) is illustrated by the example. The draft is arranged to turn always on the first or the tenth heald, and the lifting plan on the first or the tenth vertical space. The squares where the first and tenth ends and picks intersect in the weave A in *Figure 4.9*, are therefore taken as centres, and the twill line of float is cut across as shown. Therefore, instead of the floats joining together small spots are formed at each place where the twill lines cross one another in *Figure 4.8*. In order that the general effect may be clearly seen the complete weave is shown only on the first 18 ends and picks of the design.

It is very necessary for the weave, which is used as the basis of the lifting plan, to be systematically constructed in order to ensure that a symmetrical design will result. For the purpose of further illustrating this point two fancy twill weaves are given at B and C in *Figure 4.9* which are suitable for the draft of *Figure 4.8*. A single line of marks is first inserted diagonally, as shown by the dotted squares in B and C, then the first and tenth threads (on which the

Figure 4.8

draft reverses) are taken as centres, and a weave is built up which will reverse either in the direction of the warp or the weft without forming an increase in the float. Also the remainder of the weave is constructed in the same manner on each side of the centre line of marks.

In the second method of constructing point-drafted diamond designs a pointed draft is first indicated on the required number of healds, as shown at A or B in *Figure 4.10*, which are arranged on nine healds. Marks are then inserted in reverse order, as shown at C or D, and the repeat, which is on two threads less than twice the number of healds in the draft, is thus divided by the base marks into two diamond spaces. The base marks, which serve as a guide in building up the design, may be converted into distinct lines that cross one another, as shown at E; or a weave may be indicated only in the diamond

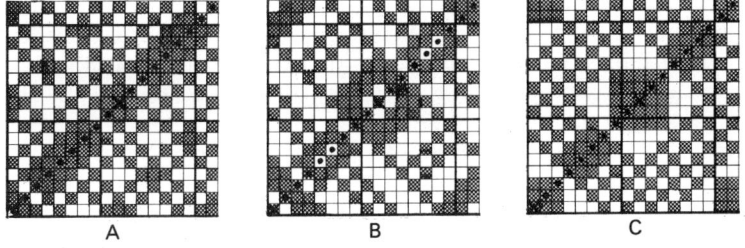

Figure 4.9

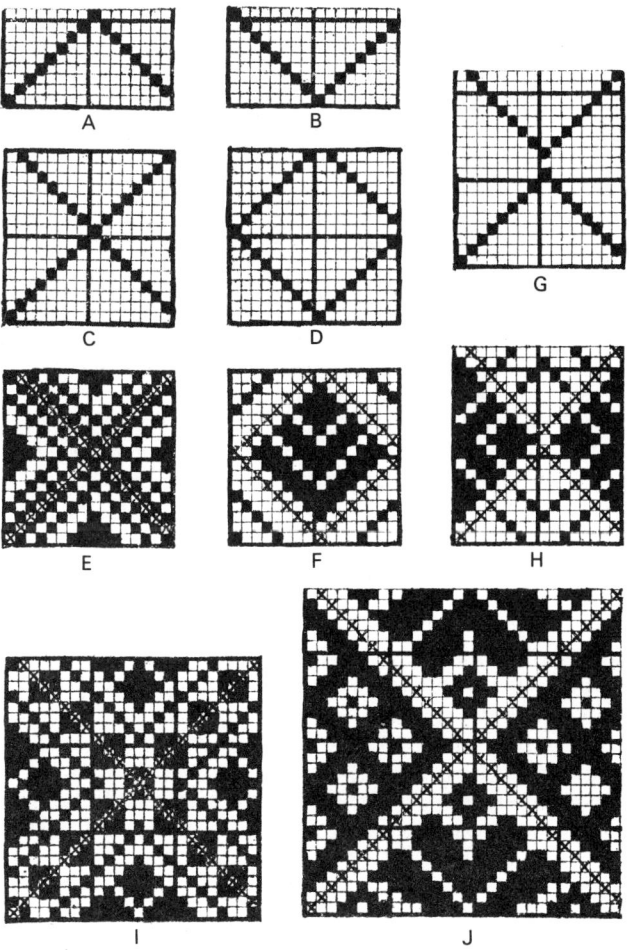

Figure 4.10

spaces, as represented at F. The two diamond spaces may be filled in in the same manner, as shown in E, or different effects may be inserted, as indicated in F, which shows one diamond space in weft float, and the other in warp float. In each case, however, it is necessary for the threads to work alike on each side of the centre ends.

In constructing diamond designs in which the sections are equal in size and exactly the reverse of each other, the repeat should be made two threads larger in one direction than the other. The method is illustrated at G and H in *Figure 4.10*; G showing how the diamond base is arranged, and H a design in which the warp float in one space exactly corresponds with the weft float in the other space.

If a hopsack weave is employed, the small squares should be arranged to reverse properly from the centre, as shown in the design given at I in *Figure 4.10*, which is constructed on the basis of a point draft on 13 healds.

The design J shows an elaborate style that is weavable on a 16-heald point draft.

Construction of diaper designs

The simplest weaves of this type are produced as a further development of the herringbone twill, in which the principle of opposing a warp float on one side of the design by a weft float on the other, is extended in both directions, i.e. horizontally and vertically. In this manner a design is formed in which the typical herringbone *cut* splits the design into four quarters, the diagonally opposite quarters being similar. Simple, even-sided twills such as the 2-and-2, or 3-and-3 produce well balanced diaper effects as shown at A and D in *Figure 4.11*. These structures are frequently employed as they are capable of forming large design repeats with considerable economy in the number of healds that need to be used. This is indicated at B and E where typical herringbone drafts are employed, using in the production of the diaper a number of healds which is no greater than the minimum required for a basic 2-and-2, or 3-and-3 twill. More elaborate diapers, such as that shown at F, can also be constructed on the herringbone draft basis provided that the twills from which they were originated fall into a certain specific category. The characteristics of such twills are: (1) That they are even-sided; (2) That their repeat splits into two halves each of which is symmetrical within itself; and (3) That the lifts in each of the two halves are diametrically opposite. The twill used as the base for the diaper F satisfies all three conditions stated above, which is shown graphically at H in *Figure 4.11* where the dotted line 'd' indicates that the twill splits up in the required manner. Other twills to conform with the above requirements can be easily constructed and the following two will produce good diapers with herringbone drafts on 16 and 12 healds respectively $\frac{2 \cdot 2 \cdot 4 \cdot}{\cdot 4 \cdot 2 \cdot 2}$; $\frac{1 \cdot 2 \cdot 1 \cdot 1 \cdot}{\cdot 1 \cdot 1 \cdot 1 \cdot 2 \cdot 1}$. Even sided twills containing more than two lines of floats which do not split in the manner indicated above cannot be woven with the economical herringbone draft. This is shown at I and J where the base is the $\frac{3}{1}\frac{1}{3}$ twill. Although this twill is even-sided each half of the repeat is not symmetrical and, as a result, upon herringbone reversal the succession of the warp and the weft floats is reversed. Therefore, though the twill itself requires only 8 healds its herringbone or diaper version must be constructed on 16 healds.

Warp and weft faced twills can also be used to produce diapers on the herringbone reversal as shown at K, L, and M in *Figure 4.11*, but owing to the very prominent *quartering* of the repeat a distinct check effect is produced and for this reason such effects are frequently termed *dice checks*.

In addition to the herringbone based diapers many other diaper forms can be constructed without a preconceived base. These offer greater freedom to

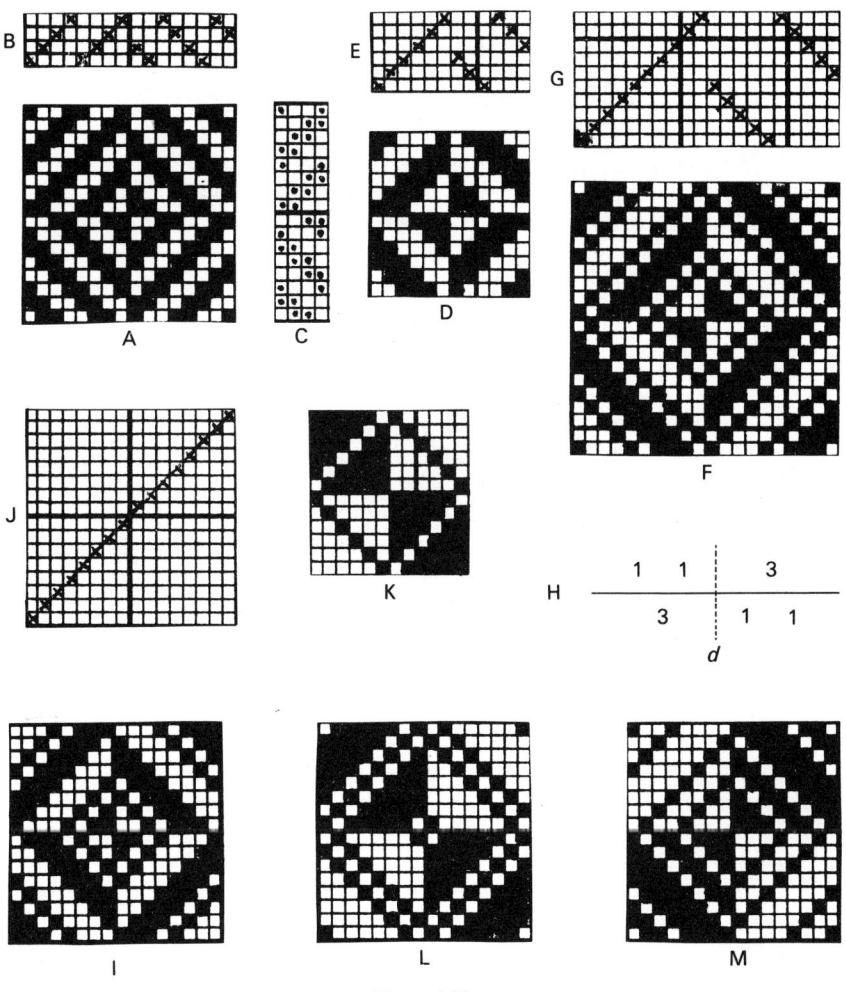

Figure 4.11

the designer, but in dobby shedding the size of their repeat is more limited as they normally cannot be woven with the same economy in the number of healds as the point or herringbone drafted designs. In this class of structures, to retain an idea of the required form, the diamond base marks may be for convenience indicated in the same manner as in the construction of pointed designs. Very interesting interlacing twill designs are produced in this system, and a convenient method of working is illustrated at A and B in *Figure 4.12*. From the centres where the diamond base lines intersect, lines of marks are inserted running to right and left alternately, as indicated by the solid squares in A. Marks are then added to the base lines to give the required length of float, as shown at B, but blank squares are left where the twills cross one another in order to break the continuity of the lines.

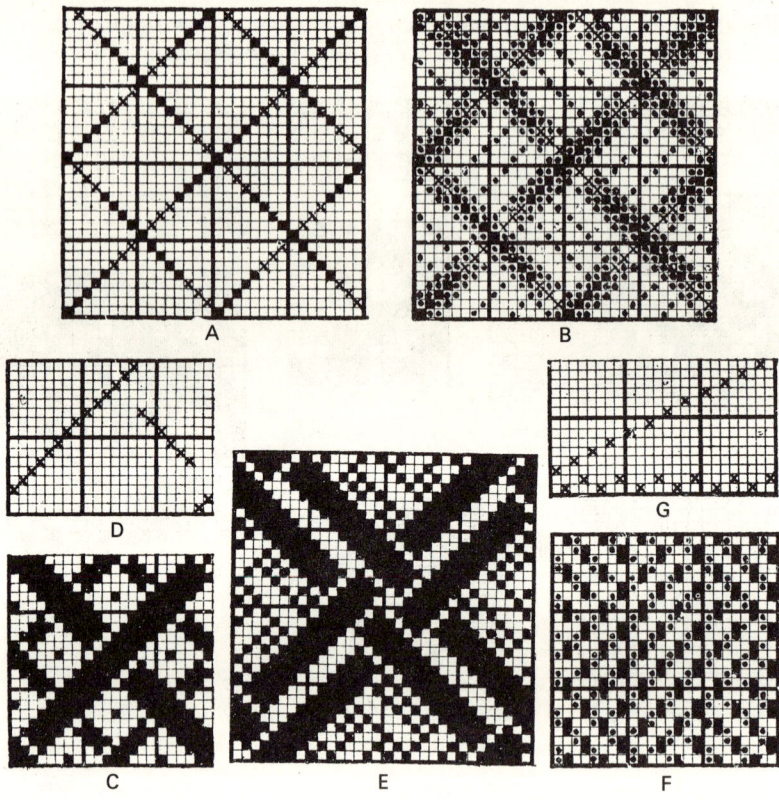

Figure 4.12

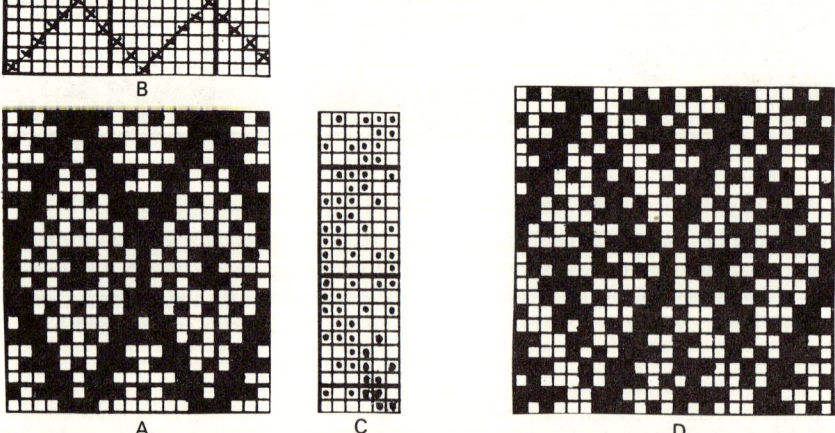

Figure 4.13

In dobby shedding, in order to obtain a larger number of threads in the repeat than the number of healds employed, an interlacing twill design may be arranged to suit a modified form of point drafting. An example is given at C in *Figure 4.12*, which repeats on 22 threads but can be drafted on 16 healds, as indicated at D.

The design E illustrates a method of interlacing the twills when two or more lines are introduced; this design cannot be drafted on to less than 29 healds, and is therefore beyond the capacity of the ordinary type of dobby.

The diamond design given at F illustrates a principle by which comparatively large effects can be woven on a small number of healds. The even ends work continuously in 2-and-2 order, as indicated by the solid marks, and can be drawn upon two healds, as shown in the draft G. The 2-and-2 twill weave is caused to run to left or to right in the design according to the position in which the marks are inserted upon the odd ends. Effects can be produced in 1-and-3 twill weave in the same manner.

Elongated and flattened diamonds and diapers

Good designs can be often obtained by extending steep and shallow twills into diamond or diaper designs. Depending upon the original twill base the resulting figure will be either elongated or flattened in appearance. Careful selection of the twills is necessary to avoid the formation of excessive length of float and some modification may on occasions be required. Both the point draft and the herringbone principle may be applied, the first method being illustrated at A, and the second at D in *Figure 4.13*, the same steep twill (shown shaded) being used as the base in each case. B shows the advantage of the point draft in dobby designing as A, which requires only 6 healds is almost as big in the area of repeat as D which needs 12 healds. Designs A and D when turned at 90° show the appearance of the flattened twills. For best effects, elongated diamonds, in common with the steep twills, should show more warp than weft on the face, whilst weft float should predominate in the flat diamonds, close setting of the threads being necessary in both to obtain sufficient firmness in the interlacing.

More elaborate diamond or diaper forms can be produced on the shaded and figured twill bases and some large diamonds suitable for jacquard designs are shown in *Figures 10.11* and *12.40* to *12.42*.

5

Miscellaneous Elementary Structures

FURTHER EXTENSION OF HOPSACK WEAVES

The mat and basket weaves, given in *Figure 3.4* can be modified in various ways with the object of obtaining further variety of pattern, and in order to make the structures firmer. Examples are given in *Figure 5.1*, in which A shows the 3-and-3 hopsack stitched in the centre of each small square, while B and C represent two methods of stitching the 4-and-4 hopsack. The small squares are not so clearly defined as in the ordinary hopsacks, but the weaves are firmer. The design D shows a modification of A obtained by extending or doubling the latter.

The design E, which is derived from the 3-and-3 hopsack, shows how a weave may be modified by reversing the float at one corner of each small square, while the design F, which is based upon the 4-and-4 hopsack, shows the floats reversed at opposite corners of each square. In both cases, the complete design results from reversing the section in which the shaded squares are indicated.

Barley-corn weaves

A mat weave also forms the foundation of each of the designs G, H, I, and J in *Figure 5.1*, to which the term 'barley-corn' is applied. The cross-twill in the designs gives a considerable degree of firmness to a cloth as compared with ordinary hopsacks of similar sizes, particularly when the cross-twill is in double lines of marks, as shown in I and J. In all the foregoing examples the floats of warp and weft cut with each other perfectly.

Stitched hopsacks

The designs K and L in *Figure 5.1* illustrate methods of imparting firmness to large weaves by the introduction of plain stitching threads. In K the plain threads are introduced only in the warp, so that the floats in the weft sections of the design are broken. In L, however, certain threads of both series inter-weave plain, and similar warp and weft sections are formed.

The design M in *Figure 5.1* is really a stitched warp rib weave that repeats on four ends, and the cloth is entirely warp faced. By colouring the ends indicated by the solid marks and the crosses 1 dark, 1 light, for 16 ends, and 1 light, 1 dark, for 16 ends, distinct squares in light and dark are formed. The cloth should contain about twice as many ends as picks per unit space, the sections then being square, so that the design looks like a hopsack.

Twilled hopsacks

The designs N to S in *Figure 5.1* are twilled hopsacks, in which the small squares, which are formed by only one series of threads (either warp or weft), run in twill order. The weaves are not so stiff as the ordinary hopsacks, and are generally more suitable than the latter for suitings and trouserings. The

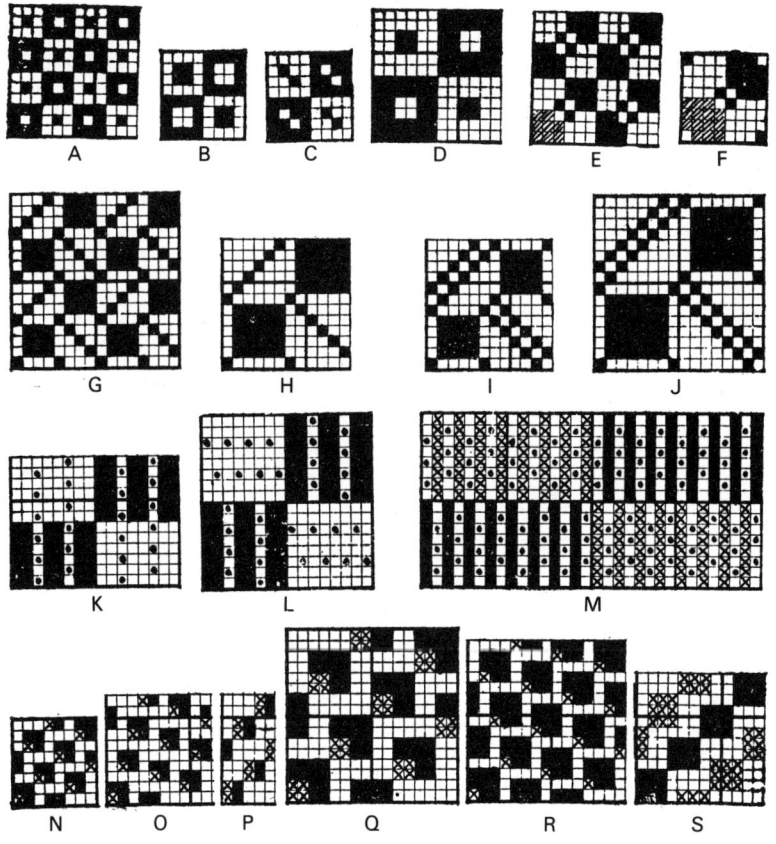

Figure 5.1

2×2 hopsack effect given at N, is based on an 8-thread sateen; that at O on a 10-thread sateen; and that at P on an extended 5-thread sateen. The 4×4 effect, given at Q, is constructed on an extended 8-thread sateen basis, or by doubling the weave N. R and S represent 3×3 twilled hopsacks, the former being constructed on a 15-thread sateen base, and the latter by inserting two rows of squares as equally distant from each other as possible on 12 threads.

CONSTRUCTION OF WEAVES BY REVERSING

The principle of construction of new weaves by reversing has been already explained in connection with the herringbone twills and the diaper effects based on such twills. In this section the principle is extended to illustrate the construction of new designs from incomplete twills and from other weaves.

The examples A to E in *Figure 5.2* illustrate a method of employing the reversing principle by which neat little check designs are formed. A small unit weave (which need not be a complete weave in itself) is first made on any suitable number of ends and picks, and the complete design is then constructed by reversing the unit vertically and horizontally. Thus, taking A as the unit weave, B is obtained by reversing the ends of A, and C by reversing the picks, while D results either from reversing the ends of C or the picks of B. Corresponding threads are connected by lines, and it will be seen that the ends of A are the reverse of the ends of B; the marks in one coinciding with the blanks in the other, while the weave is turned in opposite directions. In the same manner the picks of A are the reverse of the picks of C, the ends of C the reverse of the ends of D, and the picks of B the reverse of the picks of D. The design E, which shows the parts A, B, C, and D put together, repeats on twice as many ends and picks as the unit weave, and consists of four sections which cut with each other where they are in contact exactly like the sections of a diaper based on the herringbone twill.

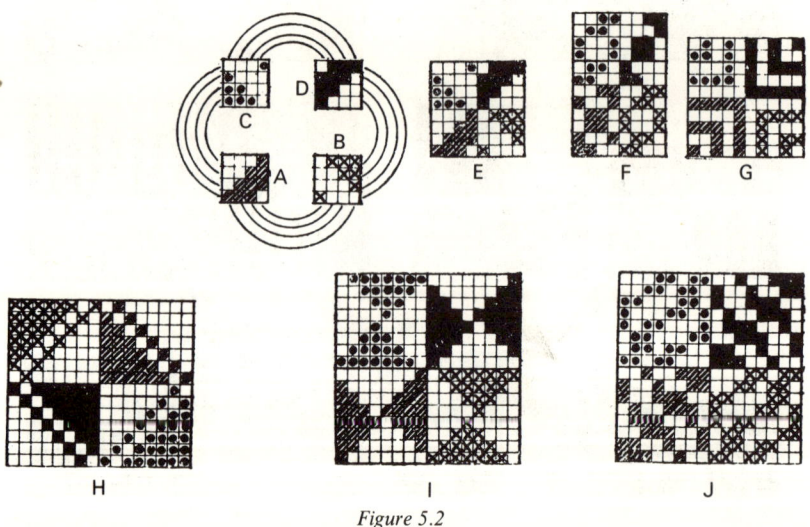

Figure 5.2

The remaining examples in *Figure 5.2* are constructed in the same manner as E, the different stages of working being represented by different marks. The unit weave of F is on four ends and six picks, and produces a design of a *crêpe* character that repeats on eight ends and twelve picks. The design G is sometimes termed a *basket* weave, and is constructed from a 5 × 5 unit, while the designs H and I, to which the term *barley-corn* is applied, result from 8 × 7, and 8 × 8 units respectively. The unit of J consists of one repeat of the Mayo weave, and this design can be used in the form shown, or each section may be extended a number of times so as to form large check designs. The construction of large check designs on the reversing principle is illustrated in *Figure 7.7*

CRÊPE WEAVES

The term crêpe is applied to weaves that contain little or no twilled or other prominent effect, and which give a cloth the appearance of being covered by minute spots or seeds, as shown in the fabric represented in *Figure 5.3*. The weaves are used alone, and in combination with other weaves in a great variety of cloths, and very frequently are employed in forming the ground

Figure 5.3

of figured fabrics. These constructions, also known as oatmeal weaves, must not be confused with crêpe cloths in which the broken surface effect is due entirely to the use of high twist yarns which, upon controlled shrinkage in the finishing, produce a highly irregular texture although woven in the plain weave. (See Appendix I.) High twist crêpe yarns are occasionally employed in conjunction with the crêpe weaves and this combination results in cloths very markedly pebbly and puckered in appearance.

Construction of crêpe weaves upon sateen bases

The weaves are constructed in a number of different ways, one of the simplest of which consists of adding marks in certain orders to some of the sateen bases. A and B in *Figure 5.4* are constructed on an 8-thread regular sateen base. In the former both the warp and the weft are floated, the same effect being produced on both sides of the cloth, whereas the latter, in which chiefly the ends are brought to the surface, is arranged to suit a cloth in which the warp is better material than the weft. C is constructed on a 10-thread sateen basis, and contains equal floats of warp and weft; the term 'sponge' is applied to this weave.

The irregular sateens, because of the entire lack of twilliness, are particularly suitable to use as bases in the construction of crêpe weaves. D in *Figure 5.4* is a simple, but very useful, crêpe which is based on the 4-thread satinette, and in effect can be classed also as a 2-and-2 broken twill; E is constructed on a 6-thread irregular sateen, and F and G on 8-thread irregular sateen bases.

Combinations of a floating weave with plain threads

In this system of constructing crêpe weaves threads that work plain are combined with threads of a floating weave which are arranged in sateen order. H in *Figure 5.4* illustrates one method of arrangement in which plain marks are indicated on the odd ends, as shown by the dots, and sateen marks on alternate picks of the even ends, as shown by the crosses. Marks are then added to the sateen base marks in an order which fits with the plain weave, as shown at I, in which the floating threads are arranged on the basis of a 4-thread satinette. The designs J and K are similarly constructed, the floating threads in the former being arranged upon the basis of a 5-thread satin, and in the

Figure 5.4

latter upon the basis of a 6-thread satin. In each case the design repeats upon twice as many ends and picks as the satin base that is employed. The plans L and M, which correspond with H and I, show how the floating weave may be inserted horizontally. The designs appear rather different in the two methods and by comparison it will be seen that whereas in the design I the number of healds can be reduced by drafting the plain ends on to one shaft, in design M as many healds are required as there are ends in the repeat of the design.

In the designs I, J, and K all the odd ends work alike; but good crêpe designs are also produced by operating them in opposite order, as shown at N in *Figure 5.4*, and combining the threads with similar floating weaves. Thus in the design O the floating weave is arranged in the same manner as in I, but the resulting design is quite different. A different basis of the floating weave is employed in the design P, which, however, is simply a modification of the satinette, a base mark being indicated on every pick, so that the repeat is on twice as many ends as picks. This is also the case in the design Q, which is a simple but effective crêpe that can be woven by means of a combination of 2-and-2 twill tappets, and plain tappets. The design R shows another variation in which two plain threads alternate with two floating threads, the latter being again arranged on a 4-thread satinette basis.

Crêpe weaves produced by reversing

The reversing principle of constructing designs, illustrated in *Figure 5.2*, can be employed in the construction of neat crêpe effects, and an example is given at S in *Figure 5.4* in which the shaded marks indicate the base weave. Also, weaves containing minute floats are built up in stages, as shown at T to X in *Figure 5.4*, one portion being reversed or turned in the opposite direction to another portion, as indicated by the different marks in the designs. The fabric represented in *Figure 5.3* corresponds with the design V in *Figure 5.4*.

Insertion of one weave over another

This method of constructing crêpe weaves consists of inserting two different weaves one over the other. In order to produce an irregular effect one at least

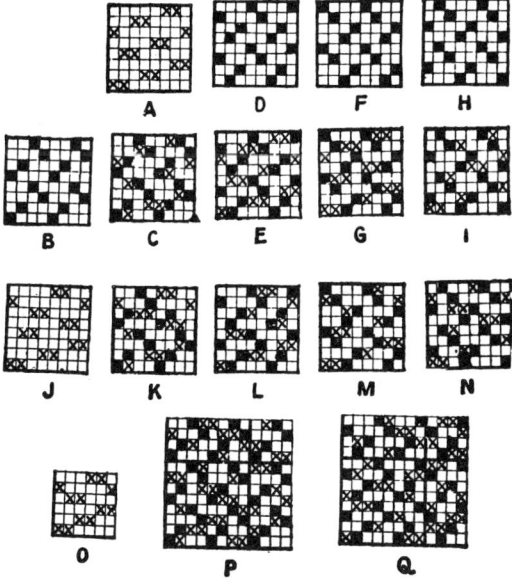

Figure 5.5

of the weaves should be irregular in construction, and it is usually better if both are irregular. The method is illustrated in *Figure 5.5*, in which A shows an 8-thread regular sateen derivative, and B the satinette; while at C the marks of both A and B are combined in the same design. As the marks of the two weaves coincide in certain places, in order to prevent confusion the weave that is marked in first should be indicated lightly, the second weave being then inserted in a different kind of mark. Afterwards the marked squares may be filled in solid in order to show the complete weave properly. In most cases, if the repeats of the two weaves have a common factor different effects are formed by changing the position of one weave. Thus by inserting the weave A in the same position each time, and changing the satinette to the positions shown at D, F, and H in *Figure 5.5*, the combinations produce the designs given at E, G, and I respectively. In the same manner, the combination of the 8-thread irregular sateen derivative, given at J, with the weaves B, D, F, and H produces the designs indicated at K, L, M, and N respectively.

The number of threads in the repeat of a design is equal to the l.c.m. of the threads in the repeats of the weaves that are combined. The combination of the 4-thread satinette B with the 6-thread weave given at O in *Figure 5.7*, thus produces a design repeating on 12 ends and 12 picks, as shown at P. The design Q shows the weave O combined with the satinette in the position indicated at D, but this is a case in which a change of position of one weave does not produce a real alteration in the resulting design, as will be evident from a careful comparison of Q and P. The method of construction can be further extended by inserting three different weaves over one another.

Armures

The term 'armure' is frequently applied to weaves of a somewhat irregular or broken character which produce more pronounced effects than crêpe weaves. In some designs a small form is arranged twice in the repeat of a

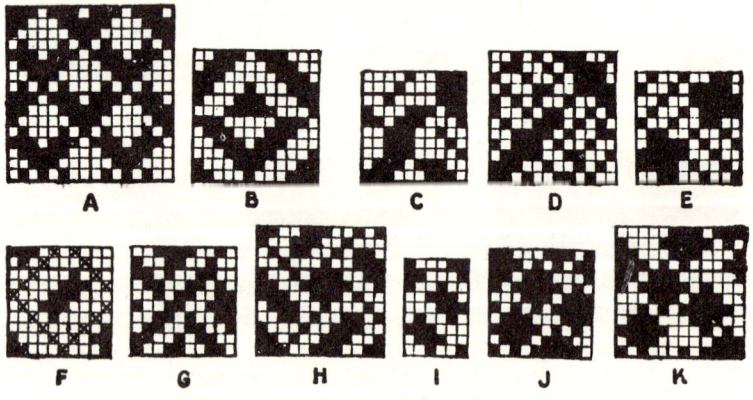

Figure 5.6

design, as shown at A and B in *Figure 5.6*. If the form is inclined it may be turned in opposite ways, as shown at C, D, and E, in each of which it will be seen that the ground weave and the figure are arranged to fit very neatly with each other. F, G, and H are arranged on small diamond bases. The form may be indicated several times in the repeat of a design; thus in the design I a small spot occurs three times in the repeat; in J, five times; and in K, six times.

HONEYCOMB WEAVES

In the cloths produced in honeycomb weaves the threads form ridges and hollows which give a cell-like appearance to the textures. Both the warp and the weft threads float somewhat freely on both sides, which, coupled with the rough structure, renders this class of fabric readily absorbent of moisture. The weaves are, therefore, suitable for towels; they are also used in various forms for bedcovers and quilts, and in combination with other weaves for fancy textures. The weaves are of two classes: (1) ordinary honeycombs which give a similar effect on both sides of the cloth; (2) Brighton honeycombs which produce the cellular formation on one side of the cloth only.

Ordinary honeycomb weaves

In most cases these can be woven in point drafts, and a method of constructing the designs on this principle is illustrated at A, B, and C in *Figure 5.7*. A point draft is indicated on the required number of healds—in this case, five,

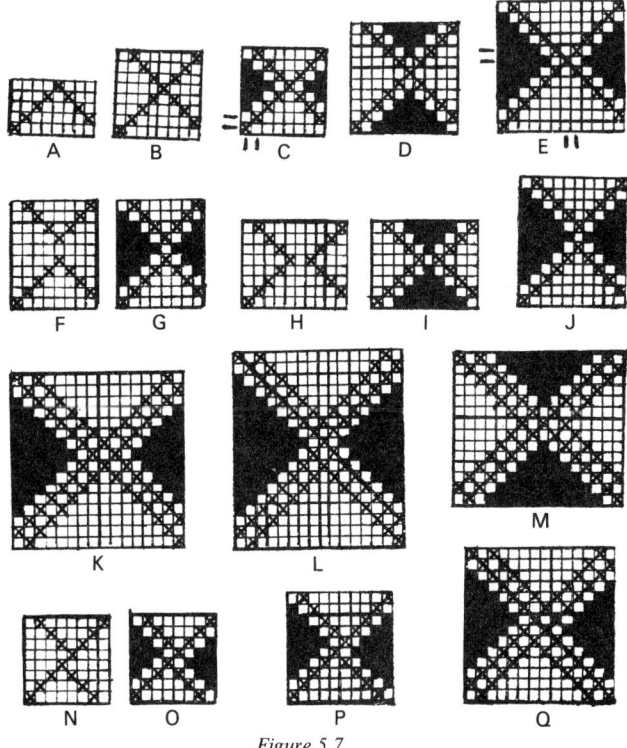

Figure 5.7

as shown at A; then the marks are reversed, as indicated at B. Afterwards, one of the diamond spaces is filled in while the other is left blank, as represented at C. D shows a similar honeycomb design which is weavable on six healds, and E a design that requires seven healds. In the foregoing system of arrangement either diamond space may be filled in, as will be seen from a comparison of D with C and E, but one yarn is floated on the surface more than the other. Thus, in the design D the weft floats are 9, 7, 5, 3, and 1, as compared with floats of 7, 5, 3, and 1 in the warp. The fabric represented in *Figure 5.8* corresponds with the design Q in *Figure 5.7*

The plan F shows a method of arranging the base so as to obtain equal warp and weft float; the resulting design repeating on two more picks than ends, as indicated at G. The basis may also be arranged on two more ends than picks,

Figure 5.8

as shown at H, the complete design for which is given at I. The latter method, however, requires a heald more than the former in producing the same length of float. The design J, which is constructed in a similar manner to G, produces the same weft float as D, and the same warp float as E. In each design G, I, and J it is necessary for the marks to be inserted in the larger diamond space.

Large honeycomb weaves are liable to be loose in structure when constructed in the ordinary manner, and in order to secure firmness of texture a double row of base marks is inserted, as shown in the design K in *Figure 5.7*, which is weavable on nine healds. The designs L and M, each of which requires the same number of healds as K, illustrate the two methods previously described, of obtaining equal warp and weft float in the firmly stitched weaves.

The plan N in *Figure 5.7* shows a base that is sometimes used in constructing honeycomb weaves; but in this system a straight draft is required. One space is filled in and the other left blank, as shown at O. The design P illustrates a similar weave which repeats on a larger number of threads, and Q a firmly stitched large weave.

In the designs given in *Figure 5.7* the ridges occur where the long floats of warp and weft are formed and the hollows where the threads interweave in plain order. Thus, in each of the designs C, E, G, J, K, and L, a warp ridge is formed by the first end, and a weft ridge by the first pick. The plain weave, about the centre of these designs, tightens the threads, and causes a depression to be formed; and although the weaves are constructed on a diamond basis, the cellular formation makes the patterns appear rectangular in the cloth. In the design D the ridges occur on the sixth end and pick, in I on the sixth end and fifth pick, and in M on the ninth end and eighth pick; while in O, P, and Q, two threads form a ridge—the first and last end, and the first and last pick in each case. Suitable weaving particulars for the design D in a heavy cloth are: 95/2 tex cotton warp and weft, 20 ends and picks per cm; and in a lighter cloth, 24/1 tex cotton warp and 33/1 tex cotton weft, 35 ends and 32 picks per cm.

Brighton honeycomb weaves

These are quite different in construction from the usual type of ordinary honeycomb, and require to be woven in straight drafts; also the number of threads in a repeat must be a multiple of four. The construction of a Brighton weave on 16 threads is illustrated at R and S in *Figure 5.9*. A diamond base is first made by inserting a single row of marks in one direction, as shown by

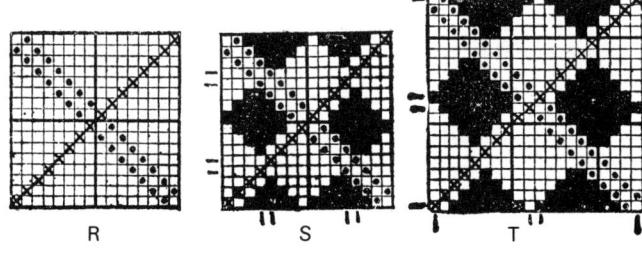

Figure 5.9

the crosses in R, and a double row in the other direction, as indicated by the dots. Marks are then added to the double rows so as to form a small warp diamond in the right and left corners of each diamond space, as shown in S; a similar weft diamond being left in the upper and lower corners. The length of float of the centre thread of each small spot is one thread less than half the number of threads in the repeat. Thus in the design S each centre float passes over $(16 \div 2) - 1 = 7$ threads, while in the design T, which shows a Brighton weave on 20 threads, each centre float passes over $(20 \div 2) - 1 = 9$ threads.

In the same manner as in ordinary honeycomb weaves, the long centre floats of warp and weft form vertical and horizontal ridges; but in the Brighton weaves two sizes of hollows are formed, a large hollow at each place where the double line of marks crosses the single line, and a small hollow in the centre of each diamond space. There is also the difference that in an ordinary honeycomb weave each repeat only forms one cell, whereas a Brighton weave produces two large and two small cells. The fabric represented in *Figure 5.10* corresponds with the design S in *Figure 5.9*. About the same weaving particulars may be employed for the design S in *Figure 5.9* as those given for the design D in *Figure 5.7*. The Brighton structure is sometimes made, however, with two thicknesses of yarn arranged in 2-and-2 order; the two thick threads being inserted where the longest floats are made.

In both classes of honeycombs there are two places where coloured threads may be effectively introduced: First, where the long floats are formed on the surface, as indicated by the position of the marks along the bottom and at the side of the design C in *Figure 5.7*, and S in *Figure 5.9*. Second, in the intermediate positions, as similarly indicated along the bottom and at the side of

Figure 5.10

E in *Figure 5.7*, and T in *Figure 5.9*. In the first position the colours follow the ridges, and show very distinctly on the surface in the form of a small check. In the second position the colours are only brought to the surface where the threads interweave plain, so that small spots of colour are formed at the bottom of the cells.

HUCKABACK WEAVES

These weaves are largely used for linen and cotton towels, glass-cloths, etc. The structure is so arranged that areas of plain weave give firmness and hard wearing qualities whilst areas of loose floats provide good moisture pick-up. The standard weaves are given at A and B in *Figure 5.11*; the former, which is termed the 6-pick or 'Devon' huck, being used for the lower grades of cloths and the latter for fine qualities.

The draft which is generally used is so arranged that the odd threads are carried by the two front healds, and the even threads by the back two healds as shown at C. A tappet shedding motion is usually employed and the lifting plan for the design A is given at E, and for the design B at F. The purpose of the special draft is to enable plain cloth to be woven in the healds (without re-drawing the warp) by coupling the healds 1 and 2 together, and 3 and 4 together, and operating them by the first and fourth tappets.

The weaves tend to draw the ends into groups of five, and, to prevent this, it is customary to place the last end of one group in the same split of the reed as the first end of the next group, while the centre three ends are placed in one split. The threads are thus dented in the order of two and three alternately, as shown at D in *Figure 5.11*.

The ordinary huckaback weaves are modified in various ways; thus G in *Figure 5.11*, which is derived from A, contains four groups of floats in the repeat; H shows a variation of B that repeats on 8 ends and picks; I repeats on 10 ends and 8 picks and produces the same effect on both sides of the cloth; while J, although not reversible, shows both warp and weft floats on each side of the cloth.

The principle of the huckaback weave is also used in the construction of designs which repeat upon a larger number of threads and contain longer floats, as shown in the design K in *Figure 5.11*. The term *honeycomb-huckaback* is applied to this weave. A further development is illustrated by the

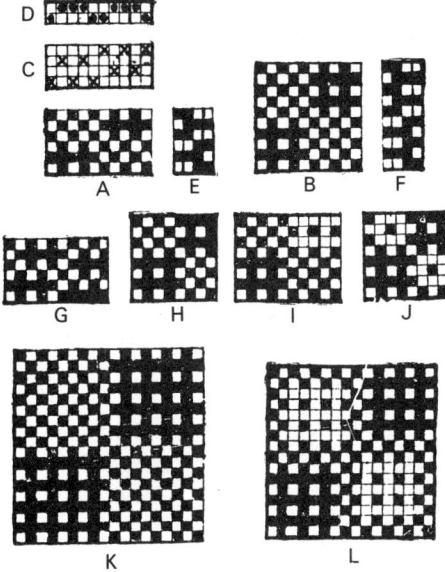

Figure 5.11

Figure 5.12

design L which, when woven in coarse yarns, belongs to a class termed 'Grecian'. *Figure 5.12* represents the appearance of the design L in the woven fabric.

MOCK LENO WEAVES

The weaves included under this head produce effects that are similar in appearance to the gauze or leno styles obtained with the aid of a doup mounting (see *Watson's Advanced Textile Design*). Two kinds of structures are produced by the weaves—(1) perforated fabrics in imitation of open gauze effects, an illustration of which in stripe form is given in *Figure 5.14*; (2) distorted thread effects in imitation of *spider* or *net* leno styles, examples of which are represented in *Figures 5.16* and *5.19*.

Perforated fabrics

Illustrations of weaves of this class are given in *Figure 5.13*, in which A, B, and C respectively show the 3 × 3, 4 × 4, and 5 × 5 imitation gauzes. Each weave is constructed by reversing a small unit, which in A, B, and C is indicated by the crosses. The weaves are in sections which oppose one another, and there is a tendency for the outer threads of adjacent sections to

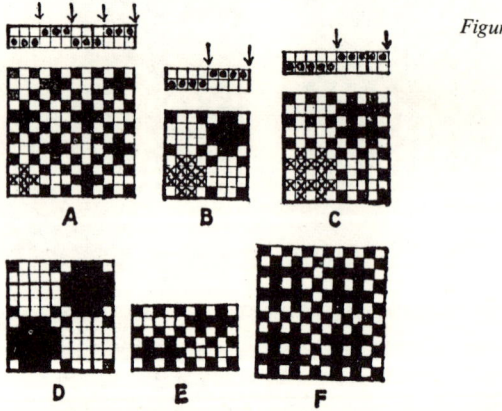

Figure 5.13

be forced apart, whereas in each section the order of interweaving permits the threads to readily approach each other. The warp threads thus run in groups with a space between, and are crossed by weft threads which are grouped together in a similar manner. The open appearance of the cloth, however, can be either improved or obscured by the system of denting that is employed. If the last end of one group is passed through the same split as the first end of the next group, the tendency of the threads to run together is counteracted; but if each group of ends is passed through a separate split the reed naturally assists in drawing the threads together in groups. Thus the designs A, B, and C should be dented 3, 4, and 5 ends respectively per split as shown above the plans. The open appearance of the weaves may be further increased by using a rather fine reed and missing alternate splits; the arrows above the denting plans in *Figure 5.13* indicating the positions of empty splits. The distance between the groups of picks can be also increased, if desired, with the aid of an interrupted take-up device but this is rarely employed as the groups of picks are quite effectively separated by the weave provided that the count and the spacing of weft yarns is selected correctly. Also, such a device is confined to an all-over open cloth and as the most common occurrence of the perforated effect is in the form of stripe or isolated figure the separation of picks over the full width of the cloth is not usually desired.

The design D in *Figure 5.13* is simply a modification of B, and E of C, and both weaves should be dented five ends per split. The design F shows a style in which the ends and picks one to five group together, and are clearly separated from the sixth end and pick. In a coarse reed the ends may be dented

Figure 5.14

five and one per split alternately; in a reed of medium fineness, five in two splits, one split missed, one per split, one split missed; while in a fine reed (16 to 20 splits per cm) a suitable order of denting is two, one, and two ends per split, one split missed, one per split, one split missed. In the design F only one yarn is floated on the surface, whereas in the other designs the warp and weft are floated equally.

The open gauze weaves are sometimes used alone, as in canvas cloths, and in cheap fabrics for window curtains; but for light dress fabrics, blouses, aprons, etc. they are, to a large extent, employed in combination with other weaves. In *Figure 5.14* the 3 × 3 imitation gauze weave, given at A in *Figure 5.13*, is shown arranged in stripe form with plain weave, while the 5 × 5 structure indicated at C, is shown as a ground weave to a figure in *Figure 12.15*. When the same threads have to form both an open effect and ordinary interlacing, as shown in *Figure 12*.15, it is, of course impracticable to leave splits of the reed empty; and in some cases, in order that the figure will be properly developed, each group of threads is placed in more than one split, but care is taken to split the groups of threads by the reed in regular order. Imitations of open leno effects are obtained in plain weave simply by missing splits in the reed; as for instance, a stripe effect might be woven in a fine reed with three plain ends in one split alternating with two splits missed.

Distorted thread effects

The imitation gauze weaves of this class may be arranged to distort certain threads in either the weft or the warp, or in both weft and warp. J in *Figure*

5.15 illustrates one of the simplest methods of producing a distorted warp effect. The ground structure is plain weave, and the fourth and eleventh ends, which are distorted, float over all the plain picks, but pass under the fourth and eleventh picks. The latter float over one group of plain ends, and under

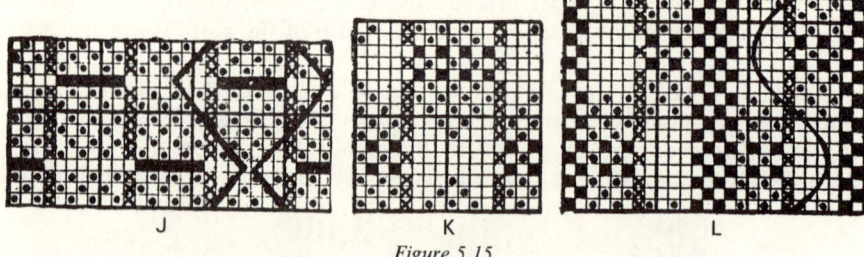

Figure 5.15

the next group in alternate order. The distorted ends are placed on a separate beam and are given in more rapidly than the ground ends, hence they are drawn towards each other where the picks four and eleven float over the ground ends. As the latter floats occur in alternate order, the ends are drawn together in pairs, and then separated, as indicated by the zig-zag lines on the right of J.

The design K in *Figure 5.15* produces a similar effect to J, but the distorted ends (5 and 13), and the picks (4, 6, 12, and 14) which float over them, are more firmly interwoven. Also the ground ends float loosely on the back of the cloth where the distorted ends are drawn together, the bending of the ends being thus facilitated. The fabric represented in *Figure 5.16* corresponds with the design K.

Figure 5.16

The design L in *Figure 5.15* shows a modification of K, in which all the distorted ends work alike, and produce independent zig-zag lines in the cloth, as indicated on the right of the design.

The distorted warp effects are chiefly used in combination with other weaves in stripe form, and an example of this is given in *Figure 5.17*. When used in stripe form the ends which form the zig-zag effect should be somewhat crowded in the reed; and in producing the above pattern, the nine ends which form each group, as indicated above the plan given in *Figure 5.17*, were dented in three splits, while the ground ends were woven two per split.

Examples of distorted weft effects are given at R and S in *Figure 5.18*. The design R is arranged with plain ground on the same principle as J in *Figure 5.15*. The floating ends pass over all the distorted picks, and alternately over

Figure 5.17

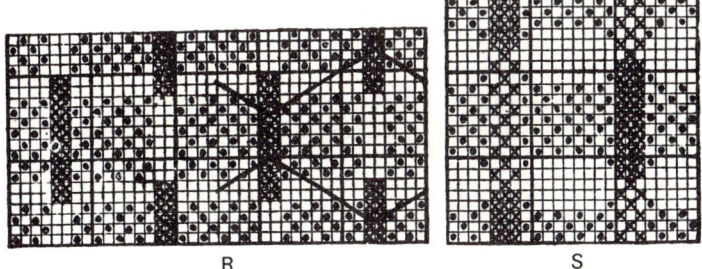

R

S

Figure 5.18

Figure 5.19

the ground picks between; therefore the distorted picks, which float over all the ground ends, are alternately drawn together and separated, as shown by the zig-zag lines on the right of R. *Figure 5.19* represents a fabric woven in the design R. In this method, the degree of distortion varies according to the difference in the shrinking of the distorted picks, which float loosely, and the ground picks, which interweave frequently; hence the best results are obtained when a ground texture is formed that shrinks considerably in width.

The design S in *Figure 5.18*, illustrates a style which is used to some extent in thick yarns. In order to develop more fully the zig-zag effect two picks are floated on both sides of each distorted pick, and the ends, which draw the floating picks together alternately float and interweave plain. The loosely-woven picks are beaten up close together so that those in the centre are forced prominently to the surface, and are in a proper position for being drawn together, and then the plain interweaving of the floating ends produces the most suitable conditions for forcing the distorted picks apart.

SIMPLE SPOT DESIGNS

Designs in which the ornament consists chiefly of small, detached spots or figures are employed in nearly all classes of yarn and yarn combinations, for dress fabrics, fancy vestings, and other textures in which elaborate figure ornamentation is not desired. Spotted effects are produced in cloths in different ways—e.g., by employing fancy threads in which spots of contrasting colour occur at intervals, and by introducing extra warp or extra weft threads which are brought to the surface where the spots are formed. In the following, however, only the system of producing spot figures is considered in which the spots are formed by floating the ordinary weft or warp threads on the surface of the cloth in an order that is in contrast with the interlacing in the ground. (The examples will be found useful as an introduction to the designing of figured fabrics, which is fully dealt with in subsequent chapters.) The figures show most prominently when the warp and weft threads are in different colours or materials; but if the two series of threads are alike the difference in the reflection of the light from the different weave surfaces is sufficient to render the figures clearly visible. Other things being equal, the weft usually forms brighter and clearer spots than the warp: (1) because it is more lustrous and bulky on account of containing less twist; and (2) because cloths generally contract more in width than in length, the weft thus being brought more prominently to the surface than the warp.

Methods of drafting spot figures

Simple spot figures are readily designed directly upon point paper, and the outline may be first lightly indicated in pencil, as represented at A in *Figure 5.20*. The squares are then filled in along the outline, as indicated at B, and this is followed by painting the figure solid, as shown at C. If the ground weave is plain, in painting the outline, the moves should be in odd numbers of squares, as shown at D, in order that the edge of the figure will fit correctly with the plain marks. If only short floats are required in the figure a simple weave (e.g., a twill or sateen) may be inserted upon it in a colour of paint that is in contrast with the first colour, as represented by the blanks in the figure shown at E. On the other hand, the binding marks may be inserted in such a manner as to give a special appearance to the figure as indicated at F. The prominence of the figure is usually reduced about in proportion to the firmness of the binding weave, but, as a rule, however pronounced a figure is required to appear, a longer float than 0·5 cm in the cloth should not be made, or the structure will be too loose.

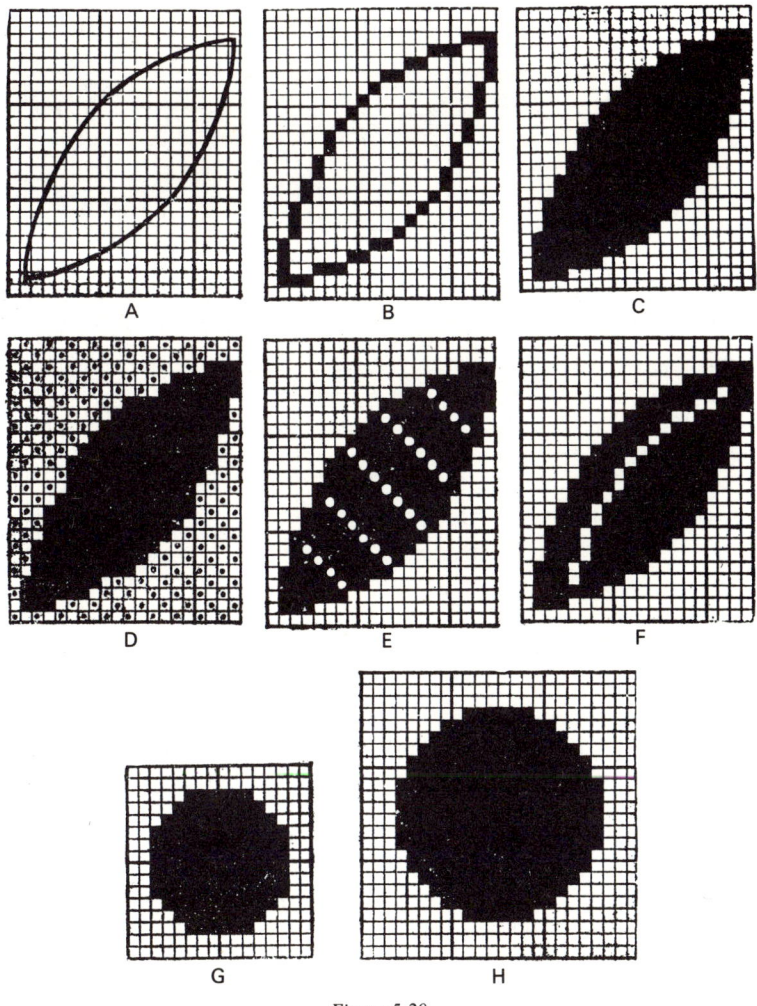

Figure 5.20

In producing a given size of figure in the cloth the number of threads, upon which it is designed, varies according to the sett of the cloth. For instance, if a spot 0·5 cm in diameter is required: For a cloth containing 24 ends and 24 picks per cm, the spot will be designed upon 12 squares in each direction, as shown at G in *Figure 5.20*; whereas for a cloth counting 36 ends and 36 picks per cm it will be designed upon 18 squares, as indicated at H. If the ends and picks per unit space are unequal, to enable the figure to be drawn in proper proportion, design paper should be used which is ruled to correspond (see *Figure 11.15*).

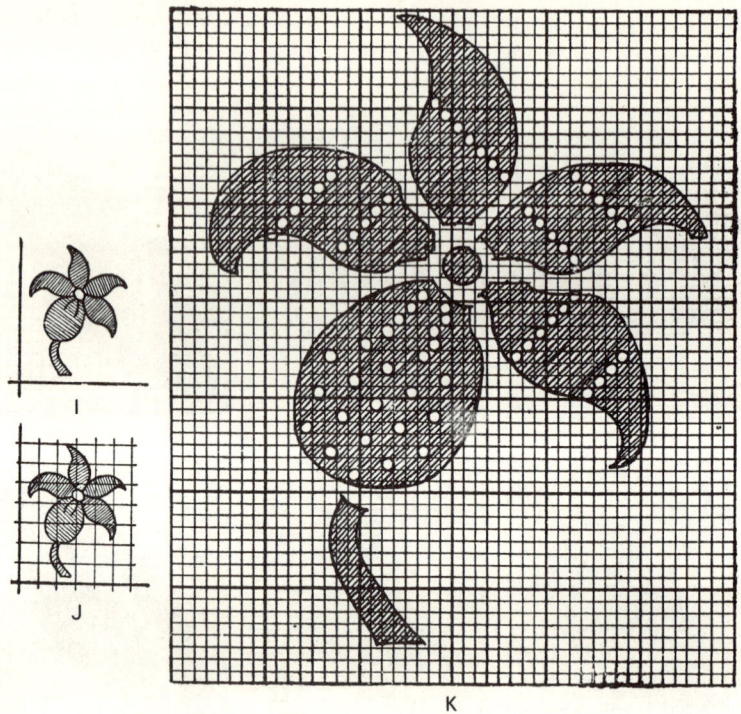

Figure 5.21

Spot figures which are rather intricate may be sketched upon plain paper, and then be drafted upon design paper in the manner illustrated at I, J, and K in *Figure 5.21*. As shown at I, two lines are drawn at right angles to each other to correspond with the direction of the warp and weft threads, the position of the lines in relation to the figure determining the angle at which the latter will be inclined in the cloth. The area over which the figure extends is then divided into equal spaces, as shown at J, each space corresponding to a number of ends and picks in the cloth. The figure is then drawn to the required scale upon the design paper, as shown at K in *Figure 5.21*, in which one large square, or eight ends and picks, correspond to one space of the sketch J. If the figure is required to appear the same size in the cloth as in the sketch, the ruling of the sketch and the number of small spaces of the design paper that each space in the sketch represents, are determined by the number of ends and picks per cm in the finished cloth. It is generally convenient, in designing small figures, to rule the lines at such a distance apart in the sketch that they correspond to the thick lines of the design paper. However, the need to sketch a figure prior to its transfer to the design paper rarely arises in dobby designs and the full procedure involved in large designs is carefully explained in the chapters on jacquard figure preparation.

Distribution of spot figures

It is only in special cases, as for instance, when a spot is arranged to fit in the centre of a coloured check, that a figure is used only once in the repeat of a design. Generally, two or more figures are contained in the repeat, and it is necessary for them to be placed at a suitable distance apart, and evenly distributed over the repeat area. The repeat must be at least so large that the figures do not encroach upon each other, and the factors which influence the number of ends and picks in a repeat are as follows: (a) The size and shape of the figure; (b) the number of figures; (c) the amount of ground space required; (d) the number of threads in the repeat of the ground weave. Even distribution of the figures is secured by employing a simple weave—such as plain and certain sateens—as the basis of the arrangement.

A method of distributing figures upon design paper, that will be found applicable to any shape of figure, is illustrated in *Figure 5.22*, which shows the spot L arranged in the order of the 5-sateen base given at M upon 30 ends and 40 picks. As shown at N, the figure is first painted in near the bottom left-hand corner of the sheet of point paper, and the square which is nearest its centre is marked, as indicated by the cross on the fifth end and sixth pick.

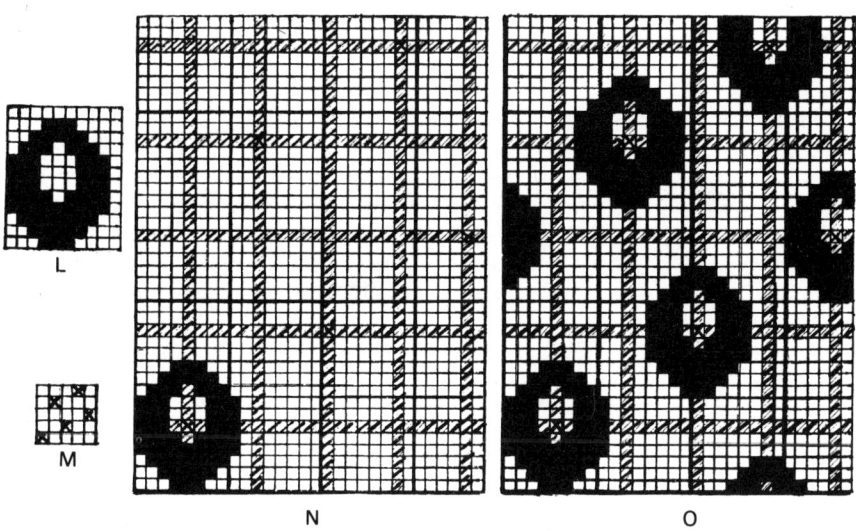

Figure 5.22

From the marked end and pick the repeat is divided in both directions into as many parts as figures to be used—in this case five; and lines are lightly ruled in pencil on the spaces, as represented by the shaded lines in N. It will be seen that the vertical lines occur at intervals of six ends and the horizontal lines at intervals of eight picks to correspond with the division into five parts each way of the repeat of 30 ends and 40 picks. Then, as indicated by the crosses in N, the squares where the divisional lines intersect are marked in the order of the sateen base. The final stage in designing the figures consists of copying the first spot square by square in the same relative position to each centre mark, as shown at O in *Figure 5.22*.

In the plain weave basis the figures are arranged in alternate order, as shown in the example given in *Figure 5.23* and the corresponding design indicated at A in *Figure 5.24*. In this case, as there are two figures in the repeat, the number of ends and picks in the design are divided into two parts from the eighth end and pick which form the centre of the first spot.

Figure 5.23

In dobby weaving point drafts enable spot figures to be produced with comparatively few healds. Thus, as shown at B in *Figure 5.24*, the design A requires only ten healds in addition to the two healds upon which the ends, which work in plain order throughout, are drawn. The lifting plan, to correspond with A and B, is given at C. With a given draft a variety of spots can be formed, and for the purpose of illustration examples are given at D, E, and F, which are suitable for the draft B.

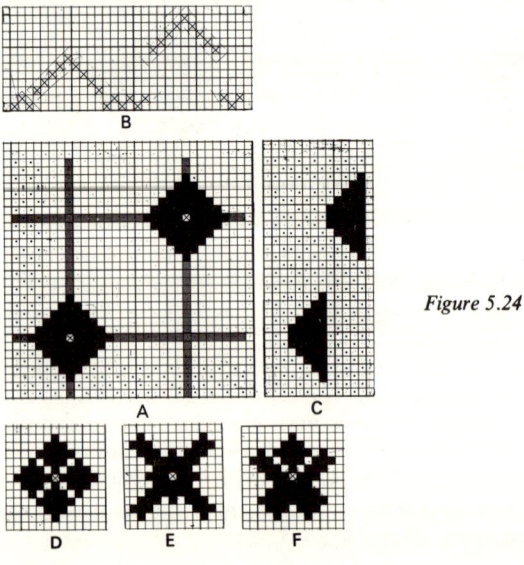

Figure 5.24

Reversing spot figures

The figures shown in *Figures 5.22* and *5.24* are symmetrical, hence they are placed the same in each position. Figures that are not symmetrical can be turned in opposite directions to each other, and in *Figure 5.25* examples are given which illustrate the different ways in which figures can be placed. In each design the centres of the figures are indicated by crosses on the ninth and twenty-fifth end and pick, and the direction in which the figures are turned is represented by a diagonal row of dots from each centre. A in *Figure 5.25* shows both figures turned the same way, a method which imparts

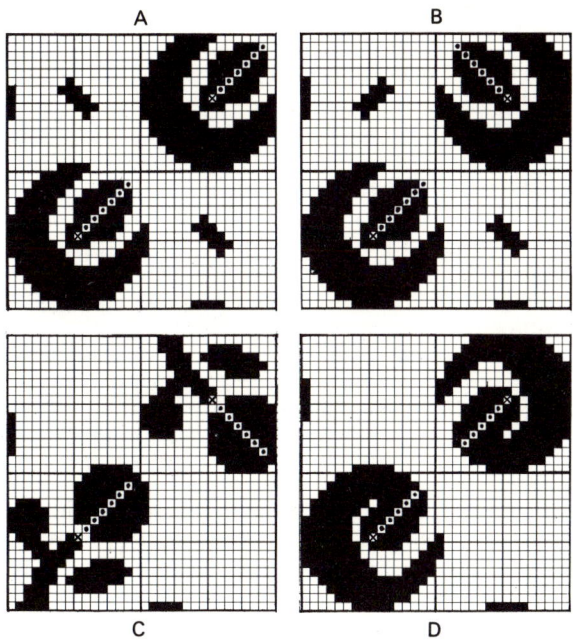

Figure 5.25

a monotonous appearance to a design, and is liable to cause the figures to fall into diagonal lines. In B and C the two figures are inclined in opposite directions, the second figure in the former design showing the first figure turned over horizontally, and in the latter design turned over vertically. In D the two figures are inclined in the same direction, but in the second position the figure is turned round 180°. The methods of reversing of elaborate figures suitable for jacquard designs are dealt with more exhaustively in Chapters 12 and 13.

Irregular sateen bases

The chief disadvantage of the regular sateen orders of distributing figures is that the systematic arrangement causes the objects to form continuous twill lines with each other in the cloth. A design appears less monotonous, and usually more pleasing, if the spots seem to be arranged indiscriminately, as

shown in the example given in *Figure 5.26*. A random appearance, com
bined with uniform distribution, can be secured by employing an irregular
sateen (see *Figure 2.16*) as the basis of the arrangement; the 8-, 10-, and

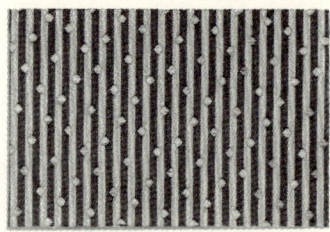

Figure 5.26

12-thread irregular weaves being particularly serviceable when the spots are
small.

Calculations relating to spot figure designing

It is sometimes necessary to arrange a given figure, or similar figures, in
different orders with the same relative amount of ground space. An indication
of the number of ends and picks in the repeat of a re-arranged design can be
found by the following formula:

$$\sqrt{(\text{ends or picks in given design})^2 \times \frac{\text{figures required}}{\text{figures given}}}$$
$$= \text{required ends or picks.}$$

For example, assuming that the spot given in *Figure 5.22* (in which five spots
are distributed upon 30 ends and 40 picks) is required to be re-arranged in
8-sateen order, with the same proportion of ground space as before:

$$\sqrt{(30 \text{ ends})^2 \times \frac{8 \text{ figures}}{5 \text{ figures}}} = 38 \text{ ends.}$$

$$\sqrt{(40 \text{ picks})^2 \times \frac{8 \text{ figures}}{5 \text{ figures}}} = 50 \text{ picks.}$$

The ascertained number of ends and picks serves only as a guide and may
need modification to suit the repeat of the ground weave and to fit in with the
new order of distribution. In the above case 40 ends × 48 picks would be
an appropriate number for the 8-sateen distribution with plain weave
ground.

   More complex designs arranged in the sateen order are given in Chapter 13,
while the method of inserting ground weaves to fit with the figure outline,
which is very important, is described in Chapter 12.

6

Special Rib and Cord Structures

In addition to simple ribs and cords produced in plain weave, or derived from the plain weave many other effects can be obtained on varying bases. Some are comparatively simple, but others are more involved in construction and belong properly to the compound structures that are beyond the scope of this volume. However, as many of the structurally more complex weaves are within the scope of tappet and dobby shedding an introduction to the principles of their construction is given in the latter part of this chapter.

FANCY RIB AND CORD WEAVES

Soleil weaves

The designs, given at A and B in *Figure 6.1*, produce a type of warp rib to which the term 'soleil' is applied. In order to more fully develop the horizontal rib lines the warp threads are sometimes arranged alternately right and left hand twist, the direction of the twist in one rib line being thus opposite to that in the next line. For piece-dyed fabrics the reverse twist yarn is usually tinted with a fugitive colour in order that it may be distinguished from the grey ordinary twist yarn during the beaming, healding, and weaving operations.

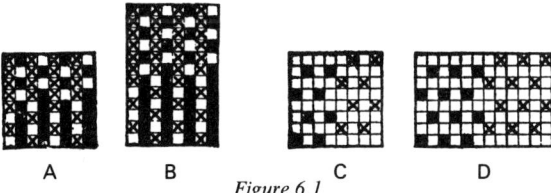

A   B   C   D

Figure 6.1

The designs C and D in *Figure 6.1* are constructed on the same principle as A and B, but in this case the surface of the cloth is covered by longitudinal weft cords. A pick-and-pick order of wefting, either in different colours, twists, or materials, may be employed.

Combination of weft cords with other weaves

The arrangement of weft cords in stripe form with another weave is illustrated by the designs A to I in *Figure 6.2*. A weft-cord stripe is produced in plain cloth by introducing one or more thick ends, or by working together several ends of the ground warp, at intervals as explained in Chapters 2 and 3. The cord ends do not take up so rapidly as the ground ends, therefore unless they are brought from a separate beam, a difficulty is liable to be caused in weaving. The design A in *Figure 6.2* shows a simple form of cord combined with plain weave, which is produced by working four ends together in one split of the reed. The four ends group together, as represented in the section given at B,

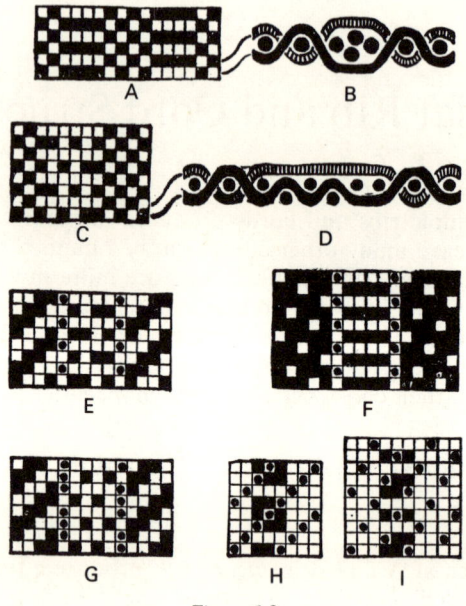

Figure 6.2

and if they are in the same colour as the weft solid narrow lines of colour are formed in the cloth. A wide cord is obtained by denting a number of ends in two or more splits of the reed, and interweaving the weft on the underside, as shown at C. The picks interweave in nearly plain order on the underside, as represented in the section D, so that the cord is kept out to the full width.

The designs E and F in *Figure 6.2* illustrate the combination of weft cords with other weaves than plain; 2-and-2 twill and 5-thread satin respectively being shown in the examples. If the cords are required to show very clearly, they should be stitched at each side with a plain end, as shown in E and F. The design G also shows a weft cord combined with 2-and-2 twill, but in this case the stitch ends at the sides are arranged to interweave with the same degree of firmness as the ground ends. The cords, however, are not so clearly defined as when the stitching ends at the sides work in plain order. The designs H and I show how weft cords may be constructed to cut with a given warp-face ground weave; the marks in this case indicating weft up.

Modified rib and cord weaves

Very neat and effective designs are constructed by commencing a rib weave in a different position in succeeding sections. Thus, in *Figure 6.3* A shows a

2-and-2 warp rib arranged in sections of 6 × 6, and B a 4-and-4 warp rib in sections of 8 × 8; while at C and D a 3-and-1 warp rib is indicated in sections of 6 × 6, and 5 × 5 respectively, the latter forming more of a warp surface than the former. The designs A to D are effectively developed by colouring the ends in the order indicated by the different marks. E shows a weft rib arranged on the same principle as D.

Longitudinal warp cords

The designs F and G in *Figure 6.3* are cord weaves which produce longitudinal cut lines at intervals of six ends. In F the first six ends interweave in plain order on the odd picks, and are raised on the even picks, while the second six ends are raised on the odd picks and interweave plain on the even picks. The

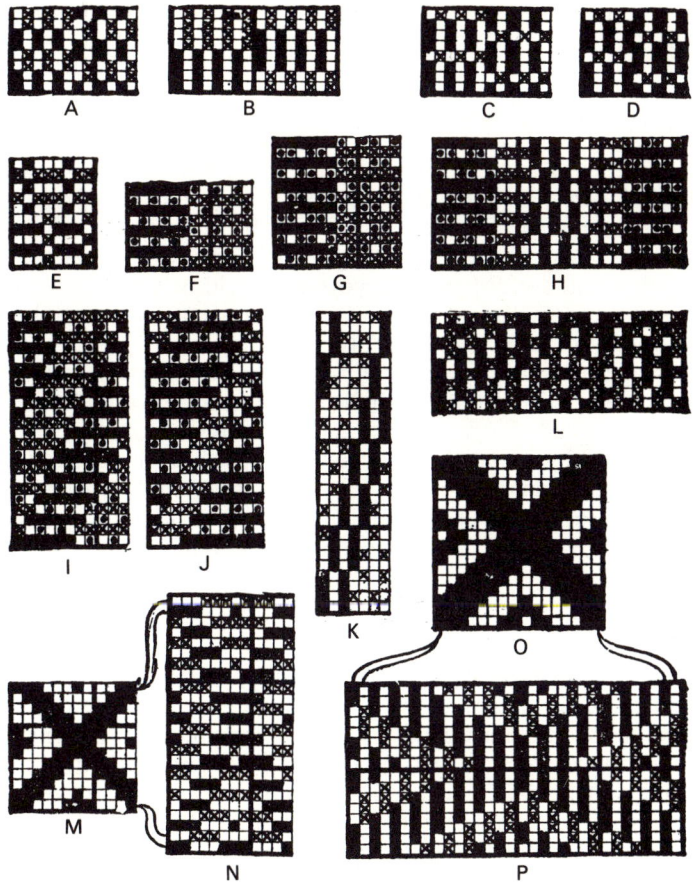

Figure 6.3

change in the interlacing of the weft from plain weave to float at the back, and vice versa, causes a fine line or cut to be made every six ends. The design G is similar to F except that the plain weave is replaced by 2-and-1 twill, which brings the warp more prominently to the surface, while the direction of the twill is reversed in succeeding sections so as to develop the cut line more clearly. The design H shows the weave given at G combined with ordinary warp and weft rib weaves.

Diagonal and waved ribs

Different methods of constructing ribbed diagonals are illustrated at I, J, and K in *Figure 6.3*. In the design I the two weaves, indicated at F, are arranged in diagonal form, while in J a weft rib is combined diagonally with one of the weaves given at F. The design K shows a very steep diagonal in which 4-and-4 warp and weft ribs are combined.

The design L in *Figure 6.3* shows a waved rib structure which is constructed on the basis of the soleil weaves given at A and B in *Figure 6.1*.

Diamond ribs

A method of constructing elaborate weft rib designs, to suit a pick-and-pick order of wefting, is illustrated by the examples M and N in *Figure 6.3*. The marks of M are indicated on the odd picks of the design N, as shown by the solid marks, then marks are inserted on the even picks, as shown by the crosses, to correspond with the blanks of M. By introducing about twice as many picks as ends per inch, the design N will produce an effect similar to M, but with a weft surface on both sides of the cloth; and if two colours of weft are employed in 1-and-1 order the same design is formed on both sides except that one colour replaces the other.

The examples O and P similarly illustrate the construction of fancy warp rib designs, the marks of O being indicated on the odd vertical spaces of P, as shown by the full squares; while marks are inserted on the even vertical spaces, as shown by the crosses, to correspond with the blanks of O. In this case about twice as many ends as picks are required, and by arranging the ends in two colours, 1-and-1, a reversible warp-faced design in two colours is formed. The colouring of cord weaves is described in Chapter 10.

Corkscrew weaves

Weaves of the corkscrew type, which are really twilled ribs, and similar in many respects to the diagonal ribs discussed above, are used either alone or in combination with other weaves for a variety of purposes. In their simplest form they produce either a warp or a weft surface; and they are most regular in construction when the repeat contains an odd number of threads. A warp corkscrew stripe fabric is represented in *Figure 10.9*, which, if turned one-quarter round, also illustrates the appearance of a weft corkscrew texture.

Warp corkscrew weaves

Ordinary weaves of this class are constructed on a sateen base counting 2 outwards, as shown at A, B, and C in *Figure 6.4*, which repeat on 7, 9, and 11 threads respectively. As many marks are added vertically to each sateen base mark as will make each vertical space contain one mark more than it contains blank squares. Thus, in the 7-thread warp corkscrew, shown at D in *Figure 6.4*, each vertical space contains four marks and three blanks; in the 9-thread weave E, five marks and four blanks; and in the 11-thread design F, six marks and five blanks. From an examination of the section given at G, which represents how the ends 1 and 2 of the design F interlace, it will be seen that the face and back of the cloth are nearly alike, the warp preponderating on both sides.

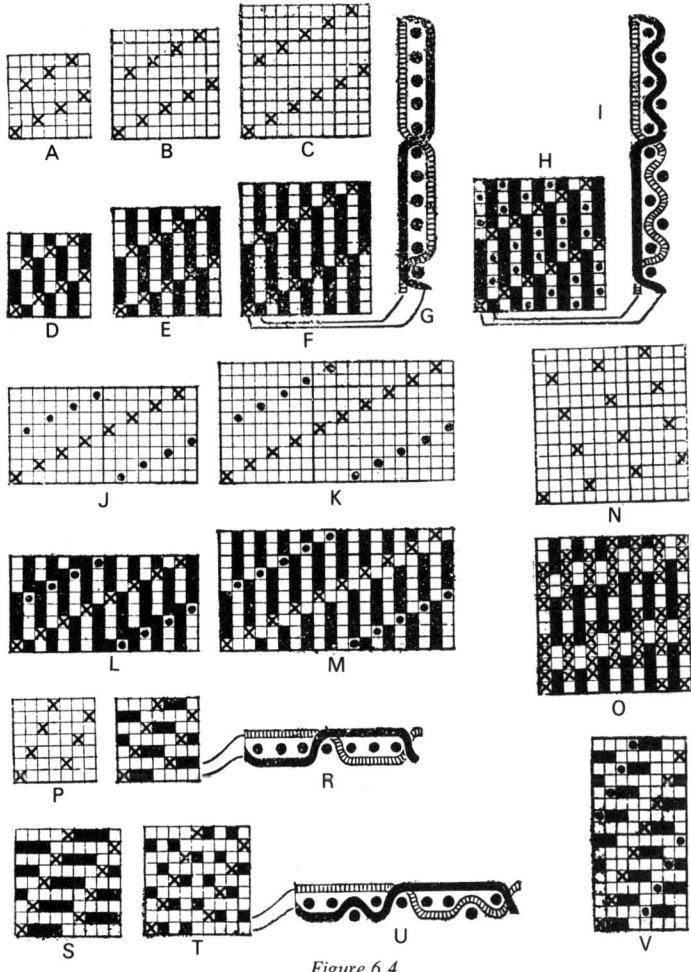

Figure 6.4

Sometimes, in order to make the weaves firmer, the floats on the back are stitched in the method indicated at H, which shows the design F modified. The threads then interlace, as represented at I, the floats on the face not being interfered with, whereas on the back the threads weave in the plain order.

In constructing warp corkscrew weaves that repeat on an even number of threads, it is necessary to employ a modification of the foregoing method. As shown at J and K in *Figure 6.4*, which represent the bases of the 8- and 10-shaft warp corkscrew weaves respectively, the repeat is upon twice as many ends as picks. A base line of marks, as shown by the crosses, is inserted on the odd vertical spaces, counting 2; then a second line—indicated by dots—is run in on the even vertical spaces, as centrally as possible. The design is completed by arranging each vertical space with two more marks than blanks, as shown at L, or with the marks and blanks equal, as represented at M. In the latter case, however, the weft shows slightly on the surface of the cloth.

The standard 13-shaft warp corkscrew, which has been extensively used for fine worsted coatings, is based on a 13-thread sateen, counting 4 outwards, as shown at N in *Figure 6.4*. Marks are added to the base marks in the order of add 4, miss 2, add 4, and miss 2, as indicated at O, and very flat twill lines are formed in the cloth, as represented by the different marks in the design.

Weft corkscrew weaves

These are exactly the opposite of the warp corkscrews, and when the repeat contains an odd number of threads, are constructed on a sateen base, counting 2 upwards. Marks are then added horizontally to the base marks, and the number of marks on each horizontal space should be one less than the number of blanks. Thus, P in *Figure 6.4* shows the basis of the 7-thread weft corkscrew, and Q the complete design; while R represents how the picks 1 and 2 interlace with the ends, a weft surface being formed on both sides. The 9-thread weft corkscrew is given at S, and the same weave with the weft stitched on the under side at T. The section U represents the interlacing of the picks 1 and 2 of T, and shows how the cloth is made firmer on the under side without the face floats being affected. The design V illustrates the method of constructing an 8-thread weft corkscrew. The systems of applying colour to corkscrew weaves, and some further modifications of the structures are described and illustrated in Chapter 10.

BEDFORD CORDS

The Bedford cord class of weave produces longitudinal warp lines in the cloth with fine sunken lines between, as shown in the fabric represented in *Figure 6.5*.

Figure 6.5

Plain-face Bedford cords

The method of constructing the *ordinary* type of Bedford cord weave is illustrated in stages by the examples A to I in *Figure 6.6*. At intervals pairs of ends work in plain order with the picks, therefore these lifts are first indicated, as shown at A, D, and G (the plain ends forming the sunken lines between the raised cords); the number of ends between the pairs of plain ends being varied according to the width of cord required. The next stage consists of inserting marks on the first and second picks of alternate cords,

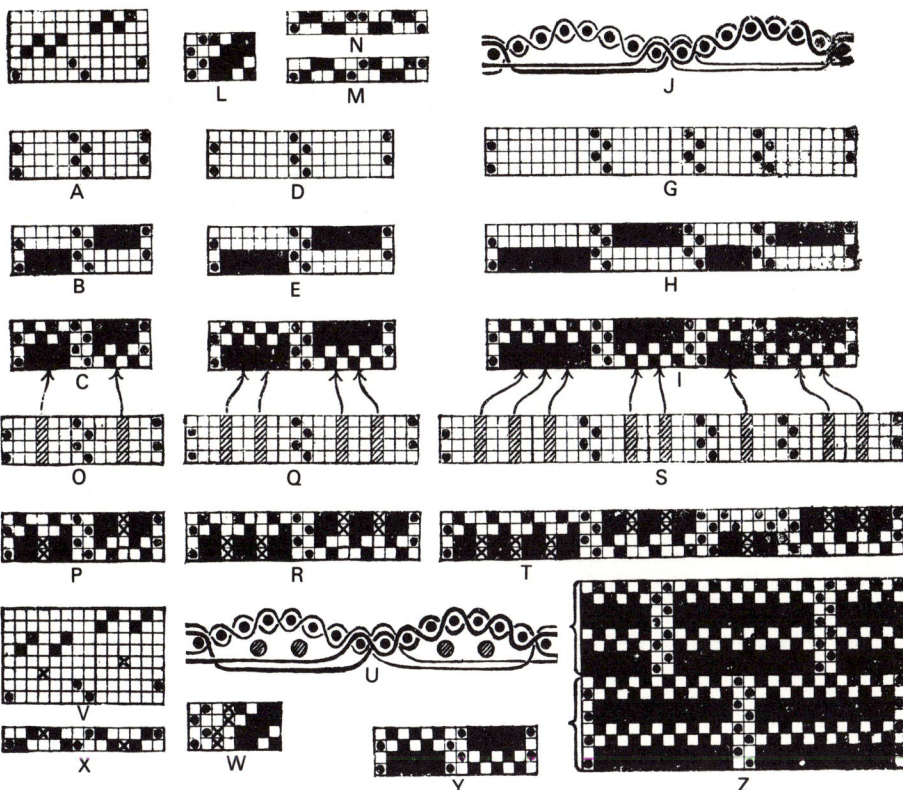

Figure 6.6

and on the third and fourth picks of the other cords, as shown at B, E, and H. The designs are then completed, as shown at C, F, and I, by inserting plain weave on the cord ends, which joins with the plain working of the pairs of ends. The cord ends float over three picks and under one, while the picks float in pairs on the back of one cord and interweave in plain order in the next cord, as shown in the section given at J, which corresponds with the design F. In the design C each cord is six ends wide, and in F eight ends wide; but I produces cords which vary in width in the order of 10, 8, 6, and 8 ends. Other widths and variations can be readily schemed.

The usual order of drafting is indicated at K in *Figure 6.6*, the plain ends being drawn on the healds at the front. The lifting plan is a combination of plain and 3-and-1 twill shedding, as shown at L. In order to develop fully the sunken lines, the plain ends should be separated by the splits of the reed, as shown in the denting plan given at M; in some cases, however, the pairs of plain ends are dented together as indicated at N. Two, three, or more ends are passed through each split according to the fineness of the cloth (two ends per split are indicated in M and N); and sometimes the plain ends are woven two per split, and the cord ends three or four per split. The number of ends in the width of a cord has some influence upon the order of denting.

Wadded Bedford cords

These structures contain thick wadding ends which lie between the rib face cloth and the weft floats on the underside; the object of the arrangement being to give greater prominence to the cords. The method of introducing wadding ends in to the designs C, F, and I is illustrated by the examples O to T in *Figure 6.6*; the arrows indicating the positions where these ends are introduced. The wadding ends, which are represented in O, Q, and S by the shaded squares, are additional to the ordinary ends. In the complete designs given at P, R, and T they are raised where the picks float at the back, as shown by the crosses, and are left down where the picks interweave in plain order. The order in which the picks interlace with the ends is illustrated by the section given at U, which corresponds with the design R. The draft for the design P is indicated at V, and the lifting plan at W; while X shows a method of denting which is based upon two ends per split, the wadding ends being dented extra. The number of wadding ends to each cord may be varied according to requirements.

The designs may be arranged with an odd number of ends (not including the wadding ends) to each cord, but it is then necessary to reverse the marks of alternate pairs of the plain ends, in order that the plain weave will join correctly. An example, without wadding ends, is given at Y in *Figure 6.6*, which contains seven ends in each cord stripe. Suitable weaving particulars of a Bedford cord are: Face warp, 20/1 tex cotton, 42 ends per cm; wadding warp, 60/2 tex cotton; weft, 16/1 tex cotton, 34 picks per cm.

Crepon Bedford cords

In both worsted and cotton cloths, hard-twisted weft is sometimes used, the shrinking of which causes the cords to stand up very prominently. The design Z in *Figure 6.6* is specially arranged to suit an order of wefting in which two picks of hard-twisted weft alternate with two picks of ordinary weft; the former floating on the underside of the cords. Each section of the design, which is enclosed by brackets, should be repeated about four times; it will be noted that the plain ends in one section are mid-way between those in the other section. In the process of finishing the hard-twisted weft floats on the under side shrink, and an irregular or *crepon* surface is imparted to the cloth.

Bedford cords, arranged with alternate picks

Bedford cords are also made with alternate picks floating at the back, in which case the pairs of plain ends require to be indicated in reverse order. An example, in which each cord is ten ends wide on the surface, is shown worked out in stages, at A to E in *Figure 6.7*. The marks of the pairs of plain ends are indicated, as shown at A; then marks, which cut with the plain marks, are inserted on alternate horizontal spaces, as represented at B. Afterwards, plain weave is inserted on the blank horizontal spaces of the cords, as indicated at C, but in this case the plain does not join perfectly with the plain

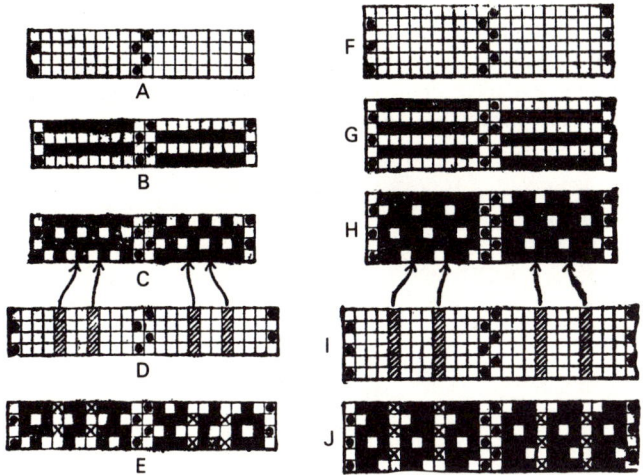

Figure 6.7

marks of the pairs of ends. If wadding ends are introduced in the positions indicated by the arrows, the complete arrangement of the ends will be as shown at D, in which the shaded marks represent the wadding ends. The complete design is given at E, in which the wadding ends are shown raised over the picks which float at the back.

Twill-faced Bedford cords

Another modification of the Bedford cord structure consists of using a warp twill instead of plain weave for the picks which interweave on the face of the cord stripes, the warp being thus brought more prominently to the surface. The examples F to J in *Figure 6.7* illustrate the different stages in designing a cord eleven ends wide on the face, in which 2-and-1 twill is employed for the face picks. H shows the complete design without wadding ends, while J shows H modified so as to include wadding ends, which are introduced in the positions indicated by the arrows below H.

WELTS AND PIQUÉS

A typical piqué structure consists of a plain face fabric composed of one series of warp and one series of weft threads, and a series of back or stitching warp threads. The stitching ends are placed on a separate beam which is very heavily weighted, whereas the face ends are kept at moderate tension. At intervals the tight stitching ends are interwoven into the plain face texture, with the result that the latter is pulled down and an indentation is formed on the surface. In order to increase the prominence of the unstitched portions of the cloth, it is customary to insert wadding picks between the tight back stitching ends and the slack face fabric.

Ordinary welt structures

The term *welt* is applied to the piqué structure when the indentations form continuous sunken lines or cuts which run horizontally in the cloth, as shown in the fabric represented in *Figure 6.8*. The number of face picks in the width of a cord is varied according to requirements, but usually the number of

Figure 6.8

consecutive picks that are unstitched should not exceed twelve. The construction of the designs is illustrated in stages in *Figure 6.9*, in which A, E, I, and M represent the first stage of weaves repeating on 6, 8, 10, and 18 picks respectively; the plain weave of the face fabric is indicated by the dots, while the position of the stitching ends is shown by the shaded squares. The ends are arranged in the order of 1 face, 1 stitching, and 1 face, in each split of the reed, or in the proportion of 2 face to 1 stitching end. The complete designs (without wadding picks), to correspond with A, E, I, and M, are given respectively at B, F, J, and N in *Figure 6.9*, the solid marks indicating the lifts of the tight stitching ends into the plain face texture on two consecutive picks. In the design B there are four picks between the indentations or cuts, in F six picks, and in J eight picks; but in the design N, which produces two sizes of cords in the cloth, there are ten and four picks alternately between the cuts.

Weft wadded welts

The designs C, G, K, and O in *Figure 6.9* illustrate the method of inserting wadding picks (the position of which is indicated by the crosses) into the respective designs B, F, J, and N; the object being to increase the prominence of the horizontal cords, and to make the cloth more substantial. Usually the wadding weft is thicker than the ground weft, and is inserted two picks at a place, as shown in C, K, and O; the looms being provided with changing shuttle boxes at one side only. Sometimes, however, the same kind of weft is used for both the face and the wadding, looms with a single box at each side being employed; and, in such a case, one wadding pick at a place may be inserted, as shown in the design G. Again, in some cloths thick wadding picks which are inserted in pairs, are supplemented by single wadding picks of the face weft. All the face ends are raised when the wadding picks are inserted, as indicated by the crosses in the designs, while the stitching ends

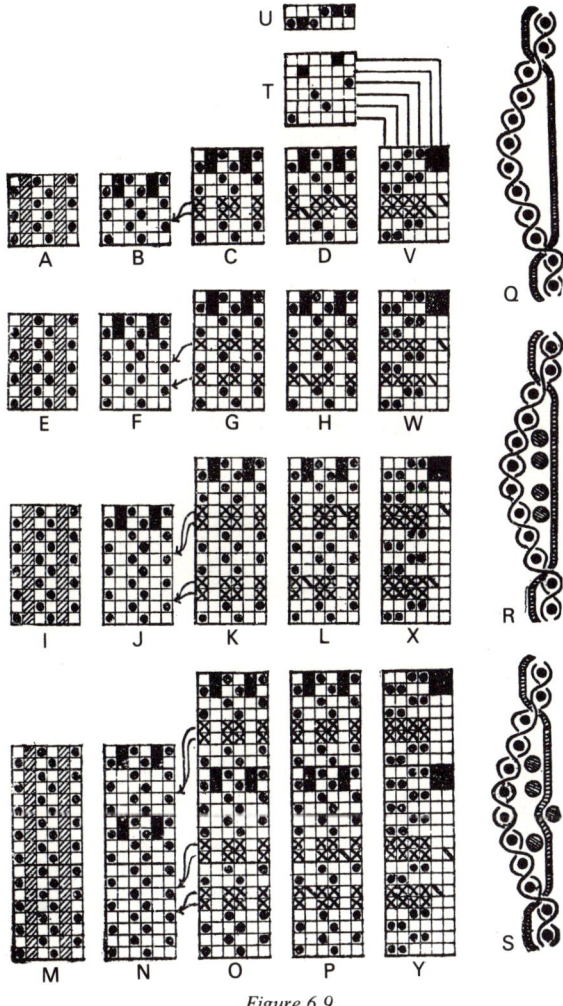

Figure 6.9

are left down. Whatever form the wadding picks take, they are inserted strictly as extra picks and the take-up motion is either rendered inoperative on wadding shots, or it is worked-out in terms of the face picks only.

Fast-back welts

In each of the foregoing designs, the stitching ends are only lifted to form the indentations, the term 'loose-back' being applied to this type of structure.

The term 'fast-back' is applied to cloths in which the stitching ends are inter-woven in plain order with all, or some, wadding picks. The reduction of the float length of the stitching ends on the back of the fabric which results from this interlacing helps to produce a more serviceable cloth less liable to acci-dental damage. The designs D, H, L, and P in *Figure 6.9* show the respective designs C, G, K, and O made fast back, the diagonal strokes indicating where the stitching threads are raised over the wadding picks. In the designs D and H all the wadding picks are used to bind-in the stitching ends, but in the design L only one of each pair, and in P only the two wadding picks in the centre of the broad cord, are so employed.

The sections Q, R, and S, in *Figure 6.9*, which respectively correspond with the designs J, K, and L, show how the threads interlace with the picks in the three types of structures, viz., loose-back without wadding picks; loose-back wadded; and fast-back welts.

The order of drafting is indicated at T in *Figure 6.9* and the denting plan at U, each split containing a stitching end between two face ends. The lifting plans for the designs D, H, L, and P, are given respectively at V, W, X, and Y.

Waved piqués

A waved piqué is a simple modification of the welt structure in which the indentations are not in a horizontal line but are arranged in alternate groups, as shown at A in *Figure 6.10*, the marks in which indicate the lifts of the stitch-ing ends on the face picks. The groups of marks do not overlap horizontally,

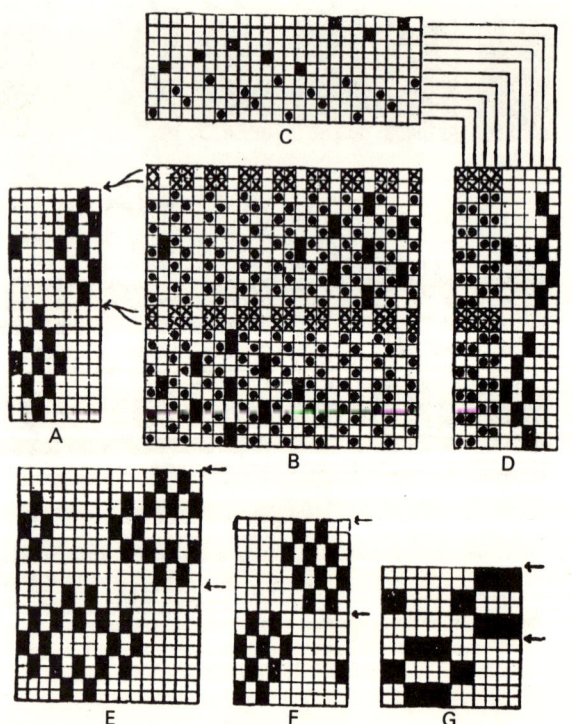

Figure 6.10

as one commences on a face pick immediately following that on which the other has finished. Between succeeding groups two wadding picks are inserted, as indicated by the arrows at the side of A. The complete design to correspond with A is given at B, in which the ends are arranged in the same order as in a welt, while there are ten face picks to two wadding picks. The lifts of the tight stitching ends force the wadding picks first in one direction and then in the other, so that waved lines are formed across the cloth. This is shown in *Figure 6.11*, which represents in the upper and lower portions respectively, the face and underside of a cloth that is similar to the design B in *Figure 6.10*. The draft of the design is given at C, and the lifting plan at D in *Figure 6.10*.

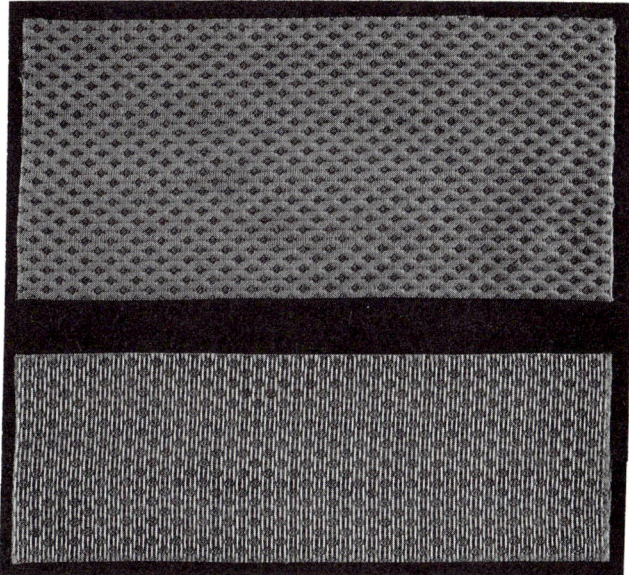

Figure 6.11

Other designs for waved piqués are given at E, F, and G, which are respectively arranged, as indicated by the arrows, to suit the introduction of 10, 8, and 6 face picks between the wadding picks. Suitable weaving particulars of a piqué cloth are: Face warp, 15/1 tex cotton, stitching warp, 21/1 tex cotton, 28 face and 14 stitching ends per cm; face weft, 12/1 tex cotton, 38 picks per cm, wadding weft, 30/1 tex cotton (wadding picks per inch dependent on the design).

7

Stripe and Check Weave Combinations

GENERAL CONSIDERATIONS INVOLVED IN COMBINING WEAVES

Stripe and check designs result from the combination, in equal or unequal spaces, of two, three, or more weaves or weave variations. Weaves that are suitable for combining in stripe form can very frequently be combined also in check form, while each transverse section of a check design, can generally be used alone in forming a stripe pattern. For these reasons, and in order to avoid repetition, the two classes of designs are described and illustrated together. The introduction of differently coloured threads may modify the appearance of both stripe and check weave combinations to a considerable extent, as shown in Chapter 10, but here only weave structure is considered.

Forms of stripes and checks

Weave combinations are employed in nearly all kinds of fabrics and in every class of material; the kind of cloth to be woven, and its purpose, largely influence the form or style of the design, and the selection of the weaves that are combined. As a rule, very diverse form is more suitable for stripes than for checks, because in the latter the surface of the cloth is more broken up by the weave changes than in the former. In both styles the form should be originated, not haphazardly, but orderly; the degree of contrast of space and of weave between the several sections being kept clearly in mind.

The examples given in *Figure 8.3*, in which the different markings may be taken to represent different weaves, illustrate a method of designing a range of stripe patterns by 'modification', a commencement being made with a simple equal stripe. Greater diversity can be obtained than is shown in the examples by combining three or more different weaves. *Figure 7.1* illustrates the various forms of weave checks that are in general use, and in this case also it will be understood that different weaves may be introduced in a more varied manner than is indicated by the different markings. Thus, the form shown at A, in which the sections are equal in size, permits of the combination of two, three, or four weaves, although two only are employed most frequently. The pattern indicated at B, in which the spaces vary in size, is particularly suitable for the combination of three weaves, the large and small squares being in

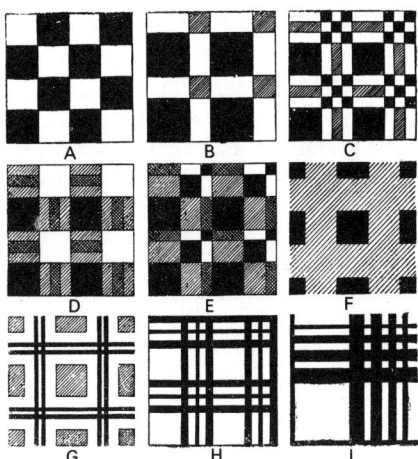

Figure 7.1

ordinary purposes, but the introduction of an overcheck, as shown at G, greatly improves the effect, particularly if the overchecking lines are emphasised. Such arrangements as those given at H and I are especially useful when it is desired to show an expensive material prominently on the surface.

Selection of weaves

In selecting weaves for combination it is necessary to take into account the nature of the cloth as to: (a) the class of material; (b) the thickness of the threads and the number of threads per unit space; and (c) the kind of finish that is applied. Either simple or elaborate weaves may be employed when the threads are smooth and even—e.g. cotton, linen, worsted, similar man-made staple yarns and all filament materials—or, if the finishing process removes the loose fibres from the surface of the cloth; because the smooth thread structure that is formed renders the weaves clearly apparent. Woollen cloths vary considerably according to the class of yarn that is used and the finish that is employed, but as the threads, in any case, are somewhat rough and uneven, weaves of a fancy character are usually unsuitable. The finest woollen cloths, which are finished with a clear face, however, admit of the combination of such weaves as twills, sateens, whipcords, ribs and corkscrews, but for similar cloths which have a raised or 'dress' face, and for rough cheviots and tweeds, only the simplest weaves are suitable. When different materials are used in a cloth weaves should be employed which will bring the better and more expensive threads chiefly to the surface.

More elaborate weaves may be employed in fine yarns and fine setts than in thick yarns and coarse setts, because in producing a given length of float more threads are passed over in the former case, which enables more detail to be introduced in the weaves.

In any material, if a raised finish is applied, the weave structure is more or less concealed by the surface fibres, and in such circumstances it is wasteful to employ elaborate weaves. A clear finish, on the other hand, develops the weaves so that a design is shown under the most favourable conditions.

Joining of weaves

It is very important to avoid the formation of long floats where the different sections of a design are in contact. Certain equal-sided twills, and weaves that are the reverse of each other, may be arranged to cut at the junctions— that is, with warp float against weft float. If the weaves will not cut they require to be carefully joined together, and, if possible, no longer float should be made at the junctions than there is in the weaves that are combined. In joining the weaves vertically the prevention of long weft floats on the face side of the cloth is of greatest importance, whereas at horizontal junctions (in check designs) chiefly the long surface warp floats have to be avoided. Long floats on the underside are of secondary importance, but they should be prevented if possible, as they may adversely affect the wearing properties of the cloth. Sometimes it is necessary to modify one or both weaves where they are in contact in order to make them join properly, and in some cases a weave with a minimum length of float—such as plain—is introduced between two weaves.

Relative firmness of the weaves

In stripe designs, if the warp is brought from one beam, the weaves that are combined should be similar in firmness. If there is much difference in the relative number of intersections in the weaves, the ends should be brought

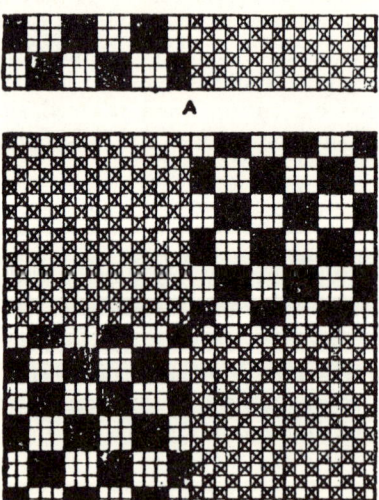

Figure 7.2

from separate beams to correspond, in order that the take-up of each series may be properly regulated. For example, the plain ends of the stripe design given at A in *Figure 7.2* will take up much more rapidly than the ends that form the 3-and-3 hopsack, hence if all the warp is brought from one beam the plain ends will become very tight, and the others slack. This will not only make it very difficult, if not impossible, to weave the cloth, but will result in the fabric having an uneven or 'cockled' appearance. In check designs similarity in the firmness of the weaves is not of the same importance, because succeeding sections of the design compensate for one another, so that the average take-up of the ends is about equal. Thus, 3-and-3 hopsack weave and plain, when combined in check form, as shown at B in *Figure 7.2*, will weave all right, except that in a heavily wefted cloth the picks tend to group together

Figure 7.3

in the hopsack sections, and to spread out in the plain sections, and, therefore, are distorted in the cloth. This is illustrated in *Figure 7.3* in which a fabric is represented that is woven in a check combination of hopsack and plain weave similar to the design B in *Figure 7.2*.

CLASSIFICATION OF STRIPE AND CHECK DESIGNS

Stripe and check weave combinations may be conveniently classified as follows:
  (1) Designs in which the same weave—usually a twill—is used throughout, but turned in opposite directions.
  (2) Designs in which the sections are in different weaves that are derived from the same base weave.
  (3) Combinations of warp and weft face weaves.
  (4) Combinations of different weaves.

Effects produced in one weave turned in opposite directions

A stripe weave of this class is shown at C in *Figure 7.4*. The dots in the design C indicate positions where coloured ends may be introduced in the cloth. The form of the stripe is similar to that shown at B in *Figure 8.3*.

Examples of check designs are given at D and G in *Figure 7.4*, the former of which is constructed in the form represented at B in *Figure 7.1*, and the latter in the form shown at A. In the design D each section consists of 3-and-3 twill, and in G of a 3-and-3 twill derivative, both designs being capable of being drafted on to six healds, as shown at E and H respectively, and both employing the principle of herringbone junction at each weave reversal line. Each draft is in two sections, and by using reversed 3-and-3 twill lifting plans, as indicated at F and I, the check designs are formed.

In fine warp-face cloths, such weaves as warp satins, warp twills, whip-cords and warp corkscrews—twilling in opposite directions—are suitable for stripe patterns when a strong contrast between the sections is not desired. Mostly, however, they are not fit for checks, because the preponderance of warp float makes it impossible, as a rule, to avoid the formation of long surface floats at the horizontal junctions. J in *Figure 7.4* shows a stripe design composed of a warp-faced 10-thread twill, while K shows a whip-cord weave arranged in stripe form.

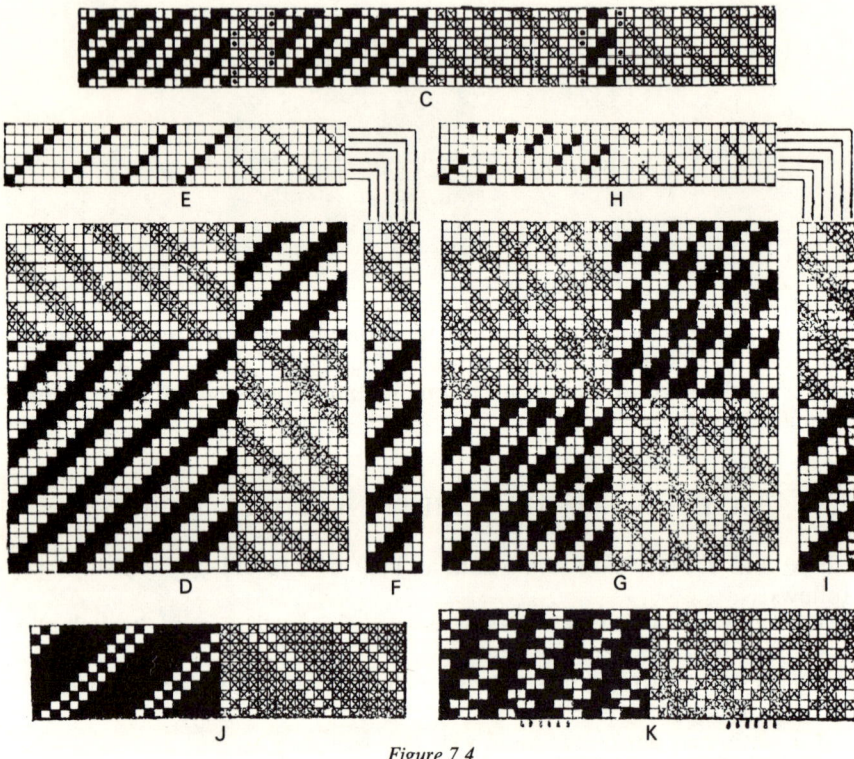

Figure 7.4

In the foregoing designs the difference of effect, due to reversing the direction of the weave, is emphasised by the twist of the yarns alternately running with and opposing the direction of the twill. A useful method of varying the appearance of the designs, particularly of the stripe patterns, consists of employing both right and left-hand twist in the threads. Thus, each section of the design K in *Figure 7.4* might be arranged in the warp in the order of 8 ends Z twist, 6 ends S twist, and 8 ends Z twist; the S twist ends occupying the positions indicated by the marks below K. The different direction of the twist modifies the prominence of the twill line and produces an additional delicate stripe usually termed *shadow stripe*.

Combinations of weaves derived from the same base weave

When the same base weave is used throughout a design, two or more different systems of drafting are employed; a stripe design resulting from a simple lifting plan, while a check design is formed by constructing the lifting plan in sections upon bases which correspond with the draft. For instance, the design given at L in *Figure 7.5*, which is based upon an 8-thread twill weave, is produced by means of a combination of straight and sateen drafting, as indicated at M. If the straight twill given in the lower portion of the plan N is used for the lifting plan, a stripe design will be formed consisting of the first 8 picks of L; whereas the complete check design results from using the whole of the plan N for the lifting plan. It will be seen that the shaded squares in N, which show the basis of the lifting plan, are arranged vertically in the same order as the marks are indicated horizontally in the draft M. The twill weave shown in the upper right-hand section of L is produced by the combination of a sateen draft and a lifting plan that is based upon the sateen. It does not necessarily follow that such a result will be obtained in all cases, as sometimes the combination simply produces another sateen re-arrangement of the twill.

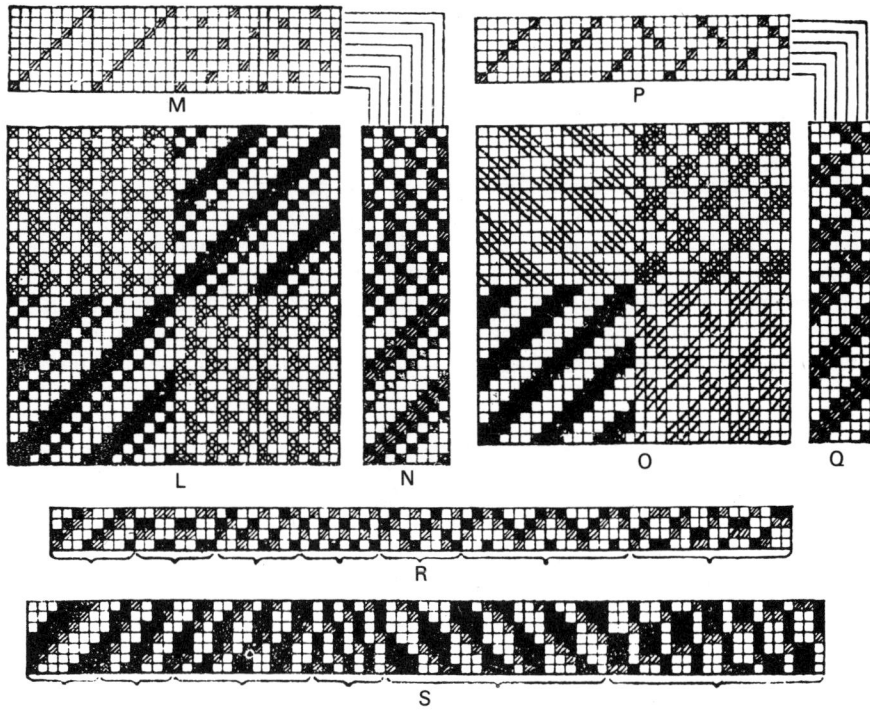

Figure 7.5

The design given at O in *Figure 7.5* illustrates the construction of a check design by combining weaves that are based upon 3-and-3 twill. The draft, which is indicated at P, is in straight and broken order alternately, and corresponds with the basis of the lifting plan given at Q. In this case the check design is composed of four different weave effects, which is due to the marks of the twill having been added horizontally to the base marks in the upper portion of the lifting plan Q. Other bases may be combined on the same principle as in the foregoing examples, but if care is not taken in selecting a suitable base weave, and in arranging the different sections, bad floats at the junctions of the weaves may readily occur, particularly in check designs.

Stripe designs which result from the combination of different orders of drafting are less liable than checks to contain bad floats at the junctions, and they, therefore, give greater scope than the latter in producing variety of effect. The examples R and S in *Figure 7.5*, in which the different sections are indicated by brackets, are given simply to show how different weaves may be constructed and combined. Two or more of the sections may be used to-gether, and each section be repeated a number of times, according to the size of pattern required. In each design the shaded squares indicate the bases of the weaves, and also the draft, while the weave in the first section forms the lifting plan. The chief advantage of this system, and also of that illustrated in *Figure 7.4*, is that the designs can be produced in a comparatively few healds; and, further, if the base weave can be woven by ordinary tappets, the stripe designs can be obtained without any modification of the loom. Check designs, however, on account of the large number of picks in the repeat, require a dobby shedding motion even though the base weave repeats on a small number of threads.

Combination of warp and weft face weaves

These produce the clearest effects in the cloth, particularly if there is a differ-ence in colour between the warp and weft yarns. Some of the possibilities of producing stripe designs on this basis have been explored in the section devoted to the warp and weft faced herringbone twills (p. 44), and further development of these into diamond forms (p. 73) has in effect resulted in the formation of *dice checks*. A simple dice check design is represented in *Figure 7.6*, and many similar effects are produced on this principle by combining

Figure 7.6

two opposite twill or sateen weaves. It is particularly necessary, in dice patterns, that the weaves cut at the junctions both vertically and horizontally in order that the sections will be firmly bound at the edges; otherwise the outermost threads, which are floated, are liable to slip over the threads in the adjacent sections.

The principle of reversing or opposing a warp float at the boundary of the figure by a weft float which has already been explained earlier (p. 43), may be employed in the construction of dice checks, but the base weave requires to be constructed very precisely in order that a uniform design will result. The marks of the base weave should be arranged in such a manner that the first and last picks are alike, and also the first and last ends, when followed in opposite directions. The examples, given at A to G in *Figure 7.7*, in which the arrows indicate the direction in which the threads should be followed, fulfil these conditions. For instance, in the plan F a mark is placed in the second square of the first pick, counting from the left, and in the second square of the last pick, counting from the right; and in the third square of the first end, counting from the top, and in the third square of the last end, counting from the bottom.

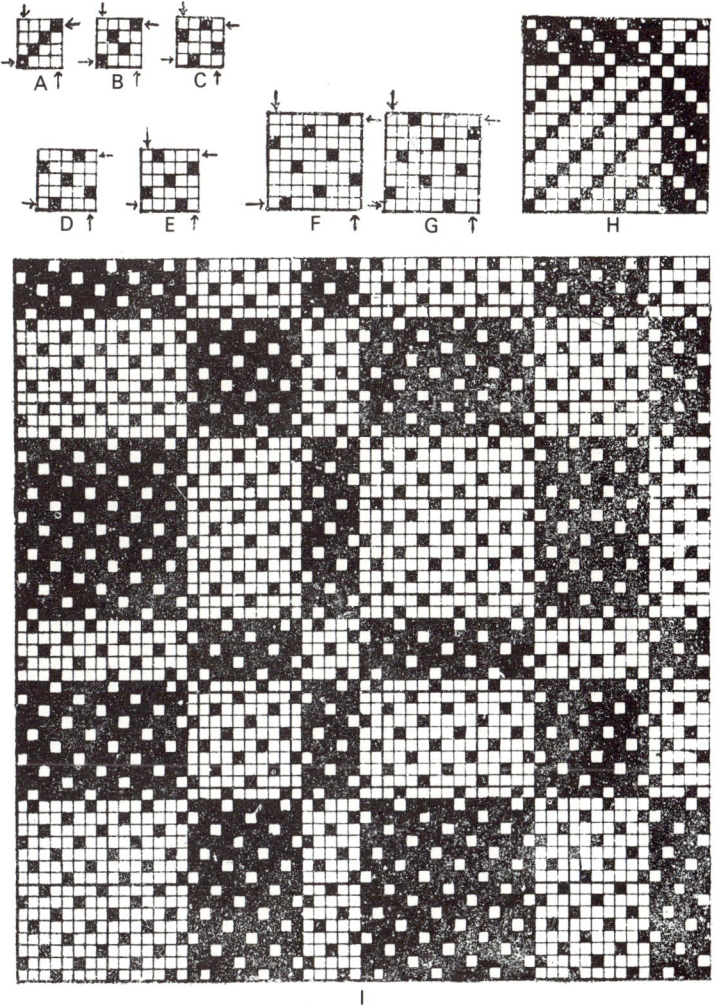

Figure 7.7

Twill base weaves are readily arranged by running a single line of marks through the centre, as shown at A in *Figure 7.7*. The 4-thread satinette may be inserted in two positions, as indicated at B and C, while the 5-thread sateen may be arranged to twill in either direction as shown at D and E. The

8-thread sateen, counting three to the right, may be indicated in two positions, as shown at F and G, and these plans, when turned one quarter round, show similar effects, counting three to the left.

The design H in *Figure 7.7*, which corresponds with the fabric represented in *Figure 7.6*, shows the combination of 4-thread warp and weft twill weaves. The large design in *Figure 7.7* shows the combination of 5-thread satin and sateen weaves, and is arranged in the form illustrated at E in *Figure 7.1*, nine different shapes of sections being formed in warp and weft.

In producing a coloured overcheck in a warp satin cloth, it is necessary to employ a weft-face weave where the specially coloured picks are required to show distinctly on the surface. The plan J in *Figure 7.8* shows how the weaves are arranged, the 5-thread satin being crossed by a 10-thread weft sateen weave (indicated in the upper portion of J) where the special picks are inserted. The cloth contains nearly twice as many ends as picks per unit space, therefore, a longer float is employed in the sateen weave than in the warp satin in order that the yarns will show about equally prominently on the surface. In example the weft sateen is carried across the corresponding colours in the warp, the arrangement enabling the design to be woven in a straight draft on ten healds. The warp weave might be carried through the corresponding weft colours, but this would complicate the draft and necessitate the use of more healds.

Warp and weft face rib or cord, and corkscrew weaves are also readily combined in stripe and check form. K in *Figure 7.8* shows a check design, which is composed of 3-and-3 warp and weft rib weaves, except that each section commences with a float of two in order that no longer float than three will be

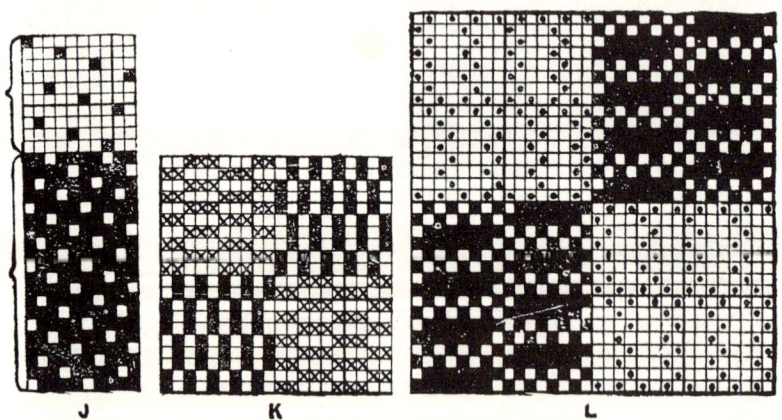

Figure 7.8

made where the weaves join. The design L in *Figure 7.8* illustrates the combination of warp and weft Bedford cord weaves, while an example of a check design that is composed of warp and weft corkscrew weaves, is given at H in *Figure 10.10*.

Combinations of different weaves

In this class of stripe and check designs, there is practically no limitation to the variety of effect that can be obtained except what is imposed by the loom and the materials employed. For fabrics such as suitings and coatings the patterns are not striking in appearance, and designs of the class shown at A, B, and C in *Figure 7.9* are employed, in each of which it will be noted that the weaves join well together. In the warp and weft rib sections of the design C,

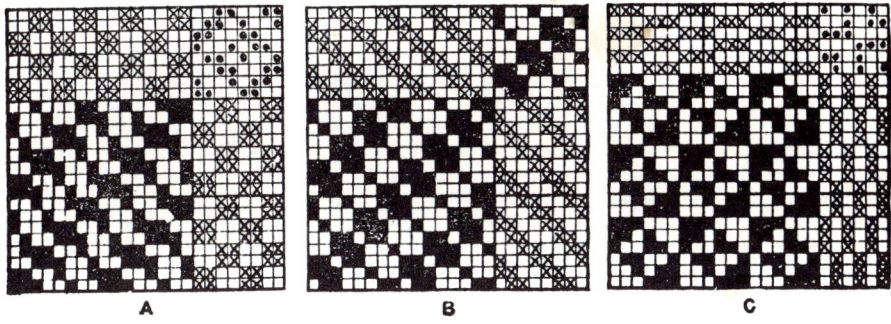

Figure 7.9

the threads should be more finely set than in the body of the check. Further combinations of different weaves in stripe form are illustrated in *Figures 10.4* and *10.5*; and in check form in *Figure 10.8*, in Chapter 10.

THE USE OF MOTIF DESIGNS

In planning the disposition of the various weaves in elaborate check designs it is usual to construct first a small motif on squared paper. Then each square of the motif is taken to represent a convenient number of ends and picks in a full design, in which different weaves are combined in an order that corresponds with the arrangement of the marks and blanks of the motif. For example, A in *Figure 7.10* shows a motif which repeats on 6 × 6, and forms the basis of the fancy dice design given at B; each square of the motif represents 8 ends and 8 picks, and the blanks and marks respectively correspond to the 4-thread weft and warp satinette that are combined in the design. The full repeat is upon 48 ends and 48 picks, but an examination will show that the design can be drafted upon 16 healds.

C in *Figure 7.10* shows how a motif may be arranged so as to represent the combination of more than two weaves. Thus, in the design D, in which 8 ends and 8 picks correspond to one square in C, the twilled hopsack sections coincide with the solid marks, the 4-thread warp twill with the dots, the Mayo weave with the crosses, and the 4-thread weft twill with the blanks of C. It is necessary for the weaves to be as carefully joined together as in any other check weave combinations. The use of motifs enables the sections of a large design to be readily arranged in advance, and there is also the advantage that several repeats of the small motif can be easily produced to judge the balance and the proper relationship of the various shapes achieved, which if attempted with a fully worked-out design would result in a lot of wasted labour, as in many cases, several trials are needed to select the most pleasing effect.

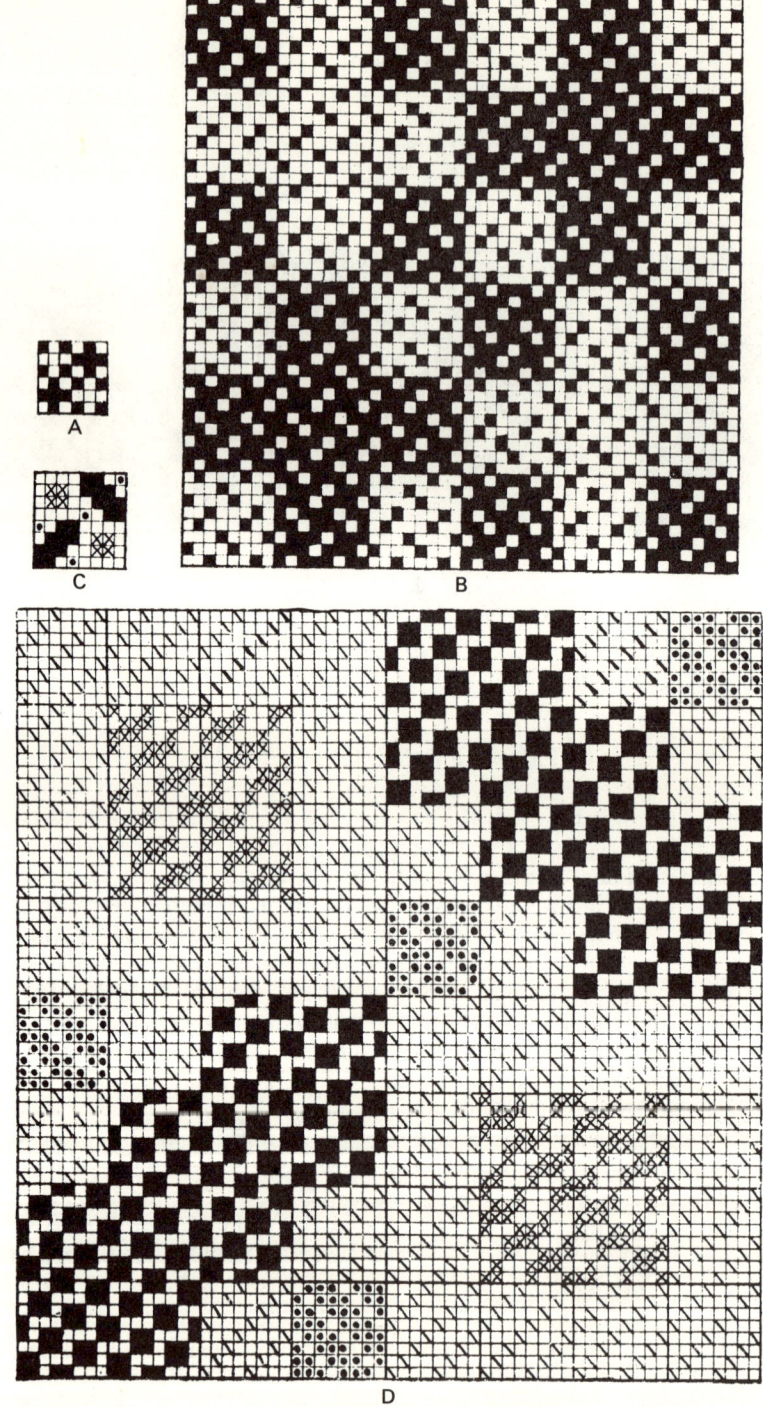

Figure 7.10

Crammed stripes and checks

The weave combinations that are used in fancy vestings, shirtings, dress and blouse fabrics, and skirtings, are frequently in much greater contrast and more elaborate than the examples given in the preceding chapter, and colours are employed more prominently in order to emphasise the form of the design. Further, the threads in certain sections of the designs are sometimes crammed —that is, there are more threads per unit space in one portion than in another

Figure 7.11

portion. The objects of cramming certain threads in a cloth are: (a) To produce a pattern in one weave by varying the density of the cloth. (b) To show a special material or colour prominently on the surface. (c) To secure firmness of structure in threads which are more loosely woven than the ground threads.

A crammed stripe fabric represented in *Figure 7.11* is composed of cotton ground warp and weft, and spun rayon crammed warp, and illustrates a style suitable for either a blouse or shirt fabric. The design for the principal stripe in this cloth with a portion of ground weave is given in *Figure 7.12*, below

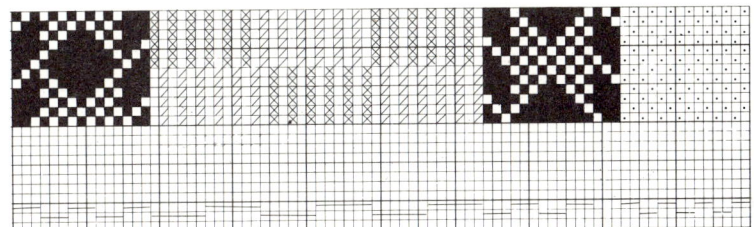

Figure 7.12

which the order of denting is indicated. The plain ground weave shown by dots is dented 2 per split, while the crammed stripe consists of a small spot with a twilled border shown in solid marks and dented 3 per split, and a warp rib (marked with crosses and diagonal marks) woven 6 per split. In between the main stripes, narrower, auxiliary crammed stripe effects are introduced.

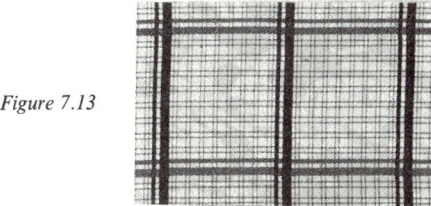

Figure 7.13

Figure 7.13 represents a crammed check fabric, the corresponding design for a portion of which is given at A in *Figure 7.14*. In this case the ground ends are dented 2 per split, and the crammed ends 4 per split, as indicated below the design, while a similar weft cram is produced by making the take-up motion inoperative on alternate picks where the brackets are indicated at the side of the design. The ground weave is plain, and the crammed weaves 8-thread satin and sateen except that the warp faced weave is doubled vertically where the crammed weft sateen is intersected. This is in order that the surface floats will be of the same length throughout the design. The system of drafting is illustrated at C in *Figure 7.14*, while B shows the corresponding lifting plan.

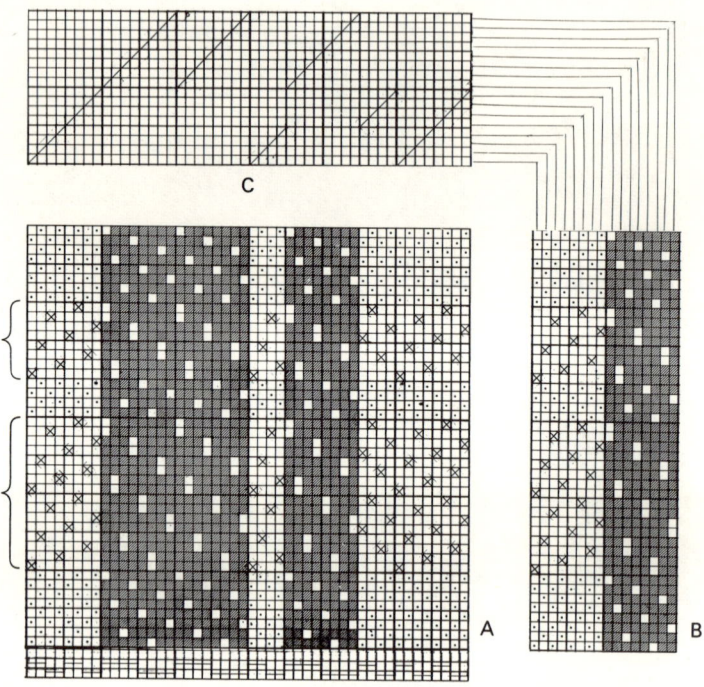

Figure 7.14

Sometimes, in order to avoid the inconvenience and added cost of weft cramming, imitation crammed effects are produced by using in sateen stripe portions a much thicker weft yarn than usual thus causing each pick to occupy about the same space as two crammed ones.

A checked dress fabric is represented in *Figure 7.15* for which the corresponding design is given at B. The design is simply a stripe combination of plain weave and crêpe, but in order to show the latter weave more prominently in the cloth it is developed in double ends and woven 4 per split, whereas the plain weave is in single ends dented 2 per split. The two sections of the design are in different colours of warp, and the checked appearance of the cloth is due to the weft being arranged in two colours to correspond with the order of warping.

Fancy weave stripes upon satin grounds

Certain features to be noted in forming a prominent fancy weave stripe upon a satin ground, are illustrated by the design given at C in *Figure 7.15*. The cloth represented is a type of cotton texture that is used for cheap skirtings, or suitings, and very frequently these fabrics, although finely set in the warp, are for economical reasons woven with proportionately only a small number of picks. It is, therefore, impossible to produce a prominent stripe effect by floating the weft, and, further, the weft should be in the same colour as the

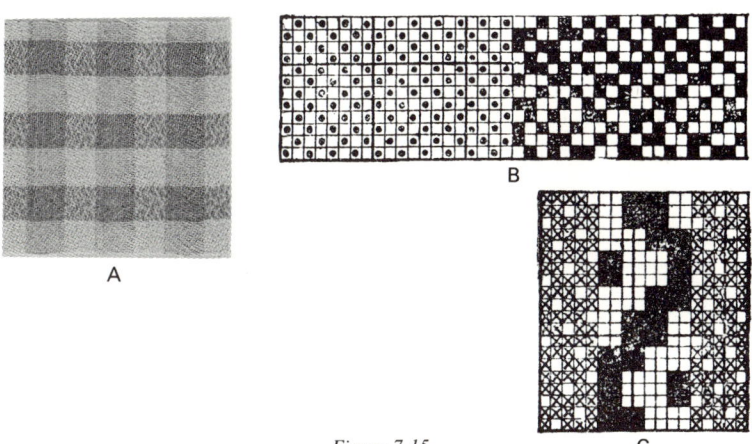

Figure 7.15

ends which form the warp satin ground in order that the latter will be quite solid in appearance. However, by employing contrasting colours in the warp, and particularly if double ends are used for the special stripe, as indicated in C, *Figure 7.15*, any required degree of prominence can be given to the fancy weave. Plain threads may be introduced to separate the different weaves, but this necessitates the use of extra healds if none of the threads in the special weave interlace in plain order. If, however, the weaves are so arranged that the satin floats do not obscure small figuring floats at the sides of the stripe, they may be placed directly in contact.

Zephyr stripes and checks

In zephyr stripes and checks, which are used for dress, blouse, and shirt fabrics, the bulk of the cloth is generally in plain weave and the pattern is very largely due to colour. Cord threads are frequently introduced, and in

Figure 7.16

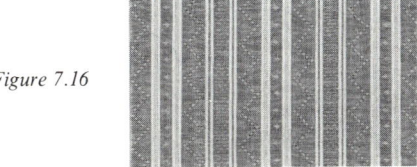

some cases certain threads are floated and brought prominently to the surface by cramming, as shown in the example given in *Figure 7.13*; while plain and crêpe weaves are combined, as indicated in the fabric represented in *Figure 7.15*. More or less elaborate figures frequently form part of the ornamentation, and a neat style of zephyr cloth is represented in *Figure 7.16*, in which a small figured effect is formed on a corded stripe. The corresponding design is given in *Figure 7.17*, in which the solid marks indicate the cord stripes each of which being produced by placing two thick white ends in one mail and one split of the reed. The bracket indicates the motif which occurs twice within the design repeat.

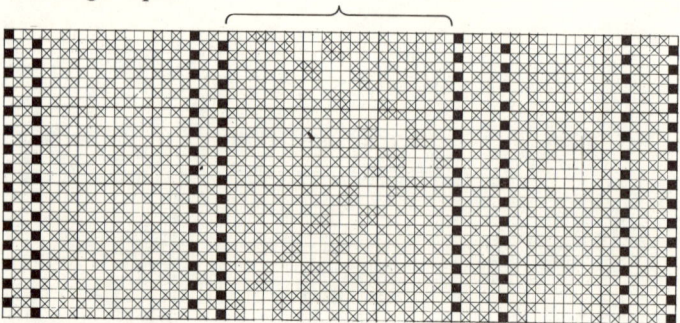

Figure 7.17

In stripe zephyrs, the weft is most frequently white, the colour being obtained in the warp, and a distinct feature is that finer weft than warp should be employed, or the cloth is liable to appear irregular or 'shady'. A fine quality may be woven in 10/2 tex cotton warp, 40 ends per cm, and 10/1 tex bleached cotton weft, 36 picks per cm; and a medium quality in 12/1 tex cotton warp, 34 ends per cm, and 10/1 tex weft, 32 picks per cm. 60/2 cotton is suitable for the cord stripes. Fine zephyrs are also made with filament rayon weft; dyed weft, both cotton and rayon, is also sometimes employed in the production of 'shot' effects.

Oxford shirting cloths

Stripe designs are also employed in Oxford shirting fabrics, and a typical example is represented in *Figure 7.18*, for which the corresponding design is given in *Figure 7.19*. The best qualities of these textures are full, soft, and somewhat lustrous, and thick weft—spun with little twist from long stapled

Figure 7.18

cotton—is employed, while the warp yarn is also made from a good grade of cotton. Standard cloths are woven with two ends per mail, with the bulk of the weave plain, but they are also made in hopsack weaves (termed matting Oxfords), in fancy mat weaves, and in plain weave with the warp composed of single ends (termed single warp Oxfords). The double-end arrangement in the warp causes the weft to be prominently displayed, so that the warp colours are subdued, whereas in single-warp Oxfords the warp colours show more distinctly while the cloth is harder in the handle. The textures are not heavily coloured, but are particularly neat and clean in appearance, a white foundation being most frequently made upon which fine lines of colour, in the form of stitch threads and small fancy weaves, are developed. In some cases, however, a coloured warp is used for the ground, but the weft is almost invariably white. In order to make a colour show clearly on a white double end foundation in the plain weave, three ends of the colour may be placed in each mail instead of two, while to get fine solid lines of colour the coloured ends may be drawn one per mail and dented four per split. The single ends in

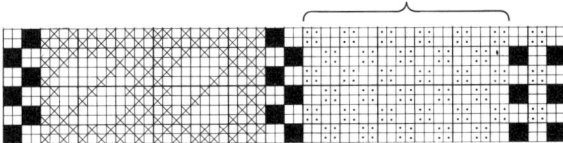

Figure 7.19

the latter arrangement take up more rapidly than the double ends, and it is, therefore, usually necessary to place them on a separate beam in order to ensure good weaving. A good quality of Oxford cloth may contain 22 double ends per cm of 16/1 tex cotton, and 20 picks per cm of 43/1 tex cotton; and a coarser cloth, 16 double ends per cm of 14/1 tex cotton, and 16 picks per cm of 60/1 tex cotton. In the design given in *Figure 7.19*, each vertical space represents two ends in the cloth, and the solid marks indicate the weave formed by the coloured threads; the bracketed portion, which consists of 2-and-2 hopsack, is repeated.

Harvard shirtings

The stripe fabric, represented at C in *Figure 7.20*, is a Harvard shirting, the corresponding design for which is shown at A. This cloth is made in single ends, and the ground weave is generally 2-and-2 twill; and, compared with

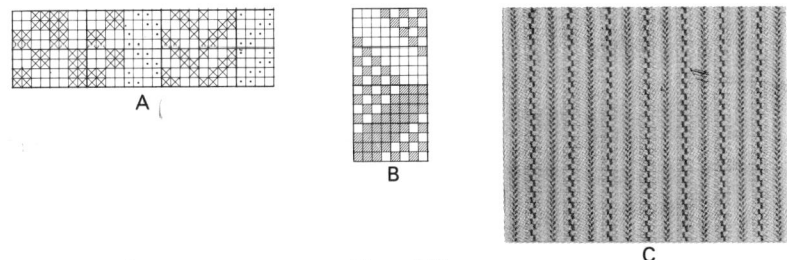

Figure 7.20

an Oxford fabric, darker colours and rather cheaper yarns are employed, the cloth being stiffer and harder, while the ornamentation is more pronounced. Sometimes, however, the Harvard cloth is made in imitation of an Oxford, as regards quality, design, and colouring, but the 2-and-2 twill ground is retained. The weft is all white, except in checked Harvards, in which a few picks of coloured weft are introduced. The weave ornamentation consists largely of variations of the 2-and-2 twill, and of mat and rib weaves working in 2-and-2, and 4-and-4 orders, by which small spot and chain effects in strong colours are formed.

Harvard cloths that are woven in dobbies are ornamented by fancy weaves and small figures along with which plain weave is generally introduced, as shown in B, *Figure 7.20*, in order that the figuring threads will be about equal in firmness to the threads which form the 2-and-2 twill ground. Very frequently the 2-and-2 twill makes a bad junction with the fancy weave, rather long white weft floats being formed, which, however, are made almost invisible by placing white ends at each side of the coloured stripe upon which the fancy weave is brought up. The 2-and-2 twill ground weave is often modified on the herringbone principle so as to produce considerable variety of effect on a small number of healds.

Wool and union shirtings

All-wool and union shirting and pyjama cloths, which are milled and raised in the finishing process, are not suitable for the combination of fancy weaves in the ordinary manner, but very elaborate colouring may be employed in the warp, as the formation of the nap on the surface greatly subdues the strength of the colours in the cloth. All wool shirtings (taffetas) may be composed in the warp of from 30/2 tex to 22/2 tex botany, and in the weft of from 22/1 tex to 13/1 tex botany with from 24 to 32 ends, and from 20 to 28 picks per cm. In a union cloth one series of threads may be composed of cotton, or wool, while the other series is a 'union', 'llama', or 'angola' yarn, which consists of a mixture of cotton and wool fibres (sometimes a mixture of wool, or cotton and nylon is employed), or both series of yarns may be union. A llama shirting is composed of union warp and weft—as for instance, 50/1 tex warp and 56/1 tex weft (worsted count) which contain 70 per cent wool, and 30 per cent cotton with 16 ends and 18 picks per cm. The colours require to be specially fast dyed in order that they will stand the milling process. As regards the weave ornamentation of these cloths, the raised surface does not prevent the development of fancy weaves in lustrous threads which are crammed in the reed, in the manner illustrated by the example given in *Figure 7.5*.

Combination of Bedford cord and piqué weaves

Bedford cords, piqués, honeycombs, and other special weaves are combined in very diverse ways in blouse fabrics, skirtings, vestings, and shirtings, with and without coloured threads. *Figure 7.21*, A, represents a cloth in which a

A

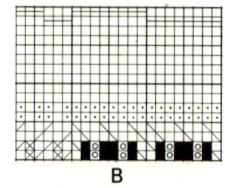

B

Figure 7.21

Bedford cord weave is combined in stripe form with piqué cords. The corresponding design is given at **B**, in which the diagonal strokes indicate the plain face weave in both structures. The cord ends in the Bedford cord section are indicated by the solid marks. The wadding ends (marked with circles), and the tight stitching ends of the piqué section (marked with crosses) are placed on the same beam (separate from the other ends). All the ends, except the stitchers are raised on picks 5 and 6, (as indicated by the dots), which form the wadding picks of the piqué stripe the take-up motion being rendered inoperative during their insertion. The order of denting is indicated above the design.

8

Elements of Colour

LIGHT AND COLOUR PHENOMENA

Lustre and colour are two associated physical phenomena which demand particular attention from the textile designer due to their prominent influence on the appearance of woven fabrics.

When light falls on a fabric some of it may be reflected at the surface of the fibres, sometimes passing through one or more fibres before being so reflected, and some may be reflected by irregularities within the fibres (Plate I-A). The former reflection may be more or less regular, as if from a mirror, and gives rise to lustre; the latter is diffuse, reducing lustre and, if the fabric is dyed, giving rise to *colour*.

The lustrous appearance of the fabric will depend upon (a) the characteristics of the fibres, (b) the way in which the fibres are arranged in the yarn, (c) the weave, and (d) the finishing technique applied. Smooth and uniform fibres, e.g. nylon and silk, act like mirrors and give a very high lustre whilst irregular and twisted fibres, e.g. cotton, give very poor lustre (mercerised cotton is more lustrous because it is rounder in cross-section than untreated cotton). In filament yarns with low twist, the fibres present long continuous surfaces to view, which give good reflection, but in staple yarns and yarns of high twist the surfaces are broken up and the lustre reduced. The degree of light reflection and, therefore, brilliance that can be achieved in some man-made continuous filament yarns is, in fact, excessive, giving rise to a harsh, metallic sheen, which may need to be muted, and such fibres may require to be delustred. The man-made staple fibres employed in circumstances in which previously natural fibres may have been used are almost invariably delustred as the sheen for such end uses is objectionable.

In common with the mechanism outlined in respect of fibres and yarns, a weave which presents large continuous areas of yarn to view, e.g. a sateen, gives a higher lustre than one where there are many thread interlacings, e.g. a plain weave or a crêpe weave. Similarly, finishes which are designed to enhance the lustre increase the uniformity and the regularity of the cloth surface, e.g. calendering, beetling etc., whilst techniques intended to destroy lustre, achieve their aim by disturbing the surface, e.g. raising.

In certain classes of fabric, which range from simple structures to elaborately figured damasks, the only ornamentation is that due to these variations in reflection from different parts of the cloth. On the other hand there are fabrics in which colour forms the predominant decorative feature, the weave simply serving as the structural element of the texture. For instance cloths with a raised surface may have the weave pattern completely concealed and in many tapestries and carpets the form produced by the weave is solely for the purpose of displaying colour. Frequently colour is of more consequence than form, since it is possible for a good scheme of colouring to redeem an otherwise uninteresting design, whereas a displeasing colour combination will render worthless a good form.

It must be realised that observations of colour effects are purely subjective and, even when free from physiological defects such as colour-blindness, no two people agree in their description of every colour effect. However, there is a wide general agreement between the descriptions given by a number of people and we can talk of an 'average observer' and use his description of what he sees.

Physical basis of colour

The simple experiment of Sir Isaac Newton determines the composition of white light and demonstrates that light is the source of colour. In the experiment a narrow beam of sunlight is intercepted by a glass prism which refracts the beam and splits it into its constituent elements, with the result that it forms a band of different colours, which may be displayed on a screen. This band is called the solar spectrum and the colours, which are arranged in the same order as those in the rainbow, are known as spectral colours. For convenience the colours are classified in six divisions, i.e., red, orange, yellow, green, blue, and violet; but every gradation of colour is shown in the spectrum, the change from one to another being imperceptible. The brightest part of the solar spectrum is in the yellow and green regions, but at the two extremes red and violet contribute very little by way of illumination.

Light is an electromagnetic wave motion—that is, like radio signals and x-rays, it is transmitted by associated vibrating electric and magnetic fields. The only difference between radio waves, light and x-rays lies in the frequency of these vibrations, which is lower for radio waves than for light and lower for light than for x-rays. Visible light waves also differ in frequency the frequency increases through the spectrum, going from red to violet and this is why the red rays are refracted less than the violet ones. Thus a spectral colour can be described by its frequency, or, more usually, by its wavelength, which decreases as frequency increases so that, frequency × wavelength = a constant (the velocity of light). Two other types of electromagnetic wave are important: the infra-red rays, which have longer wavelengths than visible light and are experienced as heat, and ultra-violet rays, which have shorter wavelengths than light and often produce fluorescence.

Any light can be analysed in the way Newton analysed sunlight and will be found to be made up of light of the different wavelengths (or colours) in different proportions (including zero). For some lights, the whole range of visible wavelengths will be present—an electric light bulb gives such a *continuous* spectrum, but with a much higher proportion of red light than in the solar spectrum: for other lights, discrete bands appear in the spectrum, e.g. a sodium street lamp gives orange-yellow light only.

Emission and absorption of light

A body emits light when some electrons in it lose energy. Energy can be given to the electrons in the first place ·by heating the body: the hotter the body, the more energy the electrons have and the greater the energy lost by the electron, the shorter the wavelength of the wave emitted. Thus all bodies emit some visible light, but only bodies above 600°C emit much visible light and the hotter the body the bluer the light it emits. Many familiar sources of light, e.g. the sun and electric light bulbs, are hot-body radiators and show continuous spectra, the electric light being richer in red light because its temperature is 3000°C whilst that of the sun is 6000°C. In recent years a different type of light source has become important—the discharge tube. In this, energy is given to the electrons in gas molecules by applying a high voltage and creating an electrical discharge through the gas. The resulting light shows, not a continuous spectrum, but narrow bands of discrete wave-lengths which are characteristic of the gas. Sodium and mercury street lights are familiar examples.

As well as emitting radiation, bodies also absorb it—some absorb every-thing which falls on them and are called *black bodies*, but others absorb only certain wavelengths and reflect the rest of the radiation. The behaviour of a body can be characterised by its *absorption spectrum*, which shows what proportion of the light of a particular wavelength is absorbed by the body. Thus a body which is not self-luminous can appear coloured because it absorbs light of some wavelengths and reflects the rest of the light which falls on it from an external source. Two theories of colour mixing depend upon these twin ideas of *reflection* and *absorption*, viz. the *light* theory and the *pigment* theory respectively. In mixing the differently coloured lights re-flected by a body the colours are added, whereas in mixing pigments, as in dyeing, the absorptions are added and, so far as colour is concerned, the process is subtractive.

Generally speaking a non-luminous body cannot reflect light of any wavelength which it does not receive and its appearance is a result of the combination of the composition of the illuminating light and its own reflection characteristics. However there are some materials which absorb at one wavelength and re-emit light at another, usually longer, wavelength—these are said to be *fluorescent*. This phenomenon is particularly important when the source is rich in ultra-violet light, e.g. a mercury discharge tube, and the now familiar fluorescent tube is a mercury discharge tube with a fluorescent coating which gives a continuous spectrum more or less like the solar one. Fluorescent materials are also used as optical brightening agents with dyes and detergents.

Colour vision and the light theory of colour

If we know the composition of the illuminating light and the absorption spectrum of a body, we can tell exactly what light the body will reflect. But this really tells us very little about what colour it will appear to be. This is because our eyes do not respond to the various wavelengths individually, but to three overlapping broad bands in the spectrum centred in the red, green,

PLATE I

A. The absorption, scattering and reflection of light in a layer of pigment

B. Colour mixtures: Light theory

C. Colour mixtures: Pigment theory

D. Ostwald colour circle

and blue regions respectively and the messages they send to the brain correspond to the proportions of these colours. Before much was known about
colour vision, however, it had been shown that most colours, including white,
could be produced by combining certain red, green and blue lights in different
proportions and many could be produced by combining only two of them.
This discovery forms the basis of the C.I.E. system of colour measurement
adopted by an international committee in 1931. The way in which these
'primary' colours, red, green, and blue, can be mixed to give other colours,
may be shown diagramatically using a triangle or a circle (Plate I-B). The
following results are obtained from the combination of coloured lights:
yellow or orange from red and green; bluish green from blue and green, and
purple (which is not found in the solar spectrum) from blue and red.

Complementary colours

Since any colour, including white, can be produced by mixing the three
primary colours, it follows that white can be produced by adding to any
colour a mixture of the three primaries in a particular proportion. This
mixture of primaries will, of course, be a colour in its own right and it is said
to be complementary to the first colour. Thus blue and yellow, green and
purple, and red and bluish green are complementary. *Complementary colours
are in the greatest possible contrast to one another.* The complement of a
colour may be determined by placing a disc of the colour upon a sheet of
white paper, looking at it intently for a time, and then transferring the gaze to
another white surface. The complementary colour will appear in the form of
the disc of the original colour, the image being termed the negative or after-
image, while the first impression is called the positive image. In explanation
of this it is supposed (the Young–Helmholtz theory) that in the retina there
are three groups of nerve fibres, one group of which is sensitive to the red
waves of light, the second to the green waves, and the third to the blue waves.
(According to other theories there are four or even seven different colour
receptors in the retina.) When a colour is looked at the corresponding nerves
are excited, and if the gaze is continued for a considerable time, become
fatigued, while the other nerves are resting. When the eye is transferred to
another surface the rested nerves produce sympathetically an after-image
which is complementary in colour to the first colour. Thus, by looking at red
the nerves that are sensitive to red become fatigued while the green and blue
groups of nerves are resting. If a white surface (which excites the red, green,
and blue groups equally) be then looked upon, the red nerves are too
exhausted to respond, whereas the green and blue groups act together, so
that a bluish green after-image appears. By looking at yellow both the red
and the green nerves are fatigued, and a blue after-image results, and so on.

The exhaustion of the colour nerves causes a colour, when looked at for
some time, to appear duller, and in examining dyed cloths, in order to avoid
this defect, it is necessary to pass from one colour to another, as for instance
from red to green or olive, or to transfer the gaze at intervals to a colour which
is complementary to the colour of the cloths. Further, the fatigue of the nerves
has an effect upon the appearance of a colour which is viewed immediately
after another colour has been looked at, and in the following list examples are
given of the changes that take place:

If red has previously been looked at—blue appears greener; yellow appears greener; orange appears yellower, and green appears bluer. If blue has previously been looked at red appears more orangy; yellow appears more intense; orange and green appear yellower. If green has previously been looked at red appears more violet; yellow appears more orange; blue appears more violet; and orange appears redder. The term 'successive contrast of colour' is applied to the effect produced by viewing colours one after the other.

The chromatic circle

Any two complementary colours are in the greatest possible contrast to one another, and *Figure 8.1* illustrates how a chromatic circle may be made which enables the colours that are complementary to be readily seen. The circle is divided into a convenient number of equal parts, in this case twelve, and at equal distances from each other the primary colours—red, green, and blue (ultramarine)—are painted in. From the red to the green the colours are

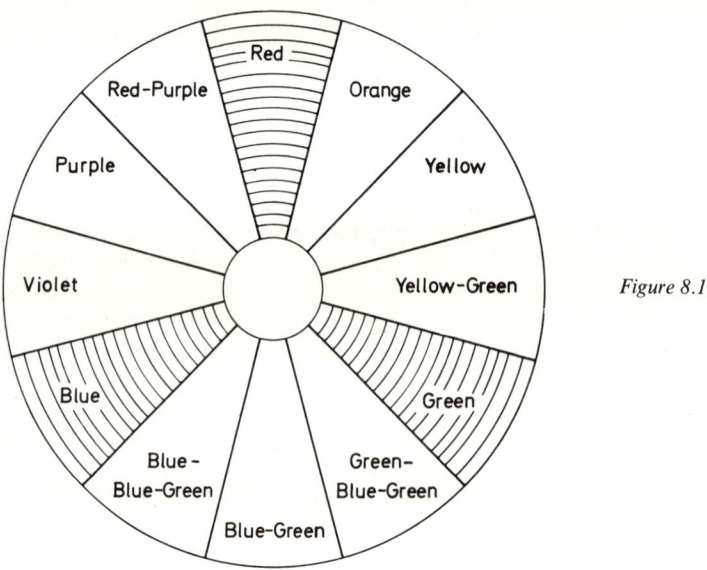

Figure 8.1

then changed through orange, yellow and yellow green; from the green to the blue through greenish blue to bluish green; and from the blue to the red through violet, purple, and reddish purple. Opposite colours in the circle are complementary and in extreme contrast to one another.

Colour measurement

When our eyes see a colour, they tell us not only what *hue* it is, but also what proportion of white light is present, i.e. what the *purity* or *saturation* of the colour is, and its *luminosity* or *brightness*. Quantitative methods of colour measurement set out to put figures to these properties: for this purpose the colours of the spectrum are accepted as being pure colours and are used as standards for comparison. In the same way that two complementary colours can be added to give white, any colour may be described as a mixture of white and a pure spectrum colour or one of the non-spectral purples which result from mixtures of spectral blues and reds. To describe the hue, therefore, all that is necessary is to state the wavelength of the spectral colour, or the wavelength of the spectral complement of the nonspectral purple. To describe the purity, it is necessary to find the proportions of the spectral colour and of white light which would be needed to match the colour: for a purple hue the calculation is slightly more complicated, but amounts to the same thing. To measure brightness, the light output has to be compared with that from a standard source. For the purposes of colourmatching it is useful to set up a series of samples of, say, the same hue and brightness, but of different purities: by doing this for different hues and for different brightnesses it is possible to build up a colour atlas such as the series of Ostwald or Munsell colour charts. By using such charts, or, more accurately, by using a spectrophotometer, it is possible to make colour matches and predict dye recipes and also to follow colour changes during fading, when hue as well as purity may change.

Pigment theory of colour

The effects obtained by mixing dyes or coloured pigments together are different from those resulting from the mixing of coloured lights. Thus, the combination of red and green lights produces yellow, and of yellow and blue lights white; whereas red and green pigments yield a dull brown, and yellow and blue pigments green. It has been previously stated that in mixing differently coloured pigments the colour effect is subtractive. A third colour is produced because colouring matter reflects colour rays other than those of its predominating colour. The *absorption spectra* of coloured bodies give the colours that are reflected by them, and it is found that both yellow and blue pigments reflect green light, so that when they are mixed the combined action of the two causes practically all the light to be absorbed except the green rays. That is, the blue absorbs the red, orange, and yellow rays of light, and the yellow absorbs the violet and blue rays, so that the reflected rays of the mixture are green. It is the reflected light rays which are common to the pigments, that govern the colour that is produced by their mixture, and the more the reflected rays of the pigments overlap the brighter is the resulting colour, while the fewer reflected rays there are in common, the duller is the colour. Both red and yellow pigments reflect orange light, red also reflects a little yellow, and yellow a little red, and the luminous orange results from their mixture. The reflected rays of red and green overlap in yellow, orange, and red light, but the quantity of each is only small, hence a dull brown hue results from the mixture.

The effects produced by mixing coloured pigments are very well explained by the Brewster theory, which is adopted in the practical application of colours in dyeing. In this theory red, yellow, and blue are taken as *simple*, or *primary* colours, because they cannot be obtained by mixing other pigment colours, whereas by their admixture in different proportions, and with the addition of black and white pigments, practically all other colours can be produced. When two of the simple colours are mixed the resultant colour is termed a *compound* colour. By mixing the primary colours in pairs *secondary* colours are formed, while the mixing of the secondary colours in pairs produces *tertiary* colours, as indicated in the following list:

CLASSIFICATION OF COLOURS

Primary	*Secondary*	*Tertiary*
Red	Green (Yellow and Blue)	Russet (Purple and Orange)
Yellow	Purple (Red and Blue)	Citron (Green and Orange)
Blue	Orange (Red and Yellow)	Olive (Green and Purple)

The tertiary colours thus result from the mixture of the three primary colours, but in each case one of the three is in excess of the other colours. Compared with the primary and secondary colours the tertiary colours are dull, the colour appearance being due to the predominating colour. Thus, red is the predominating element in russet, yellow in citron, and blue in olive. The relation of the primary, secondary, and tertiary colours to each other is shown diagrammatically in Plate I-C.

A useful diagram is also given in *Figure 8.2*, which shows the arrangement of the primary, secondary, and intermediate colours in the Brewster theory. The circle is divided into eighteen parts, and the primary colours, red, yellow, and blue are, placed equidistant from each other, with the secondary colours

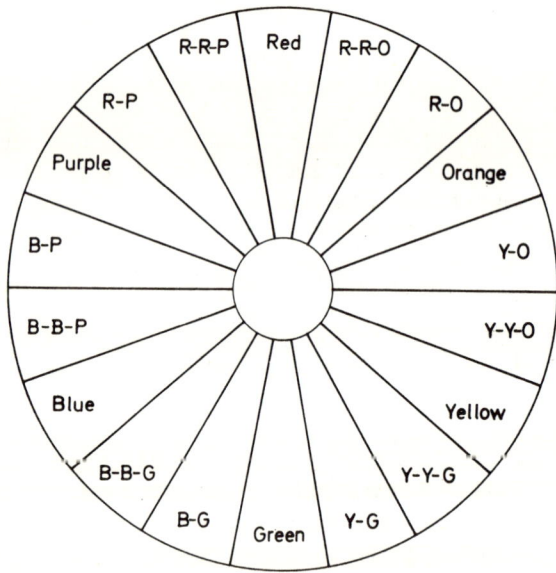

Figure 8.2

between them. Between each primary and secondary colour two intermediate colours are indicated in which the primary is in excess of the secondary in different proportions.

The term 'complementary' is used in a different sense in the light and pigment theories of colouring, as in the latter theory each primary colour and the secondary colour that results from the mixing of the *other two* primaries are considered to be complementary to each other. Thus, in the chart in

Figure 8.2 the complementary colours are furthest apart from each other on the opposite sides of the circle. A similar chart consisting of eight colours and known as the Ostwald circle is reproduced in Plate I at D. The colours in this chart are in a slightly modified relationship to one another and this is found particularly useful in establishing the greatest possible degree of contrast in colours. As in Brewster's chart the most contrasting colours are diametrically opposite to one another. It will be useful to compare C and D with B (Plate I) which illustrates the *true* complementary pairs.

Attributes of the primary and secondary colours

Different effects are produced on the mind by different colours, the impression of brightness, warmth, and nearness being conveyed by some, and of coldness and distance by others. Red is a brilliant and cheerful colour, and gives the impression of warmth. It is a very powerful colour and appears to advance slightly towards the observer. Yellow is a very luminous and vivid colour and conveys the idea of purity. It is not so warm looking as red, but appears more distinctly to advance to the eye. Blue is a cold colour and appears to recede from the eye. The qualities of the secondary colours are somewhat intermediate between the primary colours of which they are composed. Thus orange is a very strong colour and possesses warmth and brightness, but it is not so intense as yellow. Green is a retiring and rather cold colour, but appears cheerful and fresh. Purple is a beautiful rich and deep colour, and for bloom and softness is unsurpassed. The primary and secondary colours are too strong and assertive to be used in large quantities in their pure form except for very special purposes. They are chiefly employed in comparatively small spaces for the purpose of imparting brightness and freshness to fabrics; their strength being usually much reduced by mixing with black or white when they are used in large quantities as ground shades.

Modification of colours

Pigment colours may be modified in the following three ways: (1) By mixing with another colour. (2) By mixing with black. (3) By mixing with white. A scale or range of colours may be obtained by each method, or by the methods in combination. Mixing a colour with another colour produces a change in hue; thus, crimson results from adding to red a small quantity of blue, and scarlet from adding to red a small quantity of yellow. The degree of the change of hue is determined by the proportionate quantities of the colours mixed. For instance, if the yellow predominates in a mixture of yellow and blue the hue is yellowish green, but if the blue predominates a bluish green is produced. A scale of seven hues of green, running from a very yellow green at A to a very blue green at G, results from mixing yellow and blue in the proportions indicated in Table 1.

Table 1

	A	B	C	D	E	F	G
Yellow	4	3	2	1	1	1	1
Blue	1	1	1	1	2	3	4

When a colour is mixed with white or black a change of *tone* results. By mixing a colour with white in different proportions *tints* of the colour are produced; while by mixing with varying proportions of black, *shades* of the colour result. A tint is therefore a tone which is lighter, and a shade a tone which is darker, than the normal colour; and a scale of tones of a colour may

Table 2

White or Black	7	5	3	1	1	1	1
Colour	1	1	1	1	3	5	7

be obtained running from the lightest tint to the darkest shade. The relative proportions of the colour and the white or the black may be arranged on the principles illustrated in the foregoing examples, or as shown in Table 2.

Coloured greys

Certain neutral or broken colours—termed coloured greys—result from mixing a normal colour with both black and white in varying proportions. Thus, a scale of red greys, running from dark .to light results from mixing white, black, and red in the proportions given in Table 3.

Table 3

White	1	2	3	4	5	6	7
Black	7	6	5	4	3	2	1
Red	1	1	1	1	1	1	1

The white and black alone would produce a scale of seven pure greys running from dark to light, but to each of these is added the same proportion of red—i.e., one part of red to eight parts of grey. The scale thus varies às to light and shade, but is equal as to colour. In the next table a different arrangement of the proportions is given, an increasing quantity of colour being added to an equal amount of pure grey; the seven blue greys which result thus varying as to colour, but being equal as to light and shade except for the influence of the colour.

Table 4

White	4	4	4	4	4	4	4
Black	4	4	4	4	4	4	4
Blue	1	$1\frac{1}{2}$	2	$2\frac{1}{2}$	3	$3\frac{1}{2}$	4

A 'mode' shade is a broken colour in which a certain hue predominates over a pure grey.

COLOURS IN COMBINATION

Colour contrast

There are two heads under which colour combinations are classed—i.e. monochromatic contrasts, and polychromatic contrasts. Monochromatic contrasts are those in which different tones of the same colour are combined;

as, for instance, two shades of red, or three tints of blue, etc. Softly graded contrasts result which are specially suitable for such fabrics as overcoatings, suitings, and costumes. Polychromatic contrasts include all combinations of two or more different colours which may be alike or different in tone— e.g., light green and light blue, and light green and dark red. A style partakes of both classes of contrast when a ground pattern, consisting of different tones of the same colour, has bright threads of another colour introduced upon it at intervals for the purpose of improving the effect.

Two kinds of contrast may be formed by colours that are in combination— i.e., 'successive contrast' and 'simultaneous contrast'. In successive contrast the colours are such a distance apart that one is perceived after the other. In simultaneous contrast the colours are placed in juxtaposition so that both are seen at the same time. The same law governs both classes of contrast, and in each case the colours have the property of changing each other's qualities; but the change is greater when the colours are in actual contact than when they are seen separately. Colours that are in juxtaposition are subject to two kinds of contrast—'contrast of hue' and 'contrast of tone'.

Contrast of hue—In contrast of hue each colour influences its neighbour, since each appears to be tinged with the complementary hue of its neighbour. Thus, in a cloth consisting of red and blue stripes the red appears tinged with yellow—the complementary of the blue, and the blue with bluish green the complementary of the red. As a further illustration, it may be assumed that in a stripe fabric if a blue stripe is formed between two red stripes and then between two green stripes, the blue stripes, although dyed exactly the same, would appear different, because in one case the blue is tinged with bluish green—the complement of red, and in the other case with purple—the complement of green. One stripe of blue would thus appear greener, and the other more violet than is actually the case.

The change in colours due to simultaneous contrast can be readily judged by an examination of the chromatic diagram given in Plate I. It will be seen that simultaneous contrast makes the colours more unlike, and when colours that are opposite in the circle are combined the contrast between them is intensified, and, if suitably proportioned, both colours are enriched.

Contrast of tone—This comes into play when two tones of the same colour are in juxtaposition—e.g., dark blue and light blue—and when dark and light colours are placed together—e.g., dark blue and light green. The dark colour, by contrast, makes the light colour appear lighter than it actually is, while similarly, the light colour makes the dark colour appear darker than it is. On a white ground colours appear deeper and darker; on a grey ground they appear about normal; whereas on a black ground they look brighter and lighter.

Colour harmony

Harmony of colour is not governed by fixed principles, and any combination of hues that is pleasing and gives full satisfaction to the observer may be said to constitute harmony. The colour sense in different persons, however, varies —being more highly developed in some than in others—and what may appear harmonious to one may be more or less inharmonious to others. In combining colours the influence that one colour has upon another should be carefully thought out, so that they may be arranged in such a manner that they will enhance and enrich, rather than impoverish each other. Harmony is obtained when the proper hues are so associated that every particle of colour is helpful to the complete colour scheme. It is usual to distinguish between two kinds of harmony—harmony of analogy and harmony of contrast.

There are two ways of producing a harmony of analogy—(1) By the combination of tones of the same colour that do not differ widely from each other. (2) By the combination of hues which are closely related and are equal or nearly equal in depth of tone. Different tints of blue, or shades of green when combined, yield a 'harmony of analogy of tone' if the difference between them is not too marked. Tone-shaded effects are produced by combining a series or scale of tones of a colour which are so graded and arranged as to run imperceptibly one into another. In a combination of yellowish green and bluish green, yellow and blue are differentiating colours; but there is a common element in green, and if the two hues are nearly equal in depth of tone, and are harmonious when united, they form a 'harmony of analogy of hue'. Harmonies of analogy are of chief value in producing quiet effects.

There are also two ways of producing a harmony of contrast—(1) By the combination of widely different tones of the same colour. (2) By the combination of unlike colours. Thus, a pleasing combination of two tones of blue, the interval between which is marked, forms a 'harmony of contrast of tone', while the union of red and green, if harmonious, forms a 'harmony of contrast of hue'. Harmonies of contrast are useful when clear smart effects are required. As previously stated there may be analogy in tone and contrast in hue, or contrast in tone and analogy in hue in a combination.

There is also 'harmony of succession—or gradation—of hue' (which partakes somewhat of both kinds of harmony) in which there is a succession of hues that pass gradually one into the other—the spectrum being a typical example. Red and yellow, when combined, are in colour contrast; but by introducing between them a series or scale of hues of orange—running from reddish orange to yellowish orange—the two colours may be so blended one into the other that there is no sharp contrast, and an effect closely related to harmony of analogy is produced. Similarly, yellow may be passed imperceptibly into blue through a series of hues of green, and blue into red through hues of violet and purple.

Basis of colour harmony

Complementary hues are harmonious, but in their pure state they yield contrasts that are too strong. The colours still form similar complementary pairs when reduced by means of black, or white, or both, and in this condition they form most harmonious combinations. A study of the complementary hues, and their shades, tints, and broken colours, is therefore of great value as an introduction to the combining of colours, and as a basis of colour harmony.

It is not necessary, however, to select only colours that are complementary in order to produce harmony, and it is generally considered that it is better to combine hues which are from 20 to 30 degrees on one side or the other of their complements, as these are not so strongly in contrast. It will be noted that in Plate I at C (Brewster's arrangement) opposite colours are not so strongly in contrast as at D, or as in *Figure 8.1*, in which the colours are arranged according to the Young–Helmholtz theory. The effect of contrast, when complementary or near complementary colours are in contrast, is to enrich the colours.

In producing a harmony of contrast it is a good rule to select colours that are separated by at least 90 degrees on the chromatic circle, shown in *Figure 8.1*. Related colours, which are from about 30 to 90 degrees apart on the circle, such as blue and purple, etc., are in most cases inharmonious. Colours that are very near together in the chromatic circle can be combined in producing a harmony of analogy of hue.

Rood's theory of the natural order of colours, also, can be made use of as a basis of colour harmony. The order of the colours, as illustrated in *Figure 8.1*, is from violet (the darkest colour), through purple, red-purple, red, and orange to yellow (the lightest colour), then through yellow-green, green, blue-green, and blue to violet again. The natural order is for the darker colour to be deeper, or darker in tone, than the lighter colour. Thus, in a combination of red and yellow the red should be darker in tone than the yellow, while if red be combined with purple the red should be lighter in tone than the purple. A combination of light red and dark yellow, or of dark red and light purple would be discordant.

Dark grounds are more suitable for the application of bright colours, such as red, orange, and yellow, than light grounds, as their qualities of brightness and intensity are improved on the former, and diminished on the latter. On the other hand sombre colours, such as violet and purple, are deepened and enriched on light grounds and suffer on dark grounds.

Relative spaces occupied by colours

While allowing for a predominating hue it is usual to arrange the spaces occupied by the several colours in a design in accordance with the relative intensity of the hue. Too great an excess of a colour is injurious to an effect,

Table 5

(a)	2 threads black and			2 threads white.			
(b)	4	,,	,,	,,	4	,,	light grey.
(c)	8	,,	,,	,,	8	,,	mid grey.
(d)	16	,,	,,	,,	16	,,	dark grey.

or

(e)	2 threads white and			2 threads black.			
(f)	4	,,	,,	,,	4	,,	dark grey.
(g)	8	,,	,,	,,	8	,,	mid grey.
(h)	16	,,	,,	,,	16	,,	light grey.

and it is necessary to employ a strong colour more sparingly than a less intense colour. Thus, a combination of a shade of blue with intense yellow might be harmonious if the space occupied by the blue largely predominated; whereas with the yellow predominating, the effect would be displeasing on account of the blue being overpowered by the greater luminosity of the yellow.

In the same manner a few threads of bright red on a toned green foundation might prove pleasing where a large number of threads of red would appear crude.

In combining threads which are in strong contrast, the space occupied by each hue or tone should be small, but if the contrast is subdued, the space allotted to each may be large. This is illustrated in a general way by Table 5 in which the contrast is represented relatively by the terms black, grey, and white; the black and white producing a strong contrast, and the black or white with grey more subdued effects, as the grey more nearly approaches the black or the white.

Divisional colours

In many combinations the contrast has the effect of making the colours appear blurred and confused at their joining. In such a case, and when the colours are too strong in contrast, hues of a neutral character, or black, grey, or white may be employed to separate the colours. The strength of the contrast is thereby reduced, and the colours are made to appear clear and precise. When a colour is used to form the divisional line its qualities should be about intermediate between those of the two colours, or a paler tone of either colour may be suitable. Black can always be successfully used to separate two bright colours, while white and grey are useful in separating a bright and a sombre colour, or two sombre colours, grey being used instead of white when the latter forms too strong a contrast.

Although black is not so useful in separating a bright and a sombre colour as two bright colours, it can be successfully employed in combination with the sombre colours, such as blue and violet, and the darker shades of the luminous colours, in forming a harmony of analogy.

Influence of fabric characteristics on the appearance of colours

Textile materials may be dyed at various stages of manufacture, e.g. in the loose fibre state; in the sliver or top stage; in the form of the spun thread or manufactured cloth. In the case of man-made materials, in addition to the above mentioned possibilities, colour may also be added to the spinning solution prior to extrusion. The object in each instance may be to produce a solid colour effect in the cloth by employing only one colour. On the other hand, different colours may be combined at one or other stage of manufacture with the object of achieving a mixed colour effect in which the component hues may be either suffused or distinct. The exact point in the chain of production processes at which colour is introduced has a considerable bearing on the appearance of the colour in the finished cloth.

In addition to the quality of the dyestuff itself, which may be brilliant or dull, other factors which tend to modify the appearance of colours in fabrics are mainly connected with the lustre. The nature of this phenomenon was described at the beginning of this chapter and all the factors which contribute to modify lustre will have a bearing upon the colour as well. Thus, low-toned colours, which in rough fabrics may appear insipid, often look well on cloths constructed from filament materials. In smooth fibres, yarns and fabrics it is possible to achieve brightness and clarity, and though this is unlikely to be obtained in materials which have a disturbed, fibrous surface, the latter do not need to appear dull, and with a suitable choice of colour with the necessary depth of tone, a quality of fulness and softness of which such materials are capable, is frequently preferred.

The frequency of interlacing as well as the actual arrangement of the intersection points has also a very considerable effect on the appearance of colour, e.g. in plain weave fabrics in which the warp is red and the weft blue the constituent colours tend to lose their separate identities and the overall resultant hue would be purple. On the other hand, if a cloth composed of similar colours were woven in a bold 4-and-4 twill the two shades would stand apart each forming a distinct line, and although each would influence the other in conformity with the theories described earlier, neither would lose its own identity.

APPLICATION OF COLOUR

Mixed colour effects

The following methods of producing mixed colour effects are employed:
  (1) By blending differently coloured fibres which have been dyed in the raw or the sliver condition, producing 'mixture yarns'. A somewhat similar mixed colour effect is obtained in 'melange' yarns, which are produced by printing the slivers in bands of different colours that the subsequent drawing operations cause to be more or less thoroughly intermingled in the spun thread.
  (2) By introducing small tufts of dyed fibres into the slivers at the later stages of the processes preceding spinning; a thread spotted with the colour being produced.
  (3) By spinning from differently coloured rovings, producing 'marl' yarns, in which the colours are blended only to a limited extent; the resultant thread, in some cases, having almost the appearance of being composed of two differently coloured threads twisted together.
  (4) By printing the spun thread in bands of different colours.
  (5) By twisting together differently coloured threads producing various kinds of fancy twist yarns.
  (6) By combining (either as a fibre mixture or a twist) two materials in the undyed state which have different affinities for colouring matters, and submitting the woven cloth to a cross-dyeing operation.
  (7) By employing differently dyed threads, arranged one, or at most two, threads at a place, and using weaves of a crêpe or broken character.

Fibre mixture yarns

In mixtures of differently dyed fibres the degree in which the colours are intermingled varies according to the number and character of the processes which follow the blending. The mixing may be done in the later stages prior to spinning with the object of producing a colour mixture in which each colour retains its purity. On the other hand, by blending in the early stages, colour effects are produced which are quite unlike those obtained by mixing colours in any other way. The differently dyed fibres are so thoroughly intermingled that a new colour results, in which the separate colours can only be distinguished by close examination. For instance, an intimate mixture of yellow and blue fibres produces a hue of green which is quite different from any green that can be obtained by mixing yellow and blue dyes, because in the fibre mixture each colour retains, in some degree, its individuality, whereas in the dye mixture the original colours are effaced.

Various classes of fibre mixtures are included in the following list:

(1) Mixtures of white and black producing greys.
(2) Mixtures of one colour with white or black producing tones of the colour.
(3) Mixtures of different tones of the same colour.
(4) Mixtures of two or more colours.
(5) Mixtures of two or more colours with white or black.
(6) Mixtures of black and white (grey) with one or more colours producing coloured greys.

In producing a scale of hues, tones, or greys, the quantities of the different constituents may be arranged on the principle illustrated in the examples of mixing pigments.

The most suitable materials for fibre mixtures are the fairly strong and lustrous medium wools, such as are used in the manufacture of mixture serges and tweeds.

In selecting the colours to be mixed the following rules are of general application: (a) In a mixture of two tones of the same colour there should be a distinct difference between the two. (b) The colours should harmonise when laid side by side before mixing. (c) The proportionate quantities should be in accordance with the relative intensities of the hues, subdued colours, and black and white being chiefly employed, with bright colours introduced only in small quantities.

Twist yarn mixtures

In yarns composed of differently coloured threads twisted together there is no intimate intermingling of the fibres, so that each colour is seen separately, the twisting of the threads simply breaking the continuity of the colours. The prominence of an intense colour can be reduced without its purity being affected, and the yarns are, therefore, specially useful in cases in which the introduction of a self-coloured thread would cause the hue to show too strongly.

Different hues, and also different materials, can be combined in various ways in the yarns. In the grandrelle, spiral, gimp, and diamond yarns the colours appear regularly, whereas in the curl, knop, and cloud threads a special colour can be shown prominently at intervals. In the same thread combinations of two or more of the effects can be produced in diverse ways. (See: Fancy yarns—Appendix I.)

Combinations of differently coloured threads

Effects are produced by combining differently coloured threads as follows:
(a) With the warp in one colour and the weft in another colour, forming a

'shot' effect. (b) With the warp in different colours and the weft in one colour, producing a stripe. (c) With the warp in one colour and the weft in different colours, producing a cross-over effect. (d) With both the warp and the weft in different colours producing a check style.

Colour stripes and checks

An arrangement of weft threads in a cloth can also be employed for the warp threads, and vice versa; therefore, stripe and check colour combinations are considered together in the following. The patterns result from the combination, in equal or unequal spaces, of two, three, or more colours, and in their construction it is necessary to have the following in mind:

(a) Colours which harmonise, and tones that will assist harmony should be selected.
(b) Each colour or tone should be allotted a suitable extent of surface.
(c) The appearance of a colour is influenced by the weave, as different weaves break up the colours on the surface of a fabric in a varying degree; the effect, for instance, of a 2-and-2 twill being quite different from that of a 3-and-1 twill or satin. A continuous warp face weave, although suitable for a stripe, is quite inapplicable to a check. To produce a *perfect* check, weaves with equal warp and weft float should be employed and the weft threads should be similar to the warp threads as regards number, thickness, material, and colour arrangement.

Stripe and check effects may be conveniently classified into: patterns in two colours, and patterns in three or more colours; both of which may be subdivided broadly into regular and irregular orders of colouring. Arrangements of coloured threads are also classified into—simple orders, and compound orders.

Simple regular patterns

Examples of regular patterns in two colours are—4 threads dark and 4 threads light, or 16 threads dark and 16 threads light; and a three-colour style—8 threads dark, 8 threads medium, and 8 threads light. A four-colour regular pattern may be arranged—6 threads colour A, 6 threads colour B, 6 threads colour A, 6 threads colour C, 6 threads colour A, and 6 threads colour D; in which colours B, C, and D are separated from each other by the colour A. The regular arrangements do not, as a rule, yield interesting styles, but small patterns are frequently quite effective. In some cases, however, the combination of the weave with the colour scheme modifies the stiffness of the form and makes it pleasing even with large patterns. A regular order is very often employed as a ground effect in a special stripe or check design; while sometimes a slight change in a pattern is made at intervals in order to render it more interesting. For instance, a 6 × 6 order of colouring might be arranged —6 threads colour A, and 6 threads colour B five times; then 6 threads colour A, 2 threads colour B, 2 threads colour C, and 2 threads colour B. In check patterns a two-colour scheme gives three effects; the third hue being produced where the two colours cross each other. In the same manner six colour effects are produced in a three-colour scheme—i.e., colours A, B, and C separately, A and B together, A and C together, and B and C together.

Simple irregular patterns

The irregular colour arrangements permit much more detail and diversity to be introduced than the regular styles. Examples in two colours are 6 threads dark and 2 threads light, or 16 threads dark and 8 threads light; while a three-colour irregular pattern is—12 threads dark, 8 threads medium, and 4 threads light. The last example, if produced in check form, gives a variety of shapes—12 × 12, 8 × 8, 4 × 4, 12 × 8, 12 × 4, and 8 × 4.

Compound orders of colouring

A compound order of colouring is a combination of two or more simple orders, each of which is repeated a number of times. A variety of arrangements is given in Table 6.

Table 6 EXAMPLES OF COMPOUND ORDERS OF COLOURING

1	2	3
1 dark ⎱ 8 times 1 light ⎰	2 dark ⎱ 2 medium ⎬ 6 times 2 light ⎰	2 dark ⎱ 8 times 1 light ⎰
2 dark ⎱ 4 times 2 light ⎰	4 dark ⎱ 4 medium ⎬ 3 times 4 light ⎰	4 dark ⎱ 6 times 2 light ⎰
1 dark ⎱ 8 times 1 light ⎰		
4 dark ⎱ 4 times 4 light ⎰		

Example 1 is a combination of three regular simple orders in two colours; example 2, of two regular orders in three colours; and example 3, of two irregular orders in two colours.

Counter-change patterns

The term counter-change is applied to styles in which the colours change positions; one colour being allowed to predominate in one section of the pattern, and another colour in the next section in exactly the same proportion. An illustration in two colours is—8 threads dark, 2 threads light, 8 threads dark, then 8 threads light, 2 threads dark, and 8 threads light. Three colours may be introduced on this principle, as for example—12 threads dark, 4 threads medium, 12 threads dark; then 12 threads medium, 4 threads light, and 12 threads medium.

Graduated patterns

In these styles the spaces occupied by the colours are gradually increased or decreased in size, as shown in Table 7.

Example 1 illustrates 'single-shading', in which the threads are graduated in one direction only, whereas examples 2 and 3 show 'double-shading' the number of threads of each colour being gradually increased and then decreased. Example 4 illustrates inverse shading; the number of threads of one

Table 7 EXAMPLES OF GRADUATED PATTERNS

1.	Colour A	1		3		5		7		9		11	
	Colour B		2		4		6		8		10		12
2.	Colour A	2		6		10		14		10		6	
	Colour B		4		8		12		12		8		4
3.	Colour A	2		4		8		16		8		4	
	Colour B		4		8		16		8		4		2
4.	Colour A	2		4		6		8		10		12	
	Colour B		12		10		8		6		4		2
5.	Colour A	2		4		6		8		6		4	
	Colour B		3		3		3		3		3		3
6.	Colour A	1		3		5		7		7		5		3
	Colour B		2				6				6			2
	Colour C			4				8				4	

colour increasing, while those of the other are decreasing. In example 5 the first colour is double-shaded, whereas the second colour is stationary; and example 6 is illustrative of shading in three colours.

Modification of stripe and check patterns

One of the principal features in the designing of colour stripes and checks is the production of a great variety of effects by repeatedly introducing slight changes in the arrangement of the threads. The examples given in *Figure 8.3*

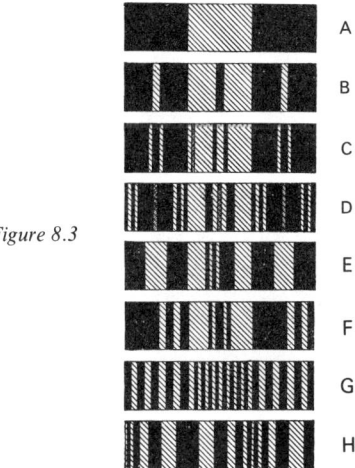

Figure 8.3

illustrate, in a general way, the system of working as applied to the modification of a stripe. Two colours only are mostly represented, but the method holds good when more colours are used. Commencing with the regular stripe, indicated at A, the first modification consists of bisecting each stripe, as shown at B, and the second by introducing two stripes in the centre, as represented at C. The stiffness of a symmetrical pattern may be reduced by introducing a line in a different colour, in the manner indicated by the differently shaded line in C. This line, in a check style, will produce an over check. Example D shows a modification which is symmetrical in form; while in each example E and F one half of the pattern is symmetrical and the other half non-symmetrical. A compound arrangement of the threads is illustrated at G and a graduated pattern at H.

Balance of contrast in pattern range designing

The examples given in *Figure 8.3* are all different in form, and each therefore constitutes a distinct style. In pattern designing, however, it is frequently necessary to produce a range of effects which will form only one style. In the latter case the arrangement of the threads requires to be exactly the same in each pattern in the range. The difference between the patterns is due to different colours being used; and it is necessary to obtain the same degree of contrast in colour and tone in each pattern. After the form of the style has been decided upon, the number of colours to be used, and their relative intensity in the different sections may be determined; the most intense colour being usually allotted to the smallest section. The colours of the first pattern may then be selected, and when found satisfactory, these are employed as the toning of every other pattern in the range. The system of working is illustrated by the following example of a range of stripes:

Table 8

Form of Stripe	A	B	C	X	Y
16 threads	Black	Black	Black	Black	Brown
4 threads	Dark Green	Dark Blue	Brown	Orange	Black
16 threads	Black	Black	Black	Black	Brown
2 threads	Red	Orange	Light Green	Dark Blue	Light Green

In each pattern A, B, and C the least intense colour or black is allotted to the largest section (16 threads), the medium colour to the next largest section (4 threads), and the brightest colour to the smallest section (2 threads). The

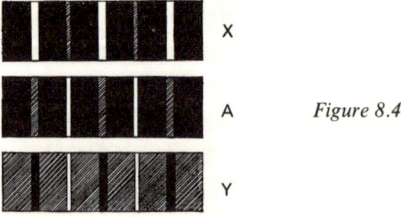

Figure 8.4

dark green, dark blue, and brown, in the medium-size section, should be equal in depth of tone, and there should be the same degree of contrast between the dark blue and the orange in pattern B, and between the brown and the light green in pattern C, as there is between the dark green and the red in the first pattern A.

Patterns X and Y in the list illustrate a wrong principle of arrangement. The same colours are employed as in the patterns B and C respectively, and the threads are arranged in the same order, but the position of the colours is changed, therefore the effects produced by X and Y would be out of balance with each other and with the first pattern. This is illustrated in *Figure 8.4*, in which the relative intensities of the colours are represented diagrammatically. In each pattern A, B, and C, in the above list, the colours would appear relatively as shown at A in *Figure 8.4*, only one style being formed; but in patterns X and Y the colours would be relatively as shown at X and Y in *Figure 8.4*, each forming a distinct style on account of the difference in the contrast between the sections.

Colour combinations in relation to weave

The weaves that are employed in conjunction with combinations of coloured threads may be broadly divided into the following three classes: (1) Weaves which bring the warp and weft threads equally, or nearly equally, to the surface of the cloth, and enable the colours to be applied in both warp and weft. This type gives the greatest scope for colour effects. (2) Warp face weaves, in which the weft is almost entirely concealed, so that it is necessary to apply the colours chiefly in the warp. (3) Weft face weaves, in which the warp is nearly concealed, and in which it is seldom possible to apply the colour except in the weft.

9

Simple Colour and Weave Effects

GENERAL CONSIDERATIONS ARISING FROM
THE COMBINATION OF WEAVE WITH COLOUR

A colour and weave effect is the form or pattern in two or more colours produced by colour and weave in combination. It is frequently quite different in appearance from either the order of colouring or the weave, because (a) the weave tends to break the continuity of the colours of warp and weft; and (b) a colour shows on the face of the fabric, whether it is brought up in warp float, or in weft float. This is illustrated in *Figure 9.1*, where, in the 3-and-3

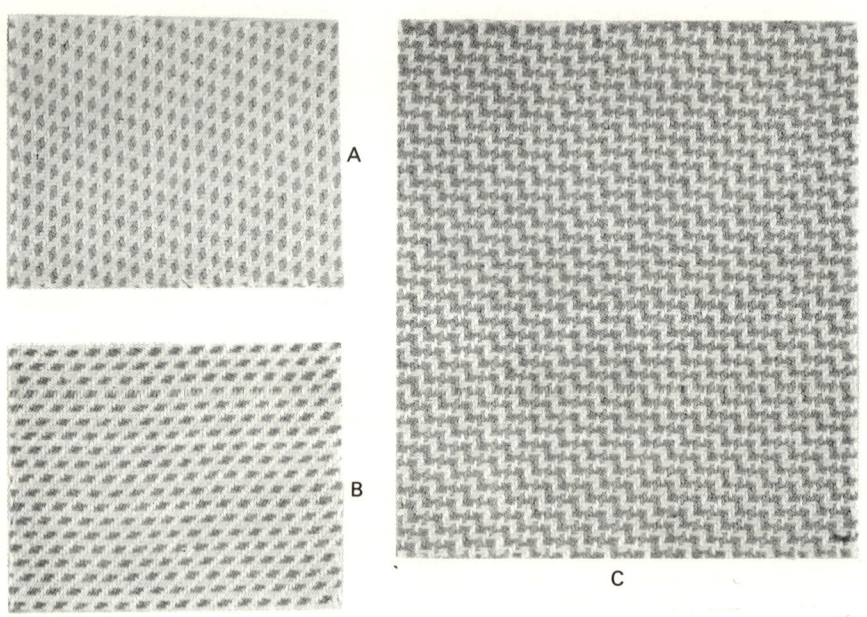

Figure 9.1

twill weave, A shows the effect produced by colouring 2 dark, 2 white in the warp, with white weft; B, 2 dark, 2 white in the weft, with white warp; and C, 2 dark, 2 white in both warp and weft. Each effect consists of a small black form on a white ground; but while in A the floating of the dark warp on the face produces the form, in B it is produced by the floating of the dark weft, and in C by the combination of dark warp float and black weft float on the surface.

Representation of colour and weave effects upon design paper

Colour and weave effects may be readily indicated upon point-paper, and for experimental purposes the method is useful, since it enables the designer to see the effect any colour plan will produce with a given weave. Three things

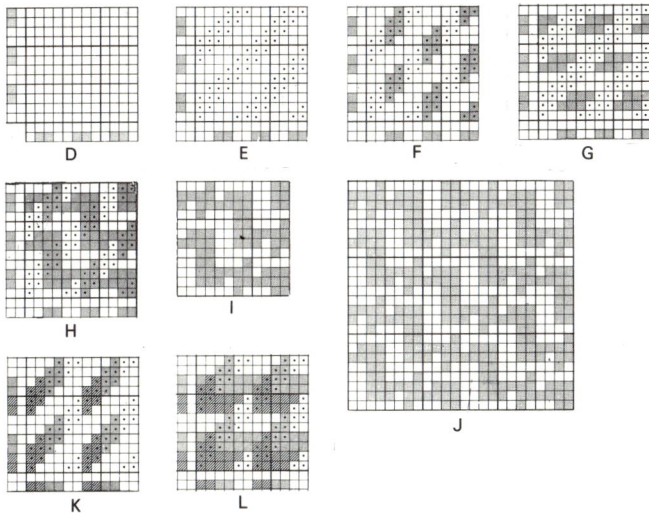

Figure 9.2

require to be known—i.e., the order of warping, the order of wefting, and the weave. The examples D and I in *Figure 9.2* illustrate in stages the working out of an effect in which the threads are arranged 2 dark, 2 light in warp and weft, while the weave is 3-and-3 twill. The example corresponds and may therefore be compared with that shown in *Figure 9.1*. The size of the repeat is obtained by finding the l.c.m. of the number of threads in one repeat of the colour plan, and in one repeat of the weave—in this case 12 ends by 12 picks. At D the arrangement of the ends as to colour is indicated along the bottom, and of the picks up the side of the reserved space. At E, the weave is inserted in the form of dots; the weave marks indicating warp float. At F the dark ends are followed vertically in successive order, and where there are weave marks— that is, where the warp is floated on the surface—the squares are filled in solid. At G the dark picks are followed horizontally in successive order, and where there are blanks in the weave—that is, where the weft is floated on the surface—the squares are filled in solid. H shows the appearance of the sketch at this stage, while I represents the complete effect with the weave marks removed. For better appreciation of the effect formed it is often necessary to show several repeats of the completed design as indicated at J.

In the plan I in *Figure 9.2* the marks represent one colour and the paper the other colour. In working out an effect in colours, the ground may be indicated in the second colour after the first colour has been painted in in the manner described; or the lighter colour may be first painted entirely over the space, and the pattern in the darker colour be afterwards indicated over it.

The method of working is similar when more than two colours are employed, as shown at K and L in *Figure 9.2*. The weave is 3-and-3 twill, and the warp and weft threads are arranged 2 dark, 2 medium, 2 light—the different colours being represented by different marks. The ends are followed first, each colour being dealt with in turn, and where there are weave marks the squares are filled in with the required colour, as shown at K. Afterwards the effect is completed by following the picks, and filling in the squares which are blank with the required colour, as shown at L. As before it is usually preferable for the sketch to be extended over two or more repeats in each direction.

Classification of colour and weave effects

A convenient classification of the orders of colouring the threads is as follows: (a) Simple warping and simple wefting; (b) compound warping and simple wefting; (c) simple warping and compound wefting; (d) compound warping and compound wefting. In (a) and (d) the order of warping may be the same, or different from the order of wefting. To each order of colouring, simple, stripe, and check weaves may be applied. The style of pattern which is produced by the combination of each order of colouring with each type of weave, is given in Table 9.

Table 9

Order of Colouring	Simple Weave	Stripe Weave	Check Weave
Simple Warping and Simple Wefting	Simple Pattern	Stripe Pattern	Check Pattern
Compound Warping and Simple Wefting	Stripe Pattern	Stripe Pattern	Check Pattern
Simple Warping and Compound Wefting	Cross-over Pattern	Check Pattern	Check Pattern
Compound Warping and Compound Wefting	Check Pattern	Check Pattern	Check Pattern

In addition to the foregoing styles, special orders of colouring and weaves are arranged to coincide with each other in such a manner as to produce special effects.

Methods of producing variety of effect in the same weave and colouring

An important factor to note in designing colour and weave effects is that different patterns can usually be obtained in one order of colouring and one weave by changing their relative positions. This is illustrated by the patterns represented in *Figures 9.3* and *9.4*. Each pattern, A to H in *Figures 9.3* and

9.4 is produced by the combination of a 4-and-4 order of warping and weft-ing, with a 2-and-2 hopsack weave. There are two ways in which the change of effect may be brought about: (1) As shown in *Figure 9.3*, the warp and weft threads may be arranged as to colour in the same manner throughout (i.e. 4 dark, 4 light), but with the weave placed in a different position in each

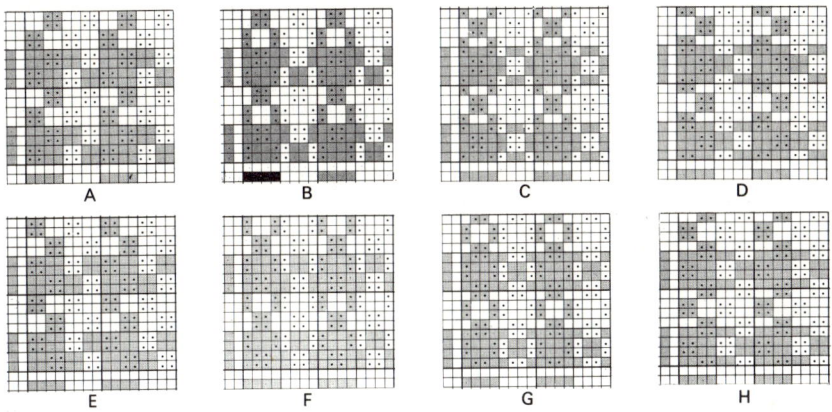

Figure 9.3

case. (2) As shown in *Figure 9.4*, the weave may be placed in the same position throughout, but with the colour pattern commencing in a different manner in each case. In the latter method either the warp, or the weft, or both the warp and the weft colours may be changed in position. It will be noted that the difference of effect in some cases is very slight, one-half of the patterns when turned over being simply duplicates of the other half. The example, however, is illustrative of the necessity in weaving of always retaining the

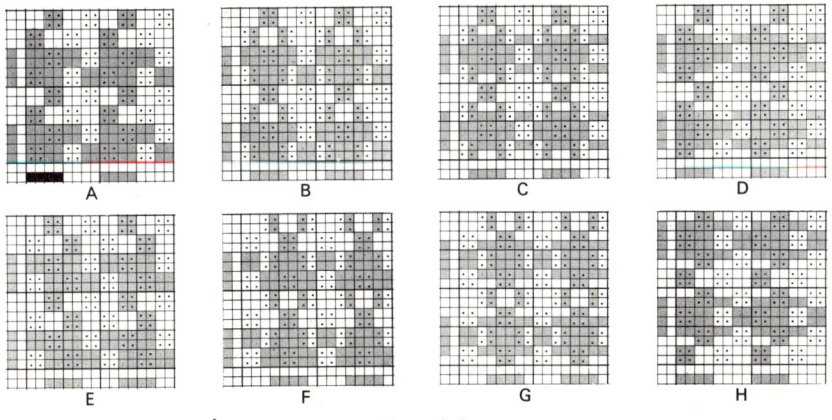

Figure 9.4

same relation between the colouring and the weave throughout the length of the cloth. In subsequent examples it is shown that the change of effect thus produced can be made use of, not only in designing small patterns, but also in the economical production of stripe and check designs in very great variety.

EXAMPLES OF SIMPLE WEAVE AND COLOUR COMBINATIONS

In these styles the arrangement of the threads as to colour may be regular (as for example, 4 dark, 4 light, or 3 dark, 3 medium, 3 light), or irregular (as, for example, 2 dark, 1 light, or 3 dark, 2 medium, 1 light). Many good effects are also obtained by arranging the weft in a different order from the warp (as, for example, 2-and-2 warping crossed with 1-and-1 wefting, or 4-and-4 warping crossed with 2-and-2 wefting).

The effects produced by applying simple weaves to simple orders of colourings comprise continuous line effects, hound's tooth patterns, bird's-eye and spot effects, step patterns, hairlines, and all-over patterns.

Continuous line effects

Examples of continuous effects, in which the lines run lengthwise of the cloth, are given in A to I in *Figure 9.5*. The weaves are dotted in, and the exact position of the dark threads in relation to the weave is indicated by the shaded marks along the bottom and at the side of the designs. All the particulars are thus given for reproducing the effects, and for the beginner it will be found good practice to work out the patterns on design paper using the technique previously described.

A in *Figure 9.5* shows the typical line effect produced by colouring the 2-and-2 twill in the order of 2 dark, 2 light; while in the effects shown at B to D the lines are more or less of a symmetrical zig-zag character. In E the lines are symmetrical and straight; in F and G they are serrated on one side, and in H and I small spots occur between the lines.

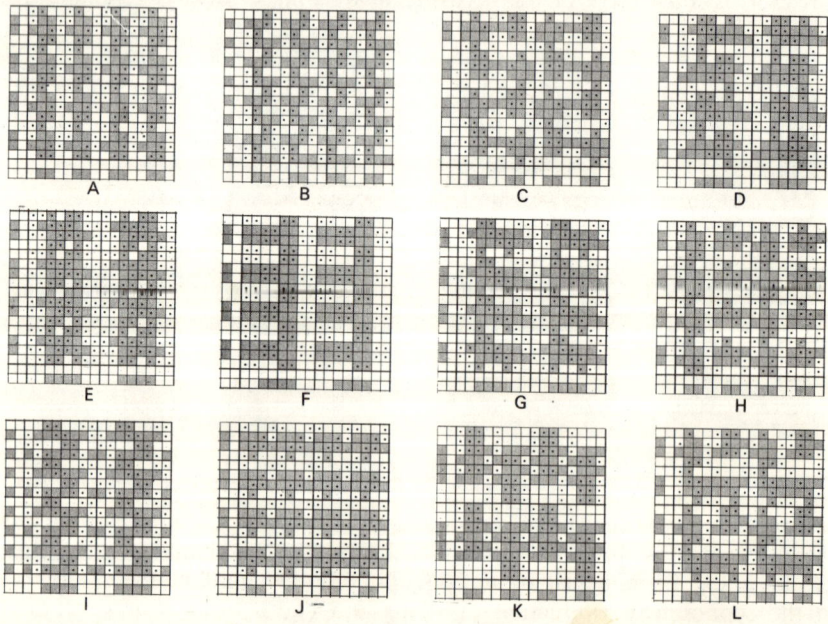

Figure 9.5

J to L in *Figure 9.5* show effects in which the lines run continuously across the piece. As a general rule, patterns in which the horizontal lines show prominently are satisfactory only when used in combination with other effects. On comparing some of the designs in *Figures 9.3* to *9.5* it will be noticed that similar weaves and colourings are employed for, both, the vertical, and the horizontal line effects, and that the change from one direction of the line to the other can be frequently accomplished by an apparently insignificant shift of the weave in respect of the colour or vice versa. (Compare A with J in *Figure 9.5*; and B with D in *Figures 9.3* and *9.4*.)

Hound's-tooth patterns

Typical examples of hound's-tooth (or, dog's-tooth) effects are shown at A and B in *Figure 9.6*. In each the order of colouring is 4 dark, 4 light in warp

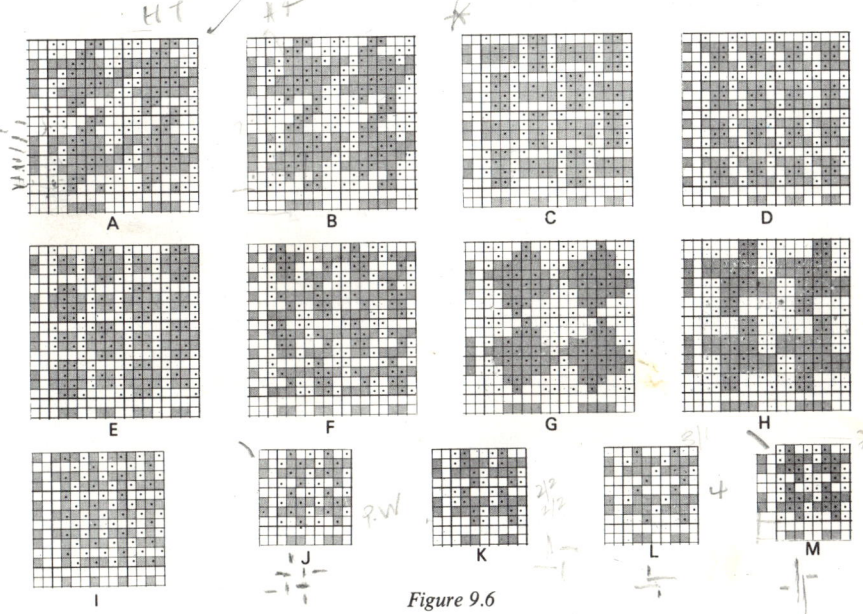

Figure 9.6

and weft, and the weave 2-and-2 twill, the slight difference between the effects being due to the weave having been placed in different positions in relation to the colouring. B in *Figure 9.7* shows a useful variation of the hound's-tooth style.

Bird's-eye and spot effects

The term bird's-eye is applied to patterns in which the surface of the cloth is covered wih distinct, small detached spots of colour. Examples are given at C to M in *Figure 9.6*. The simplest style of bird's-eye pattern is obtained by introducing the spotting yarn in the warp, and using the same shade for the weft as the ground shade of warp, as shown at A in *Figure 9.1*, and F in *Figure 9.2*.

Good spot patterns may be obtained in practically all the simple orders of warping and wefting, because where a warp colour is intersected by the same colour of weft, a spot formed of that colour appears on the surface of the cloth, whether the warp, or weft, or both are floated. Therefore, by suitably arranging the floats where different colours intersect, a required form of pattern may be produced. Thus, identical effects result from each of the arrangements given at J to M in *Figure 9.6*, a comparison of which will show that the weaves vary only where dark crosses dark, and light crosses light, but where one colour crosses the other the interlacing of the threads is the same.

Larger spot effects are shown at C to I in *Figure 9.6*. It will be noted that patterns G and I are symmetrical, which is due in each case to the centre of the weave having been arranged to coincide with the centre of either the solid dark or the solid light space.

In the effects represented at D, F, and H in *Figure 9.6* the weft is arranged in a different order from the warp, as indicated. A further series of patterns is illustrated at A to C in *Figure 9.7*, and at C the dark threads are grouped together in such a manner as to form enclosed spaces of the light colour. It will frequently be found that the grouping of the threads causes the woven effect to appear differently from the squared paper design, the small details in some cases being entirely concealed in the cloth, and in others brought out prominently.

Hairlines

These patterns consist of solid vertical or horizontal lines in 2, 3, 4, or more colours; the term hairline being specially used to distinguish effects in which each line of colour is equal to the width of one thread. By suitably arranging the weave and colouring, however, solid lines of colour may be produced which are equal in width to two or more threads. Examples of vertical hairlines are given at D to L in *Figure 9.7*, with the orders of colouring indicated by different marks alongside and at the bottom. D and E in *Figure 9.7* respectively show the single and double thread vertical hairline in two colours; the former being produced by colouring the plain weave 1 dark, 1 light in warp and weft, and the latter by colouring the 2-and-2 hopsack weave 2 dark, 2 light. Identical patterns can also be produced in the 4-thread warp satinette weave, as shown at F and G. This weave is preferred to the plain weave for the single-thread effect in some classes of fabrics, because the cloth is fuller and softer to handle and can be made heavier. Also when used for the double-thread effect, the 4-thread satinette yields a smoother and softer texture than the 2-and-2 hopsack weave, and in the latter there is, in addition, a tendency for the threads which work alike to twist round each other.

Patterns H and I in *Figure 9.7* show further examples produced in the 4-thread warp satinette weave, the effect at H being 3 dark, 1 light, and at I, 1 dark, 1 medium, 1 dark, 1 light.

The hairline effects obtainable in the satinette weave can also be produced in the 4-thread twill. Thus the patterns J to L in *Figure 9.7*, in which the 3-and-1 twill is employed, correspond respectively to F, G, and I. The satinette is usually preferable because a straight twill always results in a harsher texture than a weave of the satin type.

The plans M to Q in *Figure 9.7* are similar to D, E, F, G, J, and K except that in this case the weaves and colourings are arranged to produce horizontal hairlines. Thus, M and N respectively produce the single and double thread horizontal hairlines corresponding to D and E. Plans O and P show the 4-thread weft satinette, and plan Q the 1-and-3 twill arranged to produce horizontal effects which correspond to the vertical hairlines given at F, G, and J. On account of their barry appearance the horizontal hairlines are not much used, except in combination with the vertical hairlines and other effects in the construction of stripe, check, diagonal, and spotted patterns.

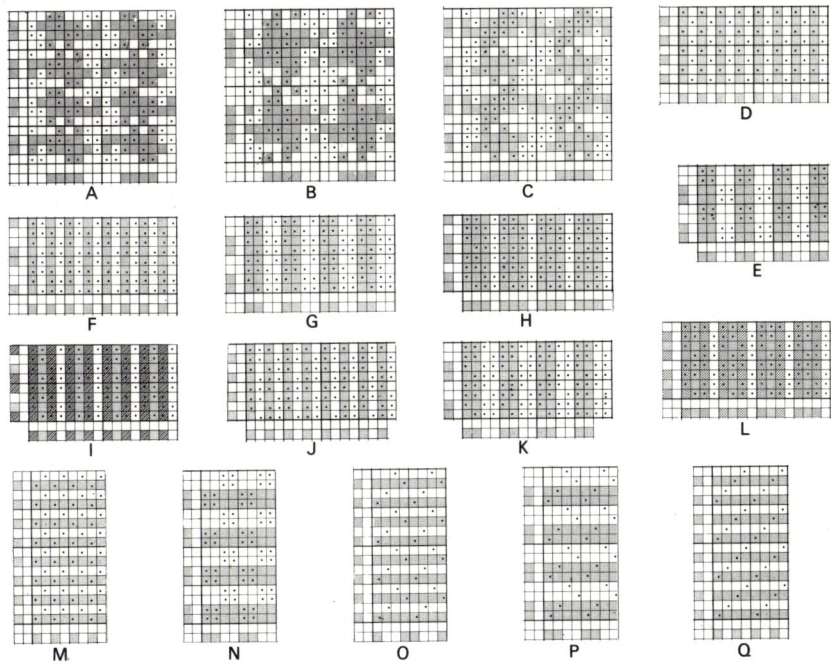

Figure 9.7

The construction of hairlines in the 3-thread twill weaves is illustrated at A to D in *Figure 9.8*, A producing a vertical effect in two colours, and B in three colours while C and D produce corresponding horizontal patterns. The plans given at E and F which are modifications of the 2-and-1 twill, will each produce a pattern in 2 dark, 2 medium, 2 light and as the modified weaves are looser in structure than the regular 3-thread twill, they permit denser settings in warp and weft and can, therefore, be used for heavier makes of cloth. The design G shows the 2-and-1 twill specially modified to produce a vertical hairline in which the colours are arranged 2 dark, 2 medium, 2 dark, 2 light. This pattern also results from the arrangement given at H which is a modification of the warp faced satinette. The plans E to H thus show how a regular weave may be modified to fit a required order of colouring when a special cloth structure is desired.

A comparison of the weaves with the orders of colouring in *Figures 9.7* and *9.8* will show that in constructing solid coloured hairline patterns the follow-ing rules are applicable: The same shades should be used for the weft as for the warp. For vertical hairlines each warp thread should pass under the corresponding colour of weft, and be raised over the other colours. For horizontal hairlines, each weft pick should pass under the corresponding colour of warp, and over the other colours. For example, assuming that a single thread vertical hairline in five colours is required, the weave must necessarily be so arranged that each end is down for one pick and up for four picks; hence the 5-thread warp twill, or, as shown at I in *Figure 9.8*, the 5-thread satin may be employed.

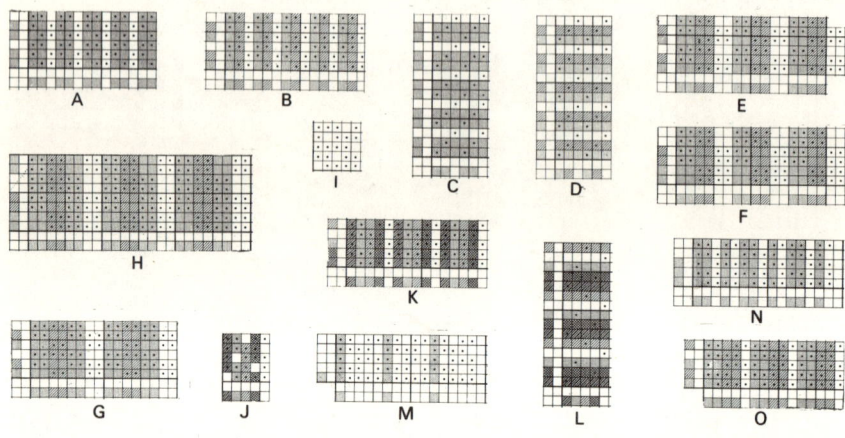

Figure 9.8

J shows the colour plan for the warp indicated along the bottom, the five shades being represented by different marks. The order of wefting, in the same five shades as the warp is obtained by noting, pick by pick, the colour of the warp thread which is depressed. Thus, as shown at K, the first pick is the same in colour as the first end, which is depressed on the first pick, the second pick is in the same colour as the fourth end; the third pick, as the second end; the fourth pick, as the fifth end; and the fifth pick, as the third end.

For the single-thread horizontal hairline in five colours, each pick must pass under one end and over four; the colour of each being determined by the colour of the end that it passes under, as shown at L in *Figure 9.8*. If the 1-and-4 twill weave is employed, however, the order of wefting is the same as the order of warping.

Other examples of vertical hairlines, obtainable in the 5-thread satin weave, are given at M to O in *Figure 9.8*, the effect at M being 1 dark, 4 light; at N, 2 dark, 1 light, 1 dark, 1 light; and at O, 2 dark, 2 medium, 1 light.

Step patterns

In these, vertical and horizontal lines unite and form zig-zag lines of colour which run in a diagonal direction, as shown in the examples given at A to F in *Figure 9.9*. They can be constructed with any ordinary twill weave in which there are two intersections, and the floats of warp and weft are equal, by arranging the colour plan on a number of threads, which is equal to half the number of threads in the repeat of the weave. Thus, at A the 2-and-2 twill is coloured 1 dark, 1 light; at B, the 3-and-3 twill is coloured 1 dark, 2 light; and at C, the 4-and-4 twill is coloured 2 dark, 2 light. A 3-shade step pattern can be produced in the 3-and-3 twill by colouring 1-and-1 in three shades, and a 4-shade in the 4-and-4 twill by colouring 1-and-1 in four shades. D shows a form of step pattern which is produced by colouring the Mayo weave 2 dark, 2 light, while the weave used in E produces exactly the same style of pattern in the 2-and-2 order of colouring as the 4-and-4 twill, and can be used in place of the latter when greater firmness of cloth is required. The 3-thread twill, when coloured 1-and-1, as shown at F, produces an interesting step

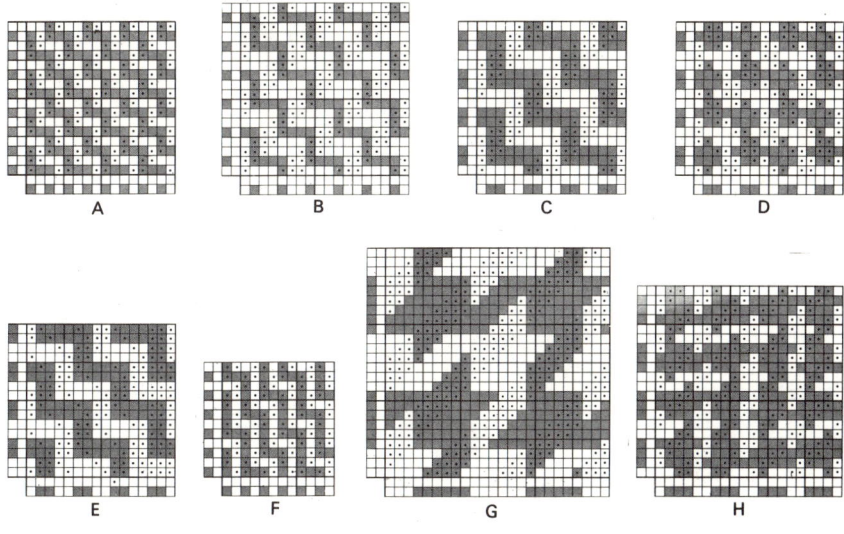

Figure 9.9

pattern, while a further variety of effects can be obtained in the 1-and-1 order of colouring by using twill weaves in which the floats are combined with the plain weave interlacing.

All-over effects

In all-over patterns the colour effect runs more or less connectedly over the surface of the cloth. They are best constructed by arranging the repeat of the colour plan and the repeat of the weave on such numbers that two or more repeats of each are required to produce one complete repeat of the pattern. For example: Assuming that the 2-and-2 twill is coloured 4 dark, 4 light, 4-dark, 3 light, fifteen repeats of the weave and four repeats of the colour plan are necessary, the complete effect being on 60 threads. Pattern G in *Figure 9.9* shows the effect produced by colouring the 4-and-4 twill 6 dark, 6 light; while pattern H shows the 2-and-2 twill coloured 3 dark, 2 light.

10

Compound Colour and Weave Effects

STRIPE COLOUR AND WEAVE EFFECTS

Changing the relative position of the weave and colouring

It has previously been shown that variety of pattern can be produced in the same weave and the same order of colouring by changing the position of one in relation to the other. The change of effect thus obtained may be made use of in the production of colour and weave stripe patterns, by modifying the warp arrangement, or the weave, in such a manner that their relative positions are different in succeeding sections of the design.

An example illustrating the method of modifying the warp colour order is given at A in *Figure 10.1*, and of modifying the weave at B. The object of preparing these and subsequent examples has been to show the different effects distinctly but in each case only a limited width of stripe is given. It

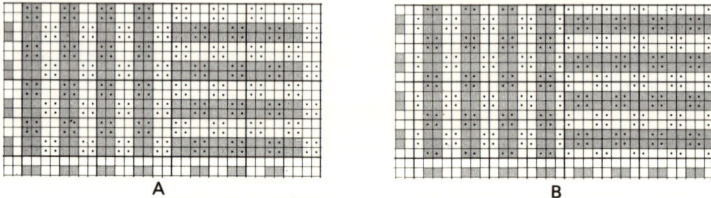

A   B

Figure 10.1

should be readily understood that a considerable diversity of form could be obtained by varying the width of each section.

It will be observed in A, *Figure 10.1* that the 2-and-2 hopsack weave is continued throughout the full width of the pattern and the change of effect is obtained by breaking the continuity of the warp colouring order. The warp, instead of being arranged continuously in the order of 2 dark, 2 light is modified by the introduction of 4 light threads at the end of each section this being sufficient to throw the colouring on to a different footing in relation to the weave. In B, on the other hand, the order of colouring is 2 dark, 2 light throughout, but while the weave is the 2-and-2 hopsack, a change of footing is made in it where the pattern changes. A comparison of A with B in *Figure 10.1* will show that the two methods produce similar styles. The first method, however, is usually the more convenient, as with a straight draft it is only necessary to modify the warp order of colouring according to the form of pattern required, whereas in the second method a special order of drafting is necessary.

In addition to the above two methods, colour and weave stripe patterns of more varied appearance can be produced in simple orders of wefting by employing: (1) simple weaves and compound orders of warping; (2) stripe weaves and simple orders of warping; (3) stripe weaves and compound orders of warping.

Simple weave and simple wefting with compound warping

Examples of this class are represented at A to H in *Figures 10.2* and *10.3*, and the three cloth samples C, D, E shown in *Figure 10.2* correspond with similarly lettered plans in *Figure 10.3*.

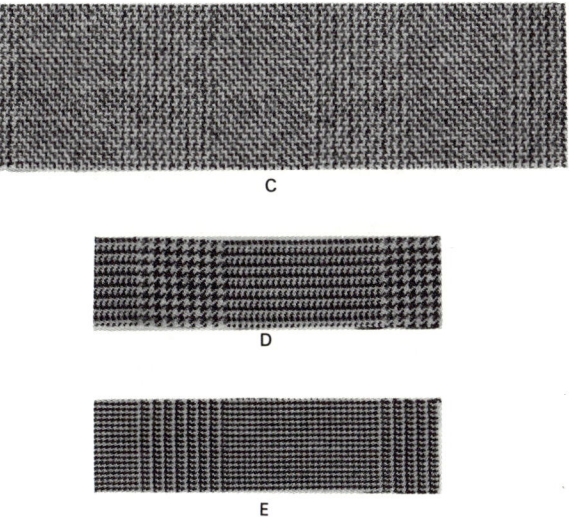

C

D

E

Figure 10.2

A and B in *Figure 10.3* show the 2-and-2 hopsack weave with identical compound warp arrangement of 2 dark, 2 light and 4 dark, 4 light orders of colouring but with different orders of wefting. At C an entirely different effect is produced in the same weave coloured 1 dark, 1 light, and 2 dark, 2 light in the warp with a simple 1 dark, 1 light arrangement in the weft (see also C in *Figure 10.2*).

The patterns given at D to H in *Figure 10.3* show the application of the 2-and-2 twill weave to a variety of compound warping plans in conjunction with several simple orders of wefting.

All the constructions given in *Figure 10.3* result from the application of only three different compound orders of warping and three simple orders of wefting to two common weaves. Very many different compound orders of warping can be, however, readily arranged, to which different weaves and orders of wefting can be applied and it will be evident that even within the limits of tappet shedding there is almost unlimited scope for the production of stripe colour and weave effects.

Stripe weave and simple wefting with simple warpings

Patterns constructed on the above basis are shown at A to F in *Figure 10.4*. In the plans A and B both the wefting and the warping consists of a simple 2 dark, 2 light colour order. The right hand sections in each of the above two patterns are also similar consisting of the 2-and-2 twill weave in which the

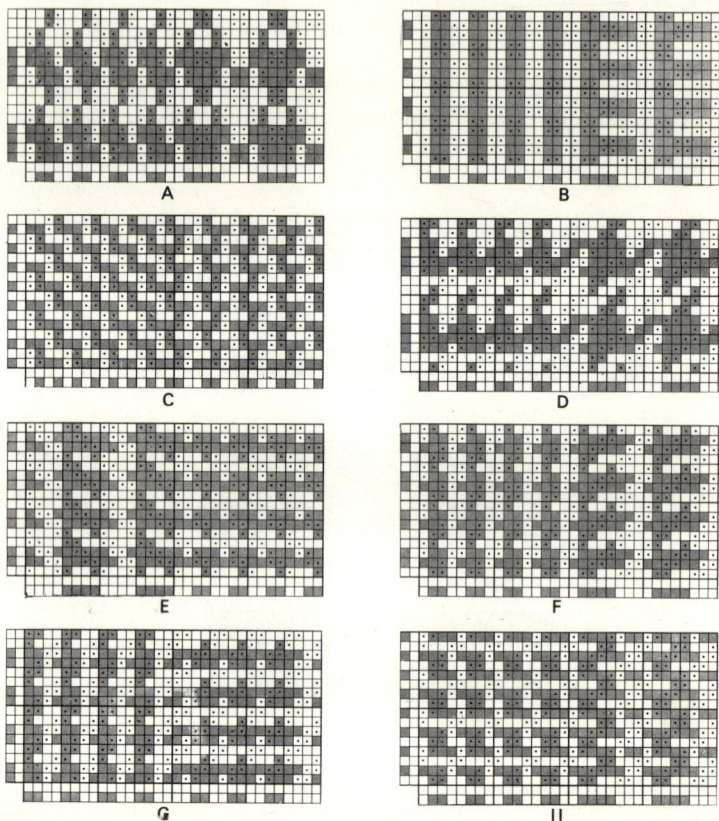

Figure 10.3

variety of effect was achieved by starting the twill on a different footing in each plan. The left hand side sections are quite varied in appearance as each has been produced in a different weave. A is constructed on a simple 2-and-2 twill diaper base, whilst B consists of a twilled hopsack.

C and D are both coloured 2 dark, 2 light in the weft and 4 dark, 4 light in the warp. In the pattern C the Mayo weave is combined with the 2-and-2 twill whilst in the pattern D a fancy 8-shaft weave is worked together with a 2-and-2 broken twill.

The bold effect achieved in the design E is due to the 4 dark, 4 light colouration in both the warp and the weft combined with the Mayo and the 2-and-2 hopsack weave arrangements.

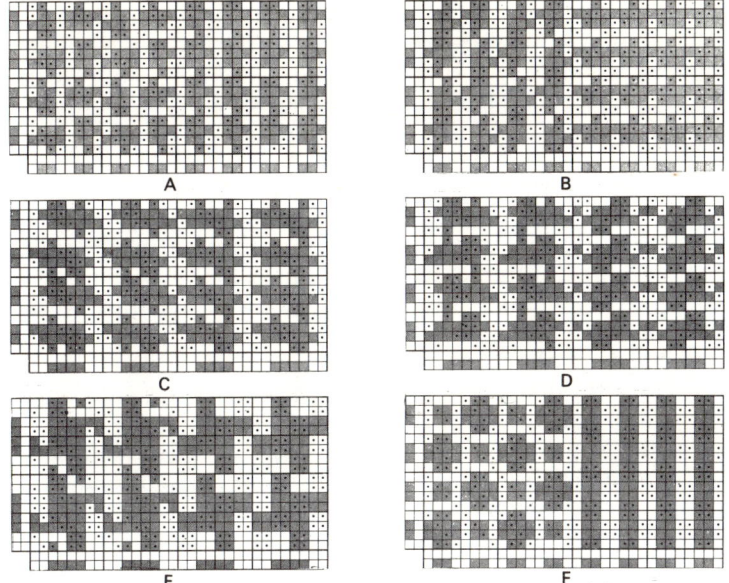

Figure 10.4

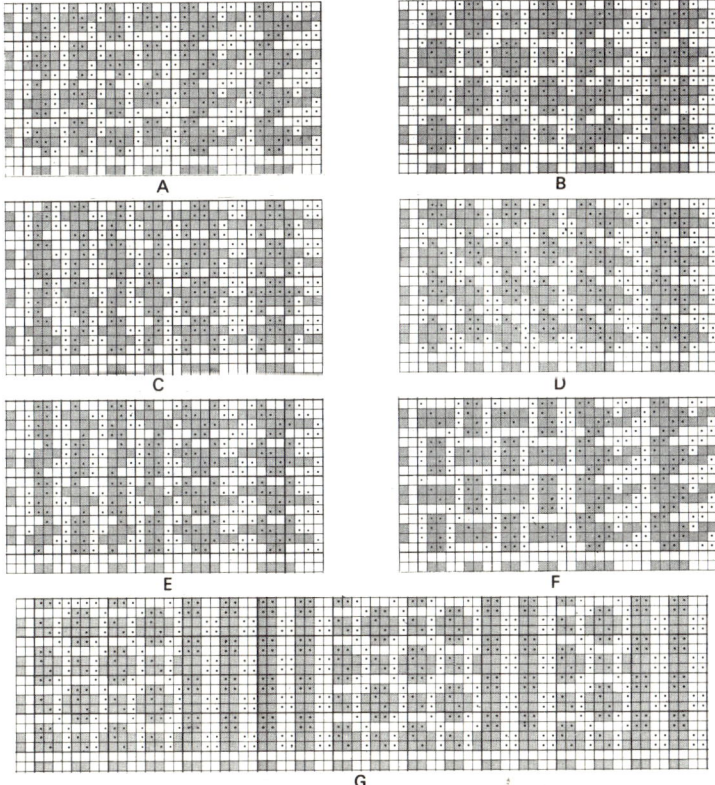

Figure 10.5

Pattern F is coloured 2 dark, 2 light in both the directions and shows a frequently employed combination of a bird's-eye effect with a double hair-line, the latter being developed in the 2-and-2 hopsack weave, whilst in the former use is made of a simple Grecian structure.

Stripe weave and simple wefting with compound warping

This type of construction is shown at A to F in *Figure 10.5*. All the examples have been produced with the same compound order of warping of 2 dark, 2 light followed by 4 dark, 4 light, and with an identical order of wefting of 2 dark, 2 light.

In A a 2-and-2 twill diaper in one section is combined with an ordinary 2-and-2 twill in the other, whilst B shows the effect of the combination of a Grecian weave with the 2-and-2 twill. In C and D the left hand section consists of the Mayo weave and the right hand sections are made with the 2-and-2 hopsack and 2-and-2 twill weaves respectively. The unusual effect at E results from the combination of a fancy 8-shaft weave and with a 2-and-2 broken twill whilst the design F is obtained with the 8-shaft diaper in one section and the 2-and-2 twill in the other.

For the sake of simplicity of presentation all the examples illustrated in *Figures 10.3* to *10.5* are shown with an equal width of stripe. However, considerable diversity of pattern could be obtained by varying the space which each stripe occupied. This is shown at G in *Figure 10.5* where the Grecian and the 2-and-2 hopsack weaves used in combination are arranged in stripes of different size, the former alternating with the latter in the order of 16, 16, 16, 8, 8, and 8 ends. This arrangement is only one of many and if further variety of effect was required more than two weaves, or more than two different orders of warping could be readily combined together.

CHECK COLOUR AND WEAVE EFFECTS

Changing the relative position of the weave and colouring

The designs given at A and B in *Figure 10.6* illustrate the method of producing check effects in one weave and one order of colouring by varying the position of one in relation to the other. In both designs each quarter consists of 2-and-2 hopsack weave and 2-and-2 warping and wefting, but it will be noted that in A while the weave is continuous, the 2-and-2 order of colouring is broken, a 4 of white occurring at each change of the effect. Thus, the change of footing in the colouring causes the relative positions of it in respect of the weave to be changed, and alternate sections of vertical and horizontal lines result. Design B produces similar style but in this case the order of colouring is continuous, the change of footing being obtained by making a break in the weave at each change of effect. An analysis of the two designs will show that each requires four healds, but the first method, illustrated by A, is more convenient and more economical than the second. Thus, while A can be produced in a regular draft by means of tappets, B requires a special draft and, on account of the large number of picks in the repeat, a dobby shedding mechanism. The boxing plan in the first method is more complex, but this

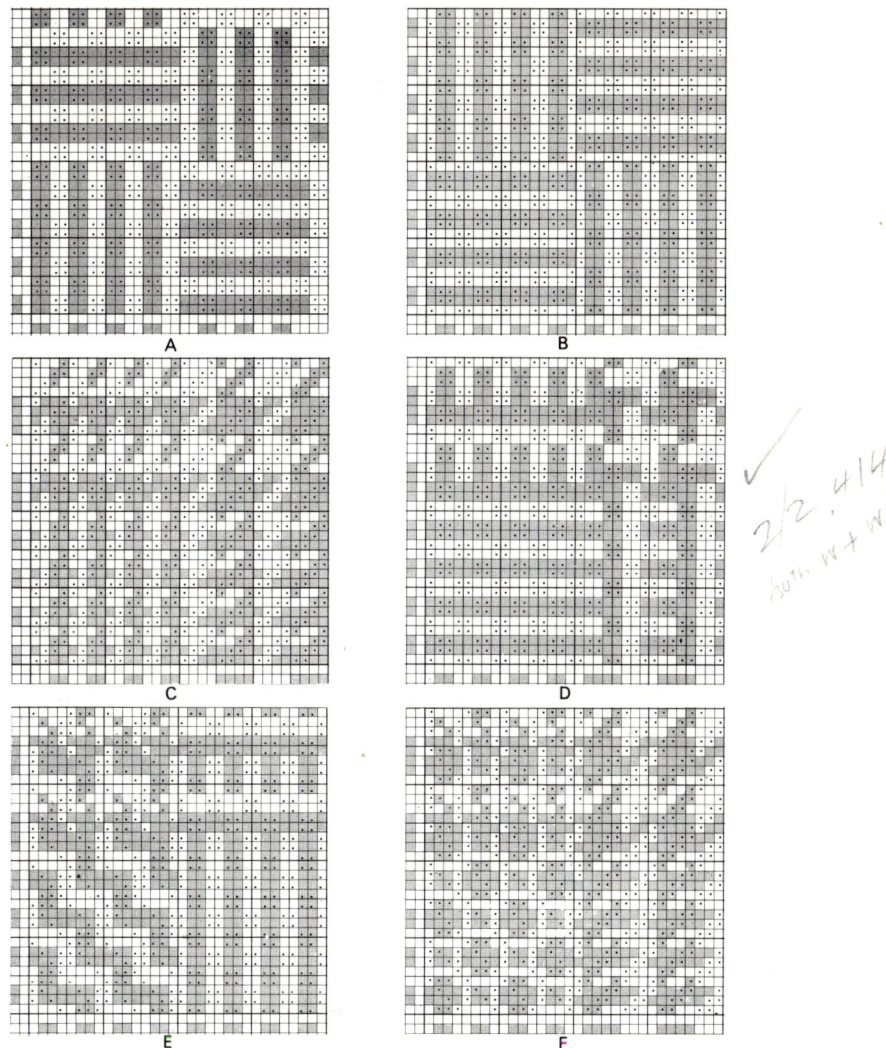

Figure 10.6

does not materially affect the question, since a check motion is required in either case. A design similar to A is represented by the fabric A in *Figure 10.7*.

In addition to the foregoing styles where checks are obtained due to changes in either weave or colour relationship, check designs are also produced in each of the combinations in Table 10.

Simple weave, compound warping and compound wefting

This combination is illustrated by the designs C and D in *Figure 10.6*, and by similarly lettered patterns in *Figure 10.7*. The order of warping and weft-ing for the two examples is the same—i.e. a compound of 2 dark, 2 white, and 4 dark, 4 white colourings as shown along the bottom and up the side of both designs. In C, the weave is 2-and-2 twill, and D, 2-and-2 hopsack.

It will be noted that both designs consist of four different effects, the reason for which will be evident if the order of colouring be compared with the weaves. Thus, in the first quarter of each design the effect is due to the 2-and-2

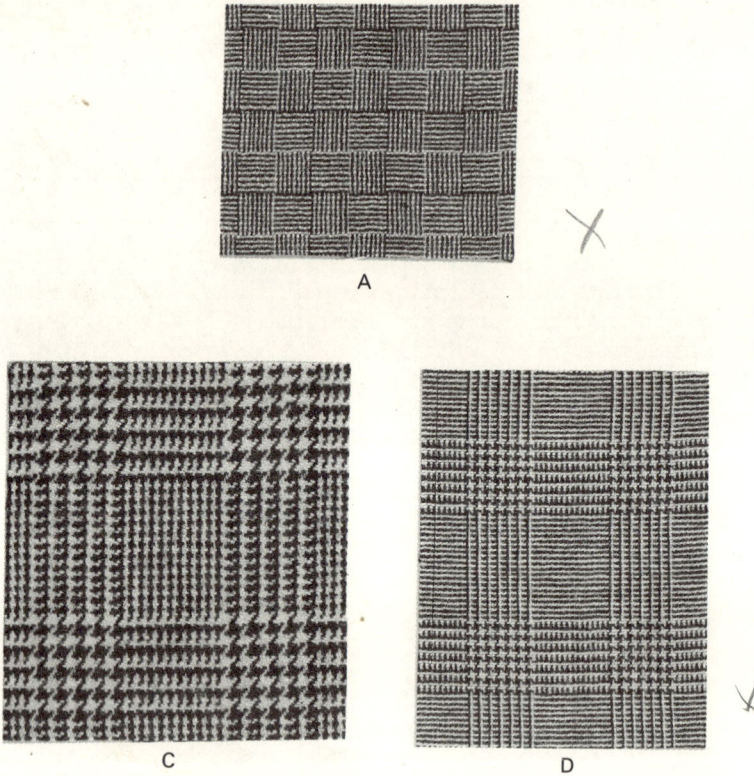

A

C

D

Figure 10.7

order of warping being crossed with 2-and-2 wefting, in the second quarter (moving clockwise) to the 2-and-2 warping with 4-and-4 wefting, in the third quarter to 4-and-4 warping with 4-and-4 wefting, and in the fourth quarter to 4-and-4 warping with 2-and-2 wefting. The best effects usually result in the quarters where the warping and wefting orders are the same. The cross effects produced where one order of colouring is crossed with another, while

Table 10

1. Simple	weave,	compound warping,		compound wefting		
2. Stripe	,,	simple	,,	,,		,,
3. ,,	,,	compound	,,	,,		,,
4. Cross-over	,,	,,	,,	simple		,,
5. ,,	,,	,,	,,	compound		,,
6. Check	,,	simple	,,	simple		,,
7. ,,	,,	compound	,,	,,		,,
8. ,,	,,	simple	,,	compound		,,
9. ,,	,,	compound	,,	,,		,,

not so good, usually give sufficient variety to make the patterns interesting. In the same manner that the pattern consists of four effects when the warping and wefting plans are compounds of two simple orders, nine effects result from compounds of three-colour schemes, and sixteen effects when the arrangement is a compound of four-colour schemes, because each warping order is crossed with all the wefting orders.

Stripe weave and compound wefting with simple and compound warping

The design marked E in *Figure 10.6* illustrates a combination in which a stripe weave is used in conjunction with a simple 2 dark, 2 light, order of warping, and a compound order of wefting in which sections of 2 dark, 2 light alternate with 4 dark, 4 light. Pattern F is also obtained in a stripe weave but in this case a compound order of colouring is employed in both, the weft and the warp. An examination of the above two designs will show that each quarter results in a different effect due to either the coincidence of varying colourings with identical weave stripes or same colourings with different weave stripes.

Cross-over weave and compound warping with simple and compound weftings

These combinations produce similar effects to those resulting from the preceding ones as shown in designs A and B in *Figure 10.8*. In both examples two simple weaves are arranged in cross-over, or horizontal stripe formation, each with the same compound order of warping of 2 dark, 2 light, followed by 4 dark, 4 light. In A the effect is achieved with the aid of a simple order of wefting while in B a compound order of wefting, identical with the warp colouring, is employed.

The chief point of difference between this method and the previous one is that with a cross-over arrangement of weaves a simple draft is required but a vertical stripe necessitates a more complex order of drafting with an advantage, however, of a much shorter lifting plan.

Check weave, simple and compound wefting with simple and compound warping

The construction of check colour and weave effects by combining a check weave with a variety of warping and wefting orders is illustrated at C to F in *Figure 10.8*. Design C results from a simple, 2 dark, 2 light, colouring in both directions.

In pattern D an identical order of wefting is retained but with a compound order of warping in which sections of 2 dark, 2 light alternate with 4 dark, 4 light. At E and F identical compound orders of wefting are employed but the order of warping is simple in the former and compound in the latter.

As previously stated, in arranging weaves in check form, the most important factor to note is that on the surface no long warp floats occur at the horizontal junctions, and no long weft floats at the vertical junctions. Considerable care is frequently necessary in getting the weaves in satisfactory relation to each other, at the same time that the desired colour-and-weave pattern is secured. Furthermore, the different portions of a check design do not have to be of the same size and a careful combination of sections of different dimensions introduces a further element of variety as illustrated by the examples C and D in *Figure 10.7*.

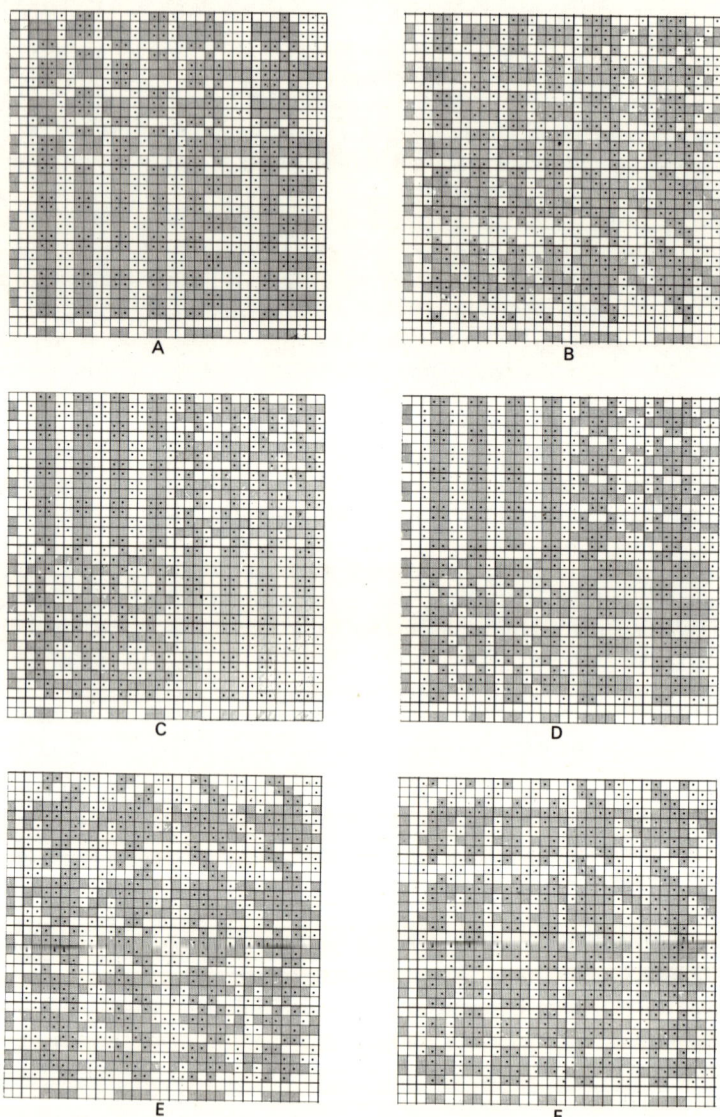

Figure 10.8

The foregoing colour-and-weave patterns illustrate standard styles, and the numerous examples that are given will, by examination and comparison, make clear how a very large variety of effects can be produced by the combination in different ways of a comparatively few units.

SPECIAL COLOUR AND WEAVE EFFECTS

Colouring of rib and corkscrew weaves

Ordinary warp rib weaves, such as are illustrated at A to F in *Figure 3.1*, and such special rib weaves as those shown at A, B, and C in *Figure 6.3*, naturally lend themselves to a 1-and-1 order of colouring in the warp. Straight and waved horizontal lines in alternate colours are respectively produced by the two classes of weaves. In the same manner, a 1-and-1 order of colouring in the weft is suitable for similar weft rib weaves, by which vertical lines in alternate colours are formed. A regular rib weave may also be coloured in sections in the manner illustrated by the design M in *Figure 6.4*, in which the order in the warp is 1 dark, 1 light for 16 threads, and 1 light, 1 dark for 16 threads; the arrangement producing a small check effect in different colours, as previously described.

The warp cord designs, shown at F and G in *Figure 6.3*, will produce solid vertical lines in alternate colours by arranging the ends—6 dark, 6 light, and the picks 1 dark, 1 light; while the Bedford cord designs, given in *Figure 6.6* will yield similar effects if the ends are arranged in sections in different colours, and a 2-and-2 order of wefting is employed. A special arrangement of coloured threads may be applied to such designs as that shown at H in *Figure 6.3*, which, for instance, may be coloured in the warp in the order of 6 dark; 3 light; 1 dark, 1 light for 6 threads; 3 dark; 6 light; and in the weft in the order of 1 dark, 1 light. The effect will be a stripe of 6 ends warp cord—solid dark; 3 ends weft rib—solid light; 6 ends warp rib—dark and light lines alternately; 3 ends weft rib—solid dark; and 6 ends warp cord—solid light. Check combinations of warp and weft rib weaves, an example of which is given at K in *Figure 7.8*, may be coloured 1-and-1 in both warp and weft, and an effect in four colours is produced by employing colours in the weft that are different from the warp colours.

Figure 10.9

Ordinary warp and weft corkscrews, which are illustrated in *Figure 6.4*, are appropriately coloured in 1-and-1 order in warp and weft respectively; twill lines being produced alternately in two colours in this case. Further, such designs as L and P in *Figure 6.3* are particularly suitable for 1-and-1 warp colouring, in the same manner that the design N in *Figure 6.3* may be very aptly coloured 1-and-1 in the weft. In most cases, particularly in warp effects—a special order of colouring can be used in conjunction with solid colouring. Thus, a warp corkscrew weave may be coloured 1-and-1 and solid alternately, so as to produce a stripe design.

Figure 10.9 represents a corkscrew fabric, in which twill lines are produced alternately in two colours, and the example also illustrates the combination of an ordinary with a special corkscrew effect. In the cloth the ordinary corkscrew weave appears like an ordinary twill, and the special effect like a broken twill.

A broken twill appearance can be produced in the corkscrew structure in two ways: (1) By modifying the corkscrew weave and using a 1-and-1 order of colouring throughout. (2) By modifying the 1-and-1 order of colouring and using an ordinary corkscrew weave throughout. For example, at A in *Figure 10.10* a 9-thread broken twill weave is indicated, while B shows the weave modified on the warp corkscrew principle to fit a 1-and-1 order of colouring, the different marks representing different colours, C on the other hand, shows a continuous 9-thread corkscrew weave in which a similar broken effect is produced by colouring the warp in the order of 1 dark, 1 light for six threads, and 1 light, 1 dark for six threads, as indicated along the bottom of the design. The usual close setting of the ends in the corkscrew weave will cause both B and C to appear similar to the basic weave A—assuming that the latter is woven in—say, dark warp and light weft.

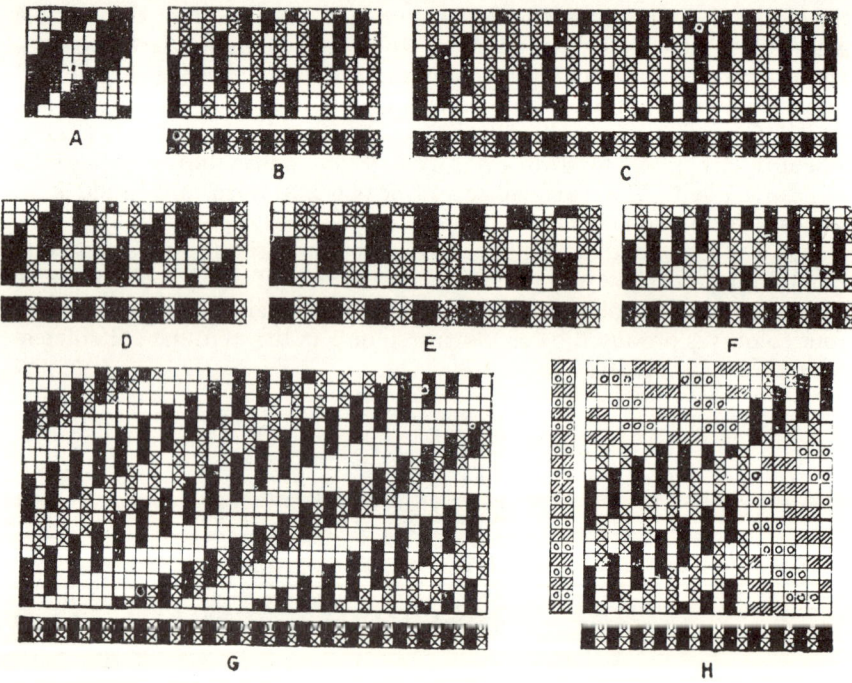

Figure 10.10

Three modifications of a warp corkscrew, which may be specially coloured and used in combination with an ordinary weave of the same class, are given at D, E, and F in *Figure 10.10*. At D the weave is arranged to coincide with a 2-and-1 order of colouring, and at E with a 2-and-2 order, while F produces a waved effect in 1-and-1 colouring.

G in *Figure 10.10* shows a form of corkscrew weave which, in 1-and-1 colouring in the warp and solid colouring in the weft, produces differently coloured twill lines of warp, brings up the weft as a third effect, and also produces a twill line in which the warp colours are intermingled.

The design H in *Figure 10.10* is a check combination of warp and weft corkscrew weaves, which if woven in two colours of warp and two different colours of weft, as indicated along the bottom and at the side respectively, will produce an effect in four colours. The example repeats upon an odd number of threads, therefore, if the order of colouring is arranged 1-and-1 throughout, the colours in certain sections will change positions in succeeding repeats. As a rule, in a combination of warp and weft corkscrew weaves, the warp-face weave forms the bulk of the design. The sections of the design H may be repeated any required number of times.

FIGURED COLOUR AND WEAVE EFFECTS

Figured weave arrangements with simple and compound orders of colouring

The check designs discussed in the preceding section of this chapter were all arranged on a rectangular base. Such arrangements, although most common, are not the only ones possible and many good colour and weave effects can be produced on a diamond base, or on a non-geometrical base, and are particularly suitable for ladies suitings and overcoatings.

Figure 10.11

Figure 10.11 illustrates one such design which is constructed upon diamond base. The diamond spaces, which in an actual cloth should occupy larger areas to show the effect to full advantage, are constructed in 2-and-2 hop-sack, 3-and-1 twill, and 1-and-3 twill with a simple 4 dark, 4 light order of warping and wefting. The design illustrates one method of arranging weaves in diamond form, their relationship to one another, and to the colouring so as to obtain a well balanced effect. Thus it will be noted that (1) the centre of each diamond space coincides with a central position of the colouring; (2) no long floats occur at the junctions of the weaves; (3) each weave is so combined with the colouring as to produce the required effect.

The design represented in *Figure 10.12* illustrates a method of producing non-geometrical figured styles in one weave and one order of colouring, by varying the position of the former in relation to the latter. The 1-and-1 order of colouring is continuous, but the plain weave which is used for the figure areas weaves on the opposite footing to the plain weave in the ground areas. As a result the figure is produced in the form of a horizontal hairline effect in clear contrast to the vertical hairline effect of the ground. Designs of this type repeat necessarily over a very large number of ends and picks and in *Figure 10.12* only a small portion of the repeat is illustrated. It is

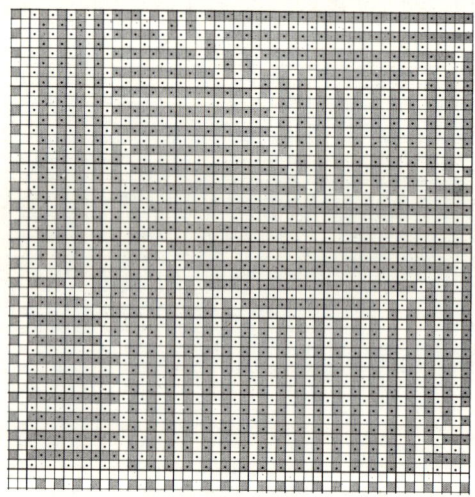

Figure 10.12

sufficient, however, to show the main constructional feature of these designs, namely a typical float of two, either of warp or weft at the points at which the figure and ground join together. It is upon the proper arrangement of these floats that the clarity of the outline of the figure depends. One of the colours—and usually, the lighter of the two is the more suitable—should form a fine line separating the figure from the ground, otherwise the form will be indefinite. Assuming that the figure is required to be outlined in the lighter shade, as in the example, the following should be observed in marking the edge of the figure: Where the floats of two are alongside each other they should be in weft float on the light picks, and in warp float on the dark picks; while, where the floats of two are one above the other, they should be in warp float on the light ends, and in weft float on the dark ends. In the case of outlining the figure in the darker shade, the conditions will be exactly the opposite.

The fabric represented in *Figure 10.13* illustrates another construction based on a simple diamond form combined with a compound order of colouring. A portion of the corresponding design given in *Figure 10.14*

Figure 10.13

Figure 10.14

shows that the weave consists of simple 2-and-2 twill diamonds and the elaborate effect is due mainly to the colouring in which sections of 2 dark, 2 light alternate with sections coloured 1 dark, 1 light in both the warp and weft directions. The use of compound orders of colouring permits the construction of intricate and varied effects on a comparatively simple weave base.

Construction of special weaves to produce distinct figured effects

The designs represented at A and B in *Figure 10.15* illustrate a special class of small figured effects produced in simple orders of colouring. Both show an identical star like form and although the colour order in each is the same (6 dark, 6 light) the weaves are different. Design A is constructed on the basis of a 3-and-3 herringbone twill, but it is only to a limited extent that modified simple weaves can be used in producing a special style of pattern. Construction of special weaves, however, allows almost unlimited scope for the production of figured effects. Example B in *Figure 10.15* illustrates the principle involved in the creation of special weaves. In this system advantage is taken of the fact that where a colour of warp is intersected by the same colour

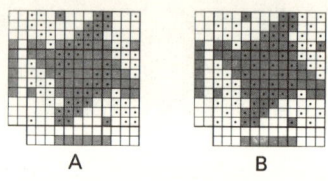

A   B

Figure 10.15

of weft, that colour will appear on the surface whatever the weave is, which enables plain or other firm weave to be employed at these places in order to give the cloth the necessary strength. Where one colour intersects another colour, either may be made to appear on the surface, in forming the required pattern, by arranging the warp and weft floats to correspond. Thus in design B, where dark ends interweave with dark picks, and light ends with light picks, plain weave is employed. Where the design is required to show dark on light picks the dark ends are raised, and where light on dark picks the light ends are raised. Where the design is required to show dark on light ends the dark weft is floated, and where light on dark ends the light weft is floated. Design B thus contains more intersections than A and may be used to produce the same effect in a cloth in which greater firmness is required.

A convenient method which may be employed to construct this type of effect is to develop the design in several stages. Assuming that a dark figure on light ground is required the first stage consists of marking the required shape lightly within the confines of the repeat. A suitable colour scheme is then indicated along the bottom and up the side of the design, the crossing points of the dark threads in the warp and in the weft coinciding with the centre of the figure. In the third stage the required weave is obtained as follows: (a) plain (or other simple weave) is inserted where each colour intersects its own colour; (b) dark ends are then followed vertically and where these cross the light picks in figure area, weave marks are inserted, but where these cross the light picks outside the marked figure area the squares are left blank; (c) dark picks are then followed horizontally and where these cross the light ends in figure areas the squares are left blank but where they cross the light ends outside the figure area weave marks are inserted. This procedure can be followed by reference to *Figure 10.17* which shows a larger design repeating upon 24 ends and picks with a 12 dark, 12 light colour pattern in both directions. *Figure 10.16* illustrates the appearance of this effect in cloth.

Figure 10.16

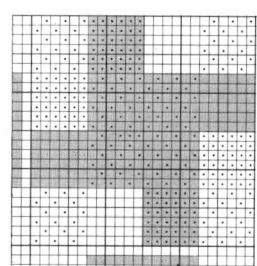

Figure 10.17

The system is not limited to the production of detached figures, as by suitably floating the threads of one colour over those of another colour, many interesting effects, consisting of interlacing lines, can be obtained. One such

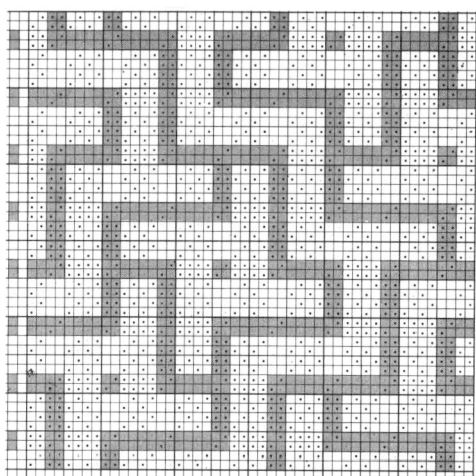

Figure 10.18

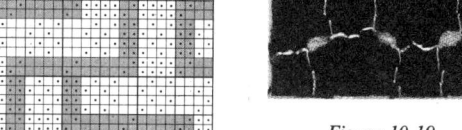

Figure 10.19

design is illustrated in *Figure 10.18* based on a simple order of colouring of 2 dark, 4 light in both directions. It has been constructed exactly according to the method outlined above and although it repeats over 48 ends and picks it can be readily produced by healds, as with careful drafting it requires the use of only 20 shafts.

Combinations of special weaves and special yarns

A special colour and weave style is represented in *Figure 10.19*, in which yarns of different materials and different thicknesses are combined, a pattern in white filament rayon and thick dark worsted being formed on a ground composed of fine light cotton threads. The arrangement in warp and weft is indicated along the bottom and at the side of the corresponding plans in *Figure 10.20*; the solid marks representing the white rayon, the shaded squares the dark worsted, and the blanks the light cotton threads. The design paper sketch in the upper portion of *Figure 10.20* represents the appearance of the effect, but it does not give a correct idea of how it will be necessary for the threads to interweave, because the structure causes considerable distortion of the thick dark threads to take place. An examination of the actual

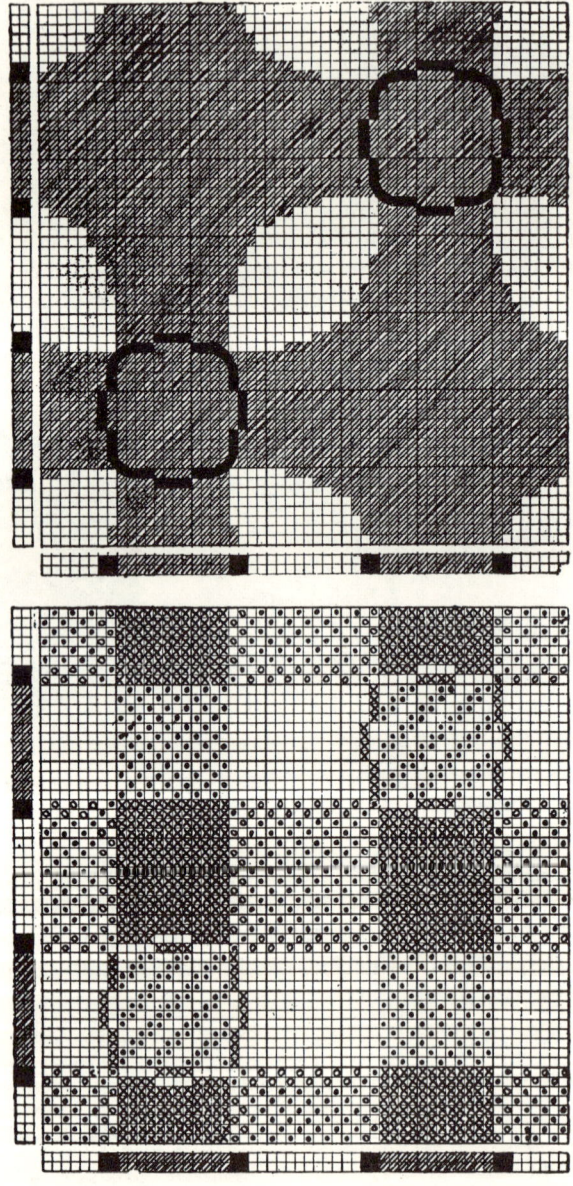

Figure 10.20

weave given in the lower portion of *Figure 10.20* will show that where the worsted ends intersect with the worsted picks, in alternate sections the weave is 2-and-2 twill surrounded by a 4-and-4 order of interweaving with the rayon threads, while in the other sections the weave is plain with the rayon threads floating on the back. The 2-and-2 twill weave is sufficiently loose to enable the thick threads to approach each other readily, and they therefore group together at these places, and are retained firmly in position by the 4-and-4 stitching of the rayon threads. Where the weave is plain, however, the intersections are too frequent for the thick threads, which therefore spread out,

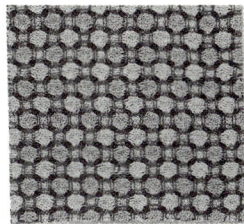

Figure 10.21

there being no obstacle to their distortion, since on every side of the plain interweaving the float is absolutely loose. The fine cotton ends and picks interweave with each other, and with the rayon threads in plain order, but the spreading out of the thick threads partly conceals them, and gives an oval shape to the rectangular space occupied by the fine threads.

The pattern shown in *Figure 10.21* illustrates another method of giving interest to a special style, as in this case not only are yarns of different materials and different counts combined, but alternate sections of the fabric are crammed. The fabric is an all rayon construction, arranged 4 dark,

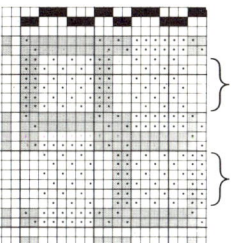

Figure 10.22

6 light in both directions, in which the dark ends and picks are considerably finer than the light ones and being crêpe twisted possess a high degree of liveliness. Where the fine, dark ends and picks interlace together a very open fabric results but the heavy, light ends and picks which are crammed produce dense solid spots in the cloth. Also the floats of the dark ends and picks are so arranged that they lift or depress alternate crammed areas inducing a degree of cloth distortion which is responsible for the attractive, 'pebbly' appearance of the texture. The complete design is represented in *Figure 10.22*, with the order of denting shown above the design and the crammed weft areas indicated by the brackets on the right.

11

Elements of Jacquard Shedding

A jacquard shedding motion is used in weaving designs that are beyond the scope of dobby shedding, i.e. designs which consist of more than about 24 different orders of interlacing. In practice, jacquards are mainly used for large and intricate figured designs with several hundreds, or even several thousands, of ends working in different fashion and repeating upon a similar number of picks. The facility with which the jacquard machine is able to cope with such large arrangements, and the comparatively small size of the machine itself, are the principal features of the system. An additional advantage is the simplicity of the draft of the warp threads and the fact that the draft does not, as a rule, require altering when the design is changed.

Although the principle of jacquard selection remains unchanged many different types can be distinguished and a preliminary division into ordinary and special jacquards is frequently made. Ordinary machines are extremely versatile and can be used to produce figured designs in almost any construction. Special jacquards are built, each, for a specific construction which limits their applicability but which may result in certain advantages within their own field of operation. These special machines include leno brocade, inverted hook, sectional harness, and self-twilling jacquards (among many others), and are described along with the structures of cloths for which they are used in *Watson's Advanced Textile Design*. In addition to this broad division the jacquards may be further classified under the following headings: (1) type of shed formed; (2) pitch; and (3) figuring capacity.

(1) Type of shed formed: (a) single lift—bottom closed shed; (b) centre shed jacquard—centre closed shed; (c) double lift single cylinder and double lift double cylinder—modified open shed; (d) double lift—open shed machine. Shed formation is dependent upon the mechanical action of the jacquard and determines largely the speed at which the machine can be operated. On occasion the shedding system may have a bearing upon the construction and for some structures one particular system may be preferable to others.

(2) Pitch: this refers to the density of setting of the selection elements in the machine which may be set in a variety of pitches broadly distinguished as the 'coarse', and the 'fine' pitch. The pitch determines the actual dimensions of the machine. Any of the jacquards classified

above under 'shed formation' could be set in any pitch, but traditionally certain types are more commonly associated with certain pitch settings than others.

(3) Figuring capacity: or the 'size' of the jacquard refers to the number of different orders of interlacing of which the machine is capable. This is normally given as a number and it may range from 100 (normally only employed in the weaving of trade names in the selvedges) to 1792.

With the exception of the figuring capacity, the variations in the ordinary jacquards do not affect the designer to any extent, but the principle of operation of the various jacquard systems should be understood thoroughly in order to exploit fully their capabilities and to comprehend exactly the meaning of such terms as 'harness ties', 'repeats', 'setts', etc.

ORDINARY JACQUARD MACHINES

Principle of operation

The design is transferred from squared paper to pattern cards in the form of holes and blanks. In ordinary jacquards a hole indicates a lift of an end and is, therefore, analogous with a mark on design paper (using the normal convention); and, by converse, a blank indicates a fall of an end into the bottom shed line and is equivalent to a blank in design paper: One card controls the selection of all the ends in the cloth for one pick. *Figure 11.1* shows the principle of operation involved. At (a) needle A is shown opposed by a hole in the card D. As the cylinder C moves in, presenting the card to the needle, the needle encountering the perforation in the card enters the

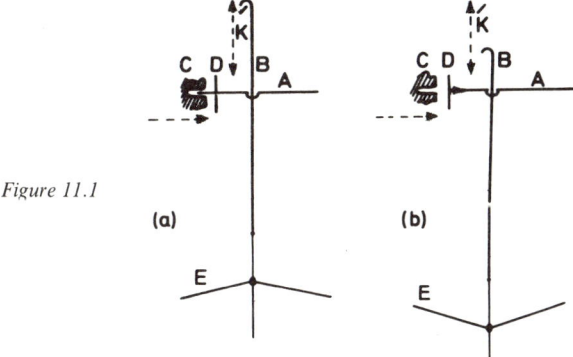

Figure 11.1

(a)   (b)

corresponding hole in the cylinder and no action takes place. This allows hook B, connected to the needle, to remain over knife K which in its upward movement takes the hook with it, thus lifting end E into the top shed line. At (b) the needle is opposed by a blank in the pattern card. As the cylinder C moves in again the blank forces the needle back and this in turn presses the hook clear of the knife just prior to the commencement of its upward movement. The knife moves up but the hook which has been pressed clear remains down and, therefore, the end controlled by this hook also stays down in the bottom shed line.

The single lift jacquard

This is the simplest type of jacquard which serves admirably to show the general arrangement of parts and to indicate the role of the selection device in achieving the control over the operation of the warp threads. The principle of selection is the same as described above and, therefore, is not repeated. The diagram in *Figure 11.2* shows the layout and the connections between the machine and the harness in a simplified, schematic manner. The horizontal needles A are each connected to a vertical hook B by forming a loop or a half-bend round the latter, and are supported by a needle-board I, through

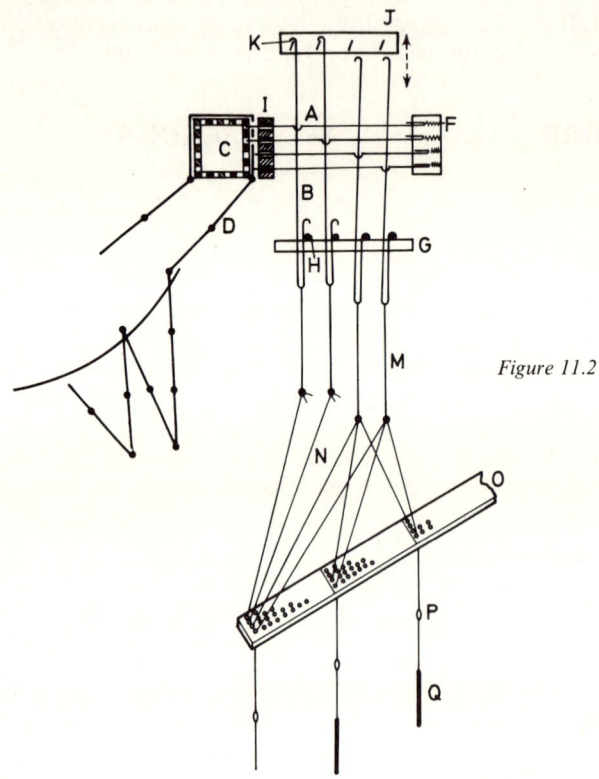

Figure 11.2

which they project slightly. The rear end of each needle, which is formed into a narrow loop is pressed by a spiral spring F to ensure the return of the needle to the original position after each selection. The hooks are prevented from turning sideways by doubling-up their lower ends and passing them through narrow slits in grate G with the bent ends resting on spindles H when the hooks are in the low position. The number of needles in each short row varies from 4 (as shown in *Figure 11.2*) to 16 and the number of short rows is multiplied to give the required size of machine. It is a general rule to connect the needles and hooks in the order shown in *Figure 11.2*, the top needle being connected to the hook nearest to, and the bottom needle to the hook farthest from the cylinder C. The same number of inclined lifting knives K are carried in an iron frame or griffe J as there are hooks B in a short row. A card-cylinder C, over which the pattern cards D pass, contains on each surface a hole opposite the end of each needle. Each face of the cylinder is provided with two pegs which act as the locating points to ensure proper registration of the card against the cylinder perforations. The cards D, the number of which is equal to the number of picks in the complete repeat of a design, are laced together at the sides and in the middle; then the last card is joined to the first so that an endless chain is formed. The pitch of the needles, and the holes in the card-cylinder, and cards is exactly the same. Long 'sets' or 'packs' of cards have to be suspended in proper position in relation to the cylinder, and in one method a wire, which is about $1\frac{1}{2}$ inches longer than a card, is tied at intervals of twelve or more cards to the twine with which the cards are laced together. By means of the wires the cards hang from a frame or 'cradle' which consists of two parallel iron bars that are rather further apart than the width of the cards, and the latter pass over supporting rollers. When long sets of cards are not used—say below 200 in a set—the cradle may consist of a curved tin channel in which the cards rest, the wires then being dispensed with.

The harness consists of neck cords M that are suspended from the hooks B; harness cords N, which are connected to the neck cords and passed separately through holes in a comber-board O; mails P; and lingoes or weights Q. The number of harness cords, mails, and lingoes, connected to each neck-cord M, varies according to the 'tie' and 'sett' of the harness. By means of the lingoes Q, the warp threads, cords, and hooks are returned to their original position after they have been raised.

The purpose of the comber-board O is to keep the harness cords in position to determine the number of cords per unit space.

Suitable connections from the loom provide the rising and falling movement to the knives, and the in-and-out movement to the cards cylinder ensuring correct synchronisation of the jacquard action with the loom cycle. The cylinder is turned one quarter of a revolution as it moves back thus presenting a new card for selection each time it moves in to press against the needles. It will be noted from *Figure 11.2* that each hook controls as many warp threads as there are harness cords connected to the corresponding neck-cord. Warp threads are moved from the bottom of the shed to the top and back again, or twice the depth of the shed at every pick; and on account of the great distance traversed by the threads and the consequent strain put upon them, and the absence of counterpoise in the machine, the single-lift jacquard is not suitable for high speeds. As a result, this system has been largely discarded being retained only in certain highly specialised fields.

The centre shed jacquard

The main difference between this and the previous type of jacquard lies in the manner of shed formation. The warp threads, when at rest, are in the centre of the shed; where there are holes in the cards the corresponding hooks are raised to the top through the action of the rising griffe, while the remaining hooks are lowered to the bottom by means of the descending griffe. The threads move only half the distance that they move in bottom closed shedding, and the rising shed is balanced by the falling shed, but as every thread is in motion a detrimental swinging movement may be set up in the harness at high speeds. Despite the above disadvantage this method of shedding is recommended for the delicate types of yarns and has been adopted as standard in the Verdol fine pitch machines which were originally developed for the silk brocade weaving, but owing mainly to their large figuring capacity they are now widely used for all types of materials, both natural and man-made.

As the Verdol system uses continuous paper roll instead of paste-board cards to operate the selection mechanism, the pressure of the pattern roll cannot be applied directly against the needles, but requires an intermediate selection device to prevent damage to the roll. The method of operation used in this system is shown in *Figure 11.3* and it will be noted that the principle of jacquard selection is basically the same here as in the previous system.

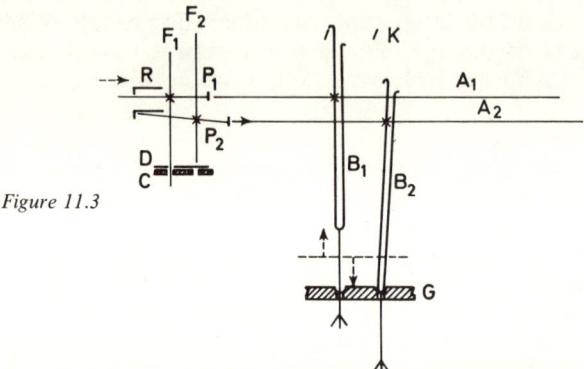

Figure 11.3

Feeler F_1 is shown opposed to a perforation in the pattern roll D which allows it to enter a corresponding hole in the cylinder plate C. The poker P_1 controlled by the feeler remains at rest and, therefore, the pusher grid R moves forward without acting upon the poker; the corresponding needle A_1 also remains undisturbed leaving the hook which it controls over the knife K. The knife in its movement upwards will take the hook and with it the harness cord and the warp end from the centre up to the top shed level. Feeler F_2 opposed by a blank raises the poker end P_2 into the path of the pusher grid which forces the poker forward against needle A_2. This movement presses hook B_2 clear off the knife and allows the hook to fall down with the top board G as it moves from the centre to the bottom shed position.

The double lift single cylinder jacquard

The term 'double lift' indicates that the jacquard has two sets of lifting knives which operate on alternate picks. Each needle controls a pair of hooks selecting one to act on odd picks in conjunction with the first set of knives, and the other to act, in conjunction with the second set of knives, on even picks. Every end, therefore, is controlled alternately by one of the hooks in a pair. The principle of selection remains unchanged and the basis of the operation is as follows: the cylinder presents the first card to the needles and whilst one set of knives implements the first selection the cylinder moves out and in again to present a fresh card for the subsequent selection; the other set of knives now commences to move up taking with it those hooks which were selected by the presentation of the second card and simultaneously the first set of knives starts moving down. This arrangement permits the formation of a modified open shed which reduces the unnecessary movements of ends in as much as any ends required to remain up for several picks in succession do not return to their original rest position between picks, but remain up except for a slight downward movement. This downward movement is due to the fact that the descending knife carries one hook of a pair, and, therefore, the corresponding end down until the other hook carried by the ascending knife is able to assume control over the end in question and return it again to the top. The transfer of the control over warp threads takes place approximately half-way through the shed. The situation described above is shown in *Figure 11.4* by the first pair of hooks A_1 and A_2. A_1 is up by virtue of the previous selection and A_2 is being selected to rise on the next pick (hole in the card), but the end controlled by this pair of hooks will fall until A_2 draws level with A_1. B_1 and B_2 show the situation when an end is required to remain down on two picks in succession where B_1 is down by virtue of the first selection and its twin is also being pressed clear of the knife (blank in the card) for the current selection. Yet another situation arises when an end which was up by previous selection is required to stay down for the following pick. This is shown at C_1 and C_2, where C_1 is at the top but its twin is being pressed off. As the two hooks are controlled by the same needle, the needle impinges upon both, and C_1 yielding to the pressure, bends to permit the deflection of C_2. Although hooks are sufficiently flexible to bend easily, this action nevertheless tends to increase the wear on cards, needles and the hooks themselves.

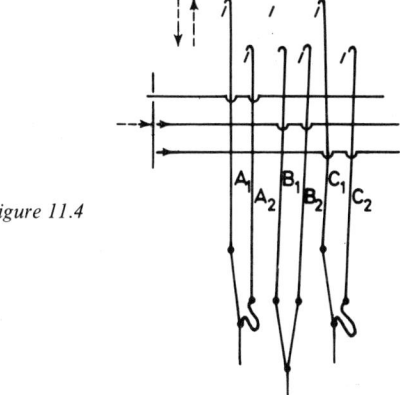

Figure 11.4

The double lift single cylinder jacquards are constructed in all sizes and pitches and can operate faster than the single lift jacquards as the sheds are formed in less time due to simultaneous movement of rising and falling threads. They also require less power as the lifting knives are compensated to some extent by those that are falling. Their main disadvantage lies in the rapid movement of the cylinder which has to provide a selection for each pick and operates at twice the speed of the knives. The violent turning movement caused the cards to be thrown off on occasion, and this led to the introduction in modern machines of pentagonal or hexagonal cylinders to reduce the angular velocity at the moment of turning.

The double lift double cylinder jacquard

This machine produces the same type of shed as the previous one and is in many aspects similar in action. The main difference is in the presence of the second cylinder which operates alternately with the first. This necessitates the separation of the pattern cards for each design into two sets laced individually, one operating the selection on odd picks, and the other on even picks. Although the system results in reducing the speed of the cylinder action it introduces the problem of correct order of card presentation and cards between the two sets are liable to get out of sequence especially during pick finding. To prevent this elaborate controls are introduced to stop the loom should the cards be incorrectly presented. A further disadvantage is the additional obstruction to light offered by the second pack of cards and the difficulty of storing two sets of cards for each design.

The open shed jacquard

This system can be regarded as a further development of the ordinary double lift principle of operation and its main advantage is that it eliminates completely any unnecessary movement of warp threads between shed forming cycles. The open shed system is nowadays employed mostly in fine pitch jacquards and these machines built with the highest degree of precision can operate successfully at speeds of up to 250 picks per minute.

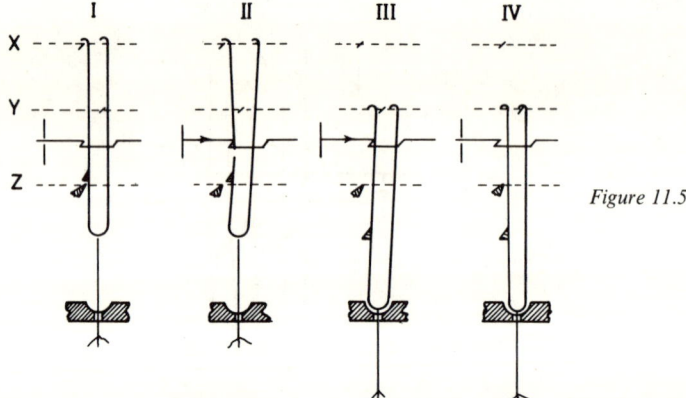

Figure 11.5

Several different methods are used to achieve the open shed and the diagram in *Figure 11.5* shows one in which a stationary griffe Z, additional to the two normal griffes X and Y, retains a double hook in the top shed position when it is required to remain up for several picks in succession (position I). At II a situation is shown in which the hook is ready to drop into the bottom shed line following the pressure by a blank opposite the needle. Position III shows the effect of two successive blanks, and at IV the end which was down by virtue of the previous selection is now ready to move up following a hole opposite the needle.

The open shed system is particularly valuable in weaving warp faced fabrics the right side up without materially increasing the power requirements of the driving mechanism.

Sizes of jacquards and cards

The English coarse pitch machines range in size from 100 to 600, and occasionally 900 hooks (in double lift machines the two hooks of a pair are counted as one). The common sizes and hook arrangements are shown in the following Table 11.

Table 11

100 size, with	26	rows of	4	hooks per row	= 104 hooks	
300 ,,	,,	38 ,,	,,	8 ,,	,, ,,	= 304 ,,
400 ,,	,,	51 ,,	,,	8 ,,	,, ,,	= 408 ,,
500 ,,	,,	51 ,,	,,	10 ,,	,, ,,	= 510 ,,
600 ,,	,,	51 ,,	,,	12 ,,	,, ,,	= 612 ,,

The fine pitch machines, of which there are several types, are normally built in much larger sizes. The Verdol pitch jacquards are made in multiples of 448 hooks, the three common sizes being 896, 1344, and 1792 hooks. In this system there are 16 hooks in each short row controlled by two rows of 8 needles, each staggered in respect of the other. The Vincenzi pitch machines are made in similar sizes in multiples of 440 hooks arranged with 16 needles and hooks per short row.

The number of hooks in the machine indicates its maximum figuring capacity, i.e. the number of warp threads that can be operated independently of each other if all the hooks are utilised. In practice not all the hooks are used for figuring and some are left empty whilst others may be employed to operate the selvedge threads, the box motion or various other devices as necessary. Usually the number of hooks tied up is a multiple of several smaller numbers as this facilitates the arrangement of various ground weaves and auxiliary figures. For instance, in the 408 size machine frequently only 384 hooks are tied-up as this figure is a multiple of 12 and 16 which permits the use of most common weaves for the ground. In addition, auxiliary motifs repeating over, say, 64, 96, or 128 ends could be fitted in with the main figure without difficulty.

When very large designs are wanted several jacquards can be combined together to work in tandem, thus further increasing the figuring capacity— e.g. 2688 size can be obtained by combining two 1344 hook machines, or 2240 size by placing a 1344 hook machine in tandem with an 896 hook model.

The cards (fully perforated) for different sizes and pitches of machines are shown in *Figure 11.6* and serve to illustrate the differences in the closeness of needle settings between the various systems. A represents 408 English coarse pitch size and measures 412 mm × 60 mm. B shows the 1320 Vincenzi pitch card which is 377 mm long × 69 mm broad, C represents the equivalent of three cards in the Verdol pitch for 896 size, each of which occupies the space of 320 mm × 27 mm. This comparison illustrates the saving which can be achieved in the weight, and also in the storage capacity when fine pitch machines are adopted instead of the coarse pitch.

With the exception of the Verdol type shown at C the cards illustrated in *Figure 11.6* show how the hooks and needles are arranged in the machines, and will make clear the meaning of the terms 'short row', and 'long row', as applied to the needles, hooks and harness cords. In looking at a fully punched card the holes (with the exception of the peg and lace holes) represent the tops of the hooks, and the ends of the needles; or, in other words, each hole

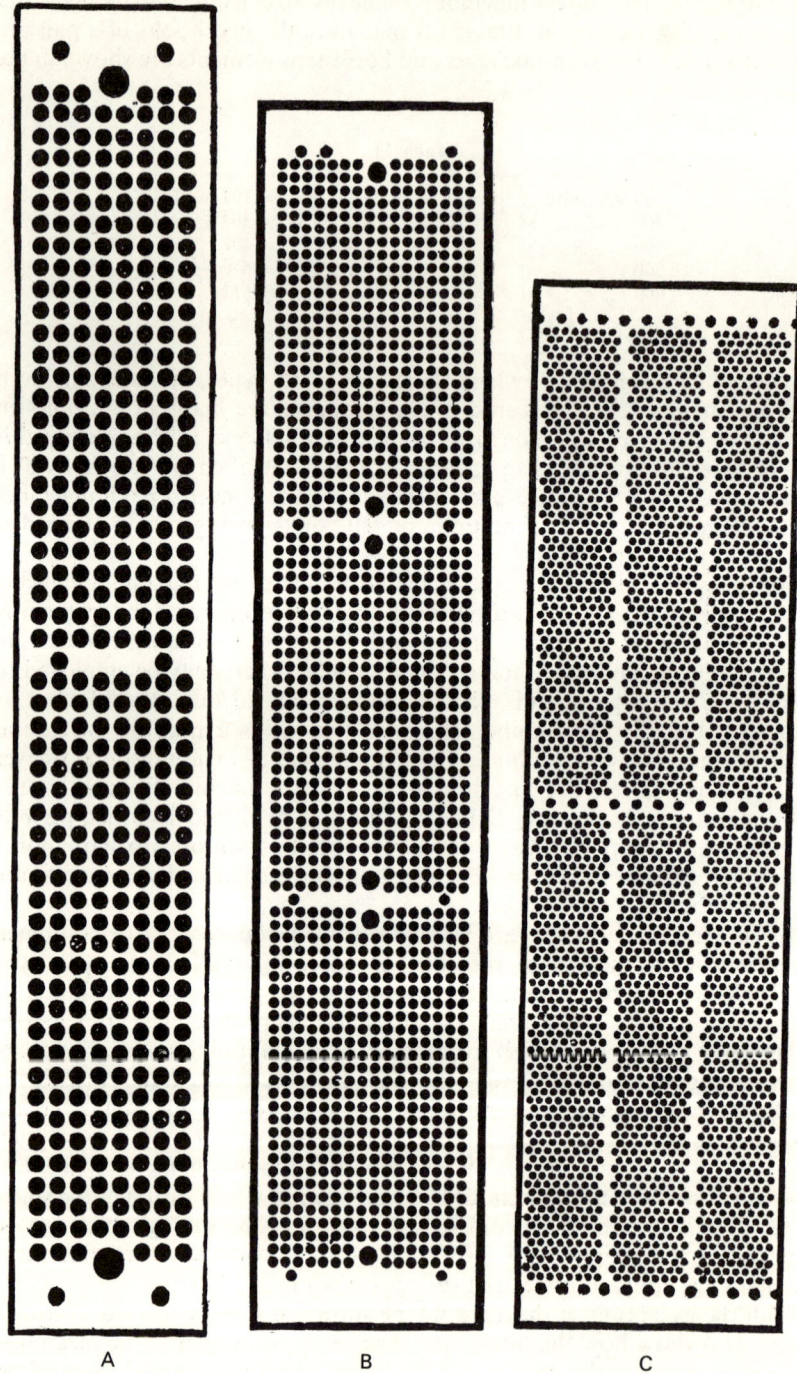

A   B   C

Figure 11.6

represents the connection of a needle to a hook (or a pair of hooks in a double-lift jacquard). Further, a card represents one pick, or one horizontal space of the design paper, and each hole (or position where a hole may be punched) a small square of a horizontal space. A card is perforated and left blank in the order indicated by the painting of the design; if certain marks represent warp up, a hole is cut to correspond with each small square thus indicated (as shown in *Figure 11.9*).

Ordinary harness ties

A jacquard may be placed in relation to the loom with the card cylinder at the right or left side, or at the back or front. If the cylinder is at one side the long rows of hooks are at right angles to the length of the comber-board, therefore the harness cords are crossed with each other in passing from the neck-cords to the holes in the comber-board. This arrangement, which is illustrated in *Figure 11.7*, is termed a London, crossed, or quarter-twist tie.

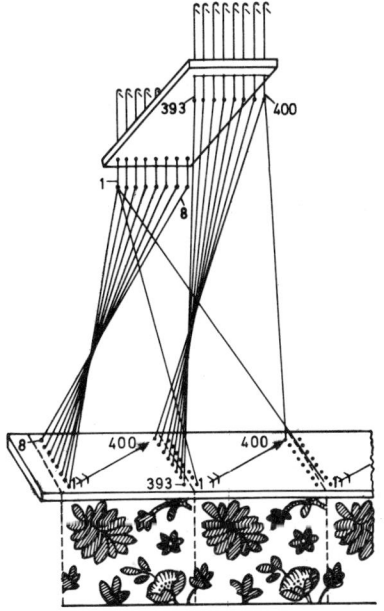

Figure 11.7

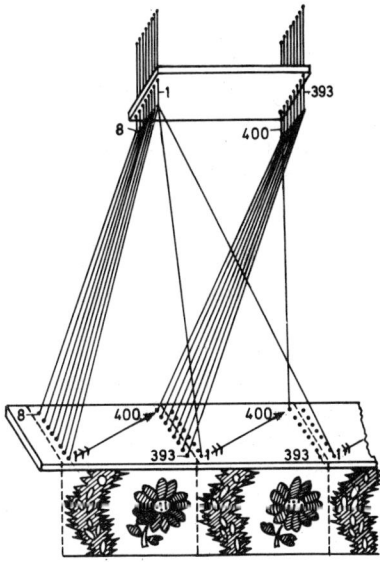

Figure 11.8

If, however, the card cylinder is at the back or front of the loom, the long rows of hooks are parallel with the length of the comber-board, so that the harness cords are not crossed. This tie is illustrated in *Figure 11.8*, and the term Norwich or straight tie is applied to the arrangement.

In tying up a harness the first hook in the row nearest the head of the cylinder (which is invariably on the right when facing the cylinder) is taken as the first hook in the machine. The other hooks in the same row follow in consecutive order from 2 to 8, as indicated by the numbers in *Figures 11.7* and *11.8*; then the hooks 9 and 16 are the first and last in the second row; the hooks 17 and 24, the first and last in the third row, and so on. If the jacquard contains as many hooks as there are figuring threads in the full width of the cloth, as, for instance, in certain classes of carpet jacquards, only one harness cord is connected to each hook, and the tie is termed a *single* tie. The most commonly used arrangement, however, is the *lay-over* or *repeating* tie, which is illustrated in *Figures 11.7* and *11.8*, and is also represented in the lower portion of *Figure 11.2*. In this tie, commencing with the first hook (or neck-cord) of the machine, the first harness cord is connected to it, the second harness cord to the second hook, the third to the third, and so on in succession until each hook has one harness cord connected to it. This gives one 'division' or 'repeat' of the harness, which occupies a certain width of the comber-board and contains as many harness cords as there are hooks tied up. The process is then repeated—commencing with the first hook, and a second harness cord is successively connected to each, a second division of the harness being thus formed in the comber-board. Again the process is repeated (and again and again if necessary) until the required width of the harness in the comber-board is obtained.

In *Figures 11.2, 11.7*, and *11.8* the divisions of the comber-board are clearly indicated, and it will be readily understood, that as in each division the harness cords are attached in exactly the same order to the hooks (or neck-cords), the figure formed by the first division will be repeated exactly by each subsequent division in the manner illustrated by the designs below the comber-boards in *Figures 11.7* and *11.8*. In the lay-over tie the number of hooks tied up gives the maximum number of threads in the repeat in width of a design; by casting out (see page 191) designs may be woven which repeat upon a lesser number, while any smaller designs repeating on the number of threads which is a factor of the total number of hooks tied-up can be accommodated.

Harness drawing in, card cutting, and card lacing

The warp threads may be drawn through the harness mails in the order shown at A in *Figure 11.9*, or as indicated at B. In the former method the first thread in a design (at the left as viewed from the front of the loom) is drawn upon a harness cord at the front of the comber-board, and if the card cylinder is at the back of the loom (which is common) the needle that controls the first thread is at the bottom of the first short row. In the latter method, under similar conditions, the first thread is drawn upon a harness cord at the back of the comber-board, and the needle which controls it is at the top of the first short row.

The construction of a design is not affected by the way in which the threads are drawn in, but a difference is made in the card-cutting. This is illustrated in *Figure 11.9* in which C shows a small design, and D portions of two cards which are cut to correspond with the first and second horizontal spaces, or picks of C—assuming that the harness draft A is employed and that the marks of the design indicate warp up. The design is placed in front of the card-cutter in the position that it has been constructed and as it is required to appear in the cloth. The bottom horizontal space corresponds with the first card, and the card-cutter follows it from left to right, each series of spaces between the thick lines of the paper coinciding with a short row of the card. If the draft indicated at B in *Figure 11.9* be employed, the design is turned one-half round, as shown at E. The first horizontal space is then at the top,

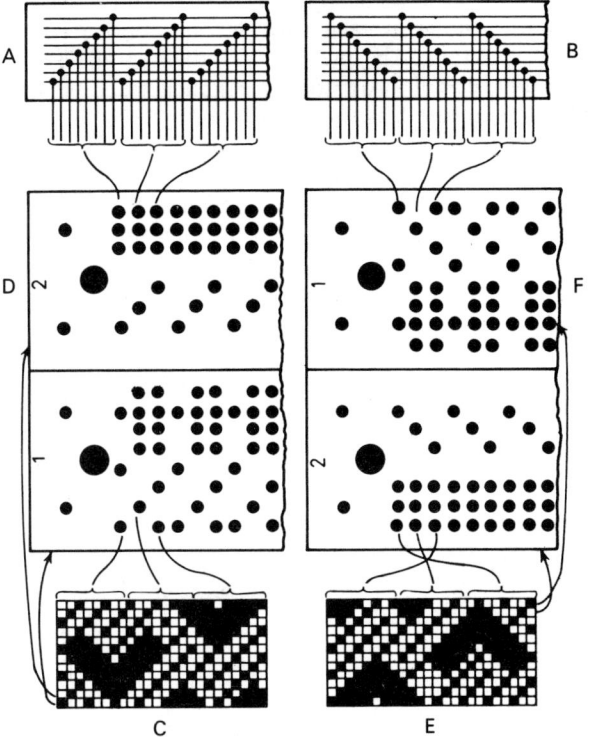

Figure 11.9

and the first card is cut from it by reading from right to left. Thus, F shows sections of cards cut from the two top horizontal spaces of E.

The cards are numbered at the end where the cutting is commenced to correspond with the numbers of the horizontal spaces of the design, and they are laced together with the numbers arranged in consecutive order. Generally the numbers follow each other from one upward in the direction shown at D in *Figure 11.9*, which is termed 'lacing forwards'. Sometimes, however, as for instance in order to reverse the direction of a twill-ground weave, they follow each other in the opposite direction as shown at F, which is termed 'lacing backwards'. As a rule the numbered ends of the cards are placed at the right (when facing the cylinder) side of the cylinder, and if the cards are laced forwards they rotate in order from the first to the last, whereas if they are laced backwards they rotate from the last to the first. An exception to this occurs when two cylinders are employed at opposite sides of the jacquard.

HARNESS AND DESIGN CALCULATIONS

Sett of the harness

The number of harness mails per unit space is decided by the rate at which the rows of holes are formed in the comber-board, and the number of holes in each row. Usually there are as many holes in each row of the comber-board as there are hooks in each short row of the jacquard. Thus, in an 8-row machine there are 8 holes in each row, and in wooden comber-boards in coarse setts, the holes may be pierced as indicated at G in *Figure 11.10*, whereas in medium setts, in order to give as much space as possible between the holes, they are staggered, as shown at H. In very fine sett harnesses, however, in order that there will be sufficient space between the rows, each row in the comber-board mostly contains twice as many holes as there are hooks in a short row of the jacquard. The arrangement for an 8-row machine is then as shown at K in *Figure 11.10*, and in tying up the harness the cords from the first row of hooks are passed through the odd holes, and from the second row through the even holes, as represented on the right of K. The

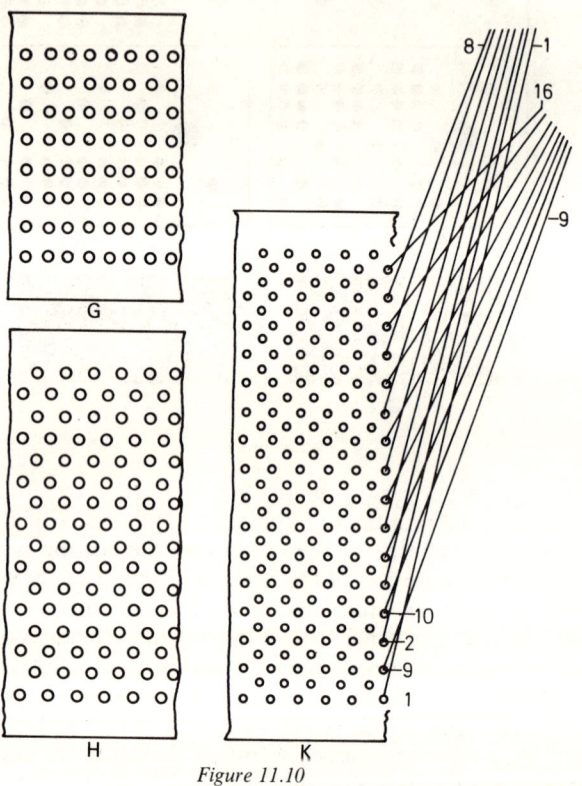

Figure 11.10

warp threads are drawn through the harness mails in corresponding order—threads 1 to 8 on the odd mails in succession, and threads 9 to 16 on the even mails, and so on.

Sometimes, for special purposes, as for instance in weaving broad crammed stripes, the comber-board is pierced at different rates to conform with the sett and width of the respective sections of the warp threads. Such an arrangement, however, is seldom necessary. For instance, a warp might be dented in the reed in the order of 200 threads, 4 per split, and 200 threads, 2 per split, but a uniform distribution of the harness cords in the comber-board would cause no difficulty in weaving, because the cords yield readily to the draw of the reed.

The number of harness cords per cm is equal to the number of rows per cm multiplied by the number of holes per row. For example, if 48 harness cords per cm are required—in an 8-row machine there will be $48 \div 8 = 6$ rows of holes per cm, and in a 12-row machine—$48 \div 12 = 4$ rows per cm.

Number of harness cords to each hook

In a lay-over or repeating tie the number of hooks tied up, and the width and sett of the harness, determine the number of harness cords to each hook. For instance, assuming that 400 hooks are tied up, 120 cm wide in the harness, with 40 harness cords per cm—the total number of harness cords in the full width $= 120 \times 40 = 4800$; and 4800 cords $\div$ 400 hooks $= 12$ harness cords to each hook. That is, the harness will be in 12 divisions, and will produce 12 repeats of a design that is constructed upon 400 threads. As a further illustration, let it be assumed that 304 hooks are tied up, 72 cm wide, with 40 harness cords per cm. In this case there will be $40 \times 72 = 2880$ cords, and $2880 \div 304 = 9$ divisions $+ 144$ cords. It is customary to tie one-half of the remainder at one side of the jacquard, and the other half at the other side, and the arrangement shown in Table 12 will therefore be suitable.

Table 12

Hooks 233 to 304	=	72	harness cords	
,, 1 to 304 × 9 repeats	=	2 736	,,	,,
,, 1 to 72	=	72	,,	,,
		2 880	,,	,,

Thus, 144 hooks will be tied up with 10 cords per hook and 160 hooks with 9 cords per hook. In the foregoing, no provision is made for the selvages, but assuming that 4 hooks are employed for the purpose, and that 24 cords are tied up at each side, each selvage hook will have $(24 + 24) \div 4$ hooks $= 12$ cords attached to it.

Casting-out in jacquards

Casting-out consists of leaving empty a portion of the mails in each repeat of the harness, and of allowing the corresponding needles, hooks, and harness cords in the machine to remain idle. The warp threads should occupy the same width in the harness as in the reed; the sett of a harness, however, is fixed when it is tied up, whereas the sett of the warp in the reed is changed according to requirements (except that it should not be finer than the sett of the harness). Casting-out may therefore be defined as a process by which a jacquard is adapted, without retying, to suit conditions that are different from those for which the harness was constructed. For instance, if a harness is tied up to 400 hooks, with 40 harness cords per cm, the conditions are perfectly suited to weaving designs repeating upon 400 threads with 40 threads per cm. It may, however, be found necessary to use the machine—(a) in weaving designs that repeat upon a smaller number of threads than 400; and (b) in weaving cloths with less than 40 threads per cm. These are the two chief purposes of casting-out; but, in addition, the process is employed to some extent in producing special effects in a straight repeating tie.

It is possible to weave designs that repeat upon any number of threads less than the number of hooks tied up, but it is obviously impossible to employ a higher number. Very small designs can be repeated across the cards a number of times—e.g., in a 400-tie, a design repeating upon 64 threads can be carried across the cards five times, with a remainder of 80 hooks cast out, or six times with 16 hooks cast out. The examples C and D, or E and F, in *Figure 11.9* illustrate the method in which a small design is repeated across the cards. Casting out 80 hooks, in a jacquard in which 400 hooks are tied up, leaves only 320 hooks in use, and under these conditions the machine is limited to designs which repeat upon 320 threads, or a number which is a factor of 320.

It is important to note that the sett of the harness is reduced in ratio proportionate to the number of hooks that are cast out; and the sett of the warp in the reed should be the same (or very nearly the same) as the reduced sett of the harness. By means of the following formula, which is of general application, an unknown factor can be readily found: The sett of the harness : the sett of the warp in the reed :: the number of hooks tied up : the number of hooks employed, or the number of threads in the design.

Two problems arise in weaving designs that repeat upon a smaller number of threads than the number of hooks tied up: (1) To find the sett of warp to suit a given sett of harness. (2) To find the sett of harness to suit a given sett of warp. In illustration of both problems let it be assumed that it is desired to weave a design repeating upon 320 threads in a 400-tie. (1) Taking the sett of the harness as 45 cords per cm, the sett of the warp should be:

$$400:320::45:36 \text{ threads per cm.}$$

(2) Taking the sett of the warp as 40 per cm, the sett of the harness should be:

$$320:400::40:50 \text{ cords per cm.}$$

When it is desired to weave a cloth with fewer threads per inch in the reed than there are harness cords per inch, it is necessary to find the number of threads in the repeat of the design relative to the number of hooks tied up. For example, assuming that a warp with 32 threads per cm in the reed, has to be woven in a 304-tie, with 40 harness cords per cm, the number of threads in the repeat of the design will be:

$$40:32::304:242 \text{ threads.}$$

In this case, however, a more convenient number is 240 threads, then the number of hooks cast out = 304 − 240 = 64.

In some special cases the hooks are cast out in long rows, which, as regards the card cutting, reduces the number of hooks in each short row—e.g., if two long rows are cast out, a 12-row machine is reduced to 10 rows, and an 8-row machine to 6 rows. Most frequently, however, the casting out is done in short rows, and if a considerable number of rows are cast out, they should be distributed as regularly as possible across the card. Also, a definite system should be employed in selecting the rows for ease of drawing-in. *Figure 11.11* illustrates a principle upon which the cast out rows may be selected. A represents one long row of a 304-card, which is in two halves, each consisting of 19 rows, and it will be understood that each black circle corresponds to a short row of eight. For a cast out of 32 hooks the 1st and 19th rows in each half are cast out, as shown at B. To increase the cast out to one of 48 hooks, the 10th row in each half is added, as indicated at C. For a cast out of 80 hooks the 7th and 13th rows in each half are also added, as shown at D; to which the 4th and 16th rows in each half are added for a cast out of 112 hooks, as shown at E. This is further increased to a cast out of 144 hooks by adding the 6th and 14th rows in each half, as represented at F.

Another important point to note in selecting the rows to be cast out is to arrange them, if possible, in such a manner that they are in the same order when counted from either end of the card. This has been kept in view in selecting the rows for the cast outs shown at B to F in *Figure 11.11*. For example, from whichever side of cast out E the rows are counted, the numbers are 1, 4, 7, 10, 13, 16, 19, in each half. The advantage of this arrangement is that the cards will fit on the cast out when turned round, which, in certain of the most common arrangements of figures, enables the cards for the second half of the design to be repeated from the cards which are cut from the first half, thus saving time both in the designing and card cutting.

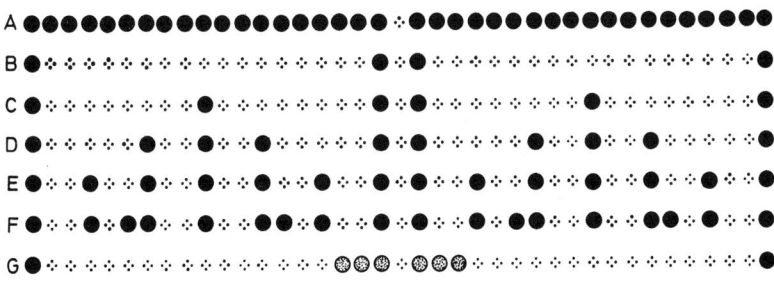

Figure 11.11

When only a given size and sett of jacquard is available for producing a design, it sometimes occurs that the proper number of ends for the repeat, obtained by calculation, is different from the number of ends in one or more repeats of the design. For example, assuming that a 33 sett warp is required to be woven in a 38 sett 304 jacquard, the correct number of ends for the repeat =

$$38 : 33 :: 304 : 264 \text{ ends}$$

and the correct cast out =

$$304 - 264 = 40 \text{ hooks.}$$

In practice, the number of ends (264) for the repeat can be varied from about 256 to 272, but a large design, repeating on, say, 288 ends, or one repeating on, say, 240 ends, will require to be modified in size to suit the size of repeat which can be obtained in the given jacquard. Small designs may also require to be modified in size, as, for example, a design repeating on 48 ends may be altered to repeat on (264 ÷ 6 repeats) = 44 ends, or (260 ÷ 5 repeats) = 52 ends. When, however, it is impossible for the repeat of a small design to be altered in size, the warp may be kept straight between the harness and the reed by casting out in the following manner.

Assuming that the calculation number of ends for the repeat is 264, and that the design repeats on 48 ends, the design is carried out on a larger number of ends than the calculation number. Thus, in this case, by repeating the design six times, the size of the repeat = 288 ends, which in the 304 jacquard gives a cast out of 16 hooks, or two rows for the card cutting. The number of harness mails (16) which are cast out in every division of the harness is then too little by (288 − 264) = 24 mails; but as the design repeats on 48 ends only, it is possible, without injury to the weaving, and without causing a break in the pattern, to cast out a block of 48 harness mails in addition to the 16 mails in any division of the harness. The number of times it will be necessary to cast out in blocks of 48 may be found as follows.

Assuming that the warp contains 3200 ends, the number of divisions which the warp requires to occupy in the harness =

$$3200 \div 264 = 12 \text{ divisions and } 32 \text{ ends.}$$

$$\frac{12 \text{ divisions} \times 24 \text{ mails cast out too little}}{48 \text{ mails in each block}} = 6 \text{ times.}$$

It is necessary to assort the 6 places regularly across the 12 divisions which the warp occupies; therefore, in this case, the odd divisions may be cast out 16, and the even divisions 16 + 48 = 64 mails. The plan of the cast-out card is shown at G, *Figure 11.11*, the shaded circles indicating a convenient position for the 48 mails or 6 rows which are cast out or filled in according to requirements. It will be understood that the cards for weaving the design must be cut as though the harness was cast out only on the first and last rows.

Size of repeat

Cloths contract in weaving and also in most cases in finishing, hence in the finished state a fabric contains more threads per unit space than are inserted in the loom. A jacquard design requires to be constructed in accordance with the finished conditions of the cloth for which it is intended, and if a cloth, when finished, contains 30 picks and 40 ends per cm, a design 16 cm long by 10 cm wide will repeat upon 30 × 16 = 480 picks or cards, and 40 × 10 = 400 ends.

The length of repeat that can be obtained in a jacquard is theoretically unrestricted, but in practice there is a limit to the number of pattern cards that can be conveniently suspended and made to work satisfactorily in a machine. In addition to mechanical considerations the question of economics is important, and it should be taken into account that the cost of a design is about in proportion to the number of cards that are required. In ordinary jacquards a separate card is required for each pick, and if it be assumed that the maximum number that can be conveniently used in a given machine is say 2000, the designer should endeavour to restrict his designs accordingly. Thus, in this case, in designing for a cloth with 40 picks per cm, the length of the repeat should not exceed 50 cm, and for a cloth containing 60 picks per cm, 33 cm; any smaller length of repeat, of course, being readily obtained. readily obtained.

The width of repeat that can be woven in an ordinary jacquard and tie is much more restricted than the length, as in the loom it cannot (in ordinary circumstances) exceed the space occupied by one division of the harness in the comber-board. The number of hooks tied up, the sett of the harness, and the contraction of the cloth, are the governing factors. For example, assuming that a cloth contracts 10 per cent from the reed width to the finished width —a 400 tie with 40 harness cords per cm will give: $(400 \div 40) - 10$ per cent = 9 cm width of repeat in the finished cloth. The result is not affected if a cloth is woven with fewer threads per inch in the reed than the number of harness cords per inch, because the hooks require to be cast out to correspond with the difference in the setts. Thus, if a cloth is woven in the foregoing tie with 30 ends per cm in the reed, there will be

$$40:30::400:300 \text{ hooks employed,}$$

and $(300 \div 30) - 10$ per cent = 9 cm width of repeat as before.

Methods of modifying the repeat in a lay-over tie

Although, in a general way it is true that the figure produced in one division of a lay-over tie will be produced exactly the same in each succeeding division, and that the width of the repeat is correspondingly limited, yet it is possible by means of special methods of drawing in and casting out to modify the size of the repeat and to obtain special effects. For instance, when the sett of the warp is not more than half the sett of the harness, the following method of casting out may be employed in order to double the size of the repeat of the jacquard. Assuming that it is required to weave a warp with 27 ends per cm in a 304-tie with 57 mails per cm, the number of mails in each division which require to be filled in =

$$57 \text{ mails}:27 \text{ ends}::304:144;$$

and the number of mails cast out in each division of the harness =

$$304 - 144 = 160.$$

Instead, however, of throwing 160 hooks entirely out of action, 288 hooks may be employed for figuring by making the design on $144 \times 2 = 288$ ends (which for the card cutting gives a cast out of $304 - 288 = 16$ ends), and by arranging the rows in the harness as follows: The first and last rows of hooks are cast out in every division of the harness; in alternate divisions of the harness half of the remaining rows, say the even rows, are cast out, and the odd rows are filled in; then in the other divisions the odd rows are cast out, and the even rows are filled in. One repeat of the figure will thus extend across two divisions of the harness. In order to cut the cards conveniently from the design the sheet of point paper may be cut into longitudinal strips and arranged with a strip from the first half alternating with a strip from the second half. Alternatively, the cutter may be instructed to cut the first half of the design on odd rows only, and then return the card back to the original starting point, and cut the second half of the design on the even rows.

This method may be employed in various ways in the production of special effects in an ordinary machine. For example, the figured skirting fabric, represented in *Figure 11.12*, was produced in an ordinary 304-jacquard by using the odd rows of hooks for the figure and the even rows for the ground. Where the border figure appears the even rows were cast out, while in the ground of the fabric the odd rows were cast out. The sett of the warp was half of that of the harness. In designing such a style the chief points to note are that the position of each part of the ornament on the point paper corresponds with the hooks which are available for its production, and that the warping plan coincides with the width and form of the border which can be obtained.

Figure 11.12

In figuring with two colours of warp arranged 1-and-1 in the harness it is possible by casting out an odd number of mails to obtain a repeat of figure which is apparently double the width of the repeat of the jacquard. For example, if one harness mail of a 304-tie be cast out, the number of ends in the repeat of the design paper plan = 303, and, as the 1-and-1 warping plan repeats on two ends, the design in the cloth will repeat on a number of ends which is common to 303 and 2—i.e., 606. The ends of the first colour will be on the odd mails in one division, and on the even mails in the next division of the harness, and correspondingly the ends of the second colour will be on

Figure 11.13

the even mails and then on the odd mails. The result of such an arrangement will be understood from an examination of the design shown in *Figure 11.13*, only half the repeat of which needs to be painted out on the design paper.

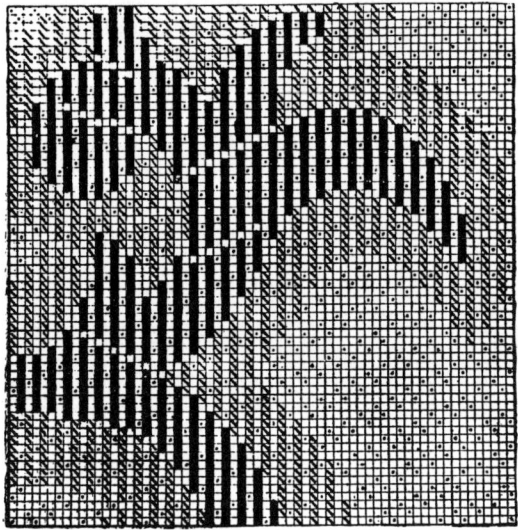

Figure 11.14

The two colours of warp, in which the figure is intended to be developed, will replace each other in succeeding divisions of the harness, hence the repeat of the design in the cloth will be on twice as many ends as the design paper plan. A portion of the design is shown at *Figure 11.14*, which illustrates the end-and-end arrangement of the figure.

Counts of design paper

Design paper is divided by thick lines usually into square blocks, each of which is subdivided into horizontal and vertical spaces. Each horizontal space corresponds to a pick of weft, and each vertical space to a warp thread and a hook of the jacquard. For convenience in the designing and card cutting the vertical ruling of the paper is arranged to coincide with the arrangement of the jacquard hooks—that is, each large square is divided vertically into as many spaces as there are hooks in a short row of the jacquard. Thus, in the design paper used for an 8-row machine there are 8 vertical spaces between each pair of thick lines, and for a 12-row jacquard, 12 spaces, so that in each case the number of vertical spaces between the vertical thick lines corresponds to one row of the card. In order to retain the correct proportions and shape of figure designs, the number of horizontal spaces in each large square requires to be in the same proportion to the number of vertical spaces as the picks are to the ends per unit space in the finished cloth. Since, however, the number of vertical spaces is fixed by the arrangement of the hooks in the jacquard, it is necessary for the number of horizontal spaces in each square to be varied according to the ratio of picks to ends in the cloth. Design paper can be purchased to suit practically any conditions, and in *Figure 11.15* a number of different rulings are illustrated. A and B represents 8 × 8 design paper which is used in designing for cloths in which the ends and picks per unit space are equal, while C shows 8 × 4 paper which is suitable for a cloth which contains twice as many ends as picks per unit space. The first number of the count of the paper indicates the vertical ruling.

In order to illustrate the necessity of using properly ruled paper a small spot is indicated at A, B, and C in *Figure 11.15*; and, assuming that the spot is required to be 0·5 cm in diameter in a cloth containing 32 ends and 32 picks per cm, it will extend over 16 ends and 16 picks, as shown at A. If, however,

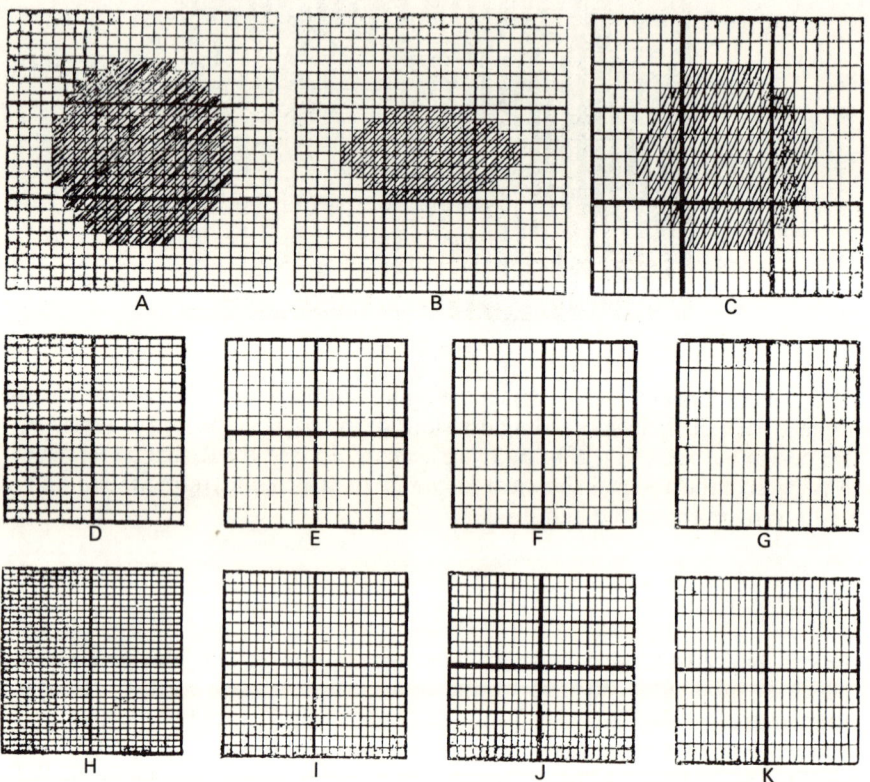

Figure 11.15

the same size of spot is required in a cloth containing 32 ends and 16 picks per cm, it will extend over 16 ends and 8 picks, as indicated at B, in which, however, the 8 × 8 paper shows the spot entirely out of proportion. On the other hand, by using paper that is ruled 8 × 4 to suit the ratio of 32 ends to 16 picks per cm in the cloth the spot is in proper proportion, as shown at C.

The proper counts of design paper to suit any given particulars of cloth (finished) may be found from the formula:

Ends per cm : Picks per cm :: Vertical spaces : Horizontal spaces.

The examples D to G in *Figure 11.15* are suitable for 8-row jacquards, and respectively show 8 × 10, 8 × 6, 8 × 5, and 8 × 3½ papers; while H to K are suitable for 12-row machines and are ruled respectively—12 × 15, 12 × 9, 12 × 8, and 12 × 5. D and H are in proper ratio, for instance, for a cloth with 40 ends and 50 picks per cm; E and I for a cloth with 48 ends and 36 picks; F and J for 44 ends and 28 picks; and G and K for 60 ends and 25 picks. In some cases 12-row paper is ruled with a line in the centre which is intermediate in thickness, as shown at J. It is generally near enough for practical purposes to take the nearest whole number for the horizontal spaces, but sometimes the paper is specially ruled to include a fraction. Thus at G the horizontal thick lines are twice as far apart as the vertical thick lines, and the paper is equivalent to 16 × 7, or 8 × 3½.

Summary of calculations

In the following, which is chiefly a summary of the foregoing in a practical form, the calculations that are involved in designing, and the conditions to be observed are illustrated. Assuming that the design represented in *Figure 11.16* (in which the lines indicate exactly one repeat) is required to be woven

Figure 11.16

in a cloth that counts, when finished, 50 ends and 38 picks per cm, and has shrunk 8 per cent from the reed width to the finished width, while the ground weave repeats upon 20 ends and 12 picks—the particulars may be ascertained as follows.

(a) Number of ends and picks (or cards) in one repeat of the design.
(b) Number of ends per inch in the reed.
(c) Suitable capacity of jacquard and sett of harness to produce the design exact in size.
(d) Counts of design paper.

(a) The repeat is 4·8 cm in width and 6 cm in length. The number of ends in the repeat—50 × 4·8 = 240.
The number of picks in the repeat—38 × 6 = 228.

(b) The number of ends per cm in the reed—50 − 8 per cent = 46.

(c) A suitable standard capacity of jacquard is an 8-row 304-tie which will require to be cast out: 304 − 240 = 64 hooks.

The sett of the harness requires to be finer than the sett of the warp, because 304 harness cords have to occupy the same width in the comber-board as 240 ends in the reed, and the proportion is therefore—

240 ends : 304 hooks : : 50 ends per cm : 63 harness cords per cm.

As it is most unlikely that, in practice, a jacquard of almost the right size will be found for every design, and as it is the modern usage to employ large jacquards to obtain the versatility of application, a more practical approach would be as follows.

A standard 1344 hook Verdol pitch jacquard is available—determine the number of hooks to be cast out and the sett of the harness. A design repeating on 240 ends will be accommodated five times by one division of the tie, therefore, the casting out calculation in this case would be:

$$1344 - (240 \times 5) = 144 \text{ hooks.}$$

Similarly, the sett of the harness would be found as follows:

1200 ends: 1344 hooks:: 50 ends per cm: 56 harness cords per cm.

(d) The count of the design paper—

50 ends: 38 picks = 8: 6.

The example may be used in further illustration of practical conditions, by assuming that the design shown in *Figure 11.16* is required to be woven in the same cloth as before, but in a 304-jacquard, which is tied up with 51 harness cords per cm. In this case the number of ends in the repeat of the design will be less than 304 in the proportion of 51 (the harness sett) to 46 (the reed sett). The number of ends is therefore—

$$51:46::304:274,$$

which it is necessary to modify to 280 to coincide with the repeat of the ground weave. This causes the repeat in width of the design to be increased from the preceding by 40 ends, and a corresponding increase in length should be made in order that the design will be in the same proportion as the original. The number of picks will therefore be—

$$240:280::228:266,$$

which, to fit with the 12 picks in the repeat of the ground weave, should be modified to 264 picks.

Irregularly dented jacquard designs

In designing figured crammed stripes, extra warp figures, etc., a suitable capacity of jacquard may be decided upon from the number of threads in the repeat of a pattern, but such calculations as the following are involved in maintaining an even balance between the harness and the reed. The calculations vary in different circumstances, but usually the factors to consider are the number of ends and splits in the repeat, and the setts of the reed and the harness.

1. With a given order of denting and a given sett of reed, to find the sett of the harness.
2. With a given order of denting and a given sett of harness to find the sett of the reed.
3. With a given sett of reed and a given sett of harness, to find the degree of cramming or number of extra threads which may be introduced.

By dividing one side into the other an unknown factor can be obtained from the formula

$$\frac{\text{Hooks tied up in jacquard} \times \text{splits per cm in reed}}{\text{Mails per cm in harness} \times \text{splits in repeat of design}}$$

In illustration, a stripe fabric is represented in *Figure 11.17*, which is dented as in Table 13.

Figure 11.17

Table 13

30 ends—spot stripe	—2 ends per split	= 15 splits	
72 ,, —figure stripe	—6 ,, ,, ,,	= 12 ,,	
30 ,, —spot stripe	—2 ,, ,, ,,	= 15 ,,	
24 ,, —plain stripe	—4 ,, ,, ,,	= 6 ,,	
12 ,, —cord	—4 ,, ,, ,,	= 3 ,,	
24 ,, —plain stripe	—4 ,, ,, ,,	= 6 ,,	
30 ,, —spot stripe	—2 ,, ,, ,,	= 15 ,,	
72 ,, —figure stripe	—6 ,, ,, ,,	= 12 ,,	
30 ,, —spot stripe	—2 ,, ,, ,,	= 15 ,,	
24 ,, —plain stripe	—4 ,, ,, ,,	= 6 ,,	
12 ,, —cord	—4 ,, ,, ,,	= 3 ,,	
24 ,, —plain stripe	—4 ,, ,, ,,	= 6 ,,	
384 ends		**114 splits**	

The design repeats on 384 ends, so that a 400s jacquard tied on 384 hooks is suitable.

1. Assuming that the reed contains 19 splits per cm, and the sett of the harness is required—

$$\frac{\text{Hooks tied up} \times \text{splits per cm in reed}}{\text{Splits in repeat of design}} = \frac{384 \times 19}{114} = 64 \text{ mails per cm.}$$

2. Assuming that the sett of the harness is 64 mails per cm and the sett of the reed is required—

$$\frac{\text{Mails per cm in harness} \times \text{splits in repeat of stripe}}{\text{Hooks tied up}} = \frac{64 \times 114}{384}$$

$$= 19 \text{ splits per cm.}$$

3. Assuming that the sett of the harness is 64 mails per cm, and the reed has 19 splits per cm, the number of extra ends may be obtained by first finding the number of splits in the width of one repeat of the harness—

$$\frac{\text{Hooks tied up} \times \text{splits per cm in reed}}{\text{Mails per cm in harness}} = \frac{384 \times 19}{64} = 114 \text{ splits in repeat.}$$

Taking the normal distribution to be 2 ends per split, the number of extra ends which may be added to form the crammed stripes = 384 hooks − (114 splits × 2) = 156. Thus the number of splits which may be arranged with 2 extra ends per split is 78; or, with 3 extra ends per split—52; or, with 4 extra ends per split—39; while a combination of one, two, three, etc., extra ends per split may be employed, so long as not more than 156 ends are added, and the total number of splits per repeat does not exceed 114.

Any smaller amount of additional ends than the 156 used in the above example may be introduced by casting out a number of hooks to correspond with the reduced number of ends.

SPECIAL HARNESS TIES

From an examination of *Figures 11.7* and *11.8* it will be readily understood that the harness cords do not necessarily require to be passed through the holes in the comber-board in the same order that they are connected to the hooks (or neck-cords), but that they may be passed from one to the other in different orders according to requirements. That is, in tying up a harness various orders of 'drafting' the cords may be employed for the purpose of enabling special forms of designs to be woven economically. The special ties must be thoroughly understood by the designer as they materially affect the designing techniques, but it should be realised that they are not very commonly employed. Of the total number of harnesses built annually all the special ties together do not account for more than about 5 per cent of the production. The decline of the special harness tie is connected with the decline of the coarse pitch machine in which the special tie was valuable as a means for increasing the comparatively small figuring capacity of that type of jacquard. The capacity of a modern fine pitch machine is so large that the special tie is, in most cases, unnecessary to increase the scope, and becomes a hindrance through curtailing the versatility of the system by limiting it to the production of only such effects for which the tie was specifically designed. In the days of rapid changes in design tastes and constant demand for novelty, such rigid system is not generally acceptable and finds its applications only in very highly specialised fields. The principal variations from the ordinary lay-over tie are: (1) centre or point ties; (2) mixed ties; (3) ties for bordered fabrics; (4) sectional ties (see *Watson's Advanced Textile Design*). Two or more of the systems may be used in combination.

Centre or point ties

This class of tie is the simplest modification of the ordinary straight tie, and is the same in principle as point-drafting in healds. The object of the arrangement is to enable bi-symmetrical designs to be woven which repeat upon twice as many ends as there are hooks in the jacquard. The cost of painting out and card cutting is comparatively small, as the full design is obtained from one-half of the width of the repeat. *Figure 11.18* illustrates the principle in reference to a 400-hook jacquard; the harness cords are tied up consecutively from the first to the last hook, and then in reverse order from the last to the first hook. The cords which are tied in reverse order are indicated by dotted lines. The figure formed in the first half of the tie is reproduced in the second half but turned the opposite way in the manner illustrated by the sketch B below the comber-board A. The fabrics represented in *Figures 12.47* and *13.6* also illustrate the form of centre tie designs. Although a 400-centre tie will produce a design repeating upon 800 ends, it is customary to leave out one end where the tie reverses, in order to avoid having two consecutive ends

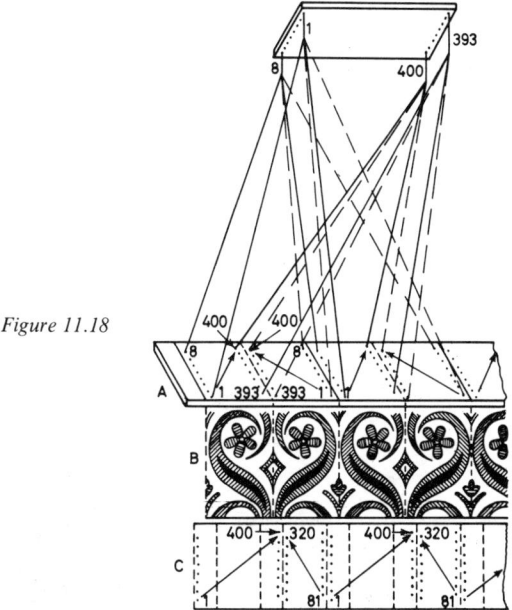

Figure 11.18

working alike. The actual full repeat is therefore 798 ends produced from a plan painted out upon 400 ends. The reversing of the tie also reverses the direction of twill and other ground weaves, and in some cases more than one thread is left out in order to prevent the formation of long floats where the ground weave is turned.

One repeat of a centre tie may extend the full width of the harness and cloth (in which case only two cords are connected to each hook) or the tie may be repeated two or more times across the width, as shown in *Figure 11.18*. The arrangement of the cords illustrated is suitable when the short rows of hooks are parallel with the short rows of holes in the comber-board (the Norwich system), but it is necessary in drawing in the warp to draw from front to back in one half of the tie, and from back to front in the other half. When, however, the short rows of hooks are at right angles to the short rows in the comber-board (the London tie—see *Figure 11.7*) it is quite convenient to connect the first hook to the front hole and the last hook to the back hole of the comber-board in both halves of the tie, which enables the ends to be drawn in in the same order throughout the full width of the harness.

In the case of designs which turn over vertically as well as horizontally (illustrations of the type are given in *Figures 11.21, 12.39,* and *12.46*), it is only necessary to paint out and cut the cards from one-fourth of the complete repeat. The figure is turned over horizontally by means of the harness tie (as previously explained), and vertically by causing the cards to turn first clockwise and then anticlockwise. In one method of accomplishing this, the last but one of the cards that form the half repeat in length, is perforated so that a special hook is raised. This, by releasing a weighted cord, causes the upper catch of the card cylinder to be made inoperative and the lower catch to be put into action, and vice versa.

Mixed ties

This class of tie is used in various ways; one useful arrangement consisting of a modification of a point tie that is employed for designs which, although partly pointed, are required to be less stiff and formal than the pure bisymmetrical patterns. Thus, a modification of the tie shown at A in *Figure 11.18* might be arranged with—say, 40 cords on each side of the middle positions tied to separate hooks, which would enable one side of each centre to be designed differently from the other side. The arrangement of the tie would then be 1 to 400, 320—81, as indicated at C in *Figure 11.18*, a design repeating upon 640 ends being obtained from a plan painted out upon 400 ends.

Figure 11.19

A mixed system of tie-up is employed for the purpose of enabling a certain portion of figure to be introduced more or less frequently than another portion. The principle is illustrated by the sketch shown in the lower portion of *Figure 11.19*, and the tie (for a 400-hook jacquard) in the upper portion. The complete design repeats upon 719 ends (allowing for casting-out one end in the centre of the bi-symmetrical stripe), and results from a plan painted out upon 400 ends.

Ties for bordered fabrics

In a bordered fabric the figure at one or both sides of the cloth is different from that formed in the centre. If the ornament in neither border nor centre is repeated, which is generally the case in the better qualities of table cloths,

Table 14

Left Border Tie	Centre Tie	Right Border Tie
Straight Hooks 1–200	Straight Hooks 201–400	Straight Hooks 1–200
Straight Hooks 1–200	Straight Hooks 201–400	Turned-over Hooks 200–1
Straight Hooks 1–200	Pointed Hooks 201–400 and 400–201	Straight Hooks 1–200
Straight Hooks 1–200	Pointed Hooks 201–400 and 400–201	Turned-over Hooks 200–1
Pointed Hooks 1–200 and 200–1	Straight Hooks 201–400	Pointed Hooks 1–200 and 200–1
Pointed Hooks 1–200 and 200–1	Pointed Hooks 201–400 and 400–201	Pointed Hooks 1–200 and 200–1

quilts, etc., an ordinary single, a pointed, or a mixed-pointed tie may be employed. Many cloths are made, however, in which the central figure is repeated a number of times, but, as a rule, only one repeat of the border figure is made at each side. The following list comprises the principal ties for cloths, with or without repeating centres, and with a similar border at each side; the

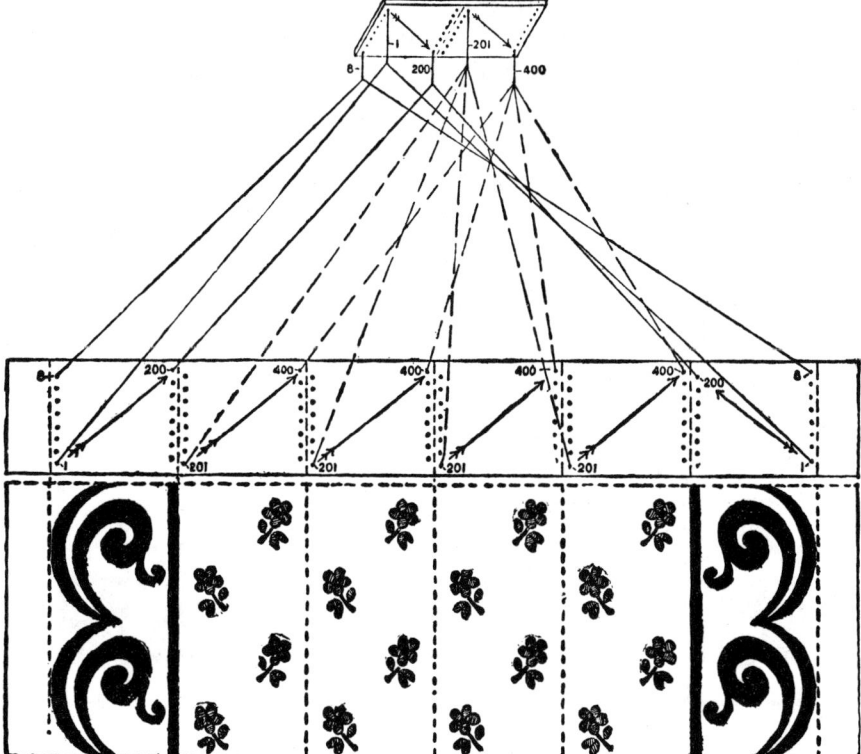

Figure 11.20

order of tying is given, assuming that a 400-hook jacquard is employed, and that one half of the hooks are employed for the borders and the other half for the centre (Table 14).

Any proportionate number of the available hooks may be employed for the border and centre—e.g., one-third for the border and two-thirds for the centre while a mixed order for tying may be introduced. Very frequently considerable ingenuity is necessary in adapting a design and the tie to suit the size of jacquard that is available.

The form of design and the tie illustrated in *Figure 11.20* corresponds with the second example in the above list. The border figure is turned over, and the centre is repeated four times, and in order that the different sections may be more readily distinguished the lines which represent the centre harness cards are shown dotted. The complete design will be formed by painting out one border and one repeat of the centre each upon 200 ends.

Figure 11.21

Figure 11.21 corresponds with the last example in the foregoing list in which both the border and the centre are pointed. In this case a square is represented in which a central repeating figure is surrounded by a border figure, and the latter by a narrow unfigured portion. Usually the unfigured portion is woven in a twill or sateen weave, and in the tie indicated in the upper portion of *Figure 11.21* the hooks 1–8 are set aside for the purpose. 200 hooks are used for the borders, and the same number for the centre, and if a plain or other selvage is also required the hooks that are in line with the peg-holes may be utilised.

Different methods are employed in weaving cross-border fabrics in which the figure is repeated several times, with the idea of using as few cards as possible. One method is to use a special cross-border jacquard made on the double-lift, single-cylinder principle with an extra cylinder upon which the border cards are placed. The centre cards act on the needles and hooks in the ordinary manner, while the border cards connected to the ordinary needles by suitable links produce the same result as if they had been placed upon the other cylinder.

The complete square, shown in *Figure 11.21*, contains, both vertically and horizontally, two repeats of the border and four repeats of the central figure. The repetition and arrangement of the different sections across the design is due to the special harness tie that is employed. A similar repetition and arrangement can be obtained lengthwise by employing two sets of cards, which are brought into action in turn. One set forms the corner and the cross-border figures, and the horizontal unfigured portions, and the other set the side-border and central figures. All the cards require to be cut to operate the selvages and the unfigured portion at the sides.

The complete square shown in *Figure 11.21* might be woven by cutting as many cross-border cards as will weave the portion indicated by the arrow A, and as many centre cards as will produce the portion represented by the arrow C. The two sets of cards are then brought into operation in turn as follows: First—the border cards turning towards the machine, as indicated by the arrow A, and then away from the machine until the border figure is completed, as indicated by the arrow B. Second—the centre cards turning alternately towards and away from the machine, as indicated by the arrows C and D respectively, for four repeats. Third—the border cards turning towards the machine to weave the figure portion, as indicated by the arrow E, and then away from the machine, as represented by the arrow F. The border cards are then retained in operation, while the first border of the next square is woven.

12

Construction and Development of Jacquard Designs

CONSTRUCTION OF SQUARED PAPER DESIGNS

The construction of jacquard designs includes the preparation of a card cutting plan on squared paper, which in most cases when an ordinary jacquard is used shows the complete working of every thread in the repeat. As opposed to the above system of detailed designing there exist forms of condensed design preparation where only the main motif is shown in block outline, and where the detailed weaves for each part of the motif are automatically introduced by the use of either, the special card cutting machines such as the Uhlig or the Dactyliseuse, or, the special jacquards. The methods of condensed design construction are explained in *Watson's Advanced Textile Design*.

In the detailed form of designing the point-paper design may be constructed from an original sketch, or from a woven sample of which the design is required to be reproduced. In either case the process generally involves an enlargement of the design, the degree of increase in size varying, in the same pitch of design paper, according to the fineness in sett of the cloth.

It is first necessary to ascertain the proper counts of the design paper and the most convenient number of ends and picks, or vertical and horizontal spaces of the design paper, upon which to draft the design, as previously described. It is shown in the calculations that the number of ends and picks, found by multiplying the ends and picks per inch respectively in the finished cloth by the width and length in inches of the repeat, may require to be modified to suit the sett and capacity of the jacquard and the repeat of the ground weave. That is, it is necessary to either select a jacquard which will give the width of repeat of the design, or to construct the design upon a number of ends that is suitable for a given jacquard. The formula

$$\frac{\text{hooks in jacquard} \times \text{sett of warp in reed}}{\text{sett of harness}}$$

gives the number of ends upon which the design should be made in order that the warp will be perfectly straight between the harness and the reed. In practice, however, the calculated number is not rigidly adhered to, as it is found that it can be varied, within limits, to suit the conditions of manufacture with practically no deteriorating effect upon the weaving of the warp.

It is a good method to decide upon a number of ends for a repeat which is a multiple of several smaller numbers, and to use this number for cloths which vary slightly in fineness. For example, a 36 sett warp is perfectly straight between the harness and the reed when woven in a 38 sett 304-tie jacquard with the design repeating on 288 ends; and designs repeating upon 288 ends, or a factor of 288, can be woven in the machine in cloths which vary in sett from 34 to 38. Again, with the same sett of harness, 240 is the calculation number for a 30-sett warp, which may be employed for cloths varying in sett from 28 to 32. The limits given are frequently exceeded in practice. This principle of working enables the same design to be applied to slightly different setts without re-making.

After the number of ends and picks required for one repeat of the design have been decided upon, the design paper work may be divided into the following processes: (1) An enlarged outline of the figure is drawn in pencil or chalk on the squared paper; (2) the figure is painted in with colour which is strong yet transparent; (3) the necessary weaves for the suitable development or binding of the figure are inserted in a second colour; (4) the ground weave is painted in. The work is frequently very tedious and occupies a large amount of time, and considerable skill and experience are required in reproducing a design to the best advantage. Much of the work, however, is almost mechanical, and ingenious methods have been adopted to reduce the amount of time and labour involved.

Process of drafting a sketch design

Previous to drawing the outline of the figure it is necessary to prepare one repeat of the design so that it can be enlarged exactly to the required scale. *Figure 12.1* illustrates the method of procedure in drafting a sketch design. It is assumed that the repeat is upon 288 ends and 352 picks, and in a square sett cloth the design paper could be 8 × 8. One exact repeat is indicated by ruling vertical and horizontal lines which respectively pass through similar parts of the figure. If the sketch has been correctly constructed, these lines are at right angles to each other. The repeat is then divided into small spaces, each of which represents a certain number of ends and picks in the cloth and of small squares on the point-paper. Any number of threads may be represented by each small space, but usually a sketch is ruled so that each space corresponds to one, two, or more of the large squares of the design paper. In designing for medium and low-sett cloths, it is very convenient to so rule the the sketch that the lines correspond with the thick lines of the design paper. With the same rate of ruling for fine-sett cloths, however, the spaces in the sketch are so small that they are difficult to follow and for cloths which count over 32 threads per cm the method illustrated in *Figure 12.1* will be found useful. The repeat of the sketch is so divided that each space represents 2 × 2 large squares, or 16 ends and 16 picks in this case. The repeat in width is thus divided into 18 spaces of 16 ends each to correspond with the repeat of 288 ends, and in length into 22 spaces of 16 picks each to correspond with the repeat of 352 picks.

The different stages of drafting a figure are illustrated in *Figure 12.2*, which corresponds with the bottom left-hand corner of *Figure 12.1*. The portion A in *Figure 12.2* shows how the outline is copied from the sketch to the scale of

16 ends and 16 picks to each space in *Figure 12.1*. The process of drawing the outline is very much facilitated by indicating distinctive lines at regular intervals in ruling the sketch, and by ruling lines at corresponding distances apart on the design paper. Thus, in *Figure 12.1* alternate lines are thicker than the others, while in *Figure 12.2* lines are lightly indicated, to correspond with the thicker lines, upon the last space of every fourth square. The distinctive

Figure 12.1

Figure 12.2

lines enable corresponding portions of the figure in the sketch and point-paper to be readily found and retained.

The second stage of working, which is illustrated at B in *Figure 12.2*, consists of painting in the small squares along the outline, and then filling in the figure solid with a wash of transparent colour. The parts lettered C illustrate the third stage in which the long floats are stopped and the figure developed by inserting marks in various orders in a colour that is in contrast with the first colour. Vermilion is chiefly used for painting the figure, and blue for the binding weaves.

Drafting designs from woven fabrics

Woven patterns are employed in two ways by the designer. In some instances the design is required to be reproduced exact in every aspect to the original and in a similar cloth; in other cases the patterns are only intended to serve as indications, the designs being modified and adapted to suit cloths which, perhaps, have very little resemblance to the original textures. In the former case it is essential that—(1) A suitable jacquard be employed to get the same size of repeat; (2) an exact copy of the form be obtained on the squared paper; (3) the weaves in the figure and ground respectively of the pattern are correctly analysed and reproduced in the new design.

The second method of using woven patterns is much more common than the first, and it is probably due to such a large variety of effects being now required for a comparatively short length of cloth that the system has recently attained such prominence. The patterns are purchased by manufacturers and merchants from firms who make a speciality of collecting the latest productions, and when a range of designs is required in a given cloth a number of suitable samples are selected to be reproduced. Only a portion of the ornament in a cloth may be used, and sometimes a portion from one sample is combined with a portion from another. From the manufacturer's point of view the question as to whether such a system should or should not be employed simply resolves itself into one of economy and expediency. The time which would otherwise be occupied in sketching new figures is saved, while a larger variety of effects can usually be obtained in any given range than when the designer's creative skill solely is relied upon. Further, the advantage to the designer of seeing and studying the various combinations of forms, colours, and materials observable in these patterns, cannot be over-estimated.

The character of the cloth in which a design is reproduced is an important factor in deciding how much resemblance there is between the new design and the original. The new cloth may be composed of different materials; it may be necessary to increase or decrease the amount of detail in drawing the outline of the figure on the point-paper; also various weave changes may be required in the figure and ground in order to adapt the design to the new texture. The result is that frequently an effect is produced in which the original design cannot be recognised.

Designs which are entirely geometrical in form, such as that shown in *Figure 12.3*, can be reproduced from woven patterns directly on to the design paper with the aid of compasses and ruler. The positions of the base lines and centres can be obtained by calculation after the number of threads in the repeat have been determined; also the number of squares to allot on the point paper for any portion of the figure can be found by measuring and calculating from the number of ends and picks per cm to which the design is being worked out. *Figure 12.4* illustrates, in a very reduced form, the method

Figure 12.3

of drawing the base lines directly upon design paper from the pattern represented in *Figure 12.3*. After these have been indicated it is only necessary to clothe the lines with the calculated size of float.

In drafting woven designs that are not geometrical in form it is necessary to divide one repeat into small spaces in the same manner as in drafting a sketch design. Different methods of accomplishing this are employed, one of

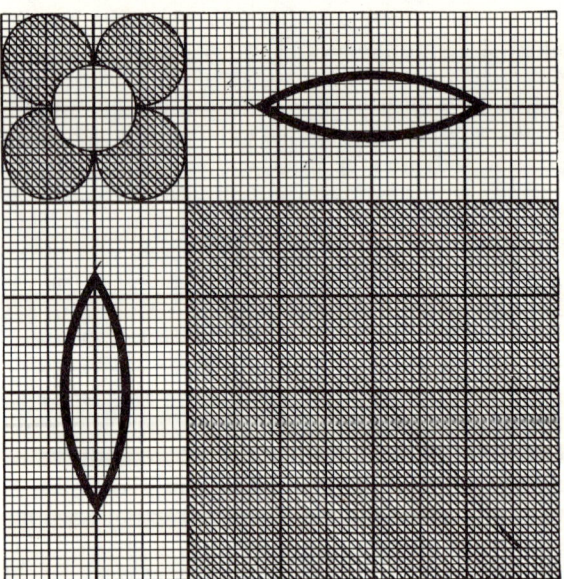

Figure 12.4

which consists of first making a sketch of the figure. A copy is readily made upon transparent tracing paper if the figure can be seen through it. If tracing paper is impracticable the method illustrated in *Figure 12.5* may be employed. The sample of cloth is pinned or pasted, at two opposite edges, on to a sheet of plain paper, and the outline of the figure is pricked round with a fine needle.

By placing a piece of carbon paper between the cloth and the sheet of paper the outline of the figure is shown in small black dots. A line is then drawn through the dots to complete the sketch, as shown in the bottom left-hand corner of *Figure 12.5*. Rather more than one repeat should be made, in order that two lines parallel with the weft and two parallel with the warp may be drawn which pass through similar parts of the figure and enclose one complete repeat. This is then divided up by drawing other lines, at regular distances apart, in the manner previously described in reference to a sketch design. It is frequently found that the warp and weft threads are not exactly

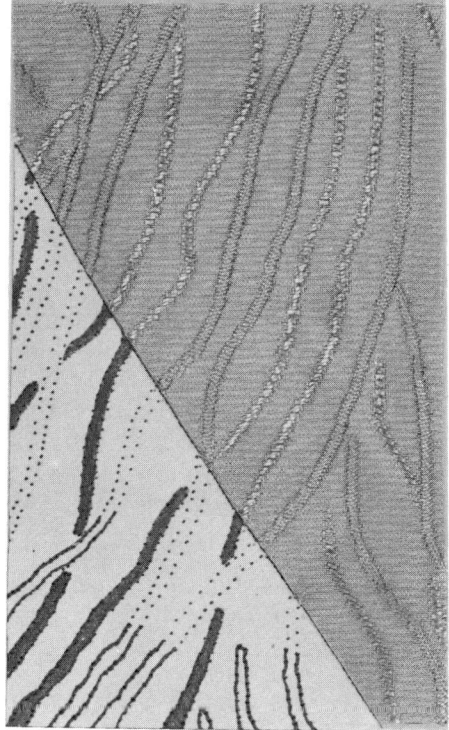

Figure 12.5

at right angles to each other, as the finishing processes have a tendency to distort the cloth, and for this reason care should be taken in dividing up the repeat to have the two series of lines parallel with the warp and weft threads respectively, or the figure will not join up correctly at the sides and at the top and bottom of the sheet of design paper. In drawing the outline on the design paper the shape of the figure should be observed in the cloth as well as in the sketch.

The construction of a sketch from a woven pattern is chiefly useful when changes in the design have to be made, and when the sketch has to be submitted for approval. If the method is used solely for the purpose of enabling a repeat to be squared out, it is really a waste of time, as other methods may be employed in which the design is made directly from the cloth.

A very quick method of squaring out woven designs is illustrated in *Figure 12.6*. An apparatus is used that consists of a wood frame A, which is nicked at regular intervals along the outer edges. Threads are passed vertically and horizontally along the under side of the frame, in such a manner that its interior is divided into small squares. The frame A rests on a flat board B, and is hinged to the latter at C, so that the opposite end of A can be raised while the pattern is placed on the board. The frame is then dropped so that

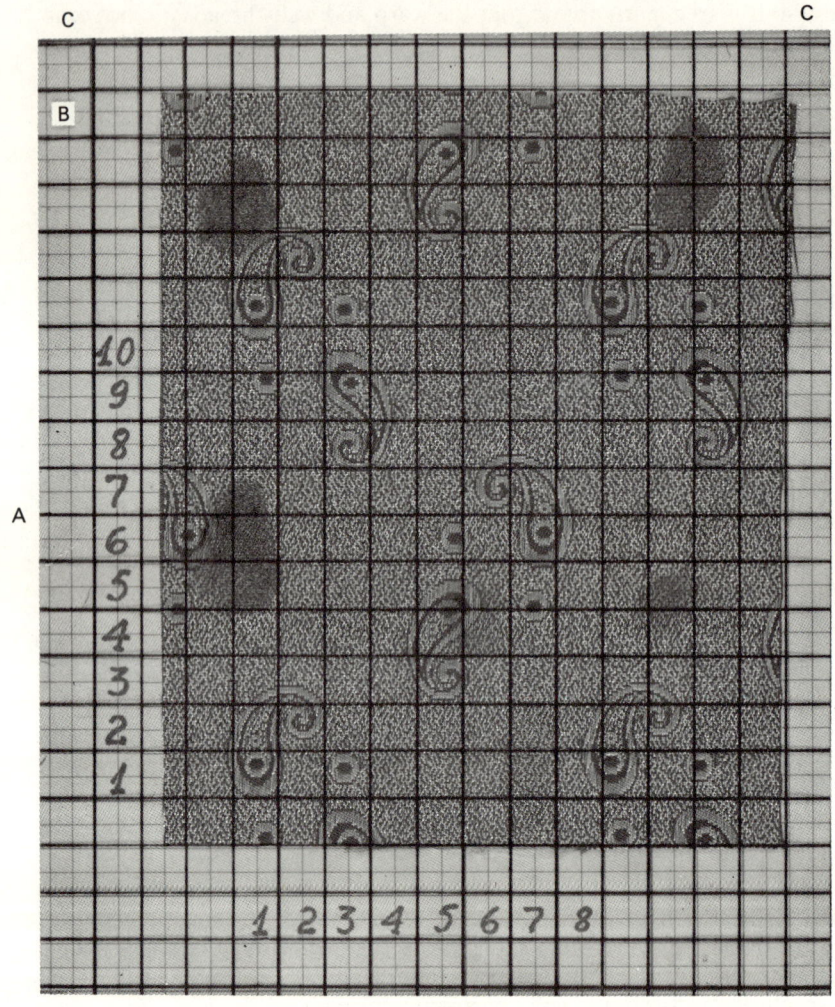

Figure 12.6

the threads rest lightly on the cloth until the latter has been drawn with a needle into such a position that the picks are parallel with the horizontal threads of the frame, and the ends parallel with the vertical threads, after which the frame is pressed down and secured with a small catch. No difficulty is found in squaring out patterns which are distorted, as the pressure of the threads retains the cloth in any position into which it has been pulled before the frame is pressed down.

The threads are wound at fixed, equal distances apart, so that surface of the cloth is divided into equal spaces. Taking the spaces to be 0·5 cm square, which is a convenient distance apart of the threads, the number of squares of the design paper, which each division of the pattern represents, may be found as follows: Assuming that a design has to be worked out at the rate of 32 ends and picks per cm, each division represents 16 squares on the design paper. Again, assuming that the pattern shown in *Figure 12.6* has to be made upon 184 ends and 174 picks—the repeat occupies $7\frac{2}{3}$ divisions in width, and $9\frac{2}{3}$ divisions in length, therefore, each division will represent $184 \div 7\frac{2}{3} = 24$ ends, and $174 \div 9\frac{2}{3} = 18$ picks. A figure is drawn on the design paper much more readily if the threads are passed across the frame in alternate colours, the design paper being then ruled, at the required intervals, with alternate colours of pencil to correspond.

DEVELOPMENT OF FIGURES

After a figure has been correctly painted in with transparent colour the next process is, usually, to insert suitable weaves upon it. The weaves should be selected with the following objects in view: (1) To produce a good texture— that is, a texture in which the threads are interwoven to such a degree that they are not liable to slip or fray when the fabric is subjected to strain and friction during wear. (2) To develop the figure in such a manner that the form is shown to the best advantage in the finished cloth.

Prevention of long floats

In some designs, of which an example is given in *Figure 12.7*, the form breaks up the mass of the figure to such a degree that no weave is required to be inserted either for stopping the floats of yarn or for developing the effect.

Figure 12.7

This condition occurs particularly when lustrous yarns are employed in forming small figures, which, if broken up too much, appear less bold and effective. *Figure 12.8* shows the squared paper design of a portion of *Figure 12.7*. The example illustrates the necessity of painting in the squares in odd numbers on the edge of a figure when plain ground, or a ground based upon plain weave, is employed, in order to ensure perfect joining of the ground weave with the figure.

When boldness of effect is required in large figures very frequently binding marks are inserted only where the floats on the face or back of the fabric will otherwise be too long. Such a method of development is illustrated by the

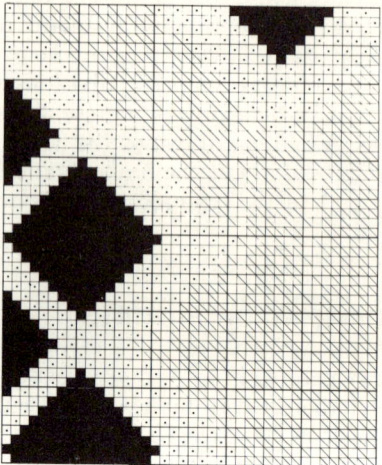

Figure 12.8

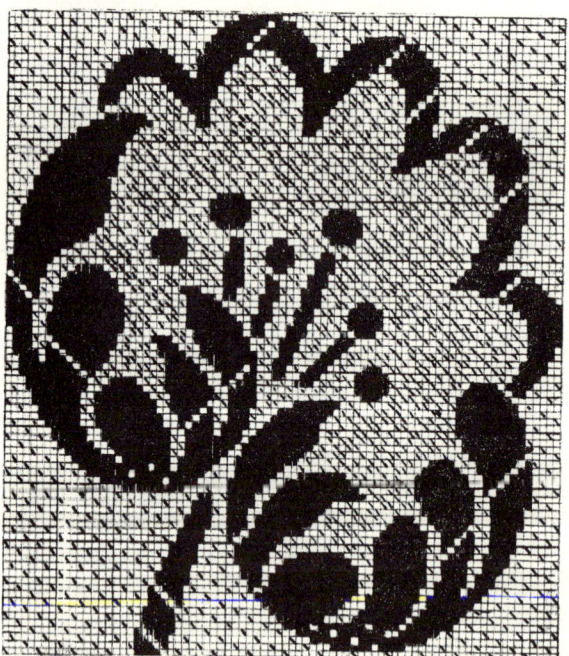

Figure 12.9

plan given in *Figure 12.9*, which represents a weft figure surrounded by warp satin ground. The example also illustrates how an open figure may be made to appear massive by inserting in the interior a weave—in this case a crêpe—which contrasts well with the ground weave (Note: marks = warp down).

Bold and flat development

In some massive styles the form can be effectively developed by inserting a large twill or sateen weave regularly over the surface of the figure, the former being employed when a lustrous and bold appearance is required, and the latter in producing a flat and less prominent effect. *Figure 12.10* shows how both twill and sateen weaves may be employed in developing the same figure,

Figure 12.10

Figure 12.11

the effect in this case being to bring out the twilled portion of each leaf more prominently and with a brighter appearance than the other portion.

Another method of developing leaves, which is similar in principle to the foregoing, is shown in *Figure 12.11*. In this example one of each pair of leaves is brought up massive and bold, while the other appears much less prominent but its distinctive shape is yet retained. The form of the bold leaf is developed (marks = warp down), by simply bringing up the veins in warp flush with a few additional binding places inserted to stop the floats which are too long. The other leaf is developed in fairly bold weft flush along the outer edges, and the interior is filled in with a four-thread weft satinette, except where the veins are shown in warp flush. This plan also shows the correct method of developing the fine lines which form the veins and stems. It is important that these show up distinctly and at the same time that they do not detract from the prominence of the main feature of the design, which in this case, is formed by the leaves.

Development of large figures

The pattern shown in *Figure 12.12* illustrates how a large number of weaves may be employed in developing a massive figure. The contrast in the appearance and the variation in the light and shade of the different weaves give interest to the effect, and assist in showing up the parts of the form clearly.

Figure 12.12

Figure 12.13

A design paper plan of a figure of this type is given in *Figure 12.13* (convention reversed). Such a combination of weaves in one figure is specially suitable for fabrics composed of dull warp and lustrous weft, which, if woven with plain ground, should be set with from 24 to 32 ends and picks per cm to show the detail clearly.

The design shown in *Figure 12.14* is in decided contrast to the preceding example as here only one weave is employed in developing the figure. Such a weave can only be suitably applied to a massive style, in which considerable latitude may be taken in following the outline. A portion of squared paper design given in *Figure 12.15* shows clearly that the figure is developed in the form of solid areas of plain weave separated from each other by a loose and open outline obtained through the use of mock leno structure. The general

Figure 12.14

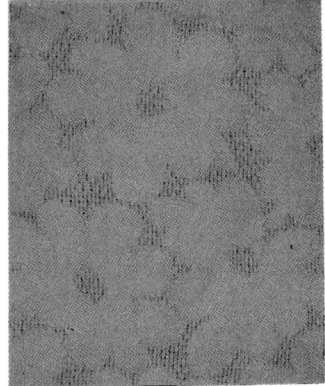

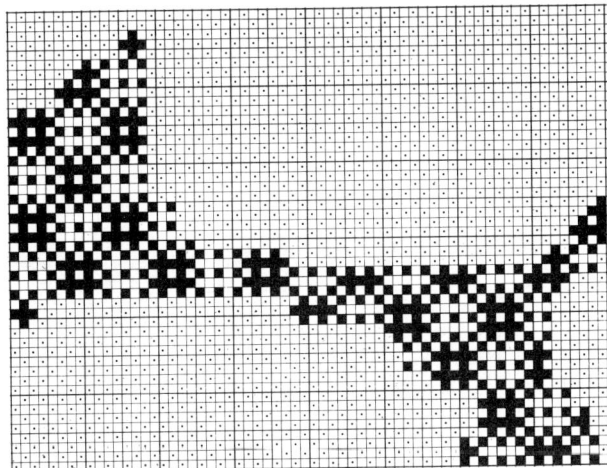

Figure 12.15

effect is that of an opaque figure on transparent ground, and the manner of development employed achieves a distinctly flat appearance which is characteristic of all designs in which only two weaves arranged in well defined areas are utilised.

Use of warp and weft float in figure development

The development of a figure in both warp and weft float is illustrated in *Figure 12.16*. This method is particularly applicable to cloths in which there is a good degree of contrast between the colours of warp and weft. A squared paper design of a portion of *Figure 12.16* is given in *Figure 12.17*. In drafting a figure formed in warp and weft float, the outline is drawn in the ordinary way, then the warp float is indicated in one colour and the weft float is either left blank, or, it may be painted in another colour. In the example given the warp figure is indicated by solid marks and the weft figure by shaded squares.

Figure 12.16

Floats of excessive length in either the warp or the weft faced areas are stopped by the opposite marks and the ground weave, or weaves, are indicated by colours or marks which are different from those used for the figure. It will be appreciated that as in *Figure 12.17* all marks, except the shaded squares, indicate warp up the card cutting instructions will be: cut all marks except the shaded squares.

It will be observed from *Figures 12.16* and *12.17* that the ground weave in this cloth is an 8-shaft warp satin (indicated by dots), and as this is a warp

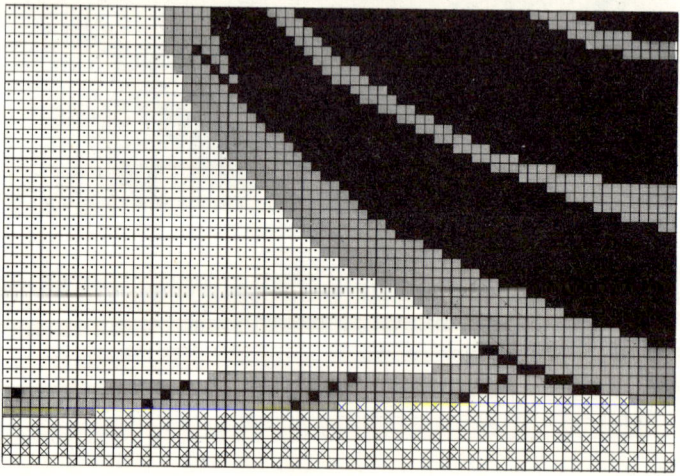

Figure 12.17

faced structure it must be rigidly separated from the warp float figure in order to achieve the necessary clarity of effect. This is achieved by ensuring that the outer outline of the figure is invariably composed of the weft float. An auxiliary effect in a rib weave surrounds the main figure and this is indicated by the crosses in *Figure 12.17*.

Figure shading

The shaded development of figures enables different degrees of light and shade to be obtained in a graduated manner, so that a natural form—flower, leaf, etc., can be represented in a natural way. In *Figure 12.18* the petals of a flower and the body of a bird are shaded so as to form a subdued but pleasing contrast with the parts which are developed in bold floats. The principle is applied most successfully to fine textures composed of smooth and even yarns.

Figure 12.18

The most common forms of shading are produced by using a twill or sateen weave as the base and varying the floats of weft and warp, as shown in *Figures 12.19* and *12.20*. For instance, a 6-thread twill basis enables five changes to be made i.e., 1-and-5, 2-and-4, 3-and-3, 4-and-2, and 5-and-1, as shown at A in *Figure 12.19*. The space to be shaded, in this case 36 ends, is divided into five sections, and the 1-and-5 twill is marked in, as shown by the crosses. The first section is left as it is, one mark is added in the 2nd section, two marks in the 3rd, three marks in the 4th, and four marks in the 5th, with the result that the weft float is gradually reduced, and the warp float correspondingly increased, and 5 degrees of light and shade are produced.

In the method shown at A in *Figure 12.19*, the warp and weft are brought about equally to the surface of the cloth, hence both series of threads should be of good quality. B illustrates a shaded weave, based upon six threads, which is suitable for shading a cloth in which, taking the marks to indicate warp, the warp is better material than the weft. There is less variation in light and shade, however, than in the former method. The 1-and-5 twill, indicated by the crosses, is changed to the 1-and-2, 2-and-1, 5-and-1, and 11-and-1 twills in succeeding sections. The last weave is suitable to use in forming the edge of a figure when a prominent outline is required.

C in *Figure 12.19* shows, in the first three sections, how a 4-thread twill may be changed from weft to warp surface, and, in the 4th section, to 7-and-1 twill.

In the form of shading shown at D in *Figure 12.19*, the floats on the face are arranged to fit with plain ground. This method is suitable for fabrics in which only one yarn shows prominently on the face. The end section shows how the 4-thread twill may be changed to the 8-thread satin.

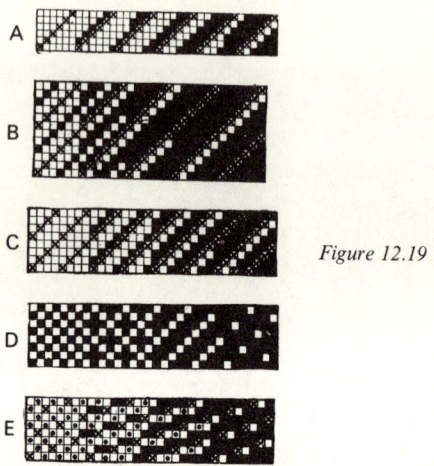

Figure 12.19

E in *Figure 12.19* illustrates the principle of shading the 8-thread satin to fit with plain ground. The 10-thread satin may be shaded in a similar manner.

F and G in *Figure 12.20* show two methods of shading the 8-thread sateen weave, each of which gives seven degrees of light and shade. The sateen base weave is indicated by the crosses; in F the marks are added at the top, and in

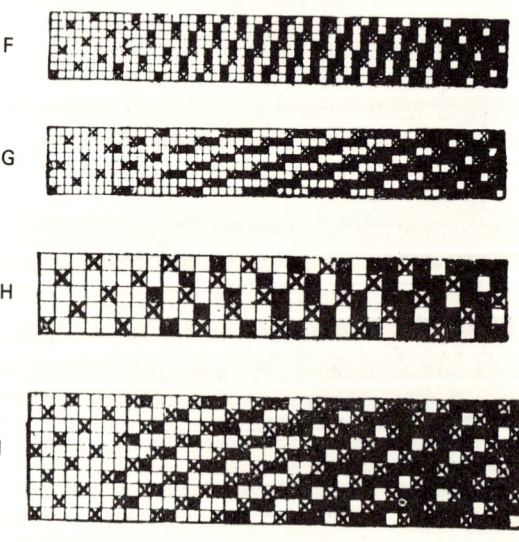

Figure 12.20

G at the side of the base marks. A comparison of the warp and weft floats in the centre five sections of F and G will show that the method of adding the marks influences the appearance of the weave. In F the marks are arranged mainly in the vertical direction and, therefore, this method is used when it is intended to display the warp on the surface, whilst the method shown in G is employed when it is desired to show the weft, as the horizontal arrangement of marks tends to make the weft more prominent than the warp.

H and I in *Figure 12.20* illustrate two methods of shading applied to the 5-sateen weave. In H the marks are added to the top of the base marks, and four degrees of light and shade are formed. I is similar to H except that the marks are added at the side, while the 5-sateen is changed to the 10-satin in the end section in order to give further variety.

Double shading

The examples given in *Figures 12.19* and *12.20* illustrate the principles upon which figure areas are shaded, but in the form shown, the designs may be used on their own in the production of shaded weave stripes. Only single-shading, however, is represented—that is, the weaves are shaded only in one direction, so that a complete change from weft to warp surface is made where

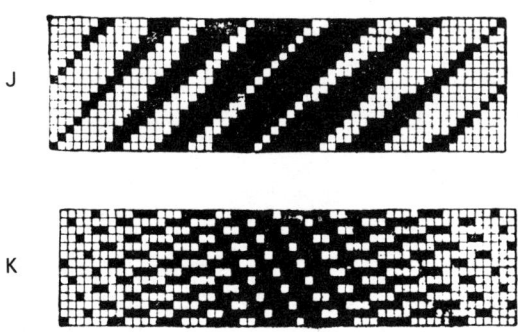

Figure 12.21

the first and last ends join. In double-shading, which is illustrated at J and K in *Figure 12.21*, the severe contrast in light and shade, produced in single-shading, is avoided, as the weaves gradually merge into each other in both directions. J shows the combination of 8-thread twills, running from 1-and-7 to 7-and-1 by adding one mark more in each section, and then back again to 1-and-7 by subtracting one mark in each section. K in *Figure 12.21* is based upon a 7-thread sateen weave, and is constructed in a similar manner to J, the additional marks being placed at the side of the base marks.

Shaded development of figures

Figure 12.22 illustrates, step by step, the method of developing a figure in 5-sateen weaves as a shaded effect after the outline of the figure has been indicated on the design paper. (1) As shown at A, the space to be shaded is divided into as many sections as there are changes in the base weave, and the latter is inserted entirely over the space. The sections need not be equal in size as the given space may be divided up unequally so as to allow either warp or weft to predominate on the surface. (2) As shown at **B**, the weave in the first section is left as it is, and a mark is added to each sateen mark in the 2nd, 3rd, and 4th sections. (3) As indicated at C, a second mark is added in the 3rd and 4th sections; and (4) as shown at D, a third mark is added in the 4th section.

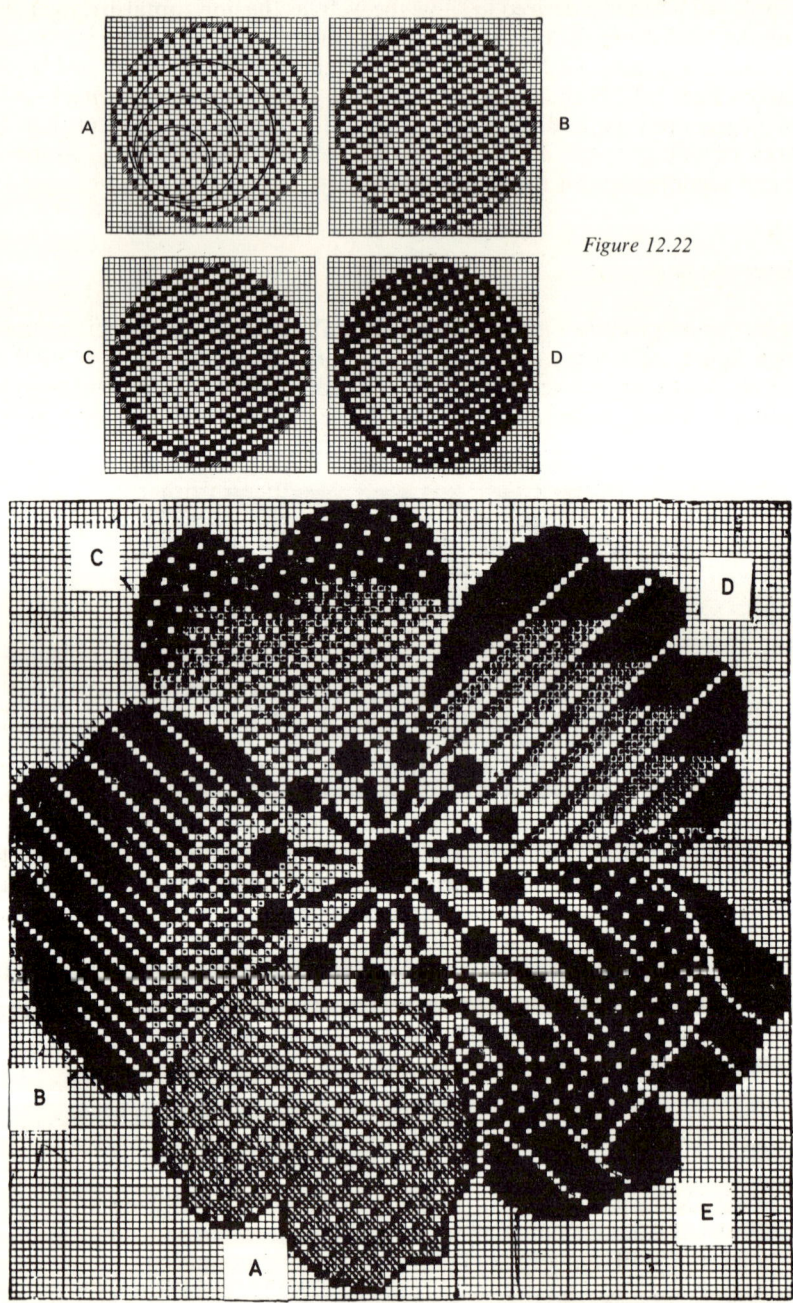

Figure 12.22

Figure 12.23

It is better to add the marks always at the same side of the base marks, and it is usually more convenient to add them gradually, as shown, than to paint over the whole of the figure in one colour, and put in the shaded weave in a second colour.

For the purpose of illustration, several different methods of shading a figure are shown in *Figure 12.23*. At A the 8-sateen weave is employed for the base, and the warp is brought mostly to the surface. The twill method of shading, indicated at B, is suitable for a somewhat coarse texture in which a plain ground, or a ground weave based upon plain, is employed. The binding of the figure in twill order brings out the effect more boldly than when a sateen weave is employed. The shading shown at C is based upon the 5 thread sateen, and as this weave is firmer in structure than the 8-thread sateen, it may be used in a lower texture than the latter. Boldness of outline and variety of effect are obtained in C by changing the 5-sateen to the 10-satin along the outer edge of the figure. At D the 6-thread twill is employed as the base; this weave being changed to the 11-and-1 twill along the outer edge of the figure. A, B, C, and D correspond with the methods illustrated in *Figures 12.19* and *12.20*; but E shows another system of development, which is sometimes employed when boldness and variety of effect are required. The 8-satin weave about the centre of E produces a rather flat effect compared with the outer edge and the shaded portion of the figure.

INSERTION OF GROUND WEAVES

The difference in appearance between the figure and ground of a design is due chiefly to contrasting weave development of the two areas; the distinction should always be sufficiently pronounced for the figure to show clearly. Therefore, it is usually necessary to avoid weaves that will produce a bold effect in the ground areas, in order that the prominence of the figure will not be reduced.

Printed ground weaves

Design paper can be purchased upon which the most commonly used ground weaves are printed in small dots, as shown at A, B, and C in *Figure 12.24*.

Figure 12.24

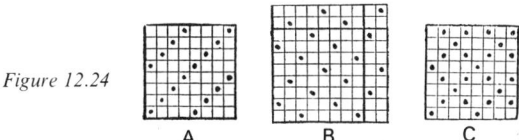

A   B   C

The 1-and-3 twill dot shown at A is chiefly employed for plain and 1-and-3 twill grounds. In addition to enabling the cards to be cut without laboriously filling in the ground weave, the dots enable the outline of the figure to be easily painted in so as to fit with the ground weave.

Joining of figure and ground

In using design paper upon which the 5-sateen weave is printed, as shown at B in *Figure 12.24*, certain of the ground dots that are in contact with the edge of the figure require to be taken out, in order that a proper junction will be made between the figure and the ground. Also, when this causes a float of more than five to be formed it is necessary for the float to be broken by the insertion of an additional mark. This is illustrated by the design shown in

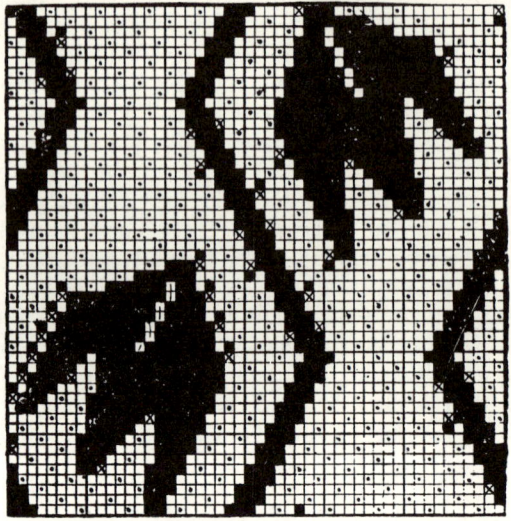

Figure 12.25

Figure 12.25, which is arranged with the lines of the figure running at different angles. The crosses indicate the dots which require to be taken out, and the full squares the marks which are then inserted to stop the long warp floats (marks = weft up) which would otherwise appear as stitching marks on the face of the cloth. In inserting any ground weave which does not fit with the moves at the edge of the figure, modifications require to be

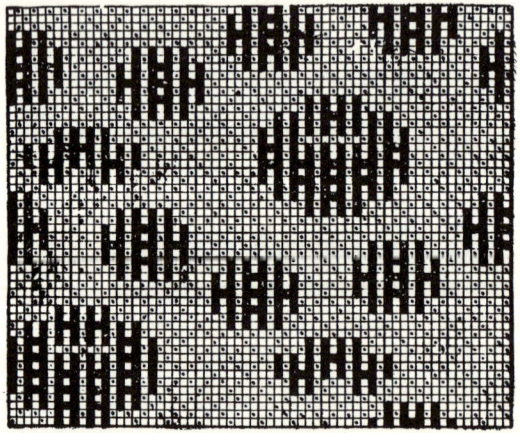

Figure 12.26

made at the junction of the figure and ground, as shown in *Figure 12.25*, in order to stop floats that are too long, and to ensure that a clear edge to the figure is formed.

The style of printed design paper, shown at C in *Figure 12.24*, is chiefly used for ordinary fabrics woven with plain ground, in place of the 1-and-3 twill dotted paper. It is, however, specially useful in designing for plain ground cloths in which alternate warp threads are composed of a special yarn which is employed in forming the figure. The dots serve as a guide in painting in the warp figure to fit with the plain ground, and also enable the figuring threads to be readily distinguished from the others. The design shown in *Figure 12.26* illustrates these points, and shows how the dots on the alternate even threads should be modified under the figure to prevent the formation of long floats of weft on the back of the cloth.

Crêpe ground weaves

The insertion of ground weaves of a crêpe character, such as those shown at D and E in *Figure 12.27*, is usually a tedious process unless a special method of working is employed. A careful examination will usually show that the weave marks have not been put together in a haphazard fashion in a crêpe,

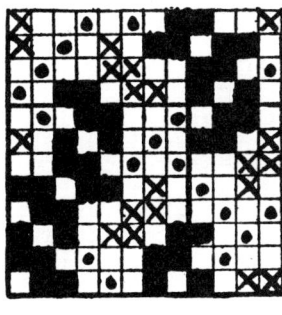

D   E

Figure 12.27

but that a definite system of construction has been employed which can be made use of in filling in the weave as a ground effect. In the examples different marks are used for the different parts of the weaves, in order that in each the basis of construction may be more readily seen. Thus both D and E are arranged on the turnover or reversed principle, and by inserting the weaves, step by step, in the order in which the different marks are indicated a complex effect may be made to appear simple, as the different parts can be put together from memory. For example, the weave shown at E may be inserted at four stages. First, that portion of the weave which is shown by the full squares is filled in over the required surface. This is followed by the portion indicated by the crosses, and the ground at this stage has a diagonal appearance, which is afterwards converted into a diamond shape by inserting the portion shown by the circles. The space which remains is then readily filled in by inserting the weave represented by the dots.

When the different parts of a figure are detached from each other, so that a fair amount of ground space is left between them, the method shown in *Figure 12.28* may be adopted with advantage in inserting a difficult weave. The ground weave is first indicated upon a separate piece of point-paper cut the full width of the design, and upon a convenient number of picks. A line is then drawn as close to the figure as is convenient for the correct joining of the figure with the ground, and the ground is inserted around the figure within the lines. Commencing with the first portion of the design the ground sheet of point paper is doubled to fit the space in which there is no ground inserted, and it is pinned to the design until the cards have been cut from this

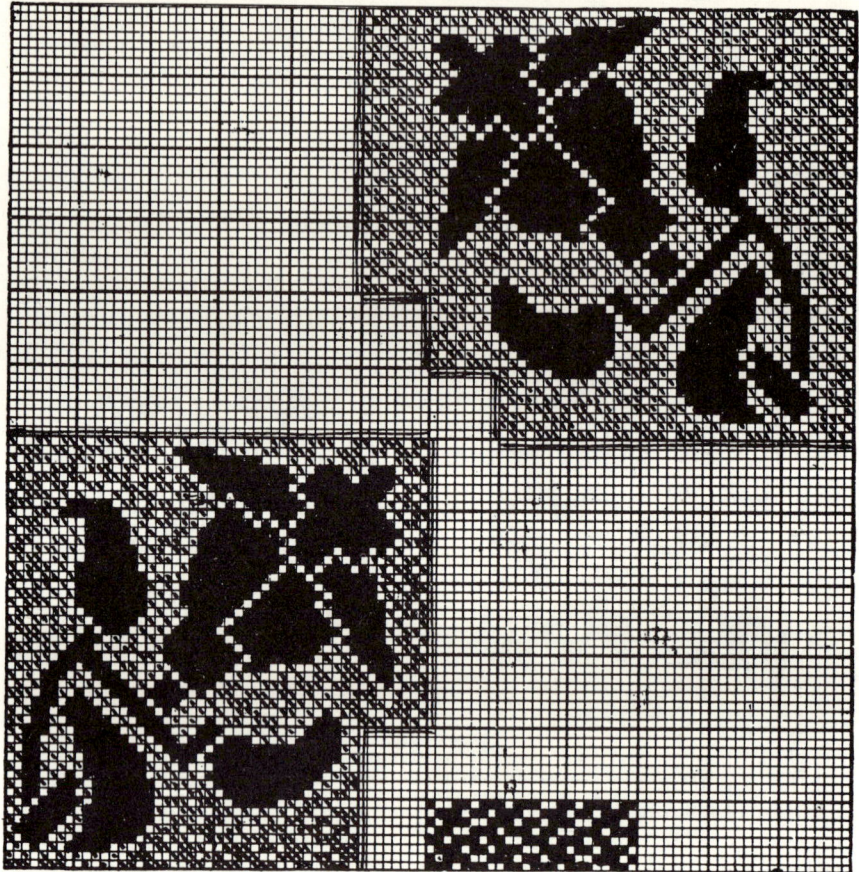

Figure 12.28

section. It is then moved to the next position, redoubled (if necessary) to fit the space between the parts of the figure, and another section of the design is cut, the process being repeated until the cutting is completed.

Stencilling ground weaves

In another method of inserting difficult ground weaves, the weave is indicated upon a separate piece of design paper, and small holes are punched in the squares where marks are shown. The separate piece is then placed on the design sheet and brushed over with a wash of colour, and the process is repeated until the whole of the ground has been stencilled in except at the edges of the figure. The joining of the ground and the figure is afterwards readily effected.

The value of an automatic arrangement for the insertion of the ground weaves will be readily appreciated at this point and in modern systems once the figure area has been carefully marked, repetition of the ground weave can be frequently left to the special card cutting machine provided with a mechanical selector.

CORRECT AND INCORRECT DESIGN DRAFTING

The chief points to note in painting in a figure on the design paper are (1) to form a good outline, and (2) to have the figure sufficiently massive and without weak places caused by fine lines. To obtain these results it is not always advisable to strictly follow the outline drawing, but to modify the form of the figure in painting it in. Typical illustrations of defective and good design paper work are given for comparison at A and B in *Figure 12.29*. In A the outline is defective because, in following the curves—say, in moving from the horizontal or the perpendicular to the angle of 45°, as shown at 1—the moves are not properly graduated. For example, commencing with the bottom pick of the figure shown at A, a float of 8 is followed by moves of 3, 4, 2, 3, 1, 2, on succeeding picks. The proper outline, as shown at B, is obtained by moves of 4, 3, 3, 2, 2, 1; that is, the distance moved at each succeeding pick is gradually reduced as the curve approaches the angle of 45°, after which the distance moved is gradually increased on succeeding ends until the perpendicular is reached.

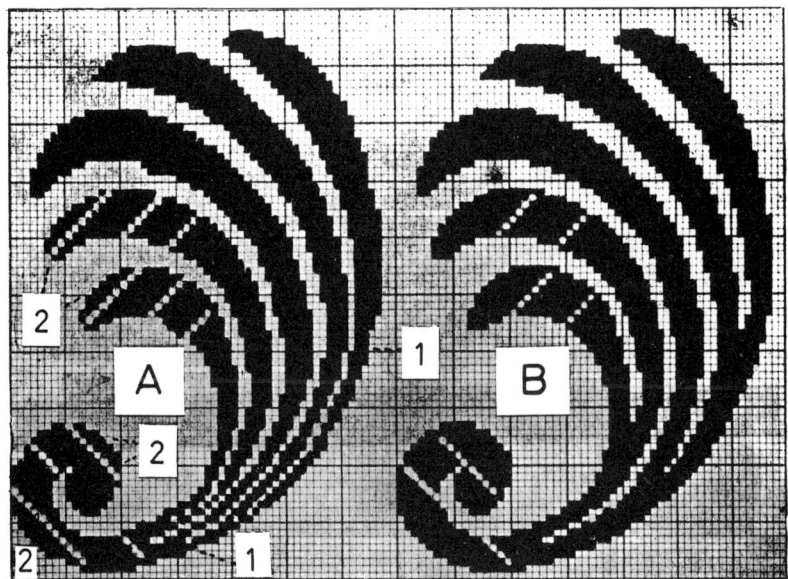

Figure 12.29

In binding the long floats of the figure in twill order, a good outline and mass may be made weak if the binding weave is inserted too near the edge of the figure. This defect is shown at the places marked 2 in A, *Figure 12.29*, whereas B shows the binding weave inserted in such positions on the figure that the outline and mass are preserved. Further, a comparison of the lower portion of A and B will show how weakness of outline and of mass, due to fine lines, may be avoided.

An unsuitable method of designing a figure on the point-paper is sometimes the cause of an otherwise well-balanced design showing a line or bar in the woven effect. This may occur under the following conditions: (1) When both the warp and weft yarns are floated in turn on the face of the fabric, or when two colours of warp or weft are used in producing the figure, without sufficient care being taken to ensure that each kind of float is regularly distributed. The defect is made more pronounced when there is a strong contrast between the figuring colours. (2) When a horizontal section of the design is given a longer float, and consequently made to show more prominently than the succeeding section, although there may be an equal amount of ornament in each section. (3) When the ground of the fabric is very firmly woven, the ground picks which precede and follow a portion of figure, tend to crowd the loosely bound picks

Figure 12.30

of the latter together, and barriness is thus promoted, because the space occupied by the figure is reduced. In the texture shown in *Figure 12.30*, a wavy bar appears, which may be said to be due to the combined influences of the preceding. In one section of the cloth the bar has been deliberately darkened in order to emphasise the effect that it produces in the design. As shown in the corresponding portion of design given in *Figure 12.31* the leaves are developed in warp float, which instead of being regularly distributed,

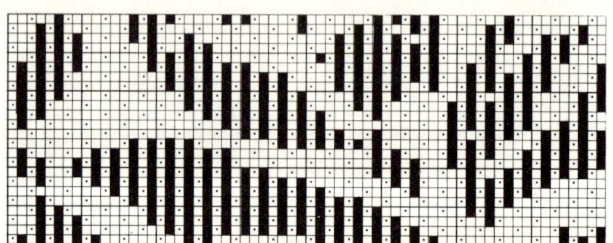

Figure 12.31

occurs in broad bands. This arrangement creates a gap between the bands, which, although undulating, shows quite distinctly. Furthermore, as the warp float along the line of the gap is all on the back of the cloth it tends to pull it up into a welt thus emphasising its presence more clearly. A suitable method of improving the design would be to incline the figure so that the gap was bridged at several points with the warp floats thus interrupting continuity of the bar.

The construction of a design upon squared paper can, in most cases, be greatly simplified by employing a method of working that is appropriate to the basis upon which the design is constructed. For this reason, in the following chapters, the designing of figures upon the recognised bases is considered along with convenient methods of design paper construction.

COMPOSITION OF DESIGNS

Methods of composing jacquard designs

There are three chief ways in which figure designs for textile fabrics are composed, viz.:
  (1) By geometric ornamentation.
  (2) By the conventional treatment of natural or artificial forms.
  (3) By the adaptation or reproduction of earlier designs.
  (1) Designs which are purely geometric in form result from the embellishment of intersecting vertical, horizontal, diagonal, circular, and radiating lines; and from the creation of spaces by the lines. Such designs may include conventionalised forms, or they may be adaptations of earlier styles.
  (2) In 'conventionalising' a natural or artificial object the form is treated in a manner that renders it a suitable ornamental feature of the texture upon which it is displayed. It is generally necessary to simplify the form of an

Figure 12.32

object, only the essential and characteristic features being abstracted; and, as a rule, the most important and beautiful parts are emphasised at the same time that they are made subservient to the general arrangement of the design. Realistic treatment in the cloth, except in such textures as 'woven pictures', should not be practised beyond what will assist in showing the form to advantage. As an example, the conventional treatment of leaves is illustrated in *Figure 12.32* (which represents a cotton furnishing fabric), in which the 'weave development' imparts a certain degree of realism to the form. The different weaves in the figure have the effect of showing the ornament more clearly by causing the light to be reflected in a varying manner from the different parts. If all the figure had been treated in the same way it would have appeared flat and uninteresting, and would have been less suitable for the purpose of the cloth. In contrast with *Figure 12.32*, the flat treatment of a flower is illustrated in *Figure 12.14*, which suits the structure and purpose of the cloth, and the means by which it has been woven.

In some cases woven forms are used to convey a meaning, as in representations of the thistle, the shamrock, a lover's knot, etc., the term 'symbolic' being then applied to the treatment. Most frequently, however, the sole object of employing conventional forms is to beautify the material, in which case, the treatment is termed 'aesthetic'. Sometimes, conventionalised natural forms are combined with forms that are 'invented', as shown in *Figure 13.4*, while again designs are sometimes composed entirely of abstract forms.

(3) The adaptation of earlier designs has been practised from the earliest periods, and it may be said that almost all modern styles have resulted from previous ones by the process of evolution. 'To adapt' is a more rational method of procedure than to endeavour to work entirely originally by putting aside all that has been previously accomplished. There are innumerable ways in which former designs may be modified and applied; by small variations new styles may be gradually evolved which finally possess few of the original features.

The term 'traditional' is applied to ornament which has been handed down from age to age without losing its original characteristics, although it may have been modified from time to time to suit the requirements of different periods. More or less exact reproductions of historic designs are yet made from famous rugs, tapestries, altar cloths, etc., while copies of recent designs are made by competitors in the same market, and when similar effects are required in cloths that are cheaper than the originals. At the present time, however, designs are most frequently adapted from cloths with the idea of reproducing the ornament in a new form.

Conditions to observe in designing figured fabrics

The following is a summary of the principal conditions that have to be observed in designing figured fabrics:

(1) The ornament should be applicable to the construction of the cloth, the nature of the materials employed, and the mechanical means of production, and be suitable for the purpose of the fabric. A style of ornament, that is appropriate to one class of cloth, may be quite unsuited to another class; the same form may, however, be suitable for different classes of cloths, but it may require to be treated in a different manner in each case.

(2) With some few exceptions, the ornament should be chiefly in solid form or mass, and not in outline. The structure of a woven texture makes it necessary for even the finest lines of a design to be massive (to a greater or lesser degree according to the cloth) in order that they will show in proper contrast with the ground.

(3) One complete repeat of a design (as in all mechanically repeated designs) must be capable of being enclosed within a rectangular space, the boundary lines of which correspond vertically and horizontally with the direction of the warp and weft threads. The rectangular shape makes it necessary for all textile designs to conform, to some extent, to a geometric basis of construction, but the ornament itself need not be geometrical.

(4) The ornament must join perfectly at the top and bottom, and at the sides of the repeat, in order that when the design is repeated longitudinally and transversely, the pattern will be continuous and unbroken. 'Woven squares', in which the ends and sides are not required to join, as in carpets and tablecloths, are an exception to this rule, but usually in these cloths a central figure is required to join to a border. In stripe designs it is only necessary to ensure that the figure joins correctly at the top and bottom of the repeat. This is illustrated in *Figure 12.44*, the dotted horizontal line in which indicates the position where repetition occurs. The width of a stripe must, however, be suitable for the repeat in width of the complete design, while the figures in each stripe must be in proper relation to those in the neighbouring stripes.

(5) The ornament should be properly balanced. A design is defective if the repetition of the figure causes vertical, horizontal, or diagonal lines to be formed in the cloth when such are not desired. Uniform distribution of the primary masses is first necessary, then any details that are added should be arranged to give even balance of the ground spaces. The analysis of good textile designs will show that the orderly arrangement of the parts is almost invariably due to certain bases or principles having been employed in their construction. Previous to sketching a design, base lines may be drawn within the rectangular repeat area in order to divide the latter into spaces in systematic order. The lines of the figure can be arranged to follow distinctly the base lines, or the latter may be partly or entirely eliminated. In the last case the use of the base lines is simply to ensure that proper balance and accurate repetition are secured.

Factors which influence woven design

In textile fabrics the style of the ornament and the way in which it should be developed are largely influenced by the following:
(1) The purpose of the cloth.
(2) The comparative smoothness, lustre, fineness, and sett (or number per unit space) of the threads.
(3) The mechanical means of production.
(4) The kind of finish that is applied to the cloth.

(1) The effect that the purpose of a cloth has upon the style of ornamentation will be readily evident from a comparison of figured textures that are in regular use such as, carpets, hangings, table-cloths, bed-covers, dress fabrics, mantles, etc. A fabric that is used to cover a flat surface, and is observed from many different points of view, requires different decorative treatment from a texture that has to hang in folds; while the necessity to cut up cloths for certain uses will render a particular style of ornament totally unfit, whereas another style is quite appropriate.

The use to which a cloth is to be applied, in many cases, largely influences its structure, and the ornament requires to be adapted to the structure as well as the use. Further, cloths that are used for similar purposes may vary extremely in structure, and different treatment of the ornament may be necessary in each case.

(2) Filament yarn fabrics, owing to the lustrous nature of the material, the smoothness and fineness of the threads, and the large number of threads per unit space that are generally employed, lend themselves in the highest degree to elaborate figure ornamentation. It is possible in these fabrics, to obtain extreme fineness of detail, but, as a general rule, the rich, lustrous quality of the material is displayed to the greatest advantage by treating the ornament boldly, and varying the weave development of the figure in the manner illustrated by the example given in *Figure 12.33*.

Figure 12.33

Elaborate ornamentation and minute weave detail of the type shown in *Figure 12.33* can also be introduced in fibre yarn fabrics that are fine in structure and finished with a clear surface. On the other hand, in coarse fabrics fine weave variations cannot be introduced. In order to illustrate how the relative number of threads per unit space in a cloth influences the weave development and the amount of detail that can be used in a design, a portion of the figure, represented in *Figure 12.33*, is shown worked out on design paper in *Figures 12.34* and *12.35*. *Figure 12.34* shows the figure drafted on 8 × 10 design paper which corresponds with the sett of 38 ends and 48 picks per cm, whereas in *Figure 12.35* the sett is taken as 26 ends and 26 picks per cm. The plans will produce exactly the same size of figure in the respective setts; but while in the finer structure it is possible to get a figure intricately developed and graceful in outline, in the coarser fabric the curves of the figure turn more rapidly, and there are fewer spaces to work upon, so that it is necessary for simpler treatment to be employed. The example, further, is illustrative of the adaptation of a design from a fine to a coarser fabric.

Certain special classes of materials require specialised treatment, e.g.—in figuring with mohair or other coarse but lustrous yarns it is desirable that the brightness of the material be developed as much as possible. These yarns are frequently employed in conjunction with cotton yarns, and the cloths are not usually fine in structure. The ornament, as a rule, should be developed boldly in fairly long floats of the lustrous threads. A cloth of this type is represented in *Figure 12.36*, and a portion of the design to correspond is given in *Figure 12.37*. The ground weave is plain which ensures that the prominence of the

Figure 12.34

main lines of the figure is not detracted from. The warp is arranged with 1 end of mercerised cotton alternating with 1 end of ordinary cotton and only the lustrous mercerised cotton ends are used in forming the figure. The ground

Figure 12.35

assumes a ribbed appearance due to lifting of the different sets of ends on alternate picks but where the figure is formed the ordinary cotton ends are made to weave plain by themselves underneath the figure to prevent the formation of unsightly weft floats on the reverse side of the fabric. In *Figure 12.37* lifts of the lustrous ends are indicated by the solid marks and lifts of the ordinary ends by the dots.

(3) The mechanical means employed in producing cloths impose very varying limitations, and an intimate knowledge of the type of loom and loom

Figure 12.36

mounting that will be employed is essential to successful designing for most classes of fabrics. Brief consideration will, in most cases, enable the limitations to be realised. For instance, in a plain box loom only one kind or colour of weft can be employed, and in a loom with changing boxes at only one end,

Figure 12.37

the picks of each kind of weft require to be inserted in even numbers; while the number of boxes limits the number of different kinds of weft that can be used.

Different types of shedding mechanism have different limitations: A dobby will operate only a certain number of healds; the size of repeat of a jacquard is limited; only a certain maximum number of ends per unit space can be woven in a given harness; a certain harness tie compels a definite form of ornamentation; a combination of healds with a harness limits the order in which certain ends can be operated; in jacquards and harnesses that are specially constructed to produce certain weave structures prescribed orders of interlacing are necessary, etc.

(4) The influence of the finish that is applied to a cloth, in deciding the style of ornament and weave development that are suitable, will be understood by comparing a figured rug which has a raised surface with a clear finished cloth. The pile or nap, formed on the surface by raising, completely conceals the thread structure, so that the introduction of fancy weaves or fine detail in the figure is useless, and only flat massive ornament is suitable.

Construction of sketch designs

In sketching a jacquard design the width of repeat that is employed should be equal to, or a factor of that of the machine in which the design will be

Figure 12.38

woven. The size of a design can be readily increased or decreased in the process of drafting the figure from the sketch, but obviously the nearer the repeat of the design is to the proper size, the truer is the resemblance of the woven effect to the original sketch. It is frequently very difficult to guard against the formation of improper stripes or bars in the cloth if only one repeat of a sketch design is made, a defect sometimes not becoming visible until the figure is repeated in width and length in the loom. As a general rule, therefore, it is advisable to roughly sketch several repeats of a design in each direction in order that the relation of the different parts of the ornament to each other in succeeding repeats may be seen. A simple illustration is given in *Figure 12.38* which will serve as a general indication of the method of preparing a sketch of a repeating figure. A number of rectangular spaces (in this case two in each direction) are first marked out by drawing lines at the proper distances apart to give the required size of repeat. A vertical waved line is used as the basis of construction in the example, and as this naturally divides the design into two similar parts, each repeat is bisected by drawing vertical and horizontal lines through the centre. The waved line is then drawn in, as shown at A, and repeated in every repeat of the sketch. The chief feature of the ornament, or the 'mass', is next introduced, as shown at B, and here great care is necessary. The lines that bisect the repeats enable the position of each mass to be correctly judged, so that approximately equal spaces, in every direction, between the masses, are obtained. When the masses have been traced into each repeat their relative positions can be still more accurately observed, and any imperfection of balance remedied. The next process is the introduction of the detail, as shown as C, and this should be less pronounced in character than the main object, in order that the prominence of the latter will not be detracted from. The detail should be added and copied into each repeat by degrees until the design is complete, care being taken that the different parts balance each other and produce a regular distribution of figure in any given straight line of the sketch.

After a rough drawing of the complete effect has been made over the given number of repeats, it is only necessary for the outline in one repeat to be filled in, as shown at D, for the purpose of indicating how the design should be developed on the squared paper. The last process is necessary only when the sketch is required to be exhibited for approval, as the necessary development can be indicated upon the figure in painting out the design on the squared paper. In the portion D of *Figure 12.38* the places where the figure may be developed in bold float have been accentuated.

Design unit and design repeat

The difference between the unit and the repeat of a design should be clearly understood. In some designs the repeat is formed of one unit. This class of design is illustrated by the example given at A in *Figure 12.39*, in which the unit, forming one complete repeat, is shown shaded. In the same manner, in the design given in *Figure 12.1*, the unit and the repeat are the same.

When a portion of figure is used two or more times in producing a complete design, the unit forms only part of the repeat. Thus, in B, *Figure 12.39*, the portion shown shaded may be taken as the unit, which is used twice in the repeat. Also the unit forms half of the repeat of the design shown in *Figure*

12.28. In C, *Figure 12.39*, the unit, which is again shown shaded, is used eight times in the repeat of the design. A unit figure may thus be used practically any number of times in forming a design, and it may be of any shape, but if it is not rectangular in shape it must be so arranged that the complete repeat of the design is rectangular.

GEOMETRIC ORNAMENTATION

All textile designs require to be so far constructed on geometrical lines as to enable one exact repeat to be enclosed within a rectangular space, at one edge of which the ornament joins correctly with that at the opposite edge. A distinction may, however, be made between the construction of designs, such

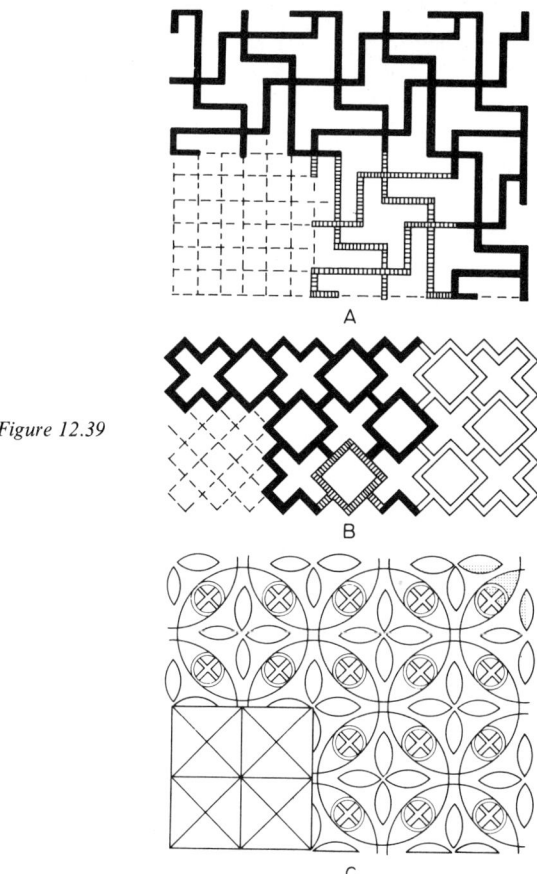

Figure 12.39

as are shown in *Figure 12.39*, which are purely geometric; and those in which the parts of the ornament consist of shapes in which no geometric form is visible, though the basis of arrangement may be of a geometric character. The purely geometric designs can be regarded, basically, as extensions of the basket, twill and diamond effects, which due to their size require the jacquard system of shedding.

At A in *Figure 12.39*, the square is used as the base of construction, as shown by the dotted lines. The design is constructed simply by thickening certain portions of the base lines and leaving other parts blank. This style of ornamentation is chiefly suitable for cloths in which special threads, arranged

Figure 12.40

at regular intervals, are employed in forming the figure. A similar design to A is given in *Figure 10.18*, while such designs as those shown in *Figures 10.19* and *10.21* are readily constructed on the square basis to fit a given order of warping and wefting.

B in *Figure 12.39* shows a simple geometrical design constructed upon a diamond basis, the lines of which are thickened and left blank in the same manner as in A. The design given in *Figure 12.40* shows sketch B fully developed, the solid black figure corresponding with the lines of the sketch,

Figure 12.41

while the grey marks illustrate a method of filling in the ground spaces to give variety to the effect at the same time achieving firmer interlacing.

C in *Figure 12.39* shows in the bottom left-hand corner, a repeat divided into rectangles, diamonds, and triangles, which, in most cases, is sufficient to enable very elaborate geometric designs to be made. The design C is constructed by describing circles and arcs of circles, with the intersecting points of the lines taken as centres.

The base lines of the design given in *Figure 12.41* correspond with the vertical, horizontal, and diagonal lines shown in the bottom left-hand corner of C in *Figure 12.39*. This example illustrates the 'counter-change' principle of construction—the weft float in one diamond space corresponding with the warp float in the other.

Figure 12.42

Figure 12.42 shows a suitable method of developing the design given at C in *Figure 12.39*. The design of a bordered fabric, shown in *Figure 11.21* is constructed upon vertical, horizontal, diagonal, and circular base lines, similar to those shown at C in *Figure 12.39*.

The use of any form of squared paper is very convenient in designing purely geometric forms, as the small spaces provide a ready means of dividing up a given size of repeat with any number of vertical, horizontal, diagonal, and circular lines, which may then be employed as the framework upon which the pattern is constructed. When design paper is used, in order to avoid having two consecutive threads working alike, the centre of a small space should be taken as the turning point where the figure reverses, as shown in *Figures 12.40, 12.41*, and *12.42*.

CONSTRUCTION OF SYMMETRICAL FIGURES

Symmetrical ornament may be arranged to form independent figures, or stripe patterns, or, as shown by the geometrical designs given at B and C in *Figure 12.39*, as continuous all-over effects. A given unit, which is used two or more times in forming a complete figure, is either reversed on opposite sides of a centre line, or is turned upon a central point. The most common arrangement is the 'bi-symmetrical' or ordinary 'turn-over' figure, the construction of which is illustrated in *Figure 12.43*. Two lines are drawn at right angles to each other, and the unit of the figure is built up on one side of the

Figure 12.43

vertical line, as shown by the portion hatched in. As the second half of the figure requires to be exactly like the first half turned over, it can be obtained by copying the unit and the vertical and horizontal lines in pencil upon tracing paper, which is then turned over and placed with the lines upon it coinciding with those of the sketch. By 'rubbing' the tracing paper the outline of the figure is transferred to the sketch. The appearance of the figure can be judged, before the second half is copied, by placing a piece of mirror

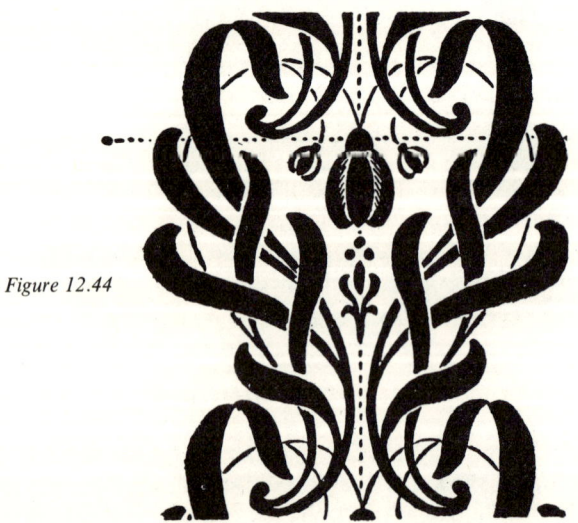

Figure 12.44

glass vertically with its lower edge along the vertical line. The arrangement of an independent bi-symmetrical figure, as a complete design, is illustrated in *Figure 13.12*.

The basis of construction of *Figure 12.44* is the same as that of *Figure 12.43*, but in the former the leaves overlap and interlace with each other in such a

Figure 12.45

manner that the figure forms a continuous stripe. The lengthwise repeat of the figure is indicated by the dotted horizontal line.

A multi-symmetrical figure is shown in *Figure 12.45*, which results from reversing a unit vertically, obliquely, and horizontally. In constructing the style two base lines are drawn crossing each other at right angles, and a

Figure 12.46

second pair crossing the first pair at 45° angle. The unit, shown by the portion hatched in, is sketched in the space of 45°, and thus forms one-eighth of the complete figure. The point where the construction lines cross one another is used as the axis upon which the unit is turned in transferring it to the various sections.

Figure 12.47

Figure 12.46 shows a multi-symmetrical figure arranged in stripe form, the unit of which is used four times in the repeat. The all-over design, given in the centre of *Figure 11.21*, is formed by 'quadruple reversing' in the same manner as *Figure 12.46*.

Figure 12.47 shows the application of the symmetrical principle of construction to a furnishing fabric in which an elaborate floral form is constructed bi-symmetrically, as shown in *Figures 12.43* and *12.44*.

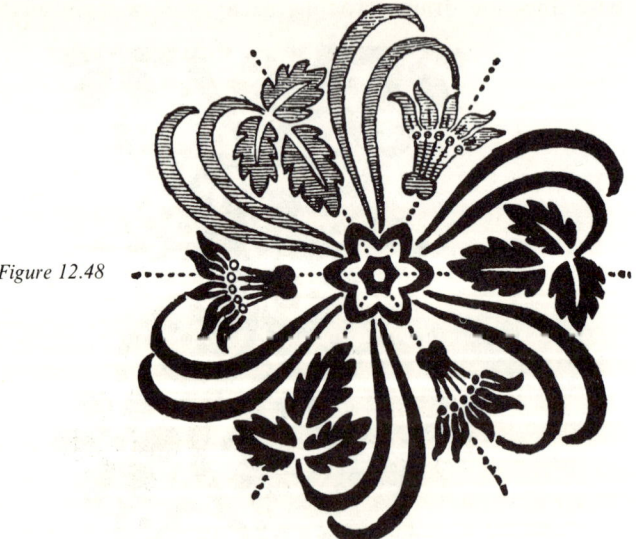

Figure 12.48

In *Figure 12.48* the unit is not turned over, but is simply turned round. Three base lines are drawn which cross each other at 60° angle, as shown by the dotted lines. The point where the lines intersect is used as the axis upon which the unit is turned, and forms the centre of the figure. The central figure and the curved lines are the same in each space of 60°, but between the curved lines the design is varied by the introduction of a leaf and a flower alternately. The complete unit of the figure thus occupies the angle of 120°, and is turned in three positions.

In the design shown in *Figure 12.49*, which is suitable for the corner of a fabric with a border all round, the unit of the figure is drawn from the corner of the square towards the centre, and is then turned round 90°, and copied in the same relative position from the remaining three corners.

Figure 12.49

In *Figure 12.50* a simple illustration is given which shows how the unit of a figure may be repeated on design paper. In this case the unit comprises one half of the complete figure, the second half being obtained by turning the unit round 180°. The centre of the figure is indicated by the crosses, and from this point the second half is copied square by square from the first half.

In constructing such styles as the foregoing, in order that the parts will fit correctly in the complete figure, it is generally necessary for the unit to be built up and copied in stages. Bi-symmetrical figures are specially suitable for

Figure 12.50

hanging fabrics, while multi-symmetrical designs are useful for textures which are viewed from every direction, as in the case of table-cloths and carpets.

REVERSING INCLINED FIGURES

When an inclined figure is used two or more times in a repeat it is customary to turn it in different ways in order to prevent it from forming twill lines, and to impart a more varied appearance to the design. *Figure 12.51* illustrates a method of placing a figure in different positions simply by turning it round, its centre being used as the axis; or, what is the same thing, by placing it each time as centrally as possible within a rectangular space.

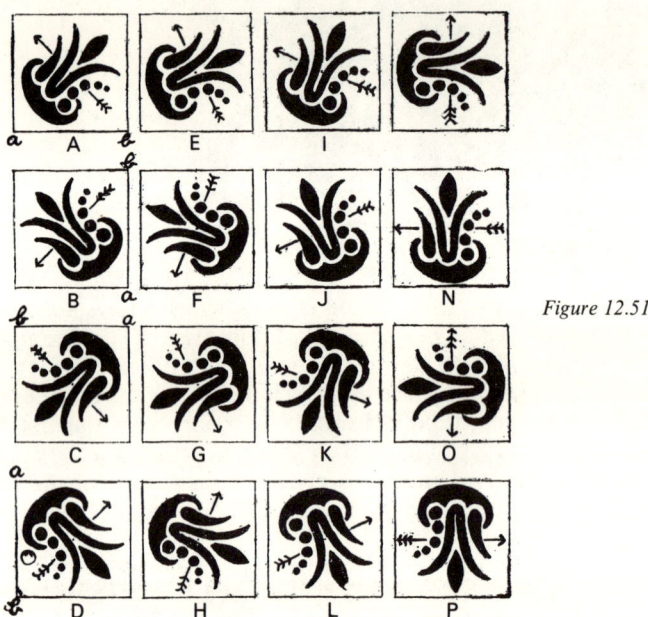

Figure 12.51

In single-ply fabrics, in which the figure is formed by interweaving the threads more loosely than in the ground of the texture, the angle of inclination has an effect upon the firmness of the cloth. The nearer the lines of figure approach the vertical or horizontal, the greater is the liability of the threads slipping or fraying when subjected to friction, while the nearer they approach the angle of 45° the firmer is the cloth structure. Of the examples given in *Figure 12.51*, A, B, C, and D, therefore, show the best positions, and M, N, O, and P the most undesirable. From an examination of A, B, C, and D, however, it will be seen that although the inclination of the figure as a whole is kept the same by turning the tracing round in each case a distance equal to 90°, the inclination of the parts of the figure is not the same in A and C as in B and D. Thus, in A and C the line formed by the small spots approaches the horizontal, and in B and D the vertical. The difference is due to the figure having been simply turned round on its centre, the line *a b* being placed in a horizontal and in a vertical direction alternately. This does not give a proper reversal of the figure.

A method of reversing is illustrated at R, S, T, and U in *Figure 12.52*, by which the same angle of inclination is obtained not only for the whole, but also for the parts of the figure. It will be seen that R and T are similar to A and C respectively in *Figure 12.51*, in which, however, no figure is placed the same as S and U. In this method S is obtained from R by turning the tracing

Figure 12.52

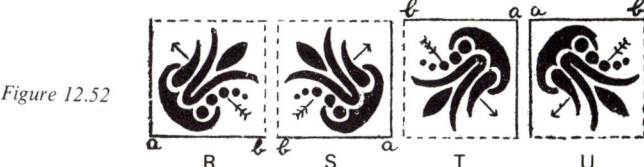

R   S   T   U

of the figure over horizontally. T is obtained from S by turning the tracing over vertically, or from R by turning the tracing round 180°. U is obtained from T by turning the tracing over horizontally, or from S by turning it round 180°, or from R by turning it over vertically. In each position the line *a b* is

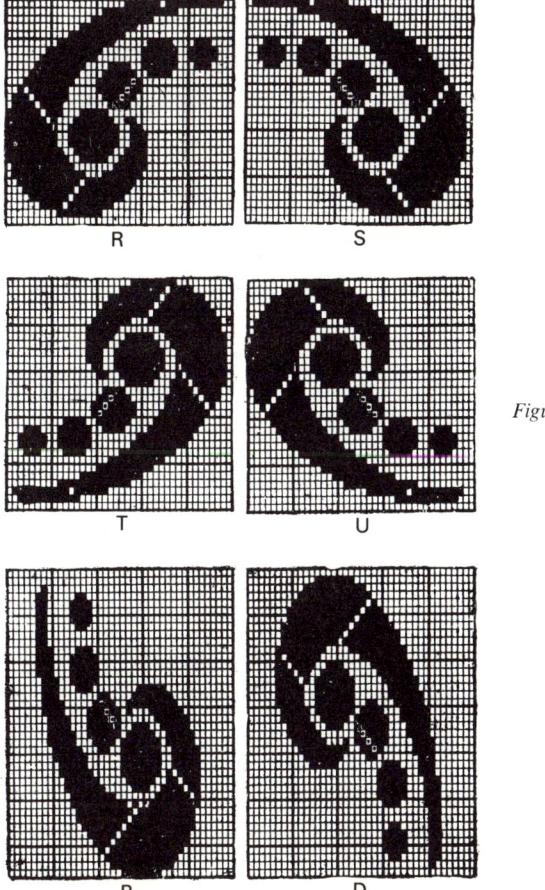

Figure 12.53

R   S

T   U

B   D

in a horizontal direction and parallel with the weft threads, therefore the parts of the figure are always in exactly the same relation to the ends and picks in the cloth. When the same figure is used a number of times in the repeat of a design, this method has the advantage that if the first figure is inclined at the most suitable angle, the remaining figures are equally correct. Also in most arrangements, the figures can be distributed over the given surface with less liability of producing lines or bars in the cloth. However, in some cases, a design appears less stiff and formal if the figure is placed in a multiplicity of different positions. For example, if there are six figures in the repeat four may be placed in different positions at 45° angle, and two at 60°; while with eight figures if four at an angle of 45° alternate with four at 30°, no two figures are placed the same.

R, S, T, and U in *Figure 12.53*, which correspond as to the angle of inclination of the figure with R, S, T, and U in *Figure 12.52*, show how a figure may be reversed on design paper by copying square by square from the first figure. For small effects this is probably the readiest method. In each case the approximate centre of the figure is indicated by the cross on the twentieth end and sixteenth pick, and a few dots are inserted diagonally from the cross to indicate the direction in which the figure is required to be inclined. The figure is reversed from the cross, the diagonal row of dots enabling the required direction to be readily obtained.

B and D in *Figure 12.53* are obtained by copying square by square from R, but in this case the figure is turned, as shown respectively at B and D in *Figure 12.51*. On square design paper the only disadvantage of thus turning the figure is that a horizontal line is changed to a vertical line, and vice versa. If, however, the cloth is not built on the square (8-by-6 paper is used in the example), this method of copying throws the figure out of its original shape, as will be seen by comparing the illustrations in *Figure 12.53*. Therefore, in changing the direction of a figure upon paper that is not square, it is necessary for the outline to be drawn or traced each time.

13

Arrangement of Figures

All designs for weaving, as already stated on numerous previous occasions, must be eventually capable of containment within a rectangular base to produce a weaver's repeat. Within the repeat, however, many different bases can be employed for the construction of figures, and the finalised shapes themselves can be placed in varying relationships one with another. Whether the design form itself is geometric, or floral, or abstract, the base lines on which it is constructed within the repeat usually take the aspect of a well-defined lattice or net. The lattice may be of varying form, and common starting points are: the rectangle, the diamond, the hexagon, the circle, etc.

When a figure is finally designed it may represent the full repeat in which case its relationship is pre-determined; or, it may represent one of many units of the repeat in which case its relationship with a number of like units within the repeat must be considered. The former situation gives rise to unit repeating, or side-by-side designs; the latter leaves the designer free to arrange the units in the most effective manner.

UNIT REPEATING DESIGNS

The term unit-repeating is applied to designs in which the unit figure and the repeat are the same. They may be constructed upon definite bases, as shown in certain of the preceding and following examples, but frequently the designs consist of combinations of different forms that are grouped together upon no particular principle, except that they fit satisfactorily together within the repeat area, and join correctly when repeated. With care, variety of effect can be produced which is free from the stiffness that sometimes characterises designs constructed upon defined bases. *Figure 13.1* is illustrative of a well-balanced, all-over, unit-repeating design, in which it will be noted that the largest form is comparatively small in relation to the size of the repeat, while the various parts of the ornament are about equally conspicuous.

If one feature of a unit-repeating design shows more prominently than the rest, the repetition of the pattern, from side to side and from end to end of the cloth, is liable to cause the leading feature to form lines in one or both directions. As a rule, when a design contains a distinct object, one or more similar objects should be used in addition, arranged according to a definite base.

Such an arrangement may still be unit-repeating, as in the examples given in *Figures 13.43* and *13.50*.

The unit-repeating principle of arrangement is very suitable for an abstract type of ornament, such as is shown in *Figure 13.2* as the indefinite system, upon which a variety of equally prominent shapes is introduced, tends to reduce the stiffness of the design. In sketching this type of design a portion of

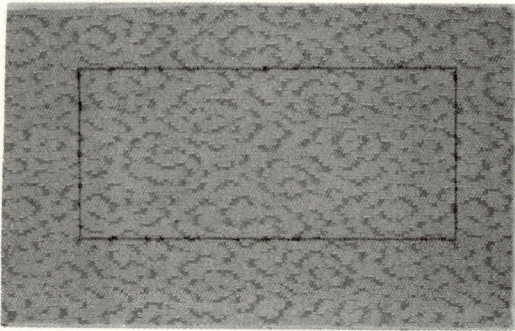

Figure 13.1   *Figure 13.2*

the figure should be drawn in and traced into corresponding positions in the repeat alongside and above the first repeat. Then, by repeating the process carefully and building up the design in stages the various parts can be made to fit correctly together at the edges of the repeat, at the same time that the formation of bars or stripes is avoided.

The unit-repeating principle is particularly applicable in the construction of designs for cloths in which a special order of introducing the warp and weft threads is employed as it enables the figure to be placed in conformity with the arrangement of the threads.

THE DROP DEVICE

This is a common device which enables the designer to place two similar units in different relationship to one another as shown at B, C, and D in *Figure 13.3*.

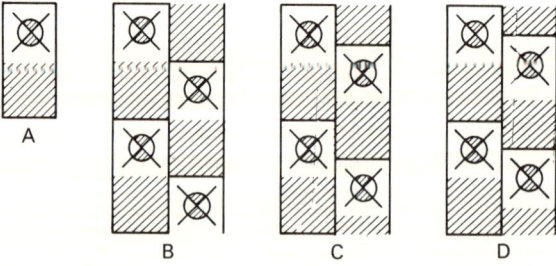

Figure 13.3

A in *Figure 13.3* shows the unit itself and B the arrangement, using the commonest and the most effective drop distance—the half-drop. C and D indicate in a schematic manner the relationship of units in the one-third, and the one-quarter drop effects respectively.

Half-drop designs

In true half-drop designs the figure in one-half of the complete repeat is exactly the same as that in the other half, and if the repeat is divided into four equal parts by bisecting it in both directions the ornament in alternate

Figure 13.4

sections is exactly the same. This is illustrated in *Figure 13.4*, in which a half-drop design is shown with the four equal-sized sections detached from each other. It will be seen that the unit-figure comprises one half of the complete design, taken either vertically or horizontally, and that one half of the repeat

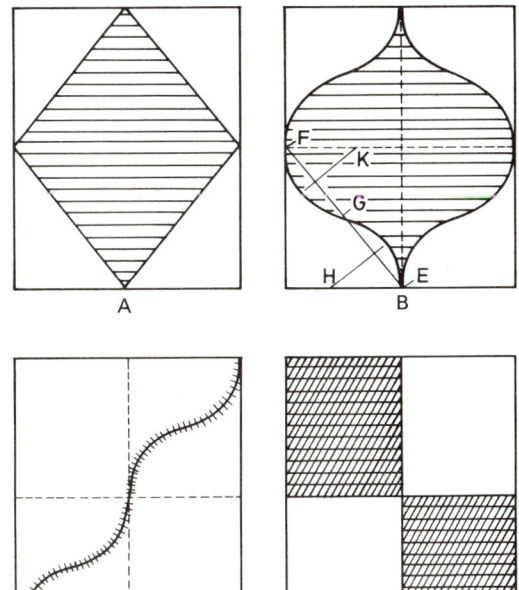

Figure 13.5

can be produced from the other half by 'half-dropping' the unit longitudinally, or, by moving the unit one half the width of the repeat.

Half-drop bases

The chief bases upon which the half-drop principle is applied are the diamond, the ogee, the diagonal waved line, and the rectangle, which are respectively indicated at A, B, C, and D in *Figure 13.5*.

The ogee base, represented at B, may be obtained as follows: The repeat is bisected in both directions, as shown by the dotted lines, and a line E F, which is drawn diagonally from corner to corner of one of the rectangles, is bisected at G. Lines are then drawn at right-angles to E F, passing through the centres of the lines E G and F G respectively, and cutting the horizontal lines at points H and K. These points form the centres from which the curves are drawn. As a rule, by using tracing paper, the ogee base lines can be drawn with sufficient accuracy freehand.

The waved line, shown at C in *Figure 13.5*, is constructed in a similar manner to the ogee In this case, however, instead of the line being turned back in order that it will join with itself in a vertical direction, it is continued in the opposite corner of the repeat, and is joined with itself diagonally.

The rectangular lattice is given at D, and in this base one half of the design is contained within a shaded and a blank section.

The diamond base

The diamond base may be employed in the construction of any form of half-drop design, but it is chiefly serviceable in the arrangement of figures that are more or less diamond-shaped. As shown in the example given in *Figure 13.6*, the leading feature, or the mass of the design is drawn within the diamond

Figure 13.6

space, which is indicated by dotted lines. The four triangular spaces at the corners of the repeat, when united form a second diamond-shaped space equal in size to the first, and the figure is traced into this space in exactly the same relative position as in the first diamond. The correct position of the second figure is obtained by marking the corners of the first diamond on the tracing paper, and then placing the paper so that the marks coincide with the corresponding corners of the second diamond. This ensures that if a line in the first diamond is crossed by a portion of the first figure the corresponding line in the second diamond will be crossed by a similar portion of the second figure in exactly the same relative position. Two or more repeats should be traced in each direction in order that it may be conveniently seen where bare places require to be filled in, or parts curtailed where the figures encroach on each other.

The ogee base

In addition to the form of ogee, illustrated at B in *Figure 13.5*, in which the base lines touch, the lines may be open, as shown at E in *Figure 13.7*; or interlacing, as indicated at F; while closed and open lines may be used in combination, as represented at G; or interlacing and open lines in combination, as shown at H.

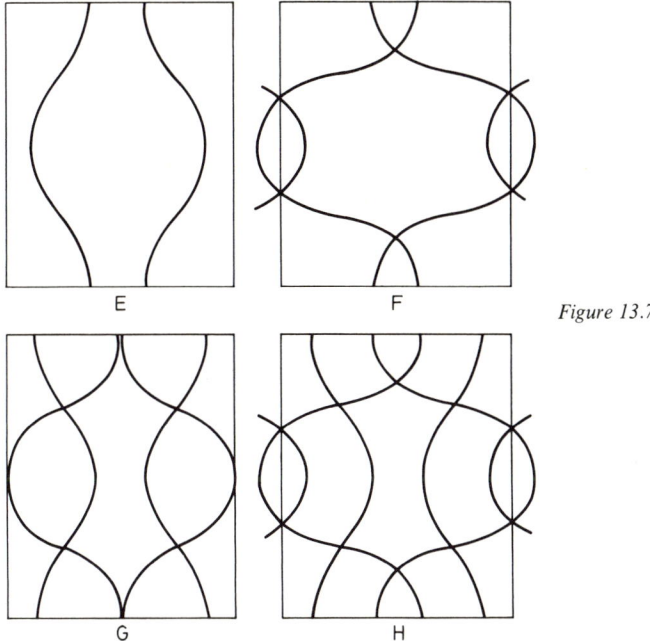

Figure 13.7

Figure 13.8 shows the application of a design to the base given at B in *Figure 13.5*. This form of ogee is merely a variation of the diamond base, the ogee lines similarly dividing the repeat into two sections, which are of the same shape and size. A similar method of constructing the sketch may therefore be employed, the figure which is placed in one space being traced into the other space in exactly the same relative position. The curved lines of the ogee are, however, better adapted than the straight lines of the diamond base for the construction of designs of a graceful flowing character. Designs based on the ogee are specially suitable for hanging fabrics on account of the effective manner in which the lines of the figure play in and out of the folds of the textures. In *Figure 13.8* the large leaves distinctly follow the base lines, and as the latter are in contact the design has a pronounced ogee appearance with the central figures closed in.

Figure 13.8

A design is given in *Figure 13.9*, which has been constructed upon an open ogee base, similar to that shown at E in *Figure 13.7*.

A design which corresponds with the basis given at G in *Figure 13.7*, is illustrated upon squared paper in *Figure 13.10*, in which a double pair of open lines are shown interlacing with a closed pair. The ogee base is naturally

Figure 13.9

adapted to the construction of drop designs of a symmetrical character, and this example illustrates a convenient method of working out such a design directly upon squared paper. The centres from which the lines are turned or reversed are found by dividing the repeat into four equal parts, as indicated by the crosses on the 1st, 17th, 33rd, and 49th squares. The ogee net, although frequently employed as a base for the half-drop arrangement of figures, can also be used in other ways, and it is not uncommon to find completely different designs used in each of the two units of the ogee base which, due to this treatment, becomes merely a part of the ornament of a unit-repeating design.

The diagonal waved line base

This base is particularly applicable to the arrangement of figures which are required to run in a diagonal direction, as shown in the design given in *Figure 13.11*. In constructing the style, the length of diagonal repeat is

Figure 13.10

Figure 13.11

indicated, and the waved line drawn in. The ornament may then be built upon the waved line before the boundary lines are indicated, because the angle of inclination of the line may be varied, within limits, to suit the form of the figure, and to fit the width of repeat that a given jacquard will give. Thus, assuming that the figure shown in *Figure 13.11* had to be inclined at a steeper angle, the repeat would be increased in length, and reduced in width, while by making the figure run at a flatter angle the length of the repeat would be reduced, and the width increased. After the boundary lines have been inserted on the sketch the parts of the figure require to be joined at the edges, and details may be added to the design, if necessary. In *Figure 13.11* one complete repeat, and its division into four equal parts, are indicated by the dotted lines, which enable the half-drop principle of arrangement to be observed.

The diagonal basis, although chiefly suitable for the diagonal arrangement of figures, can be employed in the construction of drop designs of an all-over character. There is always a tendency, however, for the diagonal line to assert itself, which allows its use as a base only for special styles.

The rectangular base

In the arrangement of given masses or detached figures upon the half-drop principle, the rectangular base, illustrated at D in *Figure 13.5*, frequently possesses distinct advantages, and except in special cases (as for example, when the ornament is required to definitely follow certain base lines) may be used with greater facility than the other bases. The chief reason for this is that in using a base such as the diamond or ogee it is necessary to indicate both the width and the length of the repeat when the sketch is commenced. With the rectangular basis, however, the length of the repeat can be varied, during the construction of the sketch, to suit the required size of mass and amount of ground space, at the same time that the width of the repeat is made to coincide with that of a given jacquard. *Figure 13.4* shows a typical example of a design which can be arranged most satisfactorily on the rectangular plan. The mass is large in proportion to the width of the repeat, therefore, in order to secure proper balance of figure and ground the length of the repeat has had to be made much greater than the width.

The method of constructing a drop design on the rectangular basis to fit a given width of repeat is shown in stages at A, B, C, and D in *Figure 13.12*. First, as shown at Λ, a horizontal line is drawn on the sheet of paper, and three vertical lines, the two outer lines having a space between them equal to the width of the repeat, while the third, which is shown dotted, divides the repeat into two equal parts. The lines should be drawn in lightly and of unlimited length.

Second, as shown at B, a tracing of the figure is made in a suitable position relative to the base line and the first vertical line. In this case, as the figure is bi-symmetrical, it is conveniently placed with the vertical line passing through its centre. The positions of this line and the horizontal line should be indicated on the tracing paper before the latter is removed, to enable the figure to be traced again in the same relative position to the other lines. A second tracing of the figure is made with the lines on the tracing paper coinciding with the horizontal line and the vertical line on the right. This ensures that the distance from one figure to the other is equal to the width of the repeat, and that the parts of the figure join correctly at the sides.

In the third stage, shown at C in *Figure 13.12*, the position of the intermediate figure is found, and the length of the repeat determined. The tracing paper, placed with the vertical line coinciding with the dotted vertical line of

Figure 13.12

the sketch, is moved in a vertical direction until it is judged that the figure occupies a suitable position in relation to the figures which have already been traced. If placed correctly the horizontal line on the tracing paper will be parallel with the base line of the sketch, and the distance between the two lines will be equal to half the repeat in length. A third tracing of the figure is made and the second horizontal line is drawn in, as shown by the dotted line; then by doubling the distance between the two horizontal lines, the position of the third horizontal line is found. When this is drawn in, the space occupied by one repeat is obtained divided into four equal rectangles.

D in *Figure 13.12* shows the completion of the sketch. Portions of the figure are traced at the top and bottom, and at the sides, and details of the design are added and traced in stages. By placing the vertical and horizontal lines on the tracing paper to coincide with the corresponding lines of the sketch the additional figure in alternate sections is readily made the same, and a correct junction formed of the parts of the figure at the edges of the repeat.

Drafting half-drop designs

In drafting a true half-drop design upon squared paper considerable time and labour can be saved by adopting a system which corresponds with the principle of construction of the design. The method is illustrated in *Figure 13.13*, which shows the lower half of the design given in *Figure 13.12* worked out in two sections lettered A and B. Each section is equal to one-fourth of the complete repeat, and they are placed alongside each other, as shown in *Figure 13.13*, while the first half of the cards is cut. Then, to enable the cards for the second half of the design to be cut, the two sections are reversed in position, A being placed on the right and B on the left. Only one half of the complete design thus needs to be painted out on the design paper, but care has necessarily to be taken that the ground weave and the figure at the top of A and B, join correctly with the bottom of B and A respectively.

Figure 13.13

A   B

In the construction of all-over designs, in which the figure is rather in-definite in character, the half-drop system is very useful, and an illustration of a design thus arranged is given in *Figure 13.14*. The designer can readily judge the balance of the figure, and the parts can be made to fit correctly together with little difficulty; while in most cases the design paper work is reduced by about one-half, as compared with a unit-repeating design.

Figure 13.14

Designs of an abstract character, such as the example given in *Figure 13.15*, are sometimes drafted directly on the squared paper without the aid of a sketch, and for this class the half-drop system of construction is very con-venient, because of the saving in time and labour that can be effected. In drawing and painting in the figure and ground, two sections of design paper are used, which together comprise one half of the complete repeat, and these are moved about, being placed alongside, and then one above the other, while the parts of the design are made to join up correctly.

Half-drop stripe designs

In stripe designs the figure is mostly placed at a different level in adjacent stripes, as shown in *Figure 13.16*, in order to prevent the masses from falling into line with each other horizontally. Therefore, although the same ornament is used in each figured stripe, a complete design extends over the width

Figure 13.15

of two stripes. In *Figure 13.16* the different position of the figure in succeeding stripes is due to dropping it one-half the length of the repeat. In sketching a stripe design, after the figure in the first stripe has been drawn in, its correct position in the second stripe is readily found on the rectangular principle by dividing the repeat horizontally into two equal parts.

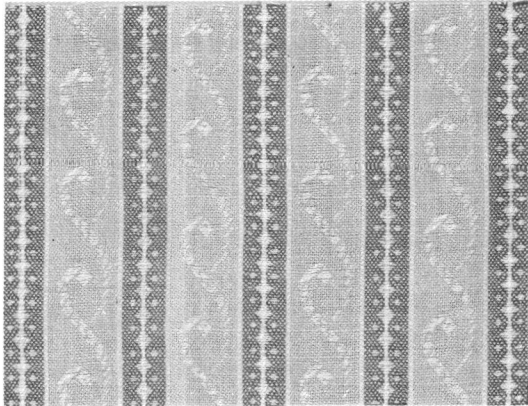

Figure 13.16

In drafting a half-drop stripe design, it is generally only necessary to fully paint out one stripe, as shown in *Figure 13.17*, which corresponds with the example given in *Figure 13.16*. The cards for the first half of the design may be cut with the upper section of *Figure 13.17* on the right, and for the second half, on the left of the lower section.

Defective half-drop designs

Figure 13.18 illustrates the defective appearance of a design in which an inclined figure is arranged on the half-drop principle. The design not only has a monotonous appearance, but the arrangement causes twill lines of

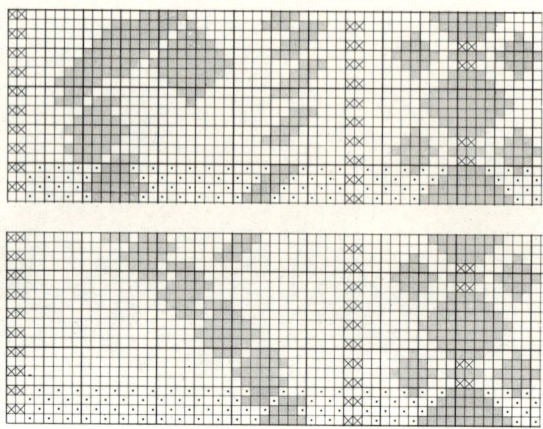

Figure 13.17

figure to show in the cloth. Unless a diagonal effect is desired, only symmetrical, or well balanced figures are suitable for the half-drop system of construction. An inclined figure requires to be turned or reversed in the intermediate position.

The half-drop principle may be employed in the arrangement of two figures which are not alike, and an illustration of the style is given in *Figure 12.1*.

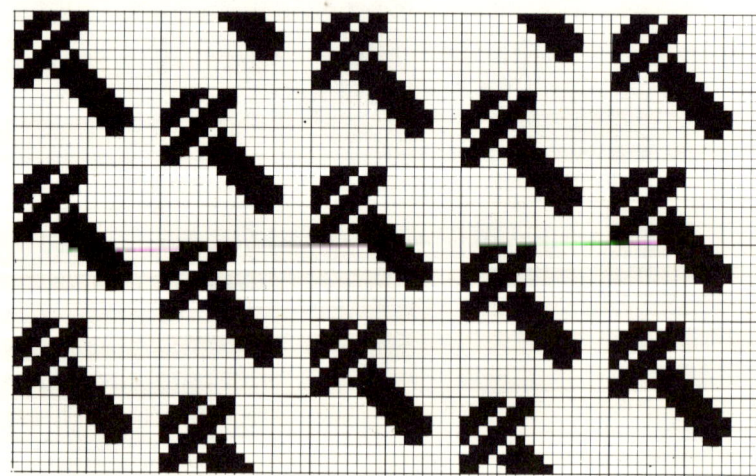

Figure 13.18

Such a design does not possess the distinctive features of a true half-drop arrangement, and it is necessary to draft it in the same manner as a unit-repeating figure.

One-third and one quarter-drop designs

As shown earlier a unit figure may be dropped each time a distance equal to
one-third or one-fourth of the length of a repeat, and be used three or four
times respectively in the complete design. The method, however, throws the
masses into twill lines, and is therefore only applicable to styles in which a

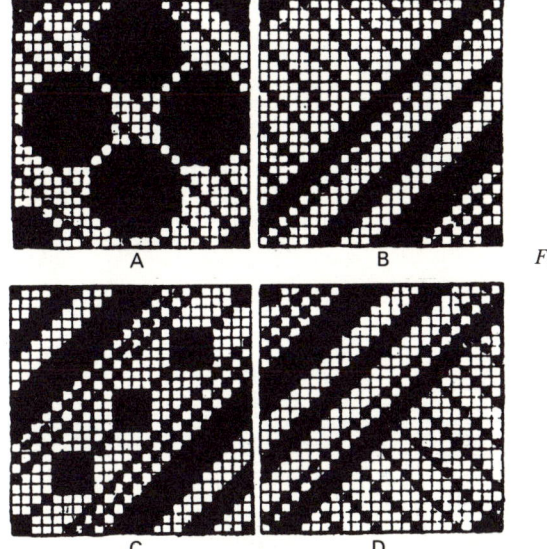

Figure 13.19

diagonal effect is not objectionable. A simple illustration is given in *Figure
13.19*, which shows how a diagonal figure may be readily designed upon
squared paper. The figure is intended to be dropped one-fourth, that is, to
repeat diagonally four times, upon 96 ends and 96 picks. One-fourth of the
design is painted out and divided into four sections, as shown by the portions
lettered A, B, C, and D. Then in cutting the cards the sections are arranged
as follows: First, A, B, C, D; second, D, A, B, C; third, C, D, A, B; fourth,
B, C, D, A.

DROP-REVERSE DESIGNS

Comparison of half-drop and drop-reverse designs

The pure drop-reverse arrangement is similar to the pure half-drop in the
respect that the unit of the design is contained twice in the repeat, the ornament in one half, in each case, being the same as that in the other half. The
essential difference between the two systems is that in the half-drop the figure
in both halves is turned the same way, whereas in the drop-reverse the figure
in one half is reversed or turned in the opposite direction to that in the other
half. The latter feature is illustrated in *Figure 13.20*, which shows the repeat of
a drop-reverse design bisected in both directions. In marking the boundary
lines of the repeat in *Figure 13.20* the vertical lines have purposely been drawn
in such positions that they pass through corresponding parts of the figure in

the upper and lower halves. Each vertical line thus indicates a position where the figure reverses, and an examination will show that the ornament in alternate sections of the design is the same, but turned the opposite way. It will also be seen that if the lower half of *Figure 13.20* be turned over from side to side and placed above the upper half with the vertical and horizontal lines coinciding, the ornament in the two halves will also coincide.

Drop-reverse bases

The chief bases upon which drop-reverse designs are constructed are the diamond, ogee, vertical waved line, and rectangle, which are indicated, in conjunction with a design, at A, B, C, and D, respectively in *Figure 13.21*.

Diamond and ogee bases

In using the diamond or ogee base the figure which is drawn in the one section is placed in the other section in exactly the same relative position to the base lines, but with the tracing turned over. Thus, in *Figure 13.21*, it will be seen

Figure 13.20

that the unit figure occupies corresponding positions in the diamond spaces of A, and in the ogee spaces of B, a portion of figure that overlaps one space similarly overlapping the other space, but turned over from side to side.

The diamond and ogee shapes are naturally best adapted to the construction of designs in which the lines of the figure follow the base lines. An

Figure 13.21

Figure 13.22

illustration is given in *Figure 13.22*, in which the central masses are reversed, but the other parts of the figure are symmetrical, and the example shows—in comparison with a style which is entirely bi-symmetrical—how the reversing method tends to reduce the stiffness of a design.

The vertical waved line base

This is a particularly suitable basis to use in the construction of designs of a graceful flowing character. From an examination of C in *Figure 13.21* it will be seen that the figure is the same on opposite sides of the line, but reversed. The principle of the arrangement is also illustrated by the example given in *Figure 12.36*.

Figure 13.23

The base can also be used with advantage in the construction of designs in which the figure runs continuously in stripe form, as shown in the example given in *Figure 13.23*. The base lines not only afford a suitable foundation upon which to arrange the parts of the ornament, but the addition of the figure, in the same relationship to each half of the line, enables a well-balanced design to be readily produced.

The rectangular base

The relation of the rectangular basis to the diamond, ogee, and vertical waved line will be understood by comparing A, B, C, and D in *Figure 13.21*, in each of which the base lines pass through corresponding parts of the figure. By examination it will be seen that the bases A, B, and C could be similarly indicated upon the design given in *Figure 13.20* in addition to the rectangular base which is shown. Further, it will be observed that *Figure 13.20* is arranged similar to D in *Figure 13.21*, except that in the former the sections which contain corresponding parts of the figure are placed alternately, while in the latter they are situated one above another. In both cases, however, the figure in the upper half exactly corresponds with that in the lower half. No matter where the boundary lines of the repeat are drawn this is a distinct feature of all true drop-reverse designs in which the unit is turned over from side to side. Because of this, and for the reason stated in reference to half-drop designs,

Figure 13.24

the rectangular system of arranging a unit figure in the drop-reverse order is frequently preferable to the other bases. Particularly is this the case when the principal figure is not well balanced, or when it is very large in comparison with the width of the repeat. In illustration of the latter point, a design is represented in *Figure 13.24*, in which the figure extends over two thirds of the width of the repeat, while the length is nearly one and a half times the width. When a large figure is arranged in a narrow repeat, an appearance is given to the design of having been woven in a larger capacity of jacquard than has actually been the case. By properly adjusting the length of the repeat, practically any size of figure, so long as it does not encroach on itself when repeated, can be arranged on the rectangular drop-reverse principle.

The method of arranging a figure (the figure given in *Figure 13.25* is used) to fit a given width of repeat, is illustrated at A and B in *Figure 13.26*. As shown at A, a horizontal base line E F, and two vertical lines E G and F H, are drawn of unlimited length; the distance between the latter being equal to the width of the repeat. The figure is inclined at a suitable angle, and a tracing is made as shown at 1, and the relative positions of the base lines to the figure are indicated on the tracing paper. The figure is then copied as shown at 2, one repeat distant from the first tracing, in a similar position relative to the vertical and horizontal lines.

B in *Figure 13.26* shows how the position of the intermediate figure is found. The tracing of the figure is turned over from side to side, and is moved about (the base lines of the sketch and tracing being kept parallel) until it is judged

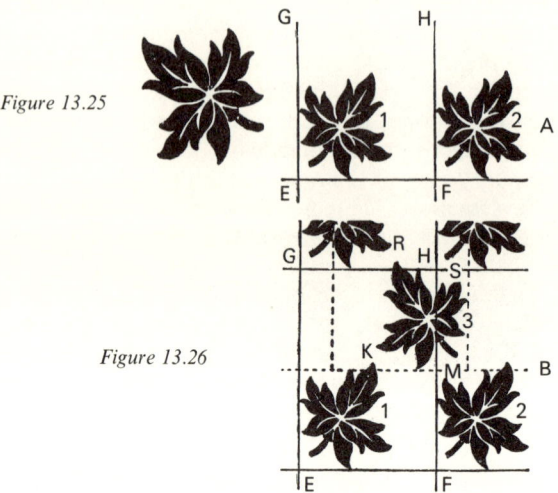

Figure 13.25

Figure 13.26

that the reversed figure is in the most suitable position in relation to the figures 1 and 2. Then a third tracing is made, as shown at 3, and the positions of the base lines are transferred lightly to the sketch, as indicated by the dotted lines. The reversed figure is usually in the best position when there is an approximately equal space between the figures at K and M; a smaller overlap, if necessary, being allowed on one side than on the other in order to counteract one side of the figure being heavier than the other side. The position of the

Figure 13.27

third horizontal line G H is found by doubling the distance between E F and the dotted horizontal line, and when this is drawn one complete repeat is enclosed within the rectangle E G H F. The main feature is again copied above the repeat, as shown, then, if correctly placed, the figures are in exactly the same relation to each other at R as at K, and at S as at M.

As shown in *Figure 13.27*, the sketch is completed by adding the details of the design in one half, and reversing them in the same relative position in the other half. A distinct advantage of this method of arrangement is that, if a proper balance of the ornament is obtained in one half of the design, a similar balance is ensured in the other half.

Systems of drafting drop-reverse designs

Different methods of constructing the squared paper design of a true drop-reverse figure may be employed either in working from a sketch or a woven pattern. One method consists of drawing the complete outline of the figure on the design paper in the same manner as in drafting a unit-repeating design. In another method one half of the design (the unit) is drawn and painted on the design paper; then a starting point of the second half is found, and the figure is copied in the reverse direction, square by square, from the first half. Thus, in *Figure 13.28*, which shows the design given in *Figure 13.27* worked out upon 96 ends and 118 picks, the position lettered A corresponds with that lettered B. The latter, therefore, shows a suitable place to commence the copy of the figure in the reversed position and it will be seen that the number of picks from A to B is half of the total number of picks in the repeat. In a third method the first half of the design is drawn on the squared paper, and a copy is made upon tracing paper. Then the tracing is turned over from side to side, placed in the proper position on the design paper, and a reversed copy of the figure made by rubbing. In each of the foregoing methods the boundary lines of the repeat may be drawn in any position in relation to the figure.

A fourth method is illustrated by *Figures 13.27* and *13.28*, in which the special features of the drop-reverse arrangement—described in reference to *Figure 13.20*—are taken advantage of to reduce the amount of work in drafting a design. The first vertical boundary line of the repeat is drawn in such a position that the figure is cut in the same relative position in each half, as shown by the line T W in *Figure 13.27*. (The position of the line T W is exactly between the line E G and the first dotted line in B, *Figure 13.26*.) The lower half of the repeat, taken from left to right, is thus made to exactly coincide with the upper half, taken from right to left. In *Figure 13.28* the two halves of the design, which are shown detached from each other, correspond with the arrangement of the repeat shown in *Figure 13.27*, and it will be seen, by comparing the picks in succession, that the marks and blanks in the lower half, read from left to right, are the same as in the upper half, read from right to left. It will therefore be clear that it is quite possible to cut all the cards from one half of a plan such as that given in *Figure 13.28*. Sometimes the half-repeat is worked out on transparent design paper, which enables the cards for the second half of the design to be cut by turning the paper over, but ordinary design paper can be used quite conveniently.

The foregoing system is only applicable to designs in which the ground weave can be arranged to read the same from each side, and it is necessary to make the design upon a number of picks which is suitable for the reversing of the ground weave. Thus, in *Figure 13.28* each half of the repeat is made with an odd number of picks in order to fit with plain ground. A number of examples are given in *Figure 13.29*, which will reverse properly at the half-repeat if the design contains an odd number of repeats of the ground weave in each case.

The preceding method is quite as applicable in constructing the design from a woven sample as from a sketch. If a thread arrangement is used in dividing up the design (see *Figure 12.6*), the sample is adjusted, as shown in *Figure 13.30*, so that a vertical thread cuts the figure in the same relative position in both halves of the repeat, this thread being taken as the commencement of the design paper plan.

Figure 13.28

When the ground weave does not reverse it is necessary for the complete design to be made, and a method is illustrated in *Figures 13.30* and *13.31*, which enables the outline of the figure to be drawn in very readily. The example is a pure drop-reverse, and in *Figure 13.30* the figure reverses from

Figure 13.29

the vertical line A B; that is, the figure in the lower half of the repeat is in the same relative position to the line as the figure in the upper half, but on opposite sides. The line A B corresponds with the first end of *Figure 13.31*, and the line C D with the first pick, the position of the latter line, however, being immaterial. The design is divided into spaces (as previously explained in reference to *Figures 12.1* and *12.6*) commencing with the lines A B and C D.

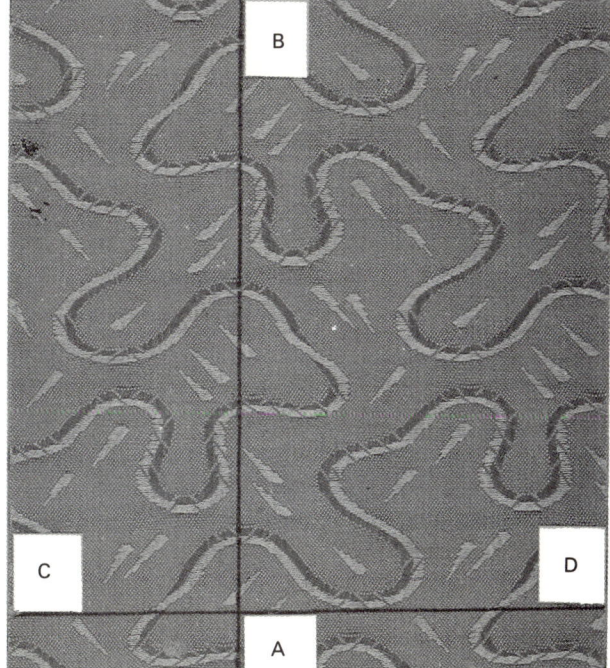

Figure 13.30

Two sheets of design paper are used, each containing one-half, or rather more than one-half, of the number of picks in the full repeat, and one sheet is turned over horizontally and placed below the other sheet so that the ruled surfaces are on the outside. (By pricking two holes in corresponding positions in each sheet, which are made to coincide when the sheets are put together the squares of the lower sheet can be placed directly below the squares of the upper sheet.) The sheets are secured by pins, and carbon paper is placed below them with the carbon side upward. As the outline of the figure in the first half of the design is drawn on the upper sheet of point-paper, an exact copy is produced at the same time on the under side of the lower sheet. Then, as shown at *Figure 13.31*, when the lower sheet is turned over, the figure upon

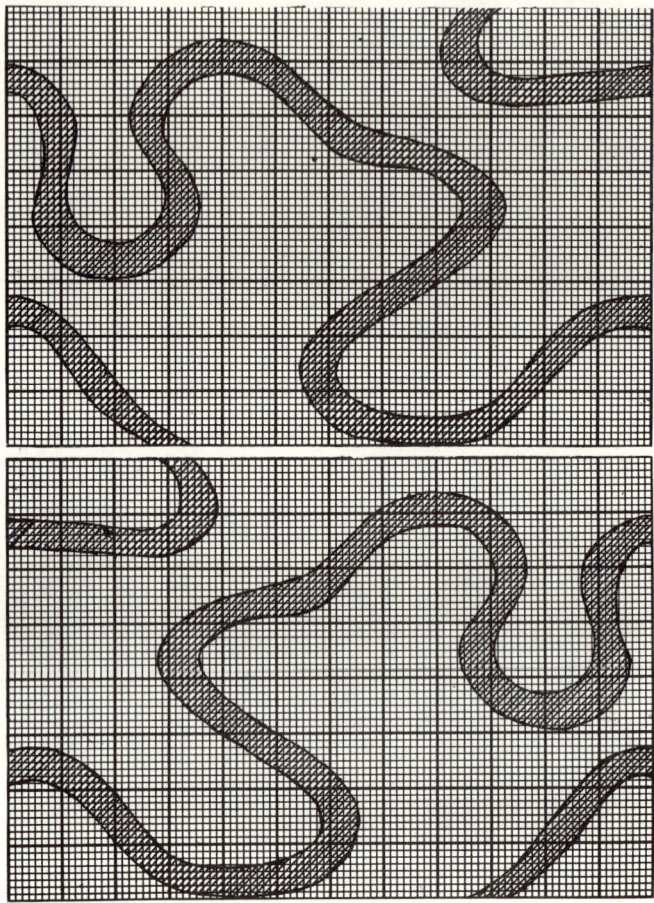

Figure 13.31

it is reversed, as in the second half of the design, and is approximately in the correct position in relation to the figure in the first half when the sheets are placed together. Some little adjustment of the outline may be necessary where the sheets join.

Drop-reverse stripe designs

In each stripe of the design given in *Figure 13.32* the figure is dropped one-half of the repeat, and turned over from side to side. Also, the ornament in the second stripe is dropped one-fourth of the repeat from its position in the first stripe, the complete repeat in width thus extending over two stripes. The mass in one stripe is brought opposite the space between the masses in the other stripe, and the barriness, which would have resulted if the figure in both stripes had been placed on the same level, is avoided. The dotted horizontal lines, which divide the repeat of *Figure 13.32* into four equal parts, show how correct distribution of the figure is secured.

Figure 13.32

A ready method of drafting the style of design illustrated in *Figure 13.32* is indicated in *Figure 13.33*. The complete design of one stripe only is made, but the sheet of squared paper is divided into four equal parts, as shown at A, B, C, and D. The full design is produced by cutting the cards with the parts placed alongside each other as follows: First, A and B; second, B and C; third, C and D; and fourth, D and A.

The method illustrated above can be readily adapted to designs repeating over three or four stripes with one-third or one-quarter drop arrangements by the division of the repeat into suitable segments.

Vertical reversing of figures

The style of figure, which is much heavier on one side than the other, is frequently very difficult to arrange on the drop-reverse principle by turning it over from side to side. It is impossible to get a proper balance of the ornament, on account of the heavy sides coming together in one line, and the light sides in another line.

The difficulty of arranging such a style can frequently be got over by turning the figure over from top to bottom in the second position, as shown in

Figure 13.34. The correct position of the second figure, and the length of repeat which is suitable, may be obtained as follows: A horizontal base line A B, two vertical lines A C and B D (the distance between the latter being equal to the width of the repeat), and a third vertical line E F, equidistant between A C and B D, are drawn of unlimited length. The figure is traced in a suitable position in relation to the lines A C and A B, and copied, as shown

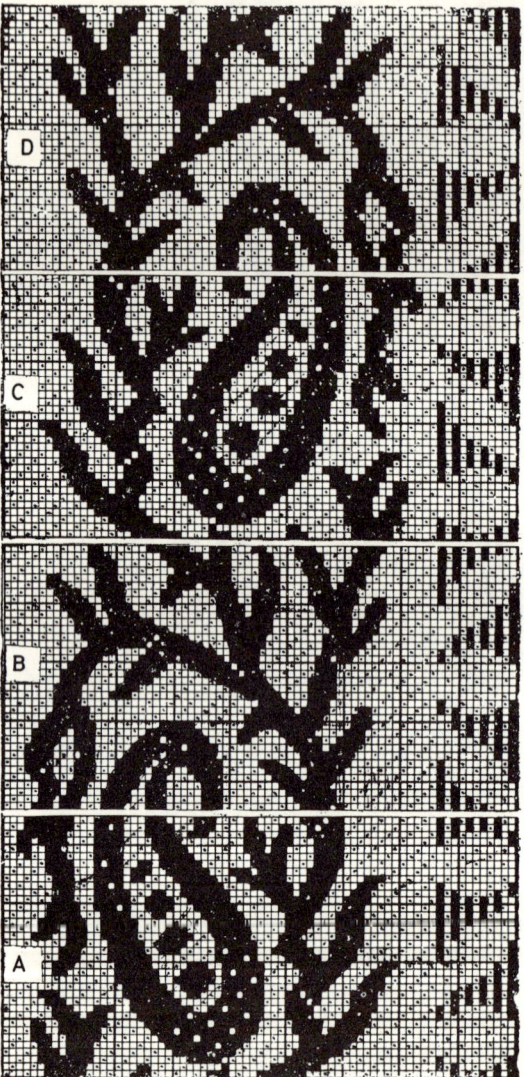

Figure 13.33

at 2, in the manner described in reference to *Figure 13.26*, care being taken that the positions of the lines A B and A C are correctly indicated on the tracing paper. The tracing is then turned over from top to bottom, and placed with the vertical line upon it coinciding with the line E F. It is moved in a vertical direction until it is judged that the reversed figure is in the best position in relation to the first two figures; and a third tracing is made, as shown at 3. The size of the repeat in length is found by turning the tracing back again, and placing it with the vertical line coinciding with the line A C extended, in such a position that there is approximately the same space between the figures at H as at G. Portions of the figure are then traced at the top, bottom, and sides, in order to show the repeat, and additional detail is added, if necessary. If the sketch is correctly constructed there will be exactly the same space between the figures at K as at G, and at M as at H.

Figure 13.34

The foregoing system is useful in cases where the figure is required to appear the same way up, when viewed from either end of the cloth. It may also be advantageously used when some prominent shape occurs at one side of the figure, as will be seen from a comparison of the sketches given in *Figures 13.35* and *13.36*. In *Figure 13.35* the figure is alternately turned over from side to side in the ordinary manner, with the result that the flowers form a pronounced line lengthwise of the design, and the leaves another line. By turning the intermediate figure over from top to bottom, as shown in *Figure 13.36*, the second figure is moved one-half the width of the repeat from the first figure, and the striped appearance is avoided. It will be noted, however, that the stems of the figure come together and form a line across the sketch, while a similar effect is produced by the tops of the leaves falling into a line. The defect, however, is less noticeable than the distinct stripe produced by the arrangement shown at *Figure 13.35*.

From this and the foregoing examples it will be understood that in using a given figure it is necessary to select a system of arrangement which is most suitable for it; while, with a given system of arrangement, the parts of the figure require to be so distributed that an evenly balanced design will result. Thus, *Figure 13.37* shows how the flowers and leaves might be re-distributed

Figure 13.35

in order to render the figure suitable for arranging on the principle illustrated in *Figure 13.35*.

In order to show the distinctive features of the design given in *Figure 13.36*, and to illustrate a convenient method of drafting the effect on squared paper,

Figure 13.36

Figure 13.37

one complete repeat of the design is enclosed within the rectangle A B D C, which is bisected by the vertical line E F. The horizontal boundary lines A B and C D cut the figure in the same relative position in each vertical half; therefore, the figure in one half of the design is exactly like that in the other half, except that it is turned over vertically. Hence, if the line A B be used as the commencement of the design, the complete outline of the figure may be

obtained on the design paper in a similar manner to that illustrated in *Figure 13.31*. In this case the sheet of point-paper is cut vertically into two equal portions, which are placed one above the other, the lower portion being turned over from top to bottom. Thus, in *Figure 13.38*, which shows the complete plan of the design, given in *Figure 13.36*, the two portions are shown detached from each other, and it will be seen that the figure in one half, followed from the bottom, exactly corresponds with that in the other half taken from the top.

Combination of half-drop and drop-reverse systems

Figure 13.39 illustrates a system of arrangement which is particularly useful in securing even distribution of the ornament when the figure is badly balanced. In the example the figure is not only heavier on one side than the other but a distinct floral shape occurs on one side at the top. The figure is used eight times in the repeat, and is turned in four directions, and the complete design is a combination of the half-drop and the drop-reverse arrangements. The multiple reversing of the figure prevents the flowers from falling

Figure 13.39

into lines, either horizontally or vertically, while the inclusion of eight figures in the repeat makes the design less stiff and formal than is the case when only two figures are used. Compared with a two-figure arrangement the chief disadvantages are that twice as many cards are required, and very large figures cannot be woven because the figuring capacity of the jacquard is practically reduced by one half. It will frequently be found, however, that the system can be employed for figures which are too large to arrange in sateen order, while it possesses many of the advantages of the sateen distribution.

The repeat of *Figure 13.39* is shown bisected by dotted lines, and it will be seen that the ornament in alternate sections is the same. In drafting the design upon squared paper, it may therefore be treated as a half-drop arrangement, so that only one-half of the effect needs to be worked out, the complete set of cards being cut from the half-repeat in the manner described in reference to *Figure 13.13*.

SATEEN SYSTEMS OF DISTRIBUTION

Comparison of regular and irregular sateen arrangements

One of the most important functions of sateen weaves is their use as bases in the distribution of figures. The most commonly used sateens are illustrated in *Figure 13.40*, in which the examples A to G are regular, and H to M, irregular sateens.

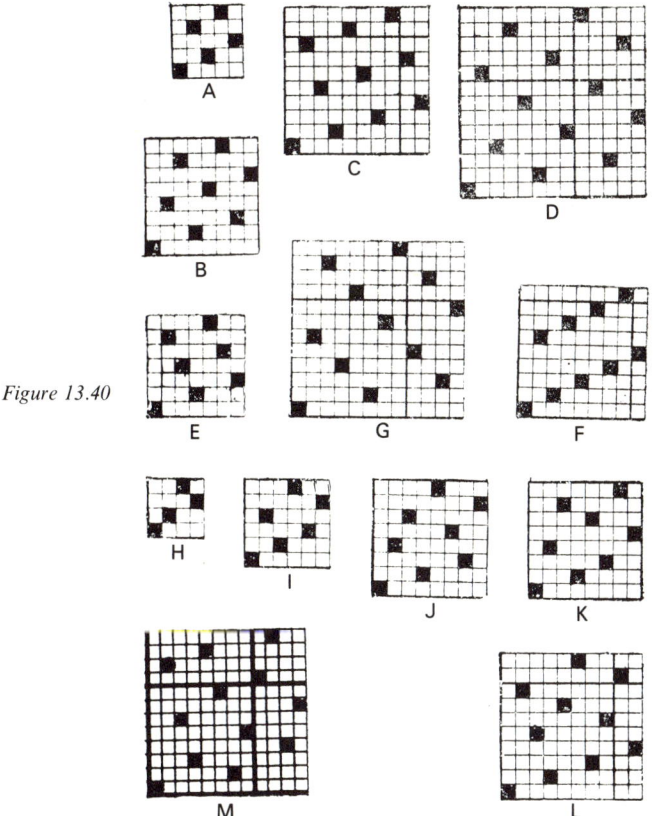

Figure 13.40

In *Figure 13.41* examples of designs are given which illustrate the comparative effects produced by using the two kinds of sateens as the bases of distribution. In the upper design the spots are arranged in the order of the 8-thread regular sateen, shown at B in *Figure 13.40*, and it will be noted that continuous diagonal lines of figure are formed. This tendency of the primary masses to fall into twill lines is occasionally an objectionable feature of the regular sateen orders of distribution. In the lower design the figures are arranged in the order of the 12-thread irregular sateen given at M in *Figure*

13.40. In this case the spots tend to run in groups of two or three, the direction of one line opposing that of another, so that there is no possibility of the figures falling into twill lines. A feature of the broken arrangements is the tendency of the figures to group in twos, threes, or fours.

Advantages of sateen bases

Compared with the half-drop and drop-reverse systems, the best sateen arrangements possess the following advantages: (1) There is less liability of stripes or bars occurring in the cloth, as uniform distribution of the primary masses is more readily secured; (2) a design is more effective be-

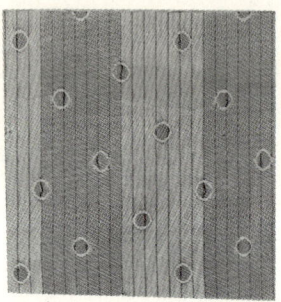

Figure 13.41

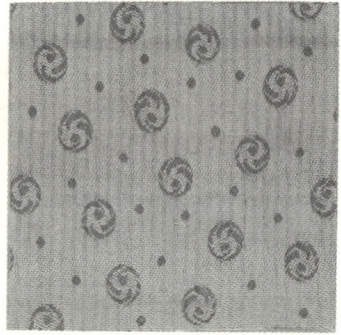

cause the main feature can be turned and reversed in diverse ways, which enables stiffness and sameness of appearance to be more readily avoided; (3) the repetition of the pattern is better concealed. The chief disadvantages are that with the same size of repeat smaller masses are necessary, or, on the other hand, with the same size of mass the capacity of the jacquard must be larger, while there is usually greater expense in cards.

Regular sateen arrangements

In using the regular sateens as bases it is important that the figures are placed at approximately uniform distances apart. Under ordinary circumstances this condition is secured by selecting a base weave in which there is a similar distance between the marks when viewed from different directions, as in the plans A, B, C, and D, in *Figure 13.40*. These are four of the best regular sateen bases, the suitability of each being due to the feature that a twill line of dots in one direction is crossed by another line about equally prominent in the other direction. Such bases as E, F, and G in *Figure 13.40*, in which the marks

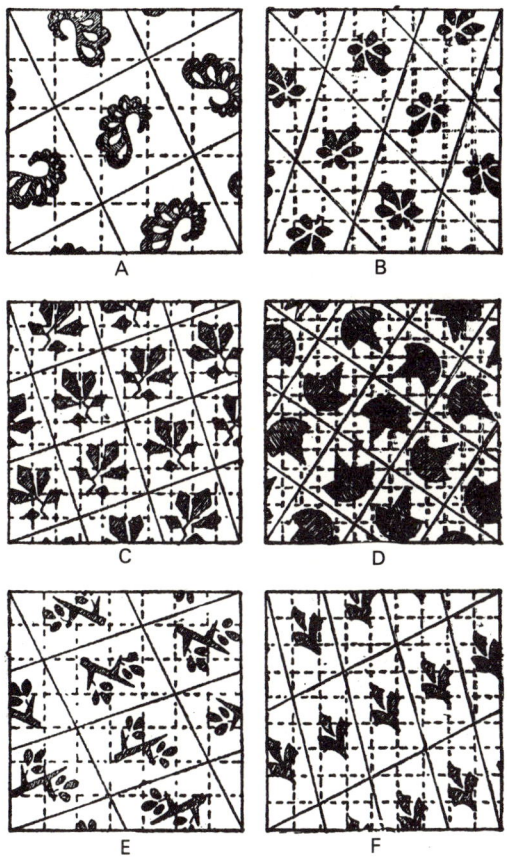

Figure 13.42

form a more prominent diagonal line in one direction than the other, are usually unsuitable. The applicability of the different sateens will be seen by comparing the examples given in *Figure 13.42*. In each design A, B, C, and D in *Figure 13.42*, the bases of which respectively correspond with the plans similarly lettered in *Figure 13.40*, there is an approximately equal space between the figures, while the twill lines, into which the figures fall, are about as prominent in one direction as another. On the other hand, designs E and F in *Figure 13.42*, the bases of which respectively correspond with E and F in *Figure 13.40*, are defective, because the spaces between the figures are unequal, and the figures form a more pronounced line in one direction than in the other. Circumstances sometimes arise, however, which render such a base as E or F necessary in order to obtain uniform distribution; as for instance, when the figure is longer in one direction than another, or when there is a considerable difference between the width and length of the repeat.

Methods of distributing the figures

In sketching designs in which the figures are arranged in sateen order, either of the two methods of dividing up the repeat illustrated in *Figure 13.42*, may be employed. In the first method the repeat is divided each way into as many parts as there are figures, as shown by the dotted lines. The number of rectangular spaces in the repeat area is equal to the square of the number of figures, and corresponds with the number of small spaces in the repeat of the sateen base weave. The correct positions of the figure are found by marking the spaces in the order of the sateen base, or by similarly marking the places where the lines intersect. B in *Figure 13.42* shows the figure placed each time as centrally as possible upon the allotted space; whereas in C in the figure is placed each time with its centre as near as possible to the selected place where a vertical and a horizontal line intersect.

In the second method, as shown by the solid lines in *Figure 13.42*, the repeat area is divided into the same number of spaces of uniform size and shape as there are figures. The spaces, in this case, indicate the relative positions of the figure which is traced as centrally as possible within each space. The method in which the positions of the intersecting diagonal lines are obtained will be readily understood by comparing the sketches with the corresponding sateen bases given in *Figure 13.40*. In each base the sateen marks form lines with each other in opposite directions, flat lines being crossed by steeper lines. By drawing lines to connect the weave marks each boundary line of the repeat is divided into a number of equal parts. Thus, to correspond with the sateen bases, in the design A in *Figure 13.42*, the points of connection are found by dividing the boundary lines of the repeat into two equal parts; in B by dividing the horizontal lines into three parts, and the vertical lines into two parts; while in D the boundary lines are divided into two and also three equal parts. On account of the designs in *Figure 13.42* having been arranged to fit the two methods of dividing up the repeat, the figures do not coincide in position with the marks in the corresponding weave bases given in *Figure 13.40*. Thus, the first horizontal series of spaces in the design A corresponds with the fifth pick of weave A, and in the design B, with the fourth pick of weave B.

Methods of reversing the figures

The manner in which a figure is turned over or reversed in a sateen distribution has a considerable influence upon the appearance of the design. A in *Figure 13.42* shows the figure inclined at a different angle in each position—a system which is chiefly suitable for such textures as carpets and table-cloths, in which the design is required to appear similar from any point of view. B in *Figure 13.42* illustrates a good system of reversing a figure in the 8-sateen order of arrangement, four positions being shown, each of which is repeated. The object is always inclined at the same angle, and is therefore retained in the same relation to the threads in the cloth. Two consecutive figures are inclined to the left and two to the right, in either the steep or the flat twill line. If the figure is inclined alternately to right and left in the 8-sateen regular distribution, cross twill lines of figure are formed, in each of which all the figures are inclined in the same direction, and the design is defective. In the 10-sateen arrangement, shown at C in *Figure 13.42*, the figure is turned in two ways, and in both the steep and the flat twill line the angle of inclination is to the left and right alternately. In the 13-sateen arrangement, given at D in *Figure 13.42*, no two figures are turned the same, which is a particularly suitable method for such a stiff figure in preventing sameness of appearance. In the design E, the figure is turned in four positions, but in F all the figures are placed the same, which not only causes the design to appear uninteresting, but the twill-line due to the unsuitable base, is accentuated.

Figure 13.43

In addition to turning the same figure in different directions in order to make a design more effective, every figure in the repeat may be different in form, as shown in the example given in *Figure 13.43*. In this design, massive figures turned in diverse ways, are arranged in 8-sateen order. All the figures possess the same characteristics but the difference in shape makes the design appear freer and more attractive.

Size of repeat

A convenient method of finding the size of repeat which is suitable for a given figure in a proposed system of arrangement is illustrated in *Figure 13.44*. The size occupied by two figures (roughly sketched in alternate order), with the necessary amount of ground space, is first found, as shown at A. Then the corresponding width and length of repeat for the sateen distribution are obtained by multiplying the ascertained dimensions by—

$$\sqrt{\frac{\text{number of figures required}}{\text{number of figures given}}}$$

This formula is applicable to all calculations on changing the number of figures while retaining the same proportion of ground space. For example, taking the repeat of A in *Figure 13.44* to be 4 cm wide by 6 cm long, the repeat for the 8-sateen distribution shown at **B** =

$$4 \text{ cm} \times \sqrt{\frac{8 \text{ figures}}{2 \text{ figures}}} = 8 \text{ cm wide.}$$

$$6 \text{ cm} \times \sqrt{\frac{8 \text{ figures}}{2 \text{ figures}}} = 12 \text{ cm long.}$$

It may be necessary for the repeat in width to be changed to fit the capacity of a given jacquard. Thus, assuming that it is necessary for the design **B** to repeat on 6 cm, the length of repeat, which will give the same proportion of ground space, will be found as follows—

$$\frac{8 \text{ cm wide} \times 12 \text{ cm long}}{6 \text{ cm wide}} = 16 \text{ cm}$$

Changing the relative width and length of the repeat in the foregoing manner is not always practicable, however, because the twill line of figures is liable to be accentuated in one direction, while it is possible that the change will cause the figures to encroach on each other.

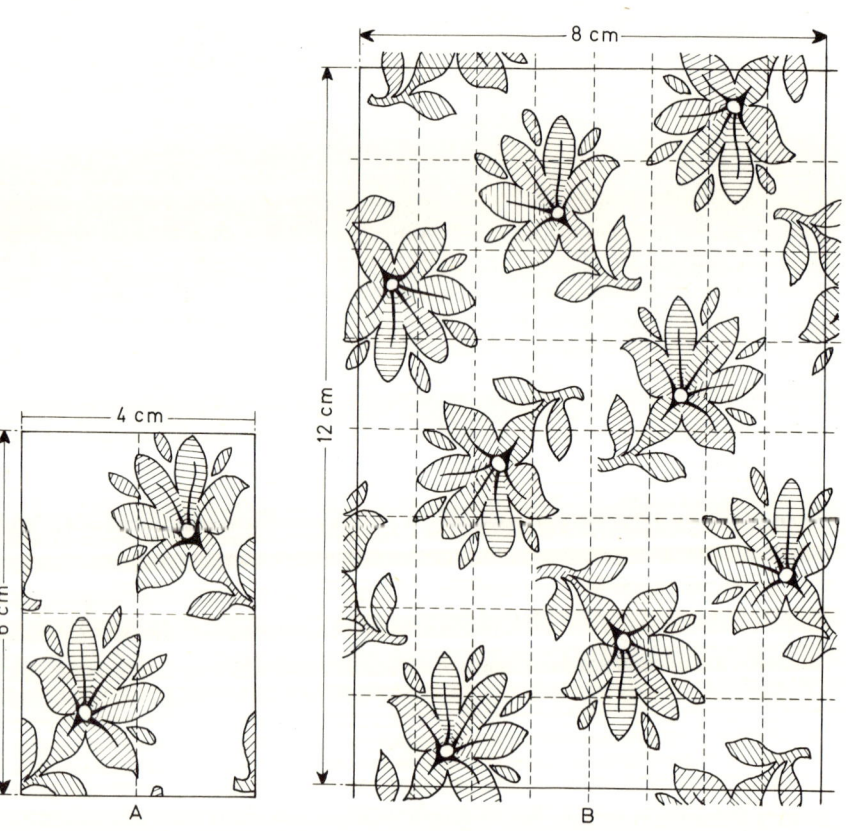

Figure 13.44

The following methods of drafting a sateen arrangement of figures from a sketch design or a woven sample can be employed: (1) The full repeat is squared out and all the figures are drawn and painted in independently upon the design paper. (2) One figure is drawn and painted on the design paper, and the remainder are copied square by square from it. (3) One figure is drawn on the design paper and the outline copied upon transparent tracing paper by means of which the remaining figures are traced. Certain of the sateen arrangements enable abbreviated methods of drafting to be employed, as shown in subsequent examples.

The 8-thread regular sateen base is one of the mose convenient to use, not only because even distribution of the figures is readily secured, but on account of the expeditious manner in which the arrangement can be drafted. This will be understood by comparing the design shown at B in *Figure 13.44* with the corresponding squared paper plan given in *Figure 13.45*. By analysis, it will be seen that the design B in *Figure 13.44* possesses two distinct features: (1) If the repeat be bisected in both directions, the figure in alternate sections is exactly the same; (2) the boundary lines of the repeat are drawn in such positions that they pass through the figure in the same way at the top and bottom, and at the sides; hence, the design appears exactly the same, whether viewed from the top or the bottom. Either feature may be taken advantage of to reduce the design paper work by one half. For example, although only half of the complete repeat is given in *Figure 13.45*, the second half of the cards can be cut from it: (a) by dividing the plan vertically into two parts, and reversing the sections; or (b) by turning the plan round. The former method can be employed for an 8-sateen arrangement whether the figure is turned in two or four directions, but the latter only when it is in four positions. Another point worthy of notice, in the latter method, is that if the rows are arranged the same from either end of the cards, both halves of the set of cards can be obtained at the same time, by cutting two cards alike from each horizontal space of the design. Thus, the half-repeat shown in *Figure 13.45*, contains 96 cards, and numbers 1 to 96, when turned round, are successively the same as numbers 192 to 97 in the full repeat. In further illustration of this, it will be seen by comparison that the upper half of the repeat of *Figure 13.44* exactly corresponds with *Figure 13.45* when the latter is turned round 180°. It is necessary, of course, for the gound weave to be commenced in such a manner that it will be continuous throughout, but as the direction of a twill line is not reversed, by thus turning the cards, it will be found that the majority of twill and sateen weaves offer no obstacle to the method.

Irregular sateen bases

Satinette arrangements

Symmetrical shapes may be arranged in satinette order without changing their angle of inclination. Usually, however, a more interesting effect is obtained if the figures are inclined in different directions as illustrated in

Figure 13.45

Figures 13.46 to *13.49.* A in *Figure 13.47* shows a figure turned in two ways and all the other illustrations show a figure turned in four ways—with a different system of reversing used in each case. The method of reversing which is most suitable is decided by the shape of the figure and its size, as compared

Figure 13.46

with the size of the repeat. A method which is convenient for one figure might produce a defective design if employed for another different shape. It will be noted in each design B, C, and D, that corresponding parts of the figures are in line with each other, and there is thus a possibility of lines showing in the cloth; but frequently this feature can be made use of to give additional interest to the grouping of the masses.

A   B   *Figure 13.47*

C   D

The positions of the figures are obtained by dividing the repeat each way into four equal parts, and marking the spaces in the order of the satinette. If each object is placed centrally on its allotted space the grouping of the figures in pairs is very noticeable, as shown in *Figure 13.46*. It is, therefore, usually better for each object to be slightly moved horizontally and vertically away from the centre of its space, in the manner illustrated by the examples given in *Figure 13.47*. The distance between the figures of each pair is thereby increased, while that between the pairs is reduced, which not only gives the design a better all-over appearance, on account of the masses being more evenly distributed, but figures can be employed which would otherwise encroach on each other.

The working out of the designs on squared paper can frequently be materially simplified if the basis of construction is taken into consideration. For example, if A and B in *Figure 13.47* are examined it will be seen that in each design the boundary lines are in such positions that the ornament in the lower half, taken from left to right, is exactly like that in the upper half taken from right to left. The designs thus possess the distinctive features of a pure drop-reverse arrangement, and a corresponding method of drafting can be employed.

In the same manner the design C in *Figure 13.47* coincides in arrangement with the examples given in *Figures 13.34* and *13.36*, in which the second half is like the first half turned over vertically.

From an examination of D in *Figure 13.47* it will be seen that the method of construction causes the design to appear the same, whether viewed from the top or the bottom. It is therefore possible, with certain ground weaves, for the complete set of cards to be cut by drafting the half repeat of the design, as shown in *Figure 13.48*, which corresponds with the lower half of D in *Figure 13.47*. The picks, from the first to the last in the given half of the design, are respectively like the last to the first in the other half, taken from opposite sides. The plan shows a fancy crêpe, that fits with plain weave, arranged so that the ground weave will be unbroken where the two halves of the repeat join.

The example given in *Figure 13.49* illustrates a method of arranging the main masses in an abstract type of design. The greater freedom of form in such designs permits unusual arrangements, and creation of uneven spaces between the figures does not present the same problems as in more formal designs. Thus, in *Figure 13.49* the four figures, each of which is slightly different, are arranged in two reversed pairs and the large spaces between the pairs are adequately filled up with meandering lines which provide additional interest without overpowering the main features of the ornament.

Irregular six-sateen arrangements

Different methods of arranging figures in 6-sateen order are illustrated in *Figures 13.50* to *13.54*. In this case the positions of the figures are found by dividing the repeat both ways into six equal parts and marking the spaces in the order of the 6-sateen weave. The masses group in threes both upward and outward, and to secure even distribution it is necessary to place each mass as centrally as possible upon its space.

Figure 13.49

Figure 13.48

Inclined figures afford considerable scope for producing diversity of effect, as a variation in the method of reversing causes a change in the relation of the masses to each other. This is illustrated by the designs shown in *Figures 13.50* to *13.52*, while many other arrangements can be made.

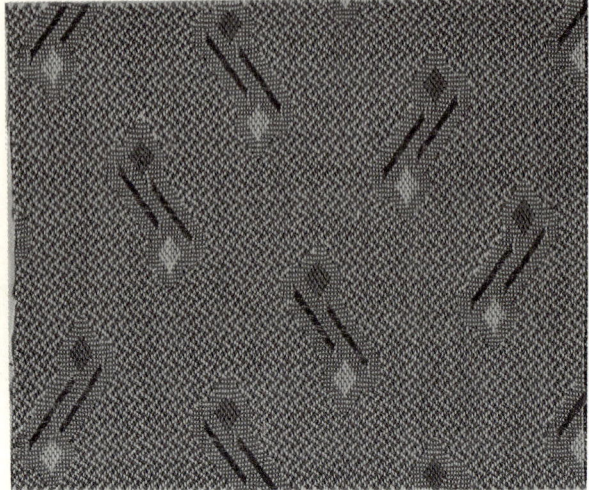

Figure 13.50

The design given in *Figure 13.53* shows how the 6-sateen order naturally permits two different forms to be introduced, one of which occupies the central position of each group of three figures. It will be noted in the example that the central figures are distributed in the drop-reverse order, and form the main features of the design; while the remaining figures are subsidiary, but in such positions that they overlap and give perfect distribution.

The design given in *Figure 13.54* shows how variety of effect may be produced by combining a satinette order with the 6-sateen. The figure in the

Figure 13.51

latter order is turned in two directions, and forms the main feature of the design; while that in the satinette order is made subsidiary and quite distinct in character, in order that the contrast will be effective. The centres of the secondary figures can be conveniently found by drawing two lines diagonally from corner to corner through three spaces, as shown, and marking off from the extremities a fourth of the length of each line.

It will be noted in each design given in *Figures 13.51* to *13.54* that instead of the first figure being placed on the first space it is placed on the sixth, the order of arrangement thus being changed from 1, 3, 5, 2, 6, 4, to 6, 2, 4, 1, 5,

Figure 13.53

Figure 13.52

Figure 13.54

Figure 13.55

3. This enables the grouping of the figures to be more readily seen, but the chief advantage is that the figures are in such positions in relation to the boundary lines of the repeat that the design can be readily made with the lower half exactly like the upper half turned over. An examination will show that *Figure 13.52* to *13.54* are thus arranged, and the feature may be made use of to simplify the construction of the design paper plan, in the same manner as in drafting a drop-reverse arrangement. Thus, *Figure 13.55* shows

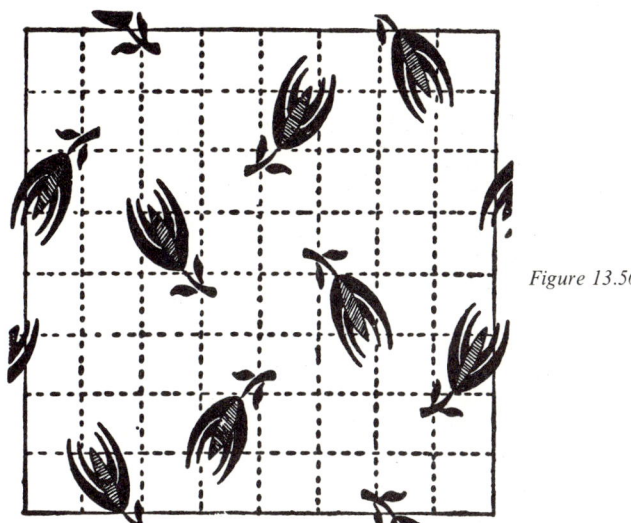

Figure 13.56

the half-repeat of *Figure 13.52* drafted upon 128 ends and 80 picks, and so far as regards the figure the marks from left to right in this half correspond with those from right to left in the second half. With ground weaves that will reverse the arrangement enables all the cards to be cut from the half-repeat, but the ground weave shown in *Figure 13.55* requires the full design to be made.

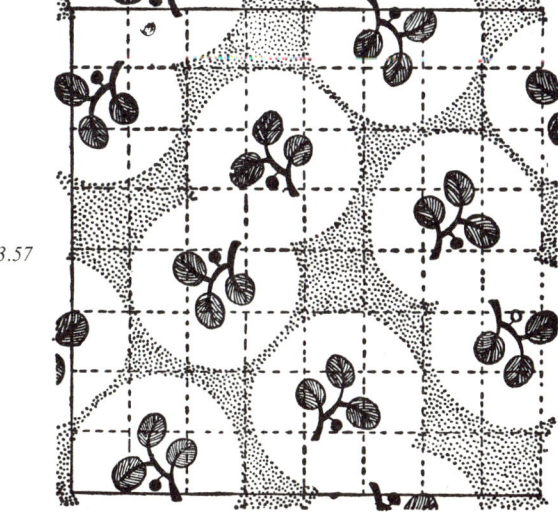

Figure 13.57

Irregular eight-sateen arrangements

Standard irregular 8-sateen arrangements are shown in *Figures 13.56* and *13.57*, the object in the former being placed on the spaces in the order of 2, 4, 8, 6, 3, 1, 5, 7, and in the latter in the order of 2, 5, 8, 3, 7, 4, 1, 6. The chief difference between the arrangements is in the manner in which the figures group in pairs. Even distribution of a given mass can be secured upon either basis, by suitably proportioning the length and width of the repeat, but the shape of the ornament generally decides which arrangement is the more suitable. Thus, in *Figure 13.56* the figures group in pairs outwardly, the

Figure 13.58

greatest distance between them being in a vertical direction, so that the arrangement is suitable for figures which are longer than they are broad. In *Figure 13.57*, on the other hand, the figures group in pairs vertically, and the greatest distance between them is in a horizontal direction, hence this arrangement is more suitable for flat figures.

The designs given in *Figures 13.56* and *13.57* are constructed in a manner that enables them to be readily drafted upon squared paper. Thus an examination of *Figure 13.56* will show that the figure is so reversed, and the boundary lines are in such positions, that the design appears the same whether viewed from the top or the bottom. Therefore if the ground weave is suitable, the design may be drafted, as illustrated by *Figure 13.48*. In *Figure 13.57* the upper half of the design is exactly like the lower half turned over, and the design can therefore be drafted in one of the methods previously described in reference to a drop-reverse arrangement. It will be appreciated, of course, that if a different shape of figure is used in each position no simplification of the point-paper work is possible.

Figure 13.58 illustrates a third grouping of the figures in the 8-sateen irregular order, which can be used to yield good results. The flowers which form the masses are placed in the order of 3, 1, 5, 2, 6, 8, 4, 7, and each unit is formed of two figures, which are reversed in such a manner that they fall into straight lines. The example illustrates that the basis readily lends itself to the production of a design of a geometrical character, which is arranged on the drop-reverse principle. *Figures 13.57* and *13.58* show, by comparison, how widely different styles can be constructed in the same basis of arrangement, the ornament in the former being as free as in the latter it is stiff.

14

Construction of Designs from Incomplete Repeats

Frequently designs have to be reproduced from small cuttings of cloth which show only a portion of the complete repeat of the figure. This is due, in many cases, to the original sample having been cut by the merchant into several pieces to enable quotations to be obtained simultaneously from different manufacturers. In some instances, it is only necessary for the ornament which is introduced to complete the design to be in keeping with the given portion of figure. In other cases, however, and particularly in certain traditional cloths, it is very necessary that as little deviation as possible be made from the original design. Good judgment, combined with an intimate knowledge of the various bases upon which designs are constructed, and of what constitutes a well-balanced design, will generally enable an accurate copy of the original figure to be obtained in an expeditious manner.

If the repeat in width is incomplete, an endeavour should be made in filling in the missing portion, to adapt the figure to the size of repeat which can be obtained in the jacquard for which the design is intended. The missing portion of figure may be added, either by making a complete sketch of the design, or by working directly on the squared paper from the sample; and the method of drafting the figure will vary according to the basis upon which it is judged that the design has been constructed.

Assuming that the figure is required to be reproduced from the small sample of cloth represented in *Figure 14.1*, a sketch of the complete design may be constructed, as shown in *Figure 14.2*. In this method an accurate copy of the outline of the given portion of figure is first made, either by tracing or by pricking round the edges, and a horizontal line is drawn parallel with the weft threads. In *Figure 14.2* the solid black figure corresponds with the portion shown in *Figure 14.1*, while the line A B indicates the direction of the weft threads in relation to the figure. From an examination of the given portions of the design it will be seen that the parts at C and D in *Figure 14.2* are the same but turned in opposite directions from which it may be judged that the design is based on the drop-reverse principle. The length of the half-repeat of the design is therefore equal to the distance in a vertical plane between similar parts of the figure, and the two half-repeats are indicated, as shown by the dotted horizontal lines. A tracing of the given figure is turned over and placed half the repeat upward, with the horizontal lines and duplicate parts of the figure coinciding, and a copy is made in the reversed position, as shown by the shaded portion of *Figure 14.2*. It is convenient to draw a vertical line, as shown at E F, in the same relative position to the parts of the figure which are alike at C and D, as the position where the figure reverses is indicated by the line. The proper width of the repeat (shown by the dotted vertical lines) is found by moving the tracing horizontally to a position in which it is judged that the chief parts of the ornament are evenly balanced. Missing portions of the figure are then drawn in, and the parts traced at the top, bottom, and sides, as shown by the outline drawing.

Figure 14.1

Having thus obtained the full design the size of repeat in terms of the total number of ends and picks per repeat can be calculated by reference to thread spacing in the sample. This provides the basis for squared paper representation of the design which can now be readily constructed by the usual method from the sketch in *Figure 14.2*. As the design is arranged on the drop-reverse principle only half the length of the repeat need be produced, the other half being obtained exactly in accordance with the rules described with reference to *Figure 13.28*.

In most cases the readiest method of drafting an incomplete design is to draw the outline of the given portion of figure to scale directly from the cloth on to the design paper, some form of thread arrangement being used for squaring out the pattern. It is also convenient, although not so expeditious,

Figure 14.2

to sketch the given portion of figure, and divide it into spaces by ruling lines. It is not, as a rule, necessary for time to be occupied in making a complete sketch of the design, as the figure can be completed on the squared paper after the given portion has been drawn and painted in. This is illustrated by the example shown in *Figures 14.3* and *14.4*. An analysis of the sketch shown in the lower portion of *Figure 14.3*, will show that the same shape of figure occurs at the positions lettered A, B, and C. Taking A as the starting-point, at B the figure is turned over from side to side, and at C from top to bottom. The distance between two horizontal lines which pass through corresponding parts of the design at A and B thus gives half the repeat in length, and similarly the distance between two vertical lines which pass through corresponding parts at A and C gives half the repeat in width. The basis on which the design has been constructed is therefore the satinette, the unit being placed and reversed as shown in the upper portion of *Figure 14.3*. The sketch in the lower portion is shown squared out in preparation for drawing the figure to scale

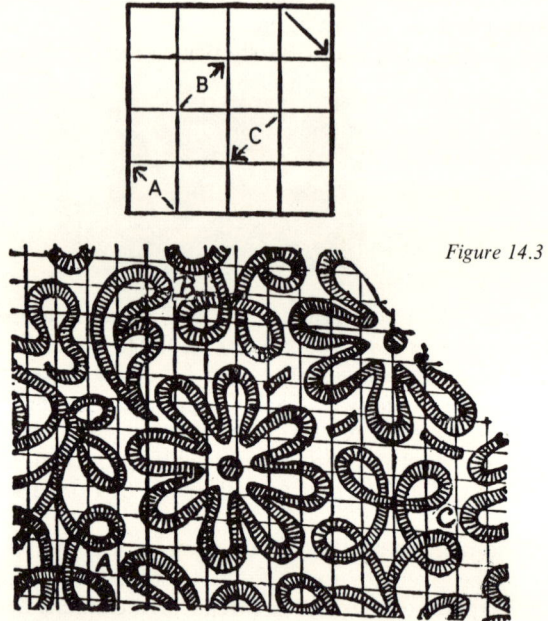

Figure 14.3

on design paper, the half repeat in width (from A to C) being divided into 11 parts, and in length (from A to B) into 10 parts. The complete paper plan is shown in *Figure 14.4*, each division of the sketch being taken to represent eight ends and picks, so that the full design repeats upon 176 ends and 160 picks. In drafting the figure on the squared paper it is first necessary to indicate the unit of the design, as shown by the portion filled in solid in *Figure 14.4*. The unit is then repeated three times, as shown by the shaded figure, either by copying square by square, or by the aid of tracing paper, the required positions being readily obtained by comparing with the pattern, and by noting that corresponding parts are half the repeat distance from each other in width or in length. A further point to note is that one vertical line (the fifth), in *Figure 14.3*, cuts similar parts of the figure in the same relative position, and is taken as the centre of the squared paper plan. The second half of *Figure 14.4*, when turned over, is therefore exactly like the first half, as in the case of a drop-reverse design.

When the given figure of an incomplete design is somewhat massive, and there is no indication of the bases of construction, a convenient method of procedure consists of arranging the mass on the drop-reverse principle. The given portion of figure is thus made full use of by being included twice in the repeat, and the style of the design is retained, while the minimum of space has to be filled in with missing figure. Inclined and non-symmetrical figures are also particularly suitable for arrangement on the drop-reverse principle and this has been amply demonstrated earlier, but they should not, as a rule, be arranged on the half-drop system which is better adapted to accommodate evenly balanced figures.

Possibly the most difficult principles of arrangement to deduce from an incomplete sample are those based on the various sateen orders. The best indication is usually the comparatively small size of each figure in relation to the total size of sample available and, secondly, the variety of slight differences in the shape and the angle of inclination of the given units as illustrated by *Figures 14.5* and 14.6 *Figure 14.5* shows four triangular units, all slightly different and all inclined at varying angles. *Figure 14.6* shows a sketch in which the four units indicated in solid black are the units copied directly from the sample. On close study of the distribution it will be observed that the figures marked 1, 2, 3, and 4 appear to occupy adjacent horizontal rows their

Figure 14.4

centres being approximately equidistant. Vertically, however, only 1 and 4 seem to occupy adjacent rows there being a gap about equal to the size of one figure between units 1 and 3, and again between 2 and 4 which suggests that at least two further figures will be required at other positions within the full repeat. Thus, it may be assumed that the area shown in the sample represents four horizontal and six vertical rows of the repeat, the full size of which is still unknown at this stage. However, it will be also noted that, counting from the right, unit 2 is displaced from unit 1 by three spaces to the left, with identical displacement also between units 3 and 4. The step or move of 3 is suggestive of sateen distribution and, considering the most likely arrangements, it could

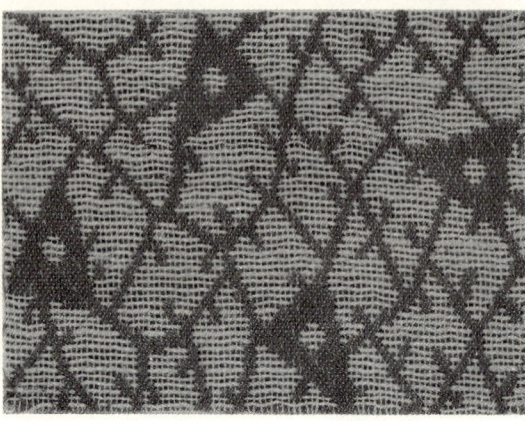

Figure 14.5

be part of a 5-, 6-, or 8-sateen order. The two lower sateen orders can be discounted as with these parts of the remaining figures would be visible within the 6 × 4 area which is available. However, on trying the 8-sateen arrangement it becomes obvious that unit 3 is also displaced from unit 2 by a step of 3 to the left and, on continuing with this step, unit 5 is placed correctly in

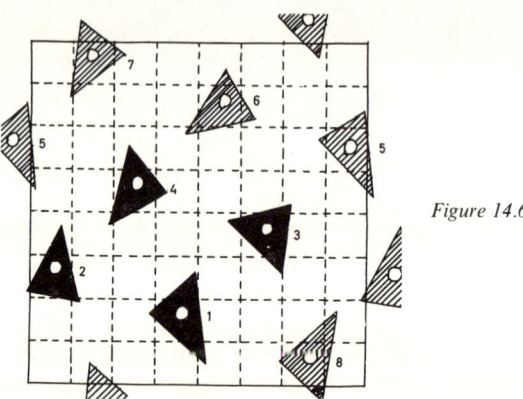

Figure 14.6

respect of unit 4, unit 6 in respect of unit 5, and so on, each fitting into its predetermined space perfectly. Before placing each unit in the proper position its angle and shape is adjusted to give the most pleasing arrangement, the main criterion being freedom from distinct twilling lines, bars or stripes. Considerable license is permissible at this stage as well as with the arrangement of any secondary ornament such as the random lines shown in *Figure 14.5*.

Appendix I

STANDARD YARNS

(See Appendix II for terms used mainly in conjunction with man-made materials)

Angola yarn See Union yarns.

Angora yarn A very soft yarn spun from the long, fine hair of the Angora rabbit, and mostly used for knitted fabrics.

Artificial silk, or **rayon** (see Appendix II).

Asbestos Yarn Asbestos is a mineral fibre found as veins in serpentine rock, the chief supply being obtained in Canada. The fibre is fine and smooth, and the yarn may consist entirely of asbestos, or a small percentage of cotton may be added in order to make the material spin better, and to increase the strength. The yarn is used single and two, three, or more fold, and in some cases a brass or copper wire thread is twisted with asbestos thread, the latter being wound round and round the wire thread so as to cover it. (See Asbestos cloth.)

Balanced twist The twist is assumed to be balanced in a two-fold yarn when half as many turns per inch have been inserted in the doubling process as were previously inserted in the opposite direction in each single thread. Theoretically, each turn of reverse twist in the doubling takes a turn out of the single twist, and in twisting together two single threads which contain, say, twenty turns per inch, the twist will be balanced when ten turns of reverse twist have been made. It is usual, however, to exceed this condition so that the twist in folded yarns more nearly approaches that of the single threads as a result of which there is very little twist left in the single threads.

Bastard cop A size of cop made at one time between the ordinary sizes of warp and weft cops.

Bleached yarns Bleaching is employed for yarns which require to be white or which it is intended to dye in light shades.

Brass bobbin yarn The thread which is wound on the thin brass bobbin, and is used as weft in the manufacture of lace cloth, the counts ranging from about 20/2 tex to about 4/2 tex.

Bundle yarn Hank yarn which is made up for transport in the form of long bundles, which are unpressed, or in short bundles in which the hanks are compressed into smaller compass in a bundling press.

Cabled yarn Term applied to yarns, such as sewing cotton (q.v.), which are produced by twisting together two or more folded yarns. The method yields a stronger, smoother, and more regular yarn than when all the single threads are twisted together at one operation.

Camel-hair yarn   See Worsted yarns and Hoisery yarns.

Carpet yarns   Fulness and resiliency are the main qualities required in a carpet pile yarn. Traditionally, Scotch blackface and East Indian wools were used along with Welsh and lower qualities of cross-bred wools. These materials are still employed extensively and are spun mainly on the woollen system although in fine Wilton and Gripper Axminster carpets worsted spun yarns are also used.

Yarns composed of man-made fibres, however, are even more extensively used than wool and in the field of non-traditionally constructed carpets they occupy a predominant position. Chief materials are certain types of viscose rayon and acrylic staple yarns as well as bulked nylon (q.v.). Fibre blends are also commonly employed, e.g. viscose rayon staple/wool; or, viscose rayon staple/wool/nylon, and, although the constitution of these blends varies, the first type is frequently encountered composed of 60 per cent viscose staple and 40 per cent wool, whilst the second type quoted is often made in the proportion of 50/30/20.

Cashmere yarn   See Worsted yarns and Hosiery yarns.

China grass or ramie yarn   Composed of fibres derived from the stems of plants of the same species as the nettle. The thread is lustrous, white, and strong and is largely used in the manufacture of gas mantles.

Chlorinated yarns   Wool in fibre, sliver, top, or yarn form is made non-shrinkable by treatment with chlorine, and at the same time is made more readily absorbent of dyes than untreated wool. (See Chlorinated cloth.)

Coir or coconut fibre yarn   Thick, coarse yarn spun from the reddish-brown fibre of which the outer covering of the coconut is composed. Used for matting (q.v.) and cordage.

Cop-and-cop doubled yarn   Two-fold yarn of which the single threads are from two different qualities or spinnings, a cop of each being twisted together in order to equalise the cost or quality of the two yarns.

Core yarn   Made with a cheap yarn in the centre round which a special kind of thread is wound in such a manner as to cover the central thread. (See Tinsel yarn.) Lastex yarn (q.v., Appendix II) has a rubber thread in the centre.

Cotton yarns   The different classes of cotton vary in length of fibre from 12 mm to about 50 mm, but the limits to which they will spin range from about 30 tex to upwards of 2 tex. The fibres are arranged somewhat straight and parallel in the thread in a very similar manner to the fibres in a worsted yarn.

Mule-spun cotton yarn   Very little cotton yarn except for the fine counts is now mule-spun. Drafting, spinning, and winding on are performed intermittently, and the twist is inserted over a long stretch of thread, so that short fibres project freely from the body of the yarn, which has a full appearance and makes a well covered cloth.

Ring-spun cotton yarn   The thread is smoother and stronger than mule-spun yarn, as the fibres are better twisted in, but it is not so elastic. Drafting, spinning, and winding on are performed continuously, and the thread has to be wound on to a substantial basis in the form of ring bobbins or strong paper tubes. About 7 tex is the limit of fineness in combed Egyptian yarn and 12 tex in carded American.

Combed cotton yarn   The short fibres, and along with them any impurities which have been left in the cotton, are separated from the long fibres by combing. The resultant yarn is, therefore, cleaner, smoother, stronger, and more lustrous than a carded (uncombed) cotton yarn, but it has less filling power, owing to the absence of the short fibres. A thread may be stated as half, ordinary, super, or double-combed, the waste taken out being respectively about 11, 15, 18, and 24 per cent. On account of the increased cost, combing is only employed to give the cotton the requisite spinning property for fine counts, and when a high-class yarn is required in medium counts.

Carded cotton yarn   Contains the short fibres and is a more fibrous or oozy thread than a combed yarn, and cannot be spun to such fine counts. A carded yarn is less costly, however, and is particularly useful when a well-covered cloth is required. In super-carded yarn the material has been specially cleaned of the very short fibres and fine impurities, to enable a superior or finer thread to be spun.

Condenser cotton yarn A thick, soft, full handling yarn, liable to contain many impurities, which is composed of soft wastes from cotton carding, combing, and drawing, and hard thread wastes from cotton spinning and weaving. These are opened out and formed into a soft, fibrous condition, and then carded on the 'roller and clearer' system, and condensed and spun on the same principle as woollen yarn.

See, also, the following Cotton yarns: *Brass bobbin, Crotchet, Doubled, Flannelette, Heald, Lace, Lisle, Mercerised, Motor tyre, Polished, Prepared hank* and *Sewing.*

Crêpe yarn Very hard twisted, single or two-fold yarn, composed of cotton, wool, silk, or rayon (q.v.). In folded yarns the twist is usually in the same direction as that of the single threads, and the high twist causes the yarn, when slack, to snarl or kink up. To set the twist and make the yarn easier to work it is subjected to humid heat, usually by steaming the yarn on bobbins. In cotton crêpe yarns the tex twist multiplier ranges from 140 to 240, but the strength gradually decreases as the multiplier rises above 130.

Crossband yarn The twist runs from right to left looking up the yarn, as shown at B in *Figure 2.12.*

Crotchet yarn A softer thread than sewing cotton, and when made at two operations of doubling the twist in the first process is in the opposite direction to that of the single twist, and in the second process is in the opposite direction to that of the folded twist.

Curled yarn See Worsted yarns.

Doubled or folded yarn Consists of two or more threads twisted together with the primary object of obtaining greater strength and evenness than can be obtained in a single yarn of the same count. Special yarns are also obtained by twisting together threads which differ in thickness, length, colour, material, etc. (see Fancy yarns). The terms flyer, ring, and twiner or mule-doubled are applied to the yarn according to the method in which the twisting is effected. (Cap doubling is employed for a certain amount of worsted yarn and tends to make a rough thread, and in the *Climax* system of doubling, the threads, wound two or more together, are twisted while passing from the twisting spindles to cheeses or warpers' bobbins, which is the reverse direction to that of ordinary doubling, a process of winding being saved.) Flyer doubling is used for high qualities of fine yarns, and for very thick doubled yarns, as a rounder and smoother thread and more regular twist is produced than in ring doubling. The latter, however, is the cheaper and more productive method, and is the one chiefly employed. In ordinary doubled yarn the direction of the folded twist is opposite to that of the single threads. This produces a softer folded yarn than if both twisting operations are in the same direction (see Twist-on-twist), because each turn of reverse twist in the folding takes a turn of twist out of each single thread. For the same reason a folded thread is usually softer than the single threads of which it is composed, and in dyeing the yarns a given tone can generally be obtained on folded threads by means of a lighter dye than is required for single threads. (See Balanced twist.)

Doubling weft (D.W.) Term applied to single cotton yarn used for doubling purposes, the amount of twist in which is between the ordinary warp and weft twist, and the direction the same as warp twist.

Wet doubled cotton yarn The single threads pass together through a trough containing water to the twisting spindles, and a smoother and stronger folded yarn is produced, because the loose fibres are laid and thoroughly twisted in. In the *English* system of wet doubling the threads simply pass under a glass rod in the water trough, whereas in the *Scotch* system the lower delivery roller revolves in the water, and the threads pass under it and then between the two rollers, by which the yarn is made much wetter than in the English system. In wet doubling fine, hard-twisted yarns the moisture does not penetrate very readily, and a wetting out agent is sometimes added to the water to improve moisture penetration.

Dry doubled yarn Threads which have to be bleached, dyed, sized, etc. are dry-doubled, as they require to be in an open condition so that they will be absorbent; also soft, full yarns such as those used for hosiery.

(See, also, *Balanced twist, Cabled, Double-throw yarn, One-throw yarn,* and *Twist-on-twist.*)

Double-throw yarn   Consists of a number of single threads, which are twisted together at two operations of doubling (see Cabled yarn).

Embroidery and **crewel yarns**   Made from silk, rayon, linen and cotton, from two to six-fold and soft twisted. The cotton yarns are mostly made from a high quality of cotton, and are gassed and mercerised to imitate silk.

Fancy, novelty or **effect yarns**   These are chiefly produced by blending different colours or materials in the fibre state; by printing or dyeing a pattern on the sliver or yarn; by introducing spots or neps of coloured fibres which are twisted in with the threads; by twisting together threads which are different in material, colour, softness, thickness, length, and amount and direction of twist; and by forming curls, snarls, lumps, knops, and thick and thin places at intervals in the yarn. The principal types of

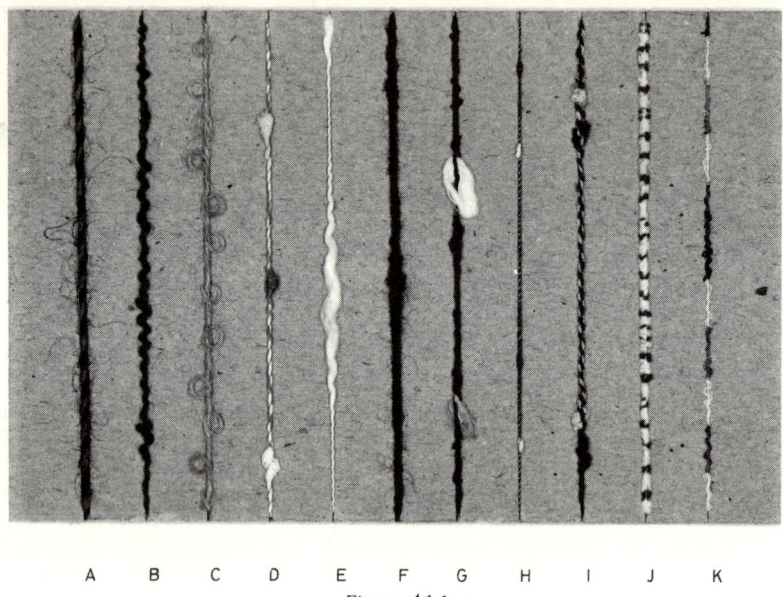

A   B   C   D   E   F   G   H   I   J   K

Figure A1.1

yarns are illustrated in *Figure A1.1*, and described in the following, but there is practically no limit to the diverse ways in which the different effects may be combined and utilised.

Grandrelle yarn   Composed of two or more differently coloured threads twisted together, which are usually about equal in thickness. A in *Figure A1.1* illustrates a two-ply yarn. In order to produce a regular effect in a cloth which is largely composed of grandrelle warp threads, each warp float on the surface should contain approximately one complete twist of the yarn, and there should, therefore, be some relation between the number of turns per inch and the length of the warp float. Thus, in a cloth with 24 picks per cm, 2-and-2 twill gives a warp float of $\frac{1}{12}$ cm, 3-and-1 twill of $\frac{1}{8}$ cm, and 5 shaft satin of $\frac{1}{6}$ cm, and the number of turns per cm of the grandrelle warp should be approximately 12, 8, and 6 for the respective weaves.

Marl yarn   Produced by spinning from two differently coloured rovings (or one white and the other coloured), a single-twist thread being made which looks similar to a two-fold grandrelle yarn, and the term mock-grandrelle is applied to it. The colours are not so distinct as in a grandrelle thread, however, and, in order to further break up the solidity of the colours, two marl threads are sometimes twisted together.

Spiral yarn   The example illustrated at B in *Figure A1.1* is a cotton yarn, and consists of a two-fold (cross-band) thread twisted cross-band with a thick soft-twisted (open-band) thread, which is given in much more quickly than the two-fold thread. The folded thread is then twisted open-band with a fine single (open-band) thread, which is held tighter than the folded thread. A worsted spiral yarn is made by twisting a thick, soft twist thread slackly with a fine, hard twist thread. This type of yarn is sometimes used in producing curl effects by heavily shrinking the cloth in which it is woven, the soft-twisted thread being thus made so slack that it forms loops on the surface.

Gimp yarn Similar to spiral yarn, but is harder twisted than the latter, and usually is finer in counts.

Corkscrew yarn Usually consists of a rather hard-twisted fine thread and a soft-twisted thick thread, the former being held tighter than the latter in the doubling process, so that the thicker thread is woven spirally round the fine thread. The yarn is sometimes similar in appearance to a spiral yarn, but the effect is not so pronounced.

Diamond yarn The yarn illustrated at D in *Figure A1.1* shows a diamond effect between the knops.

Bead yarn Contains hard lumps, like beads, at intervals, while in some cases proper beads on one thread are fixed in position by twisting another thread with the first thread.

Curl or loop yarn The example illustrated at C in *Figure A1.1* is a worsted curl yarn in which the thread that forms the curls is made with open-band twist and is folded cross-band with a double thread that has been twisted cross-band. The curl thread is much thicker than the other thread, and is slackly twisted round the latter, and the two threads are then twisted open-band with a fine open-band twist thread. The reversal of the twist in the second folding process untwists the slack curl thread, so that it forms loops at intervals. The formation of the curl may also be due to the thick thread being given in slack at regular intervals.

Snarl yarn Similar to curl yarn, but the slack thread is hard twisted, so that, instead of forming loops, it twists up and produces snarls.

Knop yarn The example illustrated at D in *Figure A1.1* consists of a dark cotton thread twisted with a light worsted thread, which at regular intervals is delivered very rapidly, so that it is wound round and round the first thread in the form of a hard knop or lump. The two threads are then twisted in the reverse direction with a second cotton thread, which acts as a binder.

Cloud yarn Illustrated at E in *Figure A1.1*. The example consists of two fine threads twisted together, and at intervals a portion of a thick, soft roving is given in and twisted with them. The threads are given in rapidly along with the roving, so that there is much less twist in the thick parts of the yarn than in the thin parts. The term cloud is also applied to a type of yarn which is mainly composed of two differently coloured threads, each of which, in turn, is wrapped round the other thread, so that the yarn shows first in one colour for a space and then in the other colour.

Slub yarn Thick slubs or lumps, as shown at F in *Figure A1.1*, are formed at intervals in the yarn. A fine thread is twisted with a thick roving, which is given in with a variable draft, so that it is made alternately fine and thick, with most of the twist running into the fine parts. A fine binding thread is then twisted with the two-fold thread in the opposite direction. The yarn is similar to a cloud yarn, except that the roving is not continuous in the latter. The thick lumps are sometimes produced by giving the roving in rapidly and winding it round and round the fine yarn (as in making a knop yarn), the roving in this case being the same thickness throughout.

Knickerbocker yarn See example G in *Figure A1.1*. Spots of colour appear in the yarn, which is usually produced on the woollen principle. Coarse and medium wools of the cheviot and cross-bred types are used for the thread, while the coloured spots are generally composed of fine wool which is introduced in small tufts during the later stage of carding, so that it remains unopened and shows as solid spots of colour.

Nub yarn An irregular thread that contains small spots or nubs, as illustrated by the yarn shown at H in *Figure A1.1*, which has been produced on the same principle as a knop yarn. The thread may also be made in the same method as a knickerbocker yarn.

Spot yarn See example I in *Figure A1.1*. Small lumps or spots, in a different colour from the ground thread, occur at regular or irregular intervals. The term spot is also applied to knop, knickerbocker, and nub yarns, which show spots of colour.

Flake yarn   Rather large patches or flakes of white or coloured material are twisted in with a differently coloured ground thread. The term flake is also applied to cloud yarns.

Chenille yarn   See example J in *Figure A1.1*. For use as a novelty yarn, chenille has a central core of threads, from which fibres project more or less all round. The yarn is formed in a weaving process in which warp threads are placed in groups at a suitable distance apart (according to the required length of the projecting fibres), and are interwoven on the gauze principle with the weft, which may be variously coloured (see *Watson's Advanced Textile Design*). The floats of weft between the groups of gauze threads are afterwards cut, and a number of chenille threads are simultaneously produced, each of which is as long as the texture which is woven in the loom. Chenille is used as a novelty yarn in both warp and weft, but it is chiefly employed as weft in chenille fabrics, and in the production of figure textures the threads are coloured to coincide with the form of the required design.

Printed yarn   In the ordinary process of printing threads one or more colours are impressed on hank or warp yarns in the form of bars, as shown at K in *Figure A1.1*, and all the threads, which are printed at the same time, are coloured alike. For chiné fabrics (q.v.) varied and elaborate colourings are printed on the warp threads.

Fast-dyed yarn   Has been so dyed that the colour will withstand without deterioration the action of such agencies as light, washing, scouring, bleaching, rubbing, etc.

Flannelette yarn   A cotton weft used for cloths which are finished with a raised surface. The thread is usually soft spun and thick, and is made from a rather short-fibred cotton of fair quality, such as Indian or similar cotton, mixed with a good class of waste fibre. Should the yarn contain too much short fibre excessive waste is made in the raising process, and if it is very soft-twisted the cloth does not wear well (see Flannelette fabric).

French or **dry-spun worsted yarn**   See Worsted yarns.

Gassed yarn   The yarn is passed through the flame of a gas burner by which the loose surface fibre is burned off. The threads appear browner after gassing, but they are made smoother and more lustrous, and the process is employed for voile and lace yarns, sewing threads, and yarns for mercerising. The usual loss in weight is about 5 per cent but threads which require to be very clear and are gassed twice may lose upwards of 8 per cent in weight. The term *genappe* is applied to gassed worsted yarn.

Hard-twist yarn   Contains more than the normal number of turns per cm, and is used for special fabrics, such as voiles, crêpes, crepons, etc.

Hemp yarn   Is naturally dark coloured, and is chiefly used for twine, cordage, and ropes, but is also employed for the backs of carpets and as a substitute for flax yarn in coarse canvas cloths.

Heald yarn   Genappe worsted heald yarn, made from long wool, is used to some extent, but Egyptian cotton yarn, ranging from 9 to 16 or more fold is more generally employed. A smooth yarn which is capable of absorbing varnish is required, and the thickness is varied according to the counts of the warp and number of ends per cm in the cloth to be woven.

Hosiery yarns   Chiefly made from wool and wool hairs, cotton, rayon, and synthetic fibres, and, as a rule, the thread should be soft-twisted, open in structure, and possess the properties of fulness and softness in a high degree. In wool a wide range of qualities is used, but a fibre which has little tendency to shrink or felt during washing is particularly serviceable. English Downs wool, which is of medium quality and length and very full handling, and fine cross-bred, are among the best knitting wools. Botany wool, which felts readily, provides a good foundation for the formation of a raised surface, but when this class of finish is not required, the material is occasionally mixed with cotton in order to reduce the shrinking property of the yarn (see Union Merino yarn). Pure Shetland wool and the fine hairs (goat, camel) possess excellent properties for hosiery yarns, and they also have a natural colour which renders them useful for many purposes without dyeing. Cotton tends to produce rather a hard thread, but when loosely twisted it can be raised so as to give a soft feel. Most frequently hosiery yarns are two or more fold in structure, and sometimes a silk or rayon thread is twisted with a wool or cotton thread.

A wide range of synthetic materials is also used in making the yarns which may be in the staple form, or in the form of continuous filament yarns either bulked or flat.

Wheeling yarn The single thread is spun on the woollen principle (see Woollen yarn), and usually two, three, or four of the threads are folded together, a somewhat heavy and coarse knitting yarn being produced.

Lambs' wool yarn Term applied to woollen-spun knitting threads made from the shorter and finer qualities of wool (not necessarily lambs' wool).

Worsted hosiery yarns (see Worsted yarn) Vary very much in quality, the longer and coarser fibres being open-drawn and flyer-spun, whereas cone-drawing along with flyer or cap spinning is employed for shorter and finer wools. Sometimes a large proportion of the short fibre is left in the yarn, and occasionally combing is entirely omitted. For under-wear yarns the best and fullest threads are obtained from fine wools by dry-combing, French drawing, and worsted mule spinning.

Fingering yarn Usually consists of two or more worsted-spun threads folded together (as distinct from a wheeling yarn, in which each thread is woollen-spun).

Cashmere hosiery yarn Made from fine Cashmere goat hair on the worsted principle.

Shetland yarn Made from soft handling natural-coloured wool (not necessarily Shetland wool), or from a mixture of white and natural-coloured wool (such as alpaca), in imitation of Shetland wool. 'Natural' wool has the advantage that it does not soil readily.

Alpaca and camel-hair knitting yarns Very soft natural-coloured yarns, spun respectively from alpaca and camel-hair fibres on the worsted principle.

Berlin wool A brightly coloured knitting yarn used chiefly for embroidery and fancy knitting by hand.

Jute yarn Is naturally yellowish-brown, and is used in coarse counts for sacks and packing sheets, but the largest proportion of the output is utilised by the carpet industry, either as ground yarns in conventional woven carpets (particularly for the weft and the stuffer warp), or in backing cloths for tufted and other unconventional types of carpetings. Jute tow yarns are made from the waste of jute.

Lace yarn High-class cotton yarn, ranging up to 5/2 tex and finer, used in the manufacture of lace (see Brass bobbin yarn). The term lace, however, is also applied to a good quality of two-fold cotton yarn in any thickness which is used for weaving purposes.

Linen or **flax yarns** Made from the fibre obtained from the stems of the flax plant by the processes of retting, scutching, hackling, drawing and spinning.

Dry-spun flax yarn The dry method of spinning is employed for thick yarns, the sizes of which are traditionally indicated by the weight in pounds per spyndle of 14 400 yards. The fibres retain their original length, and the yarn is very strong.

Demi-sec or *half-dry-spun flax yarn* The drafted rovings, after leaving the front rollers, are passed in contact with a damp roller, so that the twist is inserted in the thread while in a wet condition, the fibres being better laid and a smoother yarn produced than in dry-spinning.

Wet-spun linen yarn In wet-spinning the rovings, previous to passing between the drafting rollers, go through a trough of hot water (180° F.), by which the gum is softened that joins the ultimate fibres together, so that these are separated in the drawing process. The fine, short fibres that result are capable of being spun to very fine counts.

Boiled linen yarn Has been boiled once or twice in soda lye, which causes a loss in weight of from 5 to 10 per cent.

Creamed linen yarn Has been boiled and partly bleached, the loss in weight being about 10 or 12 per cent.

Half-bleached, three-quarter-bleached, and *full-bleached* Terms applied to linen yarn according to the length of time that the material has been subjected to the bleaching processes, and the number of times that the processes have been repeated. The yarn loses from 10 to 20 per cent in weight.

Lisle yarn Originally a linen thread (made in Lisle or Lille) used in the manufacture of lace, gloves, and hosiery, and now made of long-stapled cotton. It is a combed, rather hard-twisted, smooth, and wiry thread, with all the surface fibre removed by gassing.

Llama yarn   See Union yarns.

Mercerised cotton yarn   The yarn is passed through a cold, strong solution of caustic soda (50° to 60° Tw.), which causes it to contract considerably (about 20 per cent), and then the impregnated material is stretched to about its original length, during which the threads take on a permanent silky lustre. The caustic soda causes the flat, twisted-ribbon like fibres to swell up and become round, straight, and transparent, while the tension on the yarn (which is continued while the alkali is washed off) develops the lustre. The yarn is passed through a dilute solution of sulphuric acid to neutralise the caustic soda, and is again washed off and then dried. The most lustrous results are obtained by using a combed and gassed two-fold yarn, which contains rather less twist than ordinary two-fold, and has been spun from a high quality of cotton. Formerly no lower quality than Egyptian cotton yarn was used for mercerising, but now successful results are obtained in yarns spun from some of the better qualities of American cotton (see Mercerised cloth).

Motor tyre yarn   Heavy yarn used in the manufacture of the walls of rubber tyres. At one time constructed from high quality cotton but this though still used has been largely replaced by high tenacity rayons and by nylon. (See Appendix II.)

Mule-spun yarns   See Cotton yarns, French or dry-spun worsted yarn, and Woollen yarns.

One-throw yarn   Consists of a number of single threads, which are twisted together at one operation of doubling (see Sewing cotton).

Open-band yarn   The twist runs from left to right looking up the yarn, as shown at A in *Figure 2.12*.

Open-end spun yarns   Yarns spun by a continuous process in which the roving or sliver is separated into individual fibres which are then combined together into a yarn in a twist insertion element. Yarns of this type are loftier and have better filling capacity than ring spun yarns.

Overspun yarn   Has been spun too fine for the quality of the raw material of which it is composed, with the result that the thread is uneven in thickness, and contains weak places, or is 'twitty'.

Pack dyed yarn   Yarn dyed in a package form by forced circulation of the dye liquor through the pack. Yarn for this method of dyeing is wound on to open mesh or perforated core containers (cops, cheeses, cones, beams) and clamped upon perforated hollow spindles through which the dye liquor is circulated.

Paper yarn   A broad sheet of dried paper pulp is wound in the form of a large roll, and is then run off and mechanically cut into longitudinal flat strips, ranging upward from one-quarter of an inch in width. After a process of damping each strip has its edges turned and is passed to a twisting spindle, which twists it into the form of a round thread. It is largely employed in its natural shade, but when required coloured it is dyed in the pulp form. Its use is chiefly as weft in such fabrics as packing sheets, mats, rugs and carpets. The paper strips may be twisted round a core of fibres in order to increase their strength (see Textilose).

Pin cop   Cotton weft yarn in cop form.

Polished or **glacé yarn**   Cotton threads are passed through a special size mixture either in the hank or warp form, and then are operated upon by flat brushes carried in a large revolving cylinder, which lay the fibres. The yarn is made very hard, smooth, lustrous, and stiff, and is increased in weight from 7 to about 15 per cent. In polishing warp yarns, as many as 360 threads are treated at the same time in the form of a flat sheet, and are wound from bobbin to bobbin in the process.

Prepared hank yarn   Bobbin yarn for lace (see Brass bobbin yarn) is prepared in the hank form by a process of calendering in which the hanks are passed between heavily weighted revolving rollers. The thread is made smoother and more pliable, and during the process the hanks are continually turned, so that the treatment is uniform. To increase the flexibility of the yarn, sometimes it is lubricated by the addition of from 2 to 3 per cent of its weight of grease.

Print grandrelle   A two-fold yarn which is composed of a solid coloured thread twisted with a printed thread, the latter consisting of alternate narrow bars of white and the same colour as the solid thread. The yarn is used as warp for waterproofed over-coatings, in which the specks of white show less prominently than when the ordinary grandrelle warp is used (see Grandrelle cover fabric).

Ramie yarn See China grass yarn.

Raw material dyed yarn Spun from material which has been cleaned and then dyed in the loose fibre condition. A solid coloured thread results from using one colour of fibre, and a mixture yarn by blending two or more different colours in the fibre state. The method is extensively employed in woollen manufacture, and to a smaller extent in the cotton trade.

Reeled yarn Wound into hanks or skeins of definite length for convenience in bleach-ing, dyeing, etc., and for transport in bundle form.

Straight or *lea-reeled yarn* The thread is parallel wound, and each hank is divided into leas—usually seven—which are separated by a lease band, to which the ends of the thread are tied.

Cross-reeled yarn The thread, as it is wound, is traversed rapidly across the width of about 8 cm, so that it is crossed with itself. The thread unwinds better and with less waste, and as there is less liability of entanglement from two to four hanks may be reeled in one length.

Grant or *diamond-reeled yarn* A cross-reeled hank which shows diamond-shaped openings during the reeling process. It is wound with a wider traverse and is more open than the ordinary cross-reeled hank, and a greater number of hanks can be reeled in one continuous length.

Ring-tie reeled yarn A straight reeled cotton yarn, with 210 yards (192 m) as the length of the lea, and made one or two leas in length. It is intended to be polished in the hank, and the tie band is so arranged that it will move freely with the friction of the brushes, at the same time that the ends of the thread are indicated.

Relative twist of yarns The same relative twist is produced when the angle of twist on the surface of two different thicknesses of thread is the same. Yarns which contain the same relative twist may be used when similar effects are required in different weights of the same quality of cloth, so long as the difference in the thickness of the yarns is not extreme.

Resist-dyed yarn Has been treated in such a manner that the threads will resist the subsequent action of dyestuffs, which are applied when the yarn has been woven into cloth.

Selvedge or **selvage yarn** These are usually two-fold threads, and as long as they are sufficiently strong and of suitable thickness in relation to the warp threads of the cloth, the quality of the yarn, and regularity of twist are not important. Thus, in the manu-facture of such fabrics as cotton voiles and warp satins the selvedge yarns may be inferior to the other warp threads.

Sewing cotton Usually consists of from 6 to 12 threads, which are generally folded together at two operations of doubling. Thus, for a cable-laid 6-ply yarn, two-, or three-fold preparings are first made by twisting a corresponding number of single threads together in the same direction as the twist of the singles; then three or two preparings are twisted together in the reverse direction (see Cabled yarn). In a one-throw yarn all the single threads are twisted together at the same time in the opposite direction to the twist of the singles. Sewing thread has all the surface fibre removed by gassing, and is then polished or glazed (see Polished cotton).

Silk yarns Consist of the pale-yellow or white filaments which the silk worm spins round about itself in the form of a cocoon. The silk issues in the form of a fluid from two glands, and two other glands secrete gum, which flows through the same exit as the two fibres and cements the latter together, and the whole coagulates on contact with the air. After the filaments have been made into yarn, the gum is removed and the natural brilliance of the silk is developed, and a strong, relatively elastic, and lustrous thread is produced which dyes very readily.

Raw silk (French term—grêge) An untwisted silk thread in skein or hank form, which is produced by reeling together the filaments from several cocoons. Each filament (termed bave) consists of two fibres (termed brins), which are joined together by a coating of natural gum or sericin, and the length of the double fibre from a cocoon varies from about 500 (460 m) to 1200 yards (1100 m). Usually from three to eight cocoons are reeled from, and the sizes of raw silk range from 1 tex to about 2.5 tex. The most popular size is 1.5 to 1.7 tex, which is reeled from five cocoons, and is composed of ten continuous fibres lying side by side and gummed together. The reeled silk thread forms the raw material of the nett silk industry.

Nett or *neat silk*   A general term applied to thrown silk threads to distinguish them from spun silk threads, which are made from waste silk.

Spun silk yarns   Made from waste silk, which includes every kind of raw silk that cannot be thrown, such as defective and pierced cocoons, and the waste made in the processes of reeling, re-reeling, sorting, winding, cleaning, and throwing. The long raw fibres are cut so that the maximum length of fibre is about 25 cm, and the material by a series of processes of combing (termed dressing) is divided up into six or seven drafts, according to length. The longest drafts are then prepared, drawn, and spun in a somewhat similar manner to long lustrous wool, whereas the method employed for the shortest drafts more nearly resembles the processes used in cotton spinning. In the manufacture of British spun silk yarns the waste silk is first fully discharged or degummed (see Boiled-off silk yarn).

Douppion silk   Raw silk reeled from double cocoons, which are united owing to two worms having spun their cocoons close together. The cocoons are reeled from alternately, and where the two filaments overlap they come forward together, so that the thread is uneven.

Bright silk   Raw silk which has not been soaked with a soapy solution previous to the winding, cleaning, and throwing processes.

Washed or *steeped silk*   Raw silk which has been soaked in a solution of warm water and pure soap, in order to soften the natural gum and loosen the threads in the skeins from one another, so that the winding will be more easily performed. Sometimes advantage is taken of the steeping process to add weight to the silk, with the result that there is a greater loss in weight in the subsequent degumming operation.

Thrown silk   Raw silk which has passed through the operations of winding, cleaning, and twisting or throwing. The throwing process consists of inserting twist in the raw silk thread, and of producing a nett silk thread of the required size (two or more threads may be twisted together), which is suitable for the purpose for which it is intended.

Singles silk   Raw silk which has been wound and cleaned, and is without twist, or very slightly twisted, if required for making tram (weft), and hard-twisted if required for making organzine (warp). Certain silk fabrics are composed of singles yarn which is thrown or twisted with about 6 or 7 turns per cm, and a commonly used size of thread ranges from 1.5 to 1.7 tex. In order that the threads will retain the maximum of elasticity and strength, they are woven in the gum condition, the material being afterwards degummed and dyed in the piece. Crêpe singles, which is used for special fabrics, such as chiffon and silk crêpe, contains from 16 to 30 or more turns per cm. The term 'dumb' singles is applied to 'untwisted' singles which are used in making tram.

Tram silk   Used for weft and consists of two or more untwisted or slightly twisted singles, which are run together, and, for ordinary purposes, are twisted with one or two turns per cm. The number of singles thrown together is varied according to the required size or count of the tram, and the term two-thread, or three-thread, etc., is applied according to the number of threads twisted together. The slack twist enables the natural lustre of the fibre to be retained, but sometimes hard-twisted tram is used, for example, as weft for crêpe de chine fabrics.

Organzine silk   Used for warp, and is composed of two or more hard-twisted singles, which are wound together and hard-twisted. For example, a two-thread 3.5 tex organzine yarn may have each single thrown with 7 turns per cm, which are then twisted together in the reverse direction with 6 turns per cm. The best qualities of silk are used for organzine, but on account of the thread containing much more twist, it is not so lustrous as tram.

No-throw silk Very soft yarn, consisting of two or more untwisted singles, which are doubled together with no more twist than is necessary to bind the filaments together and prevent them from forming loops in the thread.

Hard or *gum silk* Thrown silk yarn which contains the natural gum or sericin. For textures which can be boiled off and dyed in the piece the use of silk in the hard state has the advantage that the gum makes the yarn stronger, and threads can be employed which otherwise would be too weak to bear the strain of weaving.

Boiled-off or *degummed silk yarn* Thrown silk which has had the natural gum removed by a process of boiling in hot water and soap. Before the degumming process the silk thread is harsh, stiff, and dull in appearance, and ranges from white to fawn or yellow in colour, but the boiling-off process makes the yarn soft, flexible, lustrous, and white or cream. The term 'soft' is sometimes applied to degummed silk. The 'scroop' of silk, or the characteristic rustling sound made by silk when subjected to friction, is produced by treating the degummed material with a dilute acid in the dyeing process. The extraction of the gum causes a loss in weight of from 20 to 25 per cent, frequently the loss in weight is recovered in the dyeing process by loading the thread with such substances as tannic acids or metallic salts, by means of which the weight may be increased 50 per cent or more without materially affecting the natural lustre. Along with the count of the silk, the weight to which the thread has been loaded may be stated.

Souple silk Dyed thrown silk with only a small portion of the gum removed, which makes the thread less lustrous, although stronger than when it is fully discharged.

Ecru silk Thrown silk in its natural colour and with only a small part of the gum removed.

Weighted or *loaded silk yarn* Nett silk which in the dyeing process has been weighted by means of tannic acid or metallic salts (see Boiled-off silk).

Sized silk yarns Yarns that have been tested for size or counts. The raw silk fibre varies so much in thickness that even when the singles silk contains the same number of filaments and the same number of singles are thrown together, there is considerable variation in the thickness of the resultant thread.

Lousy silk yarn A defective yarn in which some of the fibres have split and curled up, causing small specks to show cn the surface.

Crêpe silk yarns Very hard twisted silk, and may be a singles thread of 1.7 tex with from 24 to 40 turns per cm, or from two to six or more singles, twisted slackly as for tram, are twisted together with from 20 to 32 turns per cm. Before twisting gum silk is softened by soaking in a soap solution.

Crêpe de chine yarn A hard-twisted silk tram yarn, largely made by twisting from two to eight Canton singles together, with from 16 to 28 turns per cm.

Grenadine silk yarn A hard-twisted organzine silk thread (see Crêpe silk yarn) used for the warp in grenadine silk fabrics.

Marabout silk A stiff silk yarn composed of two or three untwisted singles, which are dyed in the gum condition and very hard-twisted, and used for crêpe.

Sewing or *twist silk* A small or large number of cocoon filaments may be reeled together and slightly twisted in forming the singles, two to six or more of which, according to the required size of thread, are then firmly twisted together in the reverse direction.

Embroidery silk Similar to sewing silk, but softer twisted, and made in various sizes and a great variety of colours.

Etching silk A harder twisted thread than sewing silk; used for outlining embroidered effects.

Cordonnet silk A thick, soft thread, used for crotchet work, braiding, knitting, etc., and consists of a number of singles loosely twisted together in one direction, two or more of which are then twisted together in the reverse direction.

Floss silk yarn A very thick, soft-twisted silk thread, used for embroidery purposes. A similar rayon yarn is made.

Tussah silk yarn (also termed Tussur and Tussore) Made from the cocoons spun by wild or uncultivated silk worms, which produce a thicker and less lustrous fibre than the cultivated worm. It is brown in colour, and is largely used in the natural shade in the manufacture of such fabrics as shantungs, pongees, etc. Only a small quantity of 'thrown' tussah yarn is produced, as a large proportion of the cocoons cannot be reeled, and the material is chiefly used in the making of spun silk.

Schappe silk yarn Spun silk yarn in which the natural gum is only partially removed by a process of fermentation in warm water followed by washing off in hot water, or hot water and soap. The amount of gum retained varies from 2 to 10 per cent of the weight of the yarn. Schapping is the Continental method of treating waste silk.

Bourrette silk yarn Spun silk yarn made from the shortest drafts of waste silk, which are carded, combed, and spun in a similar manner to cotton.

Silk noil yarn Made from the very short fibres (termed noil) combed out of the short drafts of waste silk, the processes of carding and spinning being similar to those employed in woollen yarn manufacture.

Sized yarn Size is added to yarns prior to weaving mainly to reduce the friction in the healds, in the reed and in the yarns themselves, to strengthen the yarn and to lubricate it. Occasionally the intention may be to increase the weight and substance of the woven cloth. Weft is only sized for special purposes, and cotton warp yarns are usually classed as light or pure, medium, and heavily sized. In light or pure sizing from 5 to 10 per cent of size (by weight) is added to the warp, solely to make it weave better, and is employed for cloths which have to be bleached or dyed or otherwise wet-finished. In medium sizing from 10 to 40 per cent is added to the weight of cotton warp yarn, in order to make the cloth heavier, while in heavy sizing the weight of the warp is increased by from 40 to upwards of 100 per cent. Sizing is also practised in weaving most of the man-made materials in staple and continuous filament form. The purpose may be to increase the strength of the yarn, to protect the yarn from the chafing action of the moving machine parts or to reduce the tendency to form static electricity effects.

The main ingredients of sizes consist of starches (natural or modified), gelatin and synthetic resins with additions of tallows, oils and waxes for the purpose of lubrication.

Slubbing-dyed yarn Worsted yarn which has been drawn and spun from wool that has been dyed in the 'top' or sliver form. For solid shades the method ensures greater cleanness and solidity of colour, while by mixing together differently dyed tops at the first stage of drawing worsted fibre mixture yarns are produced.

Soft twist yarn Contains less than the normal number of turns per cm and, according to the amount of twist, the threads are designated as soft, X soft, XX soft, XXX soft. The yarns are used for hosiery and embroidery purposes.

Textilose A composite yarn, used as a substitute for jute, and consists of a paper thread with which short waste fibres are twisted.

Tinsel or **metallic yarn** Consists of a flat thread of silver, copper, aluminium, or other metal which is used by itself or is twisted round a central thread of cotton or other fibre. It is used for church vestments, officers' uniforms, theatrical textures, banners, fringes, embroideries, lace, veils, etc. An imitation tinsel yarn is made by coating a cotton thread with metallic powder.

Tinted yarn When different threads for the same cloth are so nearly alike that they are practically indistinguishable in the grey state—as, for example, when a warp consists of both right and left twist threads arranged in a prescribed order—one of the yarns, usually that which is the reverse of the ordinary spinning, is tinted with a pale fugitive dye. This enables both series of threads to be kept in proper order during the manufacturing processes, and, as the colour readily washes out in the subsequent wet finishing operations, the appearance of the bleached and dyed cloth is not affected.

Twist Cotton warp yarn is termed twist, and unless otherwise stated it is understood that the direction of the twine is warp way (termed twist way), as shown at A in *Figure 2.12.*

Twist-on-twist Folded yarn in which the direction of the twist is the same in the doubling process as in the single threads, whereby the number of turns per cm in the latter is increased so that a harder folded yarn results than when the two twisting operations are in opposite directions. The single threads are made more solid, and if the turns per cm are not excessive, the folded thread has increased strength and elasticity, but the insertion of too much twist causes the thread to be snarly. Twist-on-twist is employed for voile yarns, and in the first doubling process of sewing cotton (q.v.).

Twist-way (T.W.) and **weft-way (W.W.) spun** Terms applied to cotton yarns to indicate the direction of the twist or twine, the former corresponding to right-hand twist and the latter to left-hand twist, looking up the thread, as shown at A and B respectively in *Figure 2.12*. While twist-way and weft-way coincide respectively with the normal direction of cotton warp and weft twist, if required warp yarn may be twisted weft-way and weft yarn twist-way, the former then being termed W.W. twist, and the latter T.W. weft. Warp, however, is much more rarely spun in the reverse direction than weft.

Twitty yarn Is irregular in size, and contains weak, brittle places, where the thread is liable to break sharply.

Union yarns Composed of two or more different classes of fibres, which may be mixed together in the fibre state, or as a 'union twist', in which a separate thread of each material is twisted together. The purpose of producing blends of fibres may be to cheapen an expensive material by adding a proportion of less expensive material, or, to obtain a superior product from the end-use point of view by combining two or more compatible materials of which each contributes a specific quality, e.g. one may be introduced for the sake of pleasant handle and appearance, and the other to improve the wearing properties. Many blended or union yarns of different types are in existence but the most common mixtures are those of wool with cotton and cotton with polyester fibre (shirtings), wool with viscose rayon staple (lightweight trouserings), and wool with acrylic or polyester fibres (suitings and overcoatings). A special reason for twisting a cotton with a wool thread is described in reference to extracted cloth (q.v.). Fibre mixtures may be produced on the woollen, cotton, and worsted systems of yarn manufacture (see Union shirtings).

Angola and *llama yarns* Composed of a mixture of wool and cotton fibres, and spun on the woollen principle. Very frequently the mixture consists of a low quality of shoddy or waste wool and waste cotton, with a small quantity of good length cotton introduced to give the necessary spinning property to the material. Sometimes, however, fairly good grades of both wool and cotton are used in producing a superior thread of this class, and for white yarns the cotton may be bleached in the fibre state. The percentages vary from about 15 of wool and 85 of cotton to 85 of wool and 15 of cotton. The yarn is used as both warp and weft in shirtings, and as weft in worsted and cotton warp cloths.

Merino yarn Produced by blending wool and cotton slivers together and drawing and spinning the material on the French worsted system. Fine, short wool is first 'dry-combed' and prepared in the form of 'tops', and these are combined, in a process termed 'melanging', with similar cotton slivers, the necessary proportions of the two being run together in the 'melangeur', according to the desired percentage of wool and cotton. In the subsequent processes of drawing and worsted mule spinning the two materials are intimately blended, and a good class of yarn is produced, as both the wool and cotton are of good quality. A common mixture is 50 per cent of each fibre, but the proportion of wool ranges from 85 per cent or more to as low as 5 per cent. Merino yarn is used in the manufacture of shirtings, and for hosiery purposes.

Alaska yarn Another term applied to a mixture of combed wool and cotton.

Vigogne Continental term for thick, soft yarn spun from waste cotton on the woollen principle, or from waste cotton with which a small quantity of waste wool has been mixed. The material is frequently dyed in the raw fibre state.

Voile yarns Made in both worsted and cotton from a high quality of material, and are combed, firmly twisted, and genapped or gassed in order to produce a round, hard thread free from projecting fibres. The yarns are mostly two-fold, with the folded twist inserted in the same direction as in the single threads (see Twist-on-twist), but single cotton voile yarns have been used with, however, less satisfactory results.

Woollen yarns Vary chiefly according to the kind of wool that is used, which may range from the finest qualities of short merino, through cross-bred and medium wools, to shoddies and wastes which are so short and low in quality that a small quantity of a longer fibre, e.g. cotton, has to be introduced to enable the material to spin. A typical woollen yarn consists of short, fine wool, and contains all the varying lengths of the fibres, which are indiscriminately mixed together so that they lie across each other in all directions. A fibrous, dull, compact, but rather uneven thread is produced, which has excellent felting properties, and when dyed takes on a soft, deep, and rich colour.

Saxony woollen yarn   A typical thread, made from fine merino wool, and used for the finest and best woollen textures.

Cheviot woollen yarn   Made from sound and strong cross-bred and medium wools, and used for cheviot and tweed cloths which require little felting.

Lustre woollen yarn   Similar to cheviot yarn, but is made from lustrous medium wool, and is used for rugs and similar pile fabrics.

Shoddy yarn   Made from re-manufactured wool and wastes, and frequently contains a proportion of cotton. The cheaper classes of woollen yarn mostly contain more or less shoddy material mixed with good wool.

Angola and *llama yarns*   Spun on the woollen principle (see Union yarns).

Ring-spun woollen yarns   Spun on the continuous system from condenser bobbins, with a special arrangement of the drafting rollers to ensure uniform drafting of the long and short fibres, and an attachment for giving a vibratory movement to the threads to impart fulness to the yarn. A satisfactory thread is produced, which, however, is somewhat inferior in softness, fulness, and felting property to a mule-spun woollen yarn.

Worsted yarns (see also Hosiery yarns)   Vary in structure and appearance according to the kind of wool used and the processes employed. A typical worsted yarn is made from long lustrous wool from which the short fibres are removed by combing, and all the processes tend to straighten the fibres. Such a yarn, therefore, is composed of fibres which do not vary extremely in length and are laid as straight and parallel as possible. The thread is smooth and lustrous, open in structure, and even in thickness, but it has little felting property, and when dyed takes on a bright colour. A typical worsted yarn is practically opposite in structure and properties to a typical woollen yarn, but this is not due to the difference in the raw material so much as to the difference in the processes through which the fibres pass. From the same class of wool two entirely different yarn structures are produced by the two different methods of construction, but certain classes of worsted yarns somewhat resemble the appearance of a woollen thread.

Flyer-spun worsted yarn   In flyer spinning the fibres are better controlled than in any other system, so that a smoother thread is produced, and the method is the most suitable for promoting the brightness of lustrous wools and wool hairs, and for obtaining a smooth yarn from coarse cross-bred wools.

Cap-spun worsted yarn   Cap spinning is much more productive than flyer spinning, and is very suitable for botany and fine cross-bred wools. The system tends to produce a thread with a large amount of fibre projecting from the surface, and is, therefore, not suitable for either lustrous or strong cross-bred wools.

Ring-spun worsted yarn   Ring spinning is employed only to a limited extent for worsted yarn, but it is a very suitable system for the finest botany threads. The fibres are under better control than in cap spinning, so that the yarn is not so wild and hairy.

Mule-spun worsted yarn   See French or dry-spun.

Lustre worsted yarn   A typical thread made from long, lustrous English wools and mohair and alpaca, by gilling, Lister-combing, open drawing, and flyer spinning, by which the brightness and smoothness of the yarn are best developed. Mohair and alpaca yarns are sometimes double-combed.

Demi-lustre worsted yarns   Made from long English and cross-bred wool, which is not so bright as lustre wool, by similar processes to those used for lustre yarns, except that Noble-combing may be employed.

Camlet yarn   A strong, rather hard-twisted worsted yarn made from demi-lustre wool (see Camlet fabric).

Serge worsted yarn   Made of medium and cross-bred wool, which is sharp and crisp to the touch, by gilling or carding (according to the length of fibre), Noble-combing, open drawing, and cap spinning. The best qualities are full handling, but have a somewhat rough and fibrous surface.

Cross-bred yarns　Range from fine to low cross-bred, the former being spun from Australian and New Zealand wools (46s to 58s quality) and used for coatings, dress fabrics, and fine hosieries. Medium cross-bred yarns are spun from wool of about 40s to 46s quality, and are used for serge and other cloths which require a firm, crisp feel, while low cross-bred yarns are spun from wools below 40s quality, and are fairly lustrous. The finer cross-bred wools are cap spun, but the lower qualities may be flyer spun, in order that the fibres will be sufficiently controlled.

Botany worsted yarn　Made of fine merino wool (60s quality or finer is termed Botany), and is a fuller, softer, and denser thread than typical worsted yarn. For fine counts the processes are carding, Holden-combing, cone drawing, and cap or ring spinning, and for coarse counts, Noble-combing, open drawing, and cap spinning. Used for the best qualities of costumes, dress fabrics, suitings, linings, shirtings, etc.

French or *dry-spun worsted yarn*　Made from short, fine wool by carding, dry-combing, French drawing, and worsted mule spinning. The system is suitable for treating the inferior classes of fine wool, as it enables shorter fibres to be left in the top, and a full, soft handling, fibrous thread is produced, which is particularly useful for soft dress and knitted fabrics. As the yarn, also, is free from oil, it is readily cleaned and dyed, and brighter, more delicate, and more even colours can be obtained than is possible in similar oil-spun yarn.

Alpaca yarn　Generally composed of a mixture of white, black, and different shades of grey and brown alpaca fibres, which is too dark to be dyed into bright colours, and the yarn is, therefore, mostly used in the natural state or is dyed black. Its chief use is as weft in dress and lining fabrics (see Bradford lustre fabrics).

Camel-hair yarn　A very soft worsted yarn made from the fine natural-coloured fibres of the camel and dromedary.

Cashmere yarn　Cashmere yarn is made from the short, fine, undercoat fibres of the Tibetan goat. It is very soft, is sometimes naturally grey or brown in colour, and is chiefly used as weft or in knitting.

Mélange yarn (French term—Vigoreaux)　A coloured mixture worsted yarn, usually made of long, lustrous wool, the colours in which are printed on the 'top' or combed sliver in the form of bars of colour. The subsequent processes of drawing and spinning cause the different colours to be thoroughly intermingled, but as each fibre may be variously coloured throughout its length, a 'melange' mixture differs in appearance from an ordinary fibre mixture in which each fibre is all one colour.

Genappe yarn　A smooth, flyer-spun worsted thread, sometimes hard-twisted, which has had all the loose fibre removed from the surface by gassing (see Gassed yarn). Used for the straight threads in rib cloths, and for braid and heald yarns.

Curled yarn　Used for astrakhans, rugs, etc., and is produced by winding together and twisting very tightly a number of worsted threads, reeling them into hanks, and setting by boiling. After untwisting and winding separately each thread is permanently curled, so that a portion that is left slack immediately curls up.

Yarn dyed　Yarn which has been dyed after the processes of spinning, doubling, etc., have been completed. The threads are reeled into hank form, or made into ball warps in readiness for dyeing, or wound into packages and dyed in that form. (See Pack dyed yarn.)

II—Standard woven fabrics

The particulars of fabrics that are given are those of actual cloths, but it will be understood that in almost every type of structure a wide range of qualities is made. Unless otherwise stated, the particulars indicate the original counts of the yarns, the ends per cm in the reed, and the picks per cm in the cloth. Most of the fabrics mentioned fall within the scope of the constructions dealt with in this work. The very wide field of compound fabrics is covered in **Watson's Advanced Textile Design,** *a companion volume to this.*

Alpaca cloth   True alpaca cloth is a Bradford lustre fabric (q.v.) in which alpaca weft is used. Normally the cloth is woven with a black cotton warp and subsequently piece dyed. Used chiefly for linings and dress goods and produced either in weft faced twill weave or in plain weave.

Amazon   A fine dress fabric, generally woven in 5-thread warp satin with worsted warp and woollen weft. The weave and the twist of the warp are so arranged that the twill lines of the satin are emphasised. The cloth is lightly milled and raised, and a full, soft handling texture with a fibrous surface is formed which, however, is not so dense as to entirely conceal the fine twill effect. 24 to 22 tex worsted warp, 72 to 48 tex woollen weft, 28 to 36 ends, and 14 to 18 picks per cm.

Appliqué   A figured texture in which the ornament is obtained by sewing or embroidering a rather opaque fabric to the surface of a thin fabric. The upper fabric is then cut away round the stitched portions so that an opaque figure is left on a light, transparent ground.

Armure   A dress fabric usually made in modified or broken warp rib weaves (see Nos. 42 and 43, *Figure A1.4*), which cause waved lines to be formed in a horizontal direction. Sometimes the warp is all alike, but the weave effect is improved by employing two kinds of warp arranged end and end, as for example—ordinary and reverse twist, mohair and botany, or wool and cotton. A botany worsted warp cloth in ordinary and reverse twists—$\pm$30/2 tex warp, 28 tex worsted weft, 38 ends, and from 23 to 28 picks per cm. If large patterns, with long warp floats on the surface, are formed, the ends are interwoven plain on the back in order to give firmness.

Asbestos cloth   A fireproof structure (see Asbestos yarn) used for such purposes as brake linings, firemen's garments, theatre curtains, etc.

Astrakhan   A cloth with a peculiar curly surface, in which the effect is largely due to the use of a thick, curled, lustrous, worsted yarn (see Curled yarn). The texture may be produced in four ways: (a) By cloth shrinkage, a non-shrinking curled yarn being floated somewhat loosely on the surface of a firmly woven ground texture which is made to contract (see Curl effects). (b) As a weft pile structure (see *Watson's Advanced Textile Design*). (c) As a warp pile fabric (see *Watson's Advanced Textile Design*). (d) As a knitted texture.

Atlas   A rich, lustrous silk fabric made in 8-thread warp satin weave, used for dress fabrics, and also for linings when woven with cotton weft.

Bag cloths   Used for flour, salt, grain, etc., cotton, plain or 2-and-2 twill, rather light and open in structure, and heavily sized in order to close up the interstices and prevent the contents from coming through (see Seamless bags). A plain cloth—about 30 tex warp, 28 tex weft, 22 ends, and 19 picks per cm in the grey cloth.

Bagging and **sacking**—The term D. W. Bagging is applied to a coarse plain woven jute fabric made with double ends in the warp and very thick weft. Jute sacking is largely woven in 2-and-1 twill, with double ends in the warp and finer set than D. W. Bagging. These structures are now also produced in polypropylene tape yarns.

Baize   A plain woven, heavily felted, woollen cloth with raised pile surface; piece dyed in bright colours, usually red or green.

Bannockburn tweed   A Scotch Cheviot woollen cloth woven with a thread of solid colour alternating with a grandrelle twist thread in warp and weft.

Barathea   A fine dress fabric with spun silk warp and botany weft, and similar in structure to 'Henrietta' (q.v.), except that the broken weft rib weave No. 16, *Figure A1.3* is used in place of 1-and-2 twill. The cloth is also made in the same weave with cotton warp similar to a cotton warp cashmere. The term 'Barathea' is also applied to a heavy worsted suiting usually made in a twilled hopsack weave similar to No. 5, *Figure A1.2*, which is an example of the weave as applied to heavy wool fabrics. In addition, a class of cotton shirting, made in a broken warp rib weave (see No. 4, *Figure A1.2*), is termed Barathea.

Batiste   The term refers chiefly to the finish of very fine, thin, plain cotton cloths, like muslin and cambric, used for dresses and linings.

Beaver cloth   A heavily milled and raised woollen overcoating fabric which is finished with a dress face (q.v.), and is made in a variety of weights, and in single, backed, and double weaves.

Beaverteen A very strong cotton fabric, with a fibrous surface on the underside, similar to but lighter than moleskin (q.v.), and is made in the same weave as the latter; or the weave given at No. 59, *Figure A1.5*, which has a weft float of four on the surface, may be employed. Used for heavy trouserings and suitings, and frequently piece-dyed. About 60/2 tex warp, 33 tex weft, 13 to 14 ends, 90 to 120 picks per cm.

Bedford cords Warp-face fabrics in worsted, linen, and cotton yarns in which rounded cord effects are formed longitudinally. Very broad cord effects can be made firmer by interweaving the picks on the underside with the wadding ends in plain order (see No. 52, *Figure A1.5*). A worsted dress fabric—28/2 tex botany warp, 32 tex botany weft, 36 ends and 32 picks per cm. Cotton Bedford cords are frequently sold under the name of 'piqué'.

The term 'London cord' is applied to twill-face cotton Bedford cords—42 tex warp, 30 tex weft, 34 ends and 31 picks per cm, wadding ends extra.

Military Bedford cords Used for riding breeches and made with two picks floating behind the cords to one on the surface (see No. 51, *Figure A1.5*). The cloth is composed of woollen yarns (except that cotton is used for the plain ends), and is very heavily milled and clear finished (see Clear woollen finish)—100 tex woollen warp, and 50/2 tex cotton warp for the plain ends, 100 tex woollen weft, 26 ends and 27 picks per cm in the loom. Contraction from 17 to 20 per cent in length and from 25 to 30 per cent in width.

Belting One class of cotton belting, woven plain, twill, or sateen, is used for the tops of skirts (see Petersham). A second class is an elastic texture, composed of cotton, wool, or silk, which is frequently richly ornamented with figures. A third class, used for power transmission, is a heavy and very strong texture, which may consist of several thicknesses of cotton duck (q.v.) cemented together, or of a solid structure in which from three to six strong, cotton fabrics are woven one above the other and firmly stitched together by special binding threads. The solid-woven beltings are specially treated and seasoned before use.

Bengaline A heavy warp rib cloth composed of silk warp and worsted or cotton weft, similar in appearance to poplin except that the rib effect is more pronounced. A 3-and-3 rib fabric—4 tex denier (2-thread) organzine warp, 30 tex worsted weft, 144 ends, and 36 picks per cm.

Bengaline de soie consists of silk in both warp and weft. Other names of ribbed silk fabrics are Cotelé, Eolienne, Epingle, Faille, Gros-de-Tours, Grosgrain, Ottoman, Poplin, etc.

Beige Originally a fine soft dress fabric made in worsted warp and weft in 2-and-2 twill weave. More recently imitated in cotton yarns. The cloth generally has a mixed colour appearance, due to the use of printed, melange, or coloured twist yarns—24 to 22 tex worsted yarns, 30 ends and 28 picks per cm.

Billiard cloth A plain woven, heavily milled woollen cloth with a fibrous finish, made from very fine merino wool and shrunk about 33 per cent in width and 25 per cent in length from the loom dimensions. About 84 to 72 tex warp and weft, 12 to 13 ends per cm, and 14 to 16 picks per cm in the loom.

Blanket range A length of cloth made as a pattern range which is woven in sections, both warp and weft way, so as to exhibit a number of designs, each of which, frequently, is only a few inches square. Satisfactory designs are selected, and a short full width length of cloth is then generally woven of each, to be again submitted for the buyer's approval or rejection.

Blankets Thick, heavily milled fabrics woven with woollen spun yarns composed entirely of wool or of wool with an admixture of cotton. The weft is soft spun, and the quality of the wool used ranges from strong and coarse fibres to fine cross-bred and merino. They are made unbordered, with coloured borders all round, or bordered only at the ends. The most important makes are known as Irish, English or Yorkshire, Witney, Ayrshire, and Cheviot or Bath blankets. Irish blankets are similar to Yorkshire except that they are made broader and shorter. Thus, a blanket might be 2540 mm × 2030 mm in a Yorkshire size compared with 2130 mm × 2410 mm in an Irish size. Typical Yorkshire blankets are woven plain and finished with a dense fibrous pile on both sides, which conceals the weave structure. The term 'Witney' can only be applied to blankets actually manufactured in Witney, but they are finished with a dense pile, and are like the Yorkshire blankets. Ayrshire blankets (not necessarily made in Ayrshire) are woven in 2-and-2 twill, which shows more or less clearly through the surface pile of fibres, and when bordered have a dark indigo-blue border all round. Cheviot or Bath blankets also are 2-and-2 twill weave, but they are raised rather more than the Ayrshire cloths, and are woven with light blue borders.

The dimensions vary extremely and range from about 1270 mm wide and 1760 mm long to 2500 mm wide and 2900 mm long, while the weights vary from about 1 kg to 3 kg. for a single blanket. A 2-and-2 twill blanket 2100 × 2150 mm—about 200 tex warp and weft, 8 ends and 10 picks per cm in the loom, 20 per cent shrinkage in width and 15 per cent shrinkage in length. A plain woven Yorkshire blanket 2000 mm × 2500 mm, about 250 tex yarns, 6 ends and 10 picks per cm in the loom; contraction about 12 per cent in length and 20 to 25 per cent in width.

Horse blankets are coarse, heavily felted woollen textures, and rug blankets (q.v.) are used in some parts of the world as articles of clothing. Cotton blankets are made with a flannelette finish, as a single cloth or as a weft backed reversible texture (see *Watson's Advanced Textile Design*).

Blankets are also made in a cellular leno construction (see *Watson's Advanced Textile Design*) using woollen, cotton or various synthetic staple yarns. Acrylic staple and polypropylene are used in the making of light-weight blankets in plain or in 2-and-2 twill constructions.

Blazer cloth   A wool flannel somewhat heavily milled and raised and finished with a fibrous surface. Used for sports jackets and caps—80 tex warp and weft, 16 ends and picks per cm.

Book muslin   The term 'book' is applied to a fine, soft, plain woven cotton muslin, and also to a very stiffly finished cotton cloth that is used for stiffening and lining clothing and millinery. The latter fabric is made of fine yarns, and is very open and flimsy as it leaves the loom, but it is heavily sized and given a board-like glossy finish. From 12 to 10 tex yarns, 13 ends and 11 picks per cm. If made with thicker yarns, like cheese cloth (q.v.), it is termed stiff book muslin (see Tarlatan and Swiss mull).

Botany twill cloths   Made in botany yarns in various weights for costumes and suitings. The 2-and-2, 3-and-3, and 4-and-4 twills are employed, and the cloths may be slightly milled to improve the feel, but they are clear finished in order that the twill effect will be clearly defined. Cloths in 2-and-2 twill range from 120/2 to 64/2 tex warp and weft, with from 13 to 20 ends and picks per cm (see Worsted Cloths).

Box cloth   A stout heavily milled woollen cloth with a dress-face finish, and a dense felt-like appearance, mostly woven in broken 2-and-2 twill. About 170 tex, wool dyed warp and weft, 13 ends and picks per cm in the loom. Contraction, 35 per cent in width and 25 per cent in length from loom dimensions.

Bradford lustre fabrics   Chiefly used for dress fabrics and linings, and are made with cotton warp and mohair, alpaca, or English lustre worsted weft, while demi-lustre is substituted for lustre weft in lower qualities of the cloths. The weft is much thicker than the warp, and in order that the brightness of the former will be developed in the highest degree, in the finishing process the cloth is drawn out in length and shrunk in width. Thus, from 63 m of warp, 127 cm wide in the reed, from 55 to 56 m of grey cloth, about 120 cm wide, is produced, and this yields about 60 m of finished cloth, 110 cm wide. In the finished fabric the ends lie almost straight with the picks bending round them, so that the structure approximates to that of a weft rib in which the warp is nearly concealed while the weft is brought prominently to the surface. In order to secure the maximum of lustre the cloths are either woven with one end per split, or if there are two ends per split in the finer setts, the loom is specially timed to obtain good cover. Very frequently the cotton warp is yarn dyed fast black or a fast colour, so that in the piece only the lustre weft requires to be dyed, but for white or light colours a bleached warp may be used.

Brilliantines, Sicilians, and *glacés*   Different makes of lustre dress fabrics chiefly woven plain or with a weft figure on plain ground. The class of weft that is used is frequently coupled with the name in order to distinguish the quality, as, for instance, a mohair brilliantine is superior to an English lustre brilliantine, etc. The term brilliantine is applied to the finer makes that range from about 20 to 28 ends per cm in the loom, and in which the weft is finer than about 38 tex worsted. A Sicilian is woven with from 14 to 19 ends per cm, and the weft is thicker than 38 tex worsted, and may be as thick as 72 tex. A glacé may be similar in structure to either a brilliantine or a silician, and the term is used to distinguish cloths in which the weft is not dyed, although the warp may be either coloured or black. Brilliantine—14/2 to 10/2 tex cotton warp, 38 to 30 tex mohair weft, 22 to 26 ends and 22 to 28 picks per cm. Sicilian glacé—14/2 tex cotton warp, 72 to 64 tex mohair or English lustre weft, 16 ends and 18 picks per cm.

Melange lustre   A fabric in which the weft has been spun from lustrous wool that has been printed in the combed sliver or top form (see Melange yarn).

Puritan   A half-mourning lustre fabric made with both bleached white and fast black cotton threads in the warp, and lustre weft which is dyed black in the piece.

Pekin stripes   Are shadow effects produced in plain lustre cloths by denting the ends irregularly, as, for example, 12 ends, two per split, 6 ends, one per split; or a section dented one per split may be arranged alternately with a section dented one per split, one split missed for a number of times.

Grenada, Florentine, and *Lorraine lustres*   Woven in the weaves given respectively at Nos. 7, 13, 17, *Figures A1.2* and *A1.3*, each of which produces a weft surface, lustre

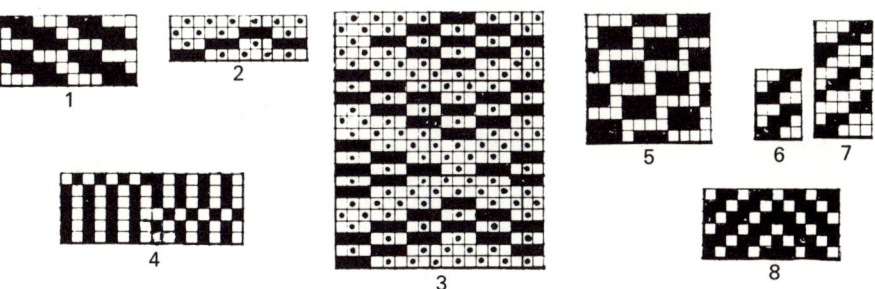

Figure A1.2

weft and cotton warp being used as in the plain lustres.

Lustre linings   Made with various weft-face twill weaves, each of which is given a distinctive name. The lining cloths are generally made lower in quality of material than the dress fabrics, single twist cotton warps, ranging from 20 to 12 tex, with from 32 to 38 ends per cm, being largely used, while the weft varies from 38 to 24 tex, of alpaca, English-lustre, and demi-lustre wool with from 28 to 40 picks per cm, according to the thickness of the weft and the firmness of the weave (see Orleans).

Brilliantine   See Bradford lustre fabrics.

Broadcloth and **plain super**   One of the oldest types of woollen cloths, made from fine merino wool in plain weave, heavily milled and finished with a dress face (q.v.). For 140 cm finished woven about 225 cm in the loom (hence the origin of the term *broad*). About 74 tex warp and weft, 12 to 13 ends and 14 to 16 picks per cm in the loom.

Brocade   Originally a heavy, rich, silk fabric ornamented with raised figures formed by extra threads or by embroidery, but now applied to any ordinary jacquard figured cloth which shows variety of effect.

Buckram   A coarse cotton fabric, woven plain, piece-dyed, and stiffened with resin or size according to the purpose for which it is intended. Thus, if employed as an underlining (see book muslin), it is not made so stiff as if used as a foundation for hats, while for use as hat shapes one class of buckram is composed of two stiffened fabrics cemented together, one of which is a rather fine muslin, and the other like cheese cloth.

Burl dyed cloth   Piece dyed woollen or worsted cloth that contains particles of undyed vegetable matter which are too numerous to be picked out, and are subjected to *burl dyeing*.

Calendered cloth   Has been subjected, in finishing, to heat while under pressure between rollers, which produces a smooth, glossy surface, and is applied to a great variety of cotton, linen, etc., fabrics.

Calico   A general term applied to various qualities of plain woven cotton cloth which are coarser than muslin.

Cambric   Originally the name of a fine linen cloth made at Cambrai in Belgium, and is now applied also to a fine bleached cotton texture which is usually given a rather stiff, bright finish and used for summer dresses. A class of cambric used for dress linings is finished soft, and is termed kid-finished cambric. 10 to 8 tex cotton warp, 8 to 6 tex cotton weft, 38 ends and about 32 to 58 picks per cm. Embroidery cambrics are made —10 to 9 tex cotton warp, 10 to 8 tex cotton weft, 32 to 40 ends and 34 to 56 picks per cm. Cotton cambrics, jaconets, lawns, mulls, nainsooks, and fine muslins are all made from a high quality of cotton yarn, and are similar cloths in the grey state, the difference between them being chiefly in the finish. Further, the finish of each class of cloth may be varied as regards softness or stiffness, and brightness or dullness, etc., according to its use, and a wide range of qualities, also, is made in each kind of cloth.

Camlet   A stout plain cloth originally made with camel-hair yarns, for which strong worsted yarns of the demi-lustre type have been substituted. 64/2 to 56/2 tex worsted warp and weft (rather hard twisted), and about 13 to 14 ends and picks per cm.

Canton   A plain cloth woven with botany warp and weft, or with cotton warp and botany weft. 12 tex combed cotton warp, 15 tex botany weft, 26 ends per cm, 30 to 36 picks per cm.

Canton flannel   A strong medium, or heavy weight, cotton flannel, woven in 2-and-2 twill, and finished with a raised surface on one side. Used for pockets, and also for underwear and dresses.

Cantoon   A strong, heavily wefted cotton fabric (see Fustian) woven in the twill weave given at No. 25, *Figure A1.3*, which repeats on six ends and twelve picks. Although the weave runs at a steep angle on design paper, in the cloth there is such a preponderance of picks over ends that a fine weft-face twill is formed running at a flat angle. The cloth is raised on the under-side, and is used for such purposes as riding breeches, jackets, etc.

Casement cloth   A plain woven cotton fabric, soft and full handling, and usually finished white or cream, made in different ways, but generally with the weft predominating on the surface. The cloth should be woven with a good quality of warp and weft, and the ends evenly spaced; sometimes mercerised in the piece. 35 tex cotton warp and 20 tex cotton weft, 18 ends and 28 picks per cm. The cloth is also made with lustre worsted weft on the same principle as Bradford lustres (q.v.), and while this texture is used for casement curtains, it is also made into summer dresses.

Cashmere   A fine botany weft face dress fabric woven in 1-and-2 twill with a larger number of picks than ends per cm. In the better qualities the warp also is botany, but for cheaper cloths cotton warp is used—20/2 to 14/2 tex cotton warp, 16 to 12 tex botany weft, with 22 to 26 ends per cm, and 52 to 64 picks per cm. Cobourgs, Henriettas, and Paramattas (q.v.) are similar in structure to cashmere, and in the finishing processes the cloths are drawn out in length and shrunk in width in order to show the weft as much as possible on the surface.

Chameleon taffeta   A rich silk fabric woven in three contrasting colours, two in the weft, arranged pick and pick, and going into the same shed, and one in the warp; gives a 3-colour shot effect (see Taffeta).

Cheese cloth   A loosely woven cotton plain cloth fabric, very light and soft, in which condition it is used for wrapping cheese and butter. This kind of cloth is also heavily sized and stiffened, and used as an underlining. About 16 tex warp and weft, 10 ends and 8 picks per cm.

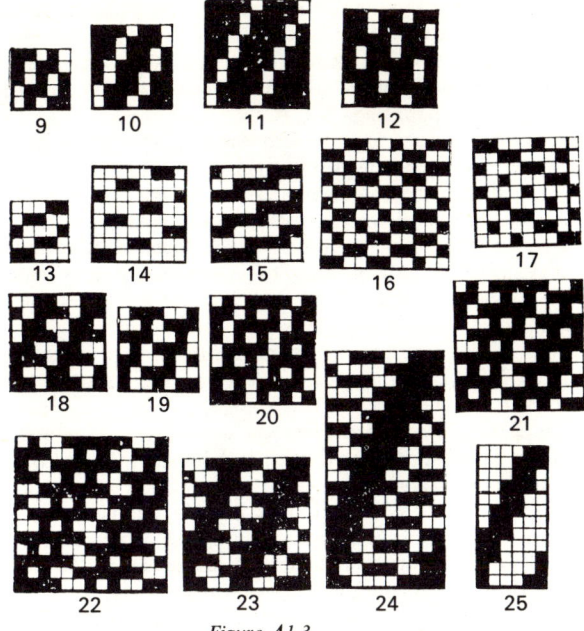

Figure A1.3

Cheviot cloth   A woollen texture made from rather thick and rough yarns, which are spun from medium wools of the Cheviot and cross-bred type. The cloth is only lightly milled and raised, and after finishing it has a crisp feel and somewhat open structure. Generally a rough fibrous surface is formed, through which the weave is more or less clearly seen, while brightness of colour is a distinct feature. Used for costumes, suitings, and overcoatings, the weight being varied according to requirements—160 to 95 tex warp and weft, 10 to 14 ends and picks per cm.

Chiffon   A very soft and filmy, plain woven silk texture, consisting of the finest singles, which are hard-twisted and woven in the gum condition, the cloth being afterwards degummed. 1.7 tex warp and weft, 40 ends and picks per cm. The term chiffon is also used in conjunction with certain silk fabrics which are finished with a soft pliable feel—e.g., 'chiffon taffeta', 'chiffon velour'.

Chiné or **chené**   Term applied to fabrics in which a design or pattern, usually of a figured character, appears that has been printed upon the warp prior to the weaving of the cloth. The cloth is most frequently woven plain, but pleasing effects are got in weaves of a crêpe character. In the weaving process the warp threads do not retain the exact relative positions that they occupied during the printing operation, so that the colours tend to run into each other and cause the edges of the different parts of the figure to be somewhat indefinite; and as the weft is not printed a much softer effect is produced than in ordinary cloth printing. The fabrics include silk, worsted, cotton, and linen structures, and are used for a variety of purposes, certain styles of designs being employed in silk ribbons, and other styles for light dress and blouse fabrics, while very large and elaborate patterns are made in furnishing textures (see Shadow cretonne).

Chintz   Cotton cloths printed with elaborately coloured designs, and used for similar purposes to cretonnes (q.v.). The cloth is usually highly glazed.

Chintzed fabric   A cloth in which one colour of weft is replaced by another colour in succeeding horizontal sections of a design so that a figure is formed in more colours than there are series of weft threads employed (see *Watson's Advanced Textile Design*).

Chlorinated cloth   The chlorination process is employed to make wool fabrics 'non-shrinkable' when they are washed. The process makes the wool brighter and harsher, and increases its affinity for dyes, but it is turned yellow and requires stoving, and the handle of the material is adversely affected.

Cleaning cloth   A coarse plain or gauze fabric employed for cleaning machinery and consisting of thick yarns spun from cotton waste. The gauze structure is generally woven by means of a gauze reed mounting.

Clear woollen finish   Applied to warp-face woollen cloths of the buckskin, venetian, and whip-cord types, and certain West of England cloths in single, backed, and double weaves in which the design and colour patterns are required to show clearly. The warp-face cloths are made with hard-twisted warp and soft-spun weft, and in twill patterns the direction of the twill and of the warp twist are arranged to show the weave distinctly. The felting of clear finished cloths is chiefly to give compactness of structure, and this is followed by dry raising or brushing, and cropping in order to remove the loose fibres from the surface.

Clip spot fabrics   Light textures, ornamented with spots or figures formed by means of extra warp or weft threads, from which the loose material, floating between the spots, is cut away (see *Watson's Advanced Textile Design*).

Cobourg   Similar to cotton warp cashmere as regards weave and yarns, but is a coarser and heavier fabric, and is used more as a lining cloth, for which purpose it is given a stiffer handle (see Cashmere).

Coco matting   Very coarse cloth composed of thick yarn made of coir fibre obtained from coconut husks. The fabrics are largely woven with two colours of warp arranged end-and-end, and fancy diamond, etc., designs are made on the warp rib principle. A similar kind of cloth is made in jute and sisal yarns.

Cord effects   The term 'cord' is applied to rib effects which run longitudinally in the cloth, and 'repp' to those which run transversely (see Repp).

Cable cord   A plain woven weft rib structure in which the weft is worsted and the warp cotton—38/2 tex cotton warp, 16 tex botany weft, 17 ends and 52 picks per cm.

Hair cord   Produced in plain cloth by introducing one thick end at a place on a ground formed of fine warp and weft, the latter being dented two ends per split and the former single. Also used to denote a 1-and-2 rib construction in which all the ends are of equal count (see D in *Figure 3.3*).

Persian cord   A 2-and-2 weft rib cloth in cotton warp and botany worsted weft, woven two ends per split, with the ends that run in pairs separated by the reed wires. 24/2 tex cotton warp, 18 tex botany weft, 30 ends and 48 picks per cm.

Russel cord   Similar in structure to Persian cord, but woven with mohair or lustre worsted weft.

Royal rib   An all-cotton, weft cord fabric woven plain with two ends per mail, and with the weft predominating over the warp—23 tex warp, 16 tex weft, 28 ends and 56 picks per cm.

Gordon cord   A botany weft and cotton warp structure made in the weave given at No. 1, *Figure A1.2*.

Metz cord   Similar structure to Gordon cord, but woven in No. 6, *Figure A1.2*.

Corduroy   Corded velveteen structures in which a weft pile forms longitudinal lines or cords, strong heavy cloths being used for trouserings, smoking jackets, and riding breeches, and lighter fabrics for dress materials. (See Fustian; also *Watson's Advanced Textile Design*.)

Corkscrew fabric   Usually a fine worsted cloth in which a warp rib twill effect is formed running at a flat angle. The 13-thread corkscrew weave (see O in *Figure 6.4*) is largely used for very fine coatings and suitings. 28/2 tex botany warp, 30 tex botany weft, 48 ends and 36 picks per cm.

Corkscrew repp   A plain woven, warp rib fabric made with fine warp and thick spiral weft, which gives an irregular, but interesting, appearance to the rib lines. 15 tex cotton warp, 120 tex cotton count spiral weft, 38 ends and 11 picks per cm.

Cotton cashmere   The term 'cashmere' is applied to all-cotton cloths woven in 1-and-2 twill, and constructed in a similar manner to botany weft cashmere. 16 tex cotton warp, 14 tex cotton weft, 26 ends and 54 picks per cm.

Cotton Georgette A cotton crêpe fabric made in imitation of silk Georgette, with hard twisted warp and weft yarns. A good cloth is woven plain with right and left twist threads arranged in 2-and-2 order in warp and weft—17/2 tex yarns, 20 ends and 18 picks per cm in the loom; contraction, about 25 per cent in width and length. In cheaper cloths the yarn is twisted all alike, and weaves with small floats of warp or weft on a plain foundation are used (see Nos. 26 and 27, *Figure A1.4*)—11/2 tex warp and weft, 24 ends and 26 picks per cm in the loom.

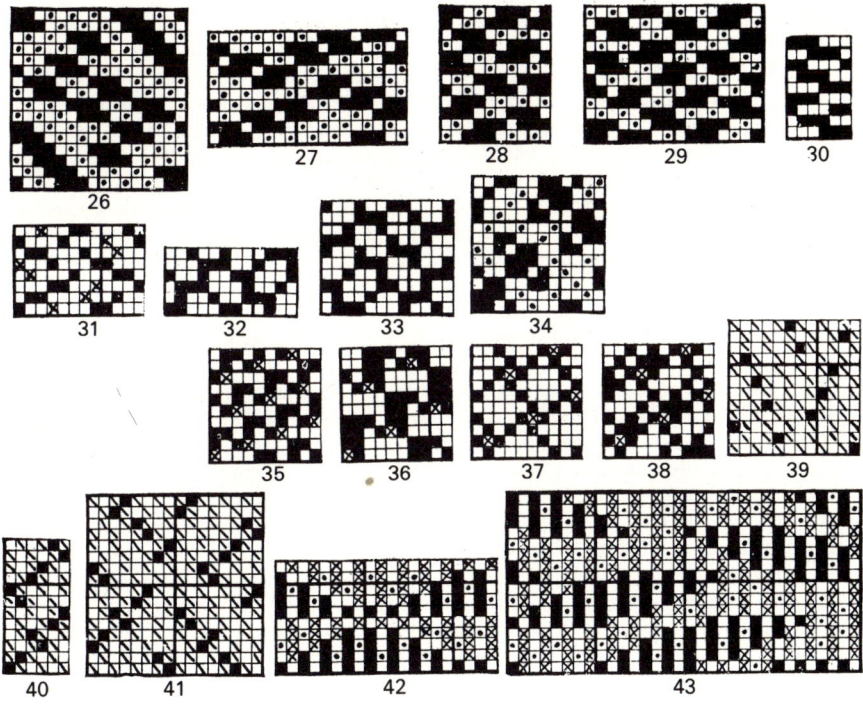

Figure A1.4

Cotton suitings and **trouserings** Made in imitation of worsted cloths as regards colouring and weave effects, very good fabrics being produced at a relatively low price, and although they lack the fulness and warmth of wool textures, they are suitable for tropical countries. The colours are mostly subdued with bright threads introduced in the form of grandrelle twists, while the weaves are simple twills, hopsacks, ribs, and the warp-face Venetian. The yarns should be spun from a good quality of cotton, and the warp doubled with less twist than ordinary, so that the threads in both directions will be full and soft. The underside of the cloth is frequently given a flannelette finish. A 2-and-2 twill fabric—38/2 tex warp, 60 to 38 tex weft, 26 ends and 19 to 26 cm picks per cm. 3-and-2 warp-face Venetian (No. 9, *Figure A1.3*)—38/2 tex warp, 38 to 30 tex weft, 30 to 36 ends and 20 to 29 picks per cm.

Cotton Venetian A cotton lining cloth made in 8-thread warp satin weave, and containing many more ends than picks per inch. It is given a finish which produces a lustrous surface similar to that of a cotton Italian, and it has the advantage over the latter that the cloth is more quickly woven as the predominating threads are in the warp. A combed and gassed Egyptian cotton warp is employed consisting usually of two-fold yarns, with the warp twist in the same direction as the twill of the satin. The weft is ordinary American or Egyptian, and the cloth is woven grey, piece-dyed, mercerised, and schreinered—20/2 to 14/2 tex warp, 24 to 16 tex weft, 58 to 66 ends and 32 to 42 picks per cm.

Coutil A strong cotton cloth, piece-dyed drab or French grey, and used for corsets (see also Nankeen). Woven in 3-thread warp-face twill, which is frequently in the form of a waved twill, 6 × 6 ends wide (see No. 8, *Figure A1.2*). A fine cloth—13/2 tex warp, 12/2 tex weft, 56 ends and 48 picks per cm.

Covert coating A light, warp-face, overcoating cloth which usually has two distinguishing features i.e., the union in the warp of coloured and white fibres and the formation of a fine, clear, steep twill effect. Olive, fawn, brown, and grey are chiefly combined with the white in the warp, and the weft is generally dyed to correspond with the warp colour. The 5-thread Venetian weave (No. 9, *Figure A1.3*) is most commonly used, but similar derivatives of satin on 7, 8, and 9 threads (see Nos. 10, 11, and 12, *Figure A1.3*), which will give a fine steep twill effect, are employed for heavier weights of cloths. The two-colour effect in the warp may be obtained in various ways, as, for example, (a) from a mixture of dyed and undyed fibres; (b) by twisting together a dyed and an undyed thread, or a dyed thread with a coloured and white marl thread; (c) from a mixture of wool and cotton fibres; (d) by twisting together a wool and a cotton thread. In (c) and (d) methods neither the wool nor the cotton is dyed before weaving, but wool weft is used and the grey cloth is piece-dyed for wool, which, by leaving the cotton in the warp unaffected, produces the two-colour effect required.

The warp yarn is most frequently worsted, or a union of worsted and cotton, and the weft worsted, but sometimes a woollen weft is used, and certain cloths are made with woollen yarn in both warp and weft. 35/2 to 30/2 tex botany or union twist warp, 45 to 38 tex botany weft, 34 to 38 ends and 22 to 26 picks per cm; or, 90 tex woollen mixture warp, 120 tex weft, 22 ends and 14 picks per cm. The worsted and cotton twist yarns usually consist of a thicker worsted than cotton thread; thus a 35/2 tex thread might be composed of 10 tex cotton and 25 tex worsted twisted together.

Covert cloths are usually shower proofed, and given a clear finish, although slight milling is generally practised in order to impart the required firmness of handle. Cloths containing woollen yarn are somewhat severely milled and raised so that the surface is covered with a short fibrous nap, which is allowed almost to conceal the weave, or, on the other hand, is cropped close enough for the weave to show clearly (see Venetian overcoating).

Crash A linen fabric with an irregular appearance due to the use of thick, uneven yarns, particularly in the weft, woven plain or in fancy crêpe weaves, largely used for towels. For the warp brown mercerised cotton is sometimes used in place of linen. Cotton crash towelling is made with waste cotton weft in weaves of an oatmeal crêpe character (see Oatmeal cloth).

Crease resist finish Applied to cotton, linen, and rayon fabrics, by which they are made strongly resistant to creasing by the incorporation of a synthetic resin within the fibres. The cloths are made heavier and stronger and they launder better.

Crêpe fabrics Have an irregular or broken surface appearance, and are produced in ordinary yarns by using such weaves as those given in *Figures 5.4* and *5.5*, and at Nos. 26 to 34, *Figure A1.4*. For weave P *Figure 5.5*—14 tex cotton warp, 32 tex lustre worsted weft, 24 ends and 22 picks per cm. For weaves Nos. 28 and 29, *Figure A1.4*— 14 tex cotton warp, 18 tex filament rayon weft, 22 ends and 20 picks per cm.

In most crêpe fabrics, however, the weave is plain and the effect is due to the use of very hard twisted threads (see Crêpe yarns), either in the weft, or warp, or both weft and warp, which, when the cloth is subjected to a wet finishing process, cause the latter to shrink considerably—from 12 to 20 per cent—in the direction of the crêpe threads. As a rule the crêpe threads are introduced in equal proportions of right and left twist, and as the cloth shrinks the differently twisted threads tend to untwist in opposite directions, so that an irregular surface results. The textures are usually dyed in the piece, and, in order that the right and left twist yarns may be distinguished during the processes of manufacture, one of them is tinted in a fugitive colour, while weft yarns are wound (in opposite directions) on to differently coloured pirns. Crêpe fabrics are light and soft to the touch, and relatively fine yarns are used with only sufficient threads per inch in the loom as will contribute to the proper shrinking of the cloth. Sometimes a more pronounced crêpe effect is obtained by using such weaves as Nos. 26 and 27, *Figure A1.4*, which show small floats on a plain foundation.

Crêpe de chine   A plain woven, lustrous and finely crinkled fabric in which a fine silk warp is woven in the gum with crêpe twisted silk weft arranged 2 × 2 of right and left twist (see Crêpe silk yarns). The cloth is degummed and dyed in the piece—6.4 tex warp, 9 tex weft, 60 ends, 34 picks per cm.

Serpentine crêpe   A plain weave cotton fabric that has almost the appearance of a crepon. The crêpe twist is used only in the weft, and is all in the same direction—10 tex warp, 23 tex weft, 23 ends and 20 picks per cm; contraction about 25 per cent from the loom width.

Crêpe cotton yarns are used very extensively not only in all-cotton cloths (see Cotton Georgette), but in combination with worsted, silk, and rayon, while crêpe botany yarns provide the shrinking element in all wool crêpe cloths, and are also used in conjunction with real silk (see Estrella) and rayon yarns. (See also, Rayon crêpe yarns and crêpe fabrics, Appendix II.)

Crepoline   A dress fabric composed of lustre or cross-bred worsted yarns, and woven in various modifications of 2-and-2 warp rib weave (see Nos. 39 to 41, *Figure A1.4*), which give a greater proportion of warp on the surface and produce an irregular effect of a crêpe character—50/2 to 38/2 tex worsted warp, 45 to 25 tex worsted weft, 26 to 30 ends and 18 to 24 picks per cm.

Crepons, crimps, and **blisters**   In the finished state these fabrics contain threads in warp, weft, or both warp and weft, which differ in length so that certain parts of the texture are slacker than other parts, and tend to cockle or form blisters on the surface. The difference in length of the threads may be obtained in three ways, as follows:

(1) A portion of the warp is placed on a separate beam, and is allowed to come in more rapidly than the warp on the ground beam. By arranging the slacker woven ends in stripe form a crimped or cockled effect is formed longitudinally, as illustrated by the fabric represented at G in *Figure 2.3*. The term 'seersucker' is also applied to the structure. A cotton fabric—45/3 tex crimp warp, 25 per cent contraction, 34 tex tight warp, 4 per cent contraction, 12 tex weft, 26 ends and 24 picks per cm.

(2) Threads are combined which naturally have different shrinking properties, so that the finishing operations cause certain threads to become much shorter while the others are scarcely affected. For example, a relatively non-shrinking mohair or English lustre worsted yarn is used in combination with either a hard twisted botany worsted yarn or a good felting woollen yarn. Plain weave may be used in producing crimped or crepon stripe or check effects, as for example by combining, say, 20 threads of 52/2 tex mohair worsted and 60 threads of 30/2 tex hard twist or crepon botany worsted.

Figured crepons or blisters are produced by employing different weave structures in conjunction with the shrinking and non-shrinking yarns. In the ground the two yarns work together and make one cloth, but where the blister structure is formed a double weave (usually double plain) is used which produces a fabric in the non-shrinking yarn above a similar fabric in the shrinking yarn. The contraction of the cloth in the finishing processes causes the non-shrinking upper fabric to become slack and a waved blister effect results.

(3) Threads which naturally have similar shrinking properties are made to contract unequally in the cloth by chemical means. Cotton yarn is, therefore, substituted for hard twisted botany in the manufacture of crepons and blisters, and the cloth is subjected to a finish, which consists of mercerising without stretching the fabric so that the shrinking of the cotton yarn has full play and may amount to 20 per cent or more. From 30/2 to 20/2 tex Egyptian cotton warp, and 14 tex cotton weft may be used in conjunction with mohair warp.

Crimp stripes and cockled effects are also produced in plain cotton fabrics by printing a caustic soda solution on the ground portions of the cloth. The printed sections contract and form a flat, even surface, while the remaining parts become slack and give the crinkled effect.

Cretonne   Used for hangings, bed valances, and upholstery purposes, and is usually ornamented by elaborate printed designs. For cloths printed in the piece plain, twill, oatmeal crêpe, and small fancy weaves are used, with thick, soft weft, which is frequently spun from waste cotton. The finish is usually dull.

Shadow cretonne is a 'chiné' or warp printed style (see Chiné), woven plain, with the warp usually predominating over the weft. The pattern has a blurred appearance, and is the same on both sides—46/2 tex cotton warp, 84 tex cotton weft, 26 ends and 13 picks per cm.

Curl effects   Produced during cloth shrinkage by arranging two kinds of yarn one or two threads of each alternately, a non-shrinking yarn being floated somewhat loosely on the surface while a yarn that shrinks readily is interwoven firmly. The cloth is heavily shrunk, but, as the floating threads do' not contract, they form curls or loops on the surface. (See *Watson's Advanced Textile Design*, and also Astrakhan.)

Damask   Originally a silk fabric (made in Damascus) with a weft sateen figure on a warp satin, or twill, or plain ground. The cloth is now extensively used for household purposes, and is made in cotton, rayon, and linen yarns with the figure and ground in opposite sateen weaves; the figure usually being in weft sateen and the ground in warp satin (see *Watson's Advanced Textile Design*). The weaves generally used are the 5- and 8-thread sateens, and the terms single and double damask are sometimes used in order to distinguish linen fabrics made in the respective weaves. The best linen damasks are woven with about 50 per cent more picks than ends per inch, and properly the term double damask should only be used for 8-thread sateen cloths which contain such an excess of picks over ends. 42 tex warp, 24 tex weft, 32 ends and 54 picks per cm.

Delaine   A plain woven fine worsted dress or blouse fabric which is usually more or less elaborately figured by printing either the warp or the cloth—20 tex botany warp, 13 tex botany weft, 26 ends and 27 picks per cm. Cotton delaine is a fine soft fabric made in imitation of wool delaine.

Denim   A strong warp face cotton cloth used for overalls, jeans, skirts, etc., largely made in 3-and-1 twill weave. The cloth is sometimes piece-dyed, but generally the warp is yarn-dyed brown or blue and crossed with white weft. The colours should be fast to washing—33 tex warp, 42 tex weft, 36 ends and 24 picks per cm.

Dhooties   Soft, light, cotton fabrics used in India for turbans, loin cloths, etc., and made traditionally in lengths of 2/5 yards, 2/6 yards, or 2/10 yards, etc., the two meaning that the cloth will be cut through the centre so as to form two garments. The body of the cloth is plain grey, and the ornamentation consists of headings and fancy borders, and in some cases of one or three prominent stripes away from the borders. In grey dhooties the border pattern is made simply by cramming grey or bleached ends in the reed (double ends in place of single ends may be employed), or by using thicker two-fold ends. Coloured dhooties are sometimes woven entirely plain with coloured ends forming border stripes, but frequently more or less elaborate figured stripes (termed flush borders) are made by means of extra threads. The borders are formed by the figure stripe which may also be introduced once at a third of the width from one side, or three times across the width at an equal distance apart—10 tex cotton ground warp, 7 tex cotton weft, 32 ground ends and 30 picks per cm in the grey cloth; 20/2 tex grey, bleached, and coloured warp for the stripe effects.

Dimity   One type of cloth, used for bed covers, is woven in 4-thread warp and weft satinette weaves, which usually form stripes equal in size, so that the pattern is the same on both sides, the warp effect having a raised appearance in each case. A common size of stripe is four threads each of warp and weft face weave (see No. 50, *Figure A1.5*), and this may form the body of the cloth with broader stripes used as a border—38 tex warp, 25 tex weft, 22 ends and 31 picks per cm, about 20 per cent shrinkage in width. The term 'dimity' is also applied to a plain-woven cotton fabric that is piece-dyed or ornamented with cord threads. About 18 tex warp and weft, 28 ends and 26 picks per cm.

Doeskin   A very fine woollen fabric composed of a high quality of merino wool, usually woven in 5-thread warp satin, a fine warp being used with the twist of the threads running in the same direction as the twill of the satin. The cloth is heavily milled and raised and finished with a dress face, and is similar to a beaver cloth, but is lighter and

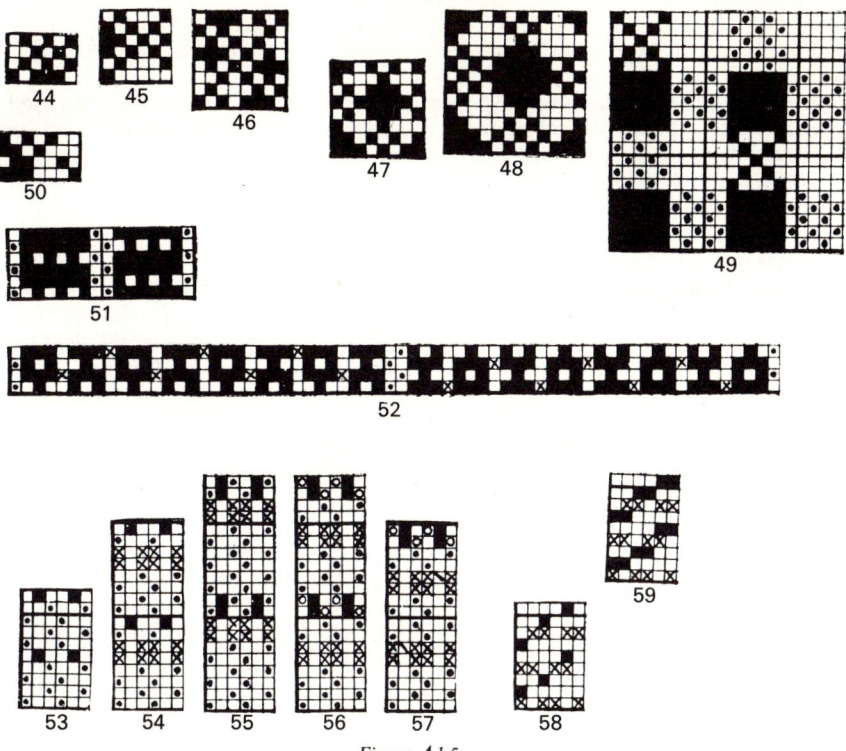

Figure A1.5

finer—95 to 75 tex warp, 180 to 135 tex weft, 20 to 26 ends and 12 to 14 picks per inch in the loom. Contraction, about 30 per cent in width and 25 per cent in length from the loom dimensions.

Domet An imitation of flannel made entirely of cotton or with cotton warp and a mixture of cotton and wool weft, and finished with a raised surface on both sides. Woven plain, and coloured in stripe form, suitable for shirtings and pyjamas (q.v.), for which it is largely used.

Donegal tweed A rough woollen cloth (similar to homespun) made from thick yarn in plain or 2-and-2 twill and finished with little or no milling. From 400 to 240 tex warp and weft, and from 4 to 8 ends and picks per cm.

Doria stripes Light, plain woven cotton cloths in which stripe patterns are formed by varying the denting of the ends, as, for example, 6 ends in six splits, 8 ends in four splits. A convenient method of making the style consists of placing the crowded ends 2 per mail and denting the mails regularly, and the above example might be woven 6 single ends in six splits, 4 double ends in four splits, 26 splits and 22 picks per cm, 10 tex cotton warp and 8 tex cotton weft.

Dress-face finished fabrics Heavily felted and raised woollen cloth, the surface of which is covered with a lustrous nap of short fibres, which are laid lengthways of the fabric and completely conceal the weave and structure. The texture is made dense and fibrous by the felting process, and the fibres are drawn on to the surface and straightened and combed in one direction by the operation of raising, while lustre is imparted to the surface by boiling the fabric. Cloths to which this type of finish is applied are doeskins, beavers, box cloths, billiard cloths, pilots, etc., which may be either wool, yarn, or piece-dyed.

Drills Warp-face fabrics largely made in cotton yarns, and woven in 3, 4, and 5-thread warp faced twills and 5-thread satin, with the twill lines running opposite to the direction of the twist of the warp yarn, in order that a prominent twill effect will be formed. It may be bleached or piece-dyed, or woven with coloured stripes in the warp with either white or dyed weft. The fineness of the yarns and the setting vary according to the weave and the weight required, satin drills being mostly made in fine yarns and setting, while a 3-and-1 twill fabric, termed Florentine, is woven with thicker yarns. In 5-thread satin—14 tex cotton warp, 16 tex cotton weft, 50 ends and 32 picks per cm or 27 tex warp, 46 tex weft, 44 ends and 28 picks per cm. In 4-thread twill—38 tex warp, 43 tex weft, 36 ends and 20 picks per cm.

The term 'pepperall drill' is applied to a very high quality of the cloth, and 'drillette' to a light make.

Duchesse satin   A very rich and lustrous silk fabric woven in 7, 8, 10, or 12-thread warp satin. 2 tex filament warp, 18 tex spun silk weft, 144 ends and 36 picks per cm.

Duck   Very heavy and strong plain woven cotton and linen canvas fabrics used for belting, sail cloth, awnings, and tents, and, when dyed black, for boot linings, etc. A heavy duck—250/6 tex cotton warp and weft, 13 ends and 10 picks per cm. A medium duck—170/5 tex cotton warp, 120/3 tex cotton weft, 18 ends and 12 picks per cm. The term 'duck' is also applied to a tropical suiting cloth woven in hopsack weaves.

Dungaree   A strong cotton fabric used for overalls, similar to denim (q.v.), but usually yarn dyed in both warp and weft—38 tex warp, 27 tex weft, 32 ends and 26 picks per cm.

Elastic webbing   A strong narrow ware fabric of special construction, and containing rubber threads in the warp; used for suspenders, belts, etc.

Eolienne   A very fine piece-dyed silk warp fabric which is crossed with thick worsted or cotton weft, a warp rib effect being formed. The warp is usually in the form of singles, somewhat loosely twisted, and woven in the gum condition, the degumming being effected in the cloth—2 tex filament silk warp, 25 tex gassed cotton weft, 60 ends and 21 picks per cm.

Epingle   A warp rib silk cloth largely used for ribbons and for making ties.

Estamene   A milled cross-bred worsted cloth, piece-dyed, and finished with a rough fibrous surface; usually woven in 2-and-2 twill, sometimes 3-and-3 twill—38/2 to 25/2 tex warp, 25 to 21 tex weft, 20 to 26 ends and 20 to 25 picks per cm.

Estrella   A crêpe de chine type of cloth (q.v.) woven plain with singles silk warp and hard-twisted botany weft, picked two right and two left twist alternately.

Faille   A fine, soft, warp rib silk fabric in which the ribs are not prominent.

Felt   The distinguishing feature of true felt is that it contains no threads, but is purely a fibrous structure. The wool fibres from a woollen carding machine are arranged layer upon layer until the desired thickness is built up the width of the card, and at the same time, by a continuous forward movement, the required length of material is obtained. This is submitted to a process of milling, while the fibres are moistened, as in the felting of woollen cloth (see Felted cloth). The fibres become interlocked and matted, and a compact texture is produced, which is used for felt hats, glove linings, table covers, floor coverings, etc., the quality and thickness varying according to its use.

Woven felt   Fibrous faced woollen cloths which have been felted to such a degree that the fibres are compactly matted together so that the thread structure does not show and the texture has the appearance of felt. The construction of a woven felt may shrink 50 per cent in width and length, and the resultant structure is stronger, firmer, and more elastic than a similar carded felt.

Felted cloth   In the felting, milling, or fulling process a wool cloth is moistened with warm soapy water, and is subjected to the intermittent application of pressure in length and in width. Under the influence of the pressure and moisture the fibres are matted and interlocked. The cloth shrinks in width and length, and from a bare thready structure as it leaves the loom it is changed to a dense, full, and compact structure. The matting and interlocking of the fibres is largely dependent on the prominence of the epithelial scale structure, and the best felting wools are the fine merinos and the poorest the smooth lustrous wools and hairs. Woollen fabrics will felt much more readily than worsted fabrics, and for heavy felting the yarns should be as soft spun as possible. As weft may be more slackly twisted than warp, the shrinkage is generally greater in width than in length, and a cloth should be set in the loom to allow for the amount of contraction that will take place in the felting process.

Flannel Plain or twill woven cloth with a very soft handle, which makes it particularly suitable for being worn next to the skin. The yarns are mostly woollen spun, and medium English wools and Colonial cross-breds are used for ordinary qualities and merino for fine textures. The cloths are milled and raised, and are usually finished with a fibrous face, but sometimes the surface is more or less clear. An ordinary plain woven flannel—95 to 80 tex warp, 84 to 74 tex weft, 10 to 11 ends and 11 to 14 picks per cm in the loom. Contraction, about 20 per cent in width and 15 per cent in length (see Molleton flannel.)

Flannelette A cotton texture largely made in plain weave, sometimes in 2-and-2 twill, and finished with a fibrous surface in imitation of wool flannel. The nap is produced almost entirely from the weft, which, usually, is soft spun and thick, in order to furnish a suitable foundation from which the surface fibre can be drawn (see Flannelette yarn). Recently harder spun weft has been used in order to produce a better wearing cloth, and to obtain a featureless texture the weft is twisted in the same direction as the warp. The cloths are mostly woven either grey (to be subsequently bleached or dyed), or in the form of coloured stripes. Sometimes the cloth is printed, the term 'velouté' being applied to printed flannelette. A plain weave cloth—25 tex warp, 50 tex weft, 20 ends and 19 picks per cm. A double-end plain cloth—27 tex warp, 46 tex weft, 38 ends and 16 picks per cm. A 2-and-2 twill cloth—25 tex warp, 40 tex weft, 27 ends and 28 picks per cm. The flannelette finish is applied to a large variety of cloths, such as cotton trouserings, rugs, blankets, dressing gown textures, in addition to ordinary underclothing fabrics, etc., which are raised on one or both sides according to requirements.

Foulard A fine, soft silk fabric, woven in 2-and-2 twill, in which a pattern is obtained by printing. Frequently the effect is a white spot upon a coloured ground—5 tex filament warp, 9 tex filament weft, 51 ends and 54 picks per cm.

French merino A similar cloth to the botany warp cashmere, except that the weave is 2-and-2 twill (see Cashmere). 15 tex botany warp, 11 tex botany weft, 24 ends and 76 picks per cm. The twill runs at a very flat angle in the cloth with the weft predominating on the surface.

Frieze A heavily felted and raised woollen fabric made of coarse or medium wools and finished with a rough fibrous surface. In ordinary friezes the surface fibres are laid in one direction, but in 'nap' friezes they are rubbed into small curls or beads. For 2-and-2 twill weave—about 270 tex warp and weft, 8 to 9 ends and picks per cm. Contraction, about 25 to 30 per cent in width and 20 per cent in length.

Fustian A generic term for velveteen, corduroy, moleskin, swansdown, beaverteen, cantoon or diagonal, and imperial cloth (q.v.). Woven with a very large number of picks per inch, the lighter structures being used for ladies' wear, and the heavier cloths for riding breeches and similar hard wearing clothing.

Gabardine A warp-face cloth, mostly woven in 2-and-2 twill, which produces a fine steep twill effect on account of the predominance of the warp over the weft, but lower qualities are sometimes made in 2-and-1 twill. Largely used for rainproof overcoatings, and made at first with botany worsted warp and cotton weft, but the warp is now more frequently composed of cotton or a blended yarn—27/2 tex botany warp, 20/2 tex cotton weft, 42 ends and 35 picks per cm. The cotton weft is yarn-dyed, but the wool warp may be dyed in the piece. A fine cotton gabardine—15/2 tex warp and weft, 64 ends and 42 picks per cm; and a lower quality—30/2 tex warp, 30 tex weft, 43 ends and 30 picks per cm. The cotton warp is frequently a 'grandrelle' yarn.

Gabardine costume cloths Have a similar warp surface to the overcoatings, but worsted warp and weft are used, and the cloth is much softer. A 3-and-1 warp twill cloth—36/2 tex botany warp, 24 tex botany or fine cross-bred weft, 40 ends and 25 picks per cm.

Gabercord A soft, all-cotton fabric, with a fine warp face twill effect (see No. 23, *Figure A1.3*), which shows very distinctly on the face—20 tex warp and 30 tex weft, soft spun, 58 ends and 24 picks per cm.

Galatea   A coloured, warp-face twill, cotton cloth, similar to a regatta (q.v.), but lighter, and usually woven in 2-and-1 twill (sometimes 3-and-1 twill). In simple stripe patterns the fabric is used for nurses' uniforms, while for dresses sometimes fancy dobby effects are introduced—23 tex warp, 28 tex weft, 36 ends and 26 picks per cm.

Gauze or **leno**   Cloths in which certain ends cross from side to side of adjacent ends. (See *Watson's Advanced Textile Design*.)

Georgette crêpe   A fine silk fabric with a crêpe appearance, due to the use of very hard twisted threads which are arranged 2-and-2 of right and reverse twist in warp and weft (see Crêpe fabrics and cotton georgette). The cloth is woven plain and degummed and dyed in the piece—1.7 tex filament 2- or 3-thread yarns, 20 to 32 turns per cm, 43 ends and picks per cm.

Gingham   A firm, plain woven, cotton fabric usually coloured in the warp, and frequently made in check form. Coarser qualities are used for aprons, etc., and finer cloths for blouses and shirtings. (See 'Zephyr'.)

Glacé   A lustre dress fabric (see Bradford lustres). Glacé is also a French term applied to cloths which give a 'shot effect' (q.v.).

Glass cloth   A good quality of linen, cotton, or linen and cotton cloth, woven grey and in stripe and check colourings, and used for drying and polishing glassware and china. 50 tex cotton or linen warp and weft, 18 ends and picks per cm.

Glen check   The full name is 'Glen Urquhart check', and is applied to a colour and weave check effect in which 2-and-2 twill weave is used in conjunction with a compound of 2-and-2 with 4-and-4 colouring. (See example C in *Figure 10.7*.)

Gloria   A strong, very firmly woven fabric composed of silk warp and worsted or cotton weft, usually made in plain weave; used for umbrella coverings and also dress goods.

Gossamer   A very soft and flexible silk gauze fabric, one end crossing one end, used for veilings—2.5 tex warp, 4 tex weft, 18 ends and 32 picks per inch.

Grenadine   A light dress fabric consisting entirely, or to a large extent, of a very open gauze structure. Stripe, check, and figured styles are formed in silk, worsted, and cotton yarns. (See *Watson's Advanced Textile Design*.)

Grey cloth   A piece of cloth in the condition in which it leaves the loom.

Grosgrain   A plain weave fabric with a prominent warp rib effect, made with fine silk warp closely set and thick silk, worsted, or cotton weft with comparatively few picks. Used for dresses and ribbons. The term 'gros' is applied to different kinds of ribbed silks e.g., *Gros de Londres* has broad and narrow ribs alternately, sometimes in different colours, while *Gros de Tours* is a heavy ribbed silk woven with two or more picks in a shed.

Gun club check   A 2-and-2 twill fabric woven in three colours in warp and weft, arranged so that the solid squares formed by two of the colours are separately surrounded by the third colour, as, for example, 4 dark, 4 light, 4 mid, 4 light; or 6 dark, 6 mid, 6 light, 6 mid.

Habit cloth   A fine woollen costume cloth largely made in 5-thread warp satin weave and finished with a dress face. A fine warp is used and rather thicker weft, as, for example, 54 tex warp, 66 tex weft, 21 ends and 13 picks per cm in the loom. Contraction about 25 per cent in width and 15 per cent in length.

Habutai   A generic term applied to many Japanese silk fabrics, which are fine, soft, closely woven in plain, twill, or fancy weaves with ungummed threads, the cloth being boiled off and dyed in the piece.

Hairline   In a true hairline the warp and weft colours are alike, and each colour of warp is intersected only by its own colour of weft, so that perfectly solid lines of colour are formed. The styles are produced in simple weaves (see *Figures 9.7* and *9.8*), and also in double plain and double twill weaves (see *Watson's Advanced Textile Design*). The term hairline is now applied rather generally to any fine, solid coloured, stripe effect.

Harris tweed   A rough, fibrous, woollen tweed, understood to be spun, woven, dyed, and finished in Harris, Lewis, and other islands of the Outer Hebrides (see Homespun). About 250 tex warp and weft, 7 ends and picks per cm.

Henrietta   Similar to cashmere (q.v.) as regards weave, weft, and relative number of picks to ends per inch, but silk warp is used in place of wool or cotton, and the cloth is finer. 10/2 to 8/2 tex spun silk warp, 12 to 11 tex botany weft, 26 to 29 ends and 62 to 66 picks per cm.

Hessian   A plain woven, strong and coarse jute cloth, made in a great variety of qualities, and used for wrapping and packing purposes. Mangled hessian is smoother and has a more glazed appearance than the ordinary cloth, and frequently is better in quality.

Holland   Plain woven linen cloth, used as furniture covering, and also as ladies' summer skirts, in the unbleached (brown) or partly bleached condition. About 51 tex warp and weft, 17 ends and picks per cm. (See Window Holland.)

Homespun   Term applied to woollen cloths composed of yarns hand spun from local wools and woven on hand looms. The weave is usually plain or 2-and-2 twill, and the yarns are coarse and uneven, and frequently consist of a mixture of fibres in the natural colours, or dyed with natural dyes obtained from local sources. The cloth is usually a rough fibrous tweed in various 'heather mixture' shades, with the weave effect showing quite clearly.

Honeycomb fabrics   Woven with honeycomb weaves (see *Figure 5.7* and Nos. 44, 45, and 46, *Figure A1.5*), which produce a cell-like appearance in the cloth. A botany dress fabric—30/2 tex warp, 30 tex weft, 36 ends and 36 picks per cm.

Huckaback cloth   An absorbent fabric, used for towels and glass cloths, mostly made in cotton yarns (see *Figure 5.11*)—74 tex warp and weft, 16 ends and 38 picks per cm.

Imperial and **imperial sateen**   See Swansdown.

Imperial cloth   A fine piece-dyed worsted coating woven in 2-and-2 twill—35/2 to 30/2 tex botany warp, 24 to 18 tex botany weft, 27 to 30 ends and 32 to 28 picks per cm. Imperial serge, which is a similar cloth, but looser woven and softer, is used for costume fabrics.

Italian cloth   A lining cloth which was originally made with a dyed cotton warp and grey botany weft, wool-dyed in the piece, and given a lustrous surface appearance in the finishing process. The brilliant lustre which can now be obtained in cotton fabrics by the operations of mercerising and schreinering has led to the substitution of cotton weft for the botany weft, and the cloths are now extensively made entirely of cotton, and woven grey and piece-dyed. A good warp and soft spun even weft are required, with many more picks than ends per inch, and the weave is 5-thread weft sateen arranged to twill in the same direction as the twist of the weft, in order that maximum smoothness of surface will be obtained. Cotton Italian—17 to 14 tex grey cotton warp, 14 tex combed and gassed Egyptian weft, 34 to 38 ends and 52 to 64 picks per cm.

Jean   2-and-1 twill cotton cloth made warp or weft face. When woven with a warp face in strong yarns a drill structure is formed (see Drills), which is used for corsets, boot linings, etc. 30 tex warp and weft, 36 ends and 26 picks per cm.

Jeanette   A name applied to 3-thread weft faced twill fabrics.

Kersey   A 2-and-2 twill cloth heavily milled and finished with a fibrous surface, and made from strong fibred Cheviot or cross-bred wool. The yarns are mostly spun on the woollen principle, but sometimes worsted yarns are used. 190 tex warp and weft, 10 ends and picks per cm. Contraction about 25 per cent in width and 15 to 20 per cent in length.

Khaki   A Persian term meaning like the earth. A yellowish-brown fabric produced from a mixture of differently dyed fibres, and largely used for military purposes on account of the difficulty of distinguishing it from natural objects. The mixture of wool fibres to produce the khaki shade has been standardised as follows: 80 per cent olive brown, 5 per cent indigo, 15 per cent white.

Lambskin   See Swansdown.

Lasting   A strong cloth used for the tops of shoes and other purposes, which was formerly composed of worsted yarns, but is now made partly or entirely of cotton and/or synthetic materials. Various weaves are used, both single and weft-backed, and the fabric is made very strong, hard, and smooth.

Lawn   Plain woven, bleached cotton cloth, very light, fine, and smooth, used for underwear and dresses. May have a soft pure finish, or be given a rather firm feel—8 to 6 tex yarns, 32 to 36 ends and picks per cm (see Cambric). Victoria lawn is a closely woven fabric with a somewhat stiff finish, Persian lawn is a soft finished cloth, while Bishop's lawn is bleached and given a bluish-white tint. Linen lawn is made of fine linen yarns.

Leno Applied generally to all classes of fabrics in which certain ends cross from side to side of other ends (see Gauze; also *Watson's Advanced Textile Design*).

Linsey A coarse fabric woven plain or 2-and-2 twill and composed of cotton warp and a union of cotton and waste wool weft. Used for heavy under-garments, and also woven in stripes across the width for use as skirts and aprons.

Limbric A plain cotton cloth with soft spun lustrous weft, thicker than the warp, and may have more picks than ends per inch. Used for dress fabrics and casement curtains.

London shrunk cloth All-wool cloth which, after the ordinary finishing operation, has been passed several times, without tension, through hot and then cold water, and afterwards slowly dried by hanging on poles in a warm chamber to make it thoroughly shrunk. In another method the cloth is folded in wet sheets, in which it lies for 24 hours, after which the wet sheets are removed, and the cloth lies for another 24 hours in a pile before it is hung up and dried. The thoroughly shrunk condition is particularly required by tailors in order that there will be no irregular shrinking of the cloth when it is damped and hot-pressed; the made-up garment also keeps its shape better during subsequent wear.

Longcloth A firm, plain woven, bleached cotton fabric, close in texture, without much size, and used for underwear—20 to 16 tex warp and weft, 28 to 32 ends and 28 to 40 picks per cm. India longcloth is a finer and softer fabric, more like cambric—12 to 9 tex warp and weft, 36 to 40 ends and 38 to 54 picks per cm.

Lump A length of cloth which is about double the usual piece length.

Madapolam Plain woven bleached cotton fabric, usually made coarser than such cloths as cambric, nainsook, lawn, etc., but it may be finished soft like nainsook—13 to 10 tex warp and weft, 27 to 34 ends, and 24 to 44 picks per cm.

Madras curtain fabrics Figured textures in which the ornamentation is produced by means of thick, soft spun, extra weft threads on a very fine and open gauze foundation. (See *Watson's Advanced Textile Design*.)

Madras handkerchiefs A plain cotton fabric woven in large coloured checks, and composed of yarns dyed with non-fast dyes which, during the finishing of the cloth, bleed, so that the different colours run into each other and give a resemblance to patterns produced by native block printing.

Madras shirting A fine, light, good quality zephyr fabric, chiefly woven in stripe patterns. The cloth has a plain foundation, and the ornamentation frequently consists of crammed silk stripes in satin weaves and extra warp spot and stripe effects (see Zephyr).

Matelasse Term now applied to boldly figured warp rib fabrics, but the real matelasse is a double or compound cloth in which wadding threads are introduced below the figure so as to give it a raised or embossed appearance.

Maud A checked woollen cloth, used as a plaid or travelling rug, in which different tones of grey yarns are used in forming the pattern.

Melange lustre See Bradford lustre fabrics.

Melton cloth A woollen cloth which is heavily milled, so as to form a firm foundation, and the fibres are drawn on to the surface by raising, but in the cropping process, which follows, the fibres are reduced in length so as to form a short, dense, non-lustrous pile. Usually woven plain or broken 2-and-2 twill—about 160 to 95 tex warp and weft, 10 to 14 ends and picks per cm in the loom. Contraction about 35 per cent in width and 25 per cent in length.

Mercerised cloth The process of mercerising cotton cloth is similar to that of mercerising cotton yarn, and consists of imparting a fine silky lustre to a fabric by subjecting it to tension while impregnated with a cold strong solution of caustic soda. Mercerised material (yarn or cloth) has a much greater affinity for dyestuffs than unmercerised cotton.

Moiré A generic term applied to 'watered' fabrics which have a distinctive wavy appearance due to the varied reflection of light from different parts of the surface of the cloth. Mostly produced in silk, cotton and rayon yarns, and the best results are obtained in fine warp and weft rib structures in which the face threads are very closely set, while the straight threads are hard and stiff. The usual process of watering consists of placing two pieces of the same texture, or folding the same piece, face to face, and subjecting the cloth while moistened with water to pressure between two heated bowls of a calendar. Where two rib lines of the cloths are against each other the surface threads are flattened, but where the rib lines of one cloth come between the rib lines of the other cloth the threads remain round. The cloth shows dark and light places which change when viewed from opposite sides, and the pattern is of a most varied character without repetition. In another method the surface of the cloth is acted upon by a roller upon which the required form of moiré design has been engraved. Polished cotton yarn is largely used for the straight threads, as it is so hard that the embossing action of the pressure rollers has full play on the surface threads so that a clearly defined watered effect results.

Moiré antique A rich silk moiré in which a very pronounced irregular effect is produced.

Moiré à retours A watered fabric in which the effect is the same in each half, but reversed, due to the cloth having been folded down the centre during the process of watering.

Moiré française A stripe moiré effect produced by means of an engraved roller.

Moirette A yarn dyed moiré, plain woven in cotton yarns, either warp or weft rib (see Moreen). Warp rib cloth—20/2 tex cotton warp, 30/2 tex polished cotton weft, 45 ends and 25 picks per cm.

Moleskin A very strong, tough, smooth, and leathery fustian cloth (q.v.), which is really an uncut cotton velveteen (see *Watson's Advanced Textile Design*), and the weave which is given at No. 58, *Figure A1.5* produces a 1-and-5 weft-face effect on the surface and a 1-and-2 weft-face twill on the underside. The system of interlacing enables a very large number of picks of thick weft to be inserted. The cloth is raised on the underside and is usually piece-dyed—72/2 to 60/2 tex warp, 38 to 33 tex weft, 14 to 16 ends, and 96 to 160 picks per cm; shrinkage in width, about 20 per cent.

Molleton flannel A high quality of 2-and-2 twill woollen flannel, heavily milled and raised, and finished with a dense fibrous nap, dyed in delicate colours, and used for such purposes as dressing gowns and jackets. About 62 tex warp and weft, 15 ends and 17 picks per cm in the loom.

Moreen Similar to 'moirette' (q.v.), except that it is piece-dyed, and in the grey state is known as grey poplin. Warp rib cloth—16/2 tex cotton warp, 60/3 tex cotton weft, 50 ends and 18 picks per cm. Weft rib cloth—60/3 tex cotton warp, 11 tex cotton weft, 17 ends and 56 picks per cm.

Moss finished cloth A soft-handling woollen cloth, mostly in fancy colourings, which is heavily milled and finished with a fibrous face through which the weave and structure show indistinctly.

Mull Very fine, plain cotton fabric, bleached and finished soft; used for dresses (see Cambric). A bluish-white, very light and fine fabric, termed sacharilla mull, is used for veils and turbans (see Swiss mull).

Muslin A generic term applied to soft, fine, open, plain woven fabrics made of silk, worsted, or cotton yarns. The most common are cotton muslins, which are woven entirely plain or are ornamented with cords and crammed stripes, and spots and figures in extra weft or warp (see *Watson's Advanced Textile Design*). Plain muslin and fabrics with simple ornamentation are used for summer dresses, aprons, etc. In Swiss muslins spotted effects are produced by embroidering the cloth after it is woven, and imitations of the fabrics are made on the clip-spot principle (see Clip spots), termed Anglo-Swiss muslin.

Nainsook A fine, light, bleached, plain woven cotton cloth, with a soft finish, and used for underwear (see Cambric). Made in many different qualities, and sometimes woven with cord stripes and used for dresses—8 tex warp and weft, 36 ends and 34 picks per cm, to 6 tex warp and weft, 44 ends and 56 picks per cm.

Diaphalene is a nainsook type of fabric, which is mercerised and dyed in delicate colours for use as underwear.

Nankeen   The term nankeen is applied to a strong 2-and-1 warp-face twill cotton cloth, firmly set in the warp, and piece-dyed drab or other colour suitable for making pockets and corsets (see also Coutil).

Nap finish   The fibres are first made to stand vertically from the foundation of a woollen cloth, as in the velvet pile finish (q.v.), and then are rubbed into the form of small curls or nubs.

Napped fabrics   Term applied to wool or cotton cloths which are finished with a raised or fibrous surface.

Narrow wares   See Small wares.

Ninon   A fine, light, soft and open silk fabric, woven plain, used for summer dresses.

Nominal   A term applied to cloths in which the actual particulars are understood to be inferior to the stated particulars. The actual width of the cloth, also, may be made rather less than the stated nominal width.

Nuns' veiling   A very light and flimsy veiling texture made of silk, worsted, or cotton, sometimes with a border on one side, and used for mourning. A heavier, plain woven fabric, made of rather hard-twisted worsted yarns, and dyed in various colours, is used for blouses and dresses—24 tex worsted warp and weft, 22 ends and picks per cm.

Oatmeal crêpe   A soft full fabric with an irregular appearance made in crêpe weaves of the type shown at Nos. 32 to 34, *Figure A1.4*, and used for costume and dress fabrics, and household purposes. Worsted, woollen, linen, or cotton yarns may be employed, but the weft should be soft spun, and sometimes condenser cotton weft is used, as, for instance, in the manufacture of printed cretonnes—30 tex cotton warp, 38 tex cotton weft, 26 ends and 28 picks per cm.

Ombré   A shaded colour effect produced by employing a number of tones of a colour, and arranging them a few threads of each in order from light to dark. Ombré patterns are also formed in different colours.

Ondule or **wave effects**   All or a portion of the ends are made to form waved lines in the cloth, by means of a deep rising and falling reed in which the wires are not placed vertically, but are arranged at varying angles. For example, 30 splits of the reed may occupy a space 2 cm wide at the bottom and 4 cm wide at the top, followed by 30 splits in the space of 2 cm at the top and 4 cm at the bottom, 60 splits thus occupying 6 cm. The arrangement is repeated across the width, and, on account of its appearance, the term fan or paquet is applied to the reed. The wires are at an equal distance apart midway between the top and bottom, and when the reed beats up in this place the ends are in the normal position. By means of a special mechanism, however, the reed is slowly raised and lowered, and the ends (except those in the central splits) are gradually moved, some to the right and others to the left of their normal position, and then back again. A V-shaped wave effect is formed, which usually extends over about 5 to 8 cm in length and width. All the warp is brought from one warp beam, so that additional strain is put on the ends which wave the most, while the straight ends in the centre contract more than they would under normal conditions.

A modification of the above style is made that is not a V-shaped effect, but all the ends wave alike in a vertical direction. A weft ondule effect, also, is sometimes made by arranging the warp in alternate sections (each, say, about 2 cm wide), under the control of two easing bars or two special sets of healds, by means of which the odd sections of ends are gradually tightened while the even sections are slowly slackened, and then vice versa. Where the warp is held tight the picks lie closer together than in the slack warp sections, hence the changes in the tension on the ends cause the picks to form a horizontal waved effect.

Organdie   A light, fine, white cotton fabric of the muslin class with a stiff, wiry, and translucent finish, and used for frilling and similar purposes—7.5 tex warp, 6 tex weft twisted warp way, about 30 ends and picks per cm.

Orleans A plain Bradford lustre fabric (q.v.) mostly used as a lining—14 tex cotton warp, 32 to 28 tex lustre or demi-lustre worsted weft, 23 ends, and 19 to 26 picks per cm.

Ottoman A heavy warp rib fabric, with broad ribs, woven in a variety of materials. The term 'Ottoman cord' is applied to a fabric made with thick warp and fine weft in which the rib lines run lengthwise.

Padded back lining A fancy figure-printed fabric which is printed solid on the reverse side in order to prevent the figure effect from showing through from the face side.

Pahpoons Plain cotton cloths woven in contrasting colours of warp and weft so as to produce shot effects, with headings in strong colour contrast with the ground, as, for instance, red warp and blue weft with bright green weft for the headings. At each side a crammed border is made, about 1 cm wide, by placing two ends in each mail.

Paisley shawl Extensively manufactured in Paisley from the beginning of the nineteenth century until about the year 1870 when the fabric went out of fashion as an article of dress. The shawls, which were hand woven, were made in imitation of the soft, fine, wool shawls from Cashmere, and although the original designs were somewhat modified, the pine patterns (signifying fertility, reproduction, abundance) remained the characteristic feature of the Paisley fabric. The figures were produced in several colours of extra weft, and for winter wear the shawls were 'filled over'—that is, the design extended over the whole of the surface, but for lighter wear the centre was made solid white, red, or black without figure. The fabrics were mostly made one-sided with the figuring wefts floating somewhat loosely on the underside, but in some cases the shawls were perfectly reversible, except that the weft colours interchanged.

Palm beach suiting A mohair cloth used for tropical suitings.

Passementerie Heavy braids and fringes which are richly ornamented with silk, tinsel, beads, etc.

Peau de soie A fine, soft, high quality, silk fabric, 5-thread warp satin surface, with a rather dull lustre, woven single, or backed with weft in 15-thread sateen order.

Pekin Term applied to striped silk fabrics in which contrasting stripes of satin, plain, rib, gauze, velvet, etc., are combined (see also Bradford lustres).

Petersham A narrow belting type of fabric, used for the tops of skirts, woven as a narrow ware (q.v.), or with a number are made side by side on the split selvedge principle (see Splits). The cloth is woven plain with thick weft and finely set warp, a warp rib structure being produced.

Piece dyed cloth Woven with the yarn in the grey condition, scoured, and then dyed, this being the most convenient and economical method of applying colour to a fabric.

Pile fabrics Cloths in which a proportion of either the weft or the warp threads is made to project from the foundation in such a manner as to form a pile or nap on the surface (see *Watson's Advanced Textile Design*).

Pilot cloth A heavily milled woollen cloth made with a nap or curl surface; dyed blue, and used for overcoats and jackets. For 2-and-2 twill weave—200 to 140 tex warp, 300 to 230 tex weft, 11 to 13 ends, and 9 to 10 picks per cm in the loom. Contraction up to 35 per cent in width and 20 to 25 per cent in length.

Pina cloth Plain woven with threads composed of pine-apple fibres which are very stiff, wiry, and lustrous, similar to polished cotton or horse hair.

Piqué Same structure as welts and may be considered as a fancy welt (q.v.).

Plain cloth Most extensively used of any fabric, and includes structures in which there is the greatest variety as regards the relative counts of warp and weft, and ends and picks per unit space. In many cloths, such as muslins, lawns, cambrics, and voiles the warp and weft are similar, and there are about the same number of ends and picks per cm, whereas in poplins, bengalines, cords, etc., there is great diversity in the warp and weft yarns and ends and picks per cm (see Rib cloths and poplin).

Plush Term applied to distinguish a pile fabric with a long pile formed in silk, worsted, or mohair. Seal plush is made with a silk pile to imitate sealskin, the pile being laid in one direction.

Plush velveteen A cotton velveteen with a long pile (see *Watson's Advanced Textile*

Design).

Poncho cloth   A stout twill, plain, or warp rib fabric frequently woven with cotton weft and worsted warp in different shades of grey and coffee brown forming bold stripes. Made about 140 cm square with an elaborate worsted fringe at each end, and worn as a cape with a slit in the centre through which the head is passed. Used in parts of South America—44/2 tex worsted warp, 39 tex cotton weft, 28 ends, and 14 picks per cm.

Pongee   A plain woven light silk fabric, usually made of wild silk in the gum condition, and is degummed in the piece. An imitation of the cloth is made in fine mercerised cotton yarns, or the fabric may be mercerised and dyed in the piece—8 to 6 tex warp and weft, 38 to 43 ends and picks per cm.

Poplin   A plain woven warp rib fabric with fine warp and thick weft (see Rib cloths). Originally made with silk in both warp and weft, but poplin is now applied to fine warp rib cloths whether made of silk, wool, cotton, or a combination of the yarns. Irish poplin is made with organzine silk warp and hard twisted and genapped worsted weft. Cotton poplin is now mostly mercerised, and this class of fabric is frequently given a moiré finish. Plain cotton poplin—14/2 tex combed and gassed Egyptian warp, 60 tex weft, 60 ends, and 14 picks per cm. Irish poplin—5 tex (2-thread) organzine warp, 68/3 tex genapped worsted weft, 80 ends and 14 to 22 picks per cm (see also Corkscrew repp).

Printers   Well made, plain, cotton cloths, with pure sized warp, largely used for printing.

Pyjama cloths   Made in silk, wool, union, and cotton yarns, and are similar in structure to many classes of shirtings (q.v.), but often woven in broader stripes and bolder colourings.

Quilts   Heavy fabrics, usually figured, mostly made of cotton yarns, and employed for counterpanes and bed and dressing table covers. The chief varieties go under the following names: honeycomb, grecian, alhambra, broché, tapestry, repp, toileting and marseilles, and patent satin.

Honeycomb quilts   Made in thick, soft-twisted, two- or three-fold warp and weft yarns. Large and bold designs are formed composed of warp and weft figure effects combined with various diamond-shaped and other forms of sections in which different sizes of ordinary and Brighton honeycombs and grecian weaves (Nos. 47 to 49, *Figure A1.5*) are used to give variety of pattern—74/2 tex cotton warp, 96/3 tex cotton weft, 18 to 22 ends, and 14 to 19 picks per cm.

Grecian quilts   Similar in structure to honeycomb quilts, but a larger proportion of the surface is formed in ordinary weaves, such as twills and sateens, so that the cloth has a smoother surface. Both honeycomb and grecian quilts consist of one warp and one weft, and are woven in ordinary jacquards. Mostly they are bleached white, but sometimes a delicate colour is used in either warp or weft. A grecian quilt in mercerised yarns—66/2 tex white warp, 66/2 tex pale yellow weft, 19 ends, and 20 picks per cm.

Alhambra quilts   The figure is formed in coloured, extra warp threads on a plain woven texture formed by a fine ground warp and a thick, soft spun, bleached weft (see *Watson's Advanced Textile Design*).

Broché and *tapestry quilts*   Elaborately coloured fabrics woven end and end in two colours with thick, soft spun, dyed weft. In the broché quilt only one weft is used, and the figuring is done mostly by the warps, although subsidiary effects may be produced in a third colour by the weft. The tapestry quilt is woven with two or three colours of weft which are different from the warp shades and all the colours are used in forming the design.

Repp quilts   A coloured cloth arranged end and end in the warp, either in two colours or a colour and white. Both warps are employed for figuring, and the same figure is formed on opposite sides of the cloth, a dark figure on one side corresponding to a light figure on the other side and vice versa, the fabric being reversible. The ground weave is plain, and, as very thick weft is used, a pronounced warp rib, or repp, ground effect is formed. 30 tex warp, woven 3-ply colour and 2-ply white, 400 tex weft, 8 ply ends each of white and colour, and 7 picks per cm; contraction of warp about 25 per cent, but very little contraction in width.

Toilet and *marseilles quilts* Compound textures, bleached in the piece, which consist of a fine, slack, plain face fabric, and tight back stitching ends, and the design is produced by the latter interweaving with the former so as to form a flat or sunk ground effect, while the unbound portion forms a raised or embossed figure (see *Watson's Advanced Textile Design*).

Patent satin quilts This type has very largely superseded the toilet quilt, and may be said to consist of two cloths—one fine and smooth and the other much coarser—which interchange with each other in forming the design (see *Watson's Advanced Textile Design*).

Ratiné A plain woven cloth with a rough surface, due to the use of thick spiral threads. Made in worsted, cotton, and union yarns, in solid and mixture colours, and in stripes and checks—about 125 tex spiral yarn in warp and weft, 7 to 8 ends and picks per cm. Also, 74/2 to 30/2 tex ordinary soft spun cotton warp, 170 to 130 tex cotton spiral weft, 10 to 16 ends, and 7 to 10 picks per cm.

Regatta A 2-and-1 warp-face twill cotton cloth, usually in stripe form, the colour being fast to washing. For use as working clothes or protective garments—27 tex cotton warp, 33 tex cotton weft, 32 ends, and 24 picks per cm.

Repp A warp rib structure in which the rib lines are prominently developed by using thick and fine threads alternately in warp and weft, and passing the thick ends over the thick picks, while the fine ends are held very tight (see Rib cloths, and diagram B in *Figure* 2.2). Repp structures are also made in such weaves as L to O in *Figure 3.1* in which two or more ends pass together over two or more picks, many more ends than picks per cm being employed (see Corkscrew repp).

Reversible cloths Similar in weave, colouring, and finish on both sides, so that either can be used as the right side. Particularly serviceable for hanging fabrics, tapestries, shawls, rugs, etc.

Reversible imperial See Swansdown.

Rib cloths Composed of bending threads in one direction and comparatively straight threads in the other direction with many more of the former threads per unit space than of the latter. The threads do not support each other the same as in ordinary cloths, and when a fabric is subjected to strain in the direction of the straight threads the bending threads tend to slide somewhat readily along the former if the cloth is not very well constructed. Broad rib effects are produced by employing warp and weft rib weaves, but the majority of rib clothes are woven in plain weave (see Poplin, also *Figure 2.2*).

Rug blankets Mostly made with cotton warp and woollen weft on the reversible weft face principle, either in solid colours or in figured styles. The cloths are woven in both coarse and fine wools and a special class of texture is made with lustre weft, and whereas the fine wool structures are mostly finished with a velvet pile surface on both sides (see Velvet pile finish), the fibres of the lustre weft are drawn on to the surface so as to form a long pile which is laid in one direction (see *Watson's Advanced Textile Design*).

Rugs All-wool travelling rugs are woven single and double in structure, and are finished with a fibrous surface on both sides. The single fabrics are largely made in twill weaves and bold check styles of colouring, while the double cloths frequently have different colour effects on opposite sides (see *Watson's Advanced Textile Design*). Woollen yarns are used composed of wools ranging from coarse cheviot and crossbred to fine crossbred and merino.

Russian cords Formed on the gauze principle, coloured crossing ends being traversed across the standard ends so as to form solid cord lines which are in strong colour contrast with the ground (see *Watson's Advanced Textile Design*).

Sarong A plain woven cotton cloth, used for women's wear in the East, and made with a rather simple coloured check pattern forming the bulk of the fabric, and a somewhat elaborate heading or 'capella', which commences about 30 cm from each end, and ranges from about 35 cm to 53 cm in depth. The pattern of the capella follows a certain definite form, and consists of two broad bars of colour with a narrow bar between followed by five narrow bars. This is repeated five times, then a division is made and usually the pattern is again repeated five times. For a woman's garment the cloth is made wide with a plain coloured border at each side, but for a girl it is made narrower with a border only at one side—20 to 16 tex warp, 19 to 15 tex weft, 22 to 24 ends, and 19 to 22 picks per cm.

Sari   Used for dresses by women of India, and woven in different widths and lengths varying from 5 to 8 m. Made with borders and broad headings at both ends, and they may be elaborately figured and coloured in the headings, borders, and centre by means of extra threads, or by large printed effects.

Sateen   A cotton fabric made in 5-thread weft face sateen, and woven like cotton Italians (see Italian cloth). Manufactured in many different qualities, and sold in the bleached, dyed, mercerised, schreinered, or printed condition. Good even yarns are required. When the direction of the sateen twill is the same as that of the twist of the weft the weave has an irregular appearance, and the term broken sateen is applied to the cloth.

Satin   Used for ribbons, trimmings, dresses, linings, etc., and originally was an all-silk fabric with a fine rich glossy surface formed in a warp satin weave (see Duchesse). The warp is much finer and more closely set than the weft, and the latter, which only shows on the under side, is frequently composed of cotton. Double faced satins are made on the reversible warp backed principle, with one side differently coloured from the other (see *Watson's Advanced Textile Design*). The term satin is also applied to fine cotton warp satins used for shirtings and linings (see Cotton venetians).

Saxony cloths   Woollen textures made from Saxony or merino quality of wool (as distinct from Cheviot cloths, which are made from coarser wool) with a fine smooth surface, soft handle, and compact structure. The fabrics are used for costumes, trouserings, suitings, and overcoatings, and are made single, backed, and double according to the weight and fineness of appearance required, and are finished clear or with varying degrees of fibre on the surface. For medium and light weight suitings in 2-and-2 twill—135 to 62 tex warp and weft, 13 to 19 ends and picks per cm in the loom.

Schreinered cloth   Cotton cloth with a very high lustre produced by subjecting it to heavy pressure by a hot steel roller which is engraved with fine parallel lines varying from 80 to 160 per cm according to the cloth to be treated and effect desired. The finish is chiefly applied to cotton venetians, linings, sateens, and printed cloths, and produces the best results on fabrics which have been mercerised. The engraved lines run diagonally across the cloth in the same direction as the twist of the surface yarn, but the angle of inclination varies according to whether the fabric has a warp or a weft surface.

Scourers or **floor cloths**   Thick, coarse fabrics used for scouring floors, woven 2-and-2 twill, and made of yarns which consist of waste wool and cotton spun on the woollen system—320 to 220 tex warp and weft, 7 to 9 ends and picks per cm.

Scrim   A very loosely woven cotton muslin type of cloth; may be as low in quality as cheese cloth (q.v.), or finer according to its use. The finer fabrics are employed for drapery and cheap window curtains, while the lower qualities are stiffened and pasted to another cloth for use as hat shapes (see Buckram).

Seamless bags   Coarse cloth woven in thick cotton or jute yarns on the double cloth principle without stitches, so that the textures are only joined at the sides, and form a tubular structure. Also produced on circular looms.

Selvedges   A good selvedge helps to finish off a fabric and gives it a neat appearance which frequently makes it sell better. The ends used for the selvedges require to be strong (see Selvedge yarns), and they generally differ in material, colour, thickness, or number per unit space from those in the body of the cloth. Very light fabrics, such as voiles and crêpes, particularly require good selvages, which are made dense and compact by cramming the ends from 0.5 cm to 2 cm wide at each side. Two-fold yarns are largely used, and mostly a few double ends (tapes) are made at the outer edges. The use of too many double ends may be the cause of slack selvedges, as these ends tend to lie straight in the cloth, and not to contract as much as the ground ends.

Serge   Twill cloth, generally understood to be of a crisp texture and somewhat rough appearance, and made of cross-bred worsted or woollen yarn.

Shadow effects   Patterns of a somewhat indistinct or elusive character produced in cloths that are in the same shade or colour throughout. The effects generally run in stripe form, although similar styles can be obtained in the direction of the weft. Most frequently produced by arranging alternate sections of *z* and *s* twist yarns in the warp, which causes light from the same position to be reflected in opposite directions. In looking at a piece-dyed cloth from one side the sections composed of *z* twist yarns appear to be much darker than the other sections, but when the cloth is looked at from the opposite side, the *s* twist sections appear to be the darker. The difference of effect is clearly seen in a plain weave fabric, but it is still more apparent in a cloth in which a continuous warp face twill or satin is employed, as in the latter case there is, in addition, the formation of a more prominent twill effect in the sections in which the direction of the twill is opposite to the direction of the warp twist (see *Figure 2.12*). When both kinds of twist are used together the reverse twist yarn is tinted with a fugitive dye in order that it may be distinguished during the processes of manufacture.

In lustre weft cloths effective shadow stripes are formed by denting the ends irregularly (see Bradford lustre fabrics), and a good check style results from using ordinary and reverse twist weft along with an irregularly dented warp. Similar subtle styles can be obtained by arranging alternate sections of threads which differ in the amount of twist, in brightness, or in fineness, or by reversing the direction of a regular warp satin weave, or by slightly reducing the length of the warp float on the surface in alternate sections.

Shantung A plain woven, rather rough fabric, made of Tussah silk yarns, in the natural brown colour, and usually containing imperfections, such as lumps, slubs, etc. About 17 tex warp and weft, 30 ends, and 29 picks per cm. Cotton and spun rayon imitations are made with a weft that is spun with rather thick soft places at irregular intervals.

Sheeting Woven in linen and cotton yarns, the latter being generally known as Bolton sheeting. Made in comparatively thick yarns, in 2-and-2 twill or plain weave, from 140 to 300 cm wide, and sold grey or bleached—2-and-2 twill cotton sheeting—49 to 42 tex warp, 60 to 49 tex weft, 18 to 20 ends, and 25 to 28 picks per cm. Plain sheeting—33 tex warp, 38 tex weft, 18 ends and 18 to 24 picks per cm. Coarser cotton sheetings are woven with thick condenser weft (see Condenser cotton yarns), while flannelette sheetings are usually made of this weft in plain weave. Fine sheetings are also woven with cotton polyester blended yarns.

Shirtings Wide variety of materials and constructions are used in the production of these cloths. The main classes are listed in the following paragraphs, but in addition to woven constructions considerable quantities of warp-knit structures are used, made chiefly in polyamide fibres. •

Plain white shirtings Better qualities of plain cotton shirtings, woven with pure sized warps, and bleached, are 27 tex warp, 38 tex weft, 22 ends, and from 26 to 28 picks per cm. Plain cotton shirtings are also mercerised in the piece or woven with mercerised yarns.

Fancy white shirtings These include cloths woven in ordinary mat weaves; mock lenos; broken warp ribs—termed Barathea—(example No. 4, *Figure A1.2*); honeycombs; Bedford cords (No. 52, *Figure A1.5*); welts and piqués (Nos. 53 to 57, *Figure A1.5*); crêpes (Nos. 26 to 34, *Figure A1.4*); sponge weaves (Nos. 35 to 38, *Figure A1.4*); and cord weaves (Nos. 2 and 3, *Figure A1.2*). The looser weaves allow fairly heavy and full handling cloths to be made, and if soft spun yarns—particularly in the weft—are used, excellent results are obtained. In 3-and-3 mat weave—24 to 18 tex cotton warp, 50 to 38 tex cotton weft, 24 to 26 ends, and 22 to 32 picks per cm. Fancy mat weave—38 tex cotton warp, 46 tex cotton weft, 25 ends, and 26 picks per cm. A light cloth in 4-and-4 mock leno weave—15 tex cotton warp and weft, 38 ends, and picks per cm. A heavy cloth in 5-and-5 mock leno weave—30 tex cotton warp, 50 tex cotton weft, 24 ends, and 22 picks per cm. Barathea or broken warp rib weave—16 tex cotton warp, 38 tex cotton weft, 48 ends, and 22 picks per cm; crêpe weave—24/2 tex mercerised cotton warp, 22 tex merino weft, 26 ends, and 25 picks per cm. Cord weave—21 tex cotton warp, 30 tex cotton weft, 32 ends, and 24 picks per cm. Diverse combinations of the preceding weaves are made, and they are also used in conjunction with stripes of warp satin, warp twill, and other effects. Such terms as the following are applied to white striped shirtings: striped Barathea, twill striped repp, striped Madras, corded cambric, corded batiste, mercerised stripe crêpe, satin striped cambric, corded lawn, embroidered lawn, mercerised stripe brocade, mercerised stripe piqué, striped ratiné, mercerised Oxford, striped cord weave, etc.

Cellular shirting An open gauze structure, largely made of cotton yarns, and, to some extent, of worsted and linen. Simple and fancy gauze effects are used alone or in combination with other weaves (see *Watson's Advanced Textile Design*).

Coloured shirtings The preceding styles, in addition to being made all white, are also ornamented by coloured threads in the form of stripe, check, and spot effects, but white or very light coloured grounds form the bulk of the surface.

The following shirtings are usually more heavily coloured, and the coloured threads require to be dyed fast to the cloth finishing processes, and to washing.

Poplin shirtings Plain weave warp-rib cloths, frequently piece-mercerised. Combed and gassed E. cotton—10/2 tex warp, 12/2 tex weft, 54 ends, 28 picks.

Zephyr shirtings Termed Madras in the United States (see Zephyr fabrics).

Oxford shirtings Double-end cotton cloths made all white in ordinary and mercerised yarns, but generally colours are introduced in the warp, and frequently fancy weave stripes are formed to give variety (see *Figures 7.8* and *7.9*). The term Oxford is now applied to other cloths than shirtings which are woven with two ends per mail.

Harvard shirtings Hard wearing cotton fabrics, with 2-and-2 twill ground on which more or less elaborate stripe effects are formed (see *Figure 7.10*)—38 to 33 tex warp and weft (both twisted warp way), 28 ends, and 26 to 29 picks per cm.

Grandrelle shirtings Largely used for workmen's shirts, and made in 5-thread warp satin weave with the bulk of the warp composed of coloured cotton twist threads (grandrelle) and white cotton weft. Single twist solid coloured and white threads are used in conjunction with the grandrelle twist threads, and in some cases the latter are replaced by mock grandrelle threads (see Marl yarns)—30/2 tex grandrelle and 30 tex single warp, 60 to 49 tex weft, 36 ends, and 26 picks per cm.

Union shirtings (see Union yarns) Usually woven plain, sometimes 2-and-2 twill, and are composed of both wool and cotton fibres, which may be introduced by employing wool yarns in one direction and cotton yarns in the other direction, or by using angola, llama, or merino yarns (q.v.) in the weft, warp, or both weft and warp. The presence of cotton in fibre mixture with wool reduces the tendency of the fabrics to shrink in washing. The same kind of finish is applied as to all-wool shirtings which are felted and raised, and the fibrous face that is formed so subdues the colours that very bold colourings can be introduced; and for the same reason fancy weaves are not suitable. For white or cream cloths the warp should be bleached in order to produce the best results, and in coloured fabrics the colours should be fast dyed to stand the felting process. The amount of wool in the cloths varies from as low as 5 per cent to 80 or 90 per cent.

Angola and *llama shirtings* Composed of woollen spun union yarns in both warp and weft, and are similar fabrics except that the llama structures are generally (but not necessarily) the finer (see angola and llama yarns)—64 tex warp, 50 tex weft, containing from 50 to 85 per cent wool, 15 ends, and 17 picks per cm.

Taffeta shirtings Very fine, plain woven, botany worsted cloths, in white, cream, or stripe colouring, and sometimes ornamented with crammed silk stripes in satin and other weaves. The cloth is also made with silk yarn in one direction and botany yarn in the other direction.

Woollen shirting Usually a moderately heavy cloth of good quality and mostly woven plain with woollen yarn in both warp and weft. A felted and raised finish is applied, and the fibrous surface that is formed enables only the simplest form of ornamentation to be introduced.

Polyester fibre/cotton shirting Fine shirtings in similar constructions to poplin are made in blended yarns containing 65 or 70% polyester fibre which imparts crease-resist properties to the cloth and improves its drying characteristics.

Shot effect A fabric woven in contrasting colours of warp and weft which are about equally on the surface, so that the cloth appears to be one colour from one point of view and the other colour from another point of view (see also Chameleon taffeta).

Showerproof cloth   Partially repellent to water by chemical treatment, or by suitable selection of materials and construction.

Sicilian   See Bradford lustre fabrics.

Silesia   A twill or satin cotton lining, heavily starched, and dyed and finished with a glossy surface, but sometimes printed in stripe form. A 2-and-2 twill cloth—27 tex warp, 18 tex weft, 24 ends, and 48 picks per cm.

Small wares   Narrow fabrics, such as tapes, braids, elastic webbing, etc., woven singly in narrow looms, or two or more side by side in broad looms, with a separate shuttle to each fabric.

Splits   Narrow cloths woven two or more alongside each other in broad looms, with the weft stretching between them, which are cut or split apart. By means of a special motion perfectly firm inner selvedges can be made, but generally the split selvedge ends are retained in position by a simple arrangement by which the outer ends are interlaced on the gauze principle. In felted cloths which require to be split, such as narrow wool shirtings woven in broad looms, the milling makes the inner selvedges sufficiently firm without other aid.

Sponge cloth   The sponge weave, given at C in *Figure 5.4*, when woven with soft yarns, produces a soft, spongy, honeycomb texture which is used for a variety of household and other purposes. In another kind of sponge cloth, employed for dress fabrics, and mostly woven plain, thick irregular nubby weft is used that is composed usually of cotton, but sometimes of wool or rayon. A sponge dress fabric, also, is made with soft irregular spiral yarns in warp and weft, and is rather similar to ratiné, but softer—about 140 tex cotton warp and weft, 7 ends, and picks per cm. A third class of sponge cloth is used for cleaning machinery, etc. (see Cleaning cloths).

Swansdown or **imperial**   Term applied to a group of heavily wefted cotton fabrics (see Fustian) that includes imperial sateen, reversible imperial, and lambskin, which are finished with a raised or fibrous surface on one or both sides. Ordinary swansdown is woven with the 2-and-3 weft venetian weave (see No. 13, *Figure A1.3*) which, because of the large number of picks, gives a weft surface on both sides, so that either side can be used for the formation of a dense nap (see Flannelette)—33 tex warp, 40 tex weft, 19 ends, and 62 picks per cm.

Imperial sateen is a heavier fabric than the ordinary swansdown, and is woven in the weave given at No. 14, *Figure A1.3*, which is based on the 8-thread sateen, and gives a weft float of six on the surface. In this case also the heavy wefting enables a soft nap to be formed on the under side.

Lambskin is the term applied to 'imperial sateen' when the cloth is raised on the face side, the compact weft surface enabling a very soft nap to be formed.

Reversible imperial is woven in the 4-and-4 weave, based on the 8-thread sateen, given at No. 15, *Figure A1.3*, which, with very heavy wefting, produces a dense weft surface on both sides of the cloth. For imperial and lambskin cloths—66/2 to 49/2 tex warp, 38 to 21 tex weft, 19 to 25 ends, and 120 to 170 picks per cm.

Swiss mull   Fine cotton muslin—8 to 6 tex warp and weft, 40 to 48 ends and picks per cm.

Swivel fabrics   Extra weft figured textures, in which the ornamentation is produced by means of a series of small swivel shuttles, each of which is capable of separately forming a figure, or part of a figure, over a certain width of the cloth. Each swivel thread is traversed from side to side and bound into the foundation cloth only where figure is formed, so that there is no waste of the extra material between the figures (see *Watson's Advanced Textile Design*).

Table felting   A thick reversible cotton fabric usually with a raised finish, made in coarse yarns, and used under an ordinary table cloth as padding.

Taffeta   Originally a plain, closely woven, silk fabric used for dress fabrics and linings, and frequently the cloth is made with thicker weft than warp, and is set so as to produce a fine warp rib structure. The term taffeta is also used in conjunction with certain effects, thus taffeta glacé indicates a 'shot' silk taffeta.

Tartan   Scotch tartans are 2-and-2 twill woollen or worsted cloths woven in more or less elaborately coloured check designs, and worn as shawls or plaids over the shoulder, and as kilts. Each Highland clan has its own particular design, and many of the clans have more than one tartan—e.g., hunting, mourning, or dress tartan. A design may be varied as regards the size of the repeat, but the different sections of the pattern require to be exactly in proportion. The cloth is made with an exact number of repeats of the colour scheme across the width of 67/70 cm, and the same tartan design may have, say, 4, 6, or 8 repeats, the smaller sizes being used for boys' or youths' wear, and the largest for men's wear—90 tex woollen warp and weft, and 16 ends and picks per cm; or 27/2 tex botany worsted, 28 ends and picks per cm. Many modifications of tartan designs have been made in cotton, rayon, etc., yarns, and crêpe and other fancy weaves have been introduced.

Terry or **turkish towelling**   A looped warp pile fabric, made in linen and cotton yarns, and used for towels, bath mats, bed covers, dressing gowns, etc. (see *Watson's Advanced Textile Design*).

Thread harness muslin   A fine, extra-weft, figured muslin fabric, woven in an ordinary jacquard which controls every warp thread. The loose floats of weft, extending between the figures, are cut away so as to leave a light, open ground (see *Watson's Advanced Textile Design*).

Ticking   A strong, somewhat stiff fabric used for mattresses and pillowcases, and made in 2-, 3-, and 4-thread twill, and 5- and 8-thread satin weaves in bold warp stripe colourings. The cloths may be all linen, or all cotton, or a combination of the two, and sometimes the coloured stripes are cotton, and the remainder of the cloth linen. 2-and-1 twill linen cloth—56 tex warp, 75 tex tow weft, 28 ends, and 19 picks per cm. 5-thread satin cotton fabric—60 tex warp, 50 tex weft, 30 ends, and 22 picks per cm.

Toiletings   (See Quilts.)

Towel fabrics   See Honeycomb, huckaback, terry, and crash.

Tow fabrics   Heavy and coarse cloths composed of flax tow yarns, which, in the weft, may be soft spun so as to produce a full handling and absorbent texture (see Crash towelling).

Tricotine   A piece dyed worsted serge costume cloth woven in a warp face weave forming fine steep twill lines (see Nos. 21 and 22, *Figure A1.3*)—34/2 tex botany warp, 28 tex worsted weft, 20 ends, and from 20 to 24 picks per cm. The term is also applied to a worsted weft and cotton warp cloth with a weft face in which fine flat twill lines are formed, and to a silk warp and cotton weft cloth, woven plain, and showing fine horizontal rib lines.

Turn back checks   A type of cloth that consists mainly of a small 2-colour check pattern, but with a border at each side in which only one of the wefts is interwoven with the warp. That is, one of the wefts 'turns back' without interweaving with a certain width of warp at each side, these ends being drawn on separate healds which are not operated when the particular weft is inserted. Thus, a fabric may be warped and wefted 2 blue and 2 white, but the blue weft 'turns back' from about 10 to 15 cm from each edge of the piece, so that the border consists of a narrow stripe effect, and the centre of a small check pattern. The border necessarily contains only half as many picks as the centre.

Tussore   Originally a light brown, fawn, or natural coloured plain woven silk fabric; also made in cotton yarns and mercerised and dyed to imitate the colour of the silk cloth. The structure is that of a plain woven warp rib (q.v.), and in some cases a few darker threads are introduced at a place so as to form stripes—30 tex cotton warp, 50 tex cotton weft, 36 ends, and 14 picks per cm.

Tweed   Term applied to a wide range of woollen cloths used for suitings, and over-coatings, which include on the one hand all kinds of cheviot fabrics and, on the other hand, fine Saxony textures, which are finished with either a dress face or a clear finish.

Utrecht velvet   A silk, or mohair, warp pile fabric which is used for upholstery purposes (see *Watson's Advanced Textile Design*).

Velours   Woollen costume cloth which has been felted and raised, and finished with a fibrous surface.

Velvet   A cut warp pile fabric with a short, soft, dense pile (see *Watson's Advanced Textile Design*).

Velveteen   A stout, heavily wefted cotton fabric, uniformly covered with a short dense pile of fibres, which is formed after the cloth has been woven by cutting certain picks of weft that float somewhat loosely on the surface (see *Watson's Advanced Textile Design*).

Velvet pile finish   The fibres form an erect pile on the surface of a woollen cloth instead of being laid in one direction, as in the dress-face finish. The texture is heavily milled and raised, and then, while stretched face down between rollers, it is beaten on the back with rods which causes the fibres to project vertically from the foundation. The cropping process follows, but this is done only to equalise the length of the fibres, and the cloth is covered with a dense vertical non-lustrous pile which conceals the weave and structure.

Venetian overcoating   Similar to covert coating (q.v.), but in addition to showing a mixture effect with a clear finish, the cloth is sometimes made in solid colour, piece dyed, and finished with a fibrous surface. The term venetian is also applied to a lustrous warp satin cotton fabric (see Cotton venetian).

Vicuna cloth   Usually a worsted warp and woollen weft cloth made backed or double in structure. A felted and raised finish is applied, but the fibres are cut sufficiently close to the surface to show the weave distinctly. The cloth is largely made double in structure with 2-and-2 twill face and plain back, the threads being arranged 2 face to 1 back in warp and weft. 35/2 tex worsted warp, 54 tex woollen weft, 36 ends, and 32 picks per cm.

Voile   A plain woven, open fabric made from hard twisted warp and weft yarn which is combed and gassed in order that the threads will be smooth, and produce a clear, crisp fabric (see Voile yarn). Made in both worsted and cotton yarns which vary extremely in thickness in different makes. A worsted voile—110/3 tex warp and weft, 9 ends and picks per cm. A cotton voile—24/2 tex warp and weft, 14 ends, and 15 picks per cm; or, 12/2 tex warp and weft, 23 ends, and 22 picks per cm. For cotton fabrics combed and gassed, hard twisted, single yarn of 12 to 10 tex has been substituted to some extent for two-fold yarn. On account of the openness of the fabric good selvedges are required, and these are frequently made 1.25 cm or more in width, an ordinary yarn being used which is crammed in the reed so as to give the necessary density. The voile ends are woven one per split, and the cloths are ornamented by means of crammed stripes, extra warp and weft figures, etc., in mercerised cotton, silk, and rayon yarns.

Voile and *rayon stripes*   The rayon ends require to be crammed in the reed, and 22 to 28 tex filament yarn is suitable to use with 12/2 tex cotton voile yarn, the former at the rate of 44 ends per cm, and the latter 22 ends per cm. Trouble is frequently found in weaving the voile and rayon ends in the same fineness of reed, on account of the former requiring to be one end per split, and reeds are therefore made to fit the warp stripe, the sections for the voile ends containing twice as many wires per unit space as the sections for the rayon ends. Thus, for the preceding example, the rayon stripe sections will have 11 splits per cm, dented 4 ends per split, and the voile sections, 22 splits per cm, dented 1 end per split.

Warp printed cloth   See Chiné or chené.

Watered fabrics   See Moire.

Waterproofed cloth   Made impervious to water by the application of a coating of rubber or other water-resisting substance to the surface of the material, or between two thin textures which are thereby cemented together.

Welts   A class of fabric, similar in structure to piques (q.v.), which is used for vestings, shirts, ties, etc. (see Nos. 53 to 57, *Figure A1.5*)—20 to 10 tex face warp, 30 to 20/2 tex back warp, 15 to 8 tex face weft, 33 to 25 tex wadding weft, 36 to 52 ends, and 38 to 64 face picks per cm, wadding picks extra.

Whip cord cloths   Show prominent steep twill lines, the warp lines forming ridges, and the weft lines furrows. The direction of the twill should be opposite to the direction of the warp twist (see Nos. 18 to 24, *Figure A1.3*).

Wigan   Medium weight cotton cloth woven plain or 2-and-2 twill, used for domestic purposes. Plain Wigan—about 50 tex warp and weft, 16 ends, and 25 picks per cm. 2-and-2 twill Wigan—about 42 tex warp and weft, 18 ends, and 33 picks per cm.

Wincey   Used for underclothing, pyjamas, and blouses. A cream underclothing fabric—23 tex bleached cotton warp, 56 to 49 tex weft containing 40 per cent wool, 25 ends and 20 to 22 picks per cm.

Window Holland   Medium weight cotton (occasionally linen) cloth used for blinds. Produced in plain weave, starch finished and frequently glazed. Piece dyed in fast to light colours.

Wool dyed cloth   Cloth in which the yarns have been spun from wool dyed in the fibre or the sliver or 'top' condition (see Slubbing dyed yarns). Each thread may be composed of fibres of one colour only, or of a mixture of differently dyed fibres (see Mixture yarns).

Woollen cloths   Composed of woollen yarns (q.v.), and the majority of the cloths are largely dependent upon the finishing operations for the density of structure, fine surface appearance, softness and flexibility, and richness of colour of the finished fabric. A cloth which on leaving the loom has a bare, thready appearance may be completely altered, and, further, the kind of finished effect that is obtained may be of a very diverse nature according to the manner in which the processes of felting, raising, and cropping are carried out (see Dress-face, velvet-pile, and clear finish, also felted, cheviot, saxony, nap, and melton cloths).

Worsted cloths (see Worsted yarns)   The brightness of colour, clearness of weave, and density of structure of most worsted cloths, as they leave the loom, are nearly the same as in the finished textures, and the finishing processes are employed to clean the fabric and to improve its appearance and handle. A few classes of worsted fabrics are milled and raised and finished with a more or less fibrous surface, but mostly the cloths are not milled, and a clear surface is formed. For certain kinds of fine worsted suitings, and overcoatings, light felting is employed, as this imparts a softness and fulness which can be obtained in no other way, but the cloths are afterwards finished clear in order to show the weave and colour pattern clearly.

Woven linings   Heavy overcoatings, etc., woven on the centre stitched double cloth principle (see *Watson's Advanced Textile Design*), with solid or simple colour effects on one side and diverse stripe and check patterns on the reverse side which forms the lining. The cloths are made in both worsted and woollen yarns, and the two sides may be alike or different in weave, fineness, material, or finish. In some cases an imitation woven lining effect is obtained by introducing extra warp and weft threads only in places where a prominent overcheck pattern is formed on the under side of a single cloth.

Yarn dyed cloth   Made from warp and weft which have been previously dyed in the yarn form.

Zephyr fabrics   Fine cotton cloths, used for shirts, blouses, and dresses, chiefly plain weave, and made with white or coloured weft and white, solid coloured, or stripe coloured warp, also in check colouring, and ornamented with cord threads, crammed effects, and simple and elaborate figures (see *Figures 7.13* to *7.17*, and *7.11*). The term 'gingham' and 'madras' are applied to Zephyr cloths, a gingham being a zephyr which is used for blouses and dresses, while a madras is a shirting fabric.

Zibeline   A heavy wool costume fabric, somewhat heavily milled and raised, and finished with a long pile of fibres on the surface laid in one direction. The weave is entirely concealed, and generally such special fibres as mohair are included in the yarns which, when drawn out on the surface, produce a characteristic appearance.

List of works for further reference:
1. *Textile Terms and Definitions*, 6th edn, The Textile Institute, 1970.
2. 'The "Mercury" Dictionary of Textile Terms', Textile Mercury Limited, 1950.

Appendix II

Man-made Textile Materials

The desirable features and properties of a textile material. Survey of the manufacture, properties and uses of man-made textile materials. Identification of textile materials. Glossary of the more important yarn terms used in respect of man-made materials.

THE DESIRABLE FEATURES AND PROPERTIES
OF A TEXTILE MATERIAL

Prior to the study of specific examples of the man-made textile materials it will be useful to postulate the desirable properties which such materials should possess, and to find out the effect which various commonly encountered agencies may have upon their performance. Knowledge of these facts enables the designer by a process of comparison and elimination to select the most suitable material for a particular end use.

The properties of special interest to the designer may be listed as follows.

Strength	Lustre
Extensibility and elastic recovery	Warmth
Fineness	Dye affinity

In addition, a designer in order to avoid the use of a material in unsuitable circumstances should be acquainted with the reaction of materials in the presence of certain agents. He should also be able to foresee whether in its intended use the material is liable to come into contact with a given agent, and if so—whether the agent is likely to have an injurious effect. The following is a list of the various agencies to the action of which most textile fibres are subjected during processing or during ordinary usage:

Heat	Alkalis
Seaming during making-up	Bleaches
Water	Dry-cleaning agents
Acids	Insects and micro-organisms

Strength   A textile material must be strong. If an article is to hold together and resist wear it needs a degree of strength. In measuring this quality in fibres or yarns, the basis on which it is quoted must be known otherwise misleading statements or claims may result. There are two ways in which strength may be measured. In one, a fixed weight of the material is taken and tested, in the other, a fixed thickness of the material is used. Where a fixed weight of the material is used, the result would be quoted against the count of the material (e.g. grams per denier) and where the fixed thickness is used, the result

343

quoted against the area of the cross-section (e.g. grams per square centimetre). Two terms are used to differentiate these methods. Tenacity is the breaking force in terms of the yarn number while tensile strength is the breaking force in terms of the unit area. Normally this point is one of little concern to the designer but with the introduction of man-made materials of lower density than the natural fibres it becomes a point of note. To take an example, the case of nylon and cotton may be quoted. If the tenacity of these materials is measured, because of the lower density of nylon and therefore greater thickness of material for a given weight, it may be that nylon would be stronger than cotton. If on the other hand, the tensile strength of the materials is obtained, because the same area of each is tested, the positions may be reversed. The designer must therefore bear in mind the end use of the fabric and if it is one where thickness of material is important then the figures for comparison of materials should be the tensile strength, but if the weight of the fabric is the criterion then tenacity would be of more value.

Extensibility and **elastic recovery**   These two features are of interest both to the manufacturer and to the consumer. From the manufacturer's view point, extensibility is a desirable property as it enables the yarns to be manipulated easily. If the material also has good elastic recovery then any stretch imparted during the processing will be recovered and the fabric performance in no way suffers. The consumer's interest concerns mainly the appearance and the serviceability. These are enhanced by the use of materials with good elastic recovery, as otherwise, such functions as bending, sitting, etc., which cause stretching would result in permanent distortion of the garment. For apparel fabrics the designer will, therefore, select materials which possess these valuable properties, but for certain special cloths which require maximum rigidity, materials which are comparatively inextensible will be employed.

Fineness   It is considered that fine fabrics can only be made from fine yarns, and in turn, fine yarns can normally be made only from fine fibres. Equally well, fine fibres can be employed also in the manufacture of heavy yarns and heavy fabrics. Fineness, therefore, is a desirable property as it does not impose any limitations on the range of applications of a given material.

The position with regard to the fineness of man-made fibres needs, however, some clarification as here it is possible to create continuous filament yarn of fine diameter either by the extrusion of mono-filament in which the fibre and the yarn are one, or, by the multi-filament extrusion process in which the yarn is composed of a number of very fine filaments. The two different yarns may be equally fine, and yet the former has no fine fibre elements in its make-up. Both can be used to produce fine fabrics, but cloths constructed from the mono-filament threads will have poorer 'cover', lower moisture absorption and poorer draping quality. For these reasons it is generally preferable to use the multi-filament yarns for apparel cloths, and the mono-filament materials in certain special circumstances where their regularity, comparative stiffness and the sheer construction are of particular value.

Lustre   With regard to consumer appeal this is a very important feature and its presence or absence frequently determines the field in which a given material can be employed. Lustre is an inherent characteristic of most man-made materials and as such it could have been a factor limiting the range of applications. Fortunately, it is possible to modify the brightness of these materials so that a complete range is available from the harsh, metallic lustre at one end of the scale to completely dull fibres at the other.

Warmth   The warmth of a fabric is dependent mainly on four features—the thermal insulation value of the material, the amount of air entrapped in the fabric, the moisture absorption of the material and the smoothness of the fabric. The thermal insulation value determines whether the material is a good insulator or a good conductor and other things being equal, the material which is a good insulator will give the warmest fabric. The amount of air entrapped is of vital importance as air itself is a good insulator so that a fabric holding a large amount of air will be warmer than one which does not. The moisture absorption while only influencing slightly the heat retaining properties of a fabric does alter the handle of a fabric considerably. Thus a material with a low moisture absorption may feel cold and clammy in humid conditions due to excess moisture condensing on the fabric while a similar fabric made of a material with a high moisture absorbing capacity in similar conditions would feel quite warm. A smooth fabric if worn near the skin will make contact with a large area of the body immediately giving a cold impression but a rougher fabric even of similar material will not make an equally intimate contact and therefore will feel warmer. Allied with this feature is the closeness of the weave itself and a closely woven fabric when used in a strong wind may be warmer than an open fabric made from a superior insulating material. The designer can do little about the thermal insulation value or the moisture absorption capacity except to choose a material giving the required values, other characteristics, however, can be altered readily to meet the exact functional requirements. For example, to entrap a large amount of air, bulked yarn can be used; to prevent close contact with the body a broken, irregular construction may be employed; and finally, if low air permeability is desired it could be achieved by close yarn settings combined with a tight interlacing.

Dye affinity An affinity for a large number of dyestuffs is a valuable asset in any fibre. It enables the designer to produce widely divergent ranges of fabrics suitable for all types of markets and for various end uses. Fortunately, with the advances in dye chemistry there are comparatively few classes of materials where the designer is not completely satisfied with the available colour ranges. In many instances the range of dyestuffs may be further supplemented by the use of pigments in the spinning solution prior to extrusion (see Spun-dyed yarns). Exclusive affinity of a material for a particular type of dyestuff offers an additional interesting possibility of cross-dyeing in the piece.

Combined with the question of dye-affinity is the question of dye fastness and close study of this aspect is essential, as in many instances colours with good fastness to some agencies, e.g. washing, may exhibit inferior fastness to others, e.g. light. Correct selection of the right class of dyestuff for a given end use will ensure satisfactory performance in the circumstances for which the fabric has been designed.

Effect of heat Apart from the question of flammability of materials the reaction to heat may take the form of melting or shrinking. The first point is of particular importance in designing cloths for children's wear, and for use in public institutions (e.g. hospitals, theatres, etc.) where greater than normal fire risks exist. In this respect most man-made materials of the synthetic type are safe, but this is the group which on the whole exhibits low stability to heat on account of the low melting point. This factor largely determines the finishing routine of such cloths and may prove a source of annoyance in the home (ironing, drying). As the synthetic materials require little ironing and dry rapidly the remedy against mishaps appears to lie in the education of the consumer and in informative labelling.

Effect of seaming This particular feature is becoming increasingly important. Prior to the advent of man-made materials, little difficulty was encountered in converting fabrics to garments as most natural materials have a good resistance to seam slippage, that is, they are sufficiently rough to grip each other and also the sewing thread firmly, thus giving a firm seam. The one exception to this was silk, but then as now, the cost of silk was such as would accommodate an extra charge to be spent on using special seams. The man-made materials are, in the main, extremely smooth and the problem is now brought down to the competitive market where additional costs for special seams may not be possible. Knowing this point, the designer can aid the garment manufacturer by altering the setting or structure of the fabric depending on the material so as to eliminate seam slippage as much as possible.

Effect of water This may be considered from two main points of view—the moisture absorption and the effect of wet treatment. In the former case the behaviour of a material depends on its intrinsic properties and it would be obviously unwise to employ hydrophobic materials in circumstances in which high moisture absorption is of advantage. Admittedly, there may be other advantages which will outweigh this consideration on certain occasions and in such cases the ability of a fabric to hold moisture may be enhanced by suitable choice of the yarn and the fabric structure.

The wet treatment may involve the use of cold water, hot water and steam, and the reaction of a fibre to such treatments must be known in order to prevent damage due to misuse of materials. Certain man-made materials become very weak when wet and the use of such materials in circumstances which demand, for instance, frequent and severe laundering should be avoided.

Effect of acids, alkalis, bleaches, and organic solvents   Knowledge of the reaction of a textile material to the above agents is necessary not only to determine the finishing routine and the cleaning methods, but also in selecting specific end uses for a given fibre. Materials which are susceptible to any agent should not be employed where such an agent is liable to be encountered. If damage is likely to occur due to an action of a common domestic cleaning agent the fabric should be clearly labelled to warn the consumer against the use of such a medium. Informative labelling would also be helpful to commercial laundries and dry cleaning establishments who could select detergents and organic solvents compatible with the processed material.

Effect of insects and micro-organisms   In general man-made fibres exhibit good resistance to biological attack and in the majority of cases such faults as, for instance, the growth of mildew may be ascribed to the sizing or finishing agent incorporated in the cloth rather than to the fibre itself. Nevertheless, as such an attack is liable to damage or discolour the fibre it should be guarded against by ensuring correct storage conditions, or by including antiseptic substances which inhibit or prevent completely the undesirable occurrences.

SURVEY OF THE MANUFACTURE, PROPERTIES AND USES OF MAN-MADE TEXTILE MATERIALS

The number of man-made textile materials available for the textile designer is already considerable and increases continually. In a survey of this type it would be impossible to deal with each fibre exhaustively and for this reason this section is devoted to a study of those that are at the moment most important. To simplify the study the whole multifarious field of man-made fibres available may be classified under the following main headings.

1. Regenerated and modified natural polymers—
   (a) rayons, (b) cellulose esters, (c) protein fibres.
2. Synthetic polymers—
   (a) polyamides, (b) polyesters, (c) polyolefines, (d) polyvinyl derivatives, (e) polyurethane elastomers.
3. Mineral based materials—
   (a) glass, (b) metallic yarns.

The above list provides a classification primarily according to the chemical base and this, as will be seen later, predetermines to some extent the mode of manufacture.

Considering the physical form of these materials they exist either in the form of continuous filaments, or as staple (cut) fibres although originally they are all extruded as filaments. Some materials may be available in the market only in one form and not in the other. Yarns made from these materials will normally consist of finer units which may be of either type the one exception being the mono-filament yarn mentioned in the previous chapter.

A continuous filament yarn is made up of a number of units equal in length to the length of the yarn itself but thinner in diameter. The actual number of units comprising a given yarn thickness may vary as the diameters of the constituent filaments can be varied themselves. This in itself will alter materially the yarn characteristics in respect of flexibility, covering power, thermal insulation value, etc., and serves to extend the range of uses and applications of these materials. A yarn of the above type requires very little twist to remain a cohesive unit and is represented at A in *Figure A2.1*.

The material required to be used in the fibre form, after extrusion as a filament, is cut or broken at intervals to provide a given staple length. The length and the thickness of the staple depends on the method of spinning which it is intended to employ subsequently. The fibre yarn (or, the discontinuous filament yarn) consists, therefore, of units which are not only finer in diameter than the yarn itself, but also shorter in length and to exist as a cohesive entity the yarn depends on the twist to hold the constituent units together. Upon untwisting the short units fall apart and the yarn disintegrates.

A   B

Figure A2.1

This type of yarn is represented schematically at B in *Figure A2.1*. Man-made materials in the staple fibre form can be employed on their own, or they can be used in blends with natural fibres or with other man-made fibres. Whichever use is made of them they are produced in the thickness and in the length determined by the spinning system to be employed and Table 15 gives some common sizes used.

Table 15

Spinning method	*Length* (mm)	*Thickness*
Cotton	37	1.7 decitex
Woollen	50	5.0 decitex
Worsted	100	3.4 decitex
Linen	100	4.4 decitex
Jute	200	8.9 decitex

It will be noted that the thickness of the fibres is quoted in the terms of 'decitex'. This provides a generally accepted and useful base for comparison, but it must be understood that the term is not strictly correct as this value does not take into account the density of the material so that two fibres of the same decitex may yet vary in respect of their thickness due to differences in density.

In the more detailed studies of the man-made materials which follow it is intended to give a survey of properties and applications of the selected members of each group. Brief references are also given in the glossary in respect of some less common materials and at the end a bibliography is provided for any designers who may require further information impossible to encompass within an Appendix to a work primarily concerned with woven cloth construction.

1. Regenerated and modified natural polymers

A study of natural fibres has shown that they are composed of long and slender molecules consisting mainly of cellulose (vegetable fibres), or protein (animal fibres). It was also found that similar molecules existed in nature in considerable abundance in non-fibrous form. In this form they were unsuitable for textile purposes because they were either combined with undesirable impurities, or were incorrectly aligned. From this knowledge an idea was conceived that if the impurities could be eliminated, or the molecules re-aligned in the required manner, artificial fibres similar to the natural ones could be produced from the non-fibrous sources. After a long period of experimental work a way was eventually found to achieve the above aims, and a number of different fibres were produced, based mainly on regenerated or modified cellulose or proteins.

(a) **Rayons** These are regenerated cellulose fibres for which the cellulose is derived either from wood pulp or from cotton linters. There are two important members of this group—the viscose rayon and the cuprammonium rayon—and although the former occupies a predominant position in respect of the quantity produced, the latter is of considerable interest to a designer in certain specialised fields. Viscose rayon is described more fully in the following paragraphs whilst cuprammonium rayon is dealt with briefly in the glossary.

Manufacture of viscose rayon The manufacture of viscose rayon may be said to date from 1892 when Cross and Bevan discovered that cellulose, when treated with alkali, reacted with carbon bisulphide to form a water soluble substance—cellulose xanthate. After many trials and errors the process as we know it today was developed. Essentially this consists of the following steps.

(1) Purifying wood pulp from spruce trees and pressing it into the form of large sheets resembling blotting paper.

(2) The sheets are soaked in caustic soda and the excess solution squeezed out. By means of 'grinding' knives, the sheets are broken down into crumbs and ripened by storing in controlled conditions. In this form the cellulose is known as alkali cellulose.

(3) Alkali cellulose is treated with carbon bisulphide to yield cellulose xanthate which still has the crumb-like appearance but is now yellow in colour.

(4) Cellulose xanthate is dissolved in a weak solution of caustic soda giving a golden brown syrupy liquid of a certain viscosity (hence the name viscose rayon).

(5) The viscose solution is filtered and stored under vacuum to remove air bubbles. When the solution has matured and is at the correct viscosity, it is ready for spinning.

(6) Spinning consists of extruding the viscose solution from the storage tank through a 'spinneret'. The spinneret is immersed in acid and as the viscose solution enters this acid bath it is coagulated into numbers of fine filaments, the number of filaments depending on the number of holes in the spinneret. The filaments are collected, washed, dried, twisted, and finally wound on to bobbins in one continuous process.

If the cut staple (fibre) form of the yarn is required, a much larger spinneret with many more holes is used, the holes being of a size suitable for the form of staple being made, e.g. for cotton spinning system 1.7 d tex, for worsted 3.4 d tex. The rope of filaments emerging from the spinneret is cut into short lengths governed by the machinery on which it will ultimately be processed—cotton 37 mm, worsted 100 mm, etc.

Modifications The viscose rayon yarn made as suggested above is capable of various modifications. A few of these are:

(a) *Delustring* The normal viscose rayon yarn has a metallic lustre and in this form is known as 'bright'. This is, however, not suitable for all purposes as sometimes a more subdued lustre is wanted. To effect this a delustring agent is added to the viscose solution prior to extrusion which after spinning is retained in the yarn as an integral part of it. This agent (titanium dioxide) has the effect of breaking up light reflection giving the rayon a soft milky lustre. This can of course be varied by altering the amount of agent in the solution. The titanium dioxide particles can be seen in a microscopical view of the filaments.

(b) *Spin dyeing* In a like manner to delustring, it is also possible to incorporate coloured pigments in the spinning solution so that the resultant filaments are coloured. The particles of pigment embedded in the yarn also exert a delustring effect so that yarns from this type of rayon tend to be softer in lustre than conventionally dyed yarns. The fastness of the colour is usually high, but the range of shades is rather limited.

(c) *Basifying* or *animalising* Viscose rayon has an affinity for certain dyestuffs, normally those which dye cotton so that when mixed with wool to form a wool/viscose blend, solid shades cause some difficulty. To aid this, it is possible to modify viscose so that it has the same affinity for dyes as wool, when it is known as basified or animalised.

(d) *Stretch spinning* In order to increase the strength of viscose rayon a stretching process is incorporated in the interval between extrusion and coagulation. This, by aligning the molecules in the filaments in a more regular order increases their strength both wet and dry. Accompanying this there is a loss of extensibility and decreased moisture absorption but for certain purposes (tyre cord fabrics) this is an advantage.

Table 16

Properties   Unless otherwise stated these figures refer to the normal type.

Tenacity: Normal	Dry 0.14 to 0.18 N/tex.
	Wet 0.06 to 0.09 N/tex.
Stretch spun	Dry 0.27 to 0.32 N/tex.
	Wet 0.17 to 0.20 N/tex.
Elongation at break:	Dry 15 to 30 per cent at 65 per cent R.H.
Normal	Wet 20 to 35 per cent.
Stretch spun	Dry 9 to 17 per cent at 65 per cent R.H.
	Wet 14 to 20 per cent.
Elastic recovery:	74 per cent at 4 per cent stretch.
	58 per cent at 14 per cent stretch.
Specific gravity:	1.52.
Regain:	11 per cent at 20°C and 65 per cent R.H.
Burning rate:	Fast.
Resistance to heat:	Decomposes rapidly at temperatures above 150°C and at lower temperatures on prolonged exposure.
Softening point:	Decomposes without melting.
Effect of age:	Slight.
Effect of sunlight:	Loses strength on prolonged exposure.
Effect of acids:	Weak solutions have little effect. Hot dilute solutions and cold concentrated solutions of strong acids will attack and disintegrate rapidly.
Effect of alkalis:	Dilute solutions have little effect but concentrated solutions of strong alkalis will cause swelling and loss of strength.
Effect of other chemicals:	Strong oxidising agents will attack but under normal conditions, hypochlorite or peroxide bleaches have little effect. In water, viscose rayon swells.
Organic solvents:	Insoluble. Soluble in cuprammonium solution and certain other selected compounds.
Dye affinity:	Generally same types as cotton, e.g. direct, vat, azoic.
Moths:	Unattacked.
Mildew:	Attacked if damp and alkaline.

Uses   Although chemically similar to cotton, the designer is well advised not to substitute viscose rayon for cotton in fabrics without first considering all the implications. On its own properties viscose is worthy of design styles and types of its own. Its fineness in filament form makes it particularly suitable for such sheer fabrics as voiles and georgettes, and as it swells to a greater degree than cotton when wet, it is of more use in crêpe fabrics. In its fibre form it cannot be spun to so fine a yarn as cotton therefore is normally found in the heavier fabrics. Losing strength when wet and being more extensible in that state suggests that care is required in washing and also that the designer should consider the amount of washing a fabric will have to withstand before suggesting viscose rayon. The fact that its lustre can be varied makes it an ideal material for a wide range of fabrics ranging from metallic lustred linings to soft sheened sharkskin and poults. Where high dry strength is important, viscose is of greater use than cotton, for example, in such things as tyre fabrics where working conditions are hot, therefore the yarns used will be dry. Untreated viscose rayon is readily creased and therefore a crease resist finish is usually given to fabrics where creasing is a possibility. This finish as well as aiding crease recovery improves dye fastness, reduces total water absorbency, combats mildew and also gives a stabilised form to the fabric.

(b) **Cellulose esters**   The group of fibres classified under this heading consists of secondary cellulose acetate and cellulose triacetate. Cotton linters are the normal raw material of both these fibres but the cellulose which still forms the basis of the fibres is modified through the replacement of hydroxyl groups in the molecule by the acetyl groups. This converts the cellulose into a cellulose acetate. The two types of acetate fibres are chemically very closely related the triacetate being a more completely acety-lated form of cellulose than the secondary acetate. Despite the close chemical similarity the physical properties of these fibres show a degree of divergence in several important aspects. Although the secondary acetate was produced commercially long before the triacetate, the significance of the latter has grown recently to such proportions that it has replaced the former in a number of important applications. For this reason it is the triacetate fibre which has been selected as the representative of this group.

Manufacture of cellulose triacetate Cotton linters are treated with acetic acid and acetic anhydride in the presence of a catalyst until acetylation is complete, i.e. until all the hydroxyl groups of the cellulose have been substituted by the acetyl groups. From the resulting solution the triacetate is precipitated, then washed and dried forming at this stage a white flake. The flake is made into spinning solution by dissolving it in methylene chloride containing some alcohol. Prior to spinning the solution is diluted, filtered and de-aerated in the usual manner. Similarly to the secondary acetate the tri-acetate is dry spun, the filaments extruded through a spinneret solidifying in the current of warm air which evaporates the solvent. The filaments are gathered together, twisted slightly and wound onto suitable packages. It is usual at this stage to lubricate the yarns with an oil mainly as an antistatic measure. Staple fibre of varying deniers can also be produced the process being similar to that described with reference to viscose rayon, but additionally the fibres are crimped permanently to assist their bulking properties.

Modifications Delustring is a common modification carried out in a manner similar to that used for viscose rayon. Bulked yarns (q.v.) are also produced in triacetate fibre.

Table 17

Properties	
Tenacity:	Dry 0.11 to 0.13 N/tex. Wet 0.06 to 0.07 N/tex.
Elongation at break:	Dry 25 to 30 per cent, wet 30 to 40 per cent.
Elastic recovery:	60 per cent at 4 per cent stretch, 30 per cent at 14 per cent stretch.
Specific gravity:	1.3.
Regain:	4.5 at 20°C and 65 per cent r.h. (after heat treatment only 2.5 to 3 per cent).
Resistance to heat:	Heat treatment stabilises the fibre dimensionally by increasing the crystallinity and molecular orientation, it increases the softening point and reduces moisture absorbency. Heat setting of triacetate fibres to retain given shape is one of the important features of this material. No appreciable loss of strength in temperatures of up to 120°C.
Softening point:	After heat treatment 225°C, fuses at approximately 300°C.
Effect of age:	Slight.
Effect of sunlight:	Slight.
Effect of acids:	Resistant to dilute acid solutions. Concentrated solutions of strong acids cause decomposition.
Effect of alkalis:	Good resistance to saponification except in the presence of strong alkalis.
Effect of other chemicals:	Good resistance to chemicals commonly encountered in processing or normal use.
Effect of organic solvents:	Soluble, or otherwise affected by a wide range of organic solvents. Completely unaffected by others—careful selection of dry cleaning agents required.
Dye affinity:	Requires special dyestuffs of the dispersed type.
Moths:	Unattacked.
Mildew:	Unaffected.

Uses Cellulose triacetate possesses many attractive features which enable it to be used for a wide variety of fabrics. One of its main attributes is the retention of shape after heat treatment. This implies also good resistance to creasing and as a result the fibre is used extensively for garments with permanent pleats and creases (skirts, slacks), and also for such articles where creasing and deformation would be particularly disadvantageous (ties, blouses, dresses). Low moisture absorption after heat treatment promotes quick drying and this combined with the previously mentioned characteristics makes it particularly suitable for garments of the 'minimum care' type. The fibre swells to only a negligible extent in water and there is, therefore, no tendency to produce the degree of relaxation shrinkage which characterises viscose rayon and secondary cellulose acetate fabrics; as a result, to arrive at the same final settings the original settings with triacetate yarns must be correspondingly higher. Combined with the low moisture absorption is the high degree of strength retention in the wet state in which aspect triacetate differs markedly from most other regenerated materials. The specific dye affinity of the fibre also lends itself to the creation of attractive cross-dyed styles.

In addition to its function as a textile fibre in its own right triacetate is extensively and advantageously employed in blends with cotton, staple viscose rayon, wool and linen. Its presence in the blend in sufficient quantity (usually 60 to 70 per cent) confers upon the blended material after heat treatment the stabilising and shape retaining properties of the triacetate. In blends it is made into suitings, light weight trouserings, summer dresses, skirts and similar articles.

(c) **Regenerated protein fibres**   Efforts have been made since the beginning of this century to produce a textile fibre from proteins. The main incentive was the possibility of using the fibre as a substitute for wool which commanded a relatively high price in comparison with most other natural materials. Between 1930 and 1950 several good fibres were produced with characteristics approaching in some respects those of the wool fibre and these were used mainly in blends with wool or cotton, especially in times when wool was in short supply. Unfortunately, no really outstanding fibres were produced in this group and their very low tenacity, particularly when wet, mitigated against wider acceptance. At present limited quantities of staple fibre based on animal casein are produced and these are used in the clothing field mainly in blends with other fibres.

2. **Synthetic polymers**

These fibres represent a significant step forward in textile technology and their origins date back mainly to the work of Carothers in the late 1920s and also to the efforts of various industrial countries during World War II to introduce synthetic materials in place of various natural products which may have been difficult to procure under wartime conditions.

Although theoretically it would be possible to synthesise these materials by starting with pure elements (mainly carbon, oxygen, hydrogen, nitrogen, and chlorine), in practice intermediate chemicals are used which often represent a half-way stage towards the finished product and thus reduce the number of operations necessary to obtain a synthetic fibre. Derivatives from coal and petroleum represent a valuable source of these intermediate chemicals.

The formation of fibrous materials depends upon the chemical being able to polymerise into long chain molecular arrangements. In this respect man imitates nature where the fibres are invariably produced in the form of long chain polymers. The process of polymerisation requires normally rigidly controlled conditions to yield the desired product and two different forms of this process are recognised—the *addition polymerisation* and the *condensation polymerisation*.

In the former type of reaction the molecules of the selected chemical, known at this stage as the monomer, literally add themselves one to another and this can be represented graphically as follows:

$$— A — A — A — A — A — A — A —$$

A in the above diagram represents the monomer which under suitable conditions has formed itself into a long chain molecule capable of producing a fibre when combined with other identical molecules. This type of reaction is typical of the polyolefines.

The *condensation polymerisation* is normally a rather more complicated reaction in which the monomer molecules combine together simultaneously eliminating a by-product molecule—usually water. This form of polymerisation occurs, amongst others, in the manufacture of polyamide fibres. In the production of these fibres two different chemical substances, capable of combining with one another, are joined together followed by subsequent junctions of the compounded substance. In simple terms the process can be represented graphically in the following manner:

$$\text{Stage I} \quad \overset{\text{Water}}{A \perp B} \rightarrow A\ B \qquad \text{Stage II} \quad A\ B \overset{\text{Water}}{\perp} A\ B \overset{\text{Water}}{\perp} A\ B \overset{\text{Water}}{\perp} A\ B \overset{\text{Water}}{\perp} A\ B -$$

The above two examples show schematically the two types of polymerisation reactions in which the single building units of the polymer are identical. Further extension of this idea includes the polymerisation of different units which results in the formation of *co-polymers*, and these can be *alternating*, e.g.

$$- X - Y - X - Y - X - Y -$$

or *block*, e.g.

$$- X - X - X - X - X - Y - Y - Y - Y - Y -$$

or *random*, e.g.

$$- X - Y - Y - X - Y - X - Y - Y - Y - X -$$

or *grafted*, in which case additional units are linked with one or the other of the existing substances to form branches or side-chains, e.g.

$$- X - X - X - X - X - X - X - \overset{\overset{\textstyle Z}{\textstyle |}}{X} - X - X -$$
$$\underset{\underset{\textstyle Z}{\textstyle |}}{X}$$

Normally, long slender molecules are preferred as these have the capacity to pack closely together during extrusion and drawing to give the necessary strength and any bulky groups at the side which would prevent the close packing are undesirable. Occasionally, however, it may be necessary to sacrifice a degree of strength to gain better extensibility or other desirable properties and in such instances side groups would be introduced deliberately. The degree of close packing or alignment of molecules along the longitudinal axis of the fibre is known as the orientation and in many fibre forming polymers a high degree of orientation is induced after extrusion by a process known as drawing without which the material may be useless from the textile point of view. As a general statement it may be said that highly orientated fibres are strong, rigid, lustrous, have low water absorption and are resistant to chemical attack and although, on the whole, the above properties are desirable an excessive propensity in any one particular direction may be objectionable, and may, therefore, require modification.

From the above general description it will be understood that many properties of the synthetic fibres are under a good measure of control and indeed, in many instances they can be modified to suit exactly a specific purpose. This permits the selection of the most suitable material for a given end use and in this respect the wealth of variety in fibres available is beneficial. It calls upon the designer, however, to possess more extensive knowledge than before, as without it the dangers of misuse are at least as considerable as are the benefits conferred by the large choice.

In view of the vast range of materials available in each major class of synthetic fibre one type only is selected and described more fully. As other members of the class are usually closely related their characteristics are frequently similar. It must not be taken for granted, however, that all the properties of the members of the same class are similar.

With the degree of fibre specialisation now possible a particular feature in a fibre may be developed to an outstanding degree and if such is the case the fibre in question may to some extent lose its identity with the other members of its own group.

(a) **Polyamides** This group encompasses several different polymers which are all products of a condensation reaction and which are commonly referred to as nylons. The polymer may be formed following a union of a diamine with a dibasic acid, or it may result from the self-condensation of an amino acid. All the fibres in this group have basically similar properties although some divergence may be expected in certain specific aspects. The numbering system which is used to describe these polymers as nylon 66, or 610, or 6, or 11, refers to the number of carbon atoms in their constituents taking the diamine (if present) first.

Manufacture of nylon 66 This was the first polyamide fibre developed on a commercial scale and it still represents a considerable proportion of the nylons produced in bulk today. It is obtained from hexamethylene diamine and adipic acid which combine together to form a salt. Upon treatment, under suitable conditions of temperature and pressure, the salt condenses to produce the nylon polymer which at this stage is extruded in the form of a long ribbon chopped after solidifying into short lengths known as 'chips'. The spinning process now follows and in the first stage the chips are melted in a heating unit. The melt is then forced through a spinneret, the filaments solidify in a cooling stream of air, and after passing through a conditioning tube are collected on a bobbin. At this stage the fibre is not yet ready for use due to poor molecular alignment, therefore, a further stage of processing known as cold drawing is introduced. In this operation the filaments are extended until the desired degree of molecular alignment has taken place and the material becomes suitable for textile purposes. The effect of cold drawing can be illustrated by Table 18.

Table 18 shows clearly that certain properties of the fibre are materially affected by the extent of drawing and this feature is used to increase the versatility of this material.

Table 18

	Strength	*Extensibility*	*Elastic Recovery*
Undrawn	Low	High	Low
Cold drawn—5 times	Medium	Medium	Medium
Cold drawn—beyond 5 times	High	Low	Low

Table 19

Properties—(The properties refer to normal nylon 66)

Tenacity:	0.43 to 0.48 N/tex.
Elongation at break:	18 to 25 per cent.
Specific gravity:	1.14.
Regain:	4 per cent at 20°C and 65 per cent r.h.
Burning rate:	Fuses.
Resistance to heat:	Loses strength if stored above 100°C.
Melting point:	250°C. Above 200°C sticking begins, at 230°C it is damaged.
Effect of age:	Slight.
Effect of sunlight:	Degraded (as all textiles) on prolonged exposure particularly when delustred.
Effect of acids:	Attacked by strong mineral acids particularly if hot. Hot or concentrated organic acids may also cause damage.
Effect of alkalis:	Very resistant to all types.
Effect of other chemicals:	Chlorine type bleaches cause degradation particularly if neutral. Hydrogen peroxide also attacks but is less severe.
Organic solvents:	Soluble in some phenols, dilute phenols may cause some shrinkage.

Table 19 continues

Table 19 *(continued)*

Dye affinity:	Disperse type as used for acetate are suitable as are also some acid and direct dyes.
Moths:	Unattacked.
Mildew:	Unattacked.

Uses   Great care is required in deciding where to use nylon, for although it has many valuable properties, it also has certain disadvantages which make it unsuitable for certain uses. These disadvantages are its low moisture absorption and its comparatively low melting point. The fact that nylon absorbs very little moisture means that after washing, garments dry rapidly. While this is of immense value especially to travellers it has the disadvantage of making fabrics feel damp or clammy in moist conditions. This might not be noticed on an outer garment, but in underwear and hose, perspiration might not be completely absorbed resulting in uncomfortable wearing conditions. Nylon is also a poor conductor of electricity and static charges are liable to collect on the fabric or garment when subjected to friction (as for example the rubbing of the leg on an underskirt). These charges attract particles of grit or dust with opposite polarity from the atmosphere so that at areas of friction, grimy marks develop. This fault is known as *fog marking* and is very difficult to remove. In the properties quoted, the groups of dyestuffs suitable for nylon were given, but as the moisture absorption is low, good absorption of the dyestuff is hindered. Deep shades are therefore not so easy to obtain as on other materials and it may be found in some mixtures that the nylon portion may dye a little lighter than the other portions. The melting point of 250°C is not so low as to cause any major difficulty in processing. Trouble may arise however once the fabric or garment reaches the consumer who is not always sufficiently careful. Obviously, nylon should not be used for fabrics or garments where under normal conditions a temperature of 250°C would be exceeded.

Despite these disadvantages, nylon has other features which make it ideal for certain purposes. It is possible to 'heat set' nylon fabrics or garments to any desired shape so that providing the setting temperature is not exceeded in any subsequent process, the fabric or garment will always return to that shape. The value of this in tie fabrics, pleated garments, stockings, etc., is unquestionable and when coupled with its good elastic recovery properties makes for garments which retain their shape over a long period. Nylon's resistance to abrasion is exceptionally high and even a small quantity mixed with other materials increases their resistance to abrasion by an appreciable amount. As its resistance to bending is also high, in fabrics or garments where abrasion and bending are normal conditions of wear, nylon has few rivals.

Particular uses where its properties are very suitable are listed below showing how wide is the range of fabrics possible from nylon, a range which can be extended further by the designer realising the full potentialities of the material and matching the properties with the consumer's requirements.

Table 20

Fineness:	Voiles, marquisettes, stockings, lace.
Smoothness:	Lining fabrics, filters.
Elasticity:	Ties, stockings, undergarments.
Strength:	Tow ropes, bead strings, fishing nets.
Ease of washing:	Shirts, underwear.
Low density:	Raincoats, foundation garments, laundry bags, body armour.
Wear resistance:	Overalls, gloves, stocking reinforcement.
Resistance to fungi:	Laces, ropes, mosquito netting for humid conditions.
Non-toxic properties:	Surgical webbing, sutures.

Nylon is also used extensively in blends with other fibres where its high abrasion resistance and excellent resiliency add materially to the performance of articles made from the blended yarns. Mixed in varying proportions with other fibres nylon is particularly valuable in the manufacture of undergarments, suitings and carpet pile yarns. The range of applications is further increased through the use of textured or bulked yarns (q.v.) which due to their construction improve the moisture absorption and the thermal insulation properties of this material.

(b) **Polyesters** The fibres in this group are also products of a condensation reaction and the polymer results usually from a combination of a dihydric alcohol with a dibasic acid. The fibre described in this group is the 'Terylene' produced by I.C.I. Ltd., and the properties and the manufacturing process of this polymer are broadly representative of the whole class.

Manufacture of Terylene The substance from which this fibre is produced is known as the polyethylene terephthalate which is obtained by combining terephthalic acid with ethylene glycol both of which are originally derived from petroleum. Chemically, polyethylene terephthalate is quite different from the polyamides but the manufacturing process of Terylene is similar to that of nylon. As in the latter, the polymer is melt-spun and solidifies in the current of cold air. The subsequent process of drawing is, however, different in as much as it is carried out at high temperature (hot drawing) but as with nylon the extent to which the filaments are drawn determines the tensile and elastic properties of the material and a wide range of qualities is possible. 'Terylene' is produced in the filament and in the cut (staple) fibre form. The latter is usually crimped to enhance its spinning and bulking properties and is made in various lengths and diameters as shown below.

Table 21

37 mm	—2.2 d tex crimped fibres for cotton system
100 mm	—4.4 d tex crimped fibres for worsted system
63 mm	—4.4 d tex crimped fibres for woollen system
100 mm	—4.4 d tex uncrimped fibres for linen system

Table 22

Properties	
Tenacity:	Normal: 0.40 to 0.50 N/tex.
	High tenacity: 0.54 to 0.63 N/tex.
Elongation at break:	Normal: 15 to 25 per cent.
	High tenacity: 7.5 to 12.5 per cent.
Elastic recovery:	85 per cent at 4 per cent stretch. 50 per cent at 14 per cent stretch.
Specific gravity:	1.38.
Regain:	0.4 per cent.
Burning rate:	Fuses.
Resistance to heat:	Very high. Shrinks at elevated temperatures in relaxed state.
Softening point:	260°C. Becomes sticky at 230 to 240°C.
Effect of age:	Slight.
Effect of sunlight:	Eventually degraded, but is equal to the best of the natural fibres.
Effect of acids:	Very high resistance. Decomposed by concentrated sulphuric acid.
Effect of alkalis:	Hydrolised by alkalis, but adequate resistance to most commercial processes except kier boiling under pressure.
Effect of other chemicals:	Excellent resistance to oxidising agents, hypochlorites and hydrosulphite.
Organic solvents:	Cold no effect except chloroform which causes some shrinkage, but hot solvents may cause shrinkage. Phenols swell or dissolve.
Dye affinity:	Disperse dyes as used for cellulose acetate and nylon, and

Table 22 continues

Table 22 *(continued)*

	azoic dyes, the latter giving good intense shades. The low moisture absorption frequently necessitates dyeing at an elevated temperature in pressurised vessels.
Moths:	Excellent resistance.
Mildew:	Excellent resistance.

Uses It is possible to heat set Terylene in a like manner to nylon thus making it very useful for fabrics or garments subjected to creasing such as ties, skirts, blouses, etc. As its resistance to abrasion is high it is suitable alone or in admixture with other materials where rubbing is likely to occur such as in stockings or raincoats. Terylene itself has a wide range of uses such as ropes, lace, ties, underwear, overalls, filter cloths, curtains, and tablecloths, but the field of applications of this fibre is considerably extended when its uses in the staple form in blends with other fibres are considered. Particularly valuable is the aspect of shape retention after heat treatment and this is fully utilised in the production of permanently pleated and creased garments (skirts, trousers) where the presence of 55–70 per cent of Terylene is sufficient to confer upon the cloth this valuable quality. Self-smoothing characteristics combined with rapid drying are the other important attributes of this fibre. Textured or bulked yarns, some of special stabilised type (q.v.) further increase the usefulness of Terylene.

(c) **Polyolefines** These are a small group of fibres which are chemically the least complex in structure of all man-made materials, and which are the product of the addition polymerisation of unsaturated hydrocarbons. Polyolefines are quite different from the other man-made fibres in two important aspects—the very low density (being the only fibres with specific gravity lower than water), and the low melting point. These features although limiting the range of applications of this type of fibre are quite valuable in certain specific circumstances.

The polyolefines are produced by a process of melt spinning followed by drawing similar to the one described in the manufacture of polyamides, and currently two chemically different materials are in production—polyethylene and polypropylene. Polyethylene may be obtained as a low density or a high density material. The former is very soft, comparatively weak and has a melting point of 115°C but actual softening of the fibre commences even before the boiling point of water is reached. The latter type is a much tougher material which has good tenacity and an improved melting point of 135°C. Unfortunately the filaments of this fibre tend to fibrillate. These disadvantages preclude the use of polyethylene in normal textile applications but it has a number of merits which make it useful in certain specialised fields. Its specific gravity is low (0.92–0.96), it has good resistance to most chemicals, is not subject to biological attack and has good abrasion and electrical resistance. In addition, it does not absorb any moisture. These special properties make it possible to employ polyethylene in washable upholstery fabrics, filter cloths, ropes, nets, insulating and surgical materials, and the low melting point makes it useful as the fusing element in laminated cloths (semi-stiff collars, etc.).

The other member of the group—the polypropylene—has a wider application and from the textile point of view is a much more promising fibre. It has all the special properties of polyethylene including the low specific gravity (0.91), is much tougher, does not fibrillate, and although its melting point of 165°C is lower than that of polyamides and polyesters it is sufficiently high to make it suitable for quite a wide range of uses. Polypropylene yarns can be bulked by the heat setting process and the fibre is also available in staple form with the usual range of thicknesses and lengths for blending with other fibres. Due to its low density the use of the system to describe the size of the filaments may be somewhat misleading and it must be remembered that for equal decitex number the polypropylene yarns will be thicker, the ratio of diameters being approximately 5:4 respectively between the propylene and most other natural and man-made materials. To overcome this difficulty the yarns may be sold at 'nominal' values. The commercially available polypropylene contains stabilisers which appreciably enhance the resistance of the fibre to light and weather. Without the stabilisers polypropylene has low resistance to the above agencies. Poor dyeing affinity due to negligible moisture absorption imposes some limitation on the range of colours available although coloured yarns can be obtained through spin-dyeing techniques.

Polypropylene fibre can be satisfactorily employed in most fields of application mentioned in respect of the polyethylene but in addition its higher melting point, bulking properties and good resiliency enable it to give very adequate performance in such fabrics as sackings, blankets and upholstery, and as pile yarns and backing cloth in carpets. Its potential cheapness will no doubt increase its range of uses.

(d) **Polyvinyl derivatives** This large group embraces rather heterogeneous materials which differ widely chemically and physically. The general title commonly adopted is perhaps rather unhappy in as much as it tends to be used to cover not only the vinyl but also vinylidene derivatives. It might be more correct to refer to these materials simply as olefine substitution products obtained by the process of addition polymerisation. Although many members of this group are valuable only within a comparatively narrow range of applications due to their highly specialised properties one class of fibre has found a very wide acceptance in many branches of the textile industry. This is the polyvinyl cyanide, perhaps better known as the polyacrylonitrile fibre obtainable commercially under the wellknown trade names of 'Orlon' and 'Acrilan', each available in a wide range of different types and qualities.

Manufacture of polyacrylonitrile fibre Melt spinning is not satisfactory in the case of this fibre and a solvent method is usually adopted. The polymer is dissolved in a suitable solvent and then extruded in a conventional manner, coagulation being effected either by a wet spinning process (similar to viscose rayon), or by a dry spinning process (similar to cellulose acetate). After spinning the yarn is stretched to improve its properties and may also be crimped. Wide variety of qualities can be produced with different tensile and elastic properties. The fibre is mainly used in staple form either by itself or in blends, and for the latter purpose it is produced in various deniers (1.7 to 6.8 d tex) and staple lengths.

Table 23

Properties	
Tenacity:	Dry: 0.16 to 0.24 N/tex.
	Wet: 0.13 to 0.22 N/tex.
Elongation at break:	Dry: 20–40 per cent.
	Wet: 25–50 per cent.
Elastic recovery:	Good.
Specific gravity:	1.17–1.20.
Regain:	1.5–1.7 per cent.
Burning rate:	Fast.
Resistance to heat:	Good.
Softening point:	Depending on type becomes sticky at between 260–450°C.
Effect of age:	High resistance.
Effect of sunlight:	High resistance.
Effect of acids:	High resistance.
Effect of alkalis:	Adequate resistance for textile purposes.
Effect of other chemicals:	High resistance to degradation by common bleaches.
Organic solvents:	Unaffected by common solvents.
Dye affinity:	Disperse, basic, vat and special dyeing technique (cuprous ion).
Moths:	Unattacked.
Mildew:	Unattacked.

Uses The high resistance of polyacrylonitrile fibres to chemical attack and their ability to withstand exposure to sunlight are the features on which many of its uses are based. It, therefore, finds applications industrially for such purposes as filter cloths, tarpaulins, sunshades, etc., and for normal domestic purposes as curtain linings, swimsuits, and window blinds. Apart from these uses the fibre can be employed for more conventional fabrics such as all types of apparel cloths either alone or in various blends, furnishing fabrics, carpets, rugs, and blankets. Its many attributes include light weight combined with good bulking, toughness and at the same time luxurious and soft hand, excellent retention of shape and dimensional stability after heat setting, with rapid drying characteristics. Although polyacrylonitrile fibres have low moisture regain they do not feel 'clammy' in wear—either due to good bulking characteristics, or, in some types, due to peculiar 'dog-bone' cross-sectional appearance which permits a degree of surface capillarity. Another interesting instance of the versatility of this class of materials is the permanently crimped bicomponent fibre (q.v.) which finds increasing use in the apparel wear.

(e) **Polyurethane elastomers**   This is a group of chemically complex fibres which have highly elastic properties and are used in applications where previously rubber threads were the only satisfactory material. The construction of these polymers consists of short rigid regions where a degree of molecular alignment exists (X in *Figure A2.2*), interspersed with completely unaligned regions where the molecules are coiled in a somewhat random fashion (Y in *Figure A2.2*). The latter uncoil to a remarkable extent upon application of strain and when released have the capacity to return to the original position, the short rigid sections acting as 'brakes' to prevent non-returnable slippage of the strained coiled fraction of the system.

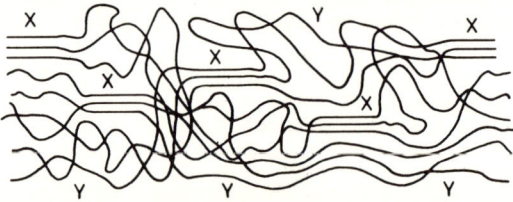

Figure A2.2

These elastomeric fibres, also known under the term spandex, are normally extruded in the form of a multifilament in which the single components immediately upon extrusion adhere to one another thus in effect producing a monofilament yarn. Spandex yarns show good sunlight and chemical resistance and do not deteriorate through oxidation. They are very light (specific gravity approximately 1.00–1.20) and have a high melting point. The disadvantages are the low tensile strength and susceptibility to certain organic solvents. The former, however, due to highly elastic properties of the material is rarely tested in use, whilst the latter can be overcome by careful selection of agents should dry-cleaning become necessary.

Spandex yarns are used extensively in all types of sportswear where freedom of movement is as essential as good fit (ski slacks, swimsuits, etc.), in foundation garments, in surgical wear and as support threads in elasticated hose tops, cuffs, etc. They can be dyed by a wide variety of dyestuffs and where shape retention is of importance the garments can be heat-set to ensure stability.

3. **Mineral based materials**   This is the smallest section of the man-made materials. The reason for this is that minerals do not generally exhibit the properties necessary for textile purposes, e.g. extensibility and elastic recovery, moisture absorption, etc. However, some of these fibres have considerable value in certain industrial applications, or as highly ornamental materials and, indeed, metallic threads (gold, silver) could be regarded as the first man-made textile material of all, having been known and used for centuries.

The modern fibres in this group could be divided into three main classes—glass, ceramic, and metallic. The first forms the most important class and is described in some detail. The ceramic fibres are mainly used for industrial purposes where high temperatures are involved as they are capable of standing up to temperatures upward of 1000°C which represents the upper safety limit for glass and asbestos fibres. Metallic threads are used mainly for decorative or protective purposes. For the ordinary range of applications the metallic thread is now often produced as a laminated material in which a thin sheet of metal foil is pressed between two layers of plastic film. The laminated sheet is then cut into thin ribbons of yarn. The width of the flat yarn thus produced may vary according to requirements and the plastic film in which the metallic strip (usually aluminium) is enclosed effectively prevents tarnishing. The threads find uses as the decorative elements in ladies' suitings, dresses, swim suits and furnishing fabrics.

Manufacture of glass fibre   The glass which is used is carefully selected and refined in order to give filaments and cut staple fibres of uniformity and with the desired qualities. It is first produced as small marbles which can then be loaded in a chute above an electrically heated furnace. The marbles are allowed to run down this chute into the furnace at a determined rate and are melted in the furnace. From the furnace the filaments flow out through a spinneret by gravity and are cooled and wound on to a drum. If cut filament form is desired, the filaments are cut by means of jets of air or steam and are then collected to form a sliver when a fibre yarn can be formed by the insertion of twist.

Table 24

Properties	
Tensile strength:	0.58 N/tex.
Elongation at break:	2 to 3 per cent.
Elastic recovery:	100 per cent.
Specific gravity:	2.54.
Regain:	0.4 per cent.
Burning rate:	None. (Note: Emulsions, etc., used in spinning may burn.)
Resistance to heat:	Begins to lose strength at temperatures over 315°C.
Softening point:	Begins to soften at 815°C.
Effect of age:	None.
Effect of sunlight:	None.
Effect of acids:	Unaffected by acids except hydrofluoric acid and phosphoric acid.
Effect of alkalis:	Attacked by hot solutions of weak alkali and cold solutions of strong alkali.
Effect of other chemicals:	Resistant to most chemicals.
Effect of organic solvents:	Insoluble in all organic solvents.
Dye affinity:	No affinity for ordinary dyes but can be coloured by resin bonded pigment dyes.
Moths:	Unattacked.
Mildew:	Unattacked.

Uses   The main uses of glass as a textile material are in fabrics where non-flammability and resistance to chemical attack other than by alkali are of prime importance. Industrially it has therefore many important uses but it is still possible to utilise it for ornamental fabrics. As it has a high tensile strength and is unaffected by age and sunlight it is obviously an ideal material for curtainings. A disadvantage here is the difficulty of dyeing but attractive fabrics are still possible using the range of colours available. It is not an easy material to launder as it absorbs little or no water and if folded and pressed too heavily, cracking may develop. Sponging in many cases is sufficient to freshen the fabric. Glass has little use in the clothing sphere as it is cold and unsympathetic to the touch but in the furnishing field it has many possibilities based on its high strength and the fact that it does not support bacteria growth.

IDENTIFICATION OF TEXTILE MATERIALS

Identification of textile materials was comparatively simple when only the natural fibres were in existence. With the advent of man-made materials the subject has become one of considerable complexity with the difficulties of identification even further compli- cated by the fact that the various fibres are not only encountered on their own but also in bi-, and tri- component blends with other fibres. In addition, the materials may contain a variety of finishing agents, themselves synthetic in origin, which may cause misleading reactions.

Obviously, in the space available in this work it is impossible to cover the whole complex field exhaustively and the main intention is to give the designer some guidance on the possibility of reaching a reasonable approximation of the identity of a material without the services of a fully equipped laboratory. The simple approach outlined in the following pages is advanced with the full knowledge that in view of the variety of materials in production it may be on occasions inadequate, and for this reason references are provided at the end of the Appendix to exhaustive books on the subject.

There are five stages in this simple scheme of identification: (1) visual examination, (2) untwisting, (3) burning test, (4) elimination, (5) summary. The methods to be followed and the reasoning adopted are given below.

(1) Visual examination. The material to be identified is examined critically and points such as lustre, whether metallic or soft, smoothness or hairiness, harsh handle or soft handle, colour, and strength noted.

(2) Untwisting. The material is untwisted and if it consists of continuous filaments then it can only be silk or one of the man-made materials. Should it prove to be of fibre construction, then it can be any textile material, both man-made and natural. As an aid to further identification, the length of the individual fibres in fibre yarns should be noted and also whether they are all of the same length or if they vary considerably. Where fibres are all of the same length then the possi- bility is that the material is man-made as natural fibres vary considerably in length and complete uniformity is rarely attained.

(3) The burning test involves taking a small quantity of the material slowly into a flame, noting how the material burns or if non-inflammable whether it melts or maintains the same shape but glows. Six distinct types of reaction may be observed:

(a) The material burns freely leaving a fine powdery ash, the smoke smelling of burnt paper.

   Any natural or man-made cellulosic material (except cellulose acetate) will give this reaction.

(b) The material burns rapidly leaving a hard tarry bead residue and a faint vinegar-like smell. Cellulose acetate is the only material with this reaction.

(c) The material recedes before the flame, but upon ignition burns freely with a smoky flame leaving a charred, tarry residue.

   This indicates a polyacrylic fibre. Similar reaction is produced by poly- urethane fibres which, however, burn with a clear, smokeless flame.

(d) The material burns with difficulty, there is a tendency towards spluttering, a crushable cinder residue remains and there is a distinct odour of burning hair or feathers. This type of burning indicates either natural protein matter (wool, silk, etc.) or any of the man-made materials based on protein.

(e) The material does not burn but as it is brought near to the flame it melts and recedes forming a bead. If brought into the flame too quickly, it may ignite. Such a reaction is typical of a number of synthetic polymers, e.g. polyamides, polyesters, polyolefines and some polyolefine substitution products.

(f) The material does not ignite but if kept in the flame it will glow and retain its shape. Mineral fibre would be indicated by this reaction.

Note: Lubricating oils or other finishing agents if present, may ignite on the surface of the non-inflammable fibres, thus confusing the observations.

(4) Elimination. The information now available is studied and materials eliminated which do not have the observed reactions. For example, burning reaction (f) eliminates all materials except the mineral based fibres.

(5) Summary. An attempt is now made to eliminate still further from the range of materials that the unknown one could be. This involves a good knowledge of textiles generally as well as the properties of materials.

The two examples given below will serve to illustrate the method.

Sample 1. Visual examination. Metallic lustred, smooth, bright coloured, medium strength yarn.

Untwisting. Filament.

Burning test. Reaction (a).

Elimination. The material cannot be cellulose acetate, any protein material, any synthetic polymer, glass or asbestos.

Summary. The material is either viscose rayon or cuprammonium rayon. If it is exceptionally fine, it is possibly cuprammonium otherwise without recourse to more involved methods of identification, this is as far as can be gone with this method.

Sample 2. Visual examination. Soft lustred, crimped, lofty, medium strength yarn.

Untwisting. Fibre yarn, fibres 75 mm long, regular.

Burning test. Reaction (c).

Elimination. The burning test eliminates all cellulose and protein materials, cellulose acetate, all synthetic polymers except acrylonitrile fibres, all mineral based fibres.

Summary. The appearance of the material and the burning reaction clearly indicate the polyacrylonitrile group and the fibre could be one of about eight or ten types available in that group. Again no closer approximation than this can be made with this simple scheme.

The scheme indicated above although not entirely positive is frequently helpful and with experience it often makes it possible to arrive at a definite conclusion bearing in mind the type of cloth in which the material was encountered, its cost, suitability, availability, etc. However, although at times positive identification is very difficult even for experts backed with formidable laboratory facilities certain aids in many instances are sufficient to provide the correct answer. Staining techniques, for example, are easy to apply and very useful in identifying undyed materials. Best known in this field are the Shirlastains and Neocarmine. A simple microscope is often quite positive as many fibres have characteristic cross-sectional or longitudinal appearance, and comparisons with known samples or with illustrations help in identifying the distinctive features. The 'difficult' group of synthetic polymers, many of which have similar microscopic appearance, can be further separated by the use of specific organic solvents, and the fact that a given material dissolves in one and not in another solvent is often sufficient to determine exactly its origin. The above indicate the simplest identification techniques but use can also be made of more sophisticated aids such as the density gradient tube, microscopic mountains with varying refractive indices, reaction to dilute or concentrated, hot or cold acids and alkalis and so on and although the difficulties of positive determination are quite real in most cases they need not be regarded as insurmountable.

GLOSSARY OF THE MORE IMPORTANT YARN TERMS USED IN RESPECT OF MAN-MADE MATERIALS

Aerated yarn   Man-made filament which contains enclosed air pockets. These may form continuous hollow centre, or they may be distributed at random as small bubbles. The presence of the air-pockets increases buoyancy and resiliency of the material and reduces its specific gravity.

Alginate fibres   The treatment of seaweed with sodium carbonate solution causes the plant to disintegrate as a thick gelatinous mass. This is diluted with water and filtered, and the filtrate, after bleaching and sterilising, is acidified with hydrochloric acid to precipitate the alginic acid which may be prepared as a spinning solution from which alginic acid rayon yarns can be spun. It is more usual, however, to neutralise the alginic acid by further treatment with sodium carbonate to produce sodium alginate solution which, when ready for spinning, may contain about 9 per cent of air-dry sodium alginate. This solution is extruded (as in the spinning of viscose rayon) into a coagulating bath containing calcium chloride, dilute hydrochloric acid, and emulsified olive oil, to produce calcium alginate rayon. The filaments are stretched during spinning, and the yarns are satisfactory in appearance, handle, tenacity (0.15 to 0.18 N/tex), extensibility and fineness (as fine as 2 decitex filaments) for weaving and knitting purposes. At this stage, however, alginate rayon is readily soluble in a dilute solution of soap and soda and must be made alkali resistant. The material in yarn form, or during the finishing of woven or knitted fabrics, is therefore treated in a bath containing metallic salts (beryllium salts leave alginate rayon uncoloured) which makes it not only alkali resistant but also non-inflammable, so that metallic alginate rayon could be useful for curtains and other furnishing fabrics. Calcium-beryllium alginate rayon is very hygroscopic, and the yarns, when wet, have about 80 per cent of the tenacity of air-dry yarns. The number of dyestuffs suitable for dyeing alginate fibres are sufficient to produce a range of colours of satisfactory fastness to light and washing.

The solubility of alginate fibres can be made use of in producing special effects in cloths. Thus a calcium alginate yarn may be twisted with a non-soluble yarn, which contains little or no twist, or is very fine, in order to give strength to the latter for weaving. The soluble yarn is then removed from the woven cloth simply by washing with soap and water, the principle being the same as in the production of 'extracted cloth' where the cotton scaffolding thread was removed by acid carbonisation process from a wool/cotton mixture.

An extra process, in which acid is used, is not required to remove the soluble alginate material, and the latter may be employed in combination with any other kind of textile fibre with no injurious result. The principle offers considerable scope for the production of special effects, as for instance: by twisting groups of fibres with the soluble yarn, or the latter may be twisted with a yarn of greater length; certain threads in a cloth may be interwoven with alginate threads, etc., so that when the soluble material is dissolved in the scouring process the groups of fibres or portions of the non-soluble threads are released and tufts, curls, loops, etc., are formed on one or both sides of the fabric.

Bi-component yarn   This yarn is achieved by fusing together longitudinally during extrusion two filaments of different chemical composition. This ensures that the twin fibres' components behave in a somewhat different manner when subjected to the influence of certain agencies. Particularly useful in this respect is the differential shrinkage property of each component when subjected to the action of heat. This property causes the development of twists and kinks in the yarn thus assisting materially in increasing its bulking properties. The heat-induced spirality is removed in water but returns again upon drying if the fabric or garment is laid out flat after washing. Thus, in each laundering cycle there is a continual movement and reconstitution of yarns in slightly different convolutions which assist in maintaining the cover, and the formation of new fibre entanglements helps to rejuvenate the fabric appearance. Other bi-component yarns may be produced as a concentric combination of a different core within a different sheath.

Bulked yarns Yarns treated in such a manner as to increase their apparent volume. Such yarns are also sometimes termed 'textured' and some have the capacity to recover fully after stretching and are known as stretch yarns. Bulked yarns improve the cover of fabrics made from them and in some instances savings of up to 40 per cent in weight are possible for cloths of similar appearance. The process also improves the thermal insulation value of the yarn and its moisture absorbency and garments produced from these yarns are lighter, fit better and are generally more comfortable in wear than similar garments produced from identical but non-bulked material.

Most processes used to produce this type of yarn depend upon thermoplastic properties of the treated fibre and the sequence of operations may be generally described as: heating to plasticise the material, deformation whilst in plastic state followed by cooling which ensures that the deformation is permanently retained. The deforming may be achieved in various ways, e.g. by passing the yarn over an edge, between toothed gears, over feeding into a stuffer box and by a twist-untwist method. In each of these processes the temperature conditions are the most critical part of the operation and any deviations at that stage will greatly affect the yarn performance and its characteristics. Most of the yarns produced in the above manner possess the ability to recover from stretch and are, therefore, also classified as stretch yarns.

Different processes are used to produce bulked yarn from non-thermoplastic materials (but can be used for thermoplastic fibres as well) and these depend upon a strong current of compressed air creating numerous loops in the individual filaments of a multi-filament yarn, combined with an overfeed principle to ensure that the filaments are free to form the loops. Yarns produced in this way increase their bulk or apparent volume but as the main core of the yarn remains undisturbed, elastic properties of the final product are largely unaffected.

Core yarn A composite yarn produced at the spinning frame by feeding-in a ready made central yarn and spinning around it an envelope or a 'wrapper' of staple fibre. The central core may be a staple fibre, or a filament yarn. These yarns are produced for decorative purposes and the central core, acting as the strengthening element during fabrication, is frequently removed during finishing by chemical action to leave a lofty, almost twistless product (see Alginate fibres). In other cases the core is allowed to remain in the yarn permanently.

Crêpe rayon yarns These have largely superseded the crêpe silk yarns (q.v.) formerly used in fine quality crêpe cloths. Viscose and cuprammonium rayons have been most popular for crêping purposes, their use as weft, in conjunction with cellulose acetate or silk warp, having been found very advantageous. Crêpe cellulose acetate yarn is produced which will give the same degree of shrinkage as the other rayons, but with ordinary twist its special properties have rendered it of particular use as the non-shrinking element of crêpe cloths. The actual counts of crêpe viscose yarn range chiefly from 84 to 110 d tex, and the turns per cm from 22 to 24, but these figures are by no means the limit, and, as a rule, the threads are composed of fine filaments. Cuprammonium crêpe yarn, as fine as 45 d tex, with about 24 turns per cm, is used for both warp and weft in fine types of Georgette crêpe cloth.

The effect of increasing the twist in rayon yarns above the normal turns per inch is, at first, to increase the strength, but beyond from 8 to 10 turns per cm in ordinary counts the additional twist tends to weaken the yarn progressively. The lustre of the yarn is reduced in proportion to the amount of twist inserted, and the thread becomes shorter and the tex count higher. A wide variation in the amount of twist in crêpe yarns results in uneven crêping, or 'river marking', as the defect is termed, in the cloth.

Previous to the crêpe twisting operation, in order that the required high degree of twist may be inserted without injury to the filaments, and to increase the flexibility of the threads, it is customary to treat the material with a light size, by which the filaments are coated with an exceedingly thin film that acts as a lubricant and assists in controlling the twist. The kind of size that is suitable varies according to the class of crêpe finish that is required in the cloth, a gelatine size being preferable for viscose crêpe yarn when a distinct pebble finish is wanted, and an oil size in order to produce a flatter surface.

In the majority of crêpe fabrics both right and left twist threads are used, and in order that the two kinds of twist may be distinguished during the preparatory and weaving processes one of the yarns is tinted, or the two kinds are tinted in contrasting colours, previous to the insertion of the crêpe twist. Also, to distinguish weft yarns further they are wound on differently coloured pirns and, in addition, the two different kinds of twist may be wound on the pirns in opposite directions (winding spindles are geared to rotate either right or left way), so that the unwinding of the threads in weaving will not increase the twist of one yarn and decrease that of the other.

The standard method of crêpe twisting single filament rayon yarn is from bobbin to bobbin, but ring twisting is now also employed. The twist may be inserted at two operations, and on a dual machine up-twisting from bobbins, etc., is now combined with down-twisting by the ring method in a continuous operation.

Staple fibre yarns, also, are crêpe twisted, the counts ranging from 38 tex to 14 tex and upwards, and the number of turns per cm from 18 to 20. 'Single-spun' staple fibre crêpe yarn has the crêpe twist inserted at the one operation of spinning, whereas the yarn is termed 'double-spun' when it is first spun with normal twist and then has the required additional turns inserted in a twisting frame in which, if required, it may be passed through water. In the second spinning the single thread is twisted round its own axis with the result that it has a more 'pebbled' appearance than the single-spun yarn. Two-fold crêpe yarns consist of two normally spun single threads which are twisted together, usually in a ring doubling frame, the direction of the twist generally being in the same direction as the twist of the singles.

After the twisting operation crêpe threads are liable to snarl or kink up, owing to the high twist, if they are held without tension, and in order to set the yarn and produce the necessary inactivity for successful working it is subjected to heated humidity. Steaming the yarn is mostly employed and the process is carried out on the material in the form in which it has been wound—in cones, cheeses, bobbins, or pirns; and the treatment requires to be uniform throughout the yarn or the pebble in the cloth will be affected. A vacuum steamer may be used in which the yarn is placed on suitable containers, and after the cover has been closed and sealed, air is withdrawn by means of a pump and the steam is admitted. Some manufacturers, however, prefer that viscose crêpe yarns on pirns are not steamed, because of the possibility that the process may be detrimental to the effect that is desired in the finished cloth.

Crimped viscose rayon Filaments produced with thicker skin on one side than the other. As this affects the moisture absorbency the fibre of this type becomes unbalanced and develops a crimp which improves its bulking properties and resiliency. Ordinary crimped viscose rayon shows the normal corrugated cross-sectional appearance but for carpets a special fibre with a smooth cross-section has been developed in order to prevent soiling and to improve the wear properties.

Cuprammonium rayon A regenerated cellulose fibre, now also known by the term cupro. In the production of this rayon, cellulose is dissolved in a cuprammonium solution, extruded into a current of water which induces a degree of stretch, and coagulated in a bath of acid. This material is more costly to produce than viscose rayon and for this reason its uses are confined to more luxurious goods. It is particularly suitable for very fine denier yarns and is made into chiffons, ninons and similar fabrics in which its excellent handle, good draping property and comparatively high tenacity are advantageously displayed.

Denier System used as the standard count for filament silk and most man-made fibres. The denier number refers to the weight in grammes of 9000 metres of yarn or filament.

Drawn yarn A man-made yarn which has been subjected after extrusion to a drawing or stretching process (non-returnable stretch) designed to induce more perfect molecular alignment within the filaments. Drawing usually increases the strength of materials but reduces their extensibility (see High tenacity yarn, also, section on Synthetic polymers).

Fancy rayon yarns   Rayon, either as filament or staple fibre yarn, may be introduced as the special thread in nearly all classes of fancy yarns (q.v.).

Boucle   A typical and popular fancy yarn in which the effect ranges from a more or less distinct curl to small spots or nubs. The yarn may be composed entirely of rayon, or the effect thread may be of rayon and the foundation threads of cotton, or wool, or both. There may be two or three foundation threads, and one effect thread which, in the twisting, has an excess delivery of from 50 to 75 cm to each metre of twist.

Random slub   A spun viscose slub yarn so produced that patterning in any width of cloth is avoided.

High tenacity yarn   Term used to denote a material with tensile strength higher than in 'normal' fibre. Produced specifically for tyre cord fabrics, conveyor belts and similar industrial applications. Can be achieved by cold or hot drawing of synthetic materials or by stretching during coagulation of viscose rayon. The higher strength is due to better alignment of molecules along the longitudinal axis of filaments. This increase is usually accompanied by reduced extensibility.

Lactron thread and **lastex yarn**   'Latex' is the water dispersion of natural rubber, or an emulsion of synthetic rubber, which is suitably prepared so as to produce a liquid of a certain degree of viscosity. 'Lactron thread' is the term applied to the round rubber filaments that are produced by extruding the prepared latex through small apertures into a coagulating bath in which they are solidified. The threads then pass to conveyors on which they are washed under water sprays, are dried and vulcanised in hot chambers, inspected while being passed across a table, and finally are wound on bobbins, all in a continuous operation. This round continuous rubber thread is used in place of the square thread of limited length which, formerly, was cut from sheet rubber. The principal sizes of fine round thread are 75s, 100s, and 125s, each number representing the number of threads that can be laid side by side in one inch; that is, 100s thread has a diameter of $\frac{1}{100}$ in. (0.254 mm).

'Lastex yarn' is produced by covering lactron thread with two layers of material by twisting two threads in opposite directions round the rubber core. The lactron thread passes through two rotating hollow spindles which respectively carry the inner and outer covering thread, and rotate in opposite directions. During the twisting operation the rubber thread is under tension in order that it will have the required degree of elongation, while care is taken that the two covering threads are given in at an equal rate so that both will subsequently permit of the same amount of stretch. The ultimate elongation of lastex yarn is limited by the covering threads, and a fabric containing the elastic yarn cannot stretch beyond the distance allowed by the non-elastic threads.

Lastex yarn is produced with an elongation that ranges from 55 per cent to 300 per cent, but usually it is from 105 per cent to 175 per cent, while the number of metres per kg in the covered form runs from 1800 to 36 000. The covering threads vary in thickness from coarse woollen counts to the finest silk and rayon; cotton covering threads, however, are most frequently employed. The latter are usually fine in counts, and the inner covering thread may be single or two-ply, and the outer thread single, two-ply, or three-ply. The lactron core may form about 30 per cent of the compound thread, with the cotton covering threads in equal proportions, or with the outer covering thread as, say, three parts to two of the inner thread.

Lastex yarn is used for corsets, bathing costumes, tight fitting under garments, waist bands, caps, and tops of socks; to impart a local grip at the end of sleeves, etc., and to form tuck and ruched effects. In woven fabrics various crêpon, undulating, and crinkled styles can be obtained by introducing one or two threads of lastex yarn at intervals. When the yarn is inserted in fabrics it has to be elongated at the time of insertion to the same degree as the finished fabric is required to be stretched. The natural latex yarns are now frequently replaced by the polyurethane elastomers in certain fields of application.

Plastic coated yarns   Cotton, rayon, fibreglass, etc., yarns are coated with exceedingly fine coverings of plastic solutions in order to make them stronger, brighter or duller, different in colour, resistant to water, chemicals, perspiration, oil and grease, and fireproof, weatherproof, and rot proof. The number of coatings that is applied varies according to the ultimate use of the thread.

Polynosic fibres These are modified viscose rayon fibres with high dry and wet tenacity, the latter being particularly valuable in achieving dimensionally stable fabrics. The crisp handle, low water imbibition (therefore reduced swelling) and good lustre make these materials very attractive. They are frequently used in applications suited for mercerised cotton which they resemble in many respects.

Split film fibre yarn A type of yarn used in twines and ropes and obtained from fibre made by splitting a sheet of film. The film is fibrillated into thin strands (usually by mechanical action), these are then gathered into bundles of suitable thickness and twisted together, thus forming a yarn. The materials particularly suitable for this process belong mostly to the polyolefines which exhibit a natural propensity towards fibrillation. Sackings and backing cloth used in the manufacture of tufted carpets are other important outlets for this type of yarn.

Spun-dyed yarns Applied to man-made materials in which colour is due to the presence of pigment particles incorporated in the spinning dope prior to extrusion. Particularly useful in fibres with poor dye affinity where it may be the only way of achieving coloured yarns. The presence of pigment particles in the fibre usually results also in the modification of the intensity of lustre.

Staple fibre Man-made fibrous material resulting from cutting or breaking of a tow (q.v.) of filaments. The choice of staple length and filament fineness is governed by the method of spinning to be subsequently employed. (Lengths produced as standard vary from 31 mm to 457 mm, counts from 0.6 d tex to 56 d tex.) Any man-made material could be produced in staple form if desired. (See varied length staple fibre yarn.)

Staplised yarn A class of mock staple fibre yarn is produced continuously from filament yarn which possesses the characteristic features of staple fibre yarn. In one method of production each group of filaments, while subjected to a downward twisting operation, is caused to balloon round the winding package and is brought in contact with an abrasive or cutting device. Only a few of the filaments are severed at a time so that the continuity of the group is retained, and a continuous product is spun which has the appearance of being composed of staple fibre. By the preceding method the yarns retain the original thickness of the filament threads, but the principle of rupturing is now applied to continuous filaments in the form of roving of much greater count which, after staplising, merely passes through the final stages of drawing and the spinning that are customary in the spinning of a staple fibre yarn. The filaments never lose their parallel arrangement, and the final count of the yarn is determined by the amount of drafting employed.

Stretch spinning A method of spinning used to produce high tenacity yarns (q.v.) involving stretching of filaments between the coagulation and the winding-on stages.

Stretch yarn Term used to denote yarns from thermoplastic fibres which have the property of rapid recovery from stretch induced by a process of deformation followed by heat setting (see Bulked yarns).

Tow A large number of filaments collected after extrusion into the form of a loose rope preliminary to the making of man-made staple fibre. The tow may be cut at intervals to supply staple of regular length in loose fibre form for subsequent spinning, or, the tow after cutting or breaking may be converted directly into a sliver in a continuous process known as the tow-to-top system.

Tyre cord yarns In Appendix I reference was made to cotton tyre yarns used in the manufacture of tyre cord fabrics. In the man-made fibre field motor car tyre industry represents one of the major outlets which is keenly sought after by both, the manufacturers of high tenacity rayon yarns and the manufacturers of nylon yarns.

Motor tyre cords, made from high tenacity viscose rayon yarns, have been found particularly serviceable, as compared with cotton cord yarns, when the tyres are run continuously for a long time at high speeds with heavy loads. Under such severe conditions the temperature in the cords tends to rise to a degree that is injurious to cotton cords, whereas, within certain limits, the strength of viscose rayon cords increases. The temperature in the tyres of heavy vehicles ordinarily rises to about 100°C and may reach 140°C, and high tenacity viscose cords have been specifically designed to withstand great strains and stresses under these conditions. Yarns which have been produced under such extreme stretching that the elongation is greatly reduced are not suitable for tyre cords.

Nylon tyre cord yarns have made their appearance in the 1950s and have captured a good proportion of the market despite the higher cost on the grounds of their excellent tenacity and elastic properties. Originally many makers favoured nylon 66 for this application as this type has a higher softening and melting point than nylon 6. The latter, however, may eventually prove to be the better suited fibre as it exhibits good thermal stability, much better adhesion to rubber and superior flex resistance. The higher cost of nylon as opposed to high tenacity rayon (about 2:1) is partially offset by the smaller quantity of nylon which needs to be used to produce an equally serviceable tyre fabric. This is due to higher strength of nylon yarns. One disadvantage of nylon based tyres is their tendency to deform temporarily when the car is parked after a long journey with the tyres quite hot. The part of the tyre on which the car rests tends to flatten out and will return to the normal shape only after several hundred yards after re-starting. This fault may eventually be eliminated either by modification in the drawing treatment, or in the chemical nature of the fibre.

Variable denier rayon yarn   Threads of varying denier are produced by modifying the speed at which the continuously issuing stream of filaments is drawn away from the extrusion device. The variations can be so controlled that the periodicity of spacing and the possibility of patterning are avoided.

Varied-length staple fibre yarn   Staple fibre that contains fibres which vary in length is produced for use in the worsted spinning industry. The distribution of the different fibre lengths is so controlled that an analysis shows the characteristic sloping shoulder of a wool top diagram. The material is provided in lots in which the length declines gradually from 152 mm to 88 mm, 127 mm to 88 mm, and 76 mm to 63 mm, but in other respects it is similar to the same class of staple fibre. It is claimed that in producing a wool and rayon mixture yarn the blending of the fibres is more thorough when the lengths of the two components are similarly varied and that a more evenly spun yarn results.

List of works for further reference:

1. Cook, J. G. *Handbook of Textile Fibres*, 4th edn. Merrow Publishing Co. Ltd., 1967.
2. *Textile Terms and Definitions*, 6th edn., The Textile Institute, 1970.
3. *Identification of Textile Materials*, 6th edn., The Textile Institute, 1970.
4. Moncrieff, R. W. *Man-Made Fibres*, 5th edn., Butterworths, 1971.
5. Press, J. J., Ed. *Man-Made Textile Encyclopaedia*, Textile Book Publishers, Inc., 1959.
6 *Review of Textile Progress*, 1954–67, Butterworths in association with The Textile Institute and The Society of Dyers and Colourists.
7. *Textile Progress*, Textile Institute Quarterly.

Appendix III

Basic Yarn and Cloth Relationships in Simple Woven Fabrics

Cloth settings in woven fabrics have evolved over a considerable number of years as a result of extensive trial and error procedures combined with practical experience and in many instances are a compromise between what is acceptable and what can be provided within a given price range. Even in standard classes of cloth they vary widely ranging from the minimum marketable quality to a desirable maximum for a particular end use. Neither the top, nor the bottom qualities represent rigid and well defined values and may vary between countries and areas due to differences in climate, fashion, habits or affluence of the various groups of people. The quality also fluctuates over a time scale and compared with clothing favoured by the Victorians which almost possessed the solidity and the permanence of heritable property, the present day constructions look decidedly flimsy.

In cloth types which use standard yarns and well known materials the traditional settings and thread counts are used which with some modifications provide wide and useful ranges of fabrics capable of satisfying most tastes and demands and there is little need for experimentation. However, when new fibres are brought into production, or when new uses for certain cloths are contemplated the trial and error procedures necessary to arrive at a correct setting may be costly and time consuming and this is a point at which a theoretical approach which gives an approximately correct starting point reduces the number and the cost of trials.

Cloth setting theories were developed in the second half of the last century with the intention of providing a designer with a ready made formula which would enable him to produce a useful cloth of a certain weight, by stipulating weaves, yarn counts or settings. The work was carried out independently by a number of workers and the investigations commenced by, amongst others, Ashenhurst and Armitage were later continued by Law and then developed by Peirce into a concept of cloth geometry.

Formulae provided for the calculation of cloth cover, or density of yarn setting depended largely on certain assumptions concerned with yarn diameters and the various constants or factors were usually calculated in terms of cotton, worsted or woollen yarn count systems. In this book all yarns are numbered according to the tex system and, therefore, this system has been adopted in all calculations which follow. The use of a direct, metric system of yarn numbering considerably simplifies the arithmetic involved and the existence of conversion tables will make it easy to compare the tex-numbers with the counts for those who are more accustomed to work on the traditional systems.

Cloth setting or density of thread spacing This is expressed as the number-of threads over a convenient linear measure such as an inch, a centimetre, or 100 mm. Two values are necessary, the first defining the number of ends, the second the number of picks per unit space.

In the previous chapters of this book the unit of one cm has been used to specify cloth settings but in this Appendix a unit of 100 mm has been adopted. This is well suited for calculations expressed in terms of the tex system and is sufficiently large to avoid fractional values which occur frequently when coarser fabrics are specified over the space of one cm. Also, being very nearly equal to 4 inches (101.6 mm), the unit provides an easy base for conversion of a given setting into threads per inch.

Yarn diameter As textile yarns are easily compressible their thickness is not usually specified as a given gauge or diameter but as a weight/length relationship known as yarn count or yarn number. However, for the purpose of calculating cloth cover, especially when dealing with new materials, new structures, or new modifications it is necessary to consider yarn diameter.

In the tex system the yarn number, N tex, indicates the weight in grammes of 1000 m of yarn, therefore, assuming constant yarn density, it will be proportional to the area of yarn cross-section. If circular cross-section is assumed the yarn can be imagined as a cylinder whose diameter can be obtained from the following relationship:

$$\text{Area of cross section} = \frac{\text{volume}}{\text{length}}$$

$$\text{or,} \qquad \pi r^2 = \frac{\pi d^2}{4} = \frac{v}{l}$$

$$\therefore \qquad d^2 = \frac{4v}{\pi l}$$

$$\text{and,} \qquad d = \sqrt{\frac{4v}{\pi l}}$$

The length is fixed at 1000 m so to find a numerical value for d it is necessary to find the volume of the yarn and this could be obtained if the density or the specific volume of the yarn were known. Densities of the textile fibres are known and the specific volume of any *fibre* can be accurately determined as it is a reciprocal of density. Yarn, however, is a composite of fibres and air, and the relative amounts of air and fibre within a yarn will vary depending on the density of the material (or materials, in blended yarns), fibre thickness, fibre alignment, degree of twist and the amount of tension applied. Peirce in his experimental work on cotton yarns estimated that the specific volume of such yarns under moderate pressures (such as can be expected to exist in a cloth) is of the order of 1.1 cm³/g. As the density of cotton is 1.52 g/cm³, and its specific volume 0.658 cm³/g, the specific volume of 1.1 cm³/g represents a yarn composed of approximately 60 per cent fibre and 40 per cent air space. In the tex system the actual volume of yarn equals *tex × specific volume* and, therefore, assuming the specific volume of 1.1 cm³/g, the formula for yarn diameter may be given as:

$$d = \sqrt{\frac{4 \times N \times 1.1}{1000\pi}}$$

From this it is possible to calculate a constant to simplify the formula to:

$$d = \sqrt{\frac{N}{F}}$$

which for yarns of specific volume of 1.1 cm³/g would be:

$$d \text{ mm} = \sqrt{\frac{N}{26.7}}$$

or, otherwise, the formula could be employed for yarns of any specific volume, V, in the following manner:

$$d \text{ mm} = \frac{\sqrt{V \times N}}{28}$$

The specific volume of 1.1 cm³/g established for cotton yarns is surprisingly close for most other fibre and multi-filament yarns irrespective of the material content but it would be inappropriate to use it for mono-filament and bulked yarns on account of vastly different fibre to air space ratios, or for poly-olefine and certain mineral yarns due to considerable differences between the densities of these materials and most of the other textile fibres. Where closer approximations to actual specific volumes are known these should, of course, be used in preference to 1.1 cm³/g.

In the above calculations a circular yarn cross-section has been assumed. This would be true in respect of monofilament and very hard twisted yarns but most of the other types of yarns tend to flatten to some extent and some workers have proposed an elliptical or a race-track cross-section as being closer to the actual appearance of yarn in a cloth. Apart from the intrinsic yarn characteristics the degree of flattening is dependent on the density of setting, which determines the amount of space available for spreading, and the tension exercised by the transverse yarn members, and should be preferably specified separately for each situation rather than used as a general proposition.

Cloth cover   The diagrams in *Figure A3.1* show projected views of two woven cloths of different construction. At A the warp and the weft threads cover the area of the cloth only partially, but at B the cloth area is covered completely with no spaces left between

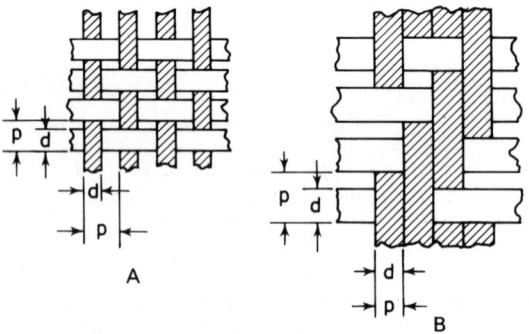

Figure A3.1

the adjacent warp yarns, and it will be seen that the relative closeness of yarns in a woven cloth is dependent upon the ratio of yarn diameter, d, to yarn spacing, p. This ratio known as relative cover, can be defined as the proportion of a projected view of a given area of cloth which is covered by threads, and will have a scale from 0 to 1, although it may also be expressed as percentage cover with a scale from 0 to 100 per cent.

$$\frac{d}{p} = \text{relative cover} \qquad \frac{d \times 100}{p} = \text{percentage cover}$$

It is preferable to express warp and weft relative cover separately, as the cumulative value of cloth cover does not indicate the comparative importance of each set of yarns which is essential for the determination of certain cloth characteristics.

From the relationship shown above it will be obvious that if $d = p$, the value of relative cover is one, and this is regarded as the theoretical maximum cover. In practice, however, this value can be exceeded considerably in any one direction, either through yarn distortion, or, by forcing the threads into different planes, especially if the relative cover of the opposite set of threads is reduced correspondingly.

The relative cover for one thread system can be calculated as follows by considering an area of 100×100 mm:

$$\text{Area per thread} = 100 \times d$$

$$\text{Area covered by } n \text{ threads of one system} = n \times 100 \times d$$

$$\therefore \text{Relative cover} = \frac{n \times 100 \times d}{100 \times 100} = \frac{n \times d}{100}$$

Examples: (1) The cloth represented at A in *Figure A3.1* is specified as follows: Warp—25 tex cotton, 267 ends/100 mm; weft—36 tex cotton, 334 picks/100 mm. Find the relative warp and weft cover. (Subscript 1 refers to warp, subscript 2 to weft.)

$$\text{Warp relative cover} = \frac{n_1 \times d_1}{100}$$

$$= \frac{267 \times \frac{\sqrt{25}}{26.7}}{100} = 0.50$$

$$\text{Weft relative cover} = \frac{n_2 \times d_2}{100}$$

$$= \frac{334 \times \frac{\sqrt{36}}{26.7}}{100} = 0.75$$

(2) Find the relative warp and weft cover of the cloth represented at B in *Figure A3.1*, which is specified as follows: Warp—64 tex cotton, 334 ends/100 mm; weft—81 tex cotton, 198 picks/100 mm.

$$\text{Warp relative cover} = \frac{334 \times \frac{\sqrt{64}}{26.7}}{100} = 1.00$$

$$\text{Weft relative cover} = \frac{198 \times \frac{\sqrt{81}}{26.7}}{100} = 0.67$$

In most circumstances the cumulative value for cloth cover is of little use, but in some special cases, such as in considering air permeability, or porosity of cloths it may be of considerable interest, and should be specified. Simple addition of the relative warp and weft covers does not give the correct result because in this way the areas where one set of threads crosses the other are counted twice. These areas equal to

$$n_1 \times n_2 \times d_1 \times d_2, \text{ hence}$$

$$\text{Relative cloth cover} = (\text{Relative warp cover} + \text{relative weft cover})$$

$$- (\text{Relative warp cover} \times \text{relative weft cover}).$$

For the fabric represented at A in *Figure A3.1* the relative cloth cover would, therefore, be:

$$(0.50 + 0.75) - (0.50 \times 0.75) = 0.88$$

Expressed as a percentage it would indicate that 88 per cent of the total cloth surface was covered by yarn, with the remaining 12 per cent of the area consisting of open spaces.

The calculations involving the degree of yarn cover in cloth can be simplified considerably if an index or cover factor is derived which will obviate the need for the cumbersome calculation of yarn diameter which is necessary to establish the relative cover value. This can be achieved in the following manner:

$$d \text{ mm} = \frac{\sqrt{N}}{26.7} \quad \text{(for yarns of specific volume 1.1 cm}^3/\text{g)}$$

$$p \text{ mm} = \frac{100}{n} \quad \text{(where } n \text{ is the number of threads per 100 mm)}$$

$$\frac{d}{p} = \text{relative cover and this has a value of 1.00 when } d = p.$$

From the above the following relationship can be established:

$$\frac{d}{p} = \frac{\sqrt{N}}{26.7} \div \frac{100}{n} = \frac{n\sqrt{N}}{2670}$$

If the numerical factor is now eliminated a cover factor, K, can be expressed as: $K = n\sqrt{N}$. the value of K being 2670 when $d = p$, i.e. when the maximum theoretical cover value is reached. In this way a direct relationship is established between the cover factor, K, the number of threads per 100 mm, and the tex yarn number, N, to the exclusion of yarn diameter calculation provided that only yarns of specific volume of 1.1 cm^3/g are considered. It will be appreciated that for the relative cover of 0.50, K has the value of 1335; for relative cover of 0.33 it has the value of 890, and so on.

Many authorities consider that the figure of 2670 is too unwieldy as a factor and, therefore, it has been recommended that the value of 267 be accepted as the tex cover factor, which will be correct for the relationship derived above if n is taken to equal the number of threads per 10 mm. The exact numerical value of K has no particular significance as long as it is understood what it represents.

Examples:

(1) It is required to produce a cloth with 50 per cent warp cover using 25 tex multifilament rayon yarn. How many ends per 100 mm should be employed?

$$n = \frac{K}{\sqrt{N}} = \frac{1335}{\sqrt{25}} = 267$$

(2) It is desired to achieve the relative weft cover of 0.67 in a cloth woven with 178 picks of cotton yarn per 100 mm. What yarn number should be used?

$$\sqrt{N} = \frac{K}{n} = \frac{1780}{178} = 10, \therefore 100 \text{ tex yarn should be used.}$$

(3) What is the warp cover factor in a cloth made from 64 tex worsted warp with 220 ends per 100 mm?

$$K = n\sqrt{N} = 220 \times \sqrt{64} = 1760$$

What is the percentage warp cover in this cloth?

$$\frac{1760 \times 100}{2670} = 66 \text{ per cent}$$

Cloth Geometry In the concept of cloth cover presented above only the packing of threads parallel to each other is considered. No account is taken at this stage of the interference of the transverse threads with this relationship and the result indicates simply the ratio of a projected area of cloth covered by the threads to the total area. Even this ratio will only be accurate if the threads in question retain their circular cross-section. In practice some yarns tend to flatten and spread out and if this occurs the cloth surface will be fully covered at relative cover values below the theoretical maximum of 1.00. Apart from the possibility of yarn flattening the settings in actual cloths are affected by the frequency with which the transverse threads intersect the plane of the opposite thread system and this must be taken into account in considering the number of threads which it will be possible to place side by side.

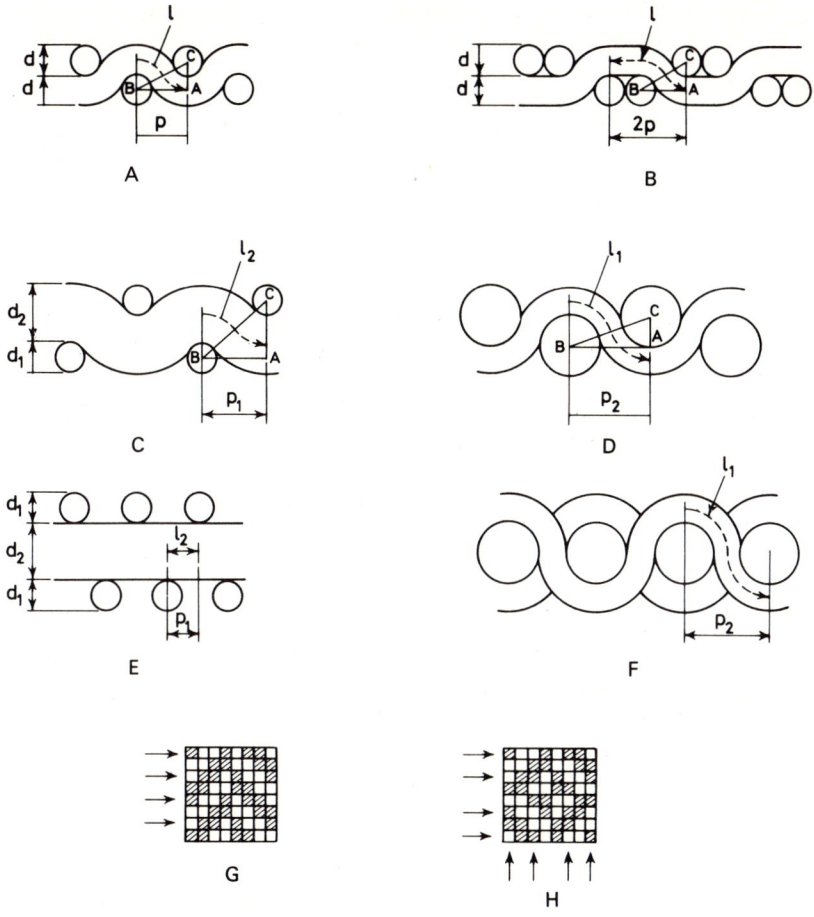

Figure A3.2

The cloth cross-section given at A, in *Figure A3.2* represents a plain weave fabric produced with identical yarns and settings in both directions. As the warp and the weft sectional views of such a fabric are the same, only one cross-section need be considered. The thread spacing represented in the diagram is the closest possible and it can be, therefore, determined that as $AC = 1d$, and $CB = 2d$, the thread spacing, p, is:

$$p = AB = \sqrt{3}d, \text{ or, } 1.732d,$$

and this represents the closest thread setting attainable without thread distortion in a square set plain weave constructed from the same yarns in both directions. The value of the cloth cover factor, K, for this cloth will be:

$$K = \frac{2670}{1.732} = 1542$$

The other important parameter obtainable from the model given at A, *Figure A3.2*, is the length, l, of the transverse thread. This, when expressed as a relationship of l/p gives the value of yarn crimp which, apart from being essential in determining the quantities of yarn to be ordered for the production of a given cloth, also determines many cloth characteristics such as tensile strength, rigidity, air permeability, etc. In the diagram the axis of the transverse thread shown as a dotted line follows an arcuate path whose length over the spacing p consists of two arcs of 60 degrees each. The radius of each arc is equal to $d(\frac{1}{2}d$ of one thread system $+ \frac{1}{2}d$ of the other), therefore the total length of the thread over the specified distance, described sometimes as the modular length, can be expressed as:

$$l = 2\frac{2\pi d}{6} = \frac{2\pi d}{3}$$

As p equals 1.732d, the ratio of l/p can be given as follows:

$$\frac{l}{p} = \frac{2\pi d}{3 \times 1.732d} = 1.209$$

or, expressed as a percentage excess of l over p, or yarn crimp, it equals to 20.9 per cent.

In practice a plain weave fabric constructed to above cover specification would be too boardy for most purposes and as a result of thread flattening it is possible to produce fully covered plain cloths at K values of between 1000 to 1400, depending on the degree of yarn spreading. Yarn flattening is also responsible for the reduction in cloth thickness and yarn crimp values from those shown in the model.

A very similar approach to the one outlined above in respect of, both, the cover factor and the yarn crimp, could be applied for other than plain weave constructions. As an example, B, in *Figure A3.2* shows a cross-sectional view of yarn intersections in a $\frac{2}{2}$ twill cloth constructed from identical yarns at a theoretical maximum square setting. The modular length, in this structure involves two adjacent parallel threads and one point of yarn intersection, the thread spacing, p, being different between the threads whose lie is not disturbed by the intersecting transverse thread, and those which the transverse thread intersects. For the sake of simplicity it is best to consider an average thread spacing, p_a, which has a value of one half of $2p$ indicated in the diagram. As the relationship of the two threads at the point of intersection is exactly the same as that calculated for the plain weave, p_a can be established as follows:

$$2p = \sqrt{3}d + d = 2.732d$$

$$\therefore \quad p_a = \frac{2.732d}{2} = 1.366d$$

and the cover factor for this cloth will have the value of:

$$K = \frac{2670}{1.366} = 1955$$

Modular length of the transverse thread for the space of $2p$ is:

$$l = \frac{2\pi d}{3} + d = 3.09$$

$$\therefore \quad \frac{l}{2p} = \frac{3.09d}{2.732d} - 1.131$$

$$\therefore \quad \text{Yarn crimp} = 13.1 \text{ per cent}$$

From the above considerations it will be clear that in all square set cloths produced with identical yarns in both directions the calculations of yarn spacing at the point of intersection will be identical and, therefore, the density of spacing will be dependent entirely on the frequency with which the intersections occur. In more complex structures in which the interval between each yarn intersection is variable it may be necessary to calculate the spacing per full repeat of the weave and to establish the average thread spacing, p_a, by dividing the repeat spacing by the number of threads in the repeat.

The solutions considered above can be extended to encompass constructions in which different settings and different yarns are used in warp and weft. As in such fabrics the warp and the weft sections are different it is necessary to show and to consider each one separately. Diagrams C and D in *Figure A3.2* show respectively the warp and the weft section of a plain cloth constructed with a fine warp yarn and a coarse weft with a maximum theoretical setting in each direction. In order to simplify the arithmetic the weft yarn diameter has been taken to be twice that of the warp ($d_2 = 2d_1$).

Warp thread spacing:

$$AC = \tfrac{1}{2}d_1 + \tfrac{3}{4}d_2 = 2d_1$$

$$BC = \tfrac{1}{2}d_1 + d_2 + \tfrac{1}{2}d_1 = 3d_1$$

$$AB = p_1 = \sqrt{5}d_1 = 2.236d_1$$

$$\therefore K_1 = \frac{2670}{2.236} = 1194$$

The low cover factor is entirely to be expected as the coarse weft will throw the adjacent ends further apart than a fine weft.

Weft thread spacing:

$$AC = \tfrac{1}{2}d_2 = d_1$$

$$BC = \tfrac{1}{2}d_2 + d_1 + \tfrac{1}{2}d_2 = 3d_1$$

$$AB = p_2 = \sqrt{8}d_1 = 2.828d_1, \text{ but } d_1 = \tfrac{1}{2}d_2,$$

$$\therefore = p_2 = 1.414d_2$$

$$\therefore K_2 = \frac{2670}{1.414} = 1888$$

A cloth of this type will also exhibit considerable differences in the warp and weft crimp values.

Weft crimp—the broken line, l_2, in diagram C is composed of two arcs, each of 48° (approx.); the radius of each arc $= \tfrac{1}{2}d_1 + \tfrac{1}{2}d_2 = 1\tfrac{1}{2}d_1$, therefore,

$$l_2 = 2\frac{3\pi d_1}{7.5} = 2.51d_1$$

$$\frac{l_2}{p_1} = \frac{2.51d_1}{2.236d_1} = 1.122$$

$$\therefore \text{ crimp} = 12.2 \text{ per cent}$$

Warp crimp—l_1 in diagram D consists of two arcs of 70° with the radii $= \tfrac{1}{2}d_2 + \tfrac{1}{2}d_1 = 1\tfrac{1}{2}d_1$, therefore,

$$l_1 = 2\,\frac{3\pi d_1 \times 70}{360} = 3.663d_1$$

$$\frac{l_1}{p_2} = \frac{3.663d_1}{1.414d_2} = \frac{3.663d_1}{2.828d_1} = 1.295$$

$$\therefore \text{ crimp} = 29.5 \text{ per cent}$$

Diagrams E and F in *Figure A3.2* represent respectively the warp and the weft sections of an unbalanced plain weave cloth of the warp rib type in which the warp yarn diameter is one half that of the weft ($d_2 = 2d_1$). As can be seen at E, $d_1 = p_1$ and, therefore, the warp cover factor in this cloth will have the value of 2670. As $l_2 = p_1$ there is no weft crimp, i.e. the weft lies perfectly straight deflecting the warp threads into two separate planes. In this situation each weft pick is separated from its neighbour by the full diameter of the warp end and, therefore:

$$p_2 = d_2 + d_1 = 1\tfrac{1}{2}d_2$$

and the maximum cover factor for weft, K_2, is:

$$K_2 = \frac{2670}{1.5} = 1760$$

The warp will exhibit a very high degree of crimp which may be given as follows:

The broken line, l_1, in diagram F is composed of two arcs of $90°$ each; the radius of each arc $= \frac{1}{2}d_2 + \frac{1}{2}d_1 = 1\frac{1}{2}d_1$, therefore:

$$l_1 = 2\frac{3\pi d_1}{4} = 4.71 d_1$$

$$\frac{l_1}{p_2} = \frac{4.71 d_1}{1.5 d_2} = \frac{4.71 d_1}{3 d_1} = 1.57$$

$$\therefore \text{ crimp } = 57 \text{ per cent}$$

The method used above in examples A to F can be readily adapted for other simple weaves and is generally applicable for constructions in which the length of float does not exceed two threads. Even in this comparatively limited range of constructions there are certain considerations which must be taken into account to avoid errors. A good example of these is the case of an ordinary 2-and-2 twill and the same twill arranged in herringbone order. An ordinary square set twill may be produced with a cover factor of 1955 as given for example B. A broad herringbone stripe in the same twill can also be produced with the same cover factor but a narrow stripe in which the direction of twill is changed after every four ends as at G, *Figure A3.2*, can only be produced at a very much reduced K value. This is due to the fact that on every alternate pick floats of one thread are occurring owing to the method of reversal. Even more severe reduction of the K value would be required in the case of 2-and-2 twill diaper given at H where floats of one occur in both directions.

In mat weaves and in weaves in which the float length exceeds two threads it is customary to add a certain fixed percentage to the calculated number of threads in order to achieve a degree of firmness corresponding to plain and 2-and-2 twill weave fabrics. The commonly used percentages are those worked out by Law which may be summarised as follows.

(1) Mat weaves—
  2-and-2 mat weave—add 4.5 per cent
  Other mat weaves—add 4.5 per cent + 9.5 per cent × (float length − 2)
(2) Twill weaves—
  Add 5 per cent × (float length − 2)
  Thus, a 4-and-4 twill warrants an addition of 10 per cent
(3) Sateen and satin weaves—
  Add 5.5 per cent × (float length − 2)
  $\therefore$ addition for 5-end satin or sateen $= 5.5 × (4−2) = 11$ per cent
  $\therefore$ addition for 6-end satin or sateen $= 5.5 × (5 − 2) = 16.5$ per cent
  $\therefore$ addition for 8-end satin or sateen $= 5.5 × (7 − 2) = 27.5$ per cent

At this point it is useful to note the discrepancy between additions required for an 8-end twill and an 8-end satin. These arise not only because the 4-and-4 twill has a shorter float but mainly because in a regular twill the thread intersections occur in a consecutive order whilst in satins they are staggered which results in a greater freedom of movement available to the floating yarns. As a result of the additions sateens and satins are usually produced with cover factors about or above the maximum value of 2670 in the direction of the face yarns, i.e. weft for sateens and warp for satins with considerably lower K values for the opposite thread direction (usually between 1400 to 1600).

Constructions in which a large variety of different weaves is employed within a repeat, such as brocades, cannot be approached in the same manner as the simple structures and in such cases the designer is guided mainly by experience and precedent. However, in figured cloths in which one weave occupies a predominant position the normal rules of cloth geometry can be applied quite successfully.

Relationship of cloth cover to cloth weight In many instances cloths are constructed to conform to a certain weight per unit area and this specification is of considerable importance not only in determining the cloth characteristics but also as a basis for costing. The weight may be expressed in ounces per running yard, ounces per square yard, or in grammes per square metre, the latter having been adopted in this chapter.

In planning a new cloth construction it is necessary to correlate all fabric parameters and for this purpose it is useful to establish a relationship between the weight and the cover of the cloth. This may be done in the following manner:

$K = n\sqrt{N}$, n being the number of threads per 100 mm.

$W = g/m^2$

Cover for warp and weft yarns $= K_1 + K_2 = n_1\sqrt{N_1} + n_2\sqrt{N_2}$

$$W = \frac{(10n_1 \times N_1) + (10n_2 \times N_2)}{1000} = \frac{n_1 N_1 + n_2 N_2}{100}$$

$\therefore 100W = n_1 N_1 + n_2 N_2$, but $n_1 = \dfrac{K_1}{\sqrt{N_1}}$, and $n_2 = \dfrac{K_2}{\sqrt{N_2}}$

therefore, the above equation could also be expressed as:

$$100W = \frac{K_1 N_1}{\sqrt{N_1}} + \frac{K_2 N_2}{\sqrt{N_2}}$$

which, when simplified:

$$100W = \frac{K_1 N_1}{\sqrt{N_1}} \times \frac{\sqrt{N_1}}{\sqrt{N_1}} + \frac{K_2 N_2}{\sqrt{N_2}} \times \frac{\sqrt{N_2}}{\sqrt{N_2}}$$

results in the following relationship:

$$100W = K_1\sqrt{N_1} + K_2\sqrt{N_2}$$

The relationship provides a useful basis for estimates but it must be realised that in this form it does not include the crimp of the threads and, therefore, the weight given would be, in fact, lower than the actual weight of cloth by a fraction equal to an aggregate value represented by the warp and weft crimps.

List of works for further reference
1. Ashenhurst, T. R. *Text. Educator*, 1888–89, 335.
2. Law, W. *Wool Record and Textile World*, 1922, 21, 968.
3. Peirce, F. T., *J.T.I.*, 1937, 28, T45.
4. *Woven Cloth Construction*; Robinson, A. T. C. and Marks, R.; Butterworths and Textile Inst., 1967.
5. *Structural Mechanics of Fibers, Yarns, and Fabrics*, Vol. I; Hearle, J. W. S., Grosberg, P. and Backer, S.; Wiley–Interscience, 1969.

Index